Feminist Consequences

GENDER AND CULTURE

CAROLYN G. HEILBRUN AND NANCY K. MILLER, EDITORS

GENDER AND CULTURE
A SERIES OF COLUMBIA UNIVERSITY PRESS

Edited by Carolyn G. Heilbrun and Nancy K. Miller

GENDER AND CULTURE READERS

Feminist Consequences

THEORY FOR THE NEW CENTURY

EDITED BY

Elisabeth Bronfen and Misha Kavka

Columbia University Press New York

COLUMBIA UNIVERSITY PRESS
Publishers Since 1893
New York   Chichester, West Sussex

Copyright © 2001 Columbia University Press
All rights reserved

Library of Congress Cataloging-in-Publication Data
Feminist consequences : theory for the new century /
edited by Elisabeth Bronfen and Misha Kavka.
p. cm. — (Gender and culture)
Includes bibliographical references and index.
ISBN 0–231–11704–3 (cloth : alk. paper)
ISBN 0–231–11705–1 (pbk : alk. paper)
1. Feminist theory. 2. Feminism.
I. Bronfen, Elisabeth. II. Kavka, Misha. III. Series.

HQ1190 .F444   2000
305.42'01—dc21   00–060141

Casebound editions of Columbia University Press books
are printed on permanent and durable acid-free paper.

Printed in the United States of America
Designed by Audrey Smith

c 10 9 8 7 6 5 4 3 2 1
p 10 9 8 7 6 5 4 3 2 1

CONTENTS

INTRODUCTION

Misha Kavka

Feminism ain't what it used to be. Perhaps with some nostalgia, many of us who call ourselves feminists look back to the peak of the second wave in the 1970s, to a feminism that in retrospect seems to have had a clear object (women), a clear goal (to change the fact of women's subordination), and even a clear definition (political struggle against patriarchal oppression). Such clarity is a trick of memory, no doubt, which reflects more on the pluralized, diversified state of feminism at the turn of the new century than it does on the actual agreements among the theorists and practitioners of the second wave. Nonetheless, the feminist work of the "long" 1980s (read late 1970s to early 1990s), in refining from ever-proliferating positions the objects, goals, and definitions of feminism, has had the effect of splintering what had been a recognizable feminist project into unrecognizability, even into a paradoxical state of visible invisibility. It is as though the more that "feminism" has become a publicly visible term, the less sense both its practitioners and its detractors have of what it is "about."

Clarity about the object, goal, and even definition of feminism now seems no longer possible or even desirable. What feminist "consciousness-raising" groups may once have considered the common object of feminism—"women" who share certain common experiences by the fact of their sex—has been exposed as a normatizing concept that performs a range of exclusions at the levels of class, race, ethnicity, nationality, and sexuality. If the putative object of feminism has turned out to be a fantasy of commonality, then the notion of a singular goal was already problematized from the outset by a disagreement between those (Marxist and materialist feminists) who strove for radical equality, or the goal of ultimately erasing the social effects of sex difference, and those (radical American feminists as well as the French theorists of "écriture féminine") who strove for radical difference, or the goal of maintaining sex difference without social detriment. Inherent to this problem of a common goal is the larger battle between feminist praxis and feminist theory (itself a debatable division), which separates feminist activists who seek to improve the social/living conditions for women through modes of direct action and feminist theorists who seek to understand and affect the structural constraints on female subjectivity. Most important, the very terms through which we might now seek to define feminism have been refined, pluralized, displaced, and/or deconstructed to the point where they hardly seem available anymore, certainly not if one claims to be defining feminism on behalf of "women." Which brings us to the paradox of being involved in a political practice that can no longer define itself as a practice, let alone define its goals.

So feminism ain't what it used to be, and the prefix "post" begins to rear its ugly head. "Postfeminism" implies, first and foremost, that there was once a time when feminists could say "we" and that that time is now gone. This is surely no more than a fantasy of retrospection, but it nonetheless threatens to mark our words on the subject with the anger, grief, denial, or resignation of those mourning at a graveside.[1] Allow me, in light of a common readership, to adopt a provisional "we" at least in terms of those readers interested enough in "feminist consequences" to be thumbing through this volume. Allow me further to define "we" as those readers/writers/thinkers/doers, engaged in different projects and struggles, who have invested and continue to invest in feminism as an enabling term. For how can feminism be dead, if the term continues to enable work built out of previous work? It's not as though we turned our backs on a coherent project and returned to it only in time to discover that the heartbeat was failing. On the contrary, the notion of a collective project with a singular history makes up both the nostalgized past and the utopian future of feminism, kept in suspense by a present that consists of multiple, ongoing kinds of feminist activity. The change marked by "post" thus happened while we were *doing* feminism; the change happened *because* we were doing feminism. The problem is not the death or the end of feminism but, rather, coming to terms with the fact that its political, strategic, and interpretive power has been so great as to produce innumerable modes of doing—whether activist, practical, theoretical, or just "quiet"—that have moved well beyond the mother term, already fractured at its origin.

Even the definition of the term "postfeminist" is under contention, with the media claiming it for the "backlash" girls of conservative feminism,[2] the Third Wave claiming it for a younger generation of culturally savvy feminists who seek "to use desire and pleasure as well as anger to fuel struggles for justice,"[3] and poststructuralist academic feminists claiming it for a pluralistic theoretical feminism that repudiates the supposed essentialism of second wave feminism.[4] In social terms, there is also a complicitous form of "postfeminism," in which women's sense of empowerment is tied directly into what could be called old patriarchal institutions, such as, in Britain, the social pressure for women to express an enthusiasm for football, or, in the United States, the bizarre hiring of Naomi Wolf by the Gore presidential campaign to advise Al Gore on his masculine image. The most worrying definition of "postfeminism," however, belongs to that group of mostly younger women, now headed toward or in the early stages of a career, who believe that feminism has already done its work by achieving as much social equality for women in the home and workplace as one could hope or even wish for.[5] In this understanding of "post" feminism has erased itself out of existence by its very success. It has thus already made either a dignified or a shrill exit, depending on your point of view, and those who continue to speak for and about it are flogging a dead horse. But surely this returns us to the problem of feminism being a set of practices without a single definition, rather than a practice that has overreached its own goal. The problem is not that the project has been completed. On the contrary, given that feminism lacks a single origin as much as a single definition, it can also have no single moment of ending. Rather, "feminism" serves as an umbrella term for an ever growing range of political projects and endeavors, themselves driven on the one hand by the tendency of feminist work to create debates and on the other hand by the capacity of social forms to retrench, always with a difference, the very constraining conditions that the second wave strove to the-matize and transform.

If feminism can no longer be defined as a coherent project, if it can no longer be considered to be about or for a singular collective of "women," if not even "postfeminism" has a common meaning or constituency, then we need to look elsewhere for the ties that bind its practitioners into collectives, strategic alliances, debates, and flat-out arguments. Calling this collection *Feminist Consequences* suggests that all we have to make us a "we," to allow us to insert ourselves into a relation to feminism, is an investment in the history and resonances of such insertions themselves. Feminism is not, how-ever, the object of a singular history but, rather, a term under which people have in different times and places invested in a more general struggle for social justice and in so doing have participated in and produced multiple histories. The emphasis on "multiple" is important here, since a too singular notion of feminism does an injustice to the differences among various struggles, differences for which acknowledgment was and still is being sought precisely in feminist projects. This is to say that, though social justice remains a universal ideal and a driving force of feminism, the content of this ideal cannot be specified in advance. If "feminism," then, begs definition and yet refuses to be singly defined, one approach is to take stock of where (rather than *what*) "feminism" is by looking back over where it has been— to consider, in other words, the work of today as the consequences of the histories accruing in the last thirty years in the name of feminism.

How do we tell the histories of the second wave and after? One approach lies in terms of what Michèle Barrett, in an article entitled "Words and Things," characterized as the "cultural turn" of feminism, from the largely materialist or social perspectives of the 1970s to the discursive concerns of literary and cultural theory prominent in the 1980s and into the 1990s.[6] Even the earlier materialist concern with "things," however, did not account for a singular approach. Under the auspices of proclaiming the sphere of the personal and the everyday to be political, "things" meant women's work as well as women's living conditions as well as women's bodies—all of which realms feminists sought to "liberate" through celebratory and incendiary politicization (sometimes literally incendiary: think of the bra-burning episodes that, though relatively few, became the photo op of a movement). While Marxist feminists looked for the source of women's subordination in material relations, focusing on women's (house)work, those who have become known as the "radical" feminists, spearheaded by the writings of

Kate Millett and Shulamith Firestone, pinpointed women's reproductive role in patriarchy as the grounds for relegating them to a biological underclass.[7] This binary between the Marxist and radical feminists is itself misleading, however, since it fails to account for theorizations of sexuality that were coming to the fore, such as the groundbreaking socio-anthropological work of Gayle Rubin, who related women's subordination in the "sex/gender system" to the inseparability of gender and reproductive sexuality, or the work of Catharine MacKinnon, who insisted that (hetero)sexuality was central to the institutionalizing of male dominance and female submission.[8] Nor does such a split account for the shading of Marxist materialism into ideological approaches, as in Juliet Mitchell's important book *Psychoanalysis and Feminism*, which took Freud's problematic theories of sexual difference as a telling description (rather than prescription) of the degree to which women's subordination is ideologically upheld.[9]

It is this ideological approach, and Mitchell's book in particular, that marks the beginning of a shift from a concern with "things" to "words," to return to Barrett. The feminist ideology critics of the '70s and '80s borrowed heavily from French structuralists—especially Lacanian psychoanalysis, Althusser's theory of ideology, and Barthes's semiotics—in order to investigate the complicity between ideology and language.[10] With the added influence of Foucault's work on sexuality in the early '80s,[11] feminist critiques by and large shifted their focus from ideology to discourse, from the notion of a possible "true" consciousness about sex and gender relations within a singular, repressive patriarchy to an understanding of sexuality as a construction, the product of differing discourses that are themselves diffuse sites and enactments of power.

Sometime between the late 1970s and the early 1990s, then, an important shift happened, a shift from explaining women's subordination in terms of a single constraining system—whether we call it capitalism, patriarchy, biology, or even language—to focusing on the discursive, material, and cultural differences that make up the being or becoming of women. This shift from systemic approaches to the passionate and sometimes agonized proliferation of difference(s) was largely the consequence of two discourses, critiques by feminists of color and by poststructuralists, that began to be voiced in feminist work from the early 1980s onwards. Though the end effect of these two discourses is the same—to deconstruct the category of "woman" as indicative of a common identity—the means are crucially different. Criticisms by feminists of color found early articulation in the United States when African

American, Latina, Native American, and Asian American women denounced the second wave feminist category of "women" as pertaining only to white, middle-class, Western women, to whom the concerns and bodies of non-white women were invisible.[12] When in 1982 Hazel Carby angrily asked, "What do you mean when you say WE?" she gave voice to the sense of exclusion experienced by many women of color from a common feminist project. Such work exposed the fantasy of commonality undergirding feminism and launched a discomfort with the use of the first-person plural that has only since increased.[13] The 1983 collection *This Bridge Called My Back*, begun in 1979, pushes the complications of the notion of "we" further, for in bringing together in one volume multiracial and multicultural perspectives, it drew attention not simply to the difference of women of color *from* the white feminist "we" but also to the operation of a range of differences *between* women. If, as these grounding volumes show, the effects and functions of race, ethnicity, and class cannot be separated from those of gender, then this makes for unstable coalitions under the umbrella term of feminism. The question of relations between women thus means constantly reconfiguring one's identity and alliances in terms of differences *within* as much as differences *from* or *of*.[14]

Poststructuralist feminism, on the other hand, makes use of philosophical poststructuralist attacks on the metaphysical assumption that there is such a thing as a coherent self grounded in an essential, knowable identity. Poststructuralist feminism thus argues that it can never be enough to say, "I am (a) woman," since gender has no more a totalizing claim on identity than any other attribute. This line of argument found its most acute articulation in Judith Butler's *Gender Trouble*, in which Butler argues that gender identity, rather than being essential to the self, is always the result of iterated, socially sanctioned performances.[15] Whether, as Butler argues, gender accrues to the body through acts, or whether one locates the function of gender elsewhere outside the self—in ideology, the Law, the unconscious, historical contexts, etc.[16]—the important point for poststructuralist feminist critics is that the category of "woman" is split by the discursive, historical, and contextual specificities of difference. In this sense, both poststructuralism and the critiques of white feminism by feminists of color have shown that we can't say "we" without a self-consciousness attentive to the essentializing and exclusionary resonances of a pronoun that can never hope to specify and contextualize the particularity of all its referents.

Together with the extension and development of these discourses of difference, the 1990s have witnessed a move across the academy as a whole to interdisciplinarity, as part of a double effort to create new objects of study and to better situate more traditional objects in local cultural contexts. This move is in no small part responsible for the diversification of feminism, both in terms of objects of investigation and methodologies. (Women's Studies departments are a good case in point, since they have borrowed from and fit themselves "in between" other disciplines.) But feminism in return shows up perhaps more clearly than any other practice how the permeability of disciplinary divisions, and hence the broadening of disciplinary range, has gone hand-in-hand with a localizing of focus by the demarcation of differences. Where second wave feminists spoke of a "we" with shared concerns based in sex/gender identity, the shift to the antiessentialism of the '80s undermined this "we" by questioning the nature of the term "women" and claiming that sexual difference was a cultural construct. The deconstruction of identity in the '80s and '90s extended the fracturing of the term "women" by drawing attention to the range of identity categories that were masked by the focus on gender. The rallying cry of materialist feminists toward the end of the '80s, "race, class and gender," became an ever longer list of formative attributes—including ethnicity, nationality, sexuality, and so on—as people became more sensitive to the multifarious complexes of identity formation.

As a logical extension of broadening the referential capacity of "women," away from a white, middle-class, Western constituency, the interdiscursiveness between feminism and postcolonialism meant that the project of inclusion-through-difference increasingly made visible feminist issues pertinent to non-Western, Third World women.[17] This project of inclusion based on difference became further complicated in the mid-'90s by a move from debates about identity and its various modes of construction to debates about *identification*. This meant that it was no longer a question of what people "were"—a formulation that carries a whiff of essentialism and hence exclusion of people's actual experience—but rather of how they imagined themselves to be and thus participated in their subjectivity construction. The shift from identity to identification was spearheaded largely by the work of queer theorists, sensitive to the role of fantasy in sorting out one's relationship to the complex of sex, desire, and sexual practice.[18] At the same time, it was developed in tandem by postcolonial theorists discussing the complex of racial and postcolonial identifications through which people negotiate their relationship to the socially superior term of "whiteness" or "colonizer."

The effect of what Rosi Braidotti has called the proliferation of "different differences" is thus an increased awareness of and sensitivity to the problematic of identity formation as it affects and effects social relations. The result on the one hand has been that feminism has remained true, or has become even more true, to its initial political project of combating social injustice through sensitivity to those who are socially marginalized and oppressed—even as that oppression has also occurred through its own rhetoric. On the other hand, it is slowly becoming clear that something is lost when the notion of community, by definition based on exclusion, is exchanged for sensitivity to differences in the name of inclusion or at least recognition of otherness. What Ranjana Khanna in this collection calls "the fetishization of the local at the expense of coalition" indicates the problem, not of divisiveness exactly but of the distantiation that results when no one is willing to *speak up for* another because that would involve the dubious act of *speaking for* an other. As Khanna points out, this reification of difference leads to noncommunication between separate ethical spheres. To say, then, as Linda M. G. Zerilli does, that "the category of women [has collapsed] as the ground of political action"[19] indicates only part of the problem facing feminism—albeit a very important part, since it calls into question what kind of politics is possible without a shared basis for political action. The difficulty that has now developed is the question of relationality, or how we understand and effect relations with one another that manifest a sense of social responsibility beyond the limits of the group based on a set of shared differences. In order to address the problem of how to do politics in an age of "different differences," feminism has turned to face the multivalent problem of ethics.

While the moments I have spotlighted here might be part of anyone's understanding of feminism insofar as feminism can be considered a struggle for justice, this is still not to say that a singular history of feminism is possible. It does, however, indicate that some kind of history must be in place in order to hold on to feminism as something still worth doing, since it is precisely what feminists have been doing that provides continuity with what is being and will be done. In this sense, theory is as much a part of feminist "doing" as activism or praxis—even though they have different immediate consequences—since feminist theory belongs to and constitutes histories that themselves cannot be disentangled from feminist praxis. The forms of feminism I have addressed above are in line with the concerns of the articles in this collection: broadly put, concerns of (self)-representation, the cross-over of feeling and politics, the construction of subjectivity in a simultaneously patriarchal and posthuman world, and the ongoing realities and possible transformations of sexual, racial, and transnational discrimination. These concerns are the consequences not only of certain problems raised by feminist work but also of solutions offered that have themselves raised further problems (as can be seen with the problem now caused by an inclusiveness based on attention to differences, which itself was a solution to the exclusions performed by the category of "women").

The title of this collection indicates our concern both with the consequences *of* thirty years of second wave feminism for contemporary feminist thinking, as well as the consequences of contemporary feminism *for* further work in the new century. By choosing the word "consequences," we wish to stress that each essay in this collection is both a consequence of a certain feminist history and has consequences itself as a moment of feminist history to come. If feminism now seems to be anything but a coherent project, this is because it has never mapped itself in terms of a single developmental history; and if it does not have a single history, then the best we can do is to choose a set of consequences at the crossroads of the past and the future to mark certain trajectories of feminist thinking. In putting together this collection, we editors chose to focus on the consequences of a certain kind of history, such as I have suggested, since we could not—and would not attempt—to address all those histories in which feminism is implicated. We also mark our own historical positioning and theoretical bias by not assuming feminism to be something that can be adequately captured by a range of representative voices (i.e., the "whole" of feminism would be illuminated if only enough different positions could be included) or by a confessional mode of writing (i.e., "real" feminism would be illuminated by bringing to light marginalized or silenced voices) or even by a materialist approach that takes the "real" situation into account (i.e., feminism is first and last about the conditions of women's lives). Being in (feminist) history means that these notions of representation, self-identity, and lived experience have been subject to criticism, and this criticism has left its indelible mark on the possible further projects of feminism itself. This collection thus seeks to reflect the way that feminism has been moving on through its own self-questioning.

The authors in the collection are all feminist academics and theorists who were asked to address the questions, "Where have we come from? What characterizes feminism now?" We, the editors, had initially envisioned the collection to be loosely divided into four categories: ethnicities and race, ethics and law, sexuality and desire, and visual and textual production. These divisions represented our understanding of contemporary thematics in feminist theory, but also matched our own interests as editors. We had also thought that each category would invite work using a particular theoretical apparatus, with ethnicities and race inviting multicultural and postcolonial approaches, ethics and law inviting theories of identity (de)construction, sexuality and desire inviting psychoanalytic approaches, and visual/textual production inviting approaches to representation as worked out by film and literary theories. We saw very quickly, however, that this kind of organization did not fit the premises of work being done by feminist theorists, as one of the few shared characteristics of feminist work at the turn of the new century is precisely that neat disciplinary divisions are no longer possible. On the one hand, though thematic/disciplinary divisions can only be constructed in advance of the actual work, they are in fact backward-looking, since they are based on the subdivisions, or subcanonizations, made out of previous work in the field. Such thematic divisions thus serve to mask the creation of new modes and objects of feminism as they are coming into being. On the other hand, the theoretical impetus of feminist work in the '70s and '80s, which came about largely because feminist thinkers were interested in the extent to which "male" theory (anthropological, Marxist, psychoanalytic, philosophical, literary, etc.) could be rewritten to reflect women's concerns, has evolved into a theoretical in-mixing, an interdiscursiveness that is inseparable from the demarcation of new objects and approaches for feminism.

Our task was thus to find a different breakdown, one that would be sensitive to interdisciplinarity and interdiscursiveness, and that would suggest the consequences of previous feminist thinking while avoiding theoretical ghettoizing. To do this, we listened for resonances in the articles before us and found certain concerns appearing repeatedly across these interdisciplinary, cross-theoretical, cross-cultural essays: ethics, affect, and the incursion of pleasure into forms of agency. In line with our contention that feminism can be defined only as a set of practices that are and have consequences, and keeping in mind the resonances that we found reappearing in the essays, we have organized the collection into a four-part structure. The first section, "Whatever Happened to Feminism?," deals with past histories; the second and third sections, "The Ethics of Affect" and "The Pleasures of Agency," address the questions of ethics and agency as worked out in particular textual and cultural spaces; and the final section, "Where to Feminism?," collects together certain issues and approaches that we think will have consequences for future feminist histories.

The historical trajectory outlined by the collection is of necessity a loose one. The first section, "Whatever Happened to Feminism?," is meant neither to lament the disappearance of a "proper" feminism nor to reproach the transformations that such a feminism has undergone but, rather, to indicate the need to think contemporary feminism in terms of the consequences of its distant as well as more recent history. Thus, Juliet Mitchell retraces the encounter between psychoanalysis and feminism in Britain and the United States from the postwar period to poststructuralism, asking whether psychoanalysis has in effect syphoned off the political thrust of the feminist project. Jane Gallop, recalling her own initial heady encounter with feminism in the early '70s, exposes the changing meaning of sexual harassment from its origins in a '70s feminism that celebrated sexual liberation and condemned sexual discrimination, to its alignment with discrimination issues and antisex rhetoric in the '90s. Rey Chow addresses the increasing awareness in work of the '80s and '90s of the problematic conflation between the two meanings of representation—aesthetic and political—when it comes to representing the bodies of women as racial or sexual "others." And Beatrice Hanssen traces the recent history of debates around feminist theory, both between poststructuralist and Frankfurt School theorists and between "theory" and "praxis" itself.

If, in broad terms, this first section traces histories of feminist thinking in terms of psychoanalysis, sexuality, representation, and theory, then the following two sections mark the consequences of such histories in terms of what I have called the resonances of ethics, affect, and pleasurable agency. Part 2, "The Ethics of Affect," brings together four related meanings of affect. Ranjana Khanna positions affect as the psychic burden borne by a (postcolonial) community. Lauren Berlant finds it in the collective sentiment responsible for nation making. Claire Kahane explores the feelings associated for later generations with the representation of traumatic and traumatized maternity in the Holocaust. And Valerie Smith moves from film melodrama to its recent remakings in order to highlight the conflicted will to class mobility and racial fluidity in narratives of passing. These four articles thus address the question of ethics, respectively, as a responsibility between subjects, a responsibility between citizens and law, a responsibility of writers and readers, and an implicit responsibility of us all as bearers of inseparable class, race, and gender identities. Part 3, "The Pleasures of Agency," then takes up the possibility of claiming agency through activities that both adopt and question the impact of pleasure in different cultural spaces. The various conjunctions set up in this section are pleasure with the law, in the form of Elisabeth Bronfen's essay on the ambivalent political purchases of cross-dressing; pleasure with shame, in the form of Anita Haya Patterson's essay on the resistance of Jamaican women's poetry to white feminist politics; and pleasure with political activism, in the form of Ann Cvetkovich's essay on the appropriation, and counterappropriation, of celebrity images for lesbian graphics activism.

The last section, "Where to Feminism?," brings together thinkers who suggest where these concerns with ethics, affect, and agency might lead. Mieke Bal considers contemporary feminist works of visual art as allegories for a possible ethical and potent feminism. Biddy Martin takes the institution of Women's Studies within the university to task for its narrow focus. Rosi Braidotti uses Deleuzian models in order to rearticulate difference as a positive measure for feminine subjects in late postmodernity. And Judith Butler reconsiders the effectivity of the notion of sexual difference for a politically viable feminism that would work in tandem with the insights of queer theory. Finally, a closing interview with Drucilla Cornell returns us to the acknowledgment that feminism both consists of particular histories and simultaneously is in history, as Cornell, through reflections on her activist and academic work, situates the past concerns of feminism within her ongoing project of delineating an "ethical feminism" against the forces of a sexually, racially, and transnationally imperialist state. In doing so, she shows the extent to which activism and theory are inseparable.

Ultimately, the essays in this collection suggest two particular consequences of second wave, or latter twentieth-century, feminism for the work of the new century: (1) that we must include in our understanding of feminism something like "postfeminist" work that has an ineradicable relationship to previous feminist thinking and remains related to this history *without* announcing the "end" of feminism, and (2) that the diversified feminist project is moving toward re-claiming universalism, though in such a way as to radically redefine "universalism" itself.

As to the first point, the work of Lauren Berlant on national sentimentalism and the essay by Rosi Braidotti on the positivity of difference can both stand in for a kind of feminist work that goes beyond addressing the position of women, social or structural, and even refuses to limit itself to "women" as such—that is, to the specific conditions of being female or of feminine subjectivity. In this sense, we might call their work postfeminist, but only to the degree that this term has a positive rather than negative meaning, since it indicates an extension of feminist history into further (what would once have been considered "other") theories, objects, and methodologies. Berlant's work, whose broad focus takes up the sentimental construction of nationhood and citizenship, could certainly not have happened without the feminist claim that "the personal is political," which, among many other consequences, opened up the space of emotions and sentiment as a field of viable inquiry and critical discourse. Conversely, Braidotti brings a feminist perspective to Deleuzian work on nongendered subjectivity, using the notion of "becoming-woman" as a testing ground for both the effectivity and the limits of marking gender on and for the late postmodern subject.

We could say of Biddy Martin's and Elisabeth Bronfen's articles that they, too, use their positioning in a feminist history to go beyond the focus on women or femininity. Martin calls for a revitalization of women's studies, not in terms of shifting or expanding the definition of "women" but, rather, by shifting our entire intellectual and pedagogical approach to take account of scientific methodologies within our antiessentialist disciplines in the humanities and social sciences. Although Bronfen takes Shakespearean heroines and Marlene Dietrich as her main icons of cross-dressing, she also moves away from gender specificity in order to underline the ambivalent relationship of cross-dressing—not just female to male, or male to female, but ultimately cyborg to human—to the law of subjectivity. These articles are all examples of the way in which "feminist" work cannot be differentiated from "postfeminist" work precisely because postfeminism can only be understood in terms of the various histories in which feminism has provided its adherents with a sense of political agency. This means that feminist thinking may now stretch beyond "women" or even gender as categories and as delimiting objects of investigation;[20] it does not, however, mean leaving these categories behind. Rather, as Biddy Martin suggests, the idea is to "suspend or defer questions about what [other objects, methodologies, or technologies] have to do with women or gender long enough to make our analyses of gender and sexuality new again and supple enough to help us intervene usefully in those developments." Postfeminism, in this sense, refers not to the end of a politics or a practice but, rather, to a suspension within it that allows such a politics to remain vital and relevant to contexts of social change. As Mieke Bal puts it in this volume, "the past is the only future we have."

The second consequence suggested by many articles in this collection comes in response to the long 1980s spent elaborating differences and ever more minutely contextualizing the local conditions and experience of (gender, sexual, racial, ethnic, national, class, . . .) identities. In the particular history of feminism I have spotlighted, I ended with feminism's turn to the question of ethics as a way of addressing the problem of intersubjective distantiation caused by the now-absolute respect paid to the "other's" difference from oneself, a distantiation that at best compartmentalizes and at worst paralyzes political action and even dialogue. Faced with this problem arising out of its own attempts at correcting earlier exclusions in the name of "women," feminist work is now beginning, somewhat cautiously, to reapproach that vilified humanist term, "universalism." In order to reclaim something such as universalism, however, the term itself needs to undergo refurbishment; it needs, in other words, to carry within itself the history of its own rejection and reappropriation. Judith Butler in this volume takes up "universality" in the name of anti-foundationalism, claiming that the universal "begins to become articulated precisely through challenges to its *existing* formulation, and this challenge emerges from those who are not covered by it . . . but who, nevertheless, demand that the universal as such ought to be inclusive of them" (original emphasis). In this definition of the term, universalism does not erase otherness; rather, it takes account of the fact that the call for universalism comes from, and thus enfolds, its "outside." Universalism in this renewed sense thus connects with human rights, or, in broader terms, with justice, which will include but extend beyond subjects who happen to be women.

Heeding the appeal of universalism understood in the terms of an ethical inclusion of the "other" is also the project of Mieke Bal, who takes the "fold" as a metaphor for the kind of connected-but-separate relationality between the self and the other that feminism should seek. Such an approach is elaborated in the context of transnational feminism by Ranjana Khanna, who asks us to imagine a relationality among women internationally that would both remain aware of the local conditions of postcolonial subjectivity and retain the more "messianic" promise of justice for women at large. Like Khanna, Juliet Mitchell also recognizes the need to refurbish a notion of universalism in the interests of returning politics to feminism, claiming that the "call to arms of the narcissism of petty differences appears only as the other side of the coin of universalism." Mitchell calls instead for a feminist *contextualization* of changing family forms that would repoliticize feminism by avoiding the narcissism of *particularization*. And Rosi Braidotti points out that the centrality of difference to our social and political thinking about identity construction implies "the confrontation with the notion of 'negative difference,' or 'pejorative others.' " She defines her project in terms of the "recomposition" of an ethical and political agency of the subject that would avoid falling into a nostalgic sense of universalism as the ground of authentic human nature but would, rather, refocus difference toward the positivity of "becoming." Though the terms and methodologies in each of these articles may be different, Butler's use of "universality" seems to reclaim a much-needed promise that "universalism" has long ago failed. At the historical juncture that follows on the effective deconstruction of "identity" and the publicly successful proliferation of difference in the name of multiculturalism (whose success can in no small part be measured by the way in which "political correctness" has been turned into a derogatory term by the Right), it now seems that the tide is turning. Without claiming commonality, since there is no longer a term that would suspend "our" disbelief in the rhetoric of inclusiveness long enough to collect "us" under its banner, many writers in this collection broach the issue of ethical relations for feminism as a way of making contact with one another without assuming each other all to be the same. Feminism has—perhaps—been through the era of differences, learned its lessons, and is moving on.

What still remains is the question of politics, especially as it relates to feminist work that exists on the page, often in the abstract terms of theory. Drucilla Cornell powerfully suggests in the closing interview that the goal of feminist theorizing at this juncture of past and future should be to make room for something like a return to collective work. Whether we think the necessity of this return in terms of the relation between personhood and the state (Berlant), or of sexuality within the Law/law (Gallop, Bronfen, Patterson), or of anti-imperialist/postcolonial coalitions (Khanna), or of the representation of identity (Chow, Kahane, Smith), or of direct activism (Cvetkovich)—all of which issues Cornell opens up—we must nonetheless realize the importance to these ongoing projects of our relations to and with one another. It is in this triple conjunction—among issues, the people who work on and for these issues, and the relations among these people—that politics lies. And this politics itself will be inseparable from the theoretical, pragmatic, and activist histories that knot together at each point of feminist articulation.

In this sense, let me suggest one more shared characteristic among the authors in this collection. There is a way in which all of the articles here both tell a history, even if only implicitly, and announce a manifesto, even if only cautiously. That is because feminism, as I have suggested, is one name for the pursuit of justice, characterized by a particular historical struggle. To forget that current conditions are the fruit of historical struggle (whether those conditions result from the civil rights movement or feminist protests or unionist action) is to forget that justice is only ever a promise, a tenuous achievement at best, which is never fully adequate or inclusive. Justice thus lies outside feminist history and propels its continued unfolding. To think, then, that feminism can be at an end because it has achieved its goal(s) is to open the door to complacency and the retrenchment of marginalizing power structures; it is, in other words, to forget that the ongoing history of doing/thinking feminism is precisely that which keeps the possibility of justice in place as a promise.

The articles in this collection thus resonate with the inseparability of history and manifesto in feminist work, and it is precisely here that I want to claim that feminism lives.

NOTES

1. For a good example of such rhetoric of mourning, see Susan Gubar, "What Ails Feminist Criticism?" *Critical Inquiry* 24, no. 4 (Summer 1998): 878–902.

2. Most well-known are Katie Roiphe, *The Morning After: Sex, Fear, and Feminism* (Boston: Little, Brown, 1993) and *Last Night in Paradise: Sex and Morals at the Century's End* (Boston: Little, Brown, 1997); Naomi Wolf, *Fire with Fire: The New Female Power* (New York: Random House, 1993) and *Promiscuities: The Secret Struggle for Womanhood* (New York: Random House, 1997); and Christina Hoff Sommers, *Who Stole Feminism? How Women Have Betrayed Women* (New York: Simon & Schuster, 1995). Roiphe's conservatism is further played out in Rene Denfield, *The New Victorians: A Young Woman's Challenge to the Old Feminist Order* (New York: Warner Books, 1995). The most recent versions of this kind of "postfeminism" can be found in Wendy Shalit, *A Return to Modesty: Discovering the Lost Virtue* (New York: Free Press, 1999), and Danielle Crittenden, *What Our Mothers Didn't Tell Us: Why Happiness Eludes the Modern Woman* (New York: Simon & Schuster, 1999).

3. Leslie Heywood and Jennifer Drake, "Introduction," in *Third Wave Agenda: Being Feminist, Doing Feminism*, ed. Leslie Heywood and Jennifer Drake (Minneapolis: University of Minnesota Press, 1997), p. 4. For other excellent "third wave" collections, see Rebecca Walker, ed., *To Be Real: Telling the Truth and Changing the Face of*

Feminism (New York: Anchor Books, 1995), and Barbara Findlen, ed., *Listen Up: Voices from the Next Feminist Generation* (Seattle: Seal Press, 1995).

4. See, for example, Ann Brooks, *Postfeminisms: Feminism, Cultural Theory, and Cultural Forms* (London: Routledge, 1997).

5. For the articulation and questioning of this kind of postfeminism, see Natasha Walter, *On the Move: Feminism for a New Generation* (London: Virago Press, 1999).

6. Michèle Barrett, "Words and Things: Materialism and Method in Contemporary Feminist Analysis," in *Destabilizing Theory: Contemporary Feminist Debates*, ed. Michèle Barrett and Anne Phillips (Stanford: Stanford University Press, 1992), pp. 201–19. For a good overview and extension of this argument, see Stevi Jackson, "Feminist Social Theory," in *Contemporary Feminist Theories*, ed. Stevi Jackson and Jackie Jones (New York: New York University Press, 1998), pp. 12–33.

7. See Kate Millett, *Sexual Politics* (Garden City, N.Y.: Doubleday, 1970), and Shulamith Firestone, *The Dialectic of Sex: The Case for Feminist Revolution* (New York: Morrow, 1970). For an overview of the materialist approach, see Annette Kuhn and Anne-Marie Wolpe, eds., *Feminism and Materialism* (London: Routledge & Kegan Paul, 1978).

8. See Gayle Rubin, "The Traffic in Women: Notes on the Political Economy of Sex," in *Toward an Anthropology of Women*, ed. Rayna R. Reiter (New York: Monthly Review Press, 1975), and Catharine MacKinnon, "Feminism, Marxism, Method, and the State: An Agenda for Theory," *Signs* 7, no. 3 (1982): 515–44.

9. Juliet Mitchell, *Psychoanalysis and Feminism* (Harmondsworth, England: Penguin Books, 1974).

10. See, in particular, the journal *m/f*, launched in 1978, ed. Parveen Adams, Beverley Brown, and Elizabeth Cowie.

11. Michel Foucault's *The History of Sexuality*, vol. 1, *An Introduction*, first appeared in English translation in 1978 (New York: Pantheon Books).

12. This exclusion is perhaps most poignantly expressed in the title of the important book *All the Women Are White, All the Blacks Are Men, But Some of Us Are Brave*, ed. Gloria T. Hull, Patricia Bell Scott, and Barbara Smith (Old Westbury, N.Y.: Feminist Press, 1983).

13. Hazel Carby, "White Women Listen! Black Feminism and the Boundaries of Sisterhood," in *The Empire Strikes Back: Race and Racism in '70s Britain*, ed. Centre for Contemporary Culture Studies, University of Birmingham (London: Hutchinson, 1982).

14. Cherrie Moraga and Gloria Anzaldúa, eds., *This Bridge Called My Back* (New York: Kitchen Table, Women of Color Press, 1983).

15. Judith Butler, *Gender Trouble* (New York: Routledge, 1990). For an account of the deconstructive sense in which Butler uses the notion of performance, see the introduction to her *Bodies that Matter: On the Discursive Limits of "Sex"* (New York: Routledge, 1993).

16. For poststructuralist approaches, see, for example, Teresa de Lauretis, "The Technology of Gender," in *Technologies of Gender* (Bloomington: Indiana University

Press, 1987); Jacqueline Rose, "Introduction–II," in *Feminine Sexuality: Jacques Lacan and the école freudienne*, ed. Juliet Mitchell and Jacqueline Rose (New York: Norton, 1985), 27–57; Cora Kaplan, *Sea Changes: Essays on Culture and Feminism* (London: Verso, 1986); and Lois McNay, *Foucault and Feminism: Power, Gender, and the Self* (Boston: Northeastern University Press, 1993).

17. As founding texts, see Gayatri Chakravorty Spivak, *In Other Worlds: Essays in Cultural Politics* (New York: Routledge, 1987), and Trinh T. Minh-ha, *Woman Native Other: Writing, Postcoloniality, and Feminism* (Bloomington: Indiana University Press, 1989).

18. See, for instance, Eve Kosofsky Sedgwick's use of the term "nonhomosexual-identified man" in "The Beast in the Closet," in *The Epistemology of the Closet* (Berkeley: University of California Press, 1990), pp. 182–212. This kind of terminology has made room for the conceptualization of all kinds of transsexual and transgender identifications, such as the male-identified lesbian or even the gay-identified heterosexual; see, for example, Judith Halberstam, "F2M: The Making of Female Masculinity," in *Literary Theory: An Anthology*, ed. Julie Rivkin and Michael Ryan (Oxford: Blackwell, 1998), pp. 759–68.

19. Linda M. G. Zerilli, "Doing Without Knowing: Feminism's Politics of the Ordinary," *Political Theory* 26, no. 4 (August 1998): 438.

20. Donna Haraway has been instrumental in expanding the notion of what could be considered "feminist" work. See her *Simians, Cyborgs, and Women* (London: Free Association Books, 1990).

Feminist Consequences

PART 1

Whatever Happened to Feminism?

Chapter 1

Psychoanalysis and Feminism
at the Millennium

JULIET MITCHELL

In the last two decades there has been an untold gain in the understanding of the psychological and representational effects of sexual difference. Yet despite this, the *politics* of the original feminist turn to psychoanalysis for a means of analysis of the internalization of women's secondary status seems finally to have run out in the sands of postmodernism. Is there something inherently apolitical in psychoanalysis? Does its self-described nonpolitical discourse draw all hopefully radical uses of it (of which there are other instances than feminism) into its apolitical, therefore potentially reactionary net? Alternatively does the recurrent, cyclical demise of feminism tempo-rally turn a radical investigatory mode, which is psychoanalysis, apolitical? Or both?

Even if articulate feminism predates psychoanalysis by at least a hundred years there is a way in which they are bedfellows. This complicates the question of politics. The contemporary relative inactivity of political fem-

inism is matched by its successful proliferation and assimilation into a natural discourse. The same is true of psychoanalysis. In both cases the weak-
ening of the radicalism of the center is the strengthening of the margins
of each. Radical, white, heterosexual feminism has become, as it were, third
world, black, or lesbian feminism; radical, heterosexual psychoanalysis has
become homosexual/lesbian psychoanalysis. Once separate, they can each
assume a new radicalism. These margins belong only to their own enterprises—there is rarely a shared constituency between, say, third world feminism and an interest in radicalizing psychoanalysis. It would seem to be
their conjuncture that draws both to a hegemonic-conservative center. This
observation suggests that an inherently conservative pull within each might
reflect something they share. The most obvious candidate would be some
conservative force within their overlapping provenance of sexuality. This
would go sharply against the frequent observation that psychoanalysis
becomes conservative when various developments within it (such as Jun-
gianism) drop the emphasis on sexuality in the hopes of making it more
acceptable. Yet, there is in fact suggestive evidence that sexuality may be the
conservative candidate in the epidemic reduction of both feminism and
psychoanalytic psychotherapy to a shared concern with whether or not
recovered memories of sexual abuse are true or false. The Recovered (or
False) Memory movements indicate that something inherently apolitical
about sexuality comes to the fore when there is an alliance of this kind. It
is not that the issue of abuse is not crucial—it clearly is. The problem is how
to make sure that the "personal is the political." All too easily it is the political that becomes the personal, with all the dangers of witch-hunting that
that implies.

There is a further contributory reflection: if both psychoanalysis and
feminism have become in-turned and self-reflective and hence conservative
in the West, another trajectory can be charted in former socialist countries.
In these there is a rising tide of interest in both feminism and psychoanalysis, as well as in sexual exploitation. Indeed the timing of this is sufficient to
make one wonder nervously if Lenin were not correct to castigate a concern with sexual emancipation, psychoanalysis, and feminism as bourgeois
enterprises. That, however, would not only be too simple but would also
only return us to its vulgarization in certain Marxist reactions against all
three. This reaction was clearly utterly inadequate, unacceptable, and unpro-
ductive. It was a part of a masculinist ideology that drew the line against anything other than production and its allied social requirements as outside the

bounds of political thought and action. The previous socialist regimes did not offer a theoretical space in which to articulate sexual difference. The official absence of discrimination militated against understanding its pervasive existence. That capitalism provides such a space is crucially important. It is no less important that this space of sexual difference opened up by capitalism is occupied by sexual exploitation, feminism, and an interest in psychoanalysis. Capitalism opens up the private but simultaneously closes the door on it as being outside the body politic. Sexuality, feminism, and psychoanalysis all march into this new area of privacy. But more than this, the ungendered citizen and worker in relation to the state occupied what space there was. Political feminism has to open the door to this—the original use of psychoanalysis was as an aid to finding the key. If the private is *not* made political, then it is a space of conservatism.

The second wave feminist turn to psychoanalysis, at least in France, England, Italy, Scandinavia, and the United States, came from a broad range of socialist concerns. In England and America the first questions addressed to psychoanalytic theory were not about sexuality but about kinship, the family, and ideology. The general context, however, in which those questions were asked was the sexual liberation of the sixties. An obvious common denominator of psychoanalysis and feminism was the place of sexuality. The original feminist enterprise became largely forgotten in the hegemonic seductions of the sexual and the representational. In the meantime there have been significant changes in Western family patterns that make the original enterprise pertinent, unless, that is, there is something inherent within "psychoanalysis and feminism" that prevents it contributing to an analysis that can be politically radical.

A Brief History: The War and Postwar Period

When it came into being during the sixties, second wave feminism inherited a situation in which the growth of what I will call "psychological motherhood" had helped to implement, indeed to promote, a postwar ideology of femininity as domestic, nurturant, expressive, intuitive, and so on—and, of course, their negatives. Psychoanalysis had been used by sociologists such as Urie Brofenbrenner in America to supplement the Parsonian functional account of the family. This argued for the need for an instrumental father negotiating the private/public divide and a mother providing the ground plan within the private sphere for emotional stability that would ensure boys would make good worker/fathers and girls good wife/mothers. British psychoanalytic object relations theory, save for a token acknowledgment of this father, focused almost exclusively on the mother's tasks and the baby's needs and emotions.

The situation in France was complicated by the oppositional role of Jacques Lacan. Lacan, returning to the radicalism of Freud, challenged Freudian orthodoxy within France but even more strongly was involved in a battle against the pervasiveness of ego psychology, particularly as it had developed within the United States. Emergent feminist analysts sided with Lacan before they deplored the phallocentrism of his reworking of Freudian theory.

The postwar use of psychoanalysis in Britain—on which I shall focus— was a humanist concern, yet some of its results were ultimately ideologically reactionary and stultifying for women. This was missed because of the combination of an unusual measure of gender equality within the psychoanalytical institutions and the overwhelming value placed on motherhood in the theory and clinical practice. The massive wartime evacuation of mothers and infants, and of children with their class teachers out of the bombed cities to the countryside shook received wisdom about families and social class. In brief, the assumption had been that improved physical conditions would be welcomed, most particularly by the poor. Until the Second World War the family was not regarded as universally important; in fact one aspect of the ideology of the family at the time almost translates into the equation that the well-to-do and the aspirant well-to-do had families while the poor had class or race. As it turned out, evacuated children overwhelmingly missed their homes, however impoverished or even dangerous these may have been. The subtle, painstaking, and thoughtful interviews of the children, analysis of the interviews, observations of behavior, interpretation of behavior, and theoretical postulates that resulted from this empirical work led to an obvious but highly problematic conclusion that still haunts us today: that in all but the most abusive situations, the family was best. There was a democratization in which everybody could and should have families. The later reaction against this must be set within this context.

The idea that the family was best was not incorrect on the obvious grounds that it was the wrong conclusion. In other words, the problem is not simply that quite clearly some families are not the best environment for their members. Rather, it was the wrong conclusion on the more radical ground that this answer missed the import of the discovery: why do children (and later it was realized this also applied to women) prefer bad families to no families? What makes a child run back to an abusive parent? And furthermore, do they continue to prefer them? The mistake was that familiarity was equated with the family and an important opportunity to test both the significance of loss and the longer-term success of adaptation to change was missed. Reading the reports today makes it clear that the distressed evacuees would seem to have been missing the all-inclusive familiar "home" rather than the specificity of the nuclear family. This is not to underestimate the significance of mothers and fathers but to suggest that they do not come alone nor only in one shape and size.

Despite the absence of depth or longitudinal research on the evacuee material, the conclusion was drawn that an infant and even a child needed a mother's attention twenty-four hours a day. This infantile need now seems so axiomatic to us that we forget how historically specific is its assumption. Because the thesis was tied in with so many humanistic and democratic reforms, questioning it was, and to an extent still is, difficult. When it was challenged by second wave feminism, it was completely inverted rather than questioned; initially, radical feminism, in particular, saw to it that the mother was thrown out with the bath water.

British psychoanalytical work, then, saw the family and within this the "good-enough" mother as crucial. Nonmedical and thus lay and women analysts were important in the psychoanalytical institutions in England. (There was a quota system operating strongly against women in medical schools, making the openness of psychotherapy training attractive.) The wartime and postwar contexts together with the predominance of women analysts who originated from a pedagogic and /or social welfare background meant that the emphasis on motherhood as psychologically crucial both for women and for babies was far greater in Britain than it was elsewhere.

In America the psychoanalytical profession was by law exclusively medical/psychiatric; it was thus male-dominated. What minimal interest there was in maternity came up against what was perceived to have been a problem with American soldiers: postwar America became obsessed by the undesirable prevalence of effete "Momism" amongst its should-be heroes. The analysis offered was that the apparently dependent, shallow personality resulted from a too indulgent mother and an insufficiently strong father. The absence of the father's protective, authoritative stance entailed that it had not been internalized as an ethical superego. American ego psychology thus emphasized the importance of the father where British object relations focused on the mother.

France had been occupied during the war. The psychoanalytical organizations had resisted the German attempt to enable them to "rescue" psychoanalysis by discarding their Jewish members. Some members had gone into exile, others had practiced in a reduced private capacity, others were killed, and a few joined the Resistance. When after the war it emerged from its dispersed or subterranean existence, it was to a psychoanalytic world dominated by the diverse but hegemonic ideologies of American practice. However, it brought its past with it. A list of the chapter headings of Elizabeth Roudinesco's *History of Psychoanalysis in France* gives us a flavor of this past: "Surrealism in the Service of Psychoanalysis"; "Marxism, Psychoanalysis, Psychology"; "Writers, Literati, Dream-Devourers"; "Jacques Lacan: A Novel of his Youth." Such a history could not, by any stretch of the imagination, be transposed to the Anglo-Saxon scene. Already political and literary, French psychoanalysis in its more radical versions just left women out of the picture. Jacques Lacan, however, had written on the family and spent some weeks in postwar London, where, strangely, he was impressed by the social engagement of British psychoanalysis. During this period of his temporary appreciation of things English, Lacan's contempt for American ego psychology intensified.

In Britain and the United States the fifties saw the war and postwar radical observations of infants and children institutionalized in a profoundly conservative and inflexible ideological form: the married (two parents), two-children (first a boy and then a girl) nuclear family. Backed by psychoanalytical work, the emphasis of sociological work was on a notional parity of different roles within the couple. The psychoanalyst John Bowlby, who had been involved in United Nations studies of maternal deprivation, turned to ethology to urge the need of mother and child for each other, with the mother offering day and night attention, as fixed forever in "nature." These ideologies did not operate in France, but in France anxiety about a chronically low birth rate led to the emplacement of many provisions to encourage and assist maternity.

However, in all the countries and overwhelmingly in Britain the demands of the economy were in unacknowledged but sharp contradiction to the promulgation of the particular fifties nuclear family as idea and practice. Although economic expansion was a stop-go affair, the dips in so-called "full-employment" were mere dimples: the economy wanted workers—whether immigrants, "foreign workers," or women.

A brief and reductive account of women's position in three of the countries where feminism was to engage prominently with psychoanalysis would run thus: the war had demanded women's work; a working woman is nevertheless disruptive of the ideology of the gender status quo. Psychoanalysis in Britain engaged with the effects of wartime disruption by producing the answer that social problems were to do with maternal deprivation that could only be remedied in the married close family. Just as after World War I, so after World War II women vacated the jobs in favor of returning soldiers and identified themselves as mothers and as wives. (Immigrants were brought in from the colonies for the leftover jobs.) For a number of reasons, by the late fifties the demand was once again for women's work and this produced the concept of "women's two roles": home-maker and paid worker.

A further factor needs to be included. Viola Klein, a sociologist using psychoanalysis and one of the few postwar scholars with an interest in women in the years before second wave feminism, argued that where once productive work was seen as a necessary evil, since the fifties work had become equivalent to one's identity.[1] If work was identity, then how could women be left out? I myself do not think that there was such a smooth transition, but Viola Klein was observing an important trend. Perhaps even more markedly in America, one was the job one did and the money one made. Certainly in epochs when, and cultures where, humanity's self-image is thus equated with activity—either mental or physical—it would seem to be more deeply marked by masculinity than when it is not. It is in such contexts that feminism arises to demand a share for women in this masculinized humanity; Mary Wollstonecraft claiming "reason" and Simone de Beauvoir the transcendence of immanence through "projects" are obvious examples. If work did become one's identity in the postwar period, then women confined to the family were living another contradiction: told to be mothers and wives, they were also "told" that these were no identities. Psychoanalysis stepped in to help: either, as in the case of ego psychology, to create these absent identities (essentially women were advised to adapt to the role of wife and mother and the personality would follow suit) or to confirm the absence of identity—as with Lacan's famous statement, "there is no such thing as the woman."

The contradiction of an idealized motherhood in a nuclear family with a labor market demanding women's work, the contradiction of an ideology that glorified femininity but made it empty of content in a world where identity was the paid work one did were both important forces behind second wave feminism. There were, then, two contradictions that came to a head in the sixties.

The Rise of Second Wave Feminism

In America, in practice and theory, psychoanalysis was, and is, a heterogeneous affair. But insofar as it was absorbed into the dominant culture it was as the practice of advising adaptation inherent in ego psychology. America was also hell-bent on leading psychoanalysis internationally. In England object relations was pursuing its subtle observations of mother-and-baby relations largely untouched by changing social realities. At the beginning of the sixties, opposition arose from the group around R. D. Laing. The ideal of the nuclear family was turned on its head; it was seen as a charnel house for the murder of the infant's "true self" and the hysterogenic or schizophrenogenic mother played a central role in the psychic devastation. Idealization had flipped to denigration. In France Lacan was waging a battle against ego psychology and orthodoxy both on the international and the French home front.

French feminism could initially ally itself with the oppositional Lacan. In England some use could be made of Laingian attacks on the family, but only at the cost of denigrating mothers—and hence women. Only in America could there be no alliance with an oppositional psychoanalysis. Not surprisingly, the earliest American feminist approaches to psychoanalysis were virulently hostile. Friedan, Millet, Firestone, Greer (Australian) attacked Freud as a representative of the patriarchy that relegated women to problematic motherhood and saw them as defined and represented by the absence of a sexual organ: the female eunuch. There were two very different, indigenous oppositional uses of psychoanalysis that were later to attract feminism: that of the emigrés from the Frankfurt School and that of Hollywood. But above all, American feminism revolted against its home-grown plant and turned to use either British object relations or Lacan and subsequently French feminism.

Despite these important national differences, there was a unifying theme. By the sixties psychoanalysis had bestowed a triple heritage of psychological understanding of women: the place of woman as mother in the family, representations of femininity, and the construction of female sexuality. This was the situation when second wave feminism emerged out of and alongside other radical movements in the latter part of the 1960s.

For women the sexual revolution of the sixties was a "world historical event" of the absolute separation of sexuality from reproduction through the pill and legalized abortion. In sexual-reproductive "theories" it was the heyday of clitoral sexuality—the exposure of the so-called Freudian myth of the vaginal orgasm and of babies as a woman's definition and destiny. Although in the sixties there were still a surprisingly large number of equal rights to be acquired, it was also evident that something over and beyond their achievement or failure of achievement relegated women to remaining the second sex. Rights had been acknowledged but not realized; what handicapped their realization? Women could no longer be defined by their statutory, legal, economic, vocational, sexual, educational, nor now sexual-reproductive deprivations, so it seemed that femininity itself must be a deprivation. What marked women's difference from men that produced this difference as deference? It was with this question—the question of what is femininity—that the tide turned.

From wherever feminists stood, they took up and developed the potential within the oppositional psychoanalytic perspectives. Thus the first positive use of psychoanalysis in America was an exploration by Chodorow, Dinnerstein, Benjamin, and others of British object relations theory with its maternal focus that, from the standpoint of American ego psychology and its patriarchal adaptational perspective, gave a welcome place to women. However, in England the focus on the family as a monolithic cave or grave for women either in the idealization (Bowlby) or the denigration (Laing/Cooper) of the mother was not where feminism wanted to be; instead we turned to Lacan. Lacan's rereading of Freud seemed to explain why women were hidden from history—why "the" woman did not exist. But in France women soon turned from Lacan to expose this conceptualization of woman as "absence" as the rhetoric of Western metaphysics (Irigaray) or to explore the pre-Oedipal territory on which British object relations had also discovered woman as "presence" (Kristeva). This work was then picked up transatlantically. The rereading of texts, above all literary and cinematic, exposed the dominance of the logos—the rational, the present, in short, the masculine—as the triumphal march of Western discourse. The logos as dominant revealed that the "other" must be repressed within. The texts of psychoanalysis themselves were read with the same brilliant scrutiny. Binary oppositions—

male/female, nature/culture—were never innocent of hierarchy. The binary itself was put in the stocks.

Toward Postmodernism

This obvious attack on the binary and the elevation of the concept of difference undercut the original feminist project in which sexual difference established to the detriment of women was constructed as one side of a binary opposition. The resultant postmodern critique of essentialism and, within the proposition of the binary, universalism entailed the implication that all previous feminism belonged to prehistory. Psychoanalysis, which had explored the binary, was criticized with the aid of new psychoanalytic insights that emphasized that all is different. "Différance" (Derrida's neologism from "difference" and "deferral"), no longer considered a product of binary division, was now considered to be repressed within an economy of "sameness." A theory of difference facilitates a practice of difference both empirically and politically. Hence postmodern feminism is a politics of relevant fragmentation. This is not in itself apolitical, but clearly, in such theoretical conditions, the center cannot hold. With no central concern, political practices must be localized or nonexistent. This is, of course, a reductive account. My concern is with the interrelationship of feminism and psychoanalysis and therefore with a selection of the parallels between them.

Where there were once the grand "modernist" schema of the Oedipus complex and the castration complex, there are now myriads of differential clinical observations and a reluctance to draw out from these any overarching schema. In one sense this shift is progressive. A return of the repressed, of femininity as what constitutes that which is different from within the sameness of masculinity, must be welcomed. However, it makes femininity dangerously analogous to a symptom. It also can rapidly descend into truism. When the notion of difference descends from the theoretical heights to the empirical lowlands, its limitations come to the fore. Did the project of psychoanalysis and feminism imply this end product?

The question of kinship that feminism had initially addressed to psychoanalysis arose first from the actual position of women and then from Marxism or, more particularly, from Engels via Althusser, who had been called in to help construct an understanding of why every analysis of sexual difference consigns women to the family but effectively leaves it at that. Engels's argument was based on anthropological work on kinship. The feminist concern returned it to that via psychoanalysis. How can feminism understand the family from the viewpoint of women? Freudian theory offered an explanation of how the sexes constructed and lived themselves differently. The premise was the differential effects of the Oedipus and castration complexes. This is not a theory of why one group is dominant over another; it is a theory about how that dominance is lived at the lowest, most generalized, common denominator. Hence it is possibly a very generalized theory of ideology in the Althusserian sense of "how one lives in the world," but that "living" only takes place within the different contexts that will show how oppression takes place.

The context of kinship was quickly ignored, and the focus was all on femininity and female sexuality. Retrospectively, the positive turning toward psychoanalysis by feminists became dominated by the issue of sexuality and sexual difference—as though in that difference was to be found an explanation of oppression. It was this project that was then criticized for its universalism. To combat the universalism, the difference within the similarity of groups of women came to the fore. Women became the problem of each other. It is at this point that the *politics* of the enterprise was short-circuited.

It is impossible to understand the oppression of women through an understanding of sexual difference. Even if Freud and Lacan have demonstrated that a repudiation of femininity is basic to humankind, it would be putting the cart before the horse and be the worst kind of psychological determinism to see this as the *cause* of oppression—although effect it may well be. The original project of seeing how women and men lived sexual difference within the specifics of diverse family and kinship groups had difference built into it. How difference became deference is another question. Is what is constituted different always the point of deference? Certainly this has been argued to be the case. Is femininity always constituted as the different? This, too, has been argued. If women are predominantly, but not exclusively, the occupants of the place of difference, then they occupy the place that is constituted inferior. No one wants that. This, however, is not the same argument as one that issues from a fundamental repudiation of femininity as such.

Contexts, however diverse, can have something in common. That commonality was contained in the notion of oppression. I am not here giving any brief for the term "oppression." It was deployed as an interim term by those on the Left who wished to recognize that the subjugation of many social groups was not coincident with exploitation. Unlike exploitation, which is clearly defined and specific, oppression is a term empty of definitional content, a term still, as it were, awaiting its own conceptualization. But in that waiting for feminism to conceptualize it, it got somewhat lost.

What happened instead was that because the Freud-Lacan account explained how sexual difference was established as denigration on the side of the feminine, that explanation substituted for an explanation of oppression. The lack that is psychologically ascribed to women became treated as an actual lack (despite Lacan's claim that "there is no lack in the real"). The psychological mode of oppression was taken as the cause of oppression. What might have been a politically useful search for a commonality of different contexts became instead, as so-called universalism, the target of an overarching criticism.

Most cultures in many contexts denigrate or idealize the category "women" and some oppress the members of that category through the use of that category. Psychoanalysis offers a particular and partial explanation of how that category is constructed. The denigratory aspect of the category is general, the oppressive realization diverse. Denigration and idealization are two sides of the same coin, so that the category "woman" may be treated either way or the category itself may be internally divided. The universalism is only the universalism of the category "woman" (or "man" or "house" or "cloud"); it is not what it was made to become—the suggestion that women's oppression was universally the same. Quite obviously it is not. Deriving the category of femininity from psychoanalysis and then analyzing the manifestations of the category both in the texts of psychoanalysis and in others entailed presenting the category back to psychoanalysis. In one sense, in that the manifestations are limitless, so are the gains in insight. But this can only be a proliferation of the endless diversity with which a universal category expresses itself. In this proliferation of differences we can see the opening toward postmodernism as a critique of the universal.

However, in order to contribute to an understanding of oppression, the thinking needed to be the other way around. As the psychiatrist-anthropologist W. H. R. Rivers with regard to another issue put it, one should not take the concept of revenge to a blood feud but, rather, look at the blood feud to understand revenge.[2] Hence the political aim had been to look at the specificities of family or kin forms to understand femininity, which in and of itself was as abstract (but as necessary as a category) as revenge.

Once the psychoanalytic understanding of the construction of female sexuality and femininity is deployed as the object of feminist analysis something happens both to the politics of feminism and to the use of psychoanalysis. Without a material context that would use and criticize its hypothesis, the politics of the alliance of feminism and psychoanalysis had to come from elsewhere; it could not be intrinsic to the project.

To a certain extent, those who have used object relations theory to show how the family becomes internalized and thus disadvantages women have managed to look at femininity within a material context. In a sense, although the idiom and intention is very different, the work could be seen as following through from Shulamith Firestone, who at the beginning of second wave feminism argued that psychoanalysis with its explanation of the Oedipus complex was just a failed feminism.[3] In this argument, a girl becomes like her mother and, as maternity is wrongly valued, women's oppression is perpetuated from one generation to the next. The problem with this project is that mental life becomes simply reflective of social life. In fact, neither mental life nor ideology can be neatly reflective. Feminist therapies also demonstrate this reflective practice. Such accounts also prevent us seeing the contradictions within those social conditions. Motherhood is highly valued in some contexts but not in others.

The other option for a political use of a psychoanalytic concept of femininity is to perceive both psychoanalysis and feminism as having been rowing the same oppositional boat. Swindells and Jardine have outstandingly demonstrated that this is what has happened with the feminist use of Lacanian analysis. They trace the lineage of the argument that British intellectual culture had always excluded psychoanalysis and this exclusion meant that "the psychoanalytic project has to be understood as a radical one."[4] However, there is an irony here: though a Freudian culture may not have been naturalized in Britain, an "object relations" culture that put the mother at the center of family life and of psychological growth was so fully a part and parcel of British intellectual life as to be completely in conformity with it. Psychoanalysis may have been excluded from other political discourses and this exclusion may have made it potentially radical on issues such as peace and disarmament. However, on the nuclear family, on issues of single parenting, on heterosexuality and homosexuality, and on women's place in general—exactly where one needs a feminist analysis—its contribution was not excluded but was in fact mainstream, and the results are both doctrinaire and in the vanguard of conformity.

Women as active practitioners and theorists, and the mother as the centerpiece, made object relations theory and practice seem and feel egalitarian. But without a feminist politics, what was in fact happening was that women were undertaking to theorize their own sphere as an enclave within the larger world. This sphere was motherhood, set up as all-fulfilling, something everyone envies. With an uncritical use of object relations theory, feminism can only buy into it, certainly benefiting from its profound insights but failing to perceive its cruel exclusions and its force for conservatism. The Western family is changing. Western societies are experiencing escalating single motherhood, lesbian and homosexual parenting, serial monogamy, and extended "reconstituted" families.

Women are offered (and subscribe to) either the "plenitude" of the family or the status of "absence" from the world of men. In the work of Lacan that "absence" found its theory. But by buying into Lacanianism at this point of absence, feminism can only gain access to a self-fulfilling prophecy. The trouble with this theory is that, though women must not be content to be "lacking," they can, as always, only "complain" or be "discontented" about this, the fate of femininity.

Psychoanalysis is not and has never claimed to be a political discourse. Feminism is nothing if it is not this. As a political practice in search of a political theory, it can use concepts and arguments from elsewhere to analyze its own object—the position of women—in the relevant contexts, but it cannot convert these concepts and arguments into political ones in and of themselves. In isolating female sexuality and femininity as the shared terrain of psychoanalysis and feminism, feminism inevitably gets drawn into the necessary apoliticism of psychoanalysis. The dominant strand of feminism selected the object of psychoanalysis as its own political object—this was, and is, a mistake. Of course, femininity and female sexuality are part of the position of women in various given situations—but not in isolation from these. Psychoanalysis, as we can see from the propagation of motherhood, does not contextualize. Any political practice must, by definition, contextualize—how else can political mobilization be contemplated, let alone achieved?

The controversies of the last decade as to universalism versus specificity are beside the point: the context will dictate whether a universal (all colonized . . . all women . . . all oppressed . . .) or a particular frame of reference is the appropriate one. Femininity and female sexuality defined by psychoanalysis, against male sexuality and masculinity, were important aspects of a feminist thrust of the seventies that argued the oppression of all women under patriarchal dominance. Its task was to create a generic identity without which no political practice makes sense. There was no way in which this difference between the sexes could be extended to include all women or all men as psychosocial groups. So thereafter, to make female sexuality or femininity of itself an object of analysis was inevitably to depoliticize it, to remove it from the political question of the general sexual difference that it addressed. This move of feminism was analogous to that of psychoanalytic object relations theory, which dealt with motherhood outside and beyond any context save that of the individual.

With femininity, female sexuality, and motherhood all on some timeless plateau, depoliticization was inevitable. The postmodern assertion of the plurality of femininities could only come into its own once the situation had been de-politicized. However, also often without contexts, this call to arms of the narcissism of petty differences appears only as the other side of the coin of universalism. The context—for the West—of powerfully changing family forms needs to be put in place.

NOTES

1. See Alva Reimer Myrdal and Viola Klein, *Women's Two Roles: Home and Work* (London: Routledge and Paul, 1956), and Klein's early work in Viola Klein, *The Feminine Character: History of an Ideology* (London: Kegan Paul, Trench, and Trubner, 1946).

2. W. H. R. Rivers, *Psychology and Ethnology* (London: Kegan Paul, Trench, and Trubner, 1926).

3. Shulamith Firestone, *The Dialectic of Sex: The Case for Feminist Revolution* (New York: Morrow, 1970).

4. Julia Swindells and Lisa Jardine, *What's Left? Women in Culture and the Labour Movement* (London: Routledge, 1989).

Chapter 2

Feminist Accused of Sexual Harassment

JANE GALLOP

1. Feminist Accused of Sexual Harassment

I am a feminist professor who was accused by two students of sexual harassment. This [work] is centered on that fact: the title is modeled after the style of tabloid headlines because of the way this fact lends itself to sensationalism. While any accusation of sexual harassment seems to promise a juicy scandal, this particular accusation is more sensational due to the newsworthy anomaly of a feminist being so accused. While sexual harassment is customarily a feminist issue, feminists usually appear on the accusers' side. For a feminist to be the accused is a dramatic reversal.

What kind of a feminist would be accused of sexual harassment?

Excerpted from Jane Gallop, *Feminist Accused of Sexual Harassment* (Durham, N.C.: Duke University Press, 1997).

I became a feminist early in 1971. It was, of course, the big moment for feminist awakenings, for young women around the country, around the world. At the time, we called it "women's liberation." Historians who remembered the women's movement of the nineteenth century called it "the second wave." And, although we baby-boomers didn't think we were second to anyone or anything, it certainly was a wave, washing over my generation, soaking us through and through in a new understanding of who we were and what we could become, changing us forever.

I was halfway through college at the time. I did college in three years, in a special post-Sputnik program that recruited promising high-school kids from around the country and stream-lined requirements to race us through; 1970–71 was the second of my three years, and I remember it all happening very fast, in a wonderful, dizzying jumble.

I was reading the books which everyone seemed to be reading, books not assigned for any course. I remember three in particular: Simone de Beauvoir's *Second Sex*, Kate Millett's *Sexual Politics*, and Shulamith Firestone's *Dialectic of Sex*. Serious, intellectual books, not unlike the books I was reading for courses. But because these were chosen, not assigned, read for reasons of social peer pressure and adolescent desire, they seemed very different.

The books were a big part of it, but I wasn't just reading, I was also going to meetings. Meetings of various sorts of women's groups, both on campus and downtown at the Women's Center. I don't remember the names of the groups or the purposes of the meetings, but I remember the feel of it all: the sense of being part of a community of women, the busy calendar, the sociability, the desire to belong, and my attraction to the strength and beauty of some of the women who went to the meetings.

The books and the meetings are inextricably jumbled together in my memory of that hectic period. There, on the fringes of my college education, I experienced an exhilarating mix of private reading and social community, which I would call learning, in the strongest sense of that word. Not only did it change me, but it vastly improved my life then and there in two essential and entwined ways.

Despite my academic "promise," which had gotten me into the fast-track foundation-funded experimental program, I was a poor student my first year of college. I got mediocre grades, did a minimum of work with little enthusiasm, cut classes, and either watched late late movies on TV or played bridge all night. My second year of school, I became a feminist, and I became a good student. Despite all the meetings, the social and political gatherings, I spent more time on my homework and attended classes more regularly. My senior year, I wrote an honor's thesis and really threw myself into that work, caring deeply about it. Somehow, feminism had made it possible for me to take my schoolwork seriously.

Freshman year, my disaffection as a student was matched by my sexual passivity. As a good soldier in the sexual revolution, I had sex often, but little pleasure and no orgasms. Although I fervently wished that all these young men I bedded would fall in love with me, all my wishing and hoping wasn't really desire.

Thanks to feminism, not only did I become a better student, but my sex life improved. In January 1971 I read de Beauvoir's *Second Sex*, learned that women could masturbate, and had my first orgasm. For me, that sea change will always be a central part of what "women's liberation" means. In no way did I lose interest in sex with other people, but now that meant bringing my sexuality into an encounter, rather than hoping some man could endow me with sexuality. I credit feminism with teaching me sexual pleasure.

Not only pleasure but also desire. A vocal if small lesbian presence was integral to the women's community on campus; this diffuse presence made the entire community seem a space of sexual possibility. I had the hots for so many of the energetic young women who went to the same meetings as I. While I actually slept with very few of them, these attractions introduced me to the feel of desire. Whereas my adolescent boy-craziness had filled me with romantic fantasies of love, when I thought about the women at the meetings I burned to touch their bodies. I walked around that year constantly in heat, energized for political activity and school work; I learned that desire, even desire unacted upon, can make you feel very powerful. And the space where I learned desire—where it filled me with energy and drive—I call feminism.

I had been a "sexually active" young woman who was, ironically, neither sexual nor active but rather awash in romance and passivity. I had been a supposedly smart girl who was deeply alienated from her own desire for knowledge. Within one whirlwind year I came into a sense of my sexual power, of my sexuality as drive and energy. In that very same year I became an active, engaged student committed to knowing as much and as well as possible. I speak of these as if they were two transformations, but they are actually two aspects of the same transformation. One and the same change made me both an engaged, productive student and a sexually energized, sexually confident woman. The disaffected, romantic, passive young woman I had been gained access simultaneously to real learning and to an active sexuality. One achievement cannot be separated from the other.

This double transformation was my personal experience of what we then called "women's liberation." This access to learning and to pleasure will always be the root meaning, my most powerful personal sense of feminism. I know there are many people for whom feminism is the opposite of sexy. And even that there are many people who presume feminism to be anti-intellectual. But for me feminism will always name the force which freed me to desire and to learn.

My initial and formative experience of feminism was this entry into a milieu bubbling indiscriminately with ideas and lusts. *Feminism turned me on*, figuratively and literally: my body and my mind began firing, pulsing with energy, an energy that did not distinguish between mind and body. Feminism made me feel sexy and smart; feminism felt smart and very sexy. When I call myself a feminist, as I have for 25 years, I necessarily refer to that milieu where knowledge and sex bubble together, to that possible community, to that possibility for women.

Perhaps that is what makes me the kind of feminist who gets accused of sexual harassment. . . .

Feminist sexual harasser seems like a contradiction in terms. I find myself positioned at the center of this contradiction. Although the position has been personally quite uncomfortable, professionally I can see it as a rare vantage point, an opportunity to produce knowledge. I have long suspected that a contradiction in terms might present an occasion to confront and rethink the terms themselves.

As a feminist theorist of sexuality, I consider it my business to understand sexual harassment. And so I'd like to take advantage of my peculiar position as an accused harasser to provide a fresh feminist view of the issue. Theorizations of harassment generally focus on what is clearly the classic scenario: the male boss uses his professional clout to force himself upon a female subordinate—sleep with me or you'll lose your job, sleep with me and you'll get a raise, a promotion. Rather than refer to this classic case, I want to produce an understanding of sexual harassment based instead upon the limit case of a feminist so accused.

The classic scenario is explicit and quid pro quo (demand for sex in exchange for professional support). The concept of harassment also includes more implicit forms, where the sexual demand or the professional threat is not stated but understood. Implicit sexual demands might ultimately include any charged talk or behavior; implicit professional threats could possibly cover the entire range of professional interaction. While these possibilities are already potentially limitless, the range of harassment is expanding in still other directions. Harassment need not be perpetrated by bosses; peers can harass, even subordinates. And gender can be a variable: increasing numbers of cases involve a man claiming to have been harassed or a woman accused of harassment.

The classic scenario—easy to recognize and deplore as sexual harassment—expands its application in every direction. I want to ground my theorizing in a limit case precisely because I believe that there should be limits to this bloated general application. I hope that my example can expose the limitations of loose analogies and impede this rampant expansion of the concept of sexual harassment.

Feminism has a special relation to sexual harassment. One could in fact say that feminism invented sexual harassment. Not of course the behavior itself, which presumably has gone on as long as men have held power over women. But, until feminism named it, the behavior had no official existence. In the mid-seventies, feminism got women to compare notes on their difficulties in the workplace; it came out that women employees all too frequently had to cope with this sort of thing. Feminism named this behavior "sexual harassment" and proceeded to make it illegal.

Today the general public knows that sexual harassment consists of some form of unwanted sexual advances and that it is some sort of crime. Inevitably people assume that it is sex which makes harassment criminal. Feminism's interest in prosecuting harassment is then chalked up to feminism's supposed hostility to sex.

But, whatever may be the feelings of individual feminists, feminism is not in principle a movement against sexuality. It is, in principle and in fact, against the disadvantaging of women. Sexual harassment is a feminist issue not because it is sexual but because it disadvantages women. Because harassment makes it harder for women to earn a living, feminists declared it a form of discrimination against women. This framing was so persuasive that, within a few years, harassment was added to the legal definition of sex discrimination. Since discrimination on the basis of sex was already illegal, once included within the category of discrimination, harassment immediately became a crime. Sexual harassment is criminal not because it is sex but because it is discrimination.

When I was charged with sexual harassment, the accusations were made on official university forms which bore the heading "COMPLAINT OF DISCRIMINATION." Under that heading, the students filed formal complaints against me, checking the box marked "Sexual Harassment." This form includes twelve such boxes, each pertaining to a type of discrimination (race or color, sex, national origin, etc.). The form itself makes it clear that harassment is treated as a subspecies of the general wrong, discrimination.

After reviewing the evidence and interviewing the witnesses, the university officer who investigated the charges against me was convinced that I had not in fact discriminated—not against women, not against men, not on the basis of sexual orientation, not on any basis whatsoever. She believed that my pedagogical practices had been, as she put it, applied in a consistent manner. Yet she nonetheless thought I probably was guilty of sexual harassment.

When it is possible to conceive of sexual harassment without discrimination, then sexual harassment becomes a crime of sexuality rather than of discrimination. There is, in fact, a recent national trend toward findings of sexual harassment where there is no discrimination. This represents a significant departure from the feminist formulation of harassment.

Although the shock value of my case resides in the supposition that it is impossible to be both a feminist and a harasser, the spectacle fascinates because it suggests the possibility that a feminist *could* be a sexual harasser—which would mean that either feminism or sexual harassment (maybe even both) are not what we assumed they were. A feminist sexual harasser is no longer a contradiction in terms; rather, it is the sign of an issue drifting from its feminist frame.

I was construed a sexual harasser because I sexualize the atmosphere in which I work. When sexual harassment is defined as the introduction of sex into professional relations, it becomes quite possible to be both a feminist and a sexual harasser.

The classic harassment scenario clearly involves both discrimination against women and sexualization of professional relations. Because people always refer to that classic case, it has been assumed that sexualizing the workplace is automatically disadvantageous to women. But if we base our thinking in the more exotic possibility of a feminist sexualizer, these two aspects of harassment no longer fit so neatly together. And sexualizing is not necessarily to women's disadvantage.

It is no coincidence that I happen to be both a feminist and someone whose professional relations are sexualized. It is because of the sort of feminist I am that I do not respect the line between the intellectual and the sexual. Central to my commitment as a feminist teacher is the wish to transmit the experience which brought me as a young woman out of romantic paralysis and into the power of desire and knowledge, to bring the women I teach to their own power, to ignite them as feminism ignited me when I was a student.

The chill winds of the current climate threaten to extinguish what feminism lit for me. What felt liberating to me as a student is today considered dangerous to my students. Today's antiharassment activism is of course a legacy of seventies feminism. But the antisexual direction of the current trend makes us forget how women's liberation turned us on. The present climate makes it easy to forget and thus crucial to remember. . . .

Twenty-five years ago, I thought Women's Studies was hot. And since that time I've devoted myself to the feminist pursuit of knowledge. After college, I went on to graduate school and wrote a feminist dissertation. In the late seventies, I got a job teaching at a university, and I've been teaching women's studies courses ever since. In the eighties, I set up and ran a Women's Studies Program at a college which did not yet have one. For more than two decades, I've been pursuing the dream of Women's Studies, led by my desire for the community which turned me on as a student.

Nowadays Women's Studies is a lot older and more established; it doesn't feel so much like a bold experiment. While it still is said in women's studies circles that feminist teachers and students ought to have a nonhierarchical relation, ought to work together as sister seekers of knowledge, in fact the relation between feminist teachers and students is not what it was when Women's Studies was young. Students and faculty are no longer discovering feminism together; today, faculty who have been feminists for decades generally teach it to students for whom it is new. We are no longer discovering books together; instead, feminist faculty teach feminist classics we've read half a dozen times to students who are reading them for the first time. Whatever lip service we might still give to an egalitarian classroom, we function as feminist authorities, trying to get our students to understand a feminism we have long known. In this context, relations between us are defined much more by our roles as teacher and student than by any commonality as feminists. These days, rather than playing with our pedagogical roles, we seem to be trapped in them, our ability to connect as women very much limited by them.

Yet my students still want a feminist education that feels like Women's Studies did to me in 1971. And so do I, deeply. I want it for them and I want it still, again, for myself.

Sometimes it works. Sometimes a class or some more informal gathering suddenly comes together, and I feel the electricity, the buzz of live knowledge, the excitement of women thinking freely together. I always try to get us to that place where learning begins to dance. When we get there, my students love me and I'm crazy for them.

But when, as is more often the case, we don't get there, we are all disappointed. And then the students are likely to blame me.

For about a decade now, students in my feminist seminars have been complaining, in their anonymous evaluations, that I am "authoritarian." They expect a feminist teacher to be different, but my authority *as a feminist* feels too much like the male professor's authority in other classrooms. This experience of the feminist teacher as authority seems to betray the very principles of feminist teaching. In the context of feminism, these complaints of authoritarianism and the complaints of sexual harassment are saying the same thing: that I abuse my power, get off on my power at the students' expense, that I am just as bad as the men.

During the time I was under investigation by the university, the two graduate students who had filed the harassment complaints called a meeting of all the grad students in the department, a predominantly feminist group. The purpose of the meeting was to get the grad students to band together so they would be strong enough to curtail my power. At this student-only meeting, in the tradition of the feminist "speak-out," students shared with each other the abuses they had suffered at the hands of faculty.

And in that context, charges of sexual harassment mingled freely with complaints about other manifestations of power. Little distinction was made between sexual harassment (the criminal charge) and authoritarianism (a complaint about teaching style). In the eyes of the students gathered together to resist me and faculty oppression, they were virtually the same crime, the crime of having power over them.

Well-versed in antiharassment rhetoric, one of the students states in her complaint against me: "it is at the level of the institutionally enforced power differential that I wish to locate my harassment charge." She found it humiliating that I had power over her and considered it a betrayal of feminism. Harassment for her in fact meant precisely experiencing what she calls "the power differential." Now that there are feminist faculty securely installed in the academy, students can experience feminist teachers as having power over them. And that makes it possible to imagine a feminist teacher as a sexual harasser.

Back when I was a student, our feminist teachers tended to be in rather tenuous institutional positions; they didn't have much institutional power. We didn't experience what power they did have as power over us, but rather as power for us—power for women, power for feminism. Bad power was men's power, the power society granted them to exploit women, impose upon women, abuse women. Twenty years later, thanks to feminism's academic success, students could look at me and see me as just like the men, just as bad as the men. And therefore worse.

A campus activist against sexual harassment, a student from another department who had never even met me, was quite willing to comment on my case to a reporter: "Jane Gallop is as bad as—*no, worse than*—the men who do this kind of thing." A woman "as bad as the men" is inevitably, *because she is a woman*, considered to be worse than the men. Although several men in my department have been accused of sexual harassment, none of those cases prompted students to rally against the accused.

Feminists often condemn the woman who is like a man as a traitor to feminism, a traitor to her sex. But the condemnation of what feminists call "the male-identified woman" bears an uncanny resemblance to a larger social prejudice, the vilification of women who are like men. Feminism has taught us a lot about that sexist image, how it works to limit and constrain women, to keep us in line, but feminists are not themselves always immune to it.

And what it means for a woman to be "just like a man" always comes down to two things: sex and power.

In 1993, at the very moment I am under investigation, Michael Crichton writes *Disclosure*, the first popular novel about sexual harassment. This novel by a best-selling author, a book that became almost immediately a Hollywood movie, marks a turning point: harassment has taken root in the culture's imagination. Sexual harassment moves from the news to the novel. And mainstream culture's first attempt to imagine harassment conjures up, not the classic scenario, but a male victim and a female predator.

Disclosure sports the epigraph, "Power is neither male nor female," and this view of power seems to be behind the choice to portray a role-reversal harassment. The epigraph is actually spoken within the novel. The woman lawyer who functions as the book's authority on harassment explains to the male vic-tim: "the figures suggest that women executives harass men in the same pro-portion as men harass women. Because the fact is, harassment is a power issue. And power is neither male nor female. Whoever is behind the desk has the opportunity to abuse power. And women will take advantage as often as men." This sounds like the moral of a story about a female sexual harasser.

Crichton is a writer known for the extensive research behind his books, and this one is no exception: *Disclosure's* understanding of harassment is very up-to-date. Explanations of sexual harassment are beginning to move away from the idea that gender is the key factor and toward a gender-neutral notion of power. While a number of feminists have embraced this move, I consider it to be a serious departure from feminism.

Sexual harassment was originally understood within a more general fem-inist analysis of sexism. Feminists saw that the specific power men exercise over individual women—as a boss or a teacher, say—is enormously magni-fied by widespread societal assumptions that men should dominate women. In a society which expects male sexuality to be aggressive and female sexu-ality submissive, a boss can sexually harass his female employee with a dev-astating combination of economic, psychological, and social coercion. The boss's pressure on his employee is backed not only by literal economic power and general psychological intimidation, but also by social expectations that relations between the sexes are supposed to be like this.

When we move beyond the gender configuration of the classic harass-ment scenario, some important things change. The link between sex and power is not always the same. Whereas male heterosexuality in our culture connotes power, both homosexuality and female sexuality tend to signify weakness and vulnerability. If we imagine a sexual harassment scenario where the victim is male or the culprit female, the abuse of power would not be reinforced by society's sexual expectations. Outside novelistic turn-abouts (and Hollywood fantasies featuring Demi Moore), a woman is much more likely to undermine than to enhance her authority by bringing her sexuality into the professional domain.

Not unlike *Disclosure*, my accuser locates harassment "at the level of the institutionally enforced power differential." Both reflect a current trend in thinking about harassment which reduces power to mere institutional position. And thus forgets the feminist insight that the most destructive abuses of power occur because of widespread, deeply-rooted social and psychological rein-forcement.

Troubled by this move to a gender-neutral understanding of sexual harassment, I take *Disclosure* as a dramatic portrayal of its real danger. Rather than worrying about male exploitation and women's disadvantage, the novel's reader is confronted with the image of an evil woman; the reader identifies with and fears for the poor man she preys upon. Under the guise of despising sexual harassment, we find ourselves once again vilifying women who presume to be sexual and powerful like men are.

Embracing a gender-neutral formulation of harassment, we leave behind the concern with sexism only to find ourselves faced with something quite traditionally sexist: an image of a woman who is evil precisely because she is both sexual and powerful. Meredith Johnson, *Disclosure's* villainess, is a single career woman who is sexy and sexually aggressive, professionally adept and successful. She corresponds to the pop cultural image of a liberated woman. Although feminists have condemned women who are just like men, society at large tends to think of women who are like men as "feminists." We might see Meredith Johnson as the fantasy of a feminist sexual harasser.

Disclosure marks a real turning point in the response to sexual harassment. Or maybe a turn of the screw. As outrage at sexual harassment becomes popular, a role-reversal fantasy allows a wide audience to embrace the feminist issue of sexual harassment and at the same time turn it against liberated women.

As the century draws to a close, it appears that the campaign against sexual harassment may in fact be *the* success story of twentieth-century feminism. At a moment when abortion rights are endangered, when affirmative action is becoming unfashionable, when everyone is jumping on the family values bandwagon, when few women want to be thought feminists, there is a broad-based consensus that sexual harassment is despicable and measures against it have become very popular.

Although feminists targeted sexual harassment in the 1970s, outrage against it did not become popular until the nineties. The Hill-Thomas hearings in late 1991 are generally credited with producing this effect. Although I have my own suspicions about the way that a black man makes it easier for Americans to see male heterosexuality as a threat to the social order, my concern here is rather with the more general question of how sexual harassment is understood at the moment when the nation finally rallies against it.

While the battle against sexual harassment has been feminism's great victory, I'm afraid that's because it has been too easy to separate the issue from feminism. Feminists took up the issue because we saw it as a form of sex discrimination, but sexual harassment is increasingly understood as having no necessary link to either discrimination or gender.

In 1990, Billie Wright Dziech, a national authority on sexual harassment, predicted that "genuine change can occur only when sexual harassment is approached as a professional rather than a gender issue." Three years later, the change Dziech was calling for seems to have occurred. Crichton's *Disclosure* approaches harassment in just that way: gender doesn't matter, what matters is who is "behind the desk." That same year, a university official finds it possible that I could be guilty of sexual harassment without having discriminated against anyone. The university's lawyer comments that they must take care to punish me as harshly as the men so that the university won't be accused of sex discrimination.

By the end of 1993, Dziech announces that the discussion of sexual harassment has entered a "new phase": the issue has moved beyond its feminist framework and taken on a life of its own. Although feminism brought the problem to public awareness, the larger public does not necessarily share the feminist assessment of the problem. Once separated from the issue of sex discrimination, harassment can be linked to other versions of socially undesirable sexuality.

As sexual harassment breaks loose from its feminist formulation, the crusade against it might even become, not just independent of feminism, but actually hostile to feminism. Dziech envisions one particularly chilling possibility: "eventually the political right will embrace protections against sexual harassment as part of its agenda for a return to traditional values." A return to traditional values always implies women returning to our proper place. And then we might see not just the odd spectacle of a feminist accused of sexual harassment but the more general prospect of feminists being so accused precisely *because* we are feminists. Once sexual harassment is detached from its feminist meaning, it becomes possible to imagine feminism itself accused as a form of sexual harassment.

2. *Consensual Amorous Relations*

Just last week, I was gossiping with a friend of mine about the department she teaches in. My friend, who is a feminist, confessed that she supported a junior colleague "even though he is a sexual harasser." Being pretty sensitive about the issue, I confronted her: "Is he really a sexual harasser, or does he just date students?"

She only meant that he dated students. Thanks to an administrative stint, my friend is very familiar with academic policy. Her casual use of the term "sexual harasser" was not aberrant but, in fact, represents a new sense of sexual harassment operative in the academy today.

Nowadays most campus sexual harassment policies include a section on "consensual relations" between teachers and students. These range from outright prohibitions of teacher-student relationships to warnings that a consensual relationship will not protect the teacher from the student's claims of harassment. Although the range suggests some uncertainty about the status of consensual relations, *their very inclusion within harassment policies* indicates that consensual relations are themselves considered a type of sexual harassment.

Sexual harassment has always been defined as *unwanted* sexual attention. But with this expansion into the realm of consensual relations, the concept can now encompass sexual attention that is reciprocated and very much welcome. This reconfigures the notion of harassment, suggesting that what is undesirable finally is not unwelcome attention but sexuality per se. Rather than some sexuality being harassing because of its unwanted nature, the inference is that sexuality is in and of itself harassment.

I have reason to be sensitive to this slippage in meaning. When I was accused of sexual harassment by two students, my relation to one of the complainants was deemed to be in violation of the university's policy on "consensual relations."

The two students charged me with classic quid pro quo sexual harassment. They both claimed that I had tried to get them to have sex with me and that, when they rejected me, I had retaliated by withdrawing professional support (in one case with negative evaluations of work, in the other with a refusal to write letters of recommendation). The university's affirmative action office conducted a lengthy investigation which resulted in a pretty accurate picture of my relations with these students. I had not tried to sleep with them, and all my professional decisions regarding them seemed clearly based in recognizable and consistent professional standards. No evidence of either "sexual advances" or "retaliations" was to be found.

What the investigation did find was that I indulged in so-called "sexual behavior" that was generally matched by similar behavior directed toward me on the part of the students. Not only did they participate in sexual banter with me, but they were just as likely to initiate it as I was. With one of the students, this banter was itself so minimal that the case was dismissed. But because my relationship with the other complainant was much more elaborate, it was determined that this mutual relationship of flirtatious banter and frank sexual discussion violated the consensual relations policy.

The woman who conducted the investigation thought that because I had a consensual "sexual relation" with a student, I should be considered guilty of sexual harassment. My lawyer argued that if this was a consensual relation, I was at most guilty of violating a university policy, not of breaking the federal law prohibiting harassment. While campus harassment policies increasingly encompass consensual relations, the laws which make harassment illegal not only do not concern themselves with such mutual relations, but would seem specifically to exclude them.

This confrontation between my lawyer and the university investigator (both specialists in the area of discrimination) demonstrates the gap opening up between a general understanding of harassment as unwanted sexual attention and this new sense of harassment operating in the academy today—which includes all teacher-student sexual relations, regardless of the student's desires.

After the investigation had been conducted, but before the findings were released, the university hired a lawyer from off-campus to head the affirmative action office. It was she who wrote the final determination of my case. This lawyer found no probable cause to believe I had sexually harassed anyone. But her determination does go on to find me guilty of violating university policy because I engaged with one of my students in a "consensual amorous relation."

The document explains the choice of "amorous" (a word which appears in the policy) as denoting a relation which was *"sexual" but did not involve sex acts.* Much less serious than quid pro quo harassment (trading professional support for sexual favors), less serious than hostile environment harassment (discrimination by emphasis on sexuality), less serious even than consensual *sexual* relations, the precise finding of "consensual amorous relations" is in fact the slightest infraction comprised within the policy.

It was as if I had been accused of "first degree harassment" and the charge had been reduced to something like "fourth degree harassment." The distinction between sexual harassment and consensual relations becomes not a difference in kind but merely a difference in degree. The university found no evidence of compromised professional judgments, or of discrimination, unwanted sexual attention, or any sort of harassment; it found I wasn't even having sex with students. But the investigation revealed that I did not in fact respect the boundary between the sexual and the intellectual, between the professional and the personal. It was as if the university, seeing what kind of relations I did have with students, felt I must be *in some way* guilty and was able, through this wrinkle in the policy, to find me *slightly guilty of sexual harassment.*

The presumption on campuses today is that any sexual relation between a teacher and a student constitutes sexual harassment. One of our most esteemed universities explains: "What might appear to be consensual, even to the parties involved, may in fact not be so." The contrast here between "appearance" and "fact" suggests that so-called "consensual relations" policies are *not in reality* about consensual relations, but about relations that are only *apparently* consensual. The policies assume that there is, in fact, no such thing as a consensual relation between a teacher and a student.

The policy of another major university elaborates: "The respect and trust accorded a professor by a student, as well as the power exercised by the professor in giving praise or blame, grades, recommendations, etc., greatly diminish the student's actual freedom of choice. Therefore, faculty are warned against even an apparently consenting relationship. The administration involved with a charge of sexual harassment shall be expected to be unsympathetic to a defense based upon consent when the facts establish that a professional power differential existed within the relationship."

Students do not have full freedom of choice; thus their consent is not true consent but merely the appearance of consent. The very existence of "a professional power differential" between the parties means a relationship will not be treated as consensual, regardless of whether consent was in fact granted. Because students cannot fully, freely, and truly consent, all teacher-student relations are presumed to be instances of sexual harassment.

As a teacher of feminist theory, I recognize this critique of consent. It is based upon a radical feminist critique of heterosexuality. Students cannot "really" consent to sex with professors for the same reasons that women cannot "really" consent to sex with men. Feminists saw that economic arrangements make heterosexuality generally "compulsory" for women. In a society where women are economically disadvantaged, most women must depend upon sexual relations with men (ranging from legal marriage to literal prostitution) for economic survival. If women need to have sex with men in order to survive, their consent to these sexual relations is not freely given.

There has been a good deal of confusion about what this critique of compulsory heterosexuality means. A few feminists have taken it to mean that no women *really want* to have sex with men. This then slides into the injunction that any woman who wants to be free *should not* have sex with men. Although only a very small number of feminists have ever taken this position, a lot of people have mistaken this extreme opinion for *the* feminist line. This confusion has resulted in widespread outrage at the idea that feminism would deny women the right to desire and enjoy men.

The feminist critique of compulsory heterosexuality was not meant to be a condemnation of heterosexuality per se but only of the way society forces men upon women without regard for our desire. Most feminists in fact understand this critique as an attempt to distinguish between socially coerced heterosexuality and women's actual desires for men. The crucial question is whether women are treated as mere sex objects or whether we are recognized as desiring subjects.

University administrators who piously intone against teacher-student sex, citing the student's impossibility to freely grant consent, would be shocked if they knew their position was based in a critique of the institution of marriage. And I don't think you could get them to agree to policies likewise prohibiting heterosexuality on the grounds that the power differential means a woman's consent is always to some extent coerced. Yet campuses around the country are formulating and enforcing policies which are the equivalent of the much-decried and seldom-embraced fringe feminist injunction against women sleeping with men.

As a feminist, I am well aware of the ways women are often compelled to sexual relations with men by forces that have nothing to do with our desire. And I see that students might be in a similar position with relation to teachers. But, as a feminist, I do not think the solution is to deny women or students the right to consent. Denying women the right to consent reinforces our status as objects rather than desiring subjects. That is why I believe the question of whether sexual advances are *wanted* is absolutely crucial.

Prohibition of consensual teacher-student relations is based on the assumption that when a student says yes she really means no. I cannot help but think that this proceeds from the same logic according to which when a woman says no she really means yes. The first assumption is protectionist;

the second is the very logic of harassment. What harassment and protectionism have in common is precisely a refusal to credit women's desires. Common to both is the assumption that women do not know what we want, that someone else, in a position of greater knowledge and power, knows better. . . .

As someone who came of age during the sexual revolution, my teens and twenties were full of short-term serious romances and an even larger number of casual sexual encounters. This variety of experience was particularly good for me as a young intellectual woman, making me feel bold and forceful as well as desirable, helping me view the world as a place of diverse possibility. Especially for women pursuing the life of the mind, desire is a blessing rather than an insult. My desire gave me drive and energy; being an object of desire made me feel admired and wanted, worthy and lovable. Now long past my twenties, I am still convinced that desire is good and that when mutual desire makes itself felt, it is a very fine thing indeed.

Prohibitions against teacher-student relations seem based in a sense of sex as inherently bad. Sex for me is not some wholly separate, nasty, debased thing, but belongs more to the world of conversation and friendship, where people make contact with others who seem interesting, forceful, attractive. Because I value human connection above all else, I regard sex as a considerable good. . . .

It is ironic that relations between teachers and students have been banned as part of the fight against sexual harassment. We fight against sexual harassment precisely because it's dehumanizing, but the ban on consensual relations is dehumanizing too. Telling teachers and students that we must not engage each other sexually ultimately tells us that we must limit ourselves to the confines of some restricted professional transaction, that we *should not treat each other as human beings.*

Around 1990 I began to take loud and public exception to the new consensual relations policies. I felt free to do so precisely because I hadn't been having sex with students since long before these policies came into existence. I thought I could risk opposing these policies because I was not in fact violating them.

This was of course before I found myself charged with sexual harassment. Two years after I started protesting these policies, the complaints against me were filed. A year after that, the university officially declared that

I had violated its consensual relations policy. Thus, I was found in violation of the very policy I had set about to protest.

I thought I was protesting a policy banning the sort of relations I used to have. I had not realized it was possible to apply the policy to the sorts of relations I still have with students.

Back in the days when I was sleeping with students, all the sex had taken place within a larger context of social and personal relations. For example, in [the] summer school class where I started dating my grad student, there was another student, a female undergrad, that I used to hang out with. She had great style, and I loved to go shopping for clothes with her. Or we'd go drinking and compare notes on the difficulties of dating men. The next year, while I rarely had sex with Scott [the grad student], I often went uptown to a bar with him and his friends to play pinball. And my relation to Micki and Diane [a student lesbian couple] began as a friendship with a couple; at the time none of us expected the couple to break up. The drinking and talking, or going out on a weekend, was not unlike relations I had with other students.

I have such relations with students to this day, although now mainly with graduate students. I socialize with students in groups and singly: we might go out to dinner, play tennis, or see a movie. Or one of my graduate advisees will tell me about his love life while I thoroughly enjoy giving him advice. Some of my best friends are students. Even though I no longer have sex with students, my relations with students have not really changed at all.

Some of these personal relations remain pretty casual; but others get intense, complicated, and sticky. The intense relations involve students who take me very seriously as a teacher. These are students who want, in some way, to be intellectuals or academics like I am. And these are the students I most care about as a teacher.

It was indeed just such a relation that landed me in violation of the school's consensual relations policy. When this graduate student took her first course from me, immediately after the second class meeting she came up and asked if we could talk. I told her to come to my office hours the next morning, but she didn't want to wait and pressed me to meet with her right then. Seeing how important it was to her, I relented and went with her to my office, despite the fact that it was 9:30 P.M. When we got there, she didn't even sit down but blurted out that she wanted me to be her advisor. She was jittery with excitement, and I was tickled to see someone who wanted that much to work with me. I immediately agreed to be her advisor; she was overjoyed and asked if we could go to the bar across the street to talk. Flattered by the ardor of her desire to work with me, I again agreed. And so began a relationship which involved not only working together in class and in my office, but going out for drinks and dinners, sometimes with other students or with her girlfriends, sometimes just the two of us.

Right from the start the relationship was not just professional, not even just social, but intensely personal and personally intense. She was, by her own admission, enamored of my work before she even met me. An ambitious woman with a flair for outrageous performance, she identified with me and thought I'd be the ideal teacher for her. I responded strongly to her desire for a career like mine. The relationship was charged with energy. And was, as such crucial relations often are, difficult. Because I believe that the most powerful educational experiences occur in an atmosphere of such intensity, I welcomed it, even though I often found it personally challenging.

I have had other teaching relationships that were as or more personal and intense. Although always tricky, they generally produce excellent results: I see the students consistently learn a lot, work really hard, and clearly benefit from working with me; I also learn a lot in such relationships and derive real satisfaction from seeing the difference I can make in the quality of their thinking and their work.

But, in this case, the relationship failed. Not because of its adventurous style but in the way so many teaching relations fall apart: more than once I told the student her work was not satisfactory; she did not accept my judgments and became increasingly suspicious and angry. And because so much passion had been invested in our relationship, the failure was particularly dramatic. The student felt let down, became outraged, and charged me with sexual harassment.

And because she did, the university had occasion to investigate my teaching practices. Although no evidence was found of the harassment the student claimed, the university looked at the pedagogical relation we had and decided it was against university rules.

As upsetting as it was to have someone I had worked so hard to help turn against me and accuse me of a loathsome crime, I am much more disturbed by the implications of the university's determination. Seeing a relation between a student enamored of a teacher's work, a student who wanted to be like that teacher, and the teacher who responded deeply to the student's desire to work with her, who wanted profoundly to help her do what she desired, the university deemed such a connection, passionate and involving so many personal hopes and dreams, an amorous relation.

And indeed it was.

In my formal response to the student's complaint, I used the psychoanalytic notion of "transference" to explain her relation to me. In psychoanalytic theory, transference is the human tendency to put people in the position our parents once held for us. It is a nearly universal response to people whose opinions of us have great authority, in particular doctors and teachers. Since our feelings about our parents include an especially powerful form of love, transference is undoubtedly an "amorous relation." But transference is also an inevitable part of any relationship we have to a teacher who really makes a difference.

In the official report on my case, the university recommends that in the future I should stop working with any student who has such a transference onto me. Which means that I would not work with any student who really believed I had something important to teach her. I would be forced to turn away precisely those students most eager to work with me, including those graduate students who come to the university where I teach expressly in order to work with me.

While I had vociferously opposed the consensual relations policies before I was accused, I never dreamed how dangerous these policies could be. My case suggests the way the category of "amorous relations" can snowball. By moving from the restricted field of romantic love to the exceedingly wide field of relationships that are either social, personal, or involve intense feelings, what was originally a policy about sexual relations could become a policy restricting and chilling pedagogical relations.

At its most intense—and, I would argue, its most productive—the pedagogical relation between teacher and student is in fact a "consensual amorous relation." And if schools decide to prohibit not only sex but "amorous relations" between teacher and student, the "consensual amorous relation" that will be banned from our campuses might just be teaching itself.

Chapter 3

Gender and Representation

REY CHOW

1

Understood in a conventional, aesthetic sense, "representation" is a word which indicates the process of the "creation of signs—things that 'stand for' or 'take the place of' something else."[1] The central concern with aesthetic representation, in the West at least, has always been mimeticism or resemblance; it is assumed that signs, which are fictive, should bear likeness to the "reality" which they represent. As is clear in this basic definition, what informs the problematic of representation is a binary structure in which one of two parts involved is supposed to be a copy, a replica, an objectified "stand-in" for the other. This binary structure remains the source of contentious debates about representations. For the presence of two parts, while logically allowing for a differentiation between them, also inevitably leads to a process of hierarchization and evaluation, so that representation is often conceived in terms of a *moral* opposition between implicit notions of absence and presence, primariness and secondariness, originality and derivation, authenticity and fakeness, and so forth, that are attributed respectively to the two parts involved. Therefore, even though it is possible, when discussing representation, to think of different representational practices—such as literature, art, music, or architecture—and also by way of theories about related representational issues such as the author, the medium, and the readers' and audiences' responses, it is virtually impossible to avoid coming to terms, sooner or later, with the value-laden implications of the two-part structure that underlies the definition of representation. Because representation can, at least in its traditional usage, indeed be reduced to mimeticist re-presentation—a derivative reproduction that imitates, that tries to resemble the thing that is represented—representation has been criticized on various fronts. In the twentieth century, for instance, the Russian Formalists' theories of art as defamiliarization (rather than reflection) of reality, the Anglo-American New Critics' focus on the ambiguities of language (rather than on the historical background of literary works), and Derridean deconstructionists' attempts to underscore the temporality and irreducibility of signification itself all stand as avant-garde subversions of the classical connotations of representation.

What does all this mean in terms of gender? Like representation, gender, when considered from a conventional, heterosexual perspective, is also a two-part structure, involving the differentiation between men and women. In this case as well, differentiation has conventionally become a process of hierarchical evaluation. The most notorious example here is the notion of "penis envy" advanced by Freud in his interpretations of feminine sexuality. In the classical Freudian framework, the possession of a particular physical organ, the penis, not only stands for the difference between boys and girls; it also becomes a mark of the girl's lack and inferiority in comparison with the boy, who is upheld as the norm. Like the controversy over representation, the most typical problem presented by gender is that one term in the binary structure is usually taken as the authentic origin and standard by which the second term is judged and found to be deficient. Once again, the process of differentiation becomes a process of value determination.

The intersection between representation as a "general" practice and gender as a "specific" system is a difficult one. The nature of this difficulty is clearest in the question of *women's relation to representation*. If representation is, by its conventional definition, a process of creating things that stand in for something else, women should be equal to men in that all human beings would be subjected to the same rules in the process of representation. Yet common experience tells a different story: not only are women often barred from taking up active positions to create the way men do (as artists, writers, composers, instigators of social reforms, runners for political offices, and so forth), but in men's acts of representation women are often used as symbols for meanings men want to convey—goddesses and femme fatales being the two extreme examples. Women, in other words, have all along been *objectified* as the very devices of representation, as the signs that bear specific moral or artistic significance in a world created by men. In his study of tribal kinship relations, for instance, anthropologist Claude Lévi-Strauss would go so far as to assert that women function, in tribal societies, as the means of exchange between different tribal groups, establishing and ascertaining relations among men.[2] Women therefore serve as the boundary markers for men in more than one sense: their physiological difference is used to confirm men's "normality" while their cultural exchangeability (between tribes) is instrumental to male sociality and bonding. In this "traffic in women,"[3] women's role in representation is not only not equal to men's but also different in value. Being the means with which men represent themselves to themselves and the world, women are made to remain, by and large, passive.

The peculiarly double nature of women's position in regard to representation is what led Freud to ask, "What does Woman want?" For, in spite of the meticulous attention thinkers such as Freud and his followers give to sexuality, it is male sexuality that is explained and little is known about the desires of women, of women in the position not of the passive symbol but of the active creator. As a way of acknowledging the complex, because a priori excluded, nature of the question of women's own desire, Jacques Lacan would define that question in terms of *jouissance*, in order to designate the area of feminine pleasure and subjectivity that is beyond the known boundaries of convention and imagination. But in thus elevating women to the realm of the nonrepresentable, Lacan seems to be repeating, albeit with good intentions, the familiar masculine habit of using women as a symbol (from *within* representation) for the meanings of excess, exoticism, or even mysticism (that are *beyond* representation).[4]

At this point, it is necessary to introduce the second major definition of representation, which does not depart from the binary structure of the one discussed so far but which shifts the sense of "standing for" from an aesthetic to a legislative and political one. Representation in this case refers to the condition of serving as the delegate, agent, or spokesperson. Legislatively and politically, what performs the function of "standing for" something is not an object or a symbol but an individual, as in the case of a "representative" speaking for or "representing" a particular electorate. Like aesthetic representation, legislative and political representation also involves the transferring of functions between different parts of a common structure, but this time the transfer is not the result of a substitution using abstract signs. Rather, it is the result of a small number of persons standing for a large group, which, presumably, has agreed to grant those persons the power to "represent" them in their absence.

Once the legislative and political definition of representation is juxtaposed with the issue of gender, it becomes possible for a different kind of question, one that focuses on agency, to emerge. And once agency emerges as an issue, the notion of the political itself must also be expanded from the formal, legislative sense of politics to that of politics as an act of power in general, involving the ability to speak for others even in realms outside the properly legalistic.

Instead of asking how women are represented or made to represent certain ideas, then, it becomes necessary to query *who* is engaged in such representations and what motivations lie behind them. For instance: in "representing" women in a certain way, are the representers being descriptive or prescriptive? Are they portraying things as they are or are they imposing on readers preconceived ideas? Are they speaking for women at the expense of women's views of themselves? From such questions it is easy to see how, for many feminists, the representations of women by many male writers, painters, musicians, philosophers, or theorists become readily suspect. Among contemporary feminist literary critics, we therefore find detailed exposures of problematic assumptions about women and female sexuality on the part of male authors.[5] Alternatively, we find continual attempts to investigate elements that are specifically feminine or feminist in aesthetic representation.[6]

The extreme case of dispute over the gendered politics of representation is conventional (heterosexual) pornography. To the opponents of pornography, the representation of women as sex objects is a violation of women's rights as subjects with their own consciousness: the women who take part in such representations, it is believed, are either economically coerced or ideologically manipulated into doing so. In other words, for those who are against pornography, no woman in her right mind could conceivably participate in such exploitative representations of womanhood, which can only be the results of men who have usurped women's rights to speak for themselves. For the most uncompromising anti-pornography critics such as Andrea Dworkin, pornography is the equivalent of sex with men, and sex with men is always rape.[7] I will return to the problematic of pornography in sections 4 and 5.

The disputes over masculinist representations of women have an intimate parallel in the disputes over Western representations of non-Western peoples and cultures. Like the feminist critics of pornography, Edward Said in his book *Orientalism* launches a powerful attack on the systematically distorted, phantasmatic depictions of non-Western cultures in the history of Western imperialism.[8] Said's point is that, like military and territorial conquests, representation, too, is a form of imperialism, but while the former conquests depend on brute force, representation works by "culture." Respectable cultural forms such as the novel become in this light a means of Western cultural hegemony. In Said's analysis, the two senses of representation are not only mutually implicated; indeed, representation in the legislative and political sense (of a small number of persons "standing for" a large group of people) is now foregrounded as a questionable privilege. In imperialist and colonialist contexts, this is to say that certain representers have been representing others (in the aesthetic sense of creating signs, making stories, drawing pictures, and producing theories about them, and so forth) *even though they have not been delegated to do so.* It is such a privilege, such an advantage of being in the position to represent (speak for others) without delegation, that allows the distorted, racist depictions of the non-West to be made under the name of objective representations (reproductions of reality). Even seemingly neutral aesthetic representations are thus seen as motivated, as acts of political representation or domination.

With the consciousness of inequality in gender and cross-cultural politics, the binary structure that is fundamental to representation takes on explosive implications. Once the emphasis shifts to representation as an intersubjective activity—involving not only signs and their creators/users but also one group of people turning another group of people into signs—it is no longer sufficient simply to seek "objective" or "accurate" representations. (Some would say that this argument applies even in the sciences.) Rather, "objective representations" and "accurate representations" tend to be viewed as oxymorons that disguise the impositions of gender- and/or culture-specific criteria by one group on another. An example of this is the habitual portrayal of "third world women" as "victims" of their own societies by Western feminist scholars. As Chandra Talpade Mohanty argues, it is, ironically, such feminist scholars' wish to discover the "third world difference"—or the "third world" as difference—that leads them to produce uniform accounts showing "third world" women as lacking all the nice things that their "first world" sisters enjoy.[9] As in the case of women being used as boundary markers for men, the "third world" is used, in such cross-cultural representations, to mark the difference and identity of the "first world," and "third world women" in particular are used to mark the difference and identity of "first world" women. Hence, Mohanty warns: "Beyond sisterhood there is still racism, colonialism and imperialism!"[10]

2

It is at this difficult juncture among representation, gender, and racial difference that *self-representation* emerges as a controversial alternative. The logic is a simple one: if even the most "objective"-looking representation of an other—be that another gender or another race—could be suspect of the lack of proper representational delegation and thus of sexual, racial, or class discrimination,[11] does that not mean that one should stop representing others altogether (in the spirit of "I must not commit the indignity of speaking for others") and only represent oneself? Does that not mean that representation must, by necessity, become self-referential?

To a large extent, these questions have already been answered in the positive by the overwhelming popularity of self-referential genres, such as autobiographies, memoirs, journals, and diaries, in contemporary cultural politics. Nor is the self-referential turn restricted to these publications only; it is increasingly being favored as well in scholarly venues such as critical essays, forums, conferences, and so forth. One explanation for this remarkable transformation in representation is provided by Jean-François Lyotard's *The Postmodern Condition*.[12] Lyotard defines postmodernity as a time when "metanarratives"—that is, the stories and theories that used to have universal explanatory power—have lost their legitimation. Instead, he argues, people's experiences and the languages that are at their disposal to comprehend these experiences have become incommensurate. The outcome of such incommensurability is an increasing relativism in representation, since, with the demise of the justifications provided by metanarratives, all experiences now *seem* to be equally valid. Such relativism finds its appropriate expression in self-referential articulations, which, by capturing the unique, the solitary, and the particularistic, and by not making general claims, have become for some the only acceptable type of representation.

And yet, even as we understand the trend of self-referentiality as the result of an epochal transformation of the ethics of representation—a transformation that questions the politics of "standing for" that divides representer from represented—the turn toward the "self," together with the accompanying claim that metanarratives no longer exist or hold relevance, is far from being unproblematic. The problems entailed are historical, technical, and political in nature.

Historically, the notion that a return to the self is "emancipatory" is a myth that is as old as the Enlightenment. According to Michel Foucault, the emergence of the "self" as such is part of a changing organization of power in Western society.[13] Whereas power in the ancient world used to be concentrated among a few persons at the top of society, it is, in modernity, widely distributed among society's members, down to the details of the care and uses of the most private areas of existence. Hence the "liberation" of the self is simultaneously the repositioning of the sources of power that methodically structure social processes. What this means is that freedom, which is always imagined as freedom from power and from domination, is strictly speaking an effect of power; the "free" or "freed" individual as such is already a representation of the changing conceptions of power from an absolute to a relative, discursive basis. This paradoxical situation is summed up by Foucault in this statement: "The 'Enlightenment,' which discovered the liberties, also invented the disciplines."[14]

To the extent that self-referentiality has acquired legitimacy as a resistant, liberatory, and thus corrective form of discourse (aimed at freeing us from the traditional fetters of representation), Foucault is perceptively precise on the representational predicament we face in the age of raised political consciousness. The alluring trap that many fall into when they turn to self-referential genres as a way "out of" metanarratives, "out of" the crime of speaking for others, is that of the age-old "realist fallacy," which allows them to attribute to self-referentiality the capacity for an unproblematic representation of reality, here the reality of the self. The fantasy is that the act of referring only to the self can finally redeem us from the fundamental and contentious binary structure of representation in which one is always (erroneously) "standing for" something or someone else. Presumed to be direct and unmediated, the act of referring to oneself has taken on the aura of a "representation" that paradoxically transcends the limits of representation, a "representation" that, no matter how trivial and self-aggrandizing, is morally justifiable because it is (thought to be) *non-representational*. Furthermore, self-representation is now equated with the expression of truth. Foucault describes this phenomenon, which he terms confession, in the following manner:

> Western man has become a confessing animal.
>
> Whence a metamorphosis in literature: we have passed from a pleasure to be recounted and heard, centering on the heroic or marvelous narration of "trials" of bravery or sainthood, to a literature ordered according to the infinite task of extracting from the depths of oneself, in between the words, a truth which the very form of the confession holds out like a shimmering mirage. Whence too this new way of philosophizing: seeking the fundamental relation to the true, not simply in oneself—in some forgotten knowledge, or in a certain primal trace—but in the self-examination that yields, through a multitude of fleeting impressions, the basic certainties of consciousness. The obligation to confess is now relayed through so many different points, is so deeply ingrained in us, that we no longer perceive it as the effect of a power that constrains us; on the contrary, it seems to us that truth, lodged in our most secret nature, "demands" only to surface; that if it fails to do so, this is because a constraint holds it in place, the violence of a power weighs it down, and it can finally be articulated only at the price of a kind of liberation. Confession frees, but power reduces one to silence; truth does not belong to the order of power, but shares an original affinity with freedom: traditional themes in philosophy, which a "political history of truth" would have to overturn by showing that truth is not by nature free—nor error servile—but that its production is thoroughly imbued with relations of power. The confession is an example of this.[15]

In Foucault's analysis, self-referential speaking is not only *not* the individual or unique way "out of" representation that it is often imagined to be; it is also, in fact, the symptom of a collective subjection. To represent, to examine, to confess about oneself are compulsive acts that imagine the self as a refuge outside power—an alibi from representation, so to speak—when the self is merely a rational systematization and a relay of institutional forces at the individual level. In the United States, illustrations of this phenomenon are found abundantly on televised talk shows, which, by staging "individual" confessions in spectacular public forums, only underscore the fact that in order for the self to make sense, certain kinds of metanarratives must somehow persist.

From the perspective of feminism and ethnicity, the logical conclusion from Foucault's analysis is, quite clearly, an unappealing and unflattering one. It demonstrates that the supposed "radicalization" performed by gender- and race-awareness on representation—by the insistence on the marginal, the local, the personal, and the autobiographical—must be modified by an understanding of the symbiotic relation between the radical and power as such. In practical terms, this means that much more care needs to be taken with the acts of self-representation. For, when women and minorities think that, by representing themselves, they are liberating themselves from the powers that subordinate them, they may actually be allowing such powers to work in the most effective way—from within their hearts and souls, in the form of voluntary, intimate confessions.

Technically, self-representation also raises once again the most tenacious problems of representation itself. These are the problems of differentiation and deferral—the temporal processes by which representation inevitably becomes *other* even in acts of referring to "itself." Another way of putting this is to say that representation, even representation of the self, would always need to come to terms with those elements of heterogeneity that render the "self" opaque rather than transparent. In spite of being imagined as the ultimate source of knowledge, the self does not necessarily "know" itself and cannot be reduced to the realm of rational cognition.

Finally, even with the most self-conscious descriptions of the self, it soon becomes necessary to ask the same *political* questions about "standing for": what privileges allow one to speak narcissistically of oneself? How far are such personal experiences supposed to be "representative" of the group from which the speaker originates? Is the act of referring to oneself not at the expense of others who may not have the opportunity to speak in the same manner? Disturbing though they may be, such questions are imperative, especially in contexts in which those who speak do so with the claim of resisting subordination on behalf of an entire group.[16] For instance, when non-white women academics resort to speaking self-referentially as a way to avoid the pitfalls of Orientalist and masculinist representations, should they be subjected to the same criticism that is made of men and Western women—the criticism that they are self-serving and representing others without delegation—or should an exception be made in their case on the basis of their gender and racial difference?[17]

3

If the refocusing on the self is not a solution to the problems of representation, how else might those problems be approached, especially in contexts where they obviously pertain to gender and ethnicity? Gayatri Chakravorty Spivak's essay "Can the Subaltern Speak?" offers an example of a useful intervention.[18] One of the most difficult works to have appeared in the field of postcolonial studies, Spivak's piece, as its title makes clear, is concerned with the question of representing underprivileged peoples of the "third world"—-the usually female figure of the subaltern (that is, a disenfranchised member of society). Spivak refers to the two senses of representation we have discussed by calling them, respectively, "portrait" and "proxy."[19] However, because the figure she is examining is a socially subordinated and deprived one, the question of representation as "proxy"—with its implications of delegation and agency—is crucial. Going far beyond most feminist arguments against misogyny and most postcolonialist arguments against Orientalism, Spivak highlights the question of representation as one of class (that is, socio-economic status). The powerlessness of the subaltern, then, becomes Spivak's means of zeroing in on the nexus of differentiation-cum-moral-evaluation that is at the heart of representation. Her essay asks: is there any representation that does not ultimately entail class privilege and inequality?

Notably also, Spivak uses the word "represent" interchangeably with the word "speak." The title of her essay could, in this light, be recast as "Can the Subaltern Represent?" Indeed, once we recast the title, the key concerns of Spivak's argument surface much more clearly. For, while the word "speak" may erroneously lend itself to a loose, imprecise definition as any mode of action or any mode of life activity, thus making it easy for people to say, "But of course the subaltern can speak," the word "represent" points much more succinctly to the question of whether the subaltern can occupy the position of the active representer, both in the aesthetic sense (as a creator of signs and symbols) and in the legislative and political sense (as a delegate and agent). Moreover, it advances the entire question one step further: if, because of her subordinated status, the subaltern cannot represent others (all of whom are presumably more powerful than she), can she at least represent herself? Can the subaltern be an autobiographer?

Spivak's response at the end of her essay is that "the subaltern cannot speak." If the subaltern can speak, she adds later in an interview, then "thank God, the subaltern is not a subaltern any more."[20] This is a chilling and sobering view of the subaltern, which means not only that the subaltern will always be represented by others, but also that she is unlikely to occupy the active position of a representer—whether of others or of herself. Foreseeably, Spivak's conclusion has sparked strong objections. Many critics, seizing the moral high ground of charging Spivak with arrogance, proceed to demonstrate, with their own speeches and writings, how different subalterns have indeed "spoken." From the perspective of the difficulties surrounding representation as outlined in the present essay, their objections are not entirely unreasonable. Implied in such objections is always the desire for liberation through the self-referential turn: even if subalterns are completely subordinated, must we not at least acknowledge them as self-representers? Are they not at least entitled to "their own" speeches, actions, performances, life activities?

By unwittingly directing her question gradually toward self-representation, however, Spivak's opponents simply confirm the very predicament of representation that is her premise. First, there is the ineluctable question of privilege: in their capacities as intellectuals bestowed with verbal and institutional power, these critics who insist that the subalterns have spoken are appointing themselves as delegates to "speak for" the subalterns. However much they want to assert the subalterns' entitlement to representation, therefore, their own position is not, legislatively or politically speaking, different from Spivak's. Second, there is the question of mediation even in the putative acts of self-representation: should a subaltern's attempt to represent herself be seen as direct, transparent, and always coinciding with itself—in brief, as a transcendent, non-representational representation—*simply because she is a subaltern?*

As a response to the second question, Spivak provides a brief reading of the final life activity of a young Hindu woman, Bhuvaneswari Bhaduri, who was a member of one of many groups involved in the armed struggle for Indian independence, and who committed suicide in North Calcutta in 1926 when she could not confront the task of a political assassination with which she was entrusted. To ensure that her suicide would not be mistaken for an expression of shame (at an illicit pregnancy), this young woman, it was revealed, had deliberately waited until the onset of menstruation before ending her own life. Her last act as a revolutionary, then, amounted to a rewriting of the major tradition of women sacrifice (*sati*) with the means of her own "unclean" female body:

> The displacing gesture—waiting for menstruation—is ... a reversal of the interdict against a menstruating widow's right to immolate herself; the unclean widow must wait, publicly, until the cleansing bath of the fourth day, when she is no longer menstruating, in order to claim her dubious privilege.

> In this reading, Bhuvaneswari Bhaduri's suicide is an unemphatic, ad hoc, subaltern rewriting of the social text of *sati*-suicide as much as the hegemonic account of the blazing, fighting, familiar Durga.[21]

Instead of having a direct autobiographical meaning, this subaltern's "self representation," in the literal form of (menstrual) blood, is an inscription saturated with the demands of history, against which the subaltern protested. But this significance of the subaltern's "speech" is redeemed only under a careful reading long after her death.

Several purposes are served by Spivak's reading. At the most obvious level, it demonstrates that "speaking for" *others* inevitably entails connotations of class in addition to gender and race. (In this case, class is evidenced in the representation of Bhuvaneswari Bhaduri, a subaltern in the "third world" who has long become silent, by Spivak, an intellectual who has a voice in the "first world.") Meanwhile, if "the subaltern cannot speak," it is not only because representation involves institutional power but also because that power cannot be successfully resisted by turning representation toward *the self*. The radical implication of Spivak's argument is thus not "the subaltern cannot speak" but that it would be naïve to assume that anyone, let alone the subaltern, can self-represent unproblematically. The utterly impoverished condition of the subaltern, that is, serves merely to underscore in an uncompromised manner a general fact. Indeed, such impoverishment makes the confrontation with (rather than avoidance of) the basics of representation a nonnegotiable one. If, as contemporary cultural politics takes pains to show, representation cannot be divorced from gender, race, class, and other differences involving hierarchy and subordination, then the message of Spivak's essay is that the reverse, too, must be heeded: even and especially a consideration of the most socially deprived, such as the female subaltern in the "third world," cannot ignore the materialities of representation—those structural, figurative elements that mediate signification and that cannot simply be reduced to the positivistic permutations of law and economics.

4

So far, I have focused on the problems arising from representation's *subjective* turn. If the case of the female subaltern indicates that even a retreat to the most impoverished self is not a solution to the theoretical impasses of representation, then the other end of the spectrum—of representation as insistent *objectification*—should also be rethought.

Typically, representation as objectification is conducted in the name of knowledge: to represent something in objectified form is assumed as a way of "knowing" it. The extreme case of such representation is conventional, heterosexual pornography, in which lurid, tabooed images of sex are accompanied by narratives of exploration and discovery, of the curiosity to reveal the secrets or truths about the human body. From the perspective of a feminism invested in giving women "agency," pornography is a thorny issue, for what can be more opposed to the fight for women's rights to speak as subjects than the practice of staging women as sex objects?

A highly interesting text on pornography is Linda Williams's *Hard Core: Power, Pleasure, and the "Frenzy of the Visible."* [22] Following Foucault's analysis of power as discursive, Williams bases her inquiry on the question: how is pornography as a type of "knowledge" produced? Instead of assuming that there is an authentic male or female body which exists before the institutionalized apparatuses of knowledge production, Williams proceeds by examining those apparatuses themselves. In the terms of our discussion, she begins not with actual bodies but with the codes of representation. Arguing that pornography is in part a logical outcome of the steadily enhanced techniques of cinematic vision, which have since the beginning been relying on strategies of fetishization, Williams shows that the *generic* development within pornography is crucial for an understanding of the ambiguous relation between the representation and "knowledge" of women as such.

For instance, while the knowledge associated with female sexuality is conventionally conceived in terms of a tactile penetration of the "secret wonders" of the female body, the technological possibilities offered by cinema, which specialize in maximizing visibility, mean that knowledge (about the female body) is now produced differently—as what can and must be seen. In the "stag film" or dirty movie, then, the exploration and revelation of sexual "truths" encounters the problem precisely of what it means to "know": while making the female body increasingly visible, the enhanced techniques of visual representation nonetheless run up against the fact that that body has not become more knowable. On the contrary, it is as though the act of seeing now becomes the very limit imposed on the knowability of the represented object. In other words, we can see but not necessarily know. This problem—of the noncoincidence between seeing and knowing—is then generically solved by the "money shot," the convention which, by focusing on penile ejaculation as the climactic moment of sexual pleasure, seems to have succeeded in maximizing visibility *and* knowledge at the same time. And yet, as Williams argues, to "know" sexual pleasure in this manner is also to become complicit with an ideological division between male and female bodies, a division that renders "female pleasure" invisible except insofar as it is "the same" as male pleasure. Moreover, this male pleasure is single-mindedly mapped onto the penis as a transparent sign. Williams's argument is worth citing in detail:

Each shot—"meat" or "money"—is emblematic of the different "climax" of its generic form. Each shot seeks maximum visibility in its representation but encounters the limits of visibility of its particular form. The stag film, seeking to learn more about the "wonders of the unseen world," encounters its limits of visibility . . . *ante portas* in penetration: for the male performer to penetrate the wonders is to make it neatly impossible for the viewer to see what is penetrated.

The money shot, however, succeeds in extending visibility to the next stage of representation of the heterosexual sex act: to the point of seeing climax. But this new visibility extends only to a knowledge of the hydraulics of male ejaculation, which, though certainly of interest, is a poor substitute for the knowledge of female wonders that the genre as a whole still seeks. The gynecological sense of the speculum that penetrates the female interior here really does give way to that of a self-reflecting mirror. While undeniably spectacular, the money shot is also hopelessly specular; it can only reflect back to the male gaze that purports to want knowledge of the woman's pleasure the man's own climax. This climax is now rendered in glorious Eastmancolor, sometimes even on a wide screen with optical or slow-motion effects, and accompanied by all the moans, groans, and cries, synchronized or post-synched, appropriate to such activity.

. . . obviously nothing could be more conventional than a money shot: like Diderot's speaking jewels, *it is a rhetorical figure that permits the genre to speak in a certain way about sex.* (my emphasis)[23]

What are the effects of this "rhetorical figure"? In spite of the obviously maximized visibility and the seemingly "frank" revelation about sex, what the money shot accomplishes is a systematic denial of difference—the difference of the female body and its pleasures that the genre purports to want to know. As a representation that tries to discover "knowledge" by looking hard, the money shot also invents ways of not looking at all when it comes to female genitalia:

Indeed, these close-ups of remarkably long, perpetually hard, ejaculating penises might seem to be literal embodiments of this idealized fantasy phallus which Freud says we all—men and women—desire. The ejaculating penis of the money shot could, in this sense, be said to disavow castration by avoiding visual association with the woman's genitalia. This, after all, is the genius of *Deep Throat*'s gimmick. By placing the clitoris in Linda Lovelace's throat, the film constructs its narrative on the importance of this organ while at the same time never having to look at it. It is as if the male fetishistic imagination, at this point in the history of the genre's attempts to capture the hard-core "truth" of pleasure, could not countenance any vision of female difference when representing the orgasmic heights of its own pleasure.[24]

In terms of the fundamental rules of representation, the difference of female genitalia thus stands as a kind of excess outside the binary structure of the series of meanings triggered by the penis as a sign. Penile ejaculation, in its seemingly uninhibited and honest outpour, has been made to "stand in" for male pleasure; male pleasure is used to stand in for universal male pleasure; universal male pleasure is used to stand in for universal sexual pleasure, and so forth—all this, while female difference continues to be evaded. Yet the turgid anchoring of the penis is clearly momentary. As a sign of unambiguous "truth," the ejaculating penis is haunted by the difference of the female body, which it must leave behind or aside in order to fulfill its knowledge-finding mission, its responsibility to look hard. Paradoxically, precisely through its denial, the female body becomes the remainder, the leftover heterogeneity that causes this "truthful" representation to burst at its seams.

When pornography is analyzed in this manner—that is, as representation—its extreme "objectifying" tendency can lend itself to a new significance. For those who are opposed to it, of course, pornographic objectification has always meant falsification of and violence against women. Even so, in order to make such a charge, such critics must first assume that some normative or authentic (female) sexuality exists and that it can be "properly" represented. Such an assumption would return us once again to the classic debates about representation—debates as to how one thing can truly "stand for" another and as to who has the right to "speak for" whom, etc.—which, as we have seen in the previous sections, have led to major theoretical impasses. In order for pornographic objectification to lead toward a significantly different way of theorizing about representation and gender, therefore, the notion of a normative or authentic sexuality would need to be given up. Without the assumption about a fixed truth about sexuality, the lurid body parts, penile outbursts, and lewd sexual acts that constitute the *mise-en-scène* of pornography could be regarded anew—as signifiers not of an "immorality" but of a deliberate *artificiality*. In the extreme tendency of such signifiers to "objectify"—to turn the world, especially women, into objects—pornography announces itself as the practice in which the *representational* quality of representation is most explicit.

To that extent, "the body" in pornography, too, would need to be rethought. As Williams writes, the basic feature found in any pornography is a certain assumption about the body: "the body is recalcitrant; it has desires and appetites that do not necessarily conform to social expectations."[25] Like "the self" in modernity, the body in pornography has been imagined as the ultimate "subject" of truth, which must, so the practice goes, be made to own up to its unmentionable secrets. But, as Williams goes on to argue, even the seemingly involuntary and unmediated "autobiographical" confessions by the body are already parts of a social process, in which the most private, intimate sensations are also the most conventionally objectified and (re)produced, and most heavily coded by way of genre and gender. In this social process, it is the female body which bears the brunt of the demand to "confess," even though that "confession" often takes the rhetorical form of male penile pleasure. By demonstrating how the gendered body is inextricably made to "speak" through generic rules, then, Williams alerts us to the fact of *gender itself as the construct of representational labor*, whose divisions the excessive modes of pornography clarify and magnify. Meanwhile, because gender is, as the example of pornography shows, a generically codified representational system, it is artificial rather than natural and therefore subject to change.

5

The juxtaposition of the radically different cases of the subaltern-as-subject and women-as-pornographic-objects brings the two definitions of representation to a crux, involving two very different kinds of future.

In terms of the aesthetics of representation, the future will no doubt continue in the direction of an increasingly abstract world, where, with ever-perfecting computer technologies, representation will become less and less a matter of re-presentation and more and more a matter of simulation (that is, "copying" or "representing" without the original). To that extent, pornography can be seen as a precursor to the demise, in the computer age, of aesthetic representation itself: the pornographic films in which human body parts—eyes, mouths, hands, legs, feet, hair, nipples, buttocks, genitalia—are "movable" and artificially manipulable to conjure "truths" about sexual desires are, in a sense, the literal forerunners to the high-tech, computer-generated images that surround us daily in their fragmented, alienated forms, for various purposes of the production of "knowledge." Not only is it true that much of our "self"-knowledge nowadays comes from partial, foreign images—consider the technically impressive variety used by doctors to explore, examine, or operate on the normally invisible spaces of our "interiors"—it is equally true that even personal particularities associated with time-honored representational practices, particularities that are supposedly "unique" and irreproducible—such as a singer's voice, a cellist's finger movements, a painter's brush strokes, a dancer's footsteps—are now perfectly "clonable" information on the computer screen. Most radically, the very appearance of a sign on the computer screen no longer requires a base in "reality": the image of a lamp which jumps, reproduces, and mutates, for instance, is just that—an electronically generated series of lines, shapes, and movements whose reality is the image itself. When "reality" is increasingly superseded by "virtuality," what would happen to *gendered* realities such as "men" and "women," and the signs that used to represent them?

At the same time, as the vast changes in technologies of simulation tend to eliminate the cumbersome materialities of actual bodies and render the age-old aesthetic concept of representation (as a mimetic copy) obsolete, the other definition of representation, having to do with the delegation of rights and the distribution of privilege, equality, and justice, remains a compelling and urgent issue. Indeed, precisely as parts of the world turn progressively "abstract" with the availability of expensive, sophisticated computer technologies, legislative and political representation pertaining to those human multitudes who are coerced into the production of such abstraction (most typically as cheap laborers) and who continue to be denied its benefits becomes ever more vital. This essay has demonstrated some of the reasons why the challenge to representation in this second sense—of "speaking for" others—cannot simply take the facile turn toward self-representation, and that even the self-representation of the disenfranchised woman from the "third world" must be given its due recognition as a thoroughly mediated discourse.

For gender, the two different futures of representation imply the following questions: as a discourse, could gender partake of the technological and social privileges that result from the gradual disappearance of classical aesthetic representation without ultimately forsaking some of its basic "realities" such as "men" and "women"? Conversely, could gender continue to represent the disenfranchised, who include many of the world's men as well as women, without coming to terms with its own status as a metanarrative, its own implication in the technological "progress" of the world? In face of the ever-widening epistemological gap between the two ends of representation—of the uprooting of classical aesthetic representation by virtuality, which converges with material advancement, on the one hand, and the tenacity of legislative and political representation, which demands responses not only to questions of sex but also to those of race, class, and myriad additional forms of differences, on the other—much more needs to be done. In that gap, too, gender will need to negotiate its future course.

NOTES

1. W. J. T. Mitchell, "Representation," in *Critical Terms for Literary Study*, ed. Frank Lentricchia and Thomas McLauglin (Chicago: University of Chicago Press, 1990).

2. Claude Lévi-Strauss, *Elementary Structures of Kinship*, rev. ed., trans. J. H. Ball et al. (London: Eyre and Spottiswoode, 1969). (*Les Structures élémentaires de la parenté*, 1949.)

3. Gayle Rubin, "The Traffic in Women: Notes on the Political Economy of Sex," in *Toward an Anthropology of Women*, ed. Rayna R. Reiter (New York: Monthly Review Press, 1975).

4. For a discussion of women and representation in psychoanalysis, see Judith Still, "Representation," in *Feminism and Psychoanalysis: A Critical Dictionary*, ed. Elizabeth Wright (Oxford: Blackwell, 1992), pp. 377–82.

5. For an example, see Kate Millett, *Sexual Politics* (1970; rpt. New York: Ballantine Books, 1978).

6. For an example, see Hilde Hein and Carolyn Korsmeyer, *Aesthetics in Feminist Perspective* (Bloomington: Indiana University Press, 1993).

7. Andrea Dworkin, *Pornography: Men Possessing Women* (New York: Perigee Books, 1979) and *Intercourse* (New York: Free Press, 1987).

8. Edward Said, *Orientalism* (New York: Pantheon Books, 1978).

9. Chandra Talpade Mohanty, "Under Western Eyes: Feminist Scholarship and Colonial Discourses," in *Colonial Discourse and Post-Colonial Theory: A Reader*, ed. with an introduction by Patrick Williams and Laura Chrisman (New York: Columbia University Press, 1994).

10. Ibid., p. 211.

11. Linda Alcoff, "The Problem of Speaking for Others," *Cultural Critique* 20 (Winter 1991–92): 5–32.

12. Jean-François Lyotard, *The Postmodern Condition: A Report on Knowledge*, trans. Geoff Bennington and Brian Massumi, foreword by Fredric Jameson (Minneapolis: University of Minnesota Press, 1984). (*La Condition postmoderne: Rapport sur le savoir*, 1979.)

13. Michel Foucault, *Discipline and Punish: The Birth of the Prison*, trans. Alan Sheridan (New York: Vintage Books, 1979). (*Surveillir et punir: Naissance de la prison*, 1975.)

14. Ibid., p. 222.

15. Michel Foucault, *The History of Sexuality*, vol. 1, *An Introduction*, trans. Robert Hurley (New York: Vintage Books, 1980), pp. 59–60. (*La Volonté de savoir*, 1976.)

16. For a discussion of the complexities involved in such acts of speaking, see Garrett Hongo, "Introduction," in *Under Western Eyes: Personal Essays from Asian America*, ed. Garrett Hongo (New York: Anchor Books, 1995).

17. Sara Suleri, "Women Skin Deep: Feminism and the Postcolonial Condition," *Critical Inquiry* 18, no. 4 (1992): 756–69.

18. Gayatri Chakravorty Spivak, "Can the Subaltern Speak?" in *Marxism and the Interpretation of Culture*, ed. with an introduction by Cary Nelson and Lawrence Grossberg (Urbana: University of Illinois Press, 1988).

19. Ibid., p. 276.

20. Gayatri Chakravorty Spivak, *The Post-Colonial Critic: Interviews, Strategies, Dialogues*, ed. Sarah Harasym (New York: Routledge, 1990), p. 158.

21. Spivak, "Can the Subaltern Speak?" p. 308.

22. Linda Williams, *Hard Core: Power, Pleasure, and the "Frenzy of the Visible"* (Berkeley: University of California Press, 1989).

23. Ibid., pp. 93–94.

24. Ibid., p. 116.

25. Ibid., p. 31.

Chapter 4

Whatever Happened to Feminist Theory?

BEATRICE HANSSEN

To raise the question of whatever happened to feminist theory is to assume that it has come to pass, that it has come to an end, and that together with what some have called the period of *post*-feminism,[1] we now have entered the epoch of *post*-theory. To be sure, a survey of the current critical field indicates that pronouncements about theory's death or end are only half true or, to say the least, premature. The "practice of theory" is alive and well in a variety of contexts, from the literary field to political theory, from post-colonial to queer to psychoanalytic theory. Yet, whether practiced institutionally—in literature, women's studies, government, history departments—

This essay was first presented in the "Feminist Theory" seminar at Harvard's Humanities Center. I am grateful for the stimulating discussion with the seminar's participants that followed the presentation, especially Lynne Layton, Linda Nicholson, Naomi Schor, Kalpana Sheshadri-Crooks, Susan Suleiman, Sarolta Takács, and Andrea Walsh.

or invoked in the political playing field at large, "theory" has acquired a string of negative epithets. It is assumed to be: elitist, male-identified, reifying, totalizing, totalitarian, specular, spectatorial, obscurantist, apolitical, universalizing, hegemonic, occidental, imperialistic, Eurocentric, antidemocratic, violent—to cite just a few of the most commonly heard invectives. Not just so-called highbrow theory—the branch of mostly French-inspired feminism that was *en vogue* in the 1970s and 1980s—met with disfavor, but the word "theory" itself—often used as a stand-in or placeholder for poststructuralism or neo-Marxism—has reached the low level of a slur, made for name-calling. In its place have come situated terms that aim to reflect difference, pluralism, and context-dependence, such as praxis, experience, the real, narrativity, performance, body politics, new historicism, pragmatism. To be sure, it is hardly astonishing that feminist theory, not unlike theory "at large," has lately become the target of much political contestation, nor that some of its manifestations have been criticized by members from within the feminist movement. In fact, feminist theory has always elicited its share of suspicion, if not invariably for the same reasons. In the late 1970s and 1980s French feminist theory increasingly came under attack for its intrinsic essentialism, ethnocentrism, and assumed universalist standpoint, in the name, often, of a more sophisticated social constructivism. Today, it is antifoundationalist poststructuralist theory in turn that is taken to task for being counterproductive, intrinsically apolitical, not materialistic enough, or "merely cultural."[2] In that sense, the observation Judith Butler makes in *Feminist Contentions*, that we are presently in the throes of "theory wars,"[3] has lost none of its relevance.

Why, one might ask, is this the case and how exactly did we arrive at this historical juncture? And what, for that matter, do we precisely mean when we refer to "theory" or "feminist theory"? Literary theory, cultural theory, social theory, political theory? And why should the practice of theory have given rise to "wars," including, or perhaps especially, in the feminist playing field? Is all theory bad or only "pure" theory, to use nomenclature that Marx and Engels first brought into circulation through their *German Ideology*? Must theory be anathema to politics, especially a feminist emancipatory or progressive politics, or is it possible to engage in "theoretical activism"?[4] But an entirely different set of questions can be added to this list of queries, which only further compounds the issue at hand. Does theory merely mean the laying out of principles that rule practice? Is it always already normative, as is the case with a Frankfurt-style critical theory, or does poststructuralist theory elide and set adrift such claims to normativity, and, as is implied, normalization?[5] Should one distinguish between, on the one hand, "traditional" or "pure" theory, which is premised on a rigid subject-object rift, and, on the other hand, an altogether different branch of theory, a new style of ideology critique that is all too conscious of its own inevitable implication in power? Can only poststructuralist theory lay claim to such self-reflection, or is it really critical theory—as some of its adherents would affirm—that provides the most viable alternative?

What I want to do in this essay is address the present status of feminist theory by taking a particular moment in contemporary feminist debates as a starting point, namely, the collection *Feminist Contentions* (1995), the Anglo-American translation of a book that first appeared in Germany as *Der Streit um Differenz* (1993) and originally centered around the question of feminism's links to postmodernism, in line with another collection titled *Feminism/Postmodernism* (1990).[6] To be sure, as Linda Nicholson cautions in *Feminist Contentions*, the book refuses to be an anthology about the state of feminist theory at the present.[7] Instead, it reflects an extended "conversation" between feminist theorists, punctuated sometimes by misunderstandings but also by "productive conflicts." Heeding Nicholson's cautionary remarks, I would nonetheless like to take her up on the invitation extended to the reader that she offer an assessment of "what the volume is about."[8] For it seems to me that the "disputes" assembled in *Feminist Contentions* prompt a range of questions about the status, viability, or even desirability of theory for feminism and point up the theoretical controversies that have seemingly fractured the group, as to which "theory" it should embrace. The differences not only reflect on the state of critique, that is, whether feminism should embrace critical theory's normative critique or rather the antifoundationalism of poststructuralism. In addition to revealing deep-seated disagreements about fundamental, methodological assumptions, principles, and premises that infuse the shared project of feminism, *Feminist Contentions* also displays a triangulation that to some extent, it seems to me, has become defining for theoretical feminisms: the "contentious" encounter between the two poles—poststructuralist and critical theory—is mediated by feminist pragmatism or neopragmatism, which becomes an alternative, an exit way out of the deadlock. In fact, whenever attempts have been made to suture the rifts between poststructuralism and critical theory, the answer almost always has been pragmatism. In this context, theory then automatically equals a problematic universalism, pragmatism not just a corrective fallibilism but also judicious political practice. Those who abjure theory altogether have elected a pragmatic frame; others, themselves theorists, have opted for the mediating construction of a "pragmatic theory" that still remains theoretical yet, instead of being universalistic and abstract, is situated, fallibilistic, local, and therefore radically nonfoundationalist.[9] In reading *Feminist Contentions* as "representative," I would like to ask whether the volume isn't symptomatic of larger strategic shifts that have occurred in the feminist playing field but also in the critical arena at large—without, naturally, wanting to leap beyond our historically or culturally situated "now." In many ways, I will suggest, antifoundationalist postmodern and poststructuralist versions of feminist theory have had to make way for a rivaling neopragmatic antifoundationalism. Especially in the United States, the revival of pragmatism in the form of neopragmatism has presented itself as the only tenable alternative to theory, and not just, as we shall see, in the writings of Richard Rorty, though he has certainly been most vocal in exhorting feminists to leave behind so-called metaphysical representational correspondence theories and, above all, old-fashioned ideology critique. But could it be that a series of problems might threaten to go unnoticed if one cathects only on the ills or symptoms of theory? Might one overlook the dangers of a "strong" pragmatism, a position that, I would argue, could turn out to be equally limiting and perhaps as indefensible as *pure* theory?

Naturally, the present essay will not seek to reify or set in stone the debates assembled in *Feminist Contentions*, nor is it meant as a defense or apology of (pure) theory. Instead, it seeks to intervene deliberatively in some of the debates about feminist theory, in which I wish to take up the position of an interlocutor in a democratic discussion about part of what currently engages feminism. Clearly, this intervention does not want to posit that all of feminism is or should be theory, for that would amount to identifying the whole (of feminism) with only a part. But in response to critics who might peremptorily object that to focus on theory means to take away valuable time from political praxis, I want to stress that it is also high time that we take stock of the often covert discursive strategies performed under the aegis of antitheoretical charges. It is time that we look at some of the rhetorical and strategic arguments that are tendered in the service of the theory debates. What kind of perhaps untenable arguments or silent assumptions are being passed off under the rubric of the against-theory debates— arguments that concern politics, praxis, agency, or the real? Can neopragmatism—especially of the sort propagated by Rorty—really lay claim to and make good on all of the positive items it lists on its political agenda? Or might it, just as much as theory, be susceptible to contestation?

To identify oneself as a theorist, these days, means finding oneself, even before the discussion has started, in a defensive mode, having to qualify what one says with frequent disclaimers. Whenever one invokes theory lately, certain doors more easily seem to get shut.[10] For one, the demand for democracy, democratic speech, and discussion is such that one must avoid obfuscation, deviousness, manipulation, rhetorical ploys. In the interest of direct, immediate access or transparent communication, all detours must be avoided, all difficult terminology shut out. Theory, especially poststructuralist theory, has not fared well in that context.[11] In Habermas's critique of poststructuralism, the latter's alleged antidemocratic intent is said to assume the guise of mere faddish aestheticism or other modes of excessive formalism. Formalism in this setting means at least two things: a quasi-Kantian ahistorical "transcendentalism," which, regardless of historical or cultural differentials, detects the same formal laws, structural similarities, and regularities everywhere. "Transcendental"—a term borrowed from Kant—then means the retrieval of the enabling conditions of possibility that either ground or, as the case may be, "un-ground," set adrift the object under analysis, say, subject positions, agency, or sexual identities. Or, again, the allusion to poststructuralism's excessive formalism (along the form-content divide) is meant to fault it for a superficial ornamentalism that fails to heed political content. If nothing else, this essay hopes to redirect the flow of current stymied debates by challenging some of these and other entrenched presuppositions that are frequently advanced, not in the least to discount or discredit feminist theorists.

Without wanting to invalidate the distinctive, specific history of feminist theory, this study also maintains that feminist theory's ends need to be analyzed not only *internally*, that is, from within the history of feminism or women's studies, but also *relationally*, that is, in the context of broader cultural and political developments in the critical field at large.[12] Thus, in studying the history of difference within the feminist movement, one must proceed internally to demonstrate how the call for diversity helped to variegate the assumed white middle-class consensus of the movement, including the early work of second wave feminists. A contextualized reading additionally reveals that feminists in the social sciences and related disciplines were theorizing difference at the same time as corresponding developments in postmodern philosophy, epistemological antifoundationalism, and postcolonial theory were taking shape. Similarly, in examining the changed status of theory in the movement, one can proceed internally and isolate, for example, radical feminism's early criticisms of theory, made in the name of women's experience, diverse history, or the concrete exigencies of the real. If one steps outside the movement's internal history, it additionally becomes clear that the current antitheory moment in feminism is in step with a more general trend, away from theory to new historicism and neopragmatism. Thus, some strands in current antitheoretical feminisms must be situated in the wake of the more encompassing theory wars that rose to prominence in the eighties: the "fall" of deconstruction and poststructuralism as a result of the Heidegger and de Man controversies, the trade embargo on the import of foreign, especially French theory, the renewal of American pragmatism, and, quite recently, the Sokal affair.

To be sure, in the past feminist voices have often been raised against an interpretive practice that looks beyond the movement's perimeters, for fear that feminism would once again be made to look secondary, subservient to a male-identified "master"-theory or discourse. Assuming a complimentary external perspective, however, doesn't necessarily mean that one moves wholly outside of feminist theory or that one becomes dependent on a stronger discourse that a supposedly derivative feminism needs in order to be set on sound, validating footing. Such concerns have no place once we conceive of feminism as intrinsically interdisciplinary, always in dialogue with multiple interlocutors, engaged in an extensive, open-minded give-and-take. To assume such a "double take"—a double critical view, which attends to feminism's internal history *and* external relations—is to be better equipped as one assesses the full complexities of the issues at hand. For it means to take the project of dialogue seriously, not as a way of palliating difference but in the interest of coalition-building. Besides stressing the methodological necessity that exists for such a "double take," I also want to argue—in perhaps all too commonsensical terms—that we try and live multiply defined feminist roles that *can* include theory. Just as we readily acknowledge difference, multiple cultural positions, identity allegiances and alliances when we discuss subject formation across race, class, and gender, so we may need to stop casting ourselves and other feminists in single-issue either/or roles: either you're a practical activist *or* a theorist, but you can't be both. On the level of theoretical formulations, too, this means giving up dogmatic territorial delineations and delimitations, jettisoning the turf wars and factionalism that have increasingly come to define theoretical feminisms as I am writing this. Certainly, a measure of healthy *agonism*—to evoke Chantal Mouffe's conception of the term—may be warranted, but must we settle for a full-blown, crippling *antagonism* that makes all dialogue impossible? Don't we misconceive of the nature of political contestation and the struggle that are supposed to accompany progressive politics when we instate unbridgeable borders between ourselves? Don't we then internalize antagonisms under the false perception that politics amounts to polemics?[13] Contentiousness, then, surely has nothing to do anymore with the productive contestation that directs progressive political struggles. In the interest of constructive debate, dialogue, and discussion, the present essay will shuttle back and forth from analyzing claims about theory to examining claims about feminist theory. Before concentrating on the historical juncture that produced *Feminist Contentions*, I will first trace the more notable moments that have governed the antitheory climate.

Against Theory

To consider the current antitheory positions in their full complexity, one does well to emphasize that the word "theory" has come to stand for a sub-field or part that often—following the logic of synecdoche—is confounded with the whole: poststructuralist theory, including all of its offshoots, such as poststructuralist psychoanalysis.[14] Thus, poststructuralist theory is supposed to have claims and pretensions to lasting foundations, so that, if unqualified, it amounts to nothing more than a transhistorical metaphysics, quaintly archaic and out-of-time in an era of new historicism. Trapped in language, theoretical poststructuralism is said to cast unremitting doubt on the "phenomenal" and the "referential" from the perspective of its self-enclosed linguistic universe. Clearly, such critical arguments about post-structuralism are less concerned with the theoretical enterprise as such, expressed, say, in scientific theories that test general principles on the basis of evidence, make adjustments to the model in order to fine-tune or, if necessary, discard the theory under consideration. Rather, in presuming that poststructuralist theory hovers above the real, its critics in many ways hark back to the ancient theory-praxis divide, including the scholastic distinction between *vita activa* and *vita contemplativa*. For its detractors, poststructuralism fundamentally exposes a "will to theory" (to paraphrase Nietzsche-Foucault) that hopelessly remains locked in a pernicious power-knowledge model.[15] But in an even more restrictive use, theory simply stands for literary theory. When Paul de Man, for example, spoke of a resistance to theory, he literally meant literary theory—though also more—swayed as he was by the euphoria of having literature and theory operate as instruments of ideology critique. The exuberance with which theory was greeted in the 1970s partially derived from the belief that the critic could use literary theory as a tool of ideology critique, much as the bygone humanist deployed literature as a lens on the eternally human.

In the mid- to late 1980s, poststructuralist theory entered into a political crisis, augmented by historical events, above all the revelations about Heidegger's and de Man's Nazi pasts, which seemed to lend credence to the suspicion that deconstruction depended on intrinsically suspect, nihilistic premises. The critique of poststructuralism's politics, however, had started well before the full-blown political crisis came about. In the early 1980s, pragmatist critics began to equate "theory"—be it mainly literary theory—with the apolitical. The signature text that sparked considerable controversy was "Against Theory" (1982) by Steven Knapp and Walter Benn Michaels. Seemingly speaking for all of pragmatism—though confining themselves to the field of literary criticism and studies—Knapp and Michaels successfully put a string of antitheory arguments into circulation that produced ripple effects well beyond the walls of literature departments.[16] In setting the tone for the post-(French) theory climate that gained prominence in those years, they took on the ontological and epistemological misconceptions that accompanied what they called the "theoretical impulse," maintaining that the Anglo-American theory tradition had been almost exclusively concerned with knowledge production: "If the ontological project of theory has been to imagine a condition of language before intention, its epistemological project has been to imagine a condition of knowledge before interpretation."[17] In Stanley Fish's *Is There a Text in this Class?*, they detected "the theoretical impulse in its purest form," a cryptofoundationalist theory of sorts that positioned itself outside of practice.[18] Idealistic epistemology à la Fish purported to stand outside of belief, when it erroneously postulated that it could devise a "theory" about belief, while the pragmatic position, defended by Michaels and Knapp, always already understood itself to be nothing but a "belief of a belief." In reality, theory quite simply was the antipode of praxis and good leftist activism, while pragmatism could pride itself on being wholly saturated with unwavering practical commitment. In no uncertain terms, their manifesto clearly summed up the arguments that were to recur in ensuing debates, especially the polarization of theory against practice:

> In our view . . . the only relevant truth about belief is that you can't go outside it, and, far from being unlivable, this is a truth you can't help but live. It has no practical consequences not because it can never be *united* with practice but because it can never be *separated* from practice. The theoretical impulse, as we have described it, always involves the attempt to separate things that should not be separated: on the onto-logical side, meaning from intention, language from speech acts; on the epistemological side, knowledge from true belief. Our point has been that the separated terms are in fact inseparable. It is tempting to end by saying that theory and practice too are inseparable. But this would be a mistake. Not because theory and practice (unlike the other terms) really are separate but because theory is nothing else but the attempt to escape practice.[19]

The net result of such stark, undiversified statements, which cast the two terms as irreconcilable antipodes (not just propagated by the authors of this manifesto), was a far-reaching factionalism that slowly but surely took hold over not a few literature departments. At times it appeared that it would for-ever be impossible for students or scholars of literature to profess to both occupations at the same time, that is, to be simultaneously a theorist and pragmatist, or a theorist and new historicist. So ingrained is this perception of mutual exclusiveness in the critical field that one easily forgets that for founding philosophical pragmatists, such as William James, not all theory was impossible, just as long as pragmatic theories attended to the antidogmatic safeguards James favored in his day: nominalism, utilitarianism, and posi-tivism.[20] Indeed, Cornel West's "Theory, Pragmatics, and Politics" makes the point convincingly when he maintains that pragmatism need not be against theory per se—be they small or grand theories—but, rather, should eschew all forms of brazen dogmatism. Impassioned by pragmatism's seemingly exclusive claims to epistemic antifoundationalism, the authors of "Against Theory" mistakenly take *all* theory or "the theoretical enterprise as a cover for new forms of epistemic foundationalism."[21] West's own vocational, prophetic pragmatism, by contrast, largely depends on grand theories such as Marxism, which are enlisted for heuristic not dogmatic ends.[22] If one elaborates further on West's critique, it becomes clear that Knapp and

Michaels's inability to conceive of "grand" metanarratives vs. "small" theories or *récits*, foundationalist vs. nondogmatic metatheories, leads them to ignore the kind of nonfoundationalist, nondogmatic fallibilistic theories that, as we shall see, many feminists prefer.

While never referring to Knapp and Michaels explicitly, Homi Bhabha's "The Commitment to Theory" still in many ways took issue with their assumptions, when he declared that theory does not automatically and of necessity shut out the political.[23] His defense of theory's hybridity helped to dismantle the suspect protectionist, exclusive rights to political practice to which antitheorists often lay claim. But Bhabha also did decidedly more than simply debunk dubitable claims to the prerogatives of praxis. For it seems to me that his analysis enables one to understand the problematic nationalistic (perhaps even protectionistic) phantasms that increasingly have come to determine the antitheory debates. As theory was rejected for being the vehicle of a new intellectual recolonialization, prompting charges of elitism, imperialism, and Eurocentrism, postcolonial critics such as Homi Bhabha and Gayatri Spivak took issue with such wholesale denunciations and undiversified invectives, all the while acknowledging the shortcomings of "capital t Theory."[24] In his "Commitment to Theory," Bhabha plainly charged that the antitheory debates meant to polarize in order to polemicize. Criticizing the projection of the geopolitical polarity of the West and the East along a theory vs. creativity axis, he warned that theory thus threatened to become identified with the Western perspective. "Are the interests of 'Western' theory necessarily collusive with the hegemonic role of the West as a power bloc? Is the language of theory merely another power ploy of the culturally privileged Western elite to produce a discourse of the Other that reinforces its own power-knowledge equation?"[25] In his view, it was mandatory to set an end to the "popular binarism between theory and politics, whose foundational basis is a view of knowledge as totalizing generality and everyday life as experience, subjectivity or false consciousness." For "[theory] does not foreclose on the political, even though battles for power-knowledge may be won or lost to great effect. The corollary is that there is no first or final act of revolutionary social (or socialist) transformation."[26] Indeed, postcolonial theorists such as Fanon demonstrated the entwinement between theory and practice, making us aware of the hybridity or cross-fertilization that exists between cross-cultural theories.

In order to cast further light on this more recent theory-praxis split, artificially held in place by antitheory critics, one might well return to some older attempts to overcome the divide. For, pursuing this genealogy of theory in descending direction, one soon remembers that before poststructuralist theory there was critical and Marxist theory. Defining for modernity's conceptual horizon, the term "pure" theory is of Marxist coinage—though the opposition to practice is, as mentioned earlier, of much older date.[27] Indeed, in its current incarnation, the division between theory and practice unmistakably leads back to Marx and Engels's early writings, to the "Theses on Feuerbach" and the contemporaneous *German Ideology*. In that tract, Marx and Engels described the origin of ideology (the first "ideologues," according to their doctrine, being priests) and the genesis of "pure theory" as the products of an originary, problematic "division of labor" that lay at the foundation of modern society and, by extension, modernity at large.[28] "Pure theory," or ideology, was of a kind with the equally objectionable "mere criticism"—a derogative term they reserved for the Young Hegelians, on whom they tried out their new instrument of critique. True theory as ideology critique was no longer divorced from a material base but able to overcome the alienating consciousness-matter divide.[29] In an attempt to fine-tune this terminological apparatus, Max Horkheimer returned to Marxist foundations when in 1938 he wrote a manifesto, titled "Traditional and Critical Theory," which would become defining for what later was to be called the Frankfurt School. In it, he clearly differentiated between a (neo-Kantian) traditional theory, on the one hand, and a Marxist, immanent, critical theory, on the other, which no longer occupied an Archimedean position outside its object. Bad theory—to extrapolate from Horkheimer's study—is, much like his conception of traditional theory, fraught with a suspect epistemological split between object and subject, while critical theory assumes the mutual enmeshment of both, all the while being painfully aware of its own implication in power.[30] Foucault mainstreamed this insight when in an explicit return to the Frankfurt School's critical theory tradition, he posited the complication of knowledge/power, even as he was weary of all manifestations of pure theory.

If it is wrong, therefore, to identify all theory with ideology, it is equally misguided to equate all theory with ideology critique. "Theoretical activism" only works if it is thought of as immanent critique, as an effort to overcome the theory/praxis divide. To fetishize theory, by contrast, is to ascribe a magical aura to it, the energy of power, force, or simply social prestige. Theory then functions as cultural capital, whose exchange value is such that it adds cultural status and standing, a theoretical chic, to its user. Seen

from a Marxist perspective, fetishized theory is an alienated product, the naturalized version of a cultural construction, a social hieroglyphic or commodity that may end up showcasing its user's alienation from praxis. Instead
of fetishizing it, the theorist must bravely assess the critical damage done to
her theory, in order to assemble the shards and move on. Indeed, as I hope
to show, this is precisely what the assemblage of feminist theory shows us to
have been the case. For, when held against the template of the conditions
that govern sound theory-construction, the *history* of feminist theory attests
to a dynamic process in which theoretical assumptions are continuously
tested or fine-tuned, and various categories of analysis—"woman," "sex,"
"gender"—adjusted. Testing itself against the real, feminist theory over the
decades has changed in the process of an ever-evolving critical activism.

For Feminist Theory

Feminist theory only exists as a multicolored assemblage of threads, a web—
to allude to the much cherished, somewhat threadbare, yet nonetheless
effective metaphor—that draws upon but also extends beyond literary,
social, cultural, critical, or political theory. Because there is no one unitary
theory, but pluralities of theories, feminist theory's history consists of
numerous strands and diverse threads, not all of which, naturally, can be disentangled in the context of this essay. That said, perhaps it might be possible
to point to a few of the most representative discussions that have occupied
feminists, in which the dialectic between "materialism" vs. "idealism" in various manifestations seems to return. If one looks at feminist debates of the
last three decades, what becomes most clear is that feminism has moved away
from working with the implicit assumption that there exists a "consensus"
among women to the increased recognition of difference, even dissent. The
exclusive concern with a presumed ideological, if not cultural, equality
among subjects came at the expense of differences across race, class, and sexual orientation, because women's particularities were subsumed under a
totalizing or universalizing feminist agenda. To be sure, internal and external
historical forces worked together to bring about these far-reaching transformations, yielding an increased perception and awareness of difference.[31]
Second wave feminism, for example, saw its unified platform crumble, first
through radical challenges to its underlying ethnocentrism and neglect of
sexual difference, later through feminism's encounter with the antifounda-

tionalism of postmodernism and poststructuralism. To some extent, the second wave's shortcomings in recognizing the full spectrum of difference
among women were the result of inadequate levels of theorization. In her
valuable overview anthology, *The Second Wave,* Nicholson has suggested that
"differences among women were acknowledged, but minimally incorporated into the basic threads of the theory," implying that the movement's
language failed to adequately render women's diversity.[32]

Looking back, for example, at one of the most turbulent controversies
that raged in the 1970s and 1990s—the essentialism-constructionism dispute
mainly angled at French feminist theory—one sees that it was played out,
early on, along the idealism vs. materialism axis. Operating with a monolithic, Western female subject, French feminist theory, especially the poeti-
cizing *écriture féminine*, was taken on for unwittingly reproducing the falla-
cies of patriarchal discourse. It is ironic that Irigaray, one of the most astute
genealogists of what was wrong with occidental theory, eventually would
come under attack for replicating its ills. In her influential *Speculum of the
Other Woman,* she traced the roots of theory back to Plato, to the idolatry of
a "specular ocularcentrism," drawing on the etymological roots of the word
theorein, "to see." Bad or pure theory for her was of the order of "mere speculation," as expressed, for example, in her observation that "Every theory of
the 'subject' will always already have been appropriated by the 'masculin.' "
("Toute théorie du 'sujet' aura toujours été appropriée au 'masculin.' ")[33]
Read carefully, her pronouncement not only connected the manufacturing
of subjecthood to masculinity—as the line ordinarily is interpreted—but
also to the very privilege of theory-construction, that is, who gets to tinker
with theories, who not. Yet, at the same time that her work deconstructed
"high theory," it also performed it under the banner of appropriating male
discourse in order to displace it parodically. Thus, her own position in the
1970s came under scrutiny from materialist feminists, such as Christine Del-
phy and Monique Wittig, so that the theory-praxis, speculation-materialism
dualism was played out between them early on. For might not the category
of "Woman" in feminine writing refer to a problematic myth, rather than to
a historical materialist practice, implying that "women do not belong to history, and that writing is not a material production"?[34]

Not all those who criticized Irigaray's work, however, would follow Wittig's materialistic bent. Some voices of dissent seemed to be informed by a
disputable theory-creativity divide, which—much as in Bhabha's analysis of
geopolitical polarization—recast the dualism in terms of gender binarisms,

maintaining that theory always already was male-identified. Here, the old gendered dualism of feeling, affect, and emotive experience vs. rationalism threatened to rear its ugly head. While such gender-biased responses largely remained essentialistic, in some cases even biologistic, some feminist critics tendered more sophisticated critiques about the dangers of getting recuperated by a patriarchal power politics through theory. Though her own work has added significant contributions to the field of feminist theory, Rosi Braidotti, for example, maintained that radical feminism could not "result in the revalorization of the discourse of 'high theory' and especially of philosophy."[35] Taking on female theorists and intellectuals such as de Beauvoir, Irigaray, or Spivak, her *Nomadic Subjects* warned that feminism might be in danger of duplicating "one of the most ancient mental habits of patriarchy: the overinvestment of the theoretical mode, as exemplified by philosophy, with the consequent glorification of the figure of the philosopher."[36] Against the "false universalisms" of theory, one ought to hold the praxis of "nomadic questioning." "What is needed in women's studies as a practice of sexual difference in the nomadic mode is a critique of the implicit system of values conveyed by high theory in its support of a conventional image of thought and of the thinker as sovereign in its text."[37] High theory, in this argument, rightly becomes like high culture or high modernism the vehicle of power that suppresses the lower classes, while advancing the cultural elitism of the white upper class. To be sure, cast in this guise one must abjure theory, but is this the whole picture? Not all philosophy necessarily is identical with "metaphysics," especially not social or political philosophy, or, say, feminist contributions to an ethics of care.[38] In my opinion, we should, for sure, acknowledge the excesses of theoretical language, as practiced in the 1970s and 1980s and, no doubt, at present. But we must also ask whether it is true that theory is intrinsically or necessarily antidemocratic, whether it is without fail a tool of obfuscation. Must theoretical talk automatically get one into the traps of a performative contradiction, must it always be exclusionary? To me, it seems that the question of whether there can be a theoretical activism, or whether "to theorize" can be a praxis, should be answered in the affirmative for Irigaray, as well as other feminist theorists, regardless of the incontestable defects or flaws their respective models may, over the years, have exposed. When Irigaray decried women's exclusion from the discipline of philosophy, the gist of her theoretical gesture was not to set up a new republic of feminist philosophers that would exclude poets, writers, performers, politicians, partisans, guerrilla troops, amazons. Feminist theory *is* a praxis insofar as it has fundamentally and radically reshaped conceptual categories or definitions of sex, gender, oppression, identity—always in an ongoing dynamic process of debate and continued, never-ending discussion. In my mind, there doesn't need to exist a contradiction between, first, acknowledging that the critique of French feminist theory's localism, classism, or luxurious literariness is justified from the standpoint of global diversified communities and, second, celebrating it as an extraordinarily creative, rich phase in the history of feminist theory.

It is no small feat that the critique of feminism's exclusionary practices, its denial of radical difference among women, slowly but surely brought about a sea change in its theoretical foundations. For, along with the twin attacks on American radical feminism and *écriture féminine* occurred a major shift away from the category "woman"—a mark of feminism's "gynocentrism"[39]—to "gender," culminating in Butler's *Gender Trouble*. In taking on "essentialism"[40] through "constructivism" and "antifoundationalism," feminists engaged in multiple alliances and in coalition-building with postmodernism, poststructuralism, and postcolonial theory. But it is here precisely that lies the crux of some of the current stymied confrontations that are still with us. Some fear that too much theory—especially too much deconstruction of the category "woman"—will supplant the category "women" by "gender" altogether, so that the collective object as well as the common objective all feminisms minimally share will be abandoned.[41] Such an abandoning of feminisms' communal ends then will automatically precipitate the very end of feminism—despite the reassurances to the contrary of so-called postfeminist theorists. Others, mainly representatives of critical theory, instead contest poststructuralism's and postmodernism's lack of normativity, shared first principles, and regulative norms, whose absence is said to hamper its political effectiveness. Representatives of poststructuralism, by contrast, often will take on the presumed universalism and totalizing gestures that accompany normative agendas, in the name of the particularisms of identity politics. However, the difficulty the historian of feminist theory encounters in trying to map all of these differences is not only the terminological confusion that beleaguers terms such as postmodernism, poststructuralism, universalism, normativity, and antifoundationalism but also the ambivalent valence these terms have acquired. Not only have attempts been made to map these terms onto the spectrum of left- vs. right-wing politics—augmented by Habermas's undiversified negative valorization of an entire school of thought[42]—but to some degree differences also pertain as to whether one operates in the humanities or social sciences. Does antifoundationalism mean political groundlessness or merely the attempt to adopt a historical, relativistic position that is conscious of its limitations and shuns totalization? Should we shunt essentialism but retain a "strategic essentialism," lest the empirical gets elided, as Spivak has charged? Does postmodern feminist social theory risk looking uncannily similar to the value-free conservatism it was meant to correct?[43] And, how do some critical theorists seek to conjoin an antifoundationalist methodology to a normative model of social change?

Among the most cogent responses to these complicated issues are, no doubt, Jane Flax's and Sandra Harding's contributions to the postmodernism debate, included in Nicholson's *Postmodernism/Feminism*—interventions so valuable, it seems to me, because they directly consider the vexed conundrum of normativity that has split apart critical theorists and poststructuralists. Flax's commonsensical observation that to get to feminist theory we must return to its purported object—gender—still very much rings true. If the common, if you will, shared goal of all feminist theory pertains to gender relations of some sort, then it also involves thinking about gender. Consequently, feminist theory always involves a *metatheoretical* moment, according to Flax—that is, a reflection on how gender is thought and, therefore, a "thinking of thinking."[44] The plurality of women's social practices and experiences is reflected in the diversity of definitions feminists have given of gender relations—as Flax continues her all too logical argument, pointing to disagreements over the sex/gender split, patterns of gender socialization, gendered social differences, modes of embodiedness, and the public/private split.[45] But in addition to recognizing innovations coming from the fields of anthropology, ethnic studies, and history, which were successfully incorporated into feminist theory, one should not underestimate the influence of postmodernist and poststructuralist antifoundationalism. Here, it seems, lies the crux of the matter of what, according to some, might be "wrong" with contemporary feminist theory: how to prevent an *epistemological* antifoundationalism from slipping into a skepticism and relativism that eventually results in a *political* groundlessness and, consequently, paralyzing inactivism? Or, to put it quite simply, how can we judge—let alone alter—the everyday political arena, aspire to improve women's situation locally and globally, if we operate with a theory that lacks clear normative directives and values? Harding expresses the dilemma of contemporary debates cogently when she wonders whether too much postmodern or postmetaphysical theory might erode justificatory political strategies needed as "a justifiable guide to practical decisions."[46] Thus, in the social and natural sciences, she convincingly argues, it may well be necessary to adopt a feminist empiricism or standpoint theory to avoid hollowing out the strongholds of self, truth, and knowledge, which could lead to a relapse into a positivistic value-free science or interpretationism.[47]

Let me try to summarize the set of problems this current methodological dilemma raises in practical terms: feminist theory must seek to hold the balance between anti- or nonfoundationalist (epistemological) strategies that correct essentialism, without falling into a political indecisiveness. Though epistemic antifoundationalism was necessary, strategically speaking, to set an end to a problematic essentialism, it now is said to have lost its beneficial effects, to the point of producing antipolitical aftereffects. In other words, too high a dose of it may lead to skepticism and relativism—charges not unsimilar to the ones made outside the field of feminisms. However, when such points acquire the status of mantras that are simply repeated, without a detailed consideration of the position under attack, they also deserve to be challenged and, if necessary, rebutted. For, as I want to claim, it means to confound epistemology with politics, if one believes either that an epistemological antifoundationalism automatically translates into politically legitimate agendas or, quite the opposite, that a critique of foundationalism must always end in antipolitics. Put differently, an epistemological antifoundationalism need not stand in contradiction to a politically founded program (which is not the same as "foundational," that is, "totalizing" or "universalizing," at the expense of difference). Conversely, the other side of the coin also holds true: antifoundationalism does not *eo ipso* result in a correct political praxis. To posit such cause-and-effect relations may mean to get entangled in an obsessional systematic logic, when in fact it is the *dogmatism* that accompanies theoretical *no less than* antitheoretical positions that needs to be avoided. It is in an attempt to avert such false dualisms that some feminist theorists have countered the charges of a dogmatic universalism, by pointing, for instance, to a situated universalism, where provisional universalist programs are tested and corrected as seen fit.

Enter neopragmatism. That some feminists have tried to replace postmodernism and poststructuralism by neopragmatism largely seems due to the unwieldiness or negatives that these labels were unable to shed. Exchanging labels in practice meant choosing a different kind of antifoundationalism that seemed less beleaguered by the flaws or charges of neoconservatism marking the earlier intellectual traditions. Presenting itself as a more viable alternative, pragmatism thus became a new strategy to retain or rescript feminist theory. Critical theorists Nancy Fraser and Iris Marion Young have been most vocal in these efforts. Coming themselves from strong theoretical positions associated with critical theory, they have proposed some of the most pronounced defenses for the pragmatic turn, Fraser by arguing for "postmodern theory" and "neopragmatism" respectively, Young by pointing to a "pragmatic theorizing."[48] Feminist theory for Young is to presuppose a subject defined by "serial collectivity," but without the universalizing and essentializing claims that come with a totalizing theory. Postfeminism, it seems to me, becomes a moot point, once the historical category of "women" is seen, following Young, as a serial collective.

But the first real signs of this new terminological shift, not surprisingly, became apparent in the context of the feminism-postmodernism debates. Indeed, in 1988 Fraser and Nicholson published a highly influential article, titled "Social Criticism without Philosophy: An Encounter between Feminism and Postmodernism."[49] Feminism, the authors argued, had "tried to rethink the relation between philosophy and social criticism so as to develop paradigms of criticism without philosophy."[50] As is clear, they did not reject the term "theory" as such, for they evoked "feminist theory"[51] (if to detect its essentialism), while turning to the critique Lyotard and Rorty had proffered of "Philosophy with a capital P." These philosophers had established that "philosophy, *and, by extension, theory in general,* can no longer function to *ground* politics and social criticism. With the demise of foundationalism comes the demise of the view that casts philosophy in the role of *founding* discourse vis-à-vis social criticism."[52] But as the authors saw it, this also meant the replacement of a modernist by a postmodernist position, in which "criticism floats free of any universalist theoretical ground."[53] The switch away from the linguistic turn meant that criticism would become "more pragmatic, *ad hoc*, contextual, and local."[54] Thus, at the same time that they were sympathetic to the postmodern project, they also developed a staunch critique of Lyotard for advocating the "illegitimacy of several genres of social criticism," such as "large-scale historical narrative and social-theoretical analyses of pervasive relations of dominance and subordination."[55] That is, he went "too quickly from the premise that Philosophy cannot ground social criticism to the conclusion that criticism itself must be local, *ad hoc*, and nontheoretical. As a result, he throws out the baby of large historical narrative with the bathwater of philosophical metanarrative and the baby of social-theoretical analysis of large-scale inequalities with the bathwater of reductive Marxian class theory."[56] In fact, what they argued for was a "postmodern theory," but with the following caveat: "if postmodern-feminist critique must remain theoretical, not just any kind of theory will do. Rather, theory here would be explicitly historical, attuned to the cultural specificity of different societies and periods and to that of different groups within societies and periods."[57] The result would be a postmodern feminist theory that was historicist, nonuniversalist, comparativist, pragmatic, and fallibilistic. "It would tailor its methods and categories to the specific task at hand, using multiple categories when appropriate and forswearing the metaphysical comfort of a single feminist method or feminist epistemelogy. In short, this theory would look more like a tapestry composed of threads of many different hues than one woven in a single color."[58] Not simply rhetorically but clearly politically persuasive, Fraser and Nicholson's essay stipulated that feminism's claim to diversity could only be achieved through a versatile methodological apparatus that would be reconfigured or retooled as the political cause saw fit. Indeed, it is this very call for pragmatism that also returned prominently—now as the mediating position—in *Feminist Contentions*.

Contentious or Debating Feminisms?

The theoretical "antagonisms" that emerged in *Feminist Contentions* were a historical product, entirely missing from an earlier 1987 collection titled *Feminism as Critique*, which had already brought together many of the same contributors.[59] Its editors, Seyla Benhabib and Drucilla Cornell, did not make an attempt to separate factions but housed them all under the broader (Marxist) rubric "critique." Rather than defining the term "critique" unequivocally, they rerouted the question through the political trajectory of the women's movement, as it emerged "alongside and in some cases out of the New Left in Europe and North America," noting that feminist critique would bid farewell to feminism's first phase, defined by the *deconstruction* of the Western tradition, to focus now on theoretical *reconstruction*.[60] Similarly, in its dialogue with Marxism, feminist critique needed to scrutinize the Marxist paradigm of *production*, without simply replacing it by the gendered category *reproduction*, or losing sight of the need for distributive justice. But if in 1987 the term "critique" was left standing as a larger label under which a diverse collective of feminist theorists could be catalogued, then the elements of the debate shifted quite dramatically in the mid-1990s when *Feminist Contentions* appeared in print. By that time a firm polarization had sedimented between a Frankfurt-style normative critique (Benhabib), on the one hand, and a poststructuralist, performative theory of "resignification" (Butler), on the other, while Fraser sought to mediate between the two, arguing that feminism needed both. Clearly, the disagreements that emerged in full view were not merely formulaic but, rather, revelatory as to deeper, substantive differences that divided the collective. At the center of these contentions was an entire lexicon of keywords, such as critique, power/force, consent/dissent, norm/normativity, universality/particularity, foundationalism, utopia. Yet, are these differences truly as unremediably unbridgeable as some of the interlocutors intimated, or might they to a large extent be formal, perhaps even methodological, and hence subject to review? It seems worthwhile to reconsider some of the most salient differences between the participants from this new angle.

In answering her critics, Butler started off questioning the catchall nature of the label "postmodernism," whose totalizing status threatened to brush over the unwieldiness of the historical field, choosing instead a deconstructive poststructuralism. This further meant differentiating her own position from a Frankfurt-style critical tradition. For, though Fraser had coined the label "dereifying critique" for her work, Butler in one of her interventions qualified the tradition of "critique," placing the term in distancing quotation marks, while at the same time fine-tuning it: "My argument is that 'critique,' to use Fraser's term, always takes place *immanent* to the regime of discourse/power whose claims it seeks to adjudicate, which is to say that the practice of 'critique' is implicated in the very power-relations it seeks to adjudicate."[61] Regardless of the fact, however, that Butler here merely cited the term "critique"—using it parodically, as it were—her version of poststructuralism nonetheless remains faithful to (Marxist) immanent critique, as defined earlier, insofar as the object of analysis from which it cannot extract itself is power. Centrally, power here does not refer to the kind of empowering force at the disposal of autonomous individuals, precious to political liberalism, but to a Foucauldian frame of reference in which power mostly equals a "subject-ing" regime of force or symbolic violence.

But the main bones of contention, undoubtedly, were the *normative* and *universalistic* claims that infuse critical theory, which, according to Butler, risked turning it into a "metapolitical site of ultimate normativity." Taking on "normative political philosophy" for allegedly assuming a stance "beyond the play of power,"[62] Butler went on to note that it was not simply a matter, however, of pitting a poststructuralist antifoundationalism against a Frankfurt-style foundationalism, for that would merely amount to privileging the other side of the same coin. "Rather, the task is to interrogate what the theoretical move that establishes foundations *authorizes*, and what precisely it excludes or forecloses."[63] Again and again, her contribution returned to querying the "authorizing power" that is performatively lent to speaking positions.[64] Her remarks thus raised the question of legitimation, suggesting in Bourdieu-like fashion that claims to legitimacy result from authoritative speech acts, which at once feed on and performatively renew authority.[65] By contrast, deconstruction allowed for the exposure of power ploys, so that, rather than being a negating act, it disclosed a new space of possibilities: "To deconstruct is not to negate or to dismiss, but to call into question and, perhaps most importantly, to open up a term, like the subject, to a reusage or redeployment that previously has not been authorized."[66] All normativity in truth shielded itself from critical dissent, driven as it was by the "ruse of authority that seeks to close itself off from contest that is, in my view, at the heart of any radical political project."[67] Furthermore, normative values such as "subjecthood" or "universality" proved to be unfounded, literally, for the historical crisis to which they had been subjected, in postcolonial or feminist discursive arenas, patently demonstrated the loss of "ground" these terms had suffered—a loss no longer to be undone by willful reflection. Her principal target, clearly, was the term "universality." Instead of being either a *procedural* or *substantive* term, "universality" in reality amounted to a "site of insistent contest and resignification,"[68] for as a foundational (Enlightenment) norm its totalizing claims had been challenged in feminist and postcolonial discourse alike. To no small degree, Butler's argument thus also remained vested in the disputes over universalism that raged in the wake of the debates sparked by Habermas's Frankfurt lectures about the legacy of the Enlightenment in the postmodern condition.

It is clear that Butler's contestations unremittingly revolved around the vexed issue of normativity. But in postulating that all normative critique incorrigibly remained oblivious to its vested interests in power, her observations were fundamentally at odds with Benhabib's. In fact, their differences illustrated the far-reaching equivocations that have accrued around terms such as norms, normative, and normalization. In a post-Nietzschean frame of reference, distinguished by the relativism of values, all norms must merely amount to the perspectival, even forceful, imposition of values. But phrased as such, this post-Nietzschean position at the same time proves highly debatable insofar as norms can of course be agreed upon democratically and deliberatively; that is, they can reflect the acquired consensus of principles in a democratic playing field with built-in correctives to adjust or jettison defunct, obsolete, exclusive—in other words, insufficiently inclusive— norms. In this respect, Benhabib, for example, has in numerous publications acknowledged and addressed the power claims that imbue Habermas's model, no less than her own normative position. Most explicitly she has done so in her important essay "The Generalized and Concrete Other," which sought to amend the assumed universal moral perspective of Habermas et al., by drawing on Carol Gilligan's ethics of care.[69] Rather than automatically being apodictic or imposed from above, radically democratic norms can find validation and vindication in rational, even emotive discussion or be challenged through contestation, dissent, and disagreement.

Shifting the terms of the discussion considerably, Fraser sought to mediate between the interlocutors, hoping to undo the dualism or "false antitheses" by deflecting from the status of their respective theories and appealing to the negotiating work of neopragmatism. Butler's and Benhabib's positions were fundamentally "complimentary,"[70] she asserted, insofar as the former could be aligned with "the local, the discrete, and the specific," the latter with "provisional totalization."[71] In wrapping up her assessment of the factions, she suggested that "Butler's approach is good for theorizing the micro level, the intrasubjective, and the historicity of gender relations. It is not useful, in contrast, for the macro level, the intersubjective, and the normative."[72] Feminism, in that sense, needed to be informed by what she called "the eclectic spirit" of neopragmatism. "This means adopting theoretical conceptions that permit both dereifying critique and normative critique, as well as the generation of new emancipatory significations."[73] Doubting, however, that Fraser's neopragmatism was postmodern,[74] Benhabib remained unswayed in her retort, disinclined to take the step Fraser had taken, insisting on the "clash of theoretical paradigms," on "serious differences" and "genuinely different conceptual options."[75] Butler, for her part, mainly regretted the state of the debates, noting their parochialism and disputing that they were "representative," inasmuch as they excluded discussions of race but also the dynamics of the "theory wars." Looking back on the dispute's limited scope, she observed that their interactions had failed to take full stock of the "presupposed sense that theoretical reflection matters."

The debate never touched on "the rarefied status of theoretical language, the place of narrative in or as theory, the possibility of a theoretical activism, the tension between theory and empiricism, the question of whether post-structuralism is the only theory that counts as 'theory.' "[76] Indirectly, Butler thereby acknowledged that, though the contributors to the book shared a commitment to theory, they disagreed over the theoretical paradigm to be embraced as well as to the scope of its practical implications. In the end, the rigorous principles that underlay, indeed founded, these triangulated conceptual theories—whether poststructuralist, critical, or pragmatic theory—determined the disagreements that preoccupied these feminist theorists. Must we conclude, then, that the encounter merely resulted in a new impasse, or might there be ways of realigning its terms and keywords in new constellations? As a way of answering this question, let me formulate another possible response to the disputes.

First of all, it seems problematic to suggest that poststructuralist feminism, as represented by Butler's position, merely proves the cordoning off of theory, reflection, or philosophy from political struggle as such.[77] Such a claim once again returns us to the false duality between theory and praxis, which arises precisely when we assume that the theoretical and the practical stand opposed to one another, according to a Kantian model of critique, rather than a (neo-)Marxist one, moored—however unsteadily—in immanent critique. It is in positivistic models that separate pristine objects from interpretation and deny the reality of the "hermeneutical circle" that theory and practice, theory and object, must be rift from one another. Once we do not subscribe to that position, however, things become less simple than some critics would have us believe. The more pressing question that needs to be raised instead is how we define politics and the political, and whether these categories are broad enough to include multiple feminist programs and agendas—all the way from identity politics that address gay and lesbian claims to equal legal and cultural recognition, to improving the socioeconomic condition of so-called welfare mothers—to cite that highly problematic term—to showing remedial solidarity with Third World women, and, in fact, to ensuring that all of us can be subjects of political agency, not just on the receiving end. In that sense, it also seems invaluable to heed Fraser's injunction, made in her *Justice Interruptus*, that we keep both perspectives—(cultural) recognition *and* economic redistribution—in view.[78] This also means that we need to remain realistic about what single theories can do and that we acknowledge the need for an assemblage of different theories with partial, sometimes small-range objectives, rather than grand totalizing goals.

Second, like Fraser, I believe that, up to a certain point, both positions— critical theory and poststructuralism—may be able to converge, certainly more so than their representatives seem willing to concede. Granted, these feminisms differ most fundamentally as to whether or not they subscribe to a universalizing project—a Kantian universal horizon of expectation, if you will—and as to whether they assume "agreement" (deliberative agreement, Benhabib) or "disagreement" (agonistic difference and contestation, Butler) as the beginning and end-all of the political playing field. Furthermore, as I have noted earlier, the first position remains wedded to normativity, the other exposes the reputed violence or exclusionary gestures that emanate from what it sees as a normative foundationalism (collapsing the two terms). But once we look more closely at the conundrum of normativity, things again appear less simple, insofar as critical theory acknowledges historical and cultural contingency while poststructuralism, for its part, draws on a minimal "normative" program. Thus, Butler acknowledges "contingent foundations" or a "historically constrained perspective,"[79] respectively, while Benhabib amends her universalist program by recognizing "situated"—cultural and historical—"foundations." Again, as I have noted earlier, it also seems false to assume, as Butler does, that all normativity is merely a matter of "authority," "violent imposition," rather than possible democratic discussion that does not exclude dissent. Undeniably, she is right in seeing deconstruction as the opening of categories of exclusion, but perhaps she too readily collapses the difference between, on the one hand, normativity, the "normal"/the "norm," or the "mean," and, on the other, an inculcating normalization executed through performative rituals, on the model of Foucault's *Discipline and Punish*.[80] Conversely, the argument that critical theory operates with a founding normativity can also be turned back onto poststructuralism, including its feminist version. Here again it is useful to distinguish between epistemic and political levels of practice, in line with my earlier discussion in the section "Against Theory." For, despite its avowed *epistemic* antifoundationalism, deconstructive feminism adheres to a normative, *politically* founded agenda, insofar as it seeks to attain a modicum of universal justice, even if it defines it in Derridean, perhaps even quasi-messianic fashion, as a "justice to come" (*à-venir*).[81] The tensions between the epistemic and political demands of Butler's poststructuralist feminism become palpable when she asserts that deconstruction constantly rifts the term "feminism," which, for its part, needs to be "affirmed as the ungrounded ground of feminist theory."[82] It is clear that, in order to respect the full diversity of all feminisms, Butler here has recourse to the paradoxical construction of an "ungrounded ground." Arguably, this paradoxical claim fits within her epistemological framework, which ceaselessly seeks to get the better of the potentially totalizing, universalizing pretensions of her own nomenclature. Yet, the phrase hardly captures the programmatic, less than merely contingent truth of feminist politics. The problem in the foregoing passage, it seems to me, is once again one of definition. For Butler, foundationalism becomes synonymous with normativity, which is why she has recourse to the fiction of an ungrounded ground. All ideology critique, however—including feminist ideology critique—remains normative insofar as it works with a representational theory and the truth-falsehood distinction on the basis of which it measures the real against the ideal—this despite Foucault's well-intended attempt to undo the left-wing "will to knowledge" by getting rid of the term "ideology" altogether. To my mind, there can be no doubt that both Butler's and Benhabib's positions are incontestably ideology-critical *and* "utopian" in nature, that is, guided by utopian regulative ideas whose ideals are, if perhaps never to be realized fully, then maximally to be approximated by feminism. One such ideal might be a global—if you will, "universal"—justice, in other words, cross-cultural legal and cultural equality for women across the globe, which respects their multiple differences. Indeed, to believe in a justice-yet-to-come, as Butler's poststructuralist feminism does, is not to be adverse to utopianism.

Let me propose therefore that we change the terms of the encounter from contentious to debating feminisms. In order to do so, we need to revive a notion of interlocutors, rather than foes or contenders, in discourse and discussion. Discursive exchange need not be exclusively concerned with repressive power but can draw upon enabling power, without having to relapse into the pitfalls of an unreflective neoliberalism. This means opting not just for a subversive discourse but also for inclusive dialogue, without wanting to give up the incommensurability or asymmetry of difference. My point simply is that we need to see the different feminisms as standing side-by-side, ready to acknowledge a minimal division of labor, with limited objectives and tasks, so that a so-called cultural feminism that demands the recognition of identity claims can cohabit with other branches—for example, those concerned more specifically with economic redistribution. It is precisely when either one of the multiple feminisms makes grander claims than it can make true that we get into dogmatic positions that must cancel each other out. Here I am thinking specifically of the latest discussions that are symptomatic of the fracturing in left-wing ranks, notably the dispute around "conservative leftism," the topic of a conference at Santa Cruz and the label used for those feminists who have criticized poststructuralism and identarian politics in the name of materialistic redistribution. In many ways, these disputes are the latest version of what I earlier called the idealism-materialism stand-off; they are also new transformations of the earlier essentialism-constructivism controversy. Butler has rightly taken issue with the return of this old divide in new guise in her "Merely Cultural," in which she convincingly argues that a cultural feminism interested in analyzing heterosexual marital economies, for example, does not necessarily stand opposed to materialism, as it harks back to Engels's analysis of the family. Most divisive in intent, no doubt, has been Martha Nussbaum's *New Republic* review article of Butler's work.[83] Though it certainly may be healthy to enter into debate with fellow feminists, as Nussbaum encourages us to do in *Cultivating Humanity*, it is quite another matter to engage in wholesale vituperations—and not only strategically speaking, as such infightings are appropriated for the agendas of non- or antifeminists. While this is not the place to engage all the issues Nussbaum's review raises,[84] suffice it to say that she mainly faults Butler for being preoccupied with a narrowly particularistic, identarian program, over and against which she holds the only viable alternative of a universalism realized through legal and legislative transformation. Clearly, Nussbaum's demand for social change makes sense; less clear is why it needs to be couched in the undiversified indictment of another feminist. For, *pace* Nussbaum, we can't demand of our fellow feminists that we symmetrically recognize our own theories in their proposals. To demand of all feminists that they only formulate legal theories or legislative recommendations, social policy blueprints that lay claim to exclusive political transformation, is to exclude literary, poetic, performative critics, historians, or still other voices from the discussion, some of which, on the surface, may seem more descriptive, but on which the feminist legal theorist might want to draw—as indeed Nussbaum has done in *Poetic Justice*—or by which the activist is inspired. To exclude these multiplicities of views or to assume justificatory, argumentative superiority is not only to operate with a hierarchical axiology but also to assume the universal claims of one's theory, a theory that can do everything. Thus, there is a difference between a fallible theory that works with the goal of approximating universal, global justice, as hospitable versions of feminism do, and a universalizing (totalizing) theory that suppresses difference, be it in the name of universalism *or* particularism (the universalization of a particularistic standpoint).[85]

Finally, there's yet another reason why I do not necessarily deplore the discussion that ensued between the participants of *Feminist Contentions* or why I don't find cause to agree with Butler that the resulting encounter was merely parochial, so that these disputes can be dismissed for being merely academic or simply elitist. To say so may mean to downplay the pedagogical project of feminism and feminist theory, the dialogue that takes place in the classroom or on the street, the extraordinary way in which many of us have been affected by feminist theory, even if we take issue with it. To my mind, feminist theory can still function in the service of consciousness-raising or the kind of citizen learning that accompanies progressive politics and the emancipatory struggle—in which case it hasn't lost its edge of promoting political literacy. Certainly, the importance of the discussions in *Feminist Contentions* should not be blown out of proportion, but they should also not blind us to what is happening out there in the critical field.

One other vector that defines that field, to which I would like to turn now in closing, involves a question with which we started out, namely, whether pragmatism, even neopragmatism—which, unlike the old version, takes into account the operations of power[86]—should automatically be hailed as the new savior. Does the pragmatic turn provide an answer to the current impasses of theory, including feminist theory? If so, whose pragmatism does feminism need to adopt, given that today there exist as many pluralities of pragmatisms as there are theoretical feminisms? To look ahead to the argument I will develop in this essay's final section, it seems to me that feminism could, and indeed *does*, make use of a *weak*, methodological form of pragmatism, if only to establish a coalition between different voices across race, class, and sexual orientation. At the same time, it may also be necessary to heed the rhetoric of a more problematic, *strong* pragmatism, of the sort advocated, for example, by Rorty, despite the gestures to peaceful dialogue and discussion on which his model seemingly hinges. If it is safe to say that the relations between pragmatism and feminism are fairly new,[87] then it is Rorty who most avidly, but also most controversially has sought to bridge the two, while Fraser has been most theoretical in crafting a feminist neopragmatism. It therefore makes sense to turn to Rorty—first, because he is one of the few pragmatists to have made a persistent appeal to feminism, but also because his most recent work, *Achieving Our Country*, directly takes on the "cultural left," including versions of "cultural feminism," for being spell-bound by too much spectatorial theory.

The Pragmatic Turn

In an era in which the deficit of so many models, including the liberal one, has become patently apparent, a pragmatic eclecticism seems to work best, turning us all into tinkerers, handy-people, picking up tools to solve problems, discarding them as we see fit, in a grand effort to retool pluralistic, radical democracy. Pragmatism translates into concrete terms Lévi-Strauss's description of the anthropologist as *bricoleur*, a description mainstreamed by Roland Barthes. Under duress and in crisis, we all end up in the ER, or emergency room, seeking to make do with whatever life-support systems are on hand, with some even resorting to the pragmatics of triage, if need be.

Following Lyotard's *The Postmodern Condition*, our postmodern era has become the playing field par excellence for pragmatism. Yet, despite his dedication to Wittgenstein et al., Lyotard seemed to offer a "nonpragmatic" variant of pragmatism, at least, when set beside the American pragmatism advocated by Rorty and others. In Lyotard's variety, pragmatism not only assumes that there no longer exists a consensus that can be reached, only the falling apart of the grand narrative of legitimacy, but the result is a "paralogism" that spelled the end to liberalism's prospect of eventually reaching universal understanding. As a result, Lyotard's tract seemingly ended up pointing to the impossibility of all practical forms of politics that still embraced utopian scripts, demolishing the normative claims of theory altogether. Returning to Horkheimer's 1938 essay (cited earlier), Lyotard showed how traditional theory's totalizing claims needed to be situated in the context of a conception of society that was unitary, while its corrective—critical theory—was intrinsically dualistic and dialectical. In the course of twentieth-century history, especially high modernism, these dialectical tools in turn had been instrumentalized by totalizing systems, whether they were liberal or Marxist in slant. Eventually, however, as the new postmodern condition showed, *agonistic* pragmatics (not the Rortyan variant) had superseded liberalism and the dualisms of Marxism, opening onto an agonistic field of language games, where rules were immanent to the game and legitimacy was simply gained by the repetitiveness of performativity. In asserting that the end or goal of dialogue was not consensus but "paralogy," Lyotard's agonistic pragmatism clearly could not be farther removed from Habermas's universal pragmatics or even Rorty's liberal "antifoundationalism."

Of all the brands of pragmatism currently in stock, Rorty's repeated pleas for pluralistic pragmatism have seemed especially appealing, since he allows us to do away with last foundations and justifications, to discard old-model Enlightenment terms such as universalism no less than dilapidated remnants of ideology critique, even to discard the burdensome baggage of moral philosophy. No longer weighed down by the Kantian categorical imperatives of universalizable moral obligations, a community of "we's" agrees that liberalism can ensure a better good. Differences in opinion are to be settled through conversation, argumentation, dialogue, or persuasive rhetoric rather than force or violence. But in contradistinction to Habermas's universal or formal pragmatics, Rorty's pragmatism claims to be radically antifoundationalist in nature. Influenced by the language philosophy of the later Wittgenstein, author of the *Philosophical Investigations*, Rorty presents political liberalism as a contingent language game, whose truth can no longer be justified, except through circular forms of reasoning. Unlike for Habermas, for Rorty the invocation of universality or rationality as the philosophical, last, or final justification of the liberal paradigm merely describes a problem incorrectly, versed in the outmoded language of an old (philosophico-political) language that has served its time. Despite these differences, neither thinker escapes the circularity of electing political liberalism as the preferred paradigm of choice, with Rorty harping on its contingency, Habermas seeking to found it rationally, arguing that consensus-forming conversation is structured like a democratic felicitous and illocutionary speech act. But, despite assertions to the contrary, Rorty similarly retains the model of consensus in the construction of a pluralistically constituted "we." The awareness that there only exists contingency does not lead him to relativism or cause him to give up utopian hope, for he still charts a history of "progress"—though the term itself is defunct—this time on an adaptive (Darwinian) scale in which liberalism functions as a tool for attaining the "greater" good. Both pragmatists emphasize the enactment of freedom in the speech act.

Given the seductiveness of Rorty's model, with its claim to logical and argumentative superiority, it seems all the more necessary to probe how this pragmatism retains a contingent foundationalism, but foundationalism nonetheless. The "stories" Rorty's pragmatism tells, in its switch from metatheory to narrative, are justificatory theories passed off as contingent narratives or examples that, in reality, often have the status or stature of exemplarity. In that sense, his pragmatism only confirms what he observes about the ironic theorist, whose main problem is "how to overcome authority without claiming authority,"[88] since he continually may lapse into metaphysics again. Some of these recidivist dynamics come to the fore in Rorty's controversial essays "Feminism and Pragmatism" and "Feminism, Ideology, and Deconstruction." The persuasive energy Rorty unleashes in these pieces is aimed at convincing feminists how their beliefs can be fitted into pragmatism's emancipatory politics or the pragmatic "view of moral progress with relative ease,"[89] that is, on condition that the universalist, realist, as well as Marxist ideology-critical model be shunted.[90] "We have to stop talking about the need to go from distorted to undistorted perception of moral reality, and instead talk about the need to modify our practices so as to take account of new descriptions of what has been going on."[91] In other words, behavior modifications and descriptive rescripting must drop the idea of the moral law as well as the other Kantian notion that "competing groups will always be able to reason together on the basis of plausible and neutral premises." Since all justificatory scripts rely on universal essences or intrinsic attributes, feminists ought to reject them for a Deweyan-Davidsonian-Putnamian pragmatism (the linguistification of Dewey). Pragmatists "abandon the contrast between superficial appearance and deep reality in favor of the contrast between a painful present and a possibly less painful, dimly-seen, future."[92] However, because feminism's task is creative rather than descriptive, its only method is "courageous and imaginative experimentation,"[93] which means in fact that ideology-driven radical politics must give way to utopianism and the use of the imagination. Feminism, Rorty prescribes, can only be prophetic, since prophecy is left when all argument fails. Or, prophecy becomes feminism's preferred game of choice, with which it is supposed to undo the myriad other, less desirable competing nominalist language games. Norms, then, equal normalization for Rorty also, except that he lapses into a nominalism that doesn't even factor in the power balance anymore: " 'Truth' is not the name of a power which eventually wins through, it is just the nominalization of an approbative adjective."[94] Lacking any conception of normativity that can be subjected to justificatory scripts, Rorty concluded that decisions about the usefulness of certain practices become entirely ad hoc, linguistic games in which interlocutors seek to persuade each other of the merits of their own game. Clearly, this hardly means that Rorty's own strong pragmatist position is devoid of implied, unaccounted-for "norms" or, perhaps better, normalizing values. Surely, feminism may want to resist the Nietzschean read this cynical pragmatist gives us of the historical narrative of women's oppression, when he—unselfconsciously, without a dose of salutary irony—posits the following: "Neither pragmatists nor deconstructionists can do more for feminism than help rebut attempts to ground these practices on something deeper than a contingent historical fact—the fact that the people with the slightly larger muscles have been bullying the people with the slightly smaller muscles for a very long time."[95] With this quasi-Nietzschean endorsement of a history of (physical) force, Rorty is flexing the muscles of his "strong" pragmatism, which remains mired in an essentialistic, almost biologistic dualism of weak vs. strong.

The cryptonormativity Rorty's pragmatism carries along has come to the surface most recently in his *Achieving our Country*, which weds staunch invectives against the cultural left—including feminism—paralyzed by too much theory, to a new American pride that claims to be merely healthy national self-esteem without becoming pathologically nationalistic. In his programmatic defense of the Reform Left, Rorty pleads for new alliances among the left, for social hope over and against cultural pessimism, which originally belonged to the right, and for the construction of a "vision of a country to be achieved by building a consensus on the need for specific reforms,"[96] as a way, also, of reconnecting with national pride. In his exhortations against the cultural left, he takes on those mesmerized by cultural politics rather than galvanized by real politics, marked by "stigmata" and "victim politics" rather than interested in economic redistribution. Informed perhaps by Arendt's lectures on Kant, Rorty holds the cultural left's aestheticized spectatorship, produced by excessive specular theoretization, against real political agency. Unambiguously addressed also to feminism, reduced now to what for him amounts to a suspect identity politics, Rorty's manifesto has more than one aside to feminist theory. Thus, MacKinnon and Butler are asked to unite rather than fight, since they risk missing out on the real political action that goes on elsewhere.

Just as Rorty's *Contingency, Solidarity, Irony* was covertly working with the corresponding vessels "liberalism-pragmatism-freedom of speech," so his *Achieving Our Country* operates with the entwinement of national pride-America-pragmatism. Achieving our country, rekindling its patriotism becomes coterminus (or codynamical) with the pragmatic turn away from last foundations and from the quest for ultimate justification. Dewey surmised that America would be the *first nation-state* to do so. Antiauthoritari-

anism on a philosophical level, which is Dewey's rejection of the correspondence truth of theory, comes to equal poetic creation, creation *ex nihilo*,
the United States as a Romantic poem: "It is to envisage our nation-state as
both self-creating poet and self-created poem."[97] Aside from invoking such
political organicism, Rorty's exhortations against the so-called spectatorial
cultural left are mediated via a weak critique of economic globalism, which
is not decried primarily for its own sake but for the negative effects it might
have on the United States, for that which might return to the shores of the
States in the form of a backlash, the disenchanted, virtually economically
disenfranchised "proles." If other intellectuals have opted for a rootless cosmopolitanism, Rorty seems to have turned toward a new defensive national
pride. Most ironically, his manifesto suffers from a performative contradiction, insofar as it abjects the cultural left as the spectatorial, phantom other,
the Gothic double, at the same time that it purports to want to create a communal platform. Not able to embrace the universalism of the rootless cos-
mopolitan, Rorty falls for the contingency of American pride that taunts
the seriousness of identity politics, including feminism. Under the banner of
pragmatism, we end up with a displaced universalism that is no longer transcendent but located "immanently" (i.e., pragmatically) in the presumed
consensus of the speaking community, and all dissent is a deviation from
those immanent rules or veiled norms. The alleged violence imputed to
spectatorial theory is now supplanted by an enforced pragmatism that
becomes difference-obliterating.

For all these reasons it may be upon us to probe not just the consequences
of "capital t Theory" but also those that follow from a "strong," unchallenged
capitalized Pragmatism. True, respected attempts have been made to suture
the theoretical differences that mark feminist theories via neopragmatism. As
we saw, Fraser has sought to craft "a more consistent and thoroughgoing
pragmatism,"[98] which, like Rorty's, rejects a "moral realism and universalism" to embrace a historicist view. Far from being a sympathetic reader of
Rorty's,[99] Fraser regards her pronounced contentions with Rorty to
amount in reality to "a disagreement within pragmatism." Thus, her early
work, *Unruly Practices*, criticized him for assuming a gendered split between
the public and private and for promoting an aestheticized irony. Under the
latter were subsumed a depoliticized theory and public politics, which
became the privileged precinct of the (male) liberal reformist. Yet, despite
these strong misgivings, Fraser's sympathies go out to a thoroughly
revamped neopragmatism, whose mandate she defines as follows: "How can

we retrieve a version of pragmatism that is compatible with radical democracy, polylogic abnormal political discourse, and socialist-feminist discourse?"[100] This means winnowing "pragmatism from cold war liberalism"[101] to construct a "democratic-socialist-feminist pragmatism" that is no longer totalizing, but proceeds by trial and error, inspiration and conjecture. But shorn of its political utilitarianism, pragmatism ends up becoming an instrument and formalized tool, as in the playful multi-ingredient recipe Fraser concocts, which has little to do anymore with either Rorty's narrowly liberal or West's vocational, prophetic pragmatism:

> Begin with the sort of zero-degree pragmatism that is compatible with a wide variety of substantive political views, with socialist feminism as well as bourgeois liberalism. This pragmatism is simply antiessentialism with respect to traditional philosophical concepts like truth and reason, human nature and morality. It implies an appreciation of the historical and socially constructed character of such categories and of the practices from which they get their sense, thereby suggesting at least the abstract possibility of social change. This sort of zero-degree pragmatism is a useful, though hardly all-sufficing, ingredient of socialist feminism."[102]

For all the persuasive force that accompanies Fraser's defense of a new socialist feminism, it may not entirely be clear what is meant by pragmatic metatheories, nor is it apparent what, shorn of its substantive claims, such a formal, methodological neopragmatism offers beyond the structuralist's *bricolage* or the tools of antiessentialism and antifoundationalism discussed earlier—besides, perhaps, a new name, not burdened, like "theory," by years of negative valorization.

Between *pure* theory and a *strong* pragmatism lie many possibilities. We may not want to underestimate the political effects that could follow from a politicized "substantivist" pragmatism, also, and especially, for feminism; equally, we do well to hold the grand gestures of pure theory at bay. As we reviewed some of the contentious theoretical and antitheoretical positions in feminism in the course of this essay, however, it became evident that current disputes between theoretical, antitheoretical, and neopragmatic feminisms need not be cause for pessimism. To be sure, testing each other's theories and practices often means that positions are subjected to vehement critique, but *critique* need not automatically be *crisis*, just as long as we don't submit positions to destructive dissections with our critical scalpel—taking the word *critique* (from *krinein*, "to cut") all too literally. We should neither lose sight of dialogical negotiation nor present our theories as capable of doing more than they could ever accomplish. Further, negotiations need not lead to a watered-down "politics of compromise" that remains adverse to productive contestation, for they can generate a viable, enabling form of coexistence and cohabitation that recognizes feminist (theoretical) activism in all its diversity. Finally, by *historicizing* feminist theory, as I have attempted to do in this essay, it also becomes possible to peer beyond what seem to be current impasses or rutlike junctures. By looking beyond the immediacy of our historical "now," it becomes conceivable to think of feminisms, including theoretical feminisms, as engaged in an ongoing process of debate, contestation, and critical revision. Theoretical feminisms then appear as positions "with attitude," certainly not with a brazen, brash attitude but a critical, even ethical one—never a moralizing one—in line with the original meaning of that time-honored word: *ēthos*.[103]

NOTES

1. The term "postfeminism" ordinarily refers to a specific branch of post–second wave, pluralistic, theoretical feminism, which, in aligning itself with postmodernism and postcolonialism, invokes the prefix *post-* as a way of overcoming the reputed essentialism of earlier feminisms. See, for example, Ann Brooks, *Postfeminisms: Feminism, Cultural Theory, and Cultural Forms* (London: Routledge, 1997), who tries to argue for the viability of the neologism. While *post* is to have temporal, i.e., sequential implications, it seems to me hard to protect the term from getting confounded with the "end of feminism." Such an "endism" is certainly present in the terms on which the label is modeled, that is, "postmodernism" and "postcolonialism," which invoke the overcoming of modernism and colonialism respectively.

2. Judith Butler, "Merely Cultural," *Social Text* 52/53, 15, nos. 3 and 4 (Fall/Winter 1997): 265–77. See also the section, "Contentious or Debating Feminisms?" below.

3. Seyla Benhabib, Judith Butler, Drucilla Cornell, and Nancy Fraser, *Feminist Contentions: A Philosophical Exchange* (New York: Routledge, 1995), p. 132.

4. Judith Butler, "For a Careful Reading," in Benhabib et al., *Feminist Contentions*, p. 132.

5. Though the term "critical theory" is nowadays often used in a broad sense, so that it can include poststructuralism, in this essay it will refer exclusively to the Frankfurt School tradition that draws on Max Horkheimer's manifesto of the move-

ment, "Traditional and Critical Theory." For a discussion of that essay, see also the section "Against Theory," below.

6. Linda J. Nicholson, ed., *Feminism/Postmodernism* (New York: Routledge, 1990).

7. Linda Nicholson, "Introduction," in Benhabib et al., *Feminist Contentions*, pp. 1–2.

8. Ibid., p. 16.

9. This is how the term "non-" or "antifoundationalist" is used in contemporary theories of social constructivism, while its opposite, "foundationalism," refers to a- or transhistorical epistemological and political models that presume their own contingent or culturally defined standpoint to carry universal validity.

10. The present text is twice guilty, doubly so, insofar as its topic is theory—feminist theory—and insofar as it may not be able to eschew theoretical language altogether.

11. The most infamous recent incident is the so-called Bad Writing Contest, organized by the journal *Philosophy and Literature*, which in 1999 selected Homi Bhabha and Judith Butler as the prizewinners. The claim that (poststructuralist) theory produces "bad writing" also reached the mainstream media; see, for example, "When Ideas Get Lost in Bad Writing; Attacks on Scholars Include a Barbed Contest with 'Prizes,' " *New York Times*, February 27, 1999. Judith Butler's response appeared in the *New York Times* on March 20, 1999.

12. See Teresa de Lauretis, who distinguishes between intrinsic/extrinsic analyses of feminism in her important "Upping the Anti [*sic*] in Feminist Theory," in *The Cultural Studies Reader*, ed. Simon During (London: Routledge, 1993), pp. 74–89.

13. See Michel Foucault, "Polemics, Politics, and Problematizations: An Interview with Michel Foucault," in *The Foucault Reader*, ed. Paul Rabinow (New York: Pantheon Books, 1984), pp. 381ff.

14. In her capacity as one of the co-organizers of the 1998 English Institute conference, "What's Left of Theory?" Butler observed that "theory" under attack often stands as a synecdoche for poststructuralism. Importantly, she added that the resistance to theory indicated at least a double threat or risk: antitheorists fear that politics may get contaminated by theory, and, conversely, theoretical elitists (in the vocabulary of the present analysis, pure theorists) want to stave off theory from getting corrupted by politics. Judith Butler, introductory remarks to "What's Left of Theory?" English Institute, Harvard University, Fall 1998.

15. Homi K. Bhabha evokes this charge in "The Commitment to Theory," in *The Location of Culture* (London: Routledge, 1994), pp. 20ff.

16. Knapp and Michaels defined (literary) theory as "the attempt to govern interpretations of particular texts by appealing to an account of interpretation in general." Walter Benn Michaels and Steven Knapp, "Against Theory," in *Against Theory: Literary Studies and the New Pragmatism*, ed. W. J. T. Mitchell (Chicago: University of Chicago Press, 1982), p. 11.

17. Ibid., p. 25.

18. Ibid., p. 26.

19. Ibid., pp. 29–30.

20. William James, "What Pragmatism Means," in *Pragmatism: A Reader*, ed. Louis Menand (New York: Vintage, 1997), p. 98.

21. Cornel West, "Theory, Pragmatisms, and Politics," in *Keeping Faith: Philosophy and Race in America* (New York: Routledge, 1993), p. 93. See also West's full-length study of pragmatism, *The American Evasion of Philosophy: A Genealogy of Pragmatism* (Madison: University of Wisconsin Press, 1989).

22. West, *Keeping Faith*, p. 104.

23. Bhabha, "Commitment to Theory," p. 30.

24. Gayatri Chakravorty Spivak, for example, uses the term to criticize what she calls "capital t Theory within feminism" or "high feminism" in "The Intervention Interview," in *The Post-Colonial Critic: Interviews, Strategies, Dialogues* (New York: Routledge, 1990), pp. 119–20.

25. Bhabha, "Commitment to Theory" pp. 20–21.

26. Ibid., p. 30.

27. See, for example, Kant's "On the Common Saying: 'This May be True in Theory, But It Does Not Apply in Practice,' " in Immanuel Kant, *Political Writings*, ed. with an introduction by Hans Reiss (Cambridge: Cambridge University Press, 1991).

28. Karl Marx and Friedrich Engels, *The German Ideology: Critique of Modern German Philosophy According to Its Representatives Feuerbach, B. Bauer and Stirner, and of German Socialism According to Its Various Prophets*, in Marx and Engels, *Collected Works*, trans. Richard Dixon et al. (New York: International Publishers, 1975), 5:44–45. See, furthermore, Marx's "Theses on Feuerbach," in which he posits that " 'revolutionary,' 'practical-critical,' activity" overcomes the theory-practice divide still present in Feuerbach's inverted Idealism. Ibid., p. 3.

29. Put differently, the ideological divide between pure theory and mere practice was to be replaced by a new materialistic theory that overcame the alienating split. Or, the untethering of the material from the realm of consciousness is the work of metaphysical ideology. On the difference between critique and criticism in Marx's work, see especially Seyla Benhabib's comprehensive study, *Critique, Norm, and Utopia* (New York: Columbia University Press, 1986), passim.

30. That theory, taken in the sense defined by Horkheimer, need not be opposed to practice/praxis is a point Habermas indirectly underscored when he qualified theory as ideology critique. See Jürgen Habermas, *The Philosophical Discourse of Modernity: Twelve Lectures* (Cambridge: MIT Press, 1987), p. 116. West similarly makes the point that ideology-critical demystification is a theoretical activity: "Demystification is a *theoretical* activity that attempts to give explanations that account for the role and function of specific social practices" (*Keeping Faith*, p. 89).

31. Some of the important publications in this area include bell hooks, *Feminist Theory from Margin to Center* (Boston: South End Press, 1984); Teresa de Lauretis,

"Displacing Hegemonic Discourses: Reflections on Feminist Theory in the 1980s," *Inscriptions* 3, no. 4 (1988): 127–44; and Barbara Johnson, *A World of Difference* (Baltimore: Johns Hopkins University Press, 1987); for overviews, see also Linda S. Kauffman, ed., *American Feminist Theory at Century's End: A Reader* (Cambridge, Mass.: Blackwell, 1993), and Michèle Barrett and Anne Philips, eds., *Destabilizing Theory: Contemporary Feminist Debates* (Stanford: Stanford University Press, 1992).

32. Linda Nicholson, ed., *The Second Wave: A Reader in Feminist Theory* (New York: Routledge, 1997), p. 261.

33. Luce Irigaray, *Speculum de l'autre femme* (Paris: Editions de Minuit, 1974), p. 165.

34. Monique Wittig, "The Point of View: Universal or Particular?" in *The Straight Mind and Other Essays* (Boston: Beacon Press, 1992), p. 60. For a more extensive discussion of Wittig's criticism, see also Judith Butler, *Gender Trouble* (New York: Routledge, 1990), pp. 25ff.

35. Rosi Braidotti, *Nomadic Subjects: Embodiment and Sexual Difference in Contemporary Feminist Theory* (New York: Columbia University Press, 1994), p. 209.

36. Ibid., p. 210.

37. Ibid., p. 211.

38. See Carol Gilligan's influential *In a Different Voice: Psychological Theory and Women's Development* (Cambridge: Harvard University Press, 1982).

39. Linda Nicholson, "Introduction," in Nicholson, ed., *Second Wave*, p. 3.

40. On the terminologically slippery word "antiessentialism," see Gayatri Spivak's observations in the interview "In a Word," reprinted in Nicholson, ed., *Second Wave*, p. 361. As Spivak there notes, "essentialism" sometimes functions as a codeword for the empirical or the real.

41. This is a concern that has been voiced, for example, by Naomi Schor. See also her "French Feminism Is a Universalism," in *Bad Objects: Essays Popular and Unpopular* (Durham, N.C.: Duke University Press, 1995), pp. 3–27.

42. See Habermas, *Philosophical Discourse of Modernity*, passim.

43. On this point, see, for example, Seyla Benhabib, "Feminism and Postmodernism: An Uneasy Alliance," in Benhabib et al., *Feminist Contentions*, pp. 17–34.

44. Jane Flax, "Postmodern and Gender Relations in Feminist Theory," in Nicholson, ed., *Feminism/Postmodernism*, pp. 39–62.

45. Ibid., p. 43.

46. Sandra Harding, "Feminism, Science, and the Anti-Enlightenment Critiques," in Nicholson, ed., *Feminism/Postmodernism*, p. 89.

47. Ibid., pp. 90ff.

48. Iris Marion Young, *Intersecting Voices: Dilemmas of Gender, Political Philosophy, and Policy* (Princeton: Princeton University Press, 1997), p. 17.

49. Nancy Fraser and Linda J. Nicholson, "Social Criticism without Philosophy: An Encounter between Feminism and Postmodernism," in Nicholson, ed., *Feminism/Postmodernism*, pp. 19–38.

50. Ibid., p. 19.

51. Ibid., p. 20.

52. Ibid., p. 21, first italics added.

53. Ibid.

54. Ibid.

55. Ibid., p. 25.

56. Ibid. In principle, I agree with the starting point of their article, when they retain what they call "large social theories" for feminist analysis. One needs to be able to analyze sexism cross-culturally, which is different from adopting "pure metanarratives" or "ahistorical normative theories about the transcultural nature of rationality or justice." However, I don't agree when they say that "these social theories purport to be empirical rather than philosophical" (p. 27) insofar as the authors here disregard the viability of such movements as social or political philosophy, at the risk of reconfirming women's exclusion from philosophy.

57. Fraser and Nicholson, "Social Criticism without Philosophy," p. 34.

58. Ibid., p. 35.

59. Seyla Benhabib and Drucilla Cornell, eds., *Feminism as Critique: On the Politics of Gender* (Minneapolis: University of Minnesota Press, 1987).

60. Ibid., p. 1.

61. Butler, "For a Careful Reading," pp. 138–39.

62. Judith Butler, "Contingent Foundations," in Benhabib et al., *Feminist Contentions*, p. 39.

63. Ibid.

64. Ibid., p. 42.

65. In the margins, it might be noted that Butler's theory of performance does not just refer to theatrical performance but also to Austin's speech act theory and thus, indirectly, to pragmatism. That is, the performance of norms is founded in the speech community, rather than imposed on them from without or grounded metaphysically, a fact that obviously doesn't prevent individual speech acts from either being violent or metaphysical. However, Butler's theory of performativity often shuttles back and forth between claims about the (transhistorical, quasi-transcendental) performativity of *all* language and social forms of performativity, though in *Excitable Speech* she seeks to distance herself from Derrida via Bourdieu. In other words, there exists a tension between the quasi-pragmatist claims of Butler's analysis of performance and the status of "performativity" as an enabling, quasi-transcendental precondition.

66. Butler, "Contingent Foundations," p. 49.

67. Ibid., p. 41.

68. Ibid., p. 40.

69. Seyla Benhabib, "The Generalized and Concrete Other: The Kohlberg-Gilli-

gan Controversy and Moral Theory," in *Situating the Self: Gender, Community, and Postmodernism in Contemporary Ethics* (New York: Routledge, 1992).

70. Nancy Fraser, "Pragmatism, Feminism, and the Linguistic Turn," in Benhabib et al., *Feminist Contentions*, p. 164.

71. Ibid., p. 163.

72. Ibid., p. 164.

73. Ibid., p. 166.

74. Like Habermas, Benhabib limits the term "postmodernism" to its negative signification, since it is marked by excessive style and aestheticism: "what postmodernist historiography displays is an 'aesthetic' proliferation of styles which increasingly blur the distinctions between history and literature, factual narrative and imaginary creation." Seyla Benhabib, "Subjectivity, Historiography, and Politics," in Benhabib et al., *Feminist Contentions*, p. 112.

75. Ibid., p. 111.

76. Butler, "For a Careful Reading," p. 132.

77. This seems to be the case in Amanda Anderson's overview essay on the debates, which too readily pushes Butler into the a- or antipolitical camp. See Anderson, "Debatable Performances: Restaging Contentious Feminisms," *Social Text* 54 (Spring 1998): 1–24.

78. Nancy Fraser, *Justice Interruptus: Critical Reflections on the "Postsocialist" Condition* (New York: Routledge, 1997).

79. Butler, "Contingent Foundations," p. 41.

80. See also Anderson, "Debatable Performances," on this point.

81. See Jacques Derrida, "Force of Law: The 'Mystical' Foundation of Authority," in *Deconstruction and the Possibility of Justice*, ed. Drucilla Cornell, Michael Rosenfeld, and David Gray Carlson (New York: Routledge, 1992), and Judith Butler, "Universality in Culture," in *For Love of Country: Debating the Limits of Patriotism*, ed. Martha C. Nussbaum et al. (Boston: Beacon Press, 1996).

82. Butler, "Contingent Foundations," p. 50.

83. Martha C. Nussbaum, "The Professor of Parody: The Hip Defeatism of Judith Butler," *New Republic*, February 22, 1999.

84. See the letters by feminists that appeared in *The New Republic*, April 19, 1999, in response to Nussbaum's review essay.

85. I here quote Charles Taylor's observation that a difference-blind liberalism might be a "particularism masquerading as the universal" out of context. See Taylor, "The Politics of Recognition," in *Multiculturalism: Examining the Politics of Recognition*, ed. Amy Gutmann (Princeton: Princeton University Press, 1994), p. 44.

86. See on this point again, West, *Keeping Faith*, pp. 4, 89–105.

87. The broadest project to craft a pragmatic feminism is that of Charlene Haddock Seigfried, who, in addition to a special issue of *Hypatia* 8, no. 2 (Spring 1993),

has published *Pragmatism and Feminism: Reweaving the Social Fabric* (Chicago: University of Chicago Press, 1996). Seigfried's definition of pragmatism is interesting, in that she cautions that she won't reduce the term to mean "a narrow instrumentalism" (unlike Fraser). Instead, she will use it to refer to "a historically specific philosophical movement also sometimes called Classical American Philosophy"—in other words, "a range of positions originating in the classical period of American philosophy that challenge the traditional philosophical privileging of theory at the expense of practice" (277n). Though her comprehensive study approaches the topic in its many facets, it seems to lack a developed concept of what politics might mean, so that her valuable study often fails to get beyond the level of analogy as it tries to show how feminism might be regrounded in Classical American Philosophy. Democratic politics becomes coterminous with "community," a term that is automatically supposed to overcome the "individualism" of liberalism.

88. Richard Rorty, *Contingency, Irony, and Solidarity* (Cambridge: Cambridge University Press, 1989), p. 105.

89. Richard Rorty, "Feminism and Pragmatism," *Michigan Quarterly Review* 30 (Spring 1991): 236.

90. Rorty, however, gets the concept of ideology critique wrong; for example, he implies that Marxism works with a "matter-consciousness distinction," when in fact the *German Ideology* sees this distinction itself as the product of ideology. See Richard Rorty, "Feminism, Ideology, and Deconstruction: A Pragmatist View," *Hypatia* 8, no. 2 (Spring, 1993), reprinted in *Mapping Ideology*, ed. Slavoj Žižek (London: Verso, 1994).

91. Rorty, "Feminism and Pragmatism," p. 234.

92. Ibid., p. 240.

93. Ibid., p. 242.

94. Ibid., p. 250.

95. Rorty, "Feminism, Ideology, and Deconstruction," in Žižek, ed., *Mapping Ideology*, p. 233.

96. Richard Rorty, *Achieving Our Country: Leftist Thought in Twentieth-Century America* (Cambridge: Harvard University Press, 1998), p. 15. For a thorough critique of Rorty's assertion that the pragmatist should endorse "his own community" or "ethnocentrism" as a way of avoiding the charge of relativism, see Barbara Herrnstein Smith's discussion of his "Solidarity or Objectivity?" in *Contingencies of Value: Alternative Perspectives for Critical Theory* (Cambridge: Harvard University Press, 1988), pp. 166ff.

97. Rorty, *Achieving Our Country*, p. 29.

98. Nancy Fraser, "From Irony to Prophecy to Politics: A Response to Richard Rorty," *Michigan Quarterly Review* 30 (Spring 1991): 263.

99. See Nancy Fraser, "Solidarity of Singularity? Richard Rorty between Romanticism and Technocracy," in *Unruly Practices: Power, Discourse, and Gender in*

Contemporary Social Theory (Minneapolis: University of Minnesota Press, 1989), chap. 5, and "From Irony to Prophecy to Politics."

100. Fraser, *Unruly Practices*, p. 105.

101. Ibid., p. 106.

102. Ibid.

103. It is in this sense that Foucault, in his later writings, has adopted the term *ēthos* to reconceptualize the meaning of *critical attitude.* For an analysis of Foucault's conception of critical *ēthos*, see my *Critique of Violence: Between Poststructuralism and Critical Theory* (London: Routledge, 2000).

PART 2

The Ethics of Affect

Chapter 5

Ethical Ambiguities and Specters of Colonialism: Futures of Transnational Feminism

RANJANA KHANNA

The strengths of transnational feminism in the last decade have also been weaknesses. Feminism has split not only between activism and theory but also into particular feminisms that struggle with the perceived inadequacies of a feminist universalism. At the same time, the splitting of feminism has allowed for a comprehensive study of local contexts and their feminist agendas and causes. The accusation of *ethnocentrism* that feminism in the West faced in the eighties and earlier has become a central part of the discussion of local contexts, while how "to do" feminism both within the academy and in practice has been the focus of feminist ethics. But this has had more than one effect on transnational feminism. On the one hand, conflict within feminism and between women has become part of the agenda to be addressed. It has also at times resulted in paralysis, or a rather self-satisfied navel gazing on the part of some who agonize about how to be ethical when it comes to dealing with gender politics outside of one's own context. The fracturing that seems inevitable to transnational feminism also threatens feminist international coalitions.

How to address ethics has thus become a crucial part of feminism within and outside the academy. But the term itself has fractured. No longer does "ethics" have solely an idealist connotation; in its daily use, the production of which owes a great deal to feminism, ethics connotes local and grounded codes of behavior. In the workplace, we hear of a *workplace ethics*, in the hospital, of *medical ethics*; increasingly, the term has been tied to a litigious context that revolves around what is admissible or inadmissible behavior in the eyes of the *law* and how one judges one's own and others' personal behavior. The local rescripting of ethics has removed it from the realm of *justice* and in some instances placed it firmly within the realm of the *law*, while in others it has conflated the ethical with the *political*, because it is thought, probably correctly, that politics should be ethical.

But in the realm of ethics, not only has there been a shift from justice to law, but also from responsibility to another to responsibility to a set of rules. Transnational feminism has allowed us to perceive the centrality of different relations to rules. This perception has initiated a fracturing. Difference has been reified to such an extent that separate ethical universes have been produced, with the overarching imperative being that one does not comment on another context. An ethical response, then, often amounts to a nonresponse. Chandra Mohanty has called on us to understand the *complex relationality* between women transnationally; all too often this recognition results in paralyzing feelings of guilt by those who structurally and economically benefit from the impoverishment of others, rather than the respectful coalition that many feminists from Spivak to Mohanty, Lugones, and Spelman have called for. Given this situation, an ethical response that results in inactivity and the reification of difference is ambiguous and, more often than not, politically inefficacious. From fear of an overarching ethnocentric universalism of the claim of justice, a new concern arises for feminism at the end of the century. How does one respond to another, and how does one address conflict with an end in sight that allows for transnational feminist action and scholarship?[1]

The particularization of ethics into codes and laws has moved ethics from the realm of justice to that of law, as I have said. If we consider a series of relationships—justice/ethics, ethics/politics, justice/law, law/ethics—what emerges is two different concepts of justice and ethics: one is somewhat messianic, the other more pragmatic. What I want to suggest, however, is that in the context of transnational feminism (and, perhaps to some extent, feminism more generally), it is necessary to maintain the messianic concept alongside a more pragmatic one. What amounts to a contradictory position does not, however, leave us at an impasse but, rather, allows a way of dealing with the inadequacies of each concept of ethics and the justice for which it ostensibly aims. Feminism has necessarily favored a pragmatic understanding of law and politics that addresses particular and immediate concerns, inequalities, and violence directed toward women. Messianic concepts of justice often appear to address nothing at all in concrete terms except as a possible consequence of a more generalized relationship to the philosophical concept of justice or to a "God." However, the pragmatic concept of ethics as a form of social justice in the realm of transnational feminism consistently fails to account for the legacies of colonialism and empire that haunt it, particularly of course in instances when First World feminism acts upon the Third World. Like international law, and often in conjunction with it, transnational feminist activism often fails to account for the colonial legacy. This manifests itself in patronizing and ill-informed gestures (for example, urgent but sensationalist struggles against female genital mutilation) and hasty assumptions of sameness (for example, the claim that the globalization of sweatshops is universally exploitative of women without taking into account local conditions and international relations).

Paradoxically, the breakdown of a singular ethics also threatens the breakdown of transnational feminism, not because of the breakdown of boundaries national or otherwise but because of a fetishization of the local at the expense of coalition. When it becomes difficult to respond to another because of the inevitable inadequacy of that gesture, one can't help but think that the rendering of ethics as the litigious and the local fails to consider the boundaries that the feminist movement in particular has called into question: the personal and the political; the individual and the collective; the private and the public; the event and the everyday; the inside and the outside; the psychical and the social; and the ethical and the political. The emphasis on particularized ethics has made us all anonymous and concerned primarily with our own behavior rather than with the repercussions of that behavior for another. Deciding how responsibility can be most useful raises the question of whether the concept of an ethics as *useful* is flawed in and of itself. Transnational feminism is haunted by this puzzle concerning the relationship between the messianic and the pragmatic, and how to understand the relationship of ethics to politics, law, justice, and the ontology of the other as much as that of the self.

It may be the case that responding most usefully to another's needs means effectively bringing them into the eyes of the law, thus understanding justice as restitution or reparation. This necessary concept of justice assumes that both wrongdoing, and its righting, take place at a particular moment in a historical event. Clearly, crime, and wrongdoing on one level, have to be assessed in terms of what can be referenced and evidenced. But that which remains beyond the boundaries of a particular event cannot easily be accounted for in terms of restitution or in terms of rights awarded. This is the problem with the very important work performed by liberal feminism. It too often endorses the status quo by giving women the right to reap its benefits.

Let us hypothesize for the moment a concept of justice that would reach beyond the litigious realm of rights, restitution, and reparation. I will posit feminism as the gift to another of something that may be impossible to give—that is, the uncertain possibility of justice that precedes any particular law even as it actualizes the possibility of justice. If we were to think of a feminist ethics, it would probably include such a wishful impossibility: that of the gift to women of the possibility of justice where that gift itself is a kind of impossibility and is based on no concept of granting, exchange, or patronage.

In the context of transnational feminism, the concept of a gift may well set off alarm bells, because it has been associated, for good reason, with a colonialist and patronizing gesture. What I want to explore, however, is why ethics needs to be restored to feminist discourse and practice so as to maintain a distinction from politics. It is only with categories as abstract as those of justice that feminist transnational politics can take place. This is, of course, an extremely thorny area when we consider the colonial legacies of juridical systems; the institutionalized (and frequently well-meaning) racism and sexism that mark its history; and the violence attendant in so many forms of law that cross national borders today. The call for justice is difficult to claim when its *manifestation-as-law*, effectively the only manner in which it can make itself manifest, has worked in the opposite direction more often than not in the history of international gendered oppression. This has introduced ambivalence about a desire for an idealized and universal concept of justice that has frequently worked against the oppressed and the disenfranchised. Both transnational feminism, and the discourse of human rights and international law that it frequently references, are haunted by the specter of colonialism. This specter, like Derrida's when he speaks of specters of Marx, is historical even if it is not dated and casts a shadow over any imagined community.[2] We could usefully think of postcolonial nations and international relations as haunted by colonialism; thus, when we think of such things as phantom public spheres, to use Bruce Robbins's phrase, we could think of them as not simply imagined or lacking any concrete existence but as carrying secrets and traumas from the past in the language and affect of the community as made up of psychical entities.[3] This affect could haunt through generations, thus suggesting the manner in which ideological tenacities are psychically inflected, carried through a people, and extended through generations. History, in that formulation, exists in psychical affect differently from in memory and separately from the archive, even as both memory and archive are constitutive of the workings of affect. Occurrences in the past, whether everyday or major events, would thus manifest themselves in terms of the everyday as affect.[4]

Any inroad into a discussion of the *future* of transnational feminism has to find a way of accounting for such spectral overshadowing, without surrendering to the ghost. For what remains of a crime, or indeed of a haunting, once reparation is awarded? What remains once a right has been secured? What can be felt or done in the name of culture and of rights that dispels something that cannot be accounted for by a verdict, or indeed by the kind of reparation we may hear of on a group level—for example, after a war, or in instances when the only reparation offered is independence itself, as in colonialism? When we think of writing in the time of or in the aftermath of war, we may think of a restoration of women's sovereignty when that has been threatened both directly and metonymically in relation to a state or a people. And when we think of the everyday, rather than simply those major historical events that dominate our understanding of history, we could think of the difficulties of such things as reproductive technologies, domestic violence, rape, the politics of aid and economic and cultural exploitation, or the possibility of coalition. In the feminist realm, ethics and politics have for the most part been conceived together. Now, once again we may not want to reduce ethics to politics.

The specter that cannot be accounted for by the pragmatic notion of justice and ethics raises questions of the unaccountable and the nonreferential. If justice and ethics are the spectral remainder of law and pragmatics, they are not simply impossible to achieve. Rather, they constitute *the impossible*.[5]

The distinction between the two is crucial for transnational feminism, which cannot escape the specter. If the ethical (understood as the nonreferential and unaccountable responsibility toward oneself and toward another) is simply impossible then its relation to the political seems potentially irrelevant. However, if it is understood as *the impossible*, the mutually constitutive nature of the two is made apparent as experience of the necessity for and inadequacy of the law.

If questions of ethics arise most prominently in relation to a *historical event* that may or may not be the same as a *traumatic event* when the need of, for example, international intervention may be required, this leaves us potentially with little sense of how, and whether, to respond to everyday occurrences. The everyday is the category that feminism has always maintained to be central to feminists' struggle against hegemonic exploitation. An ethics formed in relation to events may not embrace the difficulties of the everyday. Conversely, an ethics of the everyday may not be adequate for *tragic* historical events involving women and all those feminized as weak and tragic victims.

In order to tackle these questions, and also to consider why transnational feminism should be the locus for conceptualizing an ethics that deals with the event and the everyday, we first need to address what we mean by transnational feminism. Feminist interaction across national borders does not simply exist because of globalization; rather, it exists because of the *idea* that women internationally are materially oppressed *because they are women*. This oppression does not usually manifest itself in the same ways, nor does it preclude the possibility that women have a complex relation to each other. Women may structurally and economically disadvantage one another and may not have anything in common simply on the basis of being women. Following the deconstruction of the sex/gender distinction in 1990s feminism, identifying something called *women* is itself problematic; the category itself holds no stable meaning, and the material figuring of women varies.[6] Talking of *women's issues* also becomes problematic, because while we may want to say that, for example, low income relative to men in the same context, reproductive technology, and rape affect women, we would also have to acknowledge that this is the case in varying degrees. It seems that the *possibility* of being put in the same position because of gender is what calls for some kind of unity; but this possibility of exploitation produces a prostration before the narrative of exploitation, and the attempt to move from that position to one in which the said exploitations may be dealt with *justly*. Let's for a moment, then, suggest that feminism is constituted through two unknowable categories—*justice* and *women*. *Justice* for *women* internationally and through transnational coalition is what we aim for in feminism. We seek justice in the context of a traumatic and /or historical *event*, in terms of the everyday, and in terms of how this everyday is partially structured through the affect of an event. Acknowledging the abstraction of the terms "justice" and "woman" places feminist coalition in the psychical and the material realms simultaneously, for the idea that we have to maintain the possibility of justice for women involves a psychical investment in that idea, and not simply a strategic aim.

Writing at the end of the century, and at the beginning of another, to consider the possibilities for a future ethics of feminism, and considering what the question of ethics has to do with that of temporality and politics, calls for a reflection back fifty years, after another major ethical quandary faced intellectuals who considered themselves engaged. European powers were losing their colonies and struggling with the fact of a new form of genocide seen in World War II. The question of how to address France's inactivity in the Resistance during World War II occupation of the country, and then how to move on from that ignoble period to address issues of the day haunts the texts of France's mid-century intellectuals in a manner that resonates with today's quandary concerning what we could call the *ambiguity of ethics* and its troublesome relationship to politics and ontology.

Simone de Beauvoir attempted to tackle how ethics and politics could be brought together in a manner that accounted for man's "tragic ambiguity": his knowledge that he and his fellow human beings are building toward death that intrudes upon and shapes the experience of the present. The first page of her *Ethics of Ambiguity* immediately deals with the notion of death, the "tragic ambiguity" of man's condition, and his subsequent inability to access truth because of the temporal unfolding unto death that dominates his relationship with both himself and others, and with the events that surround him.[7] She writes therefore of the relationship between temporality and the event in relation to ethical and political quandaries. World War II had signaled a massive ethical quandary about war and genocide that continued to maintain a hold on intellectual life. What was distinctive about much of *Ethics of Ambiguity* was its determination to respond to occurrences that seemed like everyday wrongdoings rather than only to great events such as wars. Great events, after all, are often temporalized retrospectively, leaving aside the ongoing inequalities upon which they are built.

So let us return to the time in which de Beauvoir wrote her ethics, and see whether credence can be given to the concept of *justice for women* as the aim of feminism internationally. In the story of ethics, at least in an ethics that has been associated with political engagement such as feminism or nation-building, we conventionally consider ethical behavior to include another person at least indirectly if not directly. It usually involves an ability to respond to another person or a people after analysis and decisions that clarify any ambivalent feeling toward a given situation and any ambiguity in its terms or meaning. While ethics is certainly about an assessment of a person's actions, it has usually considered these in relation to an idea of the *good*, and, at least since Benthamite utilitarian thought, the *usefulness* of that good, or how that good has come to bear on the greatest number of people. In fact, we can assess this largely by the happiness or pleasure with which the good, ethical behavior has been received. But many have argued that this concept of ethics assumes a relationship to others only, rather than also to an understanding of a structure of ethical ontology.

Sartre, in contrast to de Beauvoir, believed that his model of engaged ontology could not be a model of ethics. He considered his work *Being and Nothingness* to constitute an ontology rather than an ethics, because the drive to resist "bad faith" originates not as a result of the relative happiness of others but, rather, because of the effect the presence of an other has on one's own ontological structure.[8] The ethical concern is translated into a model of *engaged* ontology, but when Sartre attempted to derive an ethics from the general model of an engaged psychoanalytically informed philosophical position, he found it to be inadequate and did not publish the work that we know now as the fragments that make up the *Notebook for an Ethics*.[9] It was as if he implicitly agreed with his Marxist critics, for example Marcuse, who claimed that the philosophical concept of freedom, as Sartre employed it, was a solipsistic retreat into the ontological from the arena of the political; and that the political, with which Sartre attempted to engage, was inadequately addressed by the concept of freedom.[10]

By contrast to the existential dilemmas concerning the relationship between ontology, ethics, and politics, Lacan claimed in Seminar XI, *contra existentialism* and explicitly *contra Sartre*, that his psychoanalytic framework is ethical rather than ontological, a claim that resituates the psychoanalytic firmly in the realm of philosophy and that disclaims the centrality of a theory of being to be at the core of psychoanalytic thought. While various theories of being emerge from the Lacanian corpus, the "master" himself presents that being as implicated within a larger ethical framework that causes a certain figuring of guilt, antagonism, and pleasure within the subject. So a kind of reversal of expectations has occurred here: Sartre, the philosopher of freedom, has apparently rejected the possibility of allying political engagement with an ethics, while Lacan, an analyst of the psyche whom we may expect to give a theory of being, offers an ethics rather than an ontology. Sartre rejected an "engaged ethics" at least in part because of the concept of the universal it implies that does not concur with his understanding of writing for one's own time and responding with some sense of immediacy.[11] Following neither liberal teleologists such as Bentham, concerned with ends and our duty to meet them, nor deontologists such as Kant, who proffered ethics as actions we are obliged to conduct prior to local value being assigned to them, Sartre saw his concept of freedom as an ongoing ontological conflict that we have to resolve creatively in order to act toward authenticity. If we make a choice that is counter to bad faith, we work toward the freedom of ourselves and everybody else because there is a contradiction inherent in the idea that one can work toward another's freedom in a way that works against one's own. If ambiguity is resolved in a choice, then this will result in acting in a manner that works toward one's own freedom and that of others.

Lacan, on the other hand, follows Freud's ethical dilemma from *Civilization and its Discontents*:[12] Is the ethical function of the analyst to encourage a libertarianism that runs counter to the repressions of modern civilization that contribute to the development of neuroses, or alternately, work in the service of civilization and the goods it values? Lacan's extension of the dilemma is not however articulated so much in terms of the work ethic suitable for psychoanalysis as in the structure of the ethical question itself. Neither of Freud's responses is satisfactory, and both work within the logic of servicing certain ideas of what is good. According to Lacan, this idea of the "good" is premised upon the concept of happiness and therefore fails to account for desire that is unconscious and does not function as if it were possible to find satisfaction and happiness. Lacan's maxim, "Have you acted in accordance with your desire?" thus commands that complexities of desire are acknowledged so that *es* can become *ich*. The analyst's function is about getting the patient to understand the discrepancy between actions and desires often manifested in guilt, a discrepancy that reveals the duplicity of such concepts as happiness.[13] While feminism—and, I would argue—particularly postcolonial feminism, has been concerned with political and representational inequality, the turn in the 1990s toward Lacanian psychoanalysis has centered on his theory of desire with the claim that it offers a means of analyzing the social that is politically efficacious. Interestingly, in Lacanian-influenced social commentary, one of the most significant departures from most models of thought that claim to be politically pertinent is not only the rejection of the imperative of the good and of happiness but also the historical rationalizations for emerging factors in people's lives.

It is in historical work that we have seen a feminist counter to the Lacanian model. Much of the historical work has been influenced by Foucault, with some, notably Judith Butler, bringing Lacan and Foucault to bear on each other.[14] But the work of feminist Foucauldians, and particularly new historicists, has challenged both an ethics of ahistorical desire they see in Lacanian-influenced work and the ontological obsessions of an ethics in the realm of philosophy. If the ethical imperative of learning had, at one point, been "Know thyself," it now seems to be "contextualize." The fall of the transcendental spatial relation and a sovereign good to the particular context and its relative moral and political stakes has effectively meant a philosophical turn from abstractions and universals that dominate Enlightenment thought to a genealogical and contextual critique that often operates in the name of oppressed peoples whose lives cannot be analyzed in the terms of universal categories. Thus, the contextual is offered as a counter to what is understood as the universalist—a predetermined and ideological response to a political context or to a text that emerges from the very epistemologies (and perhaps the very group) that is considered to have caused the initial oppression. Specific and contextual assessments, understood thus, make for the possibility of an ethics that becomes redefined as politically responsible behavior, disconnected from absolutes and able to analyze and propose political processes and responses to the aesthetic.

The question posed by Lacanian psychoanalytic theorists of the social, for example Žižek, Copjec, and Salecl, raises questions about this, and ostensibly raises them from the left.[15] They ask if there is any way to understand ethics as linked to the aesthetic and democracy that is not about the radical contingency of space, cause and effect, and historical sequence. They question how the notion of contingency can be reconfigured so as to offer a way of understanding a located subjectivity. The argument against *historicism* in Lacanian social and cultural critique draws from a problematization of both the temporality of affect of events on people's lives and the structural lack in the subject. The emphasis on "cause" in political critique, Lacanians contend, assumes an unfolding of events that have a sequential logic. This rejection is precisely why it is difficult to conceive of how a social analysis that is politicized—such as that of the scholarship on postcoloniality or feminism, or, for our purposes, postcolonial transnational feminism—can make use of Lacanian psychoanalysis that prioritizes a structural trauma of the subject in modernity rather than a trauma in the history of the individual. Lacanians such as Žižek contend that the notion of cause and an attention to the real understood as the material is faulty because we have no access to the real even though it is a part of us. It is also, crucially, exterior to us in the manner in which the exterior is simultaneously interior; it thus follows the structure of a hole in a doughnut.

This issue of access to the real, understood in terms of this hole, is linked to the persuasive dismissal of historicism in Copjec's work also. In *Read My Desire*, she critiques the "notion of an existence without predicate, or, to put it differently, of a surplus existence that cannot be caught up in the positivity of the social."[16] While the "positive unconscious"[17] of the episteme in the early Foucault did not reject psychoanalysis, the later Foucault rejects both psychoanalysis and much semiotics; Copjec, echoing the May 1968 criticism of structuralism among Parisian students, speaks of "structures marching in the streets," but she is criticizing Foucault's post-1968 genealogical studies rather than the pre-1968 structuralism. She rejects what she sees as a reduction of society to relations of power and knowledge and takes him to task for the apparent immanence of this power—that it circulates among subjects rather than being an oppressive external force. She concludes, "we are calling historicist the reduction of society to its indwelling network of relations of power and knowledge,"[18] and offers, as a counter, that "some notion of transcendence is plainly needed if one is to avoid the reduction of social space to the relations that fill it."[19] This is a fault, according to Copjec, that can be found as much in contemporary cultural studies and historicist political critique, and she sees Foucault as the source of many of these problems. The social space cannot be understood, she contends, via Foucault unless we are going to reject subjectivity as a serious component of that space, for such a non-psychoanalytic model would be inadequate to the task of assessing how those subjects that come to constitute social space are also constituted by it. Such a delicate balance needs to be maintained if the relationship between social context and psychical affect is to be grasped. This puzzle seems to be, from very different directions, the central problem of both psychoanalysis—how is the superego or even the ego-ideal constituted in any way that would explain the socialization of groups—and Marxism—why does the individual agree to, and even defend, his or her role in a civil society that is exploitative of its members? One obvious factor is power, which is why Foucault's *genealogical* nontrajectory is so persuasive; and another is Althusser's *interpellation* that reappears, for example, in Fanon's moment of recognition on the occasion of a hailing: "Look! A Negro!"[20]

Contingency, understood psychoanalytically, has drawn most effectively from the Freudian notions of *Nachträglichkeit* and affect that posit a different notion of the temporal than that based on a causal and chronological flow.[21] Contingency, then, is translated from context to subject. Contingency understood as affect does not so much destroy the relation between the social or collective and the individual or singular; rather, it potentially allows for an understanding of the process of individuation in social contexts.

If the most consistent employment of Lacan in the postcolonial context is by Homi Bhabha, it is in Bhabha's use of the notion of affect that Lacanian psychoanalysis is most persuasive. Bhabha centralizes the distinction between postmodernism and postcolonialism, a distinction that, quite astonishingly, gets lost when resistance to political conflict is reduced to a psychical function of the modern, losing its historical particularity even as it argues for singularity. Foregrounding the concept of *Nachträglichkeit*, Bhabha reminds us that affects frequently associated with the postmodern today— such as the instability of master discourses, unstable identities, and coexistent temporal multiplicities—can be seen not only now at the moment of decolonization or postcoloniality but also at earlier moments of the North-South colonial encounters manifested as what he calls a time lag. European modernity's constitution through the colonial enterprise, however, may mark a colonial form of identity that we can retroactively read as resistance to colonial rule. Yet, it is only in a deferred manner that we can understand this form of affect in terms of resistance. The function of reading this resistance today is, I would argue, to mark it as a discrepant modern rather than as the postmodern. These moments of iteration may be understood as affect in terms of postcoloniality, but spatially they can be understood as constitutive of modernity's geographical split, the impossibility of the consistency of its European narrative even as power without hegemony was established.

Bhabha differentiates himself from Derrida and de Man through opposing the "foreign interstitial" with the "metonymic fragmentation of the 'original.' "[22] Taking his cue from Benjamin, Bhabha's challenge is that of foreign cultural translation's dislocation of the original, rather than an excess or an interruption caused by the structure of metonymy. But we could bring the two concepts together very usefully through a notion of affect as a concept that acknowledges the catachresis of the origin of a trauma and that leaves its trace on the individual. This allows for a reading of historical and political processes as instruments of violence on groups—racism, sexism, colonialism, slavery—rather than seeking an absolute origin that may posit, for example, ethnic violence as always rooted in the same psychical structure of lack; or, on the other hand, trauma as originating in a singular historical event that sidelines the everyday. As some may suggest that with the end of the Cold War and globalization we move politically from the law of the father to the regime of the brother, postcolonial *Nachträglichkeit* may well throw a spanner in the works of such reduction of the historical to the leveling of trauma and its ahistorical postmodern aftereffects and affects. The existence of different forms of globalization, its interpretation and the destructive nature of the end of the Cold War for much of the third world reasserts the validity of the historical, the political, and the specifically *modern* forms of trauma in many postcolonial contexts. Assertion and critique of the centrality of national contexts and modern processes continue, even as MTV and CNN are on the TVs of the urban elite, CD-Roms are in their PCs, and Nikes are on their feet. Increasingly, however, women cannot identify with men in this critique, for where it is initiated from anticolonial nationalisms, women's continued lack of representational possibilities has caused a disidentification following the desire for but also the loss of the ideal of national independence.

The structural figuring of subjectivity in Lacan, which is quite different from both the first topography and the second topology in Freud, creates a different status for the historical and therefore a different relationship between the subject and society and how the subject is socially and politically constituted. If Freud, in *Group Psychology and the Analysis of the Ego*, attempted to understand how people became involved in group psychologies and what appears to be collective thinking around an *ego-ideal*, and in *The Ego and the Id* introduced the concept of the regulatory *superego*, he was attempting to understand the mechanisms of identification and disidentification. His broad anthropological sweeps in *Totem and Taboo*, as well as all the work on explaining traumas, certainly problematizes temporality through the concept of *Nachträglichkeit*. It does not, however, give up cause in favor of effect, thereby implicitly arguing that a structural castration constitutes the fundamental antagonism of the subject.[23] In Lacan it is less clear how to conceive of historical occurrences that appear to cause and be caused by particular psychical traumas and identifications in spite of Lacanians' insistence on *singularity* and *contingency*. While the structural split or antagonism seems to be intrinsic to the subject in Lacan's corpus, and therefore attains the status of a universal condition, it is not clear where there is very much room for understanding how the particular, with all its historical permutations, exists alongside this universal. While the universal does not necessarily trivialize the particular, it certainly seems to in much Lacanian thought: one's mind is frequently numbed by witnessing one more prostration in front of the big Other and one more careless rendition of historical events or interpretations of them. Copjec and Žižek have suggested that written law of interactions between people based on a Benthamite principle of the greatest good for the greatest number assumes that law is an external phenomenon about which one may feel ambivalent but by whose rules one is required to live within a state. For Lacanian psychoanalysis, however, those laws are internalized, through interpellation, as the big Other, and contain within the subject what Žižek calls a *supplement* that we recognize as *desire*.[24] So Lacan's ethical question is, "Have you acted in accordance with your desire?" a question later reformulated as *l'éthique du bien dire* (have you spoken in accordance with your desire?).[25] Feelings of guilt and this disjuncture between desire and action often culminate in a sense of ambiguity or uncanniness that raises questions about political efficacy and responsibility—indeed, the Ethics of an individuated Ambiguity as a central model for a social theory.

In a recent essay, "A Leftist Plea for Eurocentrism," Žižek makes a plea that one could say clearly does not need to be made, for, as we know, Eurocentrism is alive and well both as a lens of scholarly activity and as the form of politics with which Žižek equates it. He laments the passing of communism and the self-generating nature of capitalism into a *postmodern* economy of credit, in which far from being in a period that precedes the fall of capitalism in an evolutionary sense, we are, rather, in "the domain of appearance."[26] He is quick to distinguish between this notion of *appearance*—as "symbolic fiction" that exists in the realm of the Symbolic—and *simulacra*—as the "retreat of symbolic efficiency." This blurs the distinction between real and imaginary in a manner that cannot address the value, in sociopolitical terms, of the *symbolic efficiency* of the fiction as fantasy structure. If, however, we read Žižek through the lens of coloniality, reversing the conventional direction of theorizing the third world, he appears to be Eurocentric in somewhat different terms that locate him firmly in the first and (formerly) second world. For his vision of modernity and politics as developed in the West (from Ancient Greece through to the French Revolution and beyond) fails to understand the development of the modern in Europe in relational terms—that is, as being built on and constituted by colonial exploits that continue to haunt.

Žižek has reminded us of the centrality of psychical work in political formations. Reading him in the context of coloniality we may see, however, that some notion of causality has to remain, even as it may be posited as an uncertain *event*. Even though the event may not have a singular identity and cannot be reduced to a particular occurrence, it equally cannot be reduced to the primary scene of linguistics. This has a leveling effect that simply renders more or less anything traumatic in the same degree. In the appeal to universalism, what is at stake is the historicized production of psychical conditions, as well as the question of whether the international *postmodernity* in which different identities proliferate is postmodern at all. Returning to Bhabha, we could think of affects that resemble the postmodern but carry the historical weight of colonialism in a manner that renders them both modern and politically resistant to colonialist proselytizing. The notion of the Truth-Event may well be in place as resistant to the current globalization, but from quite different quarters and with quite different means from those proffered by Žižek. These different colonial repercussions are products of the *epistemic violence* (to use Gayatri Spivak's formulation) of the European legacy, but are far from Eurocentrist in their formulation.[27]

And this brings us back to our initial concerns about the problems that have plagued feminism in the 1990s. The dispersal of energies into *differences* within the feminist movement has accompanied the problematization of the term "Woman." Part of the motivation for this was the colonialist moves of some feminists in the first world who presumed to speak *for* women elsewhere. Another involved the racist exclusions of the feminist movement, with its prioritization of white middle-class women's issues and its rendering of others' issues irrelevant. Of course, what has been decried since then is the loss of the Women's Movement and an era of postfeminism that seems to proclaim the end of feminism for no other reason than that it fails to deal with how political collectivities can cohere in an age of difference. In addition, the deconstruction of the term "Woman" has caused us to wonder what our common term may be, now that we have acknowledged that there are few common causes. The term "woman" has begun to occupy a position in the political realm akin to the term "black" in British minority politics in the 1970s. And like that term, it has eroded as a political term of collectivity in the post-Thatcher/Reagan years, in which specific ethnic differences have sought recognition and distinction from each other, both as an argument for adequate representation and as a desire to distinguish one group from another. The multi-culti hybridity celebrated as national liberalism or as postcolonial cosmopolitanism often conceals within it conflict and racism within minority cultures, as well as within feminist movements.

If ethnocentrism as Eurocentrism is actually about a relation to the concept of the universal, then it is worth considering how that universal can exist without being Eurocentric. If it is true that, as Fredric Jameson puts it, "the so-called advanced countries are sinking into full postmodernity,"[28] it is worth thinking through what temporal issues are at stake when we consider whether the postcolonial puts pressure on the concept of the postmodern. In this sense, the postcolonial modern is called upon to put pressure on its "post-" as it were and, perhaps, to emphasize the affect as well as the material of the historical and economic. This effectively maintains the trace of the critical political distinction between justice and law, as well as between the archive and memory. For even if we would want to contend that a desire to form certain memories and histories causes some documents to be deemed relevant or irrelevant, and thus to be archived or destroyed, the reduction of archive to memory fails to account for reading against the grain or indeed an incorporation (or introjection) of that material in the colonies with very different consequences.

Simone de Beauvoir's feminist argument in *The Second Sex* actively takes issue with ideologies that perpetuate the positing of woman as man's other, denying the sameness of woman's ethical ability. We could say that de Beauvoir, in her attempt to analyze how this seems to occur internationally, repeats some of that otherizing herself—of Tunisian women, for example, who cannot move in and out of their cavernous existence, unlike Tunisian men, and incidentally, unlike herself figured, as it were, as the philosopher-king.[29] While she seems to posit an argument that is based on sameness and identification, she wavers into positing a difference as well, and this is necessary for her very complex notion of freedom and liberation that is quite distinct from Sartre's. It is not only in her work on Djamila Boupacha, the young woman tortured during the Algerian war of independence, that we see how her concept of ethical behavior in the face of violence emerges. Certainly, it is encapsulated there some thirteen years after *The Second Sex*.

But de Beauvoir's early text, *The Ethics of Ambiguity*, like Fanon's early writing in *Black Skin, White Masks*, presents us with quite different models than the ones they claim to build upon. If Fanon effectively rewrote Lacan's mirror stage for the colonial context when he situated suffering as the other in the realm of historical events, economic circumstances, and biological phenomenological asymmetries, de Beauvoir rewrites Sartre's concept of freedom and gives us at least two versions. For while de Beauvoir appears to be challenging the critique of Sartre's *Being and Nothingness* as solipsistic, she actually refashions that text and situates an ambiguity and desire in the notion of freedom—for there are, she suggests, multiple freedoms, ontological and political. Sartre's notion of the freedom of other people is a threat to the ontology of the subject, even though it is also the source of the subject's recognition of *his* own being-for-others that can then propel one into the ambiguity of existence that is the tension between being-in-itself and being-for-itself. The arrival of another person and, most important, the look of that other person, is an aggression, and this is why, as Sartre puts it in *Huis Clos*, hell is other people. As Debra Bergoffen persuasively demonstrates, the key distinction between Sartre and de Beauvoir in this regard is the notion of pleasure[30]; and, I would add, the notion of each person's ontological existence in ambiguity as a kind of liberation. As de Beauvoir says, "to will man free is to will there to *be* being, it is to will the disclosure of being in the joy of existence; in order for the idea of liberation to have a concrete meaning, the joy of existence must be asserted in each one, at every instant."[31]

The idea of liberation itself, the acknowledgment that the other is also a self, commands that one asserts the necessity of each person's freedom. Both in *The Ethics of Ambiguity* and in her work on the Djamila Boupacha case, de Beauvoir asserts the coexistence of horror with the self—the other ceases to be a self if individuals are not thought to be important, and, of course, *vice versa*.[32] There is, she suggests in the early text, a kind of horror to the fact that we can look at photographs of concentration camps and be immune, or that, in the context of Algeria (and she says this in 1948) "colonists appease their conscience by the contempt in which they held the Arabs who were crushed with misery: the more miserable the latter were, the more contemptible they seemed, so much so that there was never room for any remorse" (101). But acknowledging the sameness of the Other, that is, that the other is a self, also paradoxically allows one to see that the Other is actually different and has its own history that propels it into desiring a future in which political freedom for oneself and others can be worked for alongside ontological freedom.

The possibility of such a coalition has been taken up by feminists for some time now. Irigaray's engagement with Levinas, for example, stresses the threshold between people as constitutive of a necessary call that allows for both understanding and its impossibility.[33] Coalition establishes a border between subjects even as it highlights the differences between them. Much feminist literature has resulted in refashioning genres so as to draw attention to the importance of similar forms of mediation between women—the *testimonio* of Rigoberta Menchu, the epistolary style of Mariama Ba's *So Long a Letter*, the second-person narration of Assia Djebar's *Sister to Scheherazade* and that of the translator-editor and writer in Spivak's translation of Mahasweta Devi's *Imaginary Maps*.[34] Each of these texts examines this relationship of coalition between women on the level of particulars and offers in very different ways what Irigaray examines as the centrality of mediation, which is both a hinge between subjects and between the philosophical and the political—indeed, an acknowledgement of the particulars of difference. Difference, however, is understood as allowing for the positing of an ethics of mediation.

In some ways this solves the Levinasian problem; while in his concept and in the manner in which it has been taken up by Drucilla Cornell the importance of the call of the Other is always an irreducible and ongoing presence to the Self, that Other is necessarily figured rather vaguely and always seems to be the same in its abstraction. In a sense, what we are presented with in de Beauvoir is an ethics of coalition that recognizes not only a sense of acting usefully or acting in accordance with one's desire. Rather, the ethics of coalition that exists on a day-to-day level as well as on the level of a traumatic event allows for an acknowledgment of one's pleasure and pain in acting in a certain way, and of the desire that propels it, based as it is in historical and economic circumstances that lead to a notion of the future as potentially free. "An ethics of ambiguity," de Beauvoir says, "will be one which will refuse to deny *a priori* that separate existants can, at the same time, be bound to each other, that their individual freedoms can forge laws valid for all."[35] In this formulation, the Other remains Other, even as unity is proffered.

The quandary of relating to another in the context of transnational feminism is assisted by this idea of the universal, however, only in as much as it acknowledges the differences between the two types of freedom—the political and the ontological. Transnational relationship must acknowledge the differences between, on the one hand, the ambiguity of subjectivities and, on the other hand, political ambivalences with others that frequently cause conflict. I would add to de Beauvoir's notion of ambiguity something she clearly rejects, the psychical affect carried by the subject who attempts to will being, or, we could say, will completion or will justice even as that is known to be of value as *will* rather than as *being*. And involves an understanding of the psychical weight of history and that history itself.

If we think, for example, of de Beauvoir's work during the Algerian war of independence to assist Djamila Boupacha and Gisèle Halimi in seeking legal representation, her gesture is made as much toward Boupacha as toward the nation she comes from, for France, she says, is suffering from a cancer of the imagination. She is also, and we can see this from her autobiographical writings, doing the work for herself, to mark a difference from Sartre and to move out of his shadow; and she therefore, to some extent, receives pleasure from this pain. (In a class I taught on those texts, this pleasure was taboo, as if we have an ethical responsibility to suffer for the other because they suffer, a fact that seems to me to be a form of vicarious suffering that must cause some pleasure in order to be so eagerly endorsed.) But de Beauvoir's, and Halimi's, immediate problem was to get a fair trial for Boupacha even as they were confronted with the legal system itself colluding with the torture and abuse of those whom it was supposed to protect. De Beauvoir focused on the goal of legal representation to communicate that a war was going on and that torture occurred because Boupacha was deemed to be a *terrorist* allegedly performing acts of war. The ethical quandary for de Beauvoir was to communicate Boupacha's suffering in a manner that would at once allow Boupacha to be politically represented and also to publicize her pain. Maintaining a faith in legal systems that were simultaneously the instruments of Boupacha's violation necessitated demanding a national recognition that war was enacted for the armchair colonialist. But perhaps today the quandaries are different, because even though de Beauvoir called the Algerian struggle a war in 1948, in effect making everyday struggle into war, when she wrote of Djamila Boupacha, it was in fact during a war, and when she wrote of Algeria in *The Ethics of Ambiguity*, she wrote of the horrors of complacency about national wrongdoings/passivity in World War II and did not acknowledge the exploitation of Algerians.[36]

Today, however, in the period of postcolonialism, different ethical quandaries exist because of the psychical as well as the political quandaries of colonial legacies. Whether we think of such problems as developing laws in

the United States to regulate clitoridectomy, or whether we are considering international human rights laws, the colonial legacy is still very much
in place, on both a psychical and political level. For the colonialist gesture
of outlawing clitoridectomy is a very modern commitment that became
frequently associated with nationalist movements, making the outlawing of
it all the more problematic because of nativist resurgence of the practice.
For a practice deemed reprehensible by so many women internationally
can nonetheless not be dealt with outside the acknowledgment of a prior
juridical failure on the part of colonizers, and frequently a contemporary
ethical failure on the part of well-meaning but badly informed feminists.[37]
On the other hand, letting it alone is similarly problematic, because the
issue is international and has been debated in transnational contexts. Relativism returns us to the problem with which we began and leads to a breakdown of the possibility of coalition both in everyday terms and also in
moments of crisis. An ethics that bases itself on a theory of desire is a problem; it is solipsistic because desire for subjective wholeness ultimately falls
into a kind of idealism. This is why Fanon, in *The Wretched of the Earth*, will
ultimately turn to the political realm that he saw as causing psychical damage.[38] Equally, an ethics that does not account for desire as justice is not taking into account the workings and parochializations of colonial and postcolonial modernity. The fantasy of justice and the fantasy of freedom are
not simply a type of release of desire that constitutes the collective free
will. Rather, they concern understanding demand in relation to need and
desire—a desire that cannot be satisfied and perhaps then propels us toward
the future but also allows us to see the dynamic between psychic and political contingency in the present. A psychic contingency in the present
embodies within it the persistence of history, or, as Spivakian deconstruction would have it, "the impossibility of a full undoing,"[39] not simply as
fantasy or as memory but also as archive distinct from memory. Colonialism and the ethical quandaries to which it has given rise for transnational
feminism always reinscribes the postcolonial in the transnational. This is not
simply replacing globalization with universalization; rather, it is asserting
that transnational feminism is always dealing with the thorny area of postcolonialism and that any ethics is always built upon a universal renegotiated
locally. For feminist practice, and for feminist scholarship, this has meant
underscoring the political and psychical affect of colonialism and the
modernity of postcolonialism.

The spectral nature of postcolonial modernity means that an incorporation of forms of law, of languages, and of systemic inequalities into colonized countries did not amount to an introjection, or a full psychic assimilation. This incorporation of Eurocentrism and of historical abuses in the form of an individuated violence was common to the colonial sphere. While clearly Simone de Beauvoir does not engage the important contribution of psychoanalysis to a concept of ethics, her model of an ethics of ambiguity nonetheless leaves room for the necessary coupling of the historical and the psychical in any work that involves international or transnational relations in the postcolonial era. Unfortunately, Lacan, particularly in the manner in which he is employed by Žižek when Žižek makes a leftist plea for Eurocentrism, is also inadequate to the task.

While transnational scholarship has often idealized the moment of the loss of boundaries, feminist transnational scholarship and practice, I would suggest, cannot and does not endorse this. For while globalization has initiated to some degree the breakdown of national boundaries, it also maintains neocolonial economics and often colonialist relations when it comes to such issues as, for example, nuclear arms, pharmaceuticals, or the environment. But while postcolonial feminists have frequently resisted interference from people who threaten to repeat colonial gestures, anticolonial nationalism has clearly been brought under critical scrutiny. I would suggest that even as modern political and national boundaries persist, it is for women to be vigilant, not only with a critical eye toward colonialism but also with one toward nationalism. The largely masculinist nationalisms that emerged out of the former colonies frequently put, as we know, women's issues on the back burner, even in contexts of apparently progressive thought, as in Algeria—a country that, as we know, has failed to be the avant-garde third-world nation it once promised to be, where corruption would not occur and where women would not be second-class citizens. The psychical affect caused by this loss of an ideal on the part of women, I would suggest, has brought about a sense of despair, a form of melancholia. Women carry with them incorporated traumas swallowed whole, traumas that manifest themselves as continuing symptoms and traces where the anticolonial struggle is still so new and relevant. Political failures have brought about a disidentification with the nation that failed to represent women. It is this disidentification, I would suggest, that allows for coalitions between women internationally where a concept of *justice* is forged in the full knowledge of the thorniness of the specters of colonial relations and "local" abuses of women.

NOTES

1. See Chandra Mohanty, "Cartographies of Struggle," in *Third World Women and the Politics of Feminism*, ed. Chandra Talpade Mohanty, Ann Russo, and Lourdes Torres (Bloomington: Indiana University Press, 1991), pp. 1–50; Gayatri Chakravorty Spivak, "Can the Subaltern Speak?" in *Marxism and the Interpretation of Culture*, ed. Cary Nelson and Lawrence Grossberg (Urbana: University of Illinois Press, 1988), pp. 271–313; and Maria Lugones and Elizabeth Spelman, " 'Have We Got a Theory for You!': Feminist Theory, Cultural Imperialism, and the Demand for 'the Woman's Voice,' " in *Hypatia Reborn: Essays in Feminist Philosophy*, ed. Azizah Y. Al-Hibri and Margaret A. Simons (Bloomington: Indiana University Press, 1990), pp. 573–81.

2. See Jacques Derrida, *Specters of Marx: The State of the Debt, the Work of Mourning, and the New International*, trans. Peggy Kamuf (New York: Routledge, 1994), and Benedict Anderson, *Imagined Communities: Reflections on the Origin and Spread of Nationalism*, 2d ed. (London: Verso, 1991).

3. Bruce Robbins, ed., *The Phantom Public Sphere* (Minneapolis: University of Minnesota Press, 1993), pp. vii–xxvi.

4. Such a concept of haunting draws from Nicolas Abraham and Maria Torok's understanding of the distinctions between introjection and incorporation, and transgenerational haunting through a phantom that manifests itself in language. Taking the terms "introjection" and "incorporation" from Ferenczi, they speak of them in terms of losses and their aftermath. Whereas Freud does not distinguish between introjection and incorporation when he writes about mourning and melancholia, Abraham and Torok formulate introjection as a successful assimilation of something lost into the self, a process that goes on constantly through a lifetime as psychical assimilation is always necessary. Incorporation, on the other hand, is the swallowing whole of something lost. It may appear to be assimilated, but will emerge through symptoms in language. This language, and thus this incorporation, could in theory be carried through generations, resulting in a being haunted by a secret once incorporated. And it could manifest itself at particular historical moments in which events occur that cause the phantom to emerge. In the context of coloniality, we could think, for example, of incorporated colonialist ideals apparently available but actually unavailable to colonized peoples that are mourned as a loss of an ideal. The trace of such incorporation would thus be crucial to any understanding of the present or the future because of the specters that haunt. The terms are elaborated in "Maladie du deuil," in *L'Écorce et le noyau* (Paris: Aubier-Flammarion, 1978). See pp. 233–35 in particular, where they elaborate on this idea in a subsection called "La notion ferenczienne de l'introjection des pulsions opposée à celle d'incorporation de l'objet" (*The Shell and the Kernel: Renewals of Psychoanalysis*, trans. Nicholas Rand [Chicago: University of Chicago Press, 1994], 1:125–38). For more on intergenerational haunting, see *The Wolf Man's Magic Word: A Cryptonomy*, trans. Nicholas Rand (Min-

neapolis: University of Minnesota Press, 1986). (*Cryptonomie: Le verbier de l'homme aux loups* [Paris: Flammarion, 1976].)

5. Drucilla Cornell has written about this extensively, and pits Lacan against Derrida (through Levinas) in this regard. See *The Philosophy of the Limit* (London: Routledge, 1992).

6. See, for example, Judith Butler, *Gender Trouble* (London: Routledge, 1990).

7. Simone de Beauvoir, *The Ethics of Ambiguity*, trans. Bernard Frechtman (1948; rpt. New York: Citadel Press, 1997).

8. Jean-Paul Sartre, *Being and Nothingness*, trans. Hazel Barnes (1943; rpt. New York: Pocket Books, 1956).

9. Jean-Paul Sartre, *Notebooks for an Ethics*, trans. David Pellauer (University of Chicago Press, 1992). This has recently received much attention in the field of Black Studies. See, for example, Lewis Gordon, ed., *Existence in Black: An Anthology of Black Existential Philosophy* (London: Routledge, 1997).

10. See Herbert Marcuse, "Sartre's Existentialism" (1948) and "Postscript" (1965), in *From Luther to Popper*, trans. Joris de Bres (London: Verso, 1972), pp. 157–89. Marcuse withdrew his criticism in the postscript.

11. See Jean-Paul Sartre, *What Is Literature?* trans. Bernard Frechtman (1948; rpt. Bristol: Methuen, 1967).

12. Sigmund Freud, "Civilization and Its Discontents" (1930), vol. 21 of *The Standard Edition of the Complete Psychological Works of Sigmund Freud*, ed. and trans. James Strachey (London: Hogarth Press, 1953–74).

13. Jacques Lacan, *Ethics of Psychoanalysis*, trans. Catherine Porter (1959–60; rpt. London: Routledge, 1992).

14. Most recently, see Judith Butler, *The Psychic Life of Power* (Stanford: Stanford University Press, 1997).

15. See Joan Copjec, *Read My Desire: Lacan Against the Historicists* (Cambridge: MIT Press, 1994); Renata Salecl, *The Spoils of Freedom: Psychoanalysis and Feminism After the Fall of Socialism* (London: Routledge, 1994); and Slavoj Žižek, *The Sublime Object of Ideology* (London: Verso, 1989).

16. Copjec, *Read My Desire*, p. 4.

17. Michel Foucault, *The Order of Things: An Archaeology of the Human Sciences*, trans. Alan Sheridan (London: Tavistock, 1970), p. xiii.

18. Copjec, *Read My Desire*, p. 6.

19. Ibid., p. 7.

20. Frantz Fanon, *Black Skin White Masks*, trans. Charles Lee Markmann (New York: Grove Press, 1967), p. 112. (*Peau noire, masques blancs* [Paris: Editions du Seuil, 1952].)

21. For more on the concept of *Nachträglichkeit*, see Freud, "Further Recommendations on the Technique of Psychoanalysis: Remembering, Repeating, and Working Through" (1914), in *SE* 12:145–56; Working Papers on "Psychopathology"

(1950/1895), ibid., 1: 347–59; Letters to Fliess, November and December 1896, ibid., 1: 233; and "The Wolf Man," in *The Wolf-Man: The Double Story of Freud's Most Famous Case*, ed. Muriel Gardner (New York: Basic Books, 1971), pp. 173–203; Jacques Lacan, "Function and Field of Speech and Language," in *Écrits*, trans. Alan Sheridan (New York: Norton, 1977), pp. 40–56.

22. Homi Bhabha, "How Newness Enters the World," in *The Location of Culture* (London: Routledge, 1994), p. 227.

23. Freud, *Group Psychology and the Analysis of the Ego* (1921), in *SE*, vol. 28; *The Ego and the Id* (1923), in *SE*, vol. 19; *Totem and Taboo* (1912–13), in *SE*, vol. 8.

24. Slavoj Žižek, "Fantasy as a Political Category," *Journal for the Psychoanalysis of Culture and Society* 1, no. 2 (Fall 1996): 77–86.

25. Jacques Lacan, *Ethics of Psychoanalysis*; *Télévision* (Paris: Seuil, 1973).

26. Slavoj Žižek, "A Leftist Plea for Eurocentrism," *Critical Inquiry* 24 (Summer 1998): 995.

27. Gayatri Chakravorty Spivak, "Postcoloniality and Value," in *Literary Theory Today*, ed. P. Collier and H. Geyer-Ryan (Cambridge, England: Polity Press, 1990), p. 228.

28. Fredric Jameson, *The Geopolitical Aesthetic: Cinema and Space in the World System* (Bloomington: Indiana University Press, 1995), p. 1.

29. Simone de Beauvoir, *The Second Sex*, trans. H. M. Parshley (London: Picador, 1988), pp. 115–16. (*Le Deuxième Sexe* [Paris: Gallimard, 1949].)

30. Debra Bergoffen, "Out from Under: Beauvoir's Philosophy of the Erotic," in *Feminist Interpretations of Simone de Beauvoir*, ed. Margaret Simons (University Park: Pennsylvania State University Press, 1995), pp. 179–92.

31. Simone de Beauvoir, *The Ethics of Ambiguity*, trans. Bernard Frechtman (New York: Citadel Press, 1997), p. 135.

32. Simone de Beauvoir and Gisèle Halimi, *Djamila Boupacha* (Paris: Gallimard, 1962). (*Djamila Boupacha: The Story of the Torture of a Young Algerian Girl Which Shocked Liberal Opinion*, trans. Peter Green [London: André Deutsch and Weidenfeld and Nicolson: 1962].)

33. Luce Irigaray, *Éthique de la différence sexuelle* (Paris: Editions de Minuit, 1984); *J'aime à toi: Esquisse d'une félicité dans l'histoire* (Paris: Grasset, 1992); *Je, tu, nous: Pour une culture de la différence* (Paris: Grasset, 1990).

34. Mariama Ba, *So Long a Letter* (London: Heinemann, 1981); Rigoberta Menchu, *I, Rigoberta Menchu: An Indian Woman in Guatemala* (London: Verso, 1985); Assia Djebar, *A Sister to Scheherazade* (London: Heinemann, 1993); Mahasweta Devi, *Imaginary Maps* (London: Routledge, 1994). See also Gayatri Chakravorty Spivak, "The Politics of Translation," in *Destabilizing Theory: Contemporary Feminist Debates*, ed. Michèle Barrett and Anne Phillips (Cambridge, England: Polity Press, 1992), pp. 54–85.

35. Beauvoir, *Ethics of Ambiguity*, p. 18.

36. I have written on the Djamila Boupacha case more extensively in an essay forthcoming in *Algeria In and Out of French*, ed. Anne Berger (Ithaca, N.Y.: Cornell University Press, 2001).

37. I have written on this issue more extensively in an article on Alice Walker's books and film on clitoridectomy. See Ranjana Khanna and Karen Engle, "Forgotten History: Myth, Empathy, and Assimilated Culture," in *Feminism and the New Democracy*, ed. Jodie Dean (New York: Sage Press, 1996), pp. 67–80.

38. See Frantz Fanon, "Colonial War and Mental Disorders," in *The Wretched of the Earth,* trans. Constance Farrington (New York: Grove Press, 1961), pp. 249–311. (*Les Damnés de la terre* [Paris: François Maspero, 1961].)

39. Gayatri Chakravorty Spivak, "Scattered Speculations on the Question of Value," in *In Other Worlds* (New York: Methuen, 1987), p. 154.

Chapter 6

The Subject of True Feeling:
Pain, Privacy, and Politics

LAUREN BERLANT

Liberty finds no refuge in a jurisprudence of doubt[1]

Pain

Ravaged wages and ravaged bodies saturate the global marketplace in which the United States seeks desperately to compete "competitively," as the euphemism goes, signifying a race that will be won by the nations whose labor conditions are most optimal for profit.[2] In the United States the media of the political public sphere regularly register new scandals of the proliferating sweatshop networks "at home" and "abroad," which has to be a good thing, because it produces *feeling* and with it something at least akin to *consciousness* that can lead to *action*.[3] Yet even as the image of the traumatized worker proliferates, even as evidence of exploitation is found under every rock or commodity, it competes with a normative/utopian image of the U.S. citizen who remains unmarked, framed and protected by the private trajectory of his life project, which is sanctified at the juncture where the

unconscious meets history: the American Dream.[4] In that story one's identity is not borne of suffering, mental, physical, or economic. If the U.S.
worker is lucky enough to live at an economic moment that sustains the
dream, he gets to appear at his *least* national when he is working and at his
most national at leisure, with his family or in semipublic worlds of other
men producing surplus manliness (for example, via sports). In the American
dreamscape his identity is private property, a zone where structural obstacles
and cultural differences fade into an ether of prolonged, deferred, and indi-
viduating enjoyment that he has earned and that the nation has helped him
to earn. Meanwhile exploitation only appears as a scandalous nugget in the
sieve of memory when it can be condensed into an exotic thing of momentary fascination, a squalor of the bottom too horrible to be read in its own
actual banality.

The exposed traumas of workers in ongoing extreme conditions do not
generally induce more than mourning on the part of the state and the public culture to whose feeling-based opinions the state is said to respond.
Mourning is what happens when a grounding object is lost, is dead, no
longer living (to you). Mourning is an experience of irreducible bounded-
ness: I am here, I am living, he/she is dead, I am mourning. It is a beautiful,
not sublime, experience of emancipation: mourning supplies the subject the
definitional perfection of a being no longer in flux. It takes place over a distance: even if the object who induces the feeling of loss and helplessness is
neither dead, nor at any great distance from where you are.[5] In other words,
mourning can also be an act of aggression, of social death-making: it can
perform the evacuation of significance from actually existing subjects. Even
when liberals do it, one might say, "others" are ghosted for a good cause.[6]
The sorrow songs of scandal that sing of the exploitation that is always
"elsewhere" (even a few blocks away) are in this sense aggressively songs of
mourning. Play them backward and the military march of capitalist tri-
umphalism (*The Trans-Nationale*) can be heard. Its lyric, currently crooned by
every organ of record in the United States, is about necessity. It exhorts citizens to understand that the "bottom line"[7] of national life is neither utopia
nor freedom but survival, which can be achieved only by a citizenry that eats
its anger, makes no unreasonable claims on resources or control over value,
and uses its most creative energy to cultivate intimate spheres while scrap-
ping a life together flexibly in response to the market-world's caprice.[8]

In this particular moment of expanding class unconsciousness that looks
like consciousness emerges a peculiar, though not unprecedented hero: the

exploited child. If a worker can be infantilized, pictured as young, as small, as feminine or feminized, as starving, as bleeding and diseased, and as a (virtual) slave, the righteous indignation around procuring his survival resounds everywhere. The child must not be sacrificed to states or to profiteering. His wounded image speaks a truth that subordinates narrative: he has not "freely" chosen his exploitation; the optimism and play that are putatively the right of childhood have been stolen from him. Yet only "voluntary" steps are ever taken to try to control this visible sign of what is ordinary and systemic amidst the chaos of capitalism, in order to make its localized nightmares seem uninevitable. Privatize the atrocity, delete the visible sign, make it seem *foreign*. Return the child to the family, replace the children with adults who can look dignified while being paid virtually the same revolting wage. The problem that organizes so much feeling then regains livable proportions, and the uncomfortable pressure of feeling dissipates, like so much gas.

Meanwhile, the pressure of feeling the shock of being uncomfortably political produces a cry for a double therapy—to the victim and the viewer. But before "we" appear too complacently different from the privileged citizens who desire to caption the mute image of exotic suffering with an aversively fascinated mourning (a desire for the image to be *dead*, a ghost), we must note that this feeling culture crosses over into other domains, the domains of what we call identity politics, where the wronged take up voice and agency to produce transformative testimony that depends on an analogous conviction about the *self-evidence* and therefore the *objectivity* of painful feeling.

The central concern of this essay is to address the place of painful feeling in the making of political worlds. In particular, I mean to challenge a powerful popular belief in the positive workings of something I call national sentimentality, a rhetoric of promise that a nation can be built across fields of social difference through channels of affective identification and empathy. Sentimental politics generally promotes and maintains the hegemony of the national identity form, no mean feat in the face of continued widespread intercultural antagonism and economic cleavage. But national sentimentality is more than a current of feeling that circulates in a political field: the phrase describes a longstanding contest between two models of U.S. citizenship. In one, the classic model, each citizen's value is secured by an equation between abstractness and emancipation: a cell of national identity provides juridically protected personhood for citizens regardless of anything specific about them. In the second model, which was initially organized around labor, feminist, and antiracist struggles in the United States in the nineteenth century, another version of the nation is imagined as the index of collective life. This nation is peopled by suffering citizens and noncitizens whose structural exclusion from the utopian-American dreamscape exposes the state's claim of legitimacy and virtue to an acid wash of truth-telling that makes hegemonic disavowal virtually impossible at certain moments of political intensity.

Sentimentality has long been the means by which mass subaltern pain is advanced, in the dominant public sphere, as the true core of national collectivity. It operates when the pain of intimate others burns into the conscience of classically privileged national subjects, in such a fashion that they feel the pain of flawed or denied citizenship as their pain. Theoretically, to eradicate the pain those with power will do whatever is necessary to return the nation once more to its legitimately utopian odor. Identification with pain, a universal true feeling, then leads to structural social change. In return, subalterns scarred by the pain of failed democracy will reauthorize universalist notions of citizenship in the national utopia, which involves believing in a redemptive notion of law as the guardian of public good. The object of the nation and the law in this light is to eradicate systemic social pain, the absence of which becomes the definition of freedom.

Yet since these very sources of protection—the state, the law, patriotic ideology—have traditionally buttressed traditional matrices of cultural hierarchy, and since their historic job has been to protect universal subject/citizens from feeling their cultural and corporeal specificity as a political vulnerability, the imagined capacity of these institutions to assimilate to the affective tactics of subaltern counterpolitics suggests some weaknesses, or misrecognitions, in these tactics. For one thing, it may be that the sharp specificity of the traumatic model of pain implicitly mischaracterizes what a person is as what a person becomes in the experience of social negation; this model also falsely promises a sharp picture of structural violence's source and scope, in turn promoting a dubious optimism that law and other visible sources of inequality, for example, can provide the best remedies for their own taxonomizing harms. It is also possible that counterhegemonic deployments of pain as the measure of structural injustice actually sustain the utopian image of a homogeneous national metaculture, which can look like a healed or healthy body in contrast to the scarred and exhausted ones.

Finally, it might be that the tactical use of trauma to describe the effects of social inequality so overidentifies the eradication of pain with the achievement of justice that it enables various confusions: for instance, the equation of pleasure with freedom, or the sense that changes in feeling, even on a mass scale, amount to substantial social change. Sentimental politics makes these confusions credible and these violences bearable, as its cultural power confirms the centrality of interpersonal identification and empathy to the vitality and viability of collective life. This gives citizens something to do in response to overwhelming structural violence. Meanwhile, by equating mass society with "national culture," these important transpersonal linkages and intimacies all too frequently serve as proleptic shields, as ethically uncontestable legitimating devices for sustaining the hegemonic field.[9]

Our first example, the child laborer, a ghost of the nineteenth century, taps into a current vogue to reflect in the premature exposure of children to capitalist publicity and adult depravity the nation's moral and economic decline, citing it as a scandal of citizenship, something shocking and un-American. Elsewhere I have described the ways the infantile citizen has been exploited, in the United States, to become both the inspiring sign of the painless good life and the evacuating optimistic cipher of contemporary national identity.[10] During the 1980s a desperate search to protect the United States from what seemed to be an imminently powerful alliance of parties on the bottom of so many traditional hierarchies—the poor, people of color, women, gays and lesbians—provoked a counter-insurgent fantasy on behalf of "traditional American values." The nation imagined in this reactive rhetoric is dedicated not to the survival or emancipation of traumatized marginal subjects but to freedom for the American innocent: the adult without sin, the abducted and neglected child, and above all, and most effectively, the fetus. Although it had first appeared as a technological miracle of photographic biopower in the mid-1960s, in the post-Roe era the fetus became consolidated as a political commodity, a supernatural sign of national iconicity. What constituted this national iconicity was an image of an American, perhaps the last living American, not yet bruised by history: not yet caught up in the excitement of mass consumption, or ethnic, racial, or sexual mixing, not yet tainted by knowledge, by money, or by war. This fetus was an American to identify with, to aspire to make a world for: it organized a kind of beautiful citizenship politics of good intention and virtuous fantasy that could not be said to be dirty, or whose dirt was attributed to the sexually or politically immoral.

By citizenship I refer here both to the legal sense in which persons are juridically subject to the law's privileges and protections by virtue of national identity status, as well as to the experiential, vernacular context in which people customarily understand their relation to state power and social membership. It is to bridge these two axes of political identity and identification that Dr. Bernard Nathanson, founder of the National Abortion Rights Action League (NARAL) and now a pro-life activist, makes political films starring the traumatically posticonic fetal body. His aim is to solicit *aversive identifications* with the fetus, ones that strike deeply the empathetic imaginary of people's best selves while creating pressure for the erasure of empathy's scene. First, he shows graphic images of abortion, captioned by pornographic descriptions of the procedures by which the total body is visibly turned into hideous fragmented flesh. He then calls on the national conscience to delete what he has created, an "unmistakable trademark of the irrational violence that has pervaded the twentieth century."[11] The trademark to which he refers is abortion. He exhorts the public to abort the fetal trademark so as to save the fetus itself—and by extension the national identity form and its future history. In this sense the fetus's sanctified national identity is the opposite of any multicultural, sexual, or classed identity: the fetus is a blinding light that, triumphant as the modal citizen-form, would white out the marks of hierarchy, taxonomy, and violence that seem now so central to the public struggle over who should possess the material and cultural resources of contemporary national life.

It will be clear by now how the struggle over child labor takes on the same form as fetal rights discourse: revelations of trauma, incitements to rescue, the reprivatization of victims as the ground of hope, and above all, the notion that the feeling self is the true self, the self that must be protected from pain or from history, that scene of unwelcome changing. The infantile citizen then enfigures the adult's true self, his inner child in all its undistorted or untraumatized possibility. But to say this is to show how the fetal/infantile icon is a fetish of citizenship with a double social function. An object of fascination and disavowal, it stands in for (while remanding to social obscurity) the traumatized virtuous private citizen around whom history ought to be organized, for whom there is not a good-enough world. (This currently includes the formerly tacit or "normal" citizen and the sexually and racially subordinated ones.) In addition to its life as a figure for the injured adult, the fetus has another life as a utopian sign of a just

and pleasant socius, both in pro-life, profamily values rhetoric and in adver-
tisements and Hollywood films about the state of white reproductive heterosexuality in the United States during an era of great cultural, economic,
and technological upheaval. Its two scenes of citizenship can be spatialized:
one takes place in a traumatized public and the other in a pain-free intimate zone. These zones mirror each other perfectly and so betray the fetish
form of sentimental citizenship, the wish it expresses to signify a political
world beyond contradiction.[12]

I have elaborated these basic Freudian dicta about mourning, the theory
of infantile citizenship, and this account of U.S. political culture to make a
context for four claims: that this is an age of sentimental politics in which
policy and law and public experiences of personhood in everyday life are
conveyed through rhetorics of utopian/traumatized feeling; that national-
popular struggle is now expressed in fetishes of utopian/traumatic affect
that overorganize and overorganicize social antagonism; that utopian/trau-
matized subjectivity has replaced rational subjectivity as the essential index
of value for personhood and thus for society; and that, while on all sides of
the political spectrum political rhetoric generates a high degree of cynicism and boredom,[13] those same sides manifest, simultaneously, a sanctify-
ing respect for sentiment. Thus, in the sentimental national contract antagonistic class positions mirror each other in their mutual conviction about
the *self-evidence* and *objectivity* of painful feeling and about the nation's duty
to eradicate it. In the conjuncture "utopian/traumatized" I mean to convey a logic of fantasy reparation involved in the therapeutic conversion of
the scene of pain and its eradication to the scene of the political itself.
Questions of social inequity and social value are now adjudicated in the
register not of power but of sincere surplus feeling: worry about whether
public figures seem "caring" subordinates analyses of their visions of injustice; subalternized groups attempt to forge alliances on behalf of radical
social transformation through testimonial rhetorics of true pain;[14] people
believe that they know what they feel when they feel it, can locate its origin, measure its effects.

The traffic in affect of these political struggles finds validity in those
seemingly superpolitical moments when a "clear" wrong—say, the spectacle
of children violently exploited—produces a "universal" response. Feeling
politics takes all kinds: it is a politics of protection, reparation, rescue. It
claims a hardwired truth, a core of common sense. It is beyond ideology,
beyond mediation, beyond contestation. It seems to dissolve contradiction

and dissent into pools of basic and also higher truth. It seems strong and clear, as opposed to confused or ambivalent (thus: the unconscious has left the ballpark). It seems the inevitable or desperately only core material of community.

What does it mean for the struggle to shape collective life when a politics of true feeling organizes analysis, discussion, fantasy, and policy? When feeling, the most subjective thing, the thing that makes persons public and marks their location, takes the temperature of power, mediates personhood, experience, and history, takes over the space of ethics and truth? When the shock of pain is said only to produce *clarity*, when shock can as powerfully be said to produce panic, misrecognition, the shakiness of perception's ground? Finally, what happens to questions of managing alterity or difference or resources in collective life when feeling *bad* becomes evidence for a structural condition of injustice? What does it mean for the theory and practice of social transformation when feeling *good* becomes evidence of justice's triumph? As many historians and theorists of "rights talk" have shown, the beautiful and simple categories of legitimation in liberal society can bestow on the phenomenal form of proper personhood the status of normative value, which is expressed in feeling terms as "comfort";[15] and meanwhile, political arguments that challenge the claim of painful feeling's analytic clarity are frequently characterized as causing further violence to already damaged persons and the world of their desires.

This essay will raise uncomfortable questions about what the evidence of trauma is: its desire is to exhort serious critical, but not cynical, attention to the fetish of true feeling in which social antagonism is, frequently, being worked without being worked through. My larger aim is to bring into being as an object of critique the all-too-explicit "common sense" feeling culture of national life, evident in the law, identity politics, and mass society generally: it is about the problem of trying juridically and culturally to administer society as a space ideally void of struggle and ambivalence, a place made on the model of fetal simplicity. I am not trying to posit feeling as the bad opposite of something good called thinking: as we will see, in the cases to follow politicized feeling is a kind of thinking that too often assumes the obviousness of the thought it has, which stymies the production of the thought it might become.

In particular our cases will derive from the field of sexuality, a zone of practice, fantasy, and ideology whose standing in the law constantly partakes of claims about the universality or transparency of feeling, a universality juridically known as "privacy." We begin by addressing the work of feeling in Supreme Court decisions around sexuality and privacy. But the tendency to assume the nonideological, nonmediated, or nonsocial status of feeling is shared by opponents to privacy as well, with consequences that must equally, though differently, give pause: the following section interrogates the antiprivacy revolution legal radicals have wrought via the redefinition of harm and traumatized personhood. The paradoxes revealed therein will not be easily solved by ignoring or condescending to the evidence of injustice provided by the publicized pain of subordinated populations—this essay's coda focuses on a twelve-step book about reproduction, *Peaceful Pregnancy Meditations*, whose commitment to therapy for pregnant women and whose paranoia about the world of identity politics in the present moment suggests a different, not a better, model of pain, intersubjectivity, and change. Its properly paranoid politics of intimacy rejects the mirroring logics of posttraumatic national subjectivity. It promotes, instead, a deeply felt but stubbornly uncongealed form of personhood whose way of inhabiting politics, publicness, personhood, and power is instructive for thinking about what it would mean, and what kinds of changes it would bring, to induce a break with trauma's seduction of politics, in the everyday of U.S. citizenship.[16]

Privacy

It would not be too strong to say that where regulating sexuality is concerned the law has a special sentimental relation to banality. But to say this is not to accuse the law of irrelevance or shallowness. In contrast to the primary sense of banality as a condition of reiterated ordinary conventionality, banality can also mark the experience of deeply felt emotion, as in the case of "I love you," "Did you come?" or "O Say, Can You See . . . ?"[17] But for an occasion of banality to be both utopian and sublime, its ordinariness must be thrust into a zone of overwhelming disavowal. This act of optimistic forgetting is neither simple nor easy: it takes the legitimating force of institutions—for example, the nation form, or heterosexuality—to establish the virtue of forgetting banality's banality. Take a classic instance of this process, an entirely forgettable moment in *The Wizard of Oz* that precedes an unforgettable one. Auntie Em says to Dorothy, who has been interfering with the work on the farm (no child labor there: Dorothy carries *books*): "Find yourself a place where you won't get into any trouble." Dorothy, in a trance, seems to repeat the phrase, but misrepeats it, sighing, "a place where there isn't any trouble," which leads her then to fantasize *Somewhere over the Rainbow*. Between the phrase's first and second incarnations the agency of the subject disappears and is transferred to the place: the magic of will and intention has been made a property of property.

The unenumerated relation between *the* place where *you* won't get into trouble and *a* place where, definitionally, *there is no trouble* expresses the foggy fantasy of happiness pronounced in the constitutional concept of privacy, whose emergence in sexuality law during the 1960s brought heterosexual intimacy explicitly into the antagonistic field of U.S. citizenship. Privacy is the Oz of America. Based on a notion of safe space, a hybrid space of home and law in which people will act legally and lovingly toward each other free from the determinations of history or the coercions of pain, the constitutional theorization of sexual privacy is drawn from a lexicon of romantic sentiment, a longing for a space where there is no trouble, a place whose constitution in law would be so powerful that desire would meet moral discipline there, making real the dreamy rule. In this dream the zone of privacy is a paradigmatic national space too, where freedom and desire meet up in their full suprapolitical expression, a site of embodiment that also leaves unchallenged fundamental dicta about the universality or abstractness of the modal citizen.

Much has been written on the general status of privacy doctrine in constitutional history, a "broad and ambiguous concept which can easily be shrunken in meaning but which can also, on the other hand, easily be interpreted as a constitutional ban against many things other than searches and seizures."[18] Privacy was first conceived as a constitutionally mandated but unenumerated right of sexual citizenship in *Griswold* v. *Connecticut* [381 U.S. 479 (1965)]. The case is about the use of birth control in marriage: a nineteenth-century Connecticut law made it illegal for married couples to use contraceptives for birth control (oral arguments suggest that the "rhythm method" was not unconstitutional in that state[19]); they were only allowed prophylaxis to prevent disease. To challenge this law, Esther Griswold, director of Planned Parenthood in Connecticut, and Lee Buxton, the chief physician there, were arrested, by arrangement with the district attorney, for giving "information, instruction, and medical advice to *married persons* as to the means of preventing conception."[20]

The arguments made in *Griswold* stress the Due Process clause of the 14th Amendment, because denying the sale of contraceptives "constitutes a deprivation of right against invasion of privacy."[21] This kind of privacy is allotted only to married couples: Justice Goldberg quotes approvingly a previous opinion of Justice Harlan (*Poe* v. *Ullman*, 367 U.S. 497, at 533), which states that "adultery, homosexuality, and the like are sexual intimacy which the State forbids . . . but the intimacy of husband and wife is necessarily an essential and accepted feature of the institution of marriage, an institution which the State not only must allow, but which always and in every age it has fostered and protected."[22]

We can see in Harlan's phrasing and Goldberg's citation of it the sentimental complexities of making constitutional law about sexual practice in modern America. The logic of equivalence between adultery and homosexuality in the previous passage locates these antithetical sexual acts/practices in an unprotected public space that allows and even compels *zoning* in the form of continual state discipline (e.g., *laws*):[23] in contrast, marital privacy is drawn up here in a zone elsewhere to the law and takes its authority from tradition, which means that the law simultaneously protects it and turns away its active disciplinary gaze. At this juncture of space, time, legitimacy, and the law Gayatri Spivak's distinction between "Time" and "timing" will also clarify the stakes of privacy law's optimistic apartheid where sexuality is concerned. Spivak argues that the difference between hegemonic and "colonized" conceptions of imperial legal authority can be tracked by graphing "Time" as that property of transcendental continuity that locates state power to sustain worlds in the capacity to enunciate master concepts such as liberty and legitimacy in a zone of monumental time, a seemingly postpolitical space of abstraction from the everyday. In contrast, "timing" marks the always processual, drowning-in-the-present quality of subaltern survival in the face of the law's scrutiny and subject-making pedagogy.[24] Mapped onto sexuality law here, in privacy's early and most happy conceptualization, we see that nonmarital and therefore nonprivate sex exists in the antagonistic performance of the law's present tense, while the marital is virtually antinomian, Time above fallen timing. It is not only superior to the juropolitical but apparently also its boss and taskmaster.

The banality of intimacy's sentimental standing in and above the law is most beautifully and enduringly articulated in the majority opinion in *Griswold*, written by Justice William O. Douglas. Douglas argues that a combination of precedents derived from the First, Fourth, Fifth, Ninth, and Fourteenth Amendments[25] support his designation of a heretofore unenumerated constitutional right for married persons to inhabit a zone of privacy, a zone free from police access or the "pure [State] power" for which Connecticut was arguing as the doctrinal foundation of its right to discipline immorality in its citizens.[26] The language Douglas uses both to make this space visible and to enunciate the law's relation to it shuttles between the application of *stare decisis* (the rule of common law that binds judicial authority to judicial precedent) and the traditional conventionalities of heteronormative Hallmark-style sentimentality:

> The present case, then, concerns a relationship lying within the zone of privacy created by several fundamental constitutional guarantees. And it concerns a law which, in forbidding the *use* of contraceptives rather than regulating their manufacture or sale, seeks to achieve its goals by means having a maximum destructive impact upon that relationship. Such a law cannot stand in light of the familiar principle, so often applied by this Court, that a "governmental purpose to control or prevent activities constitutionally subject to state regulation may not be achieved by means which sweep unnecessarily broadly and thereby invade the area of protected freedoms" [*NAACP* v. *Alabama*, 377 U.S. 288, 307]. Would we allow the police to search the sacred precincts of marital bedrooms for telltale signs of the use of contraceptives? The very idea is repulsive to the notions of privacy surrounding the marriage relationship. We deal with a right of privacy older than the Bill of Rights—older than our political parties, older than our school system. Marriage is a coming together for better or for worse, hopefully enduring, and intimate to the degree of being sacred. It is an association that promotes a way of life, not causes; a harmony in living, not political faiths; a bilateral loyalty, not commercial or social projects. Yet it is an association for as noble a purpose as any involved in our prior decisions.[27]

Douglas bases his view that sexuality in marriage must be constitutionally protected—being above the law, prior to it, and beyond its proper gaze—on a sense that "specific guarantees in the Bill of Rights have penumbras, formed by emanations from those guarantees that help give them life and substance."[28] A *penumbra* is generally a "partial shadow between regions of complete shadow and complete illumination," but I believe the sense in which Douglas uses this dreamy concept is more proper to its application in the science of astronomy: "the partly darkened ridge around a sunspot." In other words, privacy protections around even marital sexuality are the dark emanations from the sunspot of explicit constitutional enumeration; and the zone of privacy where marital sexuality thrives is the shadowland of the "noble" institution of marriage, with its sacred obligational emanations of social stability and continuity, intimate noninstrumentality, and superiority to the dividedness that otherwise characterizes the social. To back him up, Justices Harlan's and Goldberg's opinions remind of the state and the Court's propriety in pedagogically bolstering the institutions of traditional American morality and values: after all, the theater of marital intimacy is "older than our political parties, older than our schools."

Justice Hugo Black's dissent in *Griswold* blasts Justices Douglas, Goldberg, Harlan, and White for the unethical emotionality of what he calls the "natural law due process formula [used] to strike down all state laws which [the Justices] think are unwise, dangerous, or irrational." He feels that it introduces into constitutional jurisprudence justifications for measuring "constitutionality by our belief that legislation is arbitrary, capricious or unreasonable, or accomplishes no justifiable purpose, or is offensive to our own notions of civilized standards of conduct. Such an appraisal of the wisdom of legislation is an attribute of the power to make laws, not of the power to interpret them." He finds precedent in this critique in a Learned Hand essay on the Bill of Rights that reviles judges' tendency to "wrap up their veto in a protective veil of adjectives such as 'arbitrary,' 'artificial,' 'normal,' 'reasonable,' 'inherent,' 'fundamental,' or 'essential' whose office usually, though quite innocently, is to disguise what they are doing and impute to it a derivation far more impressive than their personal preferences, which are all that in fact lie behind the decision."[29] In this view, whenever judges enter the zone of constitutional penumbra, they manufacture euphemisms that disguise the relation between proper law and personal inclination. Patricia Williams has suggested that this charge (and the countercharge, that at the heights of feeling it is no different than reason) is at the heart of the fiction of *stare decisis* that produces postfacto justifications from judicial or social tradition for judges who inevitably impose their will on problems of law but who must, for legitimacy's sake, disavow admission of the uninevitability of their claim. The virtually genetic image legal judgment has of itself in history veils not only the personal instabilities of judges but the madness of the law itself, its instability and fictive stability, its articulation at the place where interpretive will and desire mix up to produce someone's image of a right/just/proper world.[30]

After sexual privacy was donated to the U.S. heterosexual couple in *Griswold* by way of the sentimental reason the Court adopted—through the spatialization of intimacy in a bell jar of frozen history—a judicial and political nightmare over the property of sexual privacy ensued, whose mad struggle between state privilege and private liberty is too long to enumerate here. We can conclude that the romantic banality that sanctions certain forms of intimacy as nationally privileged remains hardwired into the practice of sex privacy law in the United States. However, almost twenty years later *Planned Parenthood of Southeastern Pennsylvania* v. *Casey* [112 S. Ct. 2791 (1992)] recasts the force of its machinery remarkably, replacing the monumentality of sexual privacy *Roe* established as a fundamental condition of women's liberty with the monumentality of *Roe* itself as evidence of the Court's very authority.

In their majority opinion, Justices O'Connor, Souter, and Kennedy recognize the sovereignty of the zone of privacy as a model for freedom or liberty, returning explicitly to the method of penumbral enumeration and *stare decisis* introduced in *Griswold*. But the real originality of *Planned Parenthood v. Casey* is in the extent to which it supplants *entirely* the utopia of heterosexual intimacy on which sexual privacy law was based in the first place, putting *women's pain* in heterosexual culture at the center of the story of privacy and legal protections. In this sense the legitimating force of deep juridical feelings about the sacred pleasures of marital intimacy are here inverted and displaced onto the woman, whose sexual and political trauma is now the index of the meaning and value of her privacy and her citizenship.

Briefly, *Eisenstadt* v. *Baird*, 405 U.S. 438 (1972) extended *Griswold* to unmarried women through the equal protections clause, transforming sexual privacy from its initial scene—the two-as-one utopia of coupled intimacy—into a property of individual liberty. This muted the concretely spatial aspects of the "zone of privacy," dismantling the original homology between the marital/sexual bedroom and the citizen's sense of self-sovereignty. It placed the focus on the space of the woman's body, which includes her capacities, passions, and intentions. But the shift from reframing contraception to adjudicating abortion required the discovery of more emanations from constitutional penumbra: in *Roe* v. *Wade* [410 U.S. 113 (1973)] the right of privacy remains the *woman's* right, but here one that has internal limits at the juncture where state interest over potential "life" and social self-continuity overtakes the woman's interest in controlling her sexual and reproductive existence. Gone, from that decision, is *Griswold's* rhetoric of the Court's moral pedagogy or its chivalry toward sexually sacred precincts:

indeed Justice Blackmun writes that because of the "sensitive and emotional nature of the abortion controversy" he wants to adhere to "constitutional measurement, free of emotion and predilection."[31] (There is not a sexuality/privacy case where such a *caveat* against emotion is not passionately uttered.) *Roe* attempts to achieve its post-emotionality by deploying knowledge, plumbing the juridical and historical archive on abortion: its emphasis is not on expanding liberty by thinking the contexts of its practice but rather by massaging precedent and tradition.

Planned Parenthood v. *Casey* was widely seen as an opportunity for a new set of Justices to overturn *Roe.* The Pennsylvania Abortion Control Act of 1982 (amended in 1988–89) did not abolish abortion in the state but intensified the discursive contexts in which it happened, seeking to create around abortion a state-sanctioned, morally pedagogical *zone of publicity.* Provisions included a twenty-four-hour waiting period, minor notification of parents and wife notification of husbands, and intensified standards of "informed consent" (including a state-authored brochure condemning abortion). The majority opinion has two explicit aims: to affirm the fundamental holdings of *Roe* on behalf of the sovereignty of women's citizenship, the unity of national culture, and the status of the Court's authority; and to enumerate what it felt was underenumerated in *Roe,* the conditions of the state's sovereignty over the contexts of reproduction. In other words, as Justice Scalia's dissent argues, the Court's majority opinion seeks to affirm Roe while also significantly dismantling it. Its technical mechanism for achieving this impossible feat is the substitution of an "undue burden" rule for a whole set of other protections *Roe* provides: especially by dismantling the trimester framework that determined the woman's sovereignty over reproduction in a pregnancy's first six months and substituting for it a rule that favors the state's right to place restrictions on the woman's reproductive practice (restrictions that can then be weighed by courts that will determine whether a given law mounts egregiously burdensome obstacles to the woman's exercise of her constitutional right to abortion).

Scalia claims that the majority pulls off this impossible feat (in its claim to refuse a "jurisprudence of doubt" while making equivocal legal judgments) by disguising its own muddy impulses in a sentimental and "empty" rhetoric of intimacy:

> The best that the Court can do to explain how it is that the word "liberty" *must* be thought to include the right to destroy human fetuses is

to rattle off a collection of adjectives that simply decorate a value judgement and conceal political choice. The right to abort, we are told, inheres in "liberty" because it is among "a person's most basic decisions," *ante*, at 2806; it involves a "most intimate and personal choic[e]," *ante*, at 2807; it is "central to personal dignity and autonomy," *ibid.*; it "originate[s] within the zone of conscience and belief," *ibid*; it is "too intimate and personal" for state interference, *ante*, at 2807; it reflects "intimate views" of a "deep, personal character," *ante*, at 2808; it involves "intimate relationships," and "notions of personal autonomy and bodily integrity," *ante*, at 2810.[32]

Correctly, Scalia goes on to point out that these very same qualities meant nothing to the justices when they heard *Bowers* v. *Hardwick* [478 U.S. 186 (1986)], "because, like abortion, they are forms of conduct that have long been criminalized in American society. Those adjectives might be applied, for example, to homosexual sodomy, polygamy, adult incest, and suicide, all of which are equally 'intimate.' "[33]

But Scalia's critique is trivial, in the sense that the majority opinion does not seek to rethink sexual privacy or intimacy in any serious way. The rhetoric of intimacy in the case is part of its argument from *stare decisis*,[34] but the majority justices' originality is located in their representation of the specificity, what they call the "uniqueness," of the material conditions of citizenship for women in the United States. Because the right to sexual privacy has been individuated by *Roe*, privacy no longer takes place in a concrete zone but in a "zone of conscience"—the place where, as Nietzsche tells us, the law is painfully and portably inscribed in subjects.[35] The justices refer to women's "anxieties," "physical constraints," and "sacrifices [that] have since the beginning of the human race been endured by woman with a pride that ennobles her": they contend that a woman's "suffering is too intimate and personal for the State to insist . . . upon its own vision of the woman's role."[36] Therefore abortion definitively grounds and sustains women's political legitimacy: their "ability to participate equally in the economic and social life of the Nation has been facilitated by their ability to control their reproductive lives."[37]

The justices here cede that femininity in the United States is virtually and generically an undue burden, however ennobling it might be. The de-utopianization of sexual privacy established in *Griswold* and the installation of female citizenship at the juncture of law and suffering is further reinforced by the one part of the Pennsylvania law that the majority finds unconstitutional: the clause that commands women to notify their husbands of their intention to abort. The segment in which this happens exposes women's suffering in the zone of privacy where, it turns out, men beat their wives. They cite evidence, supported by the American Medical Association, that men are raping their wives, terrorizing them (especially when pregnant), *forcing* them to inhabit a zone of privacy that keeps secreted men's abuse of women. In short, the "gruesome and torturous" conditions of marital domesticity in battering households requires the Court *not to protect privacy* for the couple but to keep the couple from becoming the unit of modal citizenship where privacy law is concerned.[38]

Catharine MacKinnon deems privacy law a tool of patriarchal supremacy: "women in everyday life have no privacy in private. In private, women are objects of male subjectivity and male power. The private is that place where men can do whatever they want because women reside there. The consent that supposedly demarcates this private surrounds women and follows us everywhere we go. Men [in contrast] reside in public, where laws against harm exist. . . . As a legal doctrine, privacy has become the affirmative triumph of the state's abdication of women."[39]

    MacKinnon's arguments in these essays—which purport to be about "women" and "men," but which to my ear are more profoundly about heterosexuality as a virtual institution and a way of life—derive from Court practice through the late 1980s, and do not consider the work jurists such as O'Connor have done to deprivatize privacy. But it should be no surprise that the modal citizen imagined by even moderates these days is no longer a complex subject with rights, needs, reciprocal obligations to the state and society, conflicting self-interests, or prospects for happiness in realms beyond the juridical: the modal citizen now is a trauma-effect who requires protection and political reparation, whether or not that citizen can be fully described by the terms in which historically subordinated classes circulate in the United States. The Opinion of the Court in *Casey* answers the dissenters' argument—which asserts that so few women are battered in the United States that the husband notification principle stands within constitutional norms—by arguing that "the analysis does not end with the one percent of women upon whom the statute operates: it begins there."[40] Here their jurisprudence is not so far from Mari Matsuda's, when she claims that "looking to the bottom" of social hierarchy and making reparative law from there is the only politically ethical thing to do.[41]

In the twenty years between *Roe* and *Planned Parenthood* v. *Casey* the general scene of public citizenship in the United States has become suffused with a practice of making pain count politically. The law of sexual privacy has followed this change, registering with symptomatic incoherence a more general struggle to maintain the contradictory rights and privileges of women, heterosexuality, the family, the state, and patriarchalized sexual privilege. The sheer ineloquence of this jumble of categories should say something about the cramped space of analysis and praxis to which the rhetoric and jurisprudence of sexual privacy has brought us. A place where there *is* much trouble: a utopia of law.

Politics

In *Griswold*, I have argued, we see codified the assurance of some jurists that the intimate feelings of married sexual partners represent that zone of privacy and personhood beyond the scrutiny of the law whose value is so absolute that the law must protect its sovereignty. Between *Griswold* and *Roe* these intimate feelings and their relation to liberty were still assumed as the sovereign materials of the law of sexual privacy. Now, however, many of the political and juridical contexts that once sustained the fantasy of a core national culture have dissolved, threatening the capacity of sentimental politics to create feeling cultures of consensus that distract from the lived violences and fractures of everyday life in the polis. The class, racial, economic, and sexual fragmentation of U.S. society has emerged into the vision of the law and the public not as an exception to a utopian norm but as a new governing rule of the present. The legal struggles over affirmative action, welfare, abortion, and immigration the courts currently worry are also about whether the utopian or the traumatic story of national life will govern jurisprudence and the world it seeks to confirm. Trauma is winning.

Central to the legal emergence of the politics of trauma against the scene of liberal-patriotic disavowal has been a group of activists from within (mainly academic) legal studies who speak from feminist, gay and lesbian, antiracist and anticapitalist movements. They take their different but generally painful experiences of social hierarchy in the United States to require a radical rhetorical and conceptual transformation of legal scholarship that embraces "subjectivity of perspective," asserts the collective nature of subject formation (around stereotypic social identities), and refuses traditional liberal notions that organize the social optimism of law around relatively unim-peded individuality, privacy, property, and conventional values.[42] At stake in this transformation of law is the importance of antinormativity to counter-hegemonic critical theory and practice: since liberal law has long recognized a particular and traditionally sanctioned form of universal personhood as that around which society, theory, forms of discipline, and aspirational pedagogies should be organized, antiliberal activism has had strategically to *ground* law in experience (in all senses of the pun) and particular identities.

In this sense critical legal praxis is the opposite of national sentimentality, which pursues collective cohesion by circulating a universalist currency of distress. At the same time, the structure of reparation central to radical legal politics suggests an unevenness in this general tactic of making legal notions of subjectivity historically and corporeally specific. Subaltern pain is not con-sidered *universal* (the privileged do not experience it, do not live expecting that at any moment their ordinarily loose selves might be codified into a sin-gle humiliated atom of subpersonhood). But subaltern pain is deemed, in this context, universally *intelligible*, constituting objective evidence of trauma reparable by the law and the law's more privileged subjects. In other words, the universal value is here no longer a property of political personhood but a property of a rhetoric that claims to represent not the universal but the true self. But if historical contexts are incomparable across fields of simple and complex distinction, how can someone's pain or traumatized identity pro-duce such perfect knowledge? And if the pedagogies of politics were neces-sary to reframe a set of experiences, knowledges, and feelings as the kind of pain that exposes injustice, what is "true" about it, exactly?

In this political model of identity trauma stands as truth. We can't use happiness as a guide to the aspirations for social change, for the feeling of it might well be false consciousness; nor boredom, which might be depression, illness, or merely a spreading malaise. Pain, in contrast, is something quick and sharp that simultaneously specifies you and makes you generic: it is something that happens to you before you "know" it, and it is intensely indi-viduating, for surviving its shock lets you know it is your general survival at stake. Yet if the pain is at the juncture of you and the stereotype that repre-sents you, you know that you are hurt not because of your relation to his-tory but because of *someone else's* relation to it, a type of someone whose privilege or comfort depends on the pain that diminishes you, locks you into identity, covers you with shame, and sentences you to a hell of constant potential exposure to the banality of derision.

Pain thus organizes your specific experience of the world, separating you from others and connecting you with others similarly shocked (but not surprised) by the strategies of violence that constantly regenerate the bottom of the hierarchies of social value you inhabit. In this sense subaltern pain is a public form because its outcome is to make you readable, for others. This is, perhaps, why activists from identity politics generally assume pain as the only sign readable across hierarchies of social life: the subaltern is the surrogate form of cultural intelligibility generally, and negated identities are pain-effects. Know me, know my pain, you caused it: in this context paranoia would seem adaptive, and would make understandable a desire for law to be both the origin *and* end of my experience of injustice. It might even make a wish I have to see even subaltern suffering as something more mediated seem, perhaps, cold, or an effect of the leisure of privilege. Who has time, after all, to query violence between shock and the moment it becomes true meaning?

These dicta ground much current countertraditional legal argument. Take, for example, an original and impassioned work such as Robin West's *Narrative, Authority, and Law*,[43] which sees as its task the production of moral criticism and transformation of the law from the point of view of its and a society's victims. West wields narratives powerfully throughout the book that reveal the law's fundamental immorality (and therefore its fundamentally immoralizing effect on the subjects who are educated to its standards) where women's lives are concerned, and her powerful feminist arguments for the need to deprivatize women's structurally induced pain testify to the radical changes in the law and other institutions of intimacy that would have to happen if women are to attain legitimacy as social subjects. But West assumes that women's pain is already available as knowledge. To her, it *is* meaning, and the material for radical pedagogy. To think otherwise is to be either misogynist or guilty of shallow and overacademic postmodernism. Empathy is an ethical rule. Not surprisingly, as it happens, one example of pain's pure force that she uses to summarize her argument comes from a child: "We must be able to say, to quote my two-year-old, 'don't do that—you're hurting me,' and we must be able to hear that utterance as an ethical mandate to change course."[44]

Not all radical legal theorists so simplify pain as to make the emblem of true wisdom about injustice and its eradication something as sentimental and fictive (to adults) as a child's consciousness:[45] yet the desire expressed in its seeming extreme clarity signals a lost opportunity for rethinking the relation of critique and culture building at this juncture of identity politics and legal theory. Would the child build a just world from the knowledge s/he gleans from her hurt? What would the child need to know for that to happen, how could it learn to think beyond trauma, to make a context for it? It seems hard, for a few reasons, for this group of legal theorists to imagine the value of such questions. One reason may be due to the centrality of "pain and suffering" to tort law, which endorses a construction of the true subject as a feeling subject whose suffering disables a person's ability to live at his/her full capacities, as s/he has been doing, and thus requires reparations from the agents who wielded the force. A great deal has been and will be written on this general area, for feminist antipornography and antiracist hate speech litigation borrows much of their legitimation from this hoary jurisprudential domain:[46] their tactic here is to challenge local purveyors of structural violence in order to make racism and misogyny *less profitable*, even symbolically, and meanwhile to use the law to debanalize violence by making illegal that which has been ordinary practice, on the model, say, of sexual harassment law or, even more extremely, using the constitutional model of "cruel and unusual punishment" to revoke legitimation from social relations of violence traditionally authorized by the state and the law.

Kendall Thomas has made this latter point, in an essay on privacy after *Bowers*.[47] He takes up Elaine Scarry's model of torture as a vehicle for the legitimating fiction of state power and claims that the Cruel and Unusual Punishment Clause of the Eighth Amendment should be applied to state discrimination against gays and lesbians. The strength and clarity of his vision and the sense that his suggestion seems to make brings us to the second reason it seems hard for theorists who equate subjectivity in general with legal subjectivity to work beyond the rule of traumatic pain in imagining the conditions for progressive social change. Thomas's model only works if the agent of violence is the state or the law; it works only if the domain of law is deemed interchangeable with the entire field of injury and reparation and if the subject of law is fully described by the taxonomies law recognizes. This position would look awkward if it were rephrased: subjects are always citizens. But the fact is that the notion of reparation for identity-based subordination assumes that the law describes what a person is. The law's typical practice is to recognize kinds of subjects, acts, and identities: it is to taxonomize. What is the relation between the (seemingly inevitable) authoritarianism of juridical categorization and the other, looser spaces of social life and personhood that do not congeal in categories of power, cause, and effect the way the law does? Is the "cruel and unusual punishment" tactic merely a reversal in extremis that points to the sublime banality of state cruelty, or is it a policy aspiration seeking a specific reparation for the specific violation/creation of gay and lesbian identities? Would the homeopathy of law against its own toxins in this domain of state cruelty work for women or the poor African Americans, Latinas and Latinos, and immigrants who are currently being economically disenfranchised from the resources state capitalism manages?

Without making a ridiculous argument that the state is merely a mirage or a fetish that represents networks of inchoate forces that control, without constituting, the realm of society, it should be possible to say that radical counterpolitics needs to contend with notions of personhood and power that do not attain the clarity of state and juridical taxonomy, even across fields of practice and stigma. The desire to find an origin for trauma, and to rework culture at the violating origin, effectively imagines subjects only within that zone, reducing the social to that zone (in this case the state and the laws that legislate nonnormative sex) and covertly reauthorizing the hegemony of the national. The desire to use trauma as the model for the pain of subordination that gets congealed into identities forgets that trauma shockingly takes you out of your life and places you into another one, whereas structural subordination is not a surprise to the subjects who experience it, and the pain of subordination *is* ordinary life.

I have not meant to argue that identity politics has become a mode of "victim politics" too reductive to see the world clearly or to have positive effects. In its most tawdry version this accusation reads that a politics organized around publicizing pain constitutes a further degradation of subaltern selves into a species of subcivilized nonagency. The people who make this argument usually recognize structural social inequality and the devastating impacts it has on persons, but continue to believe that the United States operates meritocratically, for worthy individuals. In contrast, Wendy Brown's deconstruction of contemporary U.S. identity rhetorics places skepticism about traumatic identity in the context of imagining a more radical politics. Brown sees people who claim their pain and build collective struggles around it as potentially overidentifying with their pain, then identifying as it, becoming passive to it, becoming addicted to seeing themselves as virtuous in the face of bad, unethical power. She follows Nietzsche's dicta against a passive aggressive politics of ressentiment:

Politicized identity thus enunciates itself, makes claims for itself, only by retrenching, restating, dramatizing, and inscribing its pain in politics, and can hold out no future—for itself or others—which triumphs over this pain. The loss of historical direction, and with it the loss of futurity characteristic of the late-modern age, is thus homologically refigured in the structure of desire of the dominant political expression of the age—identity politics. . . . What if we sought to supplant the language of "I am"—with its defensive closure on identity, its insistence on the fixity of position, its equation of social with moral positioning—with the language of "I want"?[48]

The critical clarity of a subordinate population's politicized pain has provided crucially destabilizing material that disaffirms the organization of liberal national culture around a utopian form of personhood that lives in zones of privacy and abstraction beyond pain; and as a counterhegemonic *tactic* this logic of radical juridicality affirms more powerfully than anything the fragile and violent disavowals that bolster hegemonic worlds of reason and the law. But to say that the traumatized self is the true self is to say that a particular facet of subjective experience is where the truth of history lies: it is to suggest that the clarity of pain marks a political map for achieving the good life, if only we would read it. It is also to imply that in the good life there will be no pain. Brown suggests that a replacement of traumatic identity with a subjectivity articulated utopianly, via the agency of imagined demand, will take from pain the energy for social transformation beyond the field of its sensual experience. For this to happen, *psychic pain experienced by subordinated populations must be treated as ideology* not as prelapsarian knowledge or a condensed comprehensive social theory. It is more like a capital letter at the beginning of an old bad sentence that needs rewriting. To think otherwise is to assert that pain is merely banal, a story always already told. It is to think that the moment of its gestation is, indeed, life itself.

Coda: Pregnancy, Paranoia, Justice

The world I have tried to telegraph here in this story about privacy's fall from the utopia of normal intimacy finds the law articulating its subjects as public and American through their position within a hegemonic regime of heterosexuality, which involves coordination with many other normative social positions that are racially and economically coded toward privilege. I have argued that the split between the patriotic context of national meta-culture and the practical fragmentations and hierarchies of everyday life has become powerfully mediated by a discourse of trauma, which imagines "relief" through juridicalized national remedies because, in fighting against the false utopia of privacy, it imagines subjects wholly created by law.

Too often, and almost always in the work of legal radicals, the nation remains sanctified as a political "zone of privacy" in *Griswold's* sense: it holds out a promise that it can relieve specific subjects of the pain of their specificity, even as the very project of nation-formation virtually requires the public exposure of those who do not structurally assimilate to the national norm (so, if population x is relieved of the obstacles to its juridical and cultural citizenship, a given population y will almost inevitably come to bear the burden of surrogacy that expresses citizenship's status as *privilege*). Fighting for justice under the law in the face of these normative strategies is crucial, a tactic of necessity. If it means telling half-truths (that an experience of painful identity shocks a minoritized subject) in order to change juridical norms about that kind of subject, it still must be a good thing. But thinking that the good life will be achieved when there is no more pain but only (your) happiness does nothing to alter the hegemonic structures of normativity and mourning whose saturation of the diminished expectations for liberty in national life I have sketched out in this essay. The reparation of pain does not bring into being a just life.

Usually this point is made in studies of testimony and the Holocaust, the unspeakable national violence that generates horrific evidence that will always fail to represent the brutal totality of its referent and that can never be repaired, reparated.[49] The cases addressed in this essay, in contrast, are ever so banal, cruel but not unusual, an ordinary part of everyday citizenship for subordinate populations in the United States. Such a difference advises replacing the model of trauma I have been critically describing as inadequate material for world- or nation-building with a model of *suffering*, whose etymological articulation of pain and patience draws its subject less as an effect of an act of violence and more as an effect of a general atmosphere of it, peppered by acts to be sure but not contained by the presumption trauma carries, that it is an effect of a single scene of violence or toxic taxonomy. Thus where certain ordinary identity forms are concerned, the question of suffering's *differend* might be drawn and drawn out differently, without the danger of analytically diffusing any population's subordination into some parodically postmodern miasma of overdetermination and pseudo-agency. (But even "suffering" can sound too dramatic for the subordinated personhood form I am reaching toward here: imagine a word that describes a constantly destabilized existence that monitors, with a roving third eye, every moment as a potentially bad event in which a stereotyped someone might become food for someone else's hunger for superiority, and connect that to a term that considers the subjective effects of structural inequalities that are deemed inevitable in a capitalist nation. "Suffering" stands in for that compound word.)

I can provide here only a sketch of this model of pain, subjectivity, and politics. We might start in a place not defined by taxonomic identity, an image of the subject as heterotopic, distracted, or what I have called "loose." Earlier in this essay privacy law was a place of intensified gendering and sexualization: women versus fetuses, wives versus husbands, the law versus the sanctity of the marital couple. Identity was clear, it was bounded, it was opposed to counteridentity. But (as Denise Riley argues) when women are not in any kind of court defending their gender, they experience the relation between their juridicalized femaleness and other scenes of womanhood and identity-style attachment in inconsistent ways.[50] Barbara Duden, Emily Martin, and Rayna Rapp's three ethnographies of the racial, class, and ethnic contexts of reproduction in the United States tell constantly of the minoritization of pregnant women in the face of medical and state expertise about fetuses, health, cleanliness, monitoring.[51] It is as though these women are even more incompetent to the task of their survival than ordinary consumers, whose desires are at least constantly rerendered as self-expertise by the pedagogies of capitalist culture. Yet the reproducing women have created a sentimental culture of their own, which coexists with the zones of their subordination: it is not that radical, yet it is very critical, and above all skeptical about the relation between knowing about women's material struggles and making them uninevitable.

I take as an example the book *Peaceful Pregnancy Meditations* by Lisa Steele George. This 1993 book epitomizes much contemporary feminine self-help literature. It merges insights about women's expertise over their bodies from the feminist health movements of the 1970s with the expertise over intimate suffering emphasized by the sentimental feminine self-help movement of the 1980s. It takes pregnancy as the condition of ordinary femininity writ large; it uses twelve-step language to partition and make livable the predictable but excruciating changes of pregnancy; it provides on each page

space for the reader to become an author through a routine of daily affir-
mations that enable pregnant women to apportion their anxieties through a
life lived one day at a time. It actively disaffirms the political public sphere
as the source of emancipatory public-making. It is paranoid about the cease-
lessness of women's caretaking burdens in the family and affective burdens
in society. Its paranoia is entirely banal, about the conditions of women's
ordinary lives.

Peaceful Pregnancy Meditations begins with a defensive nod to the world of
fetal politics. Day 1, whose title is "Beginnings," begins: "When does pregnancy really begin? At conception? Years ago when we started yearning for
a family of our own? Yesterday when our home pregnancy test turned positive? For each mother-to-be, it is different. But no matter where we define
our beginning, we know it is truly that: a new beginning."[52] The beautiful
tautologies and open questions of this passage provide for the pregnant gender a way of negotiating a complex set of contexts for maternal paranoia
and the undue burdens of femininity in the contemporary United States.
Pregnancy advice books have long made the woman responsible for fetal
health. They have long made the woman feel that the development of her
managerial skills is crucial to the happiness of everyone who depends on her
to provide clarity for them. But the current public mistrust of women's
competence within the maternal service economy has intensified the disciplinary aspects of these discourses and made women even more defensive.

George's refusal to accede to the priority of fetal personhood or any
norm of femininity remains resolute throughout the text. What she does
prioritize is ameliorating the shame at the center of the experience of modern pregnancy. She releases women from shame about the ambivalence they
feel toward the fetus and the theft of ordinary life the fetus engenders; she
acknowledges women's ambivalence toward the couple form and supports
their need to build a social world to soften the blows and stresses of a marital intimacy that can only be enjoyed in random moments of repose. Above
all, she confirms the rationality of women's ambivalent feelings about the
pressure not to have a self that is a part of what structural pain demands of
dominated persons.

On each page of the book, which represents one day, pregnant femininity is deshamed by way of a dialectic between the anger/frustration/dis-
comfort of the reader's complicated social meaning and the assurance and
comfort of the poetic affirmation George writes on each page. The affirmation, a kind of lay prayer, enables the reader to endure that life of which

she surely is not master. Formally this is signified by: a top paragraph (with titles such as "Privacy," "Manly Pride," "Chronic Uncertainty," "Ultrasound") that expresses the zone of discomfort this day's meditation depicts; a middle paragraph that graphs an affirmation of the reader's desire not to be defeated by today's degree of pain (as in, "I try to remain positive toward those around me, seeing their attention as love")[53]; and then a bottom third made up of four empty lines for women to write on that begin with the three words "Today I Feel . . ."

The book does offer the suffering women a dependable space of feeling and temporal freedom from the cramped conditions of social value and everydayness pregnant women negotiate: women's culture, a survival mechanism that involves forming a relationship with particular commodity forms and, through them, with other women, who feel the way they feel, because they are regendered as pregnant women. In this way this book, and the culture of affectivity and opinion that produces other commodities in support of its project of consolation and buttressing, keeps maternity/femininity in America from being merely a humiliating, isolating/collectivizing scene of personal struggle, public embarrassment, and alienated nonrepresentation in the political public sphere. This is what makes it a part of sentimental culture. Its aim, however, is not to change the law but to confirm the sheer difficulty of being made its subject while existing in so many strange relations undescribable by the terms "power/powerlessness," "pain/happiness," "equality/inequality."

The suffering George represents neither clarifies into a single struggle nor confuses the immediate sources of discomfort as the totality of actual sources. She sees a whole structure and a set of different ideologies in place, situating and destabilizing women and the contexts they inhabit: she cannot imagine freedom in these contexts, but merely survival. She suffers gendering, and not just for her married self—but imagines the different contexts of struggle occupied by single mothers-to-be, lesbian mothers-to-be, working mothers-to-be, and the most conventional married mothers-to-be. Linked to each other by a collective experience of being public and scrutinized in pregnancy, they can live the unique change from the positions they were in when they were nonreproducing gendered, sexual, and economic subjects. In their intimacy with and alterity to the reduced versions of their gender, the women imagined in this book imagine no outside to history, no radically different future from the one they are presently suffering (and also finding sustenance in), but an ongoing present in which they are fragmented agents whose strange social value forces a constant improvisation and scraping together of a viable existence.

The binary trauma/reparation would not satisfy the conditions of genuine social oppression pregnant women in the United States endure. Their issue is not with the past or with events signified in the scars of trauma. Instead, their political optimism requires a future, any future that might not be more drowning in the present. In contrast, the liberal-radical solution to such positioning has been to deploy an ethics of storytelling about trauma against the normative world of the law, to change the conditions of what counts as evidence, and to make something concrete happen in response, something that pays for the past. As Derrida has recently argued, however, the dialectic between situated expression that challenges universalist norms and the categorical universalism of law itself constitutes an incommensurateness already within the law that cannot be overcome by law.[54] *Peaceful Pregnancy Meditations* suggests that the banality of a superjuridical identity discovered in a condition of suffering might reveal the ground of sustained anger, but it is not one that can or should be recongealed into the ideality of identity, which confirms the present tense as the reality people live. The everyday of struggle is a ground on which ecstasy and theory and unpredicted change can be mapped into a world that will not look like the opposite of the painful juridical one.

Who gave anyone expertise over the meaning of feelings of injustice? I was sympathetic to the cultural politics of pain until I felt the violence of sentimentality: presented as a horror at momentous mass trauma that unifies a fractured society, national sentimentality is too often a defensive response by people who identify with privilege yet fear they will be exposed as immoral by their tacit sanction of a particular structural violence that benefits them. I was a wholly sympathetic participant in practices of subaltern testimony and complaint, until I saw that the different stories of trauma wielded in the name of a population's political suffering not only tended to confirm the state and its law as the core sites of personhood but also provided opportunities to further isolate dominated populations by inciting competitions over whose lives have been more excluded from the "happiness" that was constitutionally promised by national life. Meanwhile the public recognition by dominant culture of certain sites of publicized subaltern suffering is frequently (mis)taken as a big step toward the amelioration of that suffering. It is a baby step, if that. I have suggested in contrast that the pain and suffering of subordinated subjects in everyday life is an ordinary and ongoing thing that is underdescribed by the (traumatic) identity form and its circulation in the state and the law. If identity politics is a literacy program in the alphabet of that pain, its subjects must also assume that the signs of subordination they feel also tell a story that they do not feel yet, or know, about how to construct the narrative to come.

NOTES

1. *Planned Parenthood of Southeastern Pennsylvania* v. *Casey* 112 S.Ct. 2791 (1992), at 2803.

2. See, for example, George DeMartino and Stephen Cullenberg, "Beyond the Competitiveness Debate: An Internationalist Agenda," *Social Text* 41 (1994): 11–39.

3. Take the case of the former talk show host Kathie Lee Gifford, whose clothing line at the American low-price megastore Wal-Mart generated ten million dollars of profit for her in its first year. During May and June of 1996 Gifford was exposed by Charles Kernaghan, of the National Labor Education Fund in Support of Worker and Human Rights in Central America, for allowing her clothes to be made by tragically underpaid and mistreated young Honduran children, mostly girls. A Lexis/Nexis search under the keywords "Kathie Lee Gifford/Child Labor" nets close to two hundred stories, from all over the world, reporting on this event. A few main plots emerge from these stories: it is cast as a revenge story against privilege from the ranks of the less well-off, which strips from Gifford the protection of her perky, populist, and personal persona to reveal the entrepreneurial profiteer beneath; it implicates an entire culture of celebrity-centered consumerism (Jaclyn Smith/K-Mart, The Gap, Spike Lee/Michael Jordan/Nike) that is organized around a "virtuous" role-modelesque public figure or label that seems to certify healthy conscientious social membership for consumers; it becomes an exemplum of the banality of sweatshop labor in the United States and around the world; and it makes a call to belated conscience. Through Gifford's apparent intimacy with her devoted audience a "public" outraged by child exploitation seemed instantly to emerge, which led in turn to a kind of state action, involving an intensified federal push for voluntary covenants against child labor and subminimum wages (measured by "local," not U.S. standards of remuneration). It also eventuated in the development of a new label, "No Sweat," to be put on any clothes produced by adequately paid workers (a sad substitute for the Union Label of years past). This issue has quickly joined child abuse as an ongoing zone of fascination and (mainly) impotent concern in the political public sphere. See, for a relatively unjaded extended example, Sydney Schamberg, "Six Cents an Hour," *Life*, June 1996, pp. 38–48. For a more general view of the political/media exploitation of the exploited child figure, see McKenzie Wark, "Fresh Maimed Babies: The Uses of Innocence," *Transition* 65 (Spring 1995): 36–47.

4. For more exposition on the ways political cultures that value abstract or universal personhood produce privileged bodies and identities that travel unmarked, unremarkable, and free of structural humiliation, see Lauren Berlant, "National Brands/National Bodies: *Imitation of Life*," in *The Phantom Public Sphere*, ed. Bruce Robbins (Minneapolis: University of Minnesota Press, 1993), pp. 173–208, and *The Queen of America Goes to Washington City: Essays on Sex and Citizenship* (Durham, N.C.: Duke University Press, 1997); Richard Dyer, "White," in *The Matter of Images* (New York: Routledge, 1993), pp. 141–63; and Peggy Phelan, *Unmarked: The Politics of Performance* (New York: Routledge, 1993).

5. The essay of Sigmund Freud's summarized here is "Mourning and Melancholia," in *General Psychological Theory*, introduction by Philip Rieff (New York: Collier Books, 1963), pp. 164–79.

6. The best work on the civilized barbarism of mourning has been done on AIDS discourse in U.S. culture: Douglas Crimp, "Mourning and Militancy," in *Out There: Marginalization and Contemporary Cultures*, ed. Russell Ferguson, Martha Gever, Trinh T. Min-ha, and Cornel West (Cambridge: MIT Press, 1990), pp. 233–45, and virtually every essay in Douglas Crimp, ed., *AIDS: Cultural Analysis/Cultural Activism* (Cambridge: MIT Press, 1988). Crimp is especially acute on the necessary articulation of sentimentality and politics: necessary because processes of legitimation cannot do without the production of consent and empathetic misrecognition is one tactic for creating it. The question is how, and at what cost, different kinds of subjects and contexts of empathy are imagined in the struggle for radical social transformation. See also Jeff Nunokowa, "AIDS and the Age of Mourning," *Yale Journal of Criticism* 4, no. 2 (Spring 1991): 1–12. Judith Butler's work has also been a crucial intertext here, notably its representation of heterosexual melancholia (the disavowed experience of loss heterosexuals endure as a consequence of having to divert ongoing same-sex love/identification/attachments), a condition that expresses itself through gender normativity, heterosexual hegemony, misogyny, homophobia, and other forms of disciplinary order. This opened a space for thinking about the social function of mourning in similar contexts of normative hierarchy where intimacies appear to have to be constructed, not suppressed. See her *Gender Trouble: Feminism and the Subversion of Identity* (New York: Routledge, 1990) and *Bodies that Matter: On the Discursive Limits of Sex* (New York: Routledge, 1993).

7. On the "bottom line" as a site of political articulation and struggle, see Elizabeth Alexander, " 'Can You Be BLACK and Look at This?': Reading the Rodney King Video(s)," in *The Black Public Sphere*, ed. The Black Public Sphere Collective (Chicago: University of Chicago Press, 1995), pp. 81–98.

8. On the structures and rhetorics of coercive flexibility in transnational times, see David Harvey, *The Condition of Postmodernity* (London: Blackwell, 1989); Roger Rouse, "Thinking through Transnationalism: Notes on the Cultural Politics of Class Relations in the Contemporary United States," *Public Culture* 7 (Winter 1995):

353–402; and Emily Martin, *Flexible Bodies: Tracking Immunity in American Culture: From the Days of Polio to the Age of AIDS* (Boston: Beacon Press, 1994).

9. One critic who has not underestimated the hegemonic capacities of state deployments of pain is Elaine Scarry, *The Body in Pain: The Making and Unmaking of the World* (New York: Oxford University Press, 1985). This book remains a stunning description of the ways control over actual physical and rhetorical pain provides the state and the law with control over what constitutes collective reality, the conjuncture of beliefs and the material world. See especially part 2, on pain and imagining. Like the legal theorists and jurists whose writing this essay engages, Scarry works a with a fully state- (or institutionally) saturated concept of the subject, a relation more specific and nonuniversal than it frequently seems in her representation of it.

10. See Berlant, *Queen of America*. The following paragraphs revise and repeat some arguments from this book. For an essay specifically on scandalized childhood in the contemporary United States, see Marilyn Ivy, "Recovering the Inner Child in Late Twentieth-Century America," *Social Text* 37 (1993): 227–52.

11. Nathanson speaks this line in his film *The Silent Scream* (1984).

12. This intensification of national-popular patriotic familialism has taken place at a time when another kind of privatization—the disinvestment of the state economically and culturally in promoting public life—characterizes almost all the activity of the political public sphere. The economic defederalization of citizenship downsizes the public so drastically it begins to look like "the private," its nineteenth-century antithesis (only this time mass-mediated and thus publicly sutured in a more classic Habermasean sense). Yet all too frequently the analysis of the institutions of intimacy is kept separate from the considerations of the material conditions of citizenship.

13. On cynicism and citizenship, see Slavoj Žižek, *The Sublime Object of Ideology* (London: Verso, 1989), pp. 11–53.

14. On pain's place in forming the political imagination of subjects during the epoch of U.S. identity politics, see Wendy Brown's powerful essay, "Wounded Attachments: Late Modern Oppositional Political Formations," in *The Identity in Question*, ed. John Rajchman (New York: Routledge, 1995), pp. 199–227.

15. On rights talk and normativity, see Austin Sarat and Thomas R. Kearns, eds., *Identities, Politics, and Rights* (Ann Arbor: University of Michigan Press, 1995). See especially Wendy Brown's contribution, an indispensable discussion of the ways "rights talk" enables the production of traumatized political identities: "Rights and Identity in Late Modernity: Revisiting the 'Jewish Question,' " pp. 85–130.

16. "Intimate discipline" is Richard Brodhead's phrase for the coercions of sentimental culture in the United States in the nineteenth century. See "Sparing the Rod: Discipline and Fiction in Antebellum America," in *Cultures of Letters: Scenes of Reading and Writing in Nineteenth-Century America* (Chicago: University of Chicago Press, 1993), pp. 13–47.

17. Jean Baudrillard posits banality as the affective dominant of postmodern life: see *In the Shadow of the Silent Majorities . . . Or the End of the Social and Other Essays*, trans. Paul Foss, Paul Patton, and John Johnston (New York: Semiotexte, 1983), and "From the System to the Destiny of Objects," in *The Ecstasy of Communication*, ed. Slyvère Lotringer (New York: Semiotexte, 1987), pp. 77–96. See also Achille Mbembe, "Prosaics of Servitude and Authoritarian Civilities," *Public Culture* 5 (Fall 1992): 123–48; Achille Mbembe and Janet Roitman, "Figures of the Subject in Times of Crisis," *Public Culture* 7 (Winter 1995): 323–52; and Meaghan Morris, "Banality in Cultural Studies," in *Logics of Television: Essays in Cultural Criticism*, ed. Patricia Mellencamp (Bloomington: Indiana University Press, 1990), pp. 14–43.

18. Justice Hugo Black, concurring, *Griswold v. Connecticut* 381 U.S. 479 (1965), at 509.

19. Stephanie Guitton and Peter Irons, eds., *May It Please the Court: Arguments on Abortion* (New York: New Press, 1995), p. 4.

20. Justice William O. Douglas, Opinion of the Court, *Griswold v. Connecticut* 381 U.S. 479 (1965), at 480.

21. Ibid., p. 5.

22. Justice Arthur Goldberg, concurring, *Griswold v. Connecticut* 381 U.S. 479 (1965), at 499.

23. I borrow this rhetoric of zoning, and specifically its relation to the production of normative sexuality, from Lauren Berlant and Michael Warner, "Sex in Public," *Critical Inquiry* 21 (Winter 1998): 547–66.

24. Gayatri Chakravorty Spivak, "Time and Timing: Law and History," in *Chronotypes: The Construction of Time*, ed. John Bender and David E. Wellbery (Stanford: Stanford University Press, 1991), pp. 99–117.

25. Douglas writes: "Various guarantees create zones of privacy. The right of association contained in the penumbra of the First Amendment is one, as we have seen. The Third Amendment in its prohibition against the quartering of soldiers 'in any house' in time of peace without the consent of the owner is another facet of that privacy. The Fourth Amendment explicitly affirms the 'right of the people to be secure in their persons, houses, papers, and effects, against unreasonable searches and seizures.' The Fifth Amendment in its Self-Incrimination Clause enables the citizen to create a zone of privacy which government may not force him to surrender to his detriment. The Ninth Amendment provides: 'The enumeration in the Constitution, of certain rights, shall not be construed to deny or disparage others retained by the people.' " *Griswold v. Connecticut* 381 U.S. 479 (1965), at 484. Justice Goldberg's concurring opinion, while mainly running a legal clinic on the Founders' relation to unenumerated rights, adds the Due Process Clause of the Fourteenth Amendment to this constitutional congeries. Ibid., at 488.

26. Guitton and Irons, eds., *May It Please the Court*, p. 7.

27. Justice William O. Douglas, Opinion of the Court, *Griswold* v. *Connecticut* 381 U.S. 479 (1965), at 485, 486.

28. Ibid., at 484.

29. Ibid., at 517, fn. 10.

30. Patricia J. Williams, *The Alchemy of Race and Rights* (Cambridge: Harvard University Press, 1991), pp. 7–8, 134–35.

31. Justice Blackmun, Opinion of the Court, *Roe* v. *Wade* 410 U.S. 113 (1973), at 708.

32. Justice Scalia, dissent, *Planned Parenthood* v. *Casey* 112 S.Ct.2791 (1992), at 2876–2877.

33. Ibid. Scalia also blasts Justice Blackmun (fn. 2, at 2876) for using the same intimate rhetoric that means nothing, constitutionally, at least to Scalia.

34. A passionate and creative argument about what cases constitute precedent for *Roe* takes place among Justices O'Connor, Kennedy, and Souter, Ibid., at 2808–2816, and Scalia, at 2860–2867.

35. Friedrich Nietzsche, *On the Genealogy of Morals*, ed. Walter Kaufmann (New York: Vintage, 1967), pp. 57–96. On the ways Nietzsche reproduces the individuating limits of pain-centered politics, see Brown, "Wounded Attachments."

36. Justices Sandra Day O'Connor, Anthony M. Kennedy, David H. Souter, Opinion of the Court, *Planned Parenthood* v. *Casey*, at 2807.

37. Ibid., at 2809.

38. Ibid., at 2827.

39. Catharine A. MacKinnon, "Reflections on Law in the Everyday Life of Women," in *Law in Everyday Life*, ed. Austin Sarat and Thomas R. Kearns (Ann Arbor: University of Michigan Press, 1995), pp. 117–18. See also MacKinnon, *Toward a Feminist Theory of the State* (Cambridge: Harvard University Press), pp. 184–94.

40. *Planned Parenthood* v. *Casey*, at 2829.

41. Mari J. Matsuda, "Looking to the Bottom: Critical Legal Studies and Reparations," in *Critical Race Theory: The Key Writings that Formed the Movement*, ed. Kimberlè Crenshaw, Neil Gotanda, Gary Peller, and Kendall Thomas (New York: New Press, 1995), pp. 63–80.

42. Critical legal studies, critical race theory, radical feminist legal theory, and an emergent body of work in gay and lesbian culture, power, and the law encompass a huge bibliography. Rather than dump a stupidly big omnibus footnote here, let me metonymically signal the archive via a few recent helpful anthologies or extended works: Mary Becker, Cynthia Grant Bowman, and Morrison Torrey, eds., *Cases and Materials on Feminist Jurisprudence: Taking Women Seriously* (St. Paul, Minn.: West, 1994); Dan Danielsen and Karen Engle, eds., *After Identity: A Reader in Law and Culture* (New York: Routledge, 1995); Lisa Duggan and Nan D. Hunter, *Sex Wars: Sexual Dissent and Political Culture* (New York: Routledge, 1995); Mari J. Matsuda, Charles R. Lawrence III, Richard Delgado, and Kimberlè Williams Crenshaw, *Words*

that *Wound: Critical Race Theory, Assaultive Speech, and the First Amendment* (Boulder, Colo.:Westview Press, 1993), pp. 1–15; Crenshaw, Gotanda, Peller, and Thomas. eds., *Critical Race Theory*; Richard Delgado, *Critical Race Theory: The Cutting Edge* (Philadelphia:Temple University Press, 1995); Patricia Smith, ed., *Feminist Jurisprudence* (NewYork: Oxford University Press, 1993); RobinWest, *Narrative,Authority, and Law* (Ann Arbor: University of Michigan Press, 1993);Williams, *Alchemy of Race and Rights* and *The Rooster's Egg* (Cambridge: Harvard University Press, 1995).

43.West, *Narrative, Authority, and Law.*

44. Ibid., pp. 19–20. Much the same kind of respect and critique can be given to Catharine MacKinnon's promotion of juridical reparation on behalf of women's pain under patriarchy: in her work the inner little girl of every woman stands as the true abused self who is denied full citizenship in the United States. For an analysis of antipornography rhetoric's depiction of pain's place in women's citizenship, see my "Live Sex Acts," in *Queen of America.*

45.Another instance in which a generic child's nonideological relation to justice is held as the proper index of adult aspiration is to be found inWilliams, *Alchemy of Race and Rights.*This brilliant book is fully dedicated to understanding the multiple contexts in which (Williams's) legal subjectivity inherits, inhabits, and reproduces the law's most insidious violences: its commitment to syncretic modes of storytelling about these conjunctures leaves open some questions about the relation between what she represents as the madness of inhabiting legal allegories of the self in everyday life and certain scenes of hyperclarity in which children know the true scale of justice and the true measure of pain (in contrast to adults, with their brains twisted by liberal ideologies of property and contract [pp. 12, 27, for example]). Perhaps this is because, as she says, "Contract law reduces life to fairy tale" (224).

46. See Lucinda M. Finley, "A Break in the Silence: Including Women's Issues in a Torts Course," *Yale Journal of Law and Feminism* 1 (1989): 41–73. See also Scarry, *Body in Pain*; Matsuda, "Looking to the Bottom";West, *Narrative, Authority, and Law*; Williams, *Alchemy of Race and Rights*; and MacKinnon, *Toward a Feminist Theory of the State.*

47. Kendall Thomas, "Beyond the Privacy Principle," in Danielson and Engle, eds., *After Identity*, pp. 277–93.

48. Brown, "Wounded Attachments," pp. 220, 221.

49. See Shoshana Felman and Dori Laub, *Testimony: Crises of Witnessing in Literature, Psychoanalysis, and History* (New York: Routledge, 1992), and Jean-François Lyotard, *The Differend* (Minneapolis: University of Minnesota Press, 1988).

50. Denise Riley, *"Am I That Name?": Feminism and the Category of "Women" in History* (Minneapolis: University of Minnesota Press, 1988).

51. Emily Martin, *The Woman in the Body: A Cultural Analysis of Reproduction* (Boston: Beacon Press, 1987); Rayna Rapp, "Constructing Amniocentesis: Maternal and Medical Discourses," in *Uncertain Terms*, ed. Faye D. Ginsburg and Anna Lowen-

haupt Tsing (Boston: Beacon Press, 1990), pp. 28–42, and "Chromosomes and Communication: The Discourse of Genetic Counseling," *Medical Anthropology Quarterly* 2, no. 2 (1998): 143–57; Barbara Duden, *Disembodying Women: Perspectives on Pregnancy and the Unborn* (Cambridge: Harvard University Press, 1993).

52. Lisa Steele George, *Peaceful Pregnancy Meditations: A Diary for Expectant Mothers* (Deerfield Beach, Fla.: Health Communications, 1993), p. 3.

53. Ibid., p. 167.

54. Jacques Derrida, "Force of Law: The 'Mystical Foundations of Authority,' " in *Deconstruction and the Possibility of Justice*, ed. Drucilla Cornell, Michel Rosenfeld, and David Grey Carlson (New York: Routledge, 1992), pp. 3–67, esp. 61–63.

Chapter 7

Dark Mirrors: A Feminist Reflection on Holocaust Narrative and the Maternal Metaphor

CLAIRE KAHANE

The devastation of European Jewry that has been named Holocaust, Shoah, the Event—each term evoking a different narrative context for this histori-cal trauma—has become an object of increasing cultural fascination. Pro-voked in great part by the fiftieth anniversary of the liberation of the Nazi concentration camps in the mid-nineties, in part by the awakened desire among aging survivors and their descendants to give meaning to their hor-rific history, a proliferation of publications in both historiography and liter-ary studies has raised anew critical questions about representation and its limits, questions that return us again to Adorno's often quoted remark that to write poetry after Auschwitz would be barbaric. Certainly Auschwitz has compelled us to recognize that the autonomous art-object put forth by modernist theory has a limit imposed by historical trauma, that even fifty years after the event, the sheer fact of the Holocaust impinges on any aes-thetic object that claims to represent it. Indeed, for many critics the Holocaust has put into question the very logic of narrative representation and the humanistic subject that it constructs. As Andrew Hewitt insists, "personal narrative presupposes a kind of subject that the very possibility of the camp liquidated. To perpetuate personal narrative is potentially to act as though the camps never happened."[1] Yet the contrary is also true: not to perpetuate personal narrative, not to bear witness to the barbarity of the concentration camps, whether in testimony or imaginative literature, is also to act as though the camps never happened. Thus while the Holocaust has been defined as unrepresentable, while Auschwitz itself has become the metaphor for an unspeakable aporia within the heart of Western liberal discourse, a veritable explosion of narratives about the Holocaust is now compelling us to rethink the the cultural consequences of that traumatic event.[2]

What seems to have been lost in this critical engagement with the Holocaust are the feminist questions that had over the past several decades given new currency to our investment in literature as an ethical activity. Having taken on in the seventies the critical mandate of empowering women through a feminist critique of literary discourse, many of us who were feminist-psychoanalytic critics had turned to hysteria as a useful paradigm for addressing the effects of gender in, and on, representation. Hysteria as reconfigured by feminist critics was itself a pathology of gendering, its symptoms a bodily representation of repressed conflicts induced in great part by the social construction of gender. Trauma, however, as defined by Freud in his late writings, and as subsequently theorized by contemporary analytic writers, is by definition a shattering of the subject and its boundaries, a violation of the field of representation that leaves only a void.[3] If hysteria put gender at the very center of subjectivity, trauma, in its attention to the assault on the ego and the disintegration of the subject, seems to cast gender aside as irrelevant. Is gender a relevant category in theorizing trauma and its relation to representations? As a feminist-psychoanalytic critic who had recently turned from studying hysterical narrative to the narrative representation of Holocaust trauma, this was the initial question I set out to address for this collection, and not surprisingly, it quickly proliferated. Does feminist theory of the past several decades make a difference in my reading of Holocaust narratives? If gender is inseparable from symbolic form so that representation always bears the trace of the gendered subject, how is that trace manifested in Holocaust representations? Could—and should—the Holocaust even be considered within the context of gender?[4]

Freud, we might recall, first linked trauma to sexuality in the seduction theory: hysterical symptoms were, he suggested, brought on by the memory of an actual sexual violation that could not be consciously tolerated or acknowledged. While his original formulation of *traumatic* neurosis induced by repressed *memories* yielded to the concept of *psychoneurosis* induced by repressed *wishes*—so that trauma receded from theoretical interest—it was reinvigorated during World War I when Freud was called upon to treat shell shock. In the postwar *Beyond the Pleasure Principle* Freud again describes an ego overwhelmed by stimuli that it cannot process; its protective shield breached, the self fragments, unable to register or to integrate the traumatic event as a part of its history, of its identity.[5] Without temporality, the traumatic event is never really past but remains a shadow presence, encrypted, dissociated, waiting for the contingency that will evoke its repetition and, within the parameters of *Beyond the Pleasure Principle*, the drive toward death.

Significantly, although not made part of Freud's argument, it is a well-known fact that soldiers in the midst of battle trauma often call out for their mothers. Does this call for the mother indicate that trauma involves not only a breach in the ego's shield but a break in the maternal object relation? I shall suggest that it does, that, indeed, what Freud called the ego's "protective shield" is analogous to Didier Anzieu's "maternal envelope," or Winnicott's "holding environment." These are all tropes for the archaic ego's psychic experience of containment within the heterogeneous field of impulse in which it comes into being, a containment that devolves upon the maternal object relation but that trauma ruptures.[6] Moreover, I shall suggest that gender marks both the response to this traumatic rupture as well as its representations.

Let me begin with an initial proposition: that literary representations of the Holocaust attempt a textual mimesis of trauma through tropes that most potently capture, and elicit in the reader, terror, disgust, fear, and, most of all, numbness—primal affects contiguous with the traumatic event. Psychoanalysis tells us that affect is a fundamental and powerful link to the buried past, a primary means of accessing a memory trace beyond representation, of apprehending an otherness beyond language. We know the trauma through its affect as well as its effects on the subject. Paradoxically, it is literary discourse in particular, through its semiotic strategies of encoding and conveying affect, that can make real and present the inaccessible historical past and the experience of the other. Especially in the face of the Holocaust, where signifiers seem especially inadequate to the enormity of the real

event, writers—who seek to engage readers in an act of creative identification with the subject of trauma, in an apprehension of the unspeakable, and
even in a share in its guilt and shame—seek tropes that can transmit the texture of traumatic memory.[7]

In this context, I find it significant that even a cursory survey of Holocaust narrative reveals a recurrent scene foregrounded for its affective
dimension by survivors and second-generation writers alike: the painful
spectacle of a mother and child torn from one another in an anguish of loss
with which we are asked, even compelled, to identify. One need only recall
the secret center of *Sophie's Choice* by William Styron; the climactic Babi Yar
sequence of D. M. Thomas's *The White Hotel*, with its maternal heroine
clutching the hand of her adopted son as they prepare to be killed; the horrific climax of Cynthia Ozick's "The Shawl," its protagonist-mother stifling
her scream as she witnesses her child's brutal murder. Survivor accounts as
well often put in the forefront of their narratives the memory-image of a
mother being torn from her child, a child from its mother, or the antithesis,
a mother's refusal to be separated from her child, even to the point of death.
Clearly, the profound intimacy between mother and child and its callous
violation is a powerful and moving signifier, effectively capturing the per-
version of human bonds that was a primary consequence of the Holocaust.

If we understand the first trauma of infantile life to be the trauma of
maternal loss, the use of a traumatic breach in the mother-child relation to
figure an unrepresentable historical trauma has a logical inevitability as well
as a universal affective power. Yet in looking at Holocaust narrative with
feminist eyes, I am made uncomfortable by the ubiquitous presence of
mother and child as figures of traumatic loss. Is it not perhaps too easy to
use that dyadic ideal of intimacy to evoke the reader's emotional identification with the agony of separation? Too easy once again to sacralize the
mother-and-child bond to the detriment of both women and children? Too
easy to use an image of such universal sentimental appeal to represent an
event as shockingly unique to modern history as the Holocaust? Or is such
discomfort misplaced? Moreover, if as Lacanian-oriented psychoanalysts
claim, the mother-child relation, the first object relation that attaches the
child to the world, is itself a shelter from an unrepresentable Real into which
we are born, a protective psychic envelope that shields the neonate from the
assaults of a surround of impulse, doesn't the focus on that relation in traumatic narratives itself become a kind of screen, a cover-up for the terror of
confronting the nihilistic implications of the Holocaust? If the privileged

place of the mother-child bond in Holocaust narrative is a defense against an inassimilable negativity, do we need this maternal figuration of loss to contain the primal terrors released by the Holocaust? While scenes of the violent separation of mother and child were in the forefront of the grim reality of the camps, their translation into text asks us not merely to experience their painful affect but to question their function within the context of cultural representation and the social effects of their transmission.

Holocaust literature is, of course, by no means the only literature of historical trauma to use the mother-child relation as a central trope, or to foreground the figure of the suffering mother. From Harriet Beecher Stowe's manipulation of the enforced separation of mother and child in *Uncle Tom's Cabin* to arouse public sympathy for the abolitionist cause, to *Beloved*, Toni Morrison's fiction of a mother compelled out of love to kill her child, writers depicting the trauma of slavery have used the pathos of maternal suffering and child vulnerability to transmit the devastating effects of slavery.[8] Pathos thus becomes itself the crux of a paradox: an affect often manipulated to arouse public sentiment about issues of social and political significance, its conventional link to feminine sensibility has also made it suspect in rendering the gravity of public issues. Yet as Margaret Kelleher points out in her recent study of nineteenth-century Irish famine literature, "a key strategy for those who seek to convey a traumatic event is the feminization of its effects."[9] And, I would add, of its affects as well. Kelleher notes that in famine literature the victim who is the subject of a detailed description is typically female and suggests that the image of the female in pain, the female victim, more readily compels the identification of its readers.[10] As Kelleher and other feminist critics suggest, trauma itself has been gendered female: "again and again, images of women are used to figure moments of breakdown or crisis—in the social body, in political authority, or in representation itself . . . thus expressing the 'point of impossibility' of any system."[11]

That women characteristically figure the threshold of impossibility, that place where the symbolic order breaks down, which is precisely the site of trauma, is not surprising, given that the mother is typically the first figure called upon to fill the gap that trauma opens up. What seems evident from even this cursory look is that when the unspeakable needs to be spoken, it draws upon a female image for its form and affective power; and inevitably, in that place, the female and the maternal merge into one threshold-image—the female/maternal—an ambivalent figure on the boundary of subjectivity and history, a figure of archaic dimension used as a projective screen for the displacement of larger cultural anxieties, even for the unclaimed ambivalence about Being itself that Freud charted for modern consciousness.

In short, as these introductory comments and tentative questions suggest, there are gendered implications to figuring trauma through the mother and child dyad, implications to which feminist-psychoanalytic theory over the last twenty years has particularly sensitized us. In what follows, I want to consider the use of the maternal figure by two writers—Charlotte Delbo and Tad Borowski. Both were survivors of Auschwitz; both had been political prisoners; neither was Jewish. Both Delbo's *None of Us Shall Return*, the first volume of her trilogy *Auschwitz and After*, and Borowski's story, "This Way for the Gas, Ladies and Gentlemen," were written shortly after their liberation; both texts foreground a scene between a mother and child as a central figure of Holocaust trauma. Delbo's *Days and Memory*, her last work, was published in 1985; it too foregrounds the relation between mother and child. Importantly for my purposes, both were self-conscious writers, their texts powerful *literary* articulations of their historical experience.[12] Thus I think it significant that each very differently constructs a maternal metaphor as a means of giving form to the form-shattering effects of Auschwitz; the contrast between them is instructive.

Charlotte Delbo's writings are a good place to begin since she has herself commented on the question of gender: "I must not be discussed as a woman writer. . . . I am not a woman in my writing," she told a friend, insisting that there was no "distinctive female experience of the Holocaust. . . . The camp system grants complete equality to men and women."[13] If the camp system grants a complete equality of pain, equality is not the term at issue; sameness and difference are, and for my purposes a difference manifest in the field of representation. In spite of her disclaimer, I want to argue that Delbo's rhetorical use of a maternal metaphor shapes the structure as well as the content of her texts in a particularly gendered way.

None of Us Shall Return, for example, written shortly after the liberation, is constructed as a series of brief, primarily first-person narrative sequences, each focused on a grotesque anecdote of life and more often death at Auschwitz, at times followed by a fragmentary reference to the writer's present circumstance. Interspersed among these vivid depictions of extreme deprivation and brutalities imposed on the women are verses, short imagistic condensations of narrative incidents, affective responses, meditations,

many directly addressed to the reader. The effect of this structure is to fragment the reading in a mimesis of the fragmentation of the subject—Delbo's
narrator—who vividly inscribes pieces of the horrific past. Yet there is a
consistent thematic line that runs through all the sequences, a reiteration of
an empathic bond, and a mutuality of caretaking, among Delbo's group of
friends that helps them survive and sustains the value of the human subject
for the reader. Often openly using the metaphor of a mother-child relation
to describe the relation among the women, and consistently using the first-
person plural to confirm a communal subject, Delbo suggests that the
women experience the kind of permeable boundary between self and other
that has been theorized as characteristically feminine.[14]

Moreover, Delbo represents that permeable ego boundary as performed
through a tactile intimacy associated with maternal caretaking that generates
the imago of a communal body. Thus, for example, when her friend Cecile
returns from her work frozen, Delbo relates, "We rubbed her in order to
warm her up, to stop this shuddering which communicated itself to us."[15]
In roll call each of the women stands "neck drawn into her shoulders, chest
pulled in, each places her hands under the arms of the one in front of her"
in a common bodily stance by which they futilely attempt to create some
communal warmth: "We stand pressed against each other, yet as we establish
a single circulatory system, we remain frozen, through and through" (p. 63).
When Delbo faints at the roll call, her friend Viva slaps her into consciousness, her voice piercing her despair: "Keep your chin up"; and Delbo imagines "it's my mother's voice I'm hearing" and "clings to Viva as a child to its
mother" (p. 65). When Delbo, feeling she can no longer work, is ready to
give up the struggle for survival, her friend Lulu shields her from the view
of the guards and encourages her to "have a good cry": "Lulu goes on working and stays on the look out at the same time. Occasionally, she turns
around and with her sleeve, softly, wipes my face." Delbo feels "as though I
had wept on my mother's breast" (p. 105).

If this representation errs on the side of the sentimental, it also makes
clear the efficacy of the mother-daughter structure of relations into which
the women enter to ward off despair, a structure of relations encouraged by
the sameness of the body they all share as women. But because the relation
to the maternal body is also deeply ambivalent, an ambivalence heightened
by bodily needs and deprivations in the camps, the maternal body is threatening as well as comforting. Thus, for example, Delbo describes the tormented sleep of the women prisoners crowded into one bunk, some suffer-

ing from dysentery. Although named as individuals, they become a wash of body parts that recalls the shocking photos of piles of corpses in much liberation photography that haunted postwar consciousness: "It is a tangle of bodies, a melee of arms and legs . . . and everything vanishes in the shadowy dark where Lulu's leg is moving, or Yvonne's arm, and the head resting heavily on my chest is Viva's" (p. 55). Here the perceptual boundaries that separate one body from another vanish in the dark, yielding to a grotesque body-in-pieces that is all too present; here, togetherness becomes nightmare, giving rise to dreams of disintegrating into or being strangled by corporeal excess:

> The octopi strangled us with their viscous muscles, and if we succeeded in freeing an arm it was only to be strangled by a tentacle coiling itself around our necks, tightening round our vertebrae, squeezing them until they cracked the vertebrae, the trachea, the esophagus, the larynx, the pharynx, and all the canals in the throat, squeezing them to the breaking point.
> (p. 54)

Delbo reveals in this catalogue of body parts a subject at risk because of the body and its abjection of the individual subject. Thus, while Delbo evokes a pathos that at times verges on the sentimental, she also manages to convey the body-experience of Auschwitz in a rhetoric that evokes the shudder of the Real.

Similarly, *Days and Memory*, written decades after her Auschwitz experience, also depends heavily on a maternal metaphor to contain its various forms and voices. Structured as a series of interviews with survivors, *Days and Memory* juxtaposes multiple narrative voices belonging to men and women of different ages, different nationalities, who narrate and / or comment upon their horrific experiences of Auschwitz, with poems that lyrically rearticulate or meditate on some aspect of the narrative fragments. Delbo's last text thus refuses the coherence of a single narrating subject-position and projects instead a multigenred, multivocal text; yet here again the text is held together by the common reiteration among the different voices of the importance of the maternal relation. Moreover, in its structural inclusion of retrospection—the characters recall and comment on the past—as well as narration in the present tense, *Days and Memory* imitates Delbo's distinction between what she calls "deep memory"—the vivid retention of past bodily sensory experiences that are beyond language but that she attempts semiotically to encode and transmit through sound, rhythm, sense image, and an emphatic use of present tense—and common narrative memory recollected in the past tense. Both kinds of memory-representations invoke the centrality of the maternal metaphor, but deep memory emphasizes its traumatic tie to the abject body. In short, in Delbo's writings, both the sensory horror of daily life and the sustaining maternal relation that operates alongside it come to signify the truth of the Holocaust.

The opening pages of *Days and Memory* describe the sensory assaults of the camp on Delbo: the corpses lying in frozen heaps on the ground, the vermin, the inescapable odor of feces, the taste of human ash: "In Birkenau, rain heightened the odor of diarrhea. It is the most fetid odor I know. In Birkenau, rain came down upon the camp, upon us, laden with soot from the crematoriums, and with the odor of burning flesh. We were steeped in it."[16] Here Delbo represents the borders of the tolerable as so violated, the self so invaded by excremental objects that one would expect her to collapse into this object world of pure negation, as she does in her dreams:

> Over dreams the conscious will has no power. And in those dreams I see myself, yes, my own self such as I know I was: hardly able to stand on my feet, my throat tight, my heart beating wildly, frozen to the marrow, filthy skin and bones. . . . The suffering I feel is so unbearable, so identical to the pain endured there, that I feel it physically . . . I feel death fasten on me. (p. 78)

But Delbo tells us she survives by an act of splitting, developing an "impermeable skin" of memory that encrypts and preserves her Auschwitz self, the traumatized self, alive, but separate:

> Auschwitz is there, unalterable, precise, but enveloped in the skin of memory, an impermeable skin that isolates it from my present self. . . . Alas, I often fear lest it grow thin, crack, and the camp get hold of me again. (p. 78)

The image of an internal fearsome presence "enveloped within the skin of memory" resonates with intimations of a fantasmatic pregnancy not uncommon in the catalogue of women's fears, and reinvoked under the pressure of a post-traumatic stress.

If Delbo manages to convey the sensory experience of Auschwitz in a rhetoric that evokes the shudder of the Real, at other times, the rhetoric of memory evokes a pathos that verges on the sentimental. For example, in another scene, the metaphor of encryptment is turned to a very different end as Delbo describes a "she" who bears in her arms a sister dying through the night:

> She held her dying sister in her arms, hugged her to herself in order to keep her back, prevent her from slipping out of life. Softly she blew her breath upon her sister's face to warm the lips that were turning blue, to impart her own breath to them, and when her sister's heart stopped, she was filled with anger at her own which continued to beat.   (p. 79)

While the passage refers to the loss of a sister, the scene of cradling and the fantasy of imparting life to the other is modeled after a maternal imaginary that has itself become an overly idealized trope; thus the pathos stirred by the woman's futile attempt to prevent her loss does not escape a certain level of sentimentality. Although the pathos yields momentarily to anger "at her own [heart] which continued to beat," the psychology of mourning suggests that this anger is also directed at the abandoning other. Yet anger is not something Delbo can easily represent, not something her traumatized subject can readily acknowledge.[17] Taking into herself her dead sister, internalizing the external object in a melancholic identification, Delbo's "she" thus quickly transforms anger into a specifically designated maternal tenderness as she recalls "the weight of the girl she carried out of the barracks and laid upon the snow, delicately, *maternally*, a kind of burial, a sacrament of tenderness, before that body became an object to be burned" (my emphasis). Insisting on the good mother's presence in the midst of death and defilement, Delbo's "she" both assumes a maternal identity for herself and projects it into the other women inmates, attributing her—and their—survival to a maternally inflected bonding:

> Would she be dead had the others not held her upright and got her to roll-call, kept her from falling into the ditch between the barracks and the mustering yard. . . . helped her walk upon the icy road. . . . That night she had drawn in her sister's last breath, *inside her she bore her sister, alive from now on through her alone.*   (p. 80; my emphasis)

The passage, describing the bereaved woman as a protective vessel incorporating and sustaining her sister as a beloved introject, also suggests that the other women become maternal holding vessels for her—and for one another. At the same time it reveals a kind of melancholic possession by, as well as of, the dead: "she" possesses her sister inside her, but is also possessed by that internal presence who exists "from now on through her alone." Again, the resonance of a maternal metaphor of pregnancy inflects the scene, but here it bears ethical consequences.

Indeed, this responsibility for the existence of the (dead) other becomes an ethical burden that the survivors carry out of Auschwitz, a burden that they can never rid themselves of, as they reveal in the interviews. Thus, for example, years later, a woman is tormented to learn her mother did *not* die in the gas chamber, because that meant her mother had the added suffering of knowing of her daughter's suffering, a burden the daughter would have spared her: "Today the full horror of Birkenau comes back to me through my mother."[18] This is an important sentence in uncovering the complexity of traumatic identification. *The memory of the trauma is the memory of her identification with her mother's trauma.*[19] Through a relay of identifications with maternal pain articulated by the interviewees, identifications that I would suggest are more readily accommodated in the same-sex/same-body relations of mother and daughter, Delbo, as the narrator-interviewer, relives her own Holocaust experience of pain and of maternal loss and re-members it in writing.[20] Indeed, she, in turn, continues this relay by attempting to compel the reader's identification with trauma, constructing images and scenes that play on the pathos of a maternally inflected loss, a pathos that at times cannot escape a problematic conventionality in its representation. Ultimately, the ethical burden that Delbo carries to term after Auschwitz is the burden to transmit not only symbolically but also affectively the dead others, embodied in a language of sense memory, alive from now on through us, the readers.

The dynamics of group identification in Delbo's text seems analogous to that in Freud's description of group psychology, the primary distinction being that in Delbo's text the ego ideal that serves the group is not the ideal Father but the ideal Mother. In an age in which the figure of the Symbolic Father has fallen—along with his iconic avatars—into the wastebasket of history (the ego ideal, "the Leader" of which Freud spoke in *Group Psychology*, having been inexorably debased by the Holocaust), the mother-child bond has come to fill the ideological breach as paradigm and icon of the ideal relation that gives value to the social order. If the paternal idealization that reached its climax in the late nineteenth century made the powerful

Father the source of ethical prohibitions and phallic privilege, the idealization of the Mother remains linked to a different kind of social and ethical system, based on that psychic economy of female nurturance and empathy that Carol Gilligan and Nancy Chodorow have so persuasively elaborated.[21] The idealization of the mother-child bond as the model for an ethics based on empathy, however, depends on a faith in the redemptive powers of the mother, in her ability to support a loving connection to existence, a basic trust in object relations that extends outward. One would assume that the trauma of the Holocaust damaged that basic trust, as well as the stability of the maternal object relation that subtended it—that indeed the combination of trauma and melancholic loss would lead to negation and/or rage. Yet *Days and Memory* insists that the good maternal object is still present, even in Auschwitz. "Hold on to me," a woman urges her companion who is struggling in the dark; "Where are my galoshes," one calls, and "the whole group stops, stoops over the snow, gropes unseeingly. The galoshes must be found" (pp. 81–82). Here the group is represented as one entity, grounded in a communal identification that promotes an ethics of survival, an identification that is linked to their bond to a shared maternal body.

Yet as I have suggested here, there are segments in both *Auschwitz and After* and *Days and Memory* in which empathic identification with the body of another provokes terror and guilt. In one of the most striking of such episodes, "One Day," in *None of Us Shall Return*, Delbo describes a woman half crazed with thirst who had fallen into a ditch and is unable to get out. Delbo empathically imagines the woman thinking:

> "Why don't you help me, you standing so close? Help me. Pull me up. Lean in my direction. Stretch out your hand. Oh, they don't make a move."

> And her hand writhed toward us in a desperate call for help. . . .

> We did not move. . . . We stood there motionless, several thousand women speaking a variety of languages . . . huddled together heads bowed under the snow's stinging blasts.   (p. 25)

Everyone remains frozen, including the narrator who painfully tries to defend herself against the mirroring gaze of a radical negation in the eyes of the other:

I no longer look at her. I no longer wish to look. If only I could change my place in order not to see her. Not to see the dark holes of these eye sockets, these staring holes. . . . I turn away to look elsewhere. (p. 26)

Yet the narrator does not, cannot look elsewhere; in an extended description, she gives us first the vivid physical details of the woman's grotesquely deteriorated body, and then of her death when the SS guard finally releases his dog:

All is silent as in a dream. The dog leaps on the woman, sinks its fangs in her neck. And we do not stir, stuck in some kind of viscous substance which keeps us from making the slightest gesture—as in a dream. The woman lets out a cry. . . . A single scream tearing through the immobility of the plain. We do not know if the scream has been uttered by her or by us, whether it issued from her punctured throat or from ours. I feel the dog's fangs in my throat. I scream. (p. 28)

In a similar sequence in *Days and Memory,* that alternates between empathic identification with the pain of the other and guilty paralysis, Delbo, using the second-person pronoun to promote reader identification with the body in pain, describes the women standing at the infamous roll call in the freezing cold of predawn darkness:

You see nothing, each one is enclosed in the shroud of her own skin, you feel nothing neither the person next to you, huddling against you nor that other who has fallen and is being helped up. You don't speak because the cold would freeze your saliva. Each feels she is dying, crumbling into confused images, dead to herself already, without a past, any reality, without anything. (p. 83)

As light dawns, Delbo's narrator sees "the ranks of the Gypsy women like ourselves all blue from cold." Whereas earlier the gypsies had been distinguished as "them," they now—sharing the same bodily condition—become "like ourselves" in an equality of misery.

But the identification with this body "like ourselves" in its pain—a female body—becomes even more compelling to the narrator when it is a mother whose fierce attachment to her dead infant has maddened her.

Turning toward "the spectre of a woman . . . with her bundle pressed against her chest . . . her eyes gleaming with fever, with hatred, a burning unbearable hatred," the narrator gradually takes in the details of a grotesque scene:

> She holds the bundle of rags to her, in the crook of her arm, the way a baby is held, the baby's head against its mother's breast. . . . It is an infant, that bundle of rags she is clutching . . . we see the infant's head lolling, bluish, almost black.
>
> With a gentle movement she raises the baby's head, props it in the hollow between her arm and her breast. And again she lifts.   (p. 83)

The crazed mother "hugging her bundle of rags" becomes the object of incessant fascination to the narrator who can neither let go of this drama nor assimilate it long after she knows its resolution.

> Someone saw the bundle of rags, the dead baby, on the garbage heap. . . . The Gypsy had been clubbed to death by a policewoman who'd tried to pull the dead baby away from her.   (p. 84)

The narration does not move away from this killing scene but circles back to the image of the dead mother and child on the one hand, the killer-policewoman, her antagonist, on the other, repeating the details in a broken temporal sequence as if trying to make sense of this drama that pits two women, two furies, against each other, the object of their ferocity a dead infant:

> This woman, hugging her baby to her, had fought, butting her head, kicking, protecting herself and then striking with her free hand . . . a struggle in which she had been crushed despite the hate that gave her the strength of a lioness defending her brood.
>
> The Gypsy had fallen dead in the snow. . . .
>
> The mother killed, the policewoman had torn the baby from her arms and tossed it on the garbage heap in front of which the struggle had taken place. The Gypsy woman had raced to the edge of the camp,

tightly cradling the baby in her crossed arms, had run till she was out of breath and it was when she was blocked by the garbage pile that she turned to face the fury and her club. (p. 84)

Here maternal hate is the source of the woman's strength, a hate that spills over to anyone who would separate her from the dead infant even when it has become a bundle of rags. Here the maternal metaphor has exceeded its function in Delbo's text as the source of group identification and become instead the source of instinctive antipathy to the other. What Delbo gives us in this scene is an image of a maternal attachment so primal—"a lioness defending its brood"—a maternal pain so acute in its loss, that it not only complicates the meaning of the maternal metaphor but also provokes the most intense pain in a reader who shares that maternal identification. When the object of this fierce attachment is a "bundle of rags on the garbage heap" and the subject a dead Gypsy in the snow, the abject horror of the scene is all the more potent. In its description of the irrational ferocity of a maternal attachment to one's own, this scene both satisfies a desire for maternal fidelity even beyond death and at the same time suggests a significant short-coming to any simple maternal idealization and thus to a maternally based group ethics that derives from it.

In fact, Delbo's text reveals such a shortcoming in her own group: the unwillingness to put the group—a virtual family—at risk by extending its protection to those outside it.[22] In *Auschwitz and After*, when a woman is shot, Delbo and her friends instinctively count their group: "Are we all here?" and note that "it was one of the Polish women" (p. 69). In another incident, when the women are forced to run past the SS guards who beat them, the Jewish women, believing that political prisoners are not as severely beaten as Jews, try to insert themselves among Delbo and her friends. Delbo describes her group's reaction: "They fill us with pity but we do not want to be separated from each other. We protect one another" (p. 92). Thus while Delbo's text privileges the mother-child relation as an ethical paradigm of bonding and protective care, it nevertheless represents the limitations of such empathy under duress, showing indeed that the narrating subject of *Auschwitz and After* is not only gendered but nationalized—a French woman—and that those national boundaries signify. The line of survival must be drawn somewhere, and in Delbo's narratives it is reluctantly drawn around a commonality of language and culture that, like another kind of second skin, protects the group of the same; those outside the family, the clan, the nation, must fend for themselves. We might recall that Freud criticized women's fidelity to the family as a regressive force in *Civilization and its Discontents*, and that Chodorow's *The Reproduction of Mothering*, in elaborating the daughter's desire to reproduce mothering, also points to the conservative consequences of maternal identification.

Yet Delbo clearly wants to use that identification not to repeat the past but to underpin a different political future, based on a gendered ethics that we now associate with the cultural feminism of the seventies—an ethics based on a communal identification with an idealized nurturing maternal body that sustains a relation to life. Although I am uncomfortable with this representation of the maternal as idealized nurturer—the consistent underscoring of the *goodness* of the maternal object seems to me politically untenable and psychologically suspect—Delbo's text convinces me that given the traumatic circumstances of the camps, a maternal idealization with which one identified was a necessary counter not only to the brutal dehumanization of the subject so effectively instituted by the Nazi program but also to the pervasive sense of absolute abandonment, given that most of the world remained bystanders.

It would be difficult to find a more blatant example of a consciousness more distanced from maternal identification than that represented in Tad Borowski's collection of stories, *This Way for the Gas, Ladies and Gentlemen*.[23] Unlike the multiple voices and open form of Delbo's text, the stories in *This Way for the Gas* remain framed by and within the consciousness of the single narrator, who puts us in a starkly claustrophobic world almost unbearable in the relentlessness of its brutality. In contrast to the empathic sentiment that relieves the horror in Delbo's multivocal texts, Borowski's single-voiced narrator, who bears Borowski's own name, Tadeusz, is relatively detached, without affect, numb to the events he records. Yet Tadeusz conveys a sense of trauma in the very affectlessness of his first-person voice. From the opening line of the title story, "All of us walked around naked," which refers to the twenty thousand naked men and women deportees who have just been deloused, to the sentence that ends the opening paragraph, "Now they swarm around the large yard" (p. 30)—the verb as well as the sheer number he records reducing the inmates themselves to vermin—Tadeusz observes, describes, but refrains from commentary, judgment or, for the most part, any direct affective response to the incidents he records. As a consequence, the story communicates a universe more terrifyingly ahuman than Delbo's, not only because of the arbitrary violences that assault the percipient ego—

which we get in Delbo's text as well—but because there is no indication of a mediating value or even a psychic resistance. Yet, of course, the text is not neutral; traumatic affect is carried in the rhetoric of the narration, by its allusions, horrific repetitions, and juxtapositions of incident and image that reproduce in the reader the perceptual consciousness of shock, exhaustion, terror, and ultimately, disgust—affects that are somatized in the narrator's own act of vomiting, the final sense-memory of the story that the narrator records, his body speaking the repugnance he verbally disdains.

What adds to the tension of reading Borowski's text is the problematic of identifying with a narrator who is also complicit in the horrors he delineates. A member of the Canada (those who unloaded the transports and separated the valuables for the Reich, taking for themselves as reward the food and clothing of those about to die), Tadeusz is both victim and perpetrator, a split subject through whom we must access the events and with whom we are compelled to identify. And it is not a comfortable position for narrator or reader. Insistently accumulating repugnant images of both self and other, Borowski's text conveys a negation of human value from which there seems no escape.

> The bolts crack, the doors fall open. A wave of fresh air rushes inside the train. People . . . inhumanly crammed, buried under incredible heaps of luggage, suitcases, trunks, packages, crates, bundles of every description, (everything that had been their past and was to start their future). Monstrously squeezed together, they have fainted from heat, suffocated, crushed one another. Now they push towards the opened doors, breathing like fish cast out on the sand.   (p. 37)

Thus begins the narrator's introduction to his work on the transport ramp, trapping the reader in an endless repetition of atrocious images and action. Over and over again, the trains arrive, their contents are unloaded, the "transports" stripped of their possessions, brutalized, and led off in a daze to the gas chambers. As in a hell that one might imagine as only rhetorical, but here all too vividly made literal, the sequence is repeated seemingly ad infinitum, and literally ad nauseam, recorded by an increasingly exhausted narrator who finds it increasingly difficult to maintain his equilibrium.

In an early scene preceding his work with the Canada, however, the narrator eats rather than vomits: he shares a food package sent by his mother with his buddies: "We slice the meat, loaves of bread. . . . We unwrap the bacon, the onion, we open a can of evaporated milk" (p. 30). The food package marks him as more privileged than the foreigners and Jews, but the text makes clear that his mother belongs to a world radically elsewhere, beyond-Auschwitz, that his survival at Auschwitz requires much more than what a mother can send. Indeed, in Auschwitz food comes not as a gift from the good mother but as a rapacious theft in a zero-sum universe: he and his Canada buddies eat and live as long as the transports surrender their goods and die. Although at the beginning Tadeusz tries to maintain the distinction between the privileged "we" and "them"—those slated to die—the "we" that he constructs is undermined by its very basis in his consumption of "them," who continue to arrive and yield their black fruit. Thus paradoxically, "we" the consumers can neither retain a distance from "them"—since "we" incorporate them and their possessions—nor digest "them," neither disgorge them nor swallow them whole. When Tadeusz finally does vomit, literally spitting out, symptomatically refusing to take in and be part of, what he sees—"I do not assimilate it, I expel it"— he is also spitting himself out, as well as the primal object relation to the mother—and to the other—that eating symbolically represents.

Such oral and anal psychodynamics dominate Borowski's text, underscoring the regressive nature of the concentrationary universe that the narrator is forced to inhabit, as well as its unbinding of the drives. In one of the more gruesome scenes, in which infants are reduced to excremental waste, Borowski's defensive detachment breaks open, but a maternal figure comes to his rescue:

> The train has been emptied. A thin, pockmarked SS man peers inside, shakes his head in disgust and motions to our group, pointing his finger at the door.
>
> "*Rein*. Clean it up."
>
> We climb inside. In the corners amid human excrement and abandoned wrist watches lie squashed trampled infants, naked little monsters with enormous heads and bloated bellies. We carry them out like chickens, holding several in each hand.

Told to take them to the women who have disembarked and are about to be killed themselves, the narrator explodes in a rare expression of emotion when none of the women will take "them" from his hands:

"Take them for God's sake!" I explode as the women run from me in horror, covering their eyes. (p. 40)

There is something uncanny in this excessively real description: the dead infants, the women who run away, seem all part of a phantasmagoric nightmare, over which hovers the bad abandoning mother turned real. That figure will soon literally appear, but here, when the pockmarked SS man reaches for his revolver (to shoot the women who refuse) a "greyhaired woman"—the adjective itself desexualizes and maternalizes her—steps forward and "takes the little corpses out of my hands and for an instant gazes straight into my eyes. 'My poor boy,' she whispers and smiles at me. Then she walks away, staggering along the path" (p. 40). This is the only moment of compassion in the text, and significantly, it is the compassion of a maternal figure for her "poor" boy. Although her sympathetic recognition of his need provokes Tadeusz's only explicit expression of feeling, paradoxically that feeling is rage, directed not at the SS or at himself but at his helpless victims.

"I am simply furious with these people furious because I must be here because of them. I feel no pity. I am not sorry they're going to the gas chamber. Damn them all! I could throw myself at them, beat them with my fists. It must be pathological, I just can't understand."

To which his Canada mate Henri replies with the logic of the *lager*:

"Ah, on the contrary, it is natural, predictable, calculated. The ramp exhausts you, you rebel and the easiest way to relieve your hate is to turn against someone weaker. Why, I'd even call it healthy. It's simple logic." (p. 40)

This is in fact the narrative logic of Borowski's story, a logic he reveals to, and performs for, the reader. Provoked by the ubiquitous reflection of his own helplessness, above in the form of infant-corpses but also by the reflection of his own complicity, and in contrast to the Delbo persona who turns her rage against herself for surviving, Tadeusz voices rage at all the helpless others, especially women, who, like avatars of a negative mirror, reveal only his own vulnerability and guilt.

Two subsequent scenes elaborate the way in which women function as projective containers of his cast-off feelings. In the first scene, a Jewish mother abandons her child in an effort to save herself, and in the second, a golden-haired virginal girl with beautiful breasts goes nobly to her death. Allegorical images of the cowardly and the heroic, these female figures are used to convey to the reader the perverse consequences of the Holocaust, but in contrast to Delbo's text, both are represented as totally separate from the narrating consciousness, while made to bear the burden of the narrator's projective identifications.

In the first instance, "A small child with a pink cherub's face runs after [his mother] and, unable to keep up, stretches out his little arms and cries: Mama, mama" (p. 43). The sentimental rhetoric of vulnerability and inno-cence—the "small" child, the "cherub's face," the "little arms"—is melodra-matic in spite of its excessively real context. In contrast to Delbo who does not represent children as abandoned even when they are—the presence of the mother is always imagined—Borowski wants us here to identify with the abandoned and betrayed child. But we are not allowed to remain with this pathos for long. The terrified mother's response—" 'it's not mine, sir, not mine' she shouts"—elicits the rage of a Russian Kapo. "Ah, you bloody Jew-ess," he screams at her, "So you're running from your own child! I'll show you, you whore!" (p. 43), and in a fit, as the narrator watches, he chokes her, tosses her onto a truck "like a heavy sack of grain," and then violently tosses the child at her feet. Moving from pathos to explosive violence, the narra-tive highlights a mother's betrayal of her child to signify the most egregious transgression induced by Auschwitz, and immediately punishes her instead of the guiltily complicit narrator.

But the punishment does not signify her guilt as much as it does the per-version of the categories of guilt and innocence. Thus the terrified mother, who, in the Kapo's words, has become the "whore" in order to survive, just as Tadeusz has become the whore of the Nazis through his complicit actions in the Canada, draws our sympathy when she herself becomes a victim of the Kapo, who acts out the narrator's own rage. Thus the text refuses us a position of judgment; in this mutual imbrication of guilt, rage, and vulner-ability, there is no ethical position from which to judge. The mother's vio-lently abjected end, as a sack of grain, along with that of her cherub-child, takes the reader out of the pathetic identification with the child initially elicited by her maternal betrayal, out of the symbolic itself, and through the explosion of rage at a larger maternal betrayal—the abandonment by the motherland itself—into the depths of the inassimilable.[24]

In the second instance, which follows almost immediately, it is disgust that breaks through the text through a maternal metaphor. The narrator observes another transport figure: a girl with "soft, blonde hair . . . fallen on her shoulders in a torrent" who asks him what is to happen to her.

> Here standing before me, is a girl, with enchanting blond hair, with beautiful breasts, wearing a little cotton blouse, a girl with a wise, mature look in her eyes. . . . And over there is the gas chamber: communal death, disgusting and ugly. And over in the other direction is the concentration camp: the shaved head, the heavy Soviet trousers in sweltering heat, the sickening, stale odor of dirty, damp female bodies. (p. 44)

The sudden breakthrough of strong affective rhetoric in the last sentence above is striking, as is the stark contrast between the golden-haired girl, signifying beauty, innocence, nobility on the one hand, and the two alternative destinies that await her: disgusting, communal death, or the inevitable metamorphosis into the smelly, dirty women of the camp on the other. She herself thus becomes an icon of the heroic, the virginal female image that sustains also the distance of an aesthetic ideal in contrast to the misogynistic image of negation: the sickening, stale, and pointedly *damp female odor* that permeates the boundaries the narrator tries to preserve. Recalling Freud's version of the split maternal figure—virgin and whore—the narrator's images of this disjunction between the ideal and the abject stereotypically evoke the familiar epithets that turn women into contrasting signifiers of cultural value or physical corruption. Indeed, in valuing the girl for her "enchanting blond hair" and constructing the alien other as dirty, damp, and female, Borowski unwittingly supports that very stereotype which has placed the dark female (and the dark Jew) in the position of abjected other; thus, the narrator becomes doubly complicit in perpetuating a cultural system whose binarisms have become paranoid splits logically supporting a drive for a final solution.

In the sequence that follows, the text makes explicit the way in which the female body becomes the grotesque signifier of bodily abjection and is linked again to the terrifying vulnerability of the child:

> I see four Canada men lugging a corpse. Cursing, dripping wet from the strain, they kick out of their way some stray children who have been running all over the ramp, howling like dogs. The men pick them

up by the collars, heads, arms, and toss them inside the trucks, on top
of the heaps. The four men have trouble lifting the fat corpse on to
the car, they call others for help, and all together they hoist up the
mound of meat.   (p. 45)

The insistent dehumanization, not only of the incidents but of the narrator's consciousness, is a purposively shocking commentary on the effects of
Auschwitz.

This is not to say that Borowski's fiction is better or worse than Delbo's;
Borowski's more unrelenting representation of horror and hopelessness may
indeed more truly capture the horrific affect of the concentrationary universe. But in comparing the two textual representations of Auschwitz, as dif-
férent as they are in tone and structure, the figuration of the maternal in
Auschwitz—this phrase alone seems an oxymoron—provocatively stands
out as a gendered mark of difference in the literary responses of Borowski
and Delbo to the duress of Holocaust trauma. The intimate identification of
mother and daughter through a shared fantasmatic body allows Delbo a light
in the shadow of the Holocaust; the alienation from the maternal body in
Borowski's text, and the protagonist's identification with a doomed abandoned child, encourages in him a paranoid rage at the maternal figure,
which threatens to color all human relations.[25] Indeed, his text shows more
gruesomely than Delbo's the abjection of the human, shows how Auschwitz
so dominates the image of self and other that neither can serve as a ground
for an ethics or an action. Finally, Borowski's representation of Holocaust
trauma reveals such an intolerable de-idealization that spreads from the
maternal object to the object world at large that survival seems pointless.

To return through these two readings to my initial discomfort with the
nearly ubiquitous figure of the mother-child relation in Holocaust narrative, given its place in Western literature as the general locus of pathos, can
such a signifier represent the extremity of Auschwitz? Does its familiar place
in the Western imaginary paradoxically take away from the historical
uniqueness of the Holocaust? Looking at its particular role in these narratives, one can see how well it serves as a complex barometer of trauma, and
one that shows at how profound a level the ideology of gender functions in
both the response to and the representation of trauma. But these texts also
suggest that the familiar role of the mother-child dyad as a signifier of
pathos makes it a problematic trope. Indeed, pathos itself as an affect in rep-

resentations of trauma raises a dilemma for a critical reader of Holocaust narrative, who may be caught between the horns of insensitivity—a distanced objectification of the text that ignores its affective realities—and sentimentality—an uncritical empathic identification with its affect that ignores its historical relevance. What seems most clear is that when a prior narrative stereotype—the tender relation between mother and child in Delbo, the cherubic abandoned child in Borowski—comes to fill in the gap opened up by the Holocaust, we feel that inauthenticity we call sentimental even in an otherwise powerful representation of the ultimate authentic experience. As differently conceived as are Delbo's and Borowski's representations of the Holocaust, and as differently inflected by a gendered relation to the maternal object, both of their texts suffer when they idealize the mother or the child to screen the negativity of that trauma. At their most effective, both give us through their affect-inducing images an index of the terror and pain that was not a function of the aesthetic imagination, but of the all too real.

Finally, I end with another question that has often been raised: why do we want texts to stay with the negations of Holocaust trauma? Why should they reproduce in representation the horror of that history? Why indeed should we read them? Hannah Arendt's distinction between survivors who, traumatized by the horror, can only react and those who, engaging the traumatic events vicariously, can afford to contemplate its historical and cultural significance, provides me with a tentative answer, and a temporary closure to these reflections:

> If it is true that the concentration camps are the most consequential institution of totalitarian rule, "dwelling on horrors" would seem to be indispensable for the understanding of totalitarianism. But recollection can no more do this than can the uncommunicative eyewitness. . . . Only the fearful imagination of those who have been aroused by such reports but have not actually been smitten in their own flesh, of those who are consequently free from the bestial, desperate terror which, when confronted by real, present horror, inexorably paralyzes everything that is not mere reaction, can afford *to think about horrors.*[26]
> (my emphasis)

Certainly Holocaust texts by survivor-writers who have been "smitten in their own flesh" are more than a mere reaction; on the contrary, they are a move to recuperate a self and a world, to move out of the paralysis of trauma that has been the fate of many an eyewitness. But Arendt also points to the broader cultural function of Holocaust literature: it provokes in us as readers the fearful imagination that allows us who have not been bitten by the Real to *think* about the horror of the Holocaust in the service of an ethical apprehension of history, culture, and representation. What we do with those thoughts remains to be seen.

NOTES

1. Andrew Hewitt, "The Bad Seed: 'Auschwitz' and the Physiology of Evil," in *Radical Evil*, ed. Joan Copjec (New York: Verso, 1996), p. 75.

2. See, for example, James Young's discussion of the problematics of witnessing and narrative convention in *Writing and Rewriting the Holocaust: Narrative and the Consequences of Interpretation* (Bloomington: Indiana University Press, 1988). See also the provocative discussion of Auschwitz in Adam Katz, "The Closure of Auschwitz but Not Its End," *History and Memory: Studies in Representations of the Past* 10, no. 1 (Spring 1998): 59–98. Katz first surveys the response to Auschwitz as the emblem of a postmodern ethics, and the claim for the Holocaust's epochal significance; in contradistinction, he argues for a political rather than an ethical response to Auschwitz. In this sense his argument is contiguous with Lauren Berlant's critique in this volume of a rhetoric of feeling that has come to dominate American political discourse, a rhetoric that she argues ultimately depoliticizes. Katz wants to eliminate the "subject" from consideration of Auschwitz, since a subject who has no agency is not a subject, replacing it with "the alienated space" of the other. Although it seems to me that ultimately his argument participates in the contradiction he would eliminate, he raises important issues about the juridical clarity sought in categorizing the subjects of the Holocaust into perpetrators, victims, and bystanders, a clarity that blinds one to the intersections and internalizations that blur those boundaries.

3. See Sigmund Freud, *Beyond the Pleasure Principle* (1920) in *The Standard Edition of the Complete Psychological Works of Sigmund Freud*, ed. and trans. James Strachey (London: Hogarth Press, 1953–74), and the contemporary extrapolation of Freud in Cathy Caruth, *Trauma: Explorations in Memory* (Baltimore: Johns Hopkins University Press, 1995). Caruth focuses on the impossibility of witnessing a traumatic event.

4. Recently there has been a flurry of attention to the different experience of women in the Holocaust, but little engagement with the *representation* of that experience and its gendered differences. See Carol Rittner and John K. Roth, eds., *Different Voices: Women and the Holocaust* (New York: Paragon House, 1993), for a good discussion of the arguments regarding the place of gender in Holocaust studies. See

also Dalia Ofer and Lenore J. Weitzman, eds., *Women in the Holocaust* (New Haven: Yale University Press, 1998), which also focuses primarily on the social and historical experience of Jewish women in the camps. The analysis of representation as such, however, is very limited. An exception is the discussion of gender and the unspeakable in representation in Barbara Claire Freeman, *The Feminine Sublime: Gender and Excess in Women's Fiction* (Berkeley: University of California Press, 1995). Freeman essentially defines the sublime as trauma and elaborates its parameters with reference to writings on trauma by Freud, Dori Laub, Caruth, et al.

5. Extrapolating from Freud, for example, Caruth points out that without an organizing ego "the past was never fully experienced as it occurred"; thus, a traumatic event "cannot be placed within the schemes of prior knowledge," cannot, that is to say, be integrated into the temporality of a personal narrative. See *Trauma*, pp. 151, 153.

6. To use familiar tropes of current theory, in trauma the place of the mother as the primal protective shelter (Julia Kristeva) or as protective psychic envelope (Didier Anzieu) is also a screen or firewall against the real; when "it" is suddenly empty, "she" becomes the figure of abandonment, desertion, collapse, weakness, and even the object of rage. As a consequence of disillusion—the sudden loss of the maternal ideal—the object world itself is stripped of its beneficent potential and the subject stripped of its humanity as well. See Kristeva, *Powers of Horror* (New York: Columbia University Press, 1982), and Anzieu, *Psychic Envelopes* (London: Karnac Books, 1990).

7. Charlotte Delbo coins the term "sense memory" to refer to this quality of memory, one that I am equating with affective memory. See Delbo, *Auschwitz and After* (New Haven: Yale University Press, 1995), p. xiv. Lawrence Langer notes in his introduction to Delbo's book that only sense memory "preserves and tries to transmit the physical imprint of the ordeal." The impulse to share the guilt and shame associated with the traumatic denigration of the subject is certainly one motive of witnessing through writing, and one source of its relief.

8. See Freeman's illuminating chapter on Morrison's *Beloved* in *Feminine Sublime*, pp. 105–48. As Freeman remarks in her discussion of Morrison's representation of the trauma of slavery, "The question *Beloved* addresses is the same as that which motivates the discourse of the sublime: how do we symbolize events that are defined by their very unrepresentability?" (p. 124). Morrison struggles with the issue of how to narrate a story that nobody wants to think about, in this case the story of the Middle Passage: "There is a necessity for remembering the horror, but of course there's a necessity for remembering it in a manner in which it can be digested, in a manner in which the memory is not destructive. The act of writing the book, in a way, is a way of confronting it and making it possible to remember" (Marsha Darling, "In the Realm of Responsibility: A Conversation with Toni Morrison," *Women's Review of Books* 5, no. 6 [March 1988]: 5).

9. Margaret Kelleher, *The Feminization of Famine: Expressions of the Inexpressible?* (Durham, N.C.: Duke University Press, 1997), p. 6.

10. Kelleher suggests that male readers find it easier to identify with pain when the victim is female. Is this a displacement of their masochistic desires in an image of the feminine-as-suffering-other? Does the figure of suffering necessarily effeminize the sufferer? And what of female readers? Does the figure of female suffering confirm women's experience of victimization or indulge their masochistic desires? Or all of the above? See Kaja Silverman's discussion of male masochism in *Male Subjectivity at the Margins* (New York: Routledge, 1992).

11. Kelleher, *Feminization of Famine*, p. 6.

12. Borowski was imprisoned in Auschwitz and Dachau from 1943 to 1945; that experience became the basis of a series of camp stories—the most well known being "This Way for the Gas, Ladies and Gentlemen," published in 1946 in Munich, Germany. Two other collections appeared in 1948 in Poland: *Farewell to Maria* and *A World of Stone*. Borowski was a poet before the war—his poetry appeared in a 1942 underground publication, *Whatever the Earth*—but most of his work after his liberation from Auschwitz was political journalism. Borowski committed suicide in Warsaw in 1951 by turning on a gas valve. Charlotte Delbo, on the other hand, had not been a writer before the war; she had worked as an assistant to her husband, Louis Jouvet, in the French theater. After the war, however, she felt compelled to write of her experience at Auschwitz, not as transparent testimony but as a crafted and multigenred work of prose and poetry that would make her readers *see* Auschwitz; the result was the three-volume *Auschwitz and After*, much of which was written in 1946 and 1947 but not published until 1965. Delbo's last work, *Days and Memory*, was a more retrospective work published the year of her death, 1985 (*Days and Memory*, trans. with a preface by Rosette Lamont [Marlboro, Vt.: Marlboro Press, 1990]; rpt. in *Art from the Ashes*, ed. Lawrence Langer [New York: Oxford University Press, 1995]).

13. Delbo, in Rittner and Roth, *Different Voices*, p. 99.

14. The most well-known theoretical articulation of permeable ego-boundaries and feminine ego is Nancy Chodorow, *The Reproduction of Mothering: Psychoanalysis and the Sociology of Gender* (Berkeley: University of California Press, 1979).

15. Delbo, *Auschwitz and After*, p. 39. All further page references appear in the text.

16. All page numbers to citations from *Days and Memory* refer to the excerpt collected in Langer, ed., *Art from the Ashes*.

17. See Freud's *Mourning and Melancholia* (1920) in *SE*, vol. 14, for a discussion of the melancholic's transformation of anger at the abandoning object into self-anger and self-abasement. For an elaboration of masochism, melancholy, and hatred in terms of gender difference, see Julia Kristeva, *Black Sun* (New York: Columbia University Press, 1989).

18. Delbo, *Days and Memory*, p. 89.

19. In her parable of Tancred, Caruth refers to understanding trauma as the trauma of another; the wound that speaks is the voice of the other. This is understood in two ways: the other within the self retains the memory of the trauma of one's own past, or, and this reading Caruth favors, one's own trauma is tied up with the trauma of another. Thus she remarks on "the way in which trauma may lead, therefore, to the encounter with another, through the very possibility and surprise of listening to another's wound" (*Unclaimed Experience: Trauma, Narrative, and History* [Baltimore: Johns Hopkins University Press, 1996], p. 8). Both possibilities are played out in Delbo's writings.

20. Interestingly, in another fragment that also seems to mark a difference, a **son** tells of his **gratitude** in having been at Auschwitz because it allowed him to share the Holocaust experience with his mother, to know and thus identify with the particulars of what she went through, even though she died and he survived. But the son's desire to empathize with the (m)other itself suggests a distance that he wants to close. In contrast, the daughter's desire to protect her mother from a painful knowledge of her own suffering suggests an already existing identification with a good mother, in a reversal that turns her mother into a vulnerable child-version of herself.

21. See Carol Gilligan, *In a Different Voice: Psychological Theory and Women's Development* (Cambridge: Harvard University Press, 1993), which elaborates a gender difference in ethical standards, and Chodorow, *Reproduction of Mothering*, which theorizes a difference in ego structure on the basis of a gendered relation to the maternal object. The major division in feminist theory reflects this shift: on the one hand, the demand for equal rights in an Enlightenment discourse of the universal subject that stresses the sameness between men and women (this position has been critiqued as privileging the male ego-ideal); and, on the other, a "cultural feminism" that insists on an essential difference, whether biological or culturally constructed, that privileges the feminine.

22. In this context, see Joan Ringelheim's provocative discussion of her interviews with women survivors who stressed the importance of female friendships to their survival ("Women and the Holocaust: A Reconsideration of Research," in Rittner and Roth, eds., *Different Voices*, pp. 373–405). Ringelheim first argues that although the women literally survived because the Nazis did not kill them, they lived, in the sense of remained human, through creating substitute families. But in the second and third parts of her essay, written after 1984, Ringelheim revises her earlier conclusion that women bonded more than men in families of friendship. She is particularly disturbed that her former attempt to emphasize friendship among women in the death camps may have led to the "false" conclusion that women's oppression had resulted in a good, encouraging them to develop a culture of friendship. Thus in the third part of her article, she finds that the statistics show that more women than men were deported and murdered. This, however, does not seem to me to diminish her initial conclusion that women psychologically survived better than

men. But in pointing out that "bonding was limited and exclusive," she concludes it was not sufficient to counter the terror of isolation, brutality, and death, as she had first assumed (p. 388). Yet friendships are always limited and exclusive; Delbo's text, which confirms the limitations of bonding, nevertheless insists that female friendships sustained the women. Certainly Delbo's text shows friendship as a light in the darkness of Auschwitz.

The more significant question to be asked, I think, is "Why do women feel the need to tell stories of solidarity and friendship?" The answer that we get from a close reading of Delbo's text is not only that friendship happened but also that in the midst of Auschwitz, the belief in friendship, based on an empathic group identification, served as a container of primal anxieties and a source of support. That women were already predisposed to bond under conditions of oppression, that the relational egostructures psychoanalysts find to be more characteristically feminine may indeed be a consequence of women's relative powerlessness in the dominant culture, does not diminish their value.

23. Tad Borowski, *This Way for the Gas, Ladies and Gentlemen*, trans. Barbara Vedder, introduction by Jan Kott (New York: Penguin, 1992). All further page references will appear in the text.

24. Indeed, we would expect that the political reality, that one's motherland in Poland or one's fatherland in Germany wanted to get rid of one or of the group to which one belonged, to expel or destroy one, would lead to a common fantasy of maternal abandonment, or more radically, of abortion.

25. There is an extremely interesting reference to gendered responses to traumatic violence in a recent note by Jack Raper, on the "Psyart" list-serve network; he refers to "James Glass's study of MPDs [multiple personality disorders] some years back, a book called *Shattered Selves*, a persuasive account of the way MPDs learn to split off in order to separate from the body that is undergoing abuse." This is analogous to the splitting that Delbo vividly describes that enables her to survive. The note also points out that "male victims tend to end up in prison whereas the female ones end up in mental hospitals." This difference seems to conform to the distinction between the melancholic turning of anger against the self, which leads to depression, as I discussed in Delbo's text, in contrast to the violent explosion of rage projected outward in Borowski's. But also, one would have to take into account another important asymmetry in these texts: Borowski's complicity as a member of the Canada, which adds the guilt and shame of the perpetrator to the forces that drive his rage.

26. Hannah Arendt, quoted in Hewitt, "Bad Seed," p. 76.

Chapter 8

Class and Gender in Narratives of Passing

VALERIE SMITH

Stories of racial passing have long captivated the attention of American viewers and readers.[1] These accounts of characters who are "legally" black yet light-skinned enough to live as white have fascinated the American imagination for a variety of reasons. I suspect that they compel, at least in part, because they force the reader to confront a range of conflicts that are raised but inadequately explored in the classic texts within the genre. In this article I consider some of these paradoxes as sites that reveal the interconnections among race, class, and gender in the U.S. context. I locate passing within the discourse of intersectionality because although it is generally motivated by class considerations (people pass primarily in order to partake of the wider opportunities available to those in power) and constructed in racial terms (people describe the passing person as wanting to be white, not

From *Not Just Race, Not Just Gender: Black Feminist Readings* (New York: Routledge, 1998).

wanting to be rich), its consequences are distributed differentially on the basis of gender (women in narrative are more likely to be punished for passing than are men).[2]

I begin by showing how the hierarchization of race and gender in John Stahl's *Imitation of Life* (1934) reinscribes certain conventions of the genre and manipulates spectatorial allegiances. I argue that a reading informed by the theory of intersectionality resists such a narrative and emotional logic.[3] In the second section, I discuss two more recent works that problematize the assumptions of the passing plot: Julie Dash's *Illusions* (1982) and Charles Lane's *True Identity* (1991). These newer texts presuppose to some degree the intersectionality of race and gender and thereby construct passing as a potentially subversive activity.

The narrative trajectories of classic passing texts are typically predetermined; they so fully naturalize certain givens that they mask a range of contradictions inherent within them. For instance, they presuppose that characters who pass for white are betrayers of the black race, and they depend, almost inevitably, upon the association of blackness with self-denial and suffering, and of whiteness with selfishness and material comfort. The combination of these points—passing as betrayal, blackness as self-denial, whiteness as comfort—has the effect of advocating black accommodationism, since the texts repeatedly punish at least this particular form of upward mobility. These texts thus become sites where antiracist and white supremacist ideologies converge, encouraging their black readers to stay in their places.

Jessie Redmon Fauset's 1928 novel *Plum Bun*, for example, associates the aspirations of her protagonist, Angela Murray, with crass materialism and contempt for her race. As a child, Angela often passes with her mother, Mattie, when they are out on the town for the day, although the narrator makes clear that Mattie passes only for convenience and self-indulgence; she has no desire to be white. Here the narrative betrays one of its central tensions. However innocent Mattie's intentions may appear to be, they have dire consequences. She and her husband are both killed off indirectly in the text because of her passing. Moreover, it leads Angela to decide to live her life as a white woman, a decision for which she atones throughout much of the novel.

Given her racial, class, and gender status, Angela can only gain access to white privilege through the agency and good will of a wealthy white man, in this case, a man named Roger Fielding. Fielding does not know that she is black, but he does know that she is poorer than he; as a result, he refuses to marry her and offers only to set her up as his mistress. After Roger ends their relationship and dashes Angela's hopes, she recognizes the limitations of her desires; eventually she reveals her racial identity and is allowed to share her life with the black man she loves.

In the Murray family, racial politics and narrative approbation follow loosely the distribution of pigmentation. While Angela develops an appreciation for material comforts from her light-complexioned mother, her darker father and sister (Junius and Virginia) are more concerned with using their talents to uplift the race. Angela is constructed as merely self-indulgent; Virginia is virtuous, diligent, and bold. A fiercely committed race woman, she tells a friend who considers moving to South America in order to avoid racism in the United States that:

> We've all of us got to make up our minds to the sacrifice of something. I mean something more than just the ordinary sacrifices in life, not so much for the sake of the next generation as for the sake of some principle, for the sake of some immaterial quality like pride or intense self-respect or even a saving complacency; a spiritual tonic which the race needs perhaps just as much as the body might need iron or whatever it does need to give the proper kind of resistance. There are some things which an individual might want, but which he'd just have to give up forever for the sake of the more important whole.[4]

Angela's materialistic goals jeopardize her financial stability; Virginia possesses greater security because she uses her talents productively and lives within her means. Her virtues notwithstanding, Virginia endures the humiliation of a sister who is unable to acknowledge her publicly. However, once Angela accepts her race, she and Virginia are reconciled and Virginia is reunited with her true love.

Given the legal basis of the notion of passing, it is not surprising that classic passing narratives seem ideologically self-contradictory. Narratives of passing, whether written by African-American or by white authors, presume the African-American internalization of the "one-drop" and the related "hypo-descent" rules. According to the one-drop rule, individuals are classified as black if they possess one black ancestor; the "hypo-descent" rule, acknowledged historically by the federal courts, the U.S. census bureau, and other agencies of the state, assigned people of mixed racial origin to the status of the subordinated racial group. Originally deployed as a means of supporting the slavocracy and the Jim Crow system of racial segregation, then, these "rules" were internalized by African Americans who converted them from mere signifiers of shame to markers of pride.

The accommodationist impulse that seems to unify the racist and antiracist agendas is frequently enabled through the figure of the black mother. The limited opportunities that "home" represents are often associated with the self-sacrificing maternal body, where conservative racial and gender ideologies are typically lodged in narrative. The sentimental weight this figure bears in works such as the novel and two film versions of *Imitation of Life* (the other being Douglas Sirk's 1959 remake), Oscar Micheaux's *God's Stepchildren* (1938), and Elia Kazan's *Pinky* (1949) obstructs a resistant spectatorial gaze. Because these works all conflate the light-skinned daughters' rejection of their own subordinate status with their rejection of their mothers, readers or viewers are manipulated into criticizing rather than endorsing these non-compliant light-skinned women.

Additionally, while the logic of these texts for the most part condemns passing as a strategy for resisting racism, in fact, several actually use this racialized politic specifically to restrain the options and behavior of black women. Passing male characters can either be re-educated and returned to the bosom of home and community to uplift the race, or they can remain in the white world and be constructed with some measure of condescension, ambivalence, or even approval.[5] Passing women characters, on the other hand, are either re-educated and returned to the bosom of home and community, or they receive some extreme form of punishment such as death or the sacrifice of a loved one.[6]

A more general paradox or conflict exists in the very syntax of the formulation "legally black yet physically white," for the phrase polarizes the two terms and invokes ostensibly stable categories of racial difference. Systems of racial oppression depend upon the notion that one can distinguish between the empowered and disempowered populations. Those boundaries that demarcate racial difference are best policed by monitoring the congress between members of opposite sexes of different races. Yet the bodies of mixed-race characters defy the binarisms upon which constructions of racial identity depend. Signs of the inescapable fact of miscegenation, they testify to the illicit or exploitative sexual relations between black women and white men or to the historically unspeakable relations between white women and black men. The light-skinned black body thus both invokes and transgresses the boundaries between the races and the sexes that structure the American social hierarchy. It indicates a contradiction between appearance and "essential" racial identity within a system of racial distinctions based upon differences presumed to be visible.

Black Female Spectatorship and Imitation of Life (1934)

Based on Fannie Hurst's best-selling novel of the same name, John Stahl's *Imitation of Life* enjoyed extraordinary popularity in its day. Yet its reliance upon stereotypic depictions of the black mother as mammy provoked widespread criticism on the part of its contemporaneous black and other anti-racist viewers and of early critics of black images in Hollywood film. More recently, it has attracted the attention of feminist film critics and theorists because of the way it situates race within the context of the maternal melodrama.[7]

While there may appear to be a veritable industry of *Imitation of Life* criticism, most focuses on Douglas Sirk's 1959 remake. Judith Butler's 1990 essay centers on this version as does Lucy Fischer's 1991 volume, *Imitation of Life*, which contains essays, reviews, and the continuity script. Indeed, among recent studies of the *Imitation of Life* phenomenon, only Sandy Flitterman-Lewis's "Imitation(s) of Life: The Black Woman's Double Determination as Troubling 'Other,' " and Lauren Berlant's "National Brands/National Body: *Imitation of Life*," pay equal attention to the two films.[8]

Sirk's film has attracted more notice partly because of its comparative stylistic sophistication. As Fischer has written, the film "was released during the decline of the classical cinema and the birth of the modernist movement. . . . *Imitation*, with its exaggerated generic codes, embraced the art film's ironic stance toward transparent style."[9] Indeed, critics have commented on the extent to which, in Sirk's remake, imitation becomes the dominant thematic; the self-reflexive quality of this film in particular but of his other work as well exposes the artifice of the medium as well as the decay and disintegration of the social relations that organize contemporary culture.[10] Moreover, the film's preoccupation with issues of artificiality makes it especially suitable for arguments that explore the cultural construction and contestation of gender and race.

The comparative sophistication of the 1959 *Imitation* notwithstanding, I find the 1934 version better suited to my purposes here. The cynical Sirk remake narrativizes its status as spectacle, allowing viewers and critics to keep it at arm's length, bracket their emotional responses, and read its strategies primarily as comments on the constructedness of ideologies of race, gender, sexuality, and performance.[11] In contrast, the relative "sincerity" of the Stahl film implicates viewers more directly in the effects of specific constructions of race and gender relations; a critique of the project of this film thus brings sharply into focus the work of the resistant spectator in the passing narrative.

My interest in the film derives from the relationship between the main or white plot, dominated by the top-billed white star, Claudette Colbert, as Bea Pullman, and the subordinate or black plot, which features Louise Beavers as Delilah, the black mother, and Fredi Washington as her daughter, Peola. Like the book upon which it is based and the 1959 remake, this version of *Imitation of Life* is fundamentally concerned with the problematic of the white working mother and advocates the return of white women to their domestic spaces and relations. However, these issues are raised much more explicitly both in the novel and in the 1959 remake. In the 1934 version the anxiety about Bea's career and choices remains largely absent from the plot within which she figures centrally. Here the mother-daughter relationship in the main plot is idealized, if not made comedic. Tensions surrounding motherhood, class mobility, and abandonment are displaced onto the black plot, which performs the emotional labor in the film much as Delilah in Bea's household performs the visible domestic labor. Bea, the absent, largely ephemeral white mother is reconstituted in Delilah, the hyperembodied, present black mother. Moreover, the anger reserved for women who leave their place in this film is directed at Peola, who wants more for herself than the opportunities that segregationist U.S. culture will allow her. Gender and racial ideology are thus profoundly connected; Peola's character bears the weight not only of her abandonment of Delilah, but also of Bea's "abandonment" of Jessie.

And yet, while these displacements and the content of the plots may presuppose the interdependence of the lives of the two women and their daughters, the strategies by which meaning is conveyed—structure, tonal shifts, soundtrack, and camera work—differentiate and hierarchize the two plots. This stylistic disarticulation constructs gender as tenor, race as vehicle, so that the problematics of race in the film are deployed as mere metaphors for gender relations.

I argue here that the film conflates differences within and between black and white women through the relation between the two plots. I suggest, moreover, that a resistant, black feminist reading disaggregates the film's construction of the nexus of race and gender and refuses the dominance of the putative main plot in order to expose the various ways black women's bodies are used to teach whites on both sides of the camera a lesson. This reading is consistent with Toni Morrison's discussion of the functions that Africanist characters have served in U.S. cultural discourse, for it shows how the black characters are used as "surrogates and enablers," in order to "limn out and enforce the invention and implications of whiteness" and to allow the white subject to meditate upon his or her own humanity.[12] One need only look at the uses to which African Americans are typically put in much Hollywood and independent cinema today to realize that these constructions persist.

Imitation of Life is the rags-to-riches story of Bea Pullman, a white widow and mother of a daughter named Jessie. In the opening sequence, Bea, the Colbert character, is crumbling under the conflicting demands of mothering and working in the maple syrup sales business. As the film begins, she struggles to bathe and dress Jessie and fix breakfast when she receives a call from an important customer. While she speaks on the phone, the coffee boils over, the oatmeal begins to burn, and her daughter calls out for her. The intimate opening scene thus soon gives way to a frenzy of activity; Bea races up and down a flight of stairs, juggling several responsibilities and performing none of them well. She is clearly not in her place and doesn't even seem to know what that place is.

At the precise moment when Bea seems most overwhelmed, the massive, nurturant, tireless Delilah Johnson, played by Louise Beavers, appears at her door, offering to come live with her and take care of her and her daughter in exchange for nothing more than food and shelter for herself and her fair-skinned daughter, Peola. In contrast to Bea's frenetic quality, Delilah enters the film circumscribed in her place. The shot-reverse-shot editing of the scene of their meeting underscores this observation. When Delilah rings the bell, Bea runs down the stairs to answer it. The camera focuses on Bea's face as she looks toward the doorway and then a tracking shot follows her across the kitchen to the door. The next shot quickly zooms in on Delilah's beaming face framed by the screen door against a softly lit pastoral background. The effect here is to momentarily freeze Delilah's face in a nostalgic, photographic stillness.

The camera here suggests more than simply the women's mutual acknowledgment. Rather, the matching of the tracking shot with the close-up, zoom, reverse shot contrasts the two women's positions, thereby establishing the disparate functions each serves in the film. While Bea is associated with economic mobility and progress, Delilah is immediately constructed as a figure of stability, and of timeless, mythic qualities. And of course, the myth she conjures up is that of the mammy in the plantation South. Unable to negotiate her way through the urban setting—her inability to distinguish Astor Street from Astor Avenue is what leads her to Bea's home in the first place—she is eager to assume the position of an unpaid laborer. Once Delilah joins Bea's household and assumes primary responsibility for her home and child, Bea's life becomes immediately more organized and manageable. The parallel households become one, with the two women forming, to borrow Lauren Berlant's term, "a quasi-companionate couple."[13]

But Delilah gives Bea more than domestic assistance. She shares with her the recipe for her irresistible pancakes, a product that Bea markets so successfully that in time it makes her a millionaire. As her fortunes improve, Bea "generously" bestows upon Delilah twenty percent of the Aunt Delilah Corporation, and promises her that she'll be rich. Bea offers Delilah her own house and car, and the following exchange takes place:

DELILAH: You gonna send me away, Miss Bea? I can't live wid ya? Oh, honey chile, please don' send me away—don' do that to me.
BEA: Don't you want your own house?
D.: No'm. How'm I gonna take care of you and Miss Jessie if I ain' here? Let me an' Peola stay same's we been doin.' I's you' cook an' I want to stay you' cook.
B.: Well, of course you can stay, Delilah. I only thought, now that the money's coming in,—and, after all, Delilah, it's all from your pancake flour.
D.: I gives it to you honey. I makes you a present of it. You'se welcome.

This scene is immediately followed by a shot of boxes of pancake flour, emblazoned with a picture of Delilah's beaming face, topped with a crisp chef's hat, sliding down the rollway of a packing machine and then swirling into a bin filled with thousands of these boxes. This shot then fades into one of a large neon sign that advertises the product. First it reads "Aunt Delilah's

Pancake Flour: 32,000,000 Packages sold last year." Then it flashes an image of Delilah flipping pancakes.

The juxtaposition of these two scenes is significant for a variety of reasons. The content of the conversation between Bea and Delilah recalls the static quality of Delilah's initial appearance in the film. A domestic servant in the 1930s, she is the apologists' vision of the plantation mammy revisited, devoid of any desire other than to care for her white mistress, even after emancipation. As such, she offers the perfect justification for black repression. The symbolic power of this image is underscored by the ensuing shots in which we see how fully the type has captivated the popular imagination. The repeated image of the face on the box not only signals the passage of time and marks metaphorically Bea's accomplishments. The proliferation of the image shows as well the vast marketability of the mammy as type.

Bea's business accomplishments are accompanied by personal gratification. The few glimpses we see of her interactions with her daughter indicate that the two women take great delight in each other. Moreover, at one of her gala parties, she meets ichthyologist Stephen Archer, with whom she falls passionately in love. Indeed, the romance that ensues is presented as having reawakened her sexuality and womanhood; realizing where her priorities ought to lie, she stays away from the office for weeks on end, basking in Stephen's affections.

But while Bea's life proceeds from one fulfilling experience to the next, Delilah's sufferings proliferate, due to her tortured relationship with Peola. However easily Delilah may accept her role, Peola refuses to do so. Each time the movie attempts to soar into an idyllic fantasy about Bea's charmed personal or professional future, Peola is there to return it to earth with her relentless demands for equality and acceptance.

This sort of segregation of plot function is evident even as the opening credits roll. The first piece of music we hear might be identified as Delilah's theme: the opening phrase of "Nobody knows the trouble I seen," sung by a choir. The phrase is then repeated in an orchestral arrangement, heavy with strings, up an interval of a third. The soundtrack then segues into what I call Bea's theme, a light, bouncy melody dominated by harp and arpeggios. The phrase from the spiritual conjures up a certain sadness; the refusal to complete the line (with "Nobody knows but Jesus") leaves the singer and the listener in a state of desiring. In contrast, Bea's theme demonstrates greater musical range and is allowed to reach its completion. The tension between pleasure and pain on which the narrative depends is thus anticipated by the juxtaposition of the musical themes.

In the narrative, scenes of pleasure featuring Bea and Jessie frequently alternate with those of Delilah's and Peola's suffering. For instance, after Bea has paid off all the debts she incurred in order to open her first business, she and Delilah fantasize about how they will spend their money when they become rich. Bea dreams of taking a vacation, but Delilah only wants to be able to get off her feet. The placidity of the scene in which the two women share their secret hopes is disrupted when Peola enters, crying, "I'm not black! I'm not black! I won't be black! Jessie called me that!" Despite Bea's reproaches, Delilah insists that Peola must learn to accept her place, saying, "You gotta learn to take it and you might as well begin now." When Bea asks Jessie how she could say "such a mean, cruel thing to Peola," Delilah responds, "It ain't her fault, Miss Bea. It ain't your'n and it ain't mine. I don't know rightly where the blame lies. It can't be our Lord's. It's got me puzzled." This is the first of a number of episodes in which Peola expresses her anger at her situation in the form of anger at her mother. She cries, "You! You! It's 'cause you're black! You make me black!" Of course, her accusations allude to the laws governing slavery, by which the child "followed the condition" of the mother.

The camera work in this scene contributes to the way we respond to the various characters' situations. Bea and Jessie are shot in medium two-shots, either facing each other or standing side-by-side watching Delilah console Peola. This choice distances viewers from them and, in turn, distances them from the intensity of Delilah's and Peola's interaction and Delilah's suffering, even though Jessie precipitated it. In contrast, the medium two-shots of Delilah and Peola emphasize the discord between the two: while Delilah cradles her to her capacious bosom, Peola insults her. The close-ups of Delilah register her pain at and acceptance of her daughter's verbal abuse and encourage viewers to identify with her suffering rather than with Peola's rebelliousness.

This dynamic between a sequence that celebrates Bea's achievements only to culminate in Peola's anger and violence is replicated throughout the film. It's as if Peola and Delilah are repeatedly scapegoated. Their circumstances provide the source of viewer tears. Moreover, their respective frustrations and hurts pay for Bea's yearnings to rise above her place. For instance, in the next scene when Jessie is home sick from school on a stormy day, we see Bea caring for her at her bedside in an idyllic moment of maternal nurturance. Meanwhile, Delilah goes to the school to take Peola her scarf and coat. When she arrives and asks for Peola, she learns that the child has been passing. Furious at having been found out, Peola says to her mother once outside the classroom door, "I hate you . . . I hate you."

After Bea's business has made her and Delilah wealthy and they move into a townhouse in Manhattan, Bea throws an elaborate party at which she meets the man who becomes her fiancé. Delilah vicariously enjoys the party from their downstairs apartment, but Peola's position below the stairs causes her to suffer. Here Bea's social success is intercut with the tense scenes between Delilah and Peola; Peola repeatedly refuses the comfort and company Delilah offers her. The sequence ends in a teary scene between the two women in which Peola agrees to attend a "Negro" school in the south. Delilah's stoic acceptance of her daughter's contempt and her articulation of Christian resignation make explicit the religious subtext of her characterization and enhance the sentimental appeal of her character.

The scene in which Jessie comes home from her boarding school for vacation and meets Stephen Archer for the first time promises to be another idealized moment. That encounter, too, ends abruptly when Delilah rushes in with the news that Peola has disappeared from the colored teachers' college she attends. Delilah and Bea leave immediately to find Peola, and discover her working as a cashier in a coffee shop near the school. Once again, Delilah unmasks Peola publicly. This time, after they return home, Peola announces her intention to pass, to deny her blackness and her mother. After a long, tearful scene, Delilah agrees to let her daughter go, and dies soon thereafter. A contrite, distraught Peola returns home in time for the funeral, and hurls herself upon the coffin, but the only reconciliation possible is symbolic.

In contrast, just after Delilah swears to renounce her daughter, Bea meets Jessie on the stairs and affirms the unassailability of their relationship. The movie threatens to rupture Bea and Jessie's vow. While Bea and Delilah are off looking for Peola, Jessie is falling in love with Stephen, her mother's lover. Clearly, like Peola, Jessie no doubt wishes as well to do away with her mother. But since Delilah in fact does die, there is no real need for Bea to do so. Instead, when Bea learns of this conflict, she resolves that nothing and no one can come between her and her daughter, so she breaks her engagement to Stephen. In the final shot of the film, Bea and Jessie embrace while Bea repeats the lines that Jessie speaks at the beginning of the film: "I want my quack quack. I want my quack quack." Sandy Flitterman-Lewis glosses this ending usefully when she writes:

[Bea's] nostalgic tone indicates a yearning for that untroubled unity, the simplicity of mother-daughter sharing which she has attempted to recapture through her sacrifice of romance. This circularity signifies a reassertion of the utopian maternal which in fact structures the entire film; the atavistic reference to an originary moment of dual reciprocity implies an isolation from all social context, from all difference and disturbance.[14]

Although the film constructs a symmetrical household with two single mothers and two daughters, in fact the emotional logic sets up an analogy between the white mother and the black daughter. As the novel and the 1959 film demonstrate, the situations of these two women invite comparison more easily than do those of either the two mothers or the two daughters: these are the two women who leave their rightful place; these are the two who must be returned to those places at the end of the film.

The film denies the legitimacy of both Bea's claim for a public life and Peola's for social equality. But it requires Peola's punishment to stand in for Bea's; this also explains why her desires for independence and equality are constructed as inseparable from her rejection of her mother's love. Her desire is shown to be analogous to what is seen as Bea's neglect of her daughter, Jessie, and her punishment is designed to teach both her and Bea a lesson.

In order to establish Peola's story as a metaphor for Bea's, the film glosses over the radical differences between the two women's circumstances. It's one thing for Bea to stay in her place (by the end she is a millionaire), another altogether for Peola to stay where she belongs as the daughter of a black domestic worker. Put another way, this structuring device depends simultaneously upon the spectacularization of difference—in this case, racial difference—and the denial of the meanings that historically have attached to those differences.

To the extent that the film attempts to disaggregate class and race from gender identity, a resistant, black feminist analysis of this film would refuse such a denial of the implications of class and racial difference for gender identity. This is not to say that such ideological commitments would protect an oppositional viewer from the sentimental effects that the film produces; however, redefining these connections would disrupt, at least partially, the overdetermined logic of the film.

Clearly, a resistant spectator would question the premise of the film that either Bea or Peola should remain in her place. Likewise, such a spectator would challenge the inevitability of the film's logic, that the desire for racial equality is tantamount to a desire to betray either the race or the mother. An intersectional critique emphasizes as well the extent to which race and gender are linked in both plots, witness the incommensurate distribution of consequences. Both Bea and Peola refuse to remain in the positions to which they have been relegated. But race and class privilege provide a safety net below which Bea cannot fall. Peola's class advantages ultimately cannot protect her from the power of race and gender inequities.

Contemporary Revisions of the Passing Plot

During the party at which Bea meets Stephen, Delilah and Bea meet in the hallway of the mansion in which they live. Delilah descends the stairs to her quarters and Bea goes back up to the party. Indeed, throughout the party Peola and Delilah remain in their downstairs apartment; the situation is rendered all the more problematic by the fact that Delilah is dressed in a flowing gown, as if to enjoy Bea's party vicariously. The staircase here, leading up and leading down, bifurcates the screen into Bea's realm and Delilah's. It is a visual reminder of the construction of stable racial identities and differences upon which this classic passing narrative depends.

In contrast, recent texts that center on the passing plot eschew the sorts of rigid divisions that inform their antecedents. Julie Dash's *Illusions* and Charles Lane's *True Identity* seek to emancipate passing as a phenomenon from its overdetermined plots, deploying it instead to unmask the interconnections of racial and gender ideologies. By invoking and subverting traditional uses of the narrative, the films inscribe the position of spectatorial resistance.

ILLUSIONS

Julie Dash's *Illusions* centers on Mignon Dupree, a black woman studio executive in 1940s Hollywood who uses her ability to pass in order to try to bring stories to the screen that will reveal the untold histories of people of color. Unlike her narrative antecedents, for whom passing is constructed as an all-or-nothing, reactionary proposition, Mignon passes discontinuously; the film suggests that she is motivated to pass by a desire to serve her race.

For not only does she have a black lover and remain in close contact with her family, but she works to get fair wages for Esther Jeeter, a black singer hired to match her voice to the image of a lip-synching white star. At the end of the film, Lt. Bedsford, the white male colleague who has been sexually harassing Mignon, confronts her with his discovery of her secret; however, we are left not with Mignon's humiliation, but with her passionate vow to stay in Hollywood and continue fighting.

Unlike other passing characters, whose fates are frequently marked and sealed symbolically with signs of their fallen or marginal status, Mignon is associated with signs that connect her to African American cultural history and practice.[15] When we first see her, the camera focuses on the v-shaped black and white pattern in her suit and the black veil that partially conceals her face. As Phyllis Rauch Klotman reminds us, during World War II, "for African Americans the double 'V' (official NAACP sign) meant victory over racism at home as well as victory abroad." Klotman notes further that the veil recalls Du Bois's famous metaphor for the color line, a barrier Mignon transgresses more or less at will.[16] The multiplicity of meanings that attach to these symbols point to the nuances of her characterization. Her representation contrasts with a figure such as Naomi, the protagonist of Oscar Micheaux's *God's Stepchildren*, who appears on screen twice marked with an "x"—once over her head on her hat, and once on the straps of her evening dress across her back—as if to emphasize her inability to escape her fate as a woman marked by her presumptive mixed racial origins.

The anticlimactic nature of Bedsford's accusation and the iconography associated with Mignon both signal Dash's revisionist approach to her subject. Typically in passing texts, the precariousness of the character's decision provides the central tension of the narrative. Like the character, the reader or viewer is haunted by the imminence of exposure and punishment. In *Illusions*, in contrast, passing is only one of a series of deceptions with which the film is concerned. Chief among these is the constructedness of the medium itself.

As the film begins, Mignon quotes from Ralph Ellison's *Shadow and Act*, thereby framing the film with a reminder that cinema itself is only illusory:

To direct an attack upon Hollywood would indeed be to confuse portrayal with action, the image with reality. In the beginning was not the shadow but the act, and the province of Hollywood is not action, but Illusion.

Her remarks are juxtaposed with Lieutenant Bedsford's press release about the centrality of cinema to the war effort. For Bedsford, a Signal Corps officer assigned to Hollywood to produce war films, representations of the war are as significant as is the war "itself"; he sees motion pictures as crucial to the work of the military. Unlike Ellison cum Mignon, who warns against confusing portrayal and action, he emphasizes their interdependence:

> As a grim and determined nation marshals its manpower and its vast material resources to meet the totalitarian challenge to the democratic way of life, the motion picture industry is privileged to stand in the very forefront of the united American endeavor. . . . The industry's broad sphere of service in the war effort is perhaps without parallel. The fact that no other medium is so adapted to the task of building and sustaining national morale on both the fighting and home fronts, readily attests to the motion picture's essentiality.

The point of greatest narrative interest and tension is the scene in the rerecording stage, for there the passing plot and the exploration of cinematic illusion are brought together. Mignon embodies in the extreme the way that black women in particular (and members of all disenfranchised groups in general) depend upon masquerade to protect themselves and exercise power. As if to emphasize this aspect of her character, she functions as a sort of ventriloquist throughout the film. We know about Julius, her lover, and her mother because they speak through her.[17] In this scene in the rerecording stage, where sound and image must be matched, Dash alludes to the significance of masquerade in the production of cinematic illusion as well as racial and gender identity.

In the first clip from the film on which the sound engineer and his assistant are working, white starlet Lila Grant sings and dances with two male performers. The synch here is fine, but this sequence signals the dilemma at the heart of the situation as it unfolds. Here, Lila lip synchs to a tune by Ella Fitzgerald.[18] The blond starlet's appeal is enhanced by the fact that she scoffs at the cello and songs "soft and mellow," preferring instead the power of the "rhythm man." Fitzgerald herself is of course disappeared from the frame altogether; her voice and the spontaneity to which the lyrics allude are marketable on film, but her body and bodies like it are at odds with the image of womanhood in which the medium traffics.[19]

The overdubbing of Lila's second song with Esther Jeeter's voice dramatizes the evacuation of black women's power and the mutually constitutive relations between both black and white womanhood and race and gender identity. Esther's talents and labor, both invisible within the finished product, maintain Lila's position on and off screen. To the extent that the film allows for black female subjectivity and experience, they circulate within the marketplace only when they can be packaged within a real or illusory white woman's body. Likewise, the identity of the idealized white female subject relies upon rendering invisible her dependency upon the labor and identities of black women.

Dash's dramatization of the race and gender politics of this use of over-dubbing critiques white power and visibility. However, it does not presuppose an essentialized, authentic black female subject. By choosing to have Esther herself lip synch over Fitzgerald's vocals, Dash concedes her own implication in the construction and production of black women's identity. Problematizing her own position, she reminds us that her film is no more "real" than the one on which Mignon works.

TRUE IDENTITY

Directed by Charles Lane, *True Identity* revises the passing plot to highlight the role of performance in and destabilize constructions of racial difference. *True Identity* centers on Miles Pope (played by Lenny Henry, a black British comic known for his impersonations). Miles is an aspiring actor in Manhattan who dreams of being cast as a dramatic lead and fantasizes about playing Othello. However, the limited availability of serious dramatic roles for blacks in theatre makes it hard for him to find suitable work. In an early scene, Miles first resists and then capitulates to his acting coach's insistence that he play a pimp "more black . . . more Afro-American . . . more Harlemesque." This scene questions the meaning of authentic blackness, an issue to which the film returns repeatedly. The coach attempts to prompt Miles to play the part of a "real" black person, but true blackness to him is entirely artificial, constructed out of the images that commonly circulate as black in popular representations of black culture. Miles's character in the film undermines this conception of black character; he seeks a way to perform black masculinity as something other than a crotch-grabbing pimp who lives in Harlem.

Miles's agent Harvey sends him to Florida for what Miles believes will be a starring role in a production of *A Raisin in the Sun*. But as it turns out, Miles has been cast as a California raisin in a breakfast cereal commercial. On his return flight, he discovers that he has been seated next to Leland Carver (Frank Langella), the owner of the theatre at which the current New York production of *Othello* is being staged. The plane comes close to crashing as it approaches Kennedy Airport; in the moments of panic that precede what appears to be almost certain death, Carver confesses to Miles that he is really Frank Luchino, a Mafia kingpin who is believed to have been killed in an explosion years before. Thanks to the wonders of plastic surgery, he has taken on a new life and established a new identity as Carver, a financier and arts philanthropist.

Miraculously, the plane does not crash. Carver and Miles both realize that Miles knows too much about Carver's past and that his life is now endangered. Indeed, Carver's assistant, Anthony, a hold-over from his days as a full-time mobster, tries to kill Miles before he can leave the airport.

Because the police and the FBI cannot protect him, Miles goes to his best friend, Dwayne, a makeup artist (played by director Lane), for help. Dwayne makes him up as a white man so that he can hide from Carver and his hit men; Dwayne encourages the reluctant Miles to think of this deception as "the performance for his life."

When Miles, in white face, returns to his apartment to pack his bags, he meets and accidentally kills Carver's hit man, La Motta. As he contemplates his next move, Carver's deputy, Anthony, breaks in, assumes that Miles in white face is La Motta and La Motta, whom he has never seen, is Miles's neighbor. Thus Miles's alternative identity is born. To maintain his disguise, he must feign not merely the gestures and inflections of a "white" man, but more specifically, he must imitate those associated with media representations of Italian-American gangsters.

The rest of the film is given over largely to Miles's attempts, as La Motta, to pretend to pursue himself, as Miles, while he really seeks evidence that will identify Carver as Luchino. He reveals his "true identity" to Carver's black female interior decorator, Kristi (Anne Marie Johnson), with whom he falls in love, and persuades her to help him search Carver's house. Meanwhile, Dwayne helps him stage his own murder, so that in the short run, Carver believes that Miles really is dead.

As a result of an elaborate sequence of events, Miles is cast as Othello in the production at Carver's theatre. When Carver discovers that Miles is still alive, he plots his assassination on stage during the opening night performance. But Miles, Dwayne, and the FBI successfully thwart his plan; Carver is unmasked and finally captured.

Like *Illusions*, *True Identity* dismantles several of the inevitabilities that have become associated historically with the passing plot. First, it breaks up the conventional associations of passing with the boundary between black and white to show that it is a phenomenon that may be deployed strategically within a specific racial group. Frank Luchino/Leland Carver does not simply assume the identity of a legitimate businessman. An Italian American by birth, he passes as a white Anglo-Saxon Protestant philanthropist complete with suburban mansion, sophisticated blond wife (Peggy Lipton), and restrained inflections and polished diction. His bilinguality or biculturalism is revealed during his conversations with Anthony and "LaMotta." In these scenes his gestures become more emphatic, and his speech is characterized by the dropped final "g," as well as the intonations, the sharp dentals, and the profusion of expletives associated with ethnic New York (especially Italian-American) stereotypes. This use of Luchino/Carver has the potential to complicate monolithic constructions of whiteness. However, its satiric potential is undermined by the reliance upon Italian-American stereotypes in the constitution of Luchino's "true identity," especially within a film that critiques the conflation of black stereotypes with "real" black experience.

Second, like Mignon's, Miles's passing is discontinuous; it does not conform to the all-or-nothing model upon which the passing plot typically depends. Granted, Miles's options are rather more limited than are those of his fair-skinned antecedents, since his ability to pass is entirely artificial (he only looks white when he wears a wig and makeup). Nevertheless, he is shown to have more control over his alternatives than do passing characters in earlier texts, given that he can change racial identification more or less at will.

Third, Miles's decision to pass is not associated automatically with betrayal of the race. His decision to pass is motivated by the impulse to self-preservation. Yet he remains committed to a politics of racial solidarity, as evidenced in a sequence involving two taxicabs. Shortly after Miles assumes his identity as a white man, he watches a well-dressed black man try and fail to hail a taxicab on a New York street. Miles stands behind him and raises his hand; the next cabdriver stops immediately for Miles, who yields the taxi to the darker man. This scene assures the viewer that Miles has not turned his back on the indignities to which African Americans are routinely subjected, even though he has become "white." Moreover, it gestures to "real world" racism within a context where racial identity is being per-formed.[20]

When the next taxi arrives, a white woman tries to claim that she saw it first. After a brief struggle both leap in and give the driver contradictory directions. As the taxi pulls off, the woman looks at Miles, "reads" him as white and mid-dle class, and tries to figure out why he looks familiar. Eventually she decides that she must recognize him from the offices of Merrill Lynch. Rather than trading on white skin privilege to bond with a woman who he suspects would recoil from him under other circumstances, Miles slips into "black style" and tells her he has just gotten out of prison for robbing a bank in Queens. The ter-rified woman leaps from the taxi at the next opportunity.

Although this scene is played for comic effect, it serves to mark the lim-its of Miles's commitment to his performance and it reminds us of the power of the cultural narratives of race and gender from which we can never fully escape. The fact that the protagonist is an actor and his best friend a make-up artist highlights the significance of performance in the con-struction of racial identity in the film. The media may construct blackness according to certain types which, like all stereotypes, have some basis in the historical circumstances of real people. But these images are only part of the story. Miles's performance as pimp, Othello, Darryl Brown (James Brown's fictional brother), Frank La Motta, indeed, even Lenny Henry's performance as Miles Pope himself, points to a range of black (and indeed white) types and indicates the extent to which racial identity is shaped by issues of class, region, and nation.

Although Miles chooses political and racial solidarity over assimilation, the film seems to deconstruct a unifying, authentic notion of black identity. Yet even as *True Identity* challenges the binary opposition between black and white and the association of the black underclass with racial authenticity, it allows familiar correspondences between women's appearance and subjec-tivity to persist without interrogation. The diminutive Dwayne has a pen-chant for large black women, a predilection that allows the film to return repeatedly to visual and verbal images of over-sexed, corpulent, mouthy, dark-skinned women. The women to whom the film grants intelligence and tact—Kristi and Mrs. Carver (Peggy Lipton)—conform to more conven-tional standards of black and white women's beauty. Thus, *True Identity* employs the passing plot to explore the intersectionality of race and class, but it does not confront adequately the extent to which gender identities are constituted likewise by race and class.

Conclusion

Passing narratives lend themselves to mutually contradictory interpretations. For some readers and critics, these texts are inherently conservative, for they reinscribe the dynamics of white skin privilege by focusing our readerly attention or spectatorial gaze on characters light enough to pass for white. For others, the presence and discussions of such characters are more broadly suggestive. As Hazel Carby has argued, for example, these characters may be read as markers of the space between white privilege and black disempowerment.[21]

I have tried to recuperate certain of these texts through a strategy of reading that resists equating the desire for equality (especially on the part of black women) with the desire to be white. I have been concerned with what it means to punish characters who pass. But I am finally convinced that passing narratives do not provide an unproblematic way out of the discourse of racial essentialism. Passing for white will answer neither the obstacles of misogyny nor those of racism. The conditions of passing narratives are, however, productive sites for considering how the intersectionality of race, class, and gender ideologies are constituted and denied; not only do bodies that pass function as markers of sexual and racial transgression, but they signal as well the inescapable class implications of crossing these boundaries.

NOTES

1. The idea of the "passing plot" encompasses many different kinds of stories. I use the term to refer to narratives that focus on the consequences of being genotypically black for a character or characters who pass for white, at least intermittently. I have in mind novels and films such as William Dean Howells's *An Imperative Duty* (1891), Mark Twain's *Pudd'nhead Wilson* (1894), Charles W. Chesnutt's *The House Behind the Cedars* (1890), James Weldon Johnson's *The Autobiography of an Ex-Colored Man* (1912), Jessie Fauset's *Plum Bun* (1928), Nella Larsen's *Passing* (1929), Fannie Hurst's *Imitation of Life* (1933), Oscar Micheaux's *God's Stepchildren* (1937), Willard Savoy's *Alien Land*, Alfred L. Werker's *Lost Boundaries*, and Elia Kazan's *Pinky* (all 1949).

2. Several insightful essays on the interconnections of race and gender in passing plots have informed my work here, although they focus primarily on written narratives. See especially Barbara Christian, *Black Women Novelists: The Development of a Tradition, 1892–1976* (Westport, Conn.: Greenwood Press, 1980), pp. 35–61; Cheryl A. Wall, "Passing for What?: Aspects of Identity in Nella Larsen's Novels," *Black Ameri-*

can Literature Forum 20 (1986): 97–111; Deborah E. McDowell, "Introduction," in Nella Larsen, *"Quicksand" and "Passing"* (New York: Knopf, 1929; rpt. New Brunswick, N.J.: Rutgers University Press, 1986), pp. ix–xxxvii; and David Van Leer, *The Queening of America: Gay Culture in Straight Society* (New York: Routledge, 1995).

3. I draw here on Manthia Diawara's theory of a resistant black spectator that revises earlier work by Christian Metz, Laura Mulvey, and Stephen Heath, and on bell hooks's essay on black feminist spectatorship. See Diawara, "Black Spectatorship: Problems of Identification and Resistance," *Screen* 29 (Winter 1988): 66–76, and hooks, "The Oppositional Gaze: Black Female Spectators," in *Black Looks: Race and Representation* (Boston: South End Press, 1992), pp. 115–31.

4. Jessie Redmon Fauset, *Plum Bun: A Novel Without a Moral* (New York: Frederick A. Stokes, 1928; rpt. New York: Pandora Press, 1985), p. 69.

5. Consider, for instance, Charles Chesnutt's *John Walden Warwick*, James Weldon Johnson's unnamed protagonist, or Willard Savoy's Kern Roberts.

6. I have in mind here Hurst's and Stahl's Peola, Sirk's Sarah Jane, and Larsen's Clare Kendry, for example.

7. My survey of the literature on *Imitation of Life* shows that more critical attention has been directed to the 1959 remake. Lucy Fischer has written that the 1959 *Imitation* has been the subject of much recent attention because of a heightened interest in French auteurist theory and the emergence of genre studies and an increased attention to melodrama. Moreover, as she writes, "Imitation also profited from the currency of ideological criticism. Its inclusion of dominant black characters in a period of heightened racial awareness attracted writers concerned with color and class. Its status as a 'woman's picture' (focusing on the struggles of two single working mothers) made it ripe for feminist investigation." See "Three-Way Mirror: *Imitation of Life*," in *Imitation of Life*, ed. Lucy Fischer (New Brunswick, N.J.: Rutgers University Press, 1991), p. 5.

8. Judith Butler, "Lana's 'Imitation': Melodramatic Repetition and the Gender Performative," *Genders* 9 (Fall 1990): 1–18; Sandy Flitterman-Lewis, "Imitation(s) of Life: The Black Woman's Double Determination as Troubling 'Other,' " in Fischer, ed., *Imitation of Life*, pp. 325–35; Lauren Berlant, "National Brands/National Body: *Imitation of Life*," in *Comparative American Identities: Race, Sex, and Nationality in the Modern Text*, ed. Hortense J. Spillers (New York: Routledge, 1991), pp. 110–40.

9. Fischer, "Three-Way Mirror," p. 4.

10. For example, see Charles Affron, "Performing Performing: Irony and Affect," *Cinema Journal* 20 (Fall 1980): 42–52; Michael Stern, *Douglas Sirk* (Boston: Twayne, 1979); and Butler, "Lana's 'Imitation.' "

11. Judith Butler's compelling reading of the Sirk remake explores the complexity of "the construction and contestation of the mimetic illusion," but does not critique his constructions of race in terms that exceed those that Sirk establishes.

12. Toni Morrison, *Playing in the Dark: Whiteness and the Literary Imagination* (Cambridge: Harvard University Press, 1992), pp. 51–52.

13. See Berlant, "National Brands/National Body," p. 114.

14. Flitterman-Lewis, "Imitation(s) of Life," pp. 328–29.

15. S. V. Hartman and Farah Jasmine Griffin are not as easily persuaded as I am that Dash submits the passing plot to thorough critique. See their essay, "Are You as Colored as That Negro?: The Politics of Being Seen in Julie Dash's *Illusions*," *Black American Literature Forum* 25 (Summer 1991): 361–74.

16. See Phyllis Klotman, *Screenplays of the African American Experience* (Bloomington: Indiana University Press, 1991), p. 194.

17. We hear the words of Julius's letter because she reads them in a voiceover. We learn about her mother's opinions indirectly by hearing Mignon's one-sided conversation.

18. Fitzgerald fans will recognize her voice, but the film does not identify the singer until the closing credits.

19. I thank David Van Leer for this observation.

20. The encounter with the racist taxi driver is rapidly becoming a racialized primal scene that marks the "reality" of discrimination; in autobiography, criticism, and film, it signals the moment at which subject and reader/spectator wink at each other in mutual acknowledgment that a middle-class black person (generally male) is still "black," his class position notwithstanding. See, for example, Houston A. Baker, Jr., "Caliban's Triple Play," in *"Race," Writing, and Difference*, ed. Henry Louis Gates, Jr. (Chicago: University of Chicago Press, 1986), p. 385, and Cornel West, "Preface," in *Race Matters* (Boston: Beacon Press, 1993), p. x. This kind of scene is especially striking in Alan J. Pakula's screen adaptation of John Grisham's *Pelican Brief* starring Denzel Washington. The race of the male protagonist of the novel is unidentified and thus he is presumed to be white. On the surface, Pakula's film seems to suggest that a black actor can play this part without substantially changing the story. However, Pakula marks the visibility of Washington's blackness by including a scene in which he is unable to get a taxi and by eliminating the erotic tension between the Washington and the Julia Roberts characters.

21. Hazel Carby, *Reconstructing Womanhood: The Emergence of the Afro-American Woman Novelist* (New York: Oxford University Press, 1987), p. 90.

PART 3

The Pleasures of Agency

Chapter 9

Redressing Grievances:
Cross-Dressing Pleasure with the Law

ELISABETH BRONFEN

> The notion of the subject-in-process assumes that we recognize, on the
> one hand, the unity of the subject who submits to a law—the law of
> communication, among others; yet who, on the other hand, does not
> entirely submit, cannot entirely submit, does not want to submit
> entirely. The subject-in-process is always in a state of contesting the law,
> either with the force of violence, of aggressivity, of the death drive, or
> with the other side of this force: pleasure and jouissance.
>
> —Julia Kristeva, *Interviews*

The Riddle of Dress

The double proposal scene with which Billy Wilder puts closure on the scenario of mistaken identities played through in *Some Like it Hot* continues to
fascinate not only critics writing on postwar American film comedy but,
perhaps more crucially, those engaged in the debate on the potentially subversive resignification cross-dressing entails.[1] As the plot unfolds, the two
musicians Jerald/Jeraldine (Jack Lemmon) and Jo/Josephine (Tony Curtis),
who have unintentionally become the witnesses of the St. Valentine's Day
Massacre, find that the only way they can leave Chicago and thus escape
detection is to don women's clothes and join an all-women band, which is
leaving that night on a train to Florida. Once safely installed in their new
environment, however, they discover to their horror that the gangsters they
are fleeing from have chosen for their clan meeting precisely the hotel

where their band is performing. In contrast to their first successful flight, a second escape now proves to be more complicated, because in the course of their stay at this Florida beach resort, they both have gotten involved in vexed romances. The saxophonist Jo, donning the guise of a wealthy oil-producer traveling incognito, has fallen in love with the singer of the band, Sugar (Marilyn Monroe). Jerald, in turn, is being courted by a real millionaire, Osgood (Joe E. Brown), who seemingly takes him to be a woman.[2] After initial hesitation, Jeraldine finally decides to accept the older man's offer of marriage, but only in order to get himself and his friend onto the millionaire's yacht, safely out of the reach of the irate gangsters. Thus the duped Oscar, waiting for his beloved at the pier in his motorboat, is surprised to find that Jeraldine, eagerly rushing toward him, is not only not alone but is in fact accompanied by two other women, Josephine and Sugar, who, as Jeraldine explains, are meant to serve as bridesmaid and flower girl.

Once the four lovers are safely at sea, both of the cross-dressed men decide to confess their real identity. Jo explains to Sugar that she shouldn't really want him because he is a liar and a phony, "one of those no-goodniks you keep running away from." He begs her not to give in to what can only turn into a romantic catastrophe, but Sugar, acknowledging the inevitability of her fate, simply agrees. "I know, everytime," she explains blissfully, no longer listening to the warning he gives. Or perhaps she already enjoys in advance the disaster that is about to occur, for, as Jo reminds her of the romantic disappointment she had confided to him while he was dressed as a girl, she succumbs to her romantic delusion even while she is also only too aware of the consequences. "That's right, pour it on, talk me out of it," she says, as she leans forward and kisses him. She quite self-consciously falls back on an already established pattern of romantic object choices because, though sure to cause pain, it also affords the safety of the familiar.

However, Wilder's enactment of the fact that she so willfully subjects herself to a repetition compulsion whose injurious outcome is only too clear to her need not only be read as a sign of feminine masochism. Rather, one could also understand it as the director's ironic comment on the very genre his film reiterates. For what Wilder renders visible is the way in which the happy ending of any comedy of mistaken identities necessarily implies a willing blindness on the part of the players, not least of all because the role we play in the fantasy-life of the other is always a form of disguise. Though equally supportive of the blind madness of love, Jeraldine's disclosure of her male sex serves to dismantle a different aspect of the allegedly happy couple-building that the comedy genre requires. After having offered several reasons why the marriage between herself and Osgood can not take place—because she isn't a natural blond, smokes all the time, has been living with a saxophone player, and can have no children—Jerald finally admits, "I am a man." Without looking at his beloved and instead staring blissfully out toward the sea, Osgood, undaunted by this confession, responds with the line that has haunted all discussion of cross-dressing ever since—"Nobody's perfect." This second couple-formation is, arguably, one at all costs. There must be a marriage, even if the proposed bond no longer supports the hegemonic ideology of heterosexuality.[3]

Both the manner in which Billy Wilder's plot of mistaken identities addresses the comic pleasure afforded by the disturbance of clear gender categories performed in cross-dressing, as well as the way gender differences are necessarily always recuperated into normative marriage patterns, offer a fruitful point of departure for the argument I will seek to unfold.[4] For the gender trouble that *Some Like It Hot* enacts could be read as a significant reversal of the Hegelian insight that the subject prefers to avoid the antagonism in the home that the non-commensurability between masculine and feminine desire entails, even if this calls for a flight into those simple homoerotic oppositions, which can be staged on the battlefield or in the public workplace.[5] Significant about Wilder's reinscription of this gender trouble scenario is, then, the way in which his two protagonists, by appropriating feminine attire, not only find themselves actually fleeing from the simple opposition of masculine violence, namely a scene of mob warfare, but that in so doing they are ultimately forced to confront what proves to be an irresolvable antagonism, namely the law of love. Thus Billy Wilder employs the figure of cross-dressing not simply in order to emphasize the construction of all gender performance; rather, the impasse his two cross-dressed heroes find themselves in also articulates how the fate of love, given its enmeshment within culturally prescribed gender definitions, can only be experienced as a forced choice. While Sugar's desire can only express itself in response to the codes of American postwar femininity—which though injurious, also comprise the only mode of self-fashioning available to her—Jeraldine finds that he, too, can no longer disengage his desire from the feminine identity he has usurped. Though Jack Lemmon's appropriation of a culturally codified dress of femininity may appear to us to be more ironic than Marilyn Monroe's, the love scenario they ultimately find themselves trapped in discloses how falling in love—far from signifying the return to some presymbolic affective sentience—in fact comes to be coterminous with falling into cultural laws.

On the other hand, Wilder's playful celebration of gender trouble ends with the protagonists preferring the antagonism of love, which is to say they enjoy incommensurability between how each lover fantasizes the other, along with the fact that any articulation of love can only be made within the dress of symbolic constraint. They prefer the friction of sexuality over a simple opposition—be this the scene of seduction Sugar declines when she retreats from the hotel with its bevy of gullible millionaires; be it the scene of violence staged under the auspices of clan loyalty; be it the scene of pleasurable homoerotic male camaraderie, which defines Gerald and Jo's friendship and whose murky designation of gender roles on some latent level calls forth the idea of cross-dressing in the first place.[6] Neither the delusion on the part of Sugar, who knows it is her fate to be disappointed in love and thus enjoys precisely the inevitability of her love choice, nor Jerald's equally helpless surrender to Oscar's courtship, because the latter refuses to relinquish his forbidden love object, appear to be tragic modes of self-curtailment. For Wilder incorporates an ironic protective device into the forced choice around which his double romance plot revolves. His players seem to know about their romantic misrecognitions and thus do not succumb to a sentimental belief that this state of love is true, essential, or natural. Instead, the pleasurable fantasy with which Wilder dismisses us at the end of the film is that, precisely because all four players recognize the fictionality of the romance they are about to embark upon, the love contract might actually work. Their love is, after all, declared halfway between the mainland, where mob violence rages, and the yacht, which, as Michel Foucault suggests, is one of our culturally privileged heterotopic sites of unlimited imagination[7]; it is thus, significantly, a proposal made in the liminal zone between an enjoyment of pure violence and the violence of pure enjoyment.

Discussing the cross-dressing performed by Jack Lemmon in *Some Like It Hot*, Judith Butler has argued that "there are forms of drag that heterosexual culture produces for itself . . . where the anxiety over a possible homosexual consequence is both produced and deflected within the narrative trajectory of the film." According to her, the homophobia and homosexual panic thus negotiated are perhaps less subversive than one would like to assume. Instead, she claims that "such films are functional in providing a ritualistic release for a heterosexual economy that must constantly police its own boundaries against the invasion of queerness, and that this displaced production and resolution of homosexual panic actually fortifies the het- erosexual regime in its self-perpetuating task."[8] One could, of course, argue that to a degree, subversion might well lie in the eyes of the beholder, given that it is dependent upon whether the spectator is willing simply to accept the intended reading a film offers or whether they prefer to negotiate their reading in accordance with their own narrative desire. Nevertheless what is crucial about Butler's reticence to declare *every* performance of drag to be subversive is the manner in which she insists on a fundamental contradic- tion written into the gesture of culturally produced and thus sanctioned transvestitism. For cross-dressing emerges as such a vexed issue precisely because it explores the murky interface between the resilience of individual pleasure and the constraints of public law, pitting imaginary fantasies of self- fashioning against the recognition that we are always already positioned within the parameters of behavior dictated to us by the symbolic codes of our culture.

It comes as no surprise, then, that in her discussion of the ambivalence governing drag performance, Butler should have recourse to Louis Althusser's notion of interpellation. For the primal scene of subjectivity pre- sented by Althusser involves acknowledging the way in which cultural empowerment necessarily requires a form of subjection to the ideology governing it. Let us recall that Althusser not only suggested that we conceive of ideology as representing the imaginary relationship a subject entertains toward his or her real conditions of being. Ideology, he adds, is an illusion that does not correspond to reality, even while it works as an allusion to this reality. In his famous example for how interpellation involves a move from individuality (imaginary register) to subjectivity (symbolic register), Althusser also offers a primal scene for the dialectic between transgressive enjoyment and a desire for the law: a person, walking along the street, turns around 180 degrees once he or she has been hailed by a policeman. By accepting this call, the individual defines itself in relation to the law and thus assures itself a position within the symbolic community constructed under the aegis of this law. The individual perceives itself as a subject of ideology precisely because s/he feels him/herself directly interpellated by one of its representatives, when upon hearing the call "hey, you" s/he responds by turning around so as to say, "yes, it is me you are calling." In the reflection of the interpellative law the subject recognizes him/herself and assumes a fixed position within the symbolic world precisely because to answer this inter-

pellative call means to take on the position that the figure of authority prescribes to it, which is to acknowledge this as an imaginary, not a real relation. Having assumed this ideologically prescribed location, the subject can
confirm his/her identity by adding onto the response the second part of the
sentence, "It is true, I am here."[9]

According to Butler, this call "is formative, if not *performative*, precisely
because it initiates the individual into the subjected status of the subject" by
virtue of an interpellation that implies a legal reprimand and thus the presupposition of guilt.[10] This leads her to ask whether there might not be ways
of acknowledging the law's constrictive constitution of the subject that
nonetheless disarticulates punishment from recognition. In her discussion,
cross-dressing transforms into such a strategy, because it not only allows one
to refuse a punitive law that wounds and curtails but also empowers one to
rupture this law by virtue of an ironic reappropriation. Indeed, at best, it
enables one to reformulate one's symbolic identity by resignifying given
terms, rather than fully ceding to their curtailment or fully rejecting these
cultural dictates. Crucially, then, by accepting interpellation and at the same
time renegotiating its terms, the subject can question the legitimacy of the
symbolic command, even while it does not foreclose its constitutive power.
For as Butler correctly insists, while the law can be renegotiated it can not
be relinquished, because "the 'I' draws what is called its 'agency' in part
through being implicated in the very relations of power that it seeks to
oppose."[11] The troubling contradiction at stake in subject formation is, thus,
the fact that while, on the one hand, interpellation is violating and injurious
because it implies exclusions, curtailments, and reductions, it is also precisely
a symbolic castration that enables the subject to repeatedly reformulate
itself. From this aporetic impasse Butler concludes: "Occupied by such terms
and yet occupying them oneself risks a complicity, a repetition, a relapse into
injury, but it is also the occasion to work the mobilizing power of injury, of
an interpellation one never chose."[12]

Equally seminal to a discussion of cross-dressing as a strategy of self-representation that crosses pleasure with the law, is, however, the fact that the
success of interpellation is coterminous with its failure. This is the point
Mladen Dolar has so astutely addressed with his suggestion that, though
Althusserian interpellation implies a clean cut, it actually produces a residue,
marking that part of the individual that "cannot successfully pass into the
subject" and thus comes to haunt the constituted subjectivity. "The subject,"
he argues, "is precisely the failure to become the subject" and emerges not

in the realm where interpellation fully succeeds but, rather, on the fault line where it succeeds and fails at the same time—where the punitive law and that psychic material that escapes its exclusory constraints come to merge.[13] The alien kernel that determines the individual as a symbolic subject enmeshes the externally imposed legal codes with the remainder that stays on as a representational trace, recalling the psychic material that must be relinquished for the law to take hold and fix the subject into an unequivocal position. For Dolar, then, the choice the subject makes in accepting its position within a symbolic field is a forced choice: "One is presented with a choice which is decided in advance, and by choosing, one meets with a loss. To put it roughly, the subject, in its insertion in the social, is subject of a choice, but a forced one, and one that is curtailed."[14] The subject always pays a price for entry into the symbolic.

The wager of cross-dressing may well be one of our most resilient cultural strategies of the uncanny, where in one and the same gesture the subject responds to the representative of the law by acknowledging, "This is me," even while it also insists, "This is not all of me, because there is something haunting me that radically puts into question the position I am asked to assume before the law, and that reminds me that I am more than this position." Assuming a different dress becomes coterminous with rendering visible this alien kernel, this point of extimacy, as Lacan calls it, where the most intimate touches the outermost, where subjectivity is constituted around an intimate external kernel.[15] To speak of cross-dressing as the performance of extimacy means highlighting precisely the manner in which an external and to a degree injurious law, having been internalized by virtue of interpellation (with the repetition of the symbolic call ensuring the survival of this constitutive intimate foreign kernel), is materially reenacted at the body by virtue of a gesture that clearly says of itself, "I am assuming clothes, and with these a symbolic dress not legally ascribed to me."

I want to call this an uncanny reformulation of the self not only because it blurs the boundary between masculinity and femininity, nor merely because it compels us to recognize the degree to which the other gender always inhabits the self. Importantly, cross-dressing can also be read as a performance of extimacy in the sense that it stages the murky fault line between cultural subjection and empowerment, between an appropriation and a subversion of symbolic law, a rejection and an affirmation of predetermined modes of symbolic dress. The message the cross-dresser broadcasts could be seen to address the fact that we are always implicated in the power formations that constitute us, that we can redress these but never entirely rid ourselves of these cultural garments. As Judith Butler astutely notes, while there is no necessary bond between drag and subversion, the gesture of cross-dressing embodies more than a specific practice of gay culture, because it performs the ambivalence at the heart of all symbolic interpellation, which implicates us in the regimes of power that both constitute and constrain us as cultured subjects. If, then, we speak of social roles as modes of appropriative dressing, given that the subject comes to fashion itself in response to a symbolic interpellation that it can not choose, it may be fruitful to explore both the sites at which gender trouble serves to police a rigid boundary between normal and abnormal, sanctioned and punished modes of conceiving oneself in relation to the law, as well as those cultural moments where this border, though patrolled, is left open. Indeed, we might do well to ask ourselves why Western culture has so persistently enjoyed the uncanny chatoyancy[16] between fixed gender positions that is called forth by cross-dressing, even while it uses the performance of gender indeterminacy to reinstall homogenous dictates—be they heterosexist, masculinist, or racialist. Is the displayed cross-dressing only a defense against homophobic anxiety or does it also offer a rupturing of any clearly defined desire that would seek, once and for all, to draw the boundary between heterosexual and homosexual enjoyment? Does cross-dressing mark one of those sites where desire is able to liberate itself from definitions that incarcerate it within fixed categories? Does it allow us a multiple, perhaps even a contradictory identification with the performers? Does our pleasure reside in the undecidability of the interpellation?

Cross-dressing, then, emerges as one of our most resilient, most resourceful, but also most troubled cultural articulations of the way in which the subject is governed by a radical incommensurability between the pleasure of heterogeneous self-fashioning and the acceptance of an injurious law. Precisely for this reason I want to offer a cross-mapping of three historically different sets of texts, each revolving around the vexing enmeshment of subversion and appropriation that Billy Wilder's strange proposal scene at the end of *Some Like It Hot* articulates. I will begin by discussing the structuration of desire that unfolds in Shakespearean comedies involving cross-dressed girls. My interest in these early modern texts does not so much reside in the fact that these love narratives install the heterosexual marriage plot, which continues to inform our cultural image repertoire to this day, but, rather, in the way in which the Shakespearean texts point to the moments of failure written into an interpellation or call for fixed gender identities. These texts thus culturally inscribe the birth of the uncanny as an index for the ineffaceable remainder that tarries beyond interpellation.[17] In my next section I will turn to one of our most resilient icons of gender trouble, Marlene Dietrich and her repeated performances of cross-dressing, as these illustrate not only our pleasure at the enactment of fantasy scenarios revolving around the chatoyancy of gender but also an ethics of accepting one's symbolic interpellation. My conclusion will then place the successful heterotopias that emerged in the context of postmodern urban drag culture alongside the horrific nightmare scenarios of mutating bodies devised by science fiction so as to address the toxic side effects of unlimited self-fashioning. The stakes of tracking these different articulations of gender identities as a highly unstable affair is a discussion of the cost of symbolic identification. The fact that we dress ourselves in a particular social role implies not only the loss of other modes of identification, for this also entails the appropriation of a norm we have not chosen but whose choice was forced upon us. In the act of renegotiating this forced choice, what comes to the fore is the manner in which one is always more than any one cultural designation, occupying the assigned position yet also exceeding it. By proposing this multiple cross-mapping, I am not, of course, interested in trying to provide solid evidence for any explicitly intended intertextual set of relations at work in these highly diverse cultural artifacts. Rather, following Stanley Cavell, my interest is in discovering, "given the thought of this relation, what the consequences of it might be." As he notes, speaking of his own cross-mapping of Shakespearean comedies and American film comedies of the '30s, "it is a matter not so much of assigning significance to certain events of the drama as it is of isolating and relating the events for which significance needs to be assigned."[18] How does each individual text work through the concerns that motivate a performance of cross-dressing? What modes of figuration are deployed? But also, what solution to the antagonism of gender trouble does the text ultimately propose?

Affirming the Law of the Father

Wondering why, "if boys in women's dress are so threatening, did the English maintain a transvestite theater?" in contrast to all other European cultures, Stephen Orgel speculates that the cross between seductive fascination and terrifying anxiety played through by cross-dressing on the Shake-spearean stage may well have at its core a cultural fear of women. Staging women in male attire renders them unnoticeable, even while it has recourse to a rhetorical ambivalence that can cut both ways. On the one hand the manifestation of a powerful cultural anxiety about disarming and control-ling women, cross-dressing can alternatively serve as a "performative con-struction that both reveals the malleability of the masculine and empowers the feminine, enabling the potential masculinity of women to be realized and acknowledged, if safely contained within the theater's walls."[19] This has led many critics to read cross-dressing as a subversive reinscription of the existing order, even if they do not necessarily agree whether this should ultimately be understood as a cementing of gender difference, its critical dis-ruption, or a sublation of femininity into masculinity; indeed, critics at base disagree whether the subversive potentiality was limited to the action on stage or whether it was located precisely in the female audience watching the cross-dressed boy actors.[20]

In *Twelfth Night*, Viola, who has become the literary prototype for much subsequent female cross-dressing in drama as well as in opera,[21] lands on the shores of Illyria after having been shipwrecked and forcibly separated from her twin brother, Sebastian. Though she accepts the law of fate that has so dramatically disrupted her journey to Elysium, she nevertheless has a choice in how to turn this accident to her favor, and the guise she chooses is that of a woman who hides her femininity by performing the part of a eunuch. "I prithee (and I'll pay thee bounteously)," she explains to her servant, "Conceal me what I am, and be my aid / For such disguise as haply shall become / The form of my intent" (I.ii). At the same time, Viola, like many of her cross-dressed sisters, comes in the course of the play to support, albeit implicitly, the articulation of a desire which is precisely not aimed at het-erosexual couple building. Though the happy ending of the Shakespearean comedy ultimately requires a recuperation of the distinction between the girl performing femininity and the girl performing the gendered hybridity of a eunuch, it nevertheless resonates with the loss of the far less regulated expression of sexual desire that had sustained our spectatorial enjoyment of this comedy of mistaken gendered identities. As in any other case of inter-pellation, something remains after the cut that transforms the individual into a subject, and this trace hovers, like a forlorn melancholic note, amidst the wedding bells that mark the successful recuperation of order at the end of all comic misrecognitions. While the women players once more come to

hide the scar of this violent cut that severs them from their creative masculine refigurations, by reasssuming their skirts, the fact that something must
be relinquished for the heterosexual solution to hold is given material
embodiment in those figures who must visibly be excluded from the wedding ceremonies: in *Twelfth Night* these are Malvolio, bent on revenge
because the woman he loves has chosen to wed the twin of the cross-dressed
heroine, along with Antonio, the man who, owing to his immeasurable love
for Sebastian, was willing to risk imprisonment by Count Orsino, only to
find himself disacknowledged, albeit by the twin sister whom he mistakenly
takes for her brother. He uses his speech of self-defense to explicitly accuse
Sebastian of ingratitude, and yet, obliquely, he also articulates his own
romantic disappointment: "His life I gave him, and did thereto add / My
love, without retention or restraint, / All his in dedication." Although it is
this accusation that brings about the discovery of the actual identities of the
twin-couple, and Antonio is, therefore, saved from execution, he has no further lines in the denouement of the play. He can but watch silently, as his
beloved Sebastian admits to his clandestine marriage to Olivia, and remain
equally mute when Count Orsino proposes marriage to the cross-dressed
page, the other figure he mistook for his beloved.

However, even if Viola's cross-dressing ultimately brings about a double
marriage that serves to sacrifice homoerotic desire, the uncanniness of her
performance queers precisely the law of heterosexual coupling that she will
ultimately be forced to choose for herself. Indeed, she not only appears to
be a living imitation of her brother but actually explicitly defies the law of
death, when, because she fears that he may have drowned, she decides to preserve his image on her body. One could say that by transforming herself into
him, she takes on his symbolic mandate in his absence. Explaining, "I my
brother know / Yet living in my glass" (III.iv), she addresses the specularity
that, according to Althusser, haunts the manner in which we fashion ourselves in response to an ideological interpellation. Her transformation of
herself into a boy gives voice to her imaginary refiguration of her real condition, the orphan, who is lost on a foreign island, utterly vulnerable. In the
guise of such a multiply uncanny foreign body—a woman appearing to be
a man, a sister appearing to be her brother—she allows two homoerotic scenarios to unfold. The woman whom she courts in the name of her master,
Count Orsino, falls in love with her. For the audience, who are in on the
secret of her real gender, identifying with the fantasies of Countess Olivia
means enjoying the oblique representation of a clandestine love scenario

between women. At the same time Viola falls in love with her master, and, in so far as we are also asked to identify with the fantasies of the count, what is equally represented in this triangulation of desire is the pleasure of masculine homoerotic love. The resilient fascination inhabiting this performance of cross-dressing, one could then argue, is that it calls forth an ambivalent, indeed utterly contradictory set of imaginary resignifications of the heroine's symbolic position. Cross-dressing allows Viola to usurp the position of her brother (indeed, she designates her new clothes as "my masculine usurp'd attire" [V.i]) and thus to rewrite her own position within her family genealogy. At the same time it calls forth two transgressive love scenarios that not only contradict each other but will both have to be sacrificed, along with her usurpation of the role of heir to her father's estate, so that the daughter's social position can once more be fixed as that of wife, confirming the bond between a paternal figure of authority and a chosen son-in-law. On the body of Viola, performing a mimicry of her brother, the desire for a culturally forbidden love and the paternal law that dictates the gendered roles its children are to assume are as much at cross-purposes as they are mutually implicated.

The final solution of the heterosexual couple formation prescribed by the hegemonic cultural code is, however, highly precarious. This is played through in turn on the body of precisely the figure who also serves as the deus ex machina of the plot—namely the brother, returned from the murky oblivion of a supposed death by drowning. Viola, who until then believes herself to be an orphan, explains, "I am all the daughters of my father's house, / And all the brothers too" (II.iv). This hybrid symbolic body needs once more to be divided in order for the culturally privileged bond between father and son to be reinstalled, yet only the rebirth of another uncanny figure—the twin couple, which Count Orsino calls "One face, one voice, one habit, and two persons!" (V.i)—can assure that a heterosexual marriage will be renegotiated in the end as well. At the same time, this solution is coterminous with the violent exclusion of precisely the queerness that we, the audience, have enjoyed as the plot of mistaken identities took its many turns of misrecognition. Sebastian explains to Olivia, of whom (much along the lines of my reading of Billy Wilder's Osgood) we can't be sure whether she really was duped by Viola's disguise or whether she may not actually have known she was marrying a woman dressed as a page: "So comes it, lady, you have been mistook. / But nature to her bias drew in that. / You would have been contracted to a maid; / Nor are thou therein, by my life, deceiv'd: / You are betroth'd both to a maid and man" (V.i.). In other words, even as the marriage solution offered by Shakespeare's play supports the claims of heterosexist law, it opens up the space for a different negotiation.[22] We can either follow the bias of nature and renounce a homoerotic fantasy scenario, or we can read this strange twin brother, who so miraculously appears in the fifth act, as a phantom over whose doubly encoded spectral body the chatoyant desire haunting the other lovers in the play can come to be arrested. For Olivia, as Sebastian insists, he will remain a cross-dresser, a hybrid enmeshment of maid and man, and in so doing he not only gives voice to the homoerotic desire of his future wife but, perhaps more important, to the fact that even after the marriage contract has been performed, and with it the hegemonic interpellation of heterosexual law symbolically cemented, the question of femininity and masculinity remains an unstable affair.

In a similar tone, the manner in which the count proposes marriage to Viola indicates that the recuperation of her feminine dress tames in him a highly fickle desire. For isn't it strange how willingly Orsino relinquishes his beloved Olivia to the man who uncannily resembles his page Cesario, as though he had known all along that his desire was aimed not at the woman for whom he so melancholically pines? Indeed, his object may well always have been the hybrid eunuch serving him, whom he is now able to desire with impunity because the "boy" is about to don a feminine skirt. Orsino's homoerotic declaration of love—"Boy, thou hast said to me a thousand times / Thou never should'st love woman like to me"—is transformed into a culturally sanctioned order: "Give me thy hand / And let me see thee in thy woman's weeds" (V.i). Significantly, we never see this femininity redressed. At least according to the stage directions given by Shakespeare's text, Cesario never reemerges as Viola. As in Billy Wilder's postwar comedy, the playful ambivalence of cross-dressing is preserved to the end. Or put another way, the ideology of gender that the Shakespearean text unfolds proves to be first and foremost an imaginary relation, constructed over and against the real conditions of sexual identity.

Not all Shakespearean comedies, however, employ feminine cross-dressing so as to undercut the harsh exclusions dictated by paternal law. It is, therefore, fruitful to revisit a second, earlier Shakespearean comedy, *The Merchant of Venice*, because the usurped masculinity performed by Portia addresses in a far more direct but also far more tragic manner how vexed the relation between appropriation of a foreign dress and subjection to the laws of this alterity can actually be. On the one hand this Shakespearean daughter, like Viola an orphan, explicitly denounces paternal interpellation as an act of narcissistic wounding as well as a curtailment of her agency. For her future as a lover and as a wife revolves around the fact that she must submit herself to a courtship ritual dictated to her by her dead father's will, which declares that she must marry the man who chooses the casket that contains her portrait. To her servant Nerissa, she describes this pact qua tacit under- standing between her dead father and her future husband as one in which she has no choice: "O me the word 'choose'! I may neither choose who I would, nor refuse who I dislike, so is the will of a living daughter curb'd by the will of a dead father: is it not hard Nerissa, that I cannot choose one, nor refuse none?" (I.ii). On the other hand, Portia ironically usurps masculine attire to support precisely this paternal law, which is to say, this mode of symbolic interpellation in which the only choice you have is a forced one, namely that of wounding subjection. This other appropriation of the pater- nal law involves not her marriage plot but, rather, the strife between the merchant Antonio and the Jewish money-lender Shylock, who has lent three thousand ducats to the Christian so that Antonio might help his friend Bassanio—whom Antonio loves with a selfless passion equal to that of Antonio in *Twelfth-Night*—court the rich and beautiful heiress of Belmont, Portia. Shylock, who carries a grudge against Antonio because the latter is willing to lend money without profit and in so doing undermines Shylock's business, uses the opportunity of an accident to three of his opponent's ships to take revenge. Before the court of Venice Shylock places his claim to one pound of flesh from the body of his debtor in exchange for the money the latter can not return.

Portia may not be able to speak for herself in the realm of her private apartment in Belmont and must instead watch silently as a man, known to be a spendthrift and a fortune hunter, succeeds in claiming her as his wife,[23] but she resurfaces in male attire at another site, the public courtroom in Venice. Wearing the robes of an advocate, and thus representing a symbolic mandate that was never legally bestowed upon her, she comes to redress her grievance against the harshness of her father's last will and is able to rein- troduce agency into her marriage plot by defending her future husband's benefactor. Indeed, she proves to be more adept at the law than either Anto- nio or Bassanio. If, in this public site, she can renegotiate the wounding sub- jection inflicted upon her by paternal law, she significantly does so, however, by performing a splitting of this wounding law into two agencies: on the one hand, the representative of a just, albeit harsh law of the dead father, the fully legitimized Venetian citizen she has come to defend, and, on the other hand, Shylock, as the representative of an equally harsh paternal lineage, whose law, however, will in the course of the court proceedings be determined illegal and obscene in a rhetorical sleight of hand that turns the abused citizen into a criminal.[24]

Perturbing about the plot of *The Merchant of Venice* is, however, the fact that it contains a twofold scenario of feminine cross-dressing in which both narratives revolve around the question of whether a daughter will accept or resignify an injurious paternal interpellation; moreover, the plot achieves this by crossing the question of sexual self-positioning with the question of how one chooses to position oneself in relation to the class and race designations of one's family. For one must not overlook the fact that Portia is not the only one to appropriate the masculine robe. Jessica, the daughter of Shylock, equally usurps a masculine attire to resist the claim her father makes to her loyalty as a Jew's daughter. Dressed as a page, she meets her Christian lover, Lorenzo, at midnight in front of her father's house and with him steals not only Shylock's jewels and money but also the ring her dead mother, Leah, had once given him. In contrast to Portia who, though decrying the harshness of her paternal legacy, nevertheless subjects herself to this mandate, Jessica uses her cross-dressing to flee not only from her home but also from her racial heritage. In her case the usurpation of masculine attire functions as a provisional mode of self-refashioning, as a liminal identity she must assume before she can cross over into a second, more permanent mode of cross-dressing—namely the assimilated Jew, married to a Christian, jettisoned forever from her father's home as well as from her paternal, cultural, and racial inheritance. As she exchanges her woman's weeds for the cloak of a page, Jessica also sheds her Jewish heritage so as to fully appropriate a foreign, Christian identity. She explains to Launcelot that she is fully aware of the sin that her betrayal of her paternal interpellation entails: "Alack, what heinous sin is it in me / To be ashamed to be my father's child! / But though I am a daughter to his blood / I am not to his manners: O Lorenzo / If thou keep promise I shall end this strife, / Become a Christian and thy loving wife" (II.iii). And appropriately, the night is so dark during her act of transgression that, though immediately recognizing the voice of her beloved, Jessica asks Lorenzo to give her proof of his identity. "Who are you?—tell me for more certainty," she calls out, "Albeit I'll swear that I do know your tongue" (II.vi). Indeed she is grateful to the darkness of the night because it dresses the shame she feels at the exchange she is about to undertake with its own dark cloak. It is as though she required a twofold disguise—the masculine attire and the nocturnal absence of light—to cover up her dual crime, dispossessing her father of a daughter but also stealing his money and his jewels. In response to Lorenzo, who asks her to be his torchbearer, she replies, "What, must I hold a candle to my shames? /—They in themselves (goodsooth) are too too light. / Why, 'tis an office of discovery (love), / And I should be obscur'd" (II.vi).[25]

And yet, although she will always be haunted by the paternal law whose interpellation she may consciously reject, her nocturnal cross-dressing allows her to reformulate her imaginary relationship to the crime she has committed against her father by refusing his symbolic mandate. Later, in her new home in Belmont, Jessica is able to refigure her shame into a narrative that mitigates her guilt. During a nocturnal lover's quarrel both Lorenzo and his bride interpolate their transgression into a sequence of literary nights, in which love led to catastrophe. "In such a night as this," Lorenzo begins, "Troilus methinks mounted the Trojan walls, And sigh'd his soul toward the Grecian tents where Cressid lay that night" (V.i). Jessica, in turn, evokes the night in which Thisbe did not keep her appointment with her Pyramus because she was frightened away by a lion, while Lorenzo recalls the image of Dido at the shores of Carthage, waiting in anguish for her lover to return. After Jessica responds with an evocation of how, in such a night, "Medea gathered the enchanted herbs that did renew old Aeson," Lorenzo finally includes their own nocturnal transgression, as though it were nothing other than a literary reference, dehistoricized and idealized: "In such a night did Jessica steal from the wealthy Jew, and with an unthrift love did run from Venice, as far as Belmont" (V.i). As they challenge each other about who has experienced the greater injuries in the course of this forbidden love and who has been the more cruel lover, they not only in retrospect enjoy these acts of subjugation but, more crucially, turn their crimes and delusions into a mythic scene, another mode of redressing grievances.

Portia, one could argue, follows a similar rhetoric of replaying her own psychic wounding in another register, though in her case the transposition does not involve turning herself into a heroine of ancient literary texts. She uses her cross-dressing so that she can resignify her own impotence in relation to the law of her father on the body of the Jew Shylock.[26] Astutely Portia notes to her servant, "Hanging and wiving goes by destiny," so as to point not only to the manner in which she has no choice in whom she will marry, or simply to articulate that this forced marriage marks the death of her own agency since declared wife under the auspices of her dead father's will; she is hung from the start. Portia, however, also gives voice to the fact that her marriage requires the sacrifice of someone else besides her. What makes Shakespeare's plot so resiliently disturbing is that her partner in crime, the accomplice onto whom she will ultimately project her guilt, should be the Jew Shylock. At stake, then, in the courtroom scene is the manner in which any performance of agency comes inevitably to be enmeshed with the symbolic law that necessarily curtails the subject, making claims in its name. Indeed, the interpellation by the law, which we can never refuse but only renegotiate, serves not only to make us recognize that our only choice is to accept the curtailment of the self it dictates. It also allows a fantasy scenario to be brought into circulation, in the course of which some one else will bear the burden of this forced choice, or at least share the costs of interpellation.

Together with her servant Nerissa, Portia dons a habit in which both their future husbands will think they "are accomplished in what we lack" (III, iv.), namely the masculine part, and with it the symbolic power this endows its bearer. Owing to her usurped attire, seemingly in possession of the masculine member and thus by implication a member of the symbolic community, where the antagonism of gender is transformed into a simple opposition between two different ethnic representations of the law, Portia functions as the agent of a sanctioned difference. As she transforms the accuser Shylock into the accused, she comes to perform for all those present in the courtroom the cruel consequences that are entailed when the Jewish law of revenge is pitted against the Christian law of mercy. As Shylock explains in his self-defense, "If a Jew wrong a Christian, what is his humility? revenge! If a Christian wrong a Jew, what should his sufferance be by Christian example?—why revenge! The villainy you teach me I will execute, and it shall go hard but I will better the instruction" (III, ii). This logic, one could argue, is nothing other than a radical appropriation, on the part of Shylock, of the Christian double standard, whereby the cruel injury the Venetian law habitually imposes on its Jews is redressed as an insistence that he, too, may profit from the same cultural codes. Yet against this logic— which seems to uncover precisely what is rotten in Venetian law—Portia holds the law of mercy. In other words, in one and the same gesture, she renders visible the core antagonism around which the symbolic codes of Venice revolve, even while she presents an argument that will keep this dangerous rottenness at bay by preserving the simple difference between Christian and

Jew. Shylock, she maintains, may insist on his right, indeed must receive his bond. He is fully justified in what he terms his craving for the law, but only if he is able to remain within the limits of the very condition he himself dictated to his debtor. He is ordered to take a pound of flesh from Antonio without shedding a drop of blood. In her usurped masculine attire, Portia thus transforms into an old biblical figure, into "a second Daniel!" as Gratiano notes, and thanks the Jew "for teaching me that word" (IV. i). She both gives body to the cruel harshness of the law he seeks to have affirmed in the courtroom and turns this very law against him. In this precise sense one can speak of Portia's cross-dressing as being uncanny, because she has appropriated not only her father's but also her opponent's legal code, using the latter against Shylock so as to defend herself against the subjection imposed upon her by the former. The horrific logic she exposes with her performance is that Shylock is now in her position. Like Portia in relation to her marriage plot, Shylock has no choice. He is forced to relinquish half his possessions to the state of Venice, as he must also subject himself to a forced assimilation. Particularly perturbing about this solution is not only the fact that it so cruelly highlights the cost of symbolic agency but that, in so far as it signifies a reversal of the position Portia's father dictates to her in his will, it also reveals that there is no escape from the law that wounds, even if there are sites where this law can temporarily be refigured. Dressed as a man of the law, in the Venetian courtroom, but only in this attire and only in this setting, Portia can regain the agency she has lost once and for all in her Belmont estate. The satisfaction that her wishful reversal entails resonates with the knowledge of its temporal and spatial delimitation.[27]

The multiple wedding celebrated in Belmont is marred by the fact that throughout the play we are never shown any convincing love scenes between Portia and Bassanio. Indeed, the latter is only too ready to give the ring, which Portia had asked him to preserve as a token of his loyalty, to the figure he takes for Antonio's attorney. Moreover, this marriage solution is uncanny because, along the lines discussed by Mladen Dolar, it offers an overdetermined visualization of the trace that remains after hegemonic interpellation has been successfully reinstalled. The Jew Shylock is as much excluded from the apparent bliss of Belmont as is the melancholic lover Antonio, who, like his namesake in *Twelfth Night*, can do nothing except warn his friend Bassanio, for whom he was willing to give his life, not to be reckless with the gifts of his future wife. But if Portia, by resuming her woman's weeds, seemingly relinquishes all resistance to her father's law, Jessica sits under the light of the moon and remembers the night of her paternal betrayal. Both embody the cost that successful interpellation entails, whether in the case of Portia this is the unchallenged acceptance of her position or in the case of Jessica her radical exchange of one position of subjection for another. Portia, hoping that in future her husband will be less careless with the tokens of loyalty she gives to him, is only too justified in harboring doubts about the sagacity of the father's law that so fatefully binds her to a fickle man. And yet what we are called upon to acknowledge is not just the violent psychic injuries upon which this happy ending is grounded. Recollecting both daughters' transgressions, we recognize that for a brief interim cross-dressing allowed an empowering crisis in interpellation to surface. A trace of this possibility is carried beyond the end of the plot along with our silent awe at the harshness with which the play of gender difference comes once more to be contained.[28]

Celebrating Gender Hybridity

In his autobiography, *Fun in a Chinese Laundry*, Josef von Sternberg describes the cultural practice of cross-dressing prevalent in Berlin in the 1920s:

> This ocean was seething when I was called to explore it. I lived in a quiet hotel on the river Spree, a rest house in the midst of a maelstrom, and to leave it was like shooting the rapids. At night, when I went out to dine, it was not unusual for something that sat next to me, dressed as a woman, to powder its nose with a large puff that a moment ago had seemed to be a breast. To differentiate between the sexes was, to make an understatement, confusing. Not only did men masquerade as females, wearing false eyelashes, beauty spots, rouge and veil, but the woods were full of females who looked and functioned like men. A third species, defying definition, circulated, ready to lend itself to whatever the occasion offered. To raise an eyebrow at all this branded one as a tourist.[29]

The manner in which Sternberg, in turn, came to introduce the heroine of *Morocco* (1930), Amy Jolly, to the audience sitting in a Moroccan nightclub—and concomitantly, on the extradiegetic level of the film, his star, Marlene Dietrich, to the American audience in her first Hollywood film—

begs to be read in relation to the culture of cross-dressing sanctioned by the bohemian world of Berlin. This, not least of all, because it refers to a world Dietrich decisively left behind, as she moved across the Atlantic Ocean. However, as the exploration of a "third species," performed on the stages of Berlin nightlife between the two world wars, is reencoded in the language of Hollywood and its production code, it is perhaps not incidental that the birth of Marlene Dietrich as an international star was not only played through in a scene where she dons male attire to win the admiration of her new audience but that this transformation should itself be staged in a third, liminal site, North Africa as site for a battle fought among Europeans.[30] Much has, of course, been written about the manner in which Marlene Dietrich appeared from the start to be nothing other than a creation of Josef von Sternberg, or, as Dyer notes "a pure vehicle for the latter's fantasies and formalist concerns."[31] Yet one must not forget that Sternberg is himself responsible for the idea that the icon of female seduction he had artificially constructed was, in fact, fundamentally cross-dressed, as a refiguration of his masculine self in a feminine body. Casting himself in the role of Svengali Jo, he enjoyed proclaiming, "In my films Marlene is not herself. Remember that, Marlene is not Marlene. I am Marlene, she knows that better than any-one."[32] At the same time von Sternberg was also the first to admit that, although he was the creator of the star Dietrich, he had not imposed a for-eign personality upon her. He had merely known how to dramatically emphasize those attributes that he required for the persona he wanted her to embody, while his makeover of her appearance involved suppressing all the other aspects of his favorite actress that fit neither his fantasy of femi-nine seduction nor his formal concerns.[33]

What many critics have thus focused on in relation to the scene in which Dietrich, in her role as a former hooker, presents herself for the first time on the stage of a Moroccan cabaret and thus in the field of vision of the two men who will vie for her romantic attention, is the way her cross-dressing not only comments ironically on the content of her first song—the inevitable failure of romantic love—but also raises the question of a vexed spectatorship.[34] The scene, after all, begins with the owner of the nightclub asking his audience to welcome the newcomer with their "usual discrimi-nating kindness." However, von Sternberg frames Amy's appearance on this stage with two shot sequences that embellish the highly ambivalent expec-tations of her audience. On the one hand, we hear a cynical comment made by the artist and millionaire La Bessière (Adolphe Menjou), who notes, as he smiles sadistically at his friends, that the usual welcome to newcomers is, if he recalls properly, rather unpleasant. On the other hand, we see Tom Brown (Gary Cooper), a soldier in the foreign legion, initially sitting calmly in the midst of a raucous crowd, smugly smoking his cigarette, and then nonchalantly offering a chair to the gypsy woman who has just joined him and who gesticulates dramatically as a way of excusing her lateness. He, too, gazes at the stage in an apparently sadistic manner, seemingly assured of the power of his spectatorial position. Indeed, there seems to be an invisible boundary drawn between both of these men (who are clearly positioned by von Sternberg as our point of identification) and the woman whose appearance they are so eagerly anticipating. Both men pose as empowered and invulnerable spectators, while their female companions function as pure supplements to their gaze. They are the passive accomplices in this visual game, whose source and point of control is initially marked as being masculine. Thus, even though these two men are presented as the spectators we are meant to identify with, we realize almost immediately that von Sternberg has implicitly assigned to us the role of their feminine accomplices.[35] Like the women, we are meant to watch the men watching a star, who at least on the diegetic level of the film is implicitly performing for their gaze. The voyeuristic setting, constructed by von Sternberg as a frame for Marlene Dietrich/Amy Jolly's entrance on the stage, is grounded in the expectation that the female performer will subject herself to the sadistic desire of her masculine spectators. This expected circulation of gazes casts her as an object that can be enjoyed at a distance, without any direct contact taking place between her and her audience.[36]

With the appearance of Amy Jolly on stage, however, about to sing "Quand l'amour meurt," von Sternberg ironically undercuts the very relay of gazes he had initially established to frame her performance. In other words, he dismantles the tacit presuppositions underlying the notion of an empowered masculine gaze at precisely the same moment as he produces it by virtue of his mise-en-scène. Marlene Dietrich, dressed in a tuxedo and wearing a top hot, casually saunters onto the stage and throws a cool, inquisitory gaze at the tempestuous audience that greets her with impatient shouting. At this point one could still interpret her walk as cautious, fearful, as though she were trying to convince her audience that she were dependent on their benevolent attitude toward her and, indeed, willing to do anything to please them. Sternberg cuts to a close-up of the two men gazing at her, who in the following song sequence will implicitly be the two members of the audience Amy privileges. For several seconds Tom critically judges the woman who has just appeared before him, viewing her exclusively in relation to his desire, and, having decided that she does, in fact, please him, he cedes to her seductive play. He begins to clap demonstratively; however, upon noticing that the rest of the crowd continues to shout obscenities, he becomes violent. So as to assure himself an untainted enjoyment of the scene that is about to commence, he threatens those soldiers sitting closest to him with his fist, even while he silences his companion by placing his hands around her throat, strangling her into obedience as he pushes her back onto her chair. Only then does he himself return to his own seat.

Upon closer inspection it becomes clear that, from the start, Marlene Dietrich's cool sauntering contains a calculated resistance against the subjection expected of her. In what calls out to be read as a sign of utter self-assurance and poise, Amy Jolly enters the stage holding a cigarette in her right hand, while her left hand partially sticks out from the pocket of her trousers.[37] With a clear aim in mind she heads for the chair placed in the center of the stage and slightly pulls up the leg of her left trousers with her right hand, only to sit on the arm of the chair. Leaning her left hand further along the back of the chair, she secures her position and continues to calmly smoke her cigarette, casting her gaze in an aloof manner over the excited crowd. Nothing disturbs this gaze; no impatience, no insecurity, no doubt can be discerned here. Rather, she appears like a mother, mildly smiling down at her disobedient children and clearly enjoying the fact that her favorite son valiantly defends her. As though she had all the time in the world, she waits until the excitement of the foreplay has come to an end. Only then does she calmly rise from her seat and walk toward the railing that demarcates the fault line between audience and stage. Comfortably leaning against it, she finally begins to sing. Once more Sternberg interpolates close-ups of the two men whose sadistic comments and body language von Sternberg used to frame her song—the soldier and the millionaire/artist, the embodiments of the two options Amy Jolly will have to choose from in the course of the film's romance plot. Both have leaned back in their seats, fully immersed in their respective enjoyment. Yet the doubling of the masculine gaze serves to make us recognize not only how much each one of their fantasy scenarios, revolving as it does about the woman about to sing, is a limited one. It also raises the suspicion that in this game of pleasurable gazes, there is always something that exceeds the position of the allegedly privileged, dominating masculine gaze. Indeed, the fact that von Sternberg offers us two men, absorbed in their individual pleasure, undermines the very self-assurance that this relay of gazes exchanged between audience and singer is meant to support. For what von Sternberg renders only too visible is that the woman, who by virtue of her seductive appearance is meant to support one privileged spectator's power, in fact satisfies this desire for many men. In so doing she discloses the fact that any relation between a publicly staged body and its one spectator is an imaginary one.

At the same time, von Sternberg enacts a murky scenario, given that the desire of these supposedly privileged spectators is in fact visibly undermined by the desire of the woman, playing to their gaze. Amy Jolly not only offers a performance of how perfectly she can subject herself to the masculine gaze, how skillfully she can enact what this privileged spectator desires, but she also demonstrates that she is fully in control of this performance and that nothing can deter her from the mise-en-scène she has conceived for herself. Her cross-dressing signals a hybrid appearance. While on the manifest level she appears to passively take on the submissive role expected of a night-club star, on a latent level—but one that is still part of von Sternberg's mise-en-scène—she is masterfully in control of a twofold act of cross-dressing: a seductive woman dressed as a man (Amy Jolly) and a German actress made up as a new international star (Marlene Dietrich). Amy calmly disengages herself from the touch of one of the men sitting behind the railing and, moving slightly further along this wooden barrier that divides her from her audience, she finally comes to rest. She will not allow herself to be chosen by a random spectator. Instead, self-consciously policing this boundary, she is the one who chooses, who plays an active part in her performance. Sternberg shows her smiling directly first at La Bessière, who, by virtue of the framing, now appears to be entirely isolated from his friends, self-absorbed in his solitary enjoyment. Then we are shown how she smiles at Tom Brown, who proudly begins to look around himself, signaling that his pleasure depends on his knowing that others have recognized him to be the man Amy has chosen to single out from the crowd. A play with her top hat— sometimes lifting it slightly, then again pushing it down to cover her forehead—which runs through the entire scene, further cements the tacit understanding between these two figures, in the midst of a sexually overdetermined public display where Amy oscillates between being the object and the agent of a relay of gazes that empowers as much as it subjects the players explicitly involved.

With the resolution of the song, the manner in which Marlene Dietrich's body comes to function as the site of a chatoyant play with predetermined gender designations—so as to visualize the fluid distinction between the empowered position of the spectator and the disempowered one of the gazed-at feminine body—finds a brilliant acme. First, accepting the offer of the man sitting behind her to partake of a glass of champagne with him, Amy Jolly breaks open the boundary between stage and audience. She deftly heaves herself over the railing and, after having offered a toast to the entire audience, empties the entire glass in one gulp, while her onlookers applaud her. Then, imitating the gesture of the men watching her, she in turn gazes several moments at his female companion. After having turned her upper body in precisely the same manner as Tom had while she was singing her song, she signals to her audience that the action about to take place is intended for their pleasure—she approaches the woman and takes the flower the latter is wearing behind her ear. Now the figure who had initially been introduced as an accomplice of the masculine gaze has turned into the explicit object of the entire audience's gaze and as such imitates the position Amy had occupied throughout the performance of her song. Having been singled out by Amy, she is isolated from all the other people in the crowd, the object of everyone's gaze, including that of the singer, who in contrast to the clandestine visual gestures she shared with her two privileged male spectators has openly interpellated her. At the same time, the woman continues to be assigned the position of spectator as well, though now no longer the silent accomplice of a male gaze but rather representing the mode of gazing that had initially been ascribed to La Bessière and Tom Brown. Amy, self-consciously appropriating for herself the masculine position of the active agent, once more approaches the woman and, having briefly smelled the flower, she leans forward to kiss her on the mouth. While the audience laughs benevolently, Amy moves back several steps and, again imitating Tom's body gestures, lightly touches her top hat with her right index finger, as though she were thanking the woman for the kiss, much as he had clandestinely thanked her for the song earlier on.

Only then does Amy fully turn around, take off her hat, and bow before the entire audience, as though, in the manner proposed by Althusser, her 180-degree turn signals her acknowledgment of the expectations the audience had imposed upon her for her initiation as a performer. This is, furthermore, also Dietrich's assertion that she will embody the role of the international Hollywood star von Sternberg has cast her in. On both levels of the spectacle, this turn marks the moment where the performer is clearly no longer presented as an individual, caught in imaginary processes, but, rather, as a subject, empowered in her agency because she accepts the position that is being ascribed to her as defined by the parameters of the setting she has chosen to appear in. It is only after this turn that Amy finally returns to the stage; however, rather than exiting she walks directly toward Tom, who is sitting at a table in the first row, facing the center of the stage. Still fully certain that he is her privileged spectator, which is to say the chosen object of her gaze, Tom gets up and once more claps demonstratively, even while he now directly faces her. At this point he is as conscious as she that together they form the object of the gaze of the entire audience. Amy Jolly, however, undermines the self-assurance that this public display of her seductive body is meant to afford by now drawing Tom into her performance. For she forces him into the feminine position. Briefly she once more smells the flower, only to throw it at Tom, rather than offering him a kiss. If she had imitated his body language, clearly encoded as being masculine, so as to seduce the female accomplice of the masculine gaze, with the male spectators joyfully applauding this furtive performance of lesbian desire, what Amy now illustrates is that, in the course of a performance where gender identities are rendered fluid, the male spectator can suddenly find himself to be cross-dressed as well. Tom is not only the recipient of the flower that was originally harbored behind the ear of his clandestine lover, passively watching the spectacle. Rather, he too is forced to submit helplessly to Amy Jolly's gift, though unlike the woman he is not rewarded with a direct erotic embrace. The fact that Tom now finds himself in the position of the helpless object of the gaze is confirmed by the fact that the audience, which continues to be encoded as a masculine body, applauds this spectacle as well. But one could add that Tom also has made a 180-degree turn. He too is no longer merely in the position of a narcissistic individual, absorbed in a pleasurable visual spectacle. Though it will take the entire narrative of the film for him to accept her offer of unconditional love, this gift marks the fact that in one and the same gesture Amy acknowledges her place in relation to the desire of her audience and interpellates him as a fellow subject. Together with him she will—in what could be called an ethical gesture—be able, in a scene von Sternberg stages as a moment of rebirth for both, to cast off the entire mise-en-scène of imaginary scenes and spectacles, so as to resignify herself beyond all cross-dressing, and thus beyond all social dresses, in the empty space of the African desert.[38]

In the course of this scene so clearly marked by von Sternberg as a double inaugural fantasy scenario—Amy Jolly, introduced into a romantic scene of male rivalry, and Marlene Dietrich introduced into the competitive world of Hollywood celebrities—we have a chatoyant exchange between masculinity and passive femininity, where the boundary between the active viewer and the passive performer collapses. Dietrich's cross-dressing serves to underline the gender hybridity in both of the key players of the scene, in Amy Jolly's self-empowered agency and in Tom Brown's acceptance of vulnerability. The third player, La Bessière, is removed in the course of the scene, only to be replaced by a disembodied law that emerges as the invisible source of interpellation at the end of the sequence, superseding the relay of gazes played out at the level of imaginary relations of pleasurable narcissism. For the relay played out in the course of the scene forces both Amy and Tom to accept their position in a scenario that exceeds the cabaret scene. As Amy Jolly once more turns to the entire audience and, lifting the top hat slightly, bows before them, she signals her acceptance of their interpellation: "yes, I am she, whom you have addressed"; "yes, I accept the position you have designated for me." The self-assurance of the stride with which she finally leaves the stage cements this symbolic contract. Two moments, however, disturb the recuperation of order. The men have unwittingly become her collective accomplices and as such find themselves cast into the position initially assigned to the women. At the same time, von Sternberg does not end the sequence without once more offering us a close-up of Tom. Initially confused, then angered, Tom finally accepts the gift and imitates her smelling the flower. He, too, enjoys the chatoyancy of the roles.

The rhetorical cross-dressing at work in this sequence on the formal level is such that, as viewers of this relay of gazes, we cannot be sure whose power is being displayed. Is the woman really only the passive object of the diverse men who gaze at her or must one not also speak about these spectators as the objects of the cross-dressed woman? Is the cross-dressing that Marlene Dietrich and Josef von Sternberg so dexterously play through only an obliteration of femininity or also a gesture that renders masculinity uncanny, fraught with ambivalences? For even though Amy Jolly, dressed as a man, is intended to function as a cipher for masculine empowerment—precisely because she is expected to reflect for her privileged masculine spectators the imaginary relation they entertain toward their real social conditions—she also turns into a cipher for the disturbing, uncanny kernel inherent to any gender designation. In the course of this crossover from one gender position to the other, it not only becomes ever more difficult to determine *who* seduces *whom* but also *for whom* Amy serves as a cipher—for the director Josef von Sternberg, for the star Marlene Dietrich, or for a particular type of femininity one could call the icon of seduction? Equally indeterminate is the question of which gendered desire is being satisfied by this scene.[39]

Marlene Dietrich, who throughout her life enjoyed being photographed while wearing men's clothes, argued that this preference of dress was exclusively a question of comfort. As early as 1933 she explained to a reporter,

> I simply followed up the logical consequences of the big pajama-fashion and I have to confess, that I have never felt more comfortable and better dressed. The public is always outraged about something new. First I showed my legs, and they were outraged, now I hide my legs, and they are equally outraged. I want to emphasize that I genuinely prefer men's clothes and that I don't wear them to provoke a sensation. I simply find that I appear more appealing in men's clothes. Furthermore, these clothes give one perfect freedom and comfort, which I can't say is true for women's clothes and skirts. Women's clothes require so much time, it is so fatiguing to buy them. You need hats, shoes, handbags, scarves, coats and many details that all have to fit together. That requires much thought and precise choice and for that I have neither time nor interest.[40]

Yet there are also other images of Dietrich wearing men's clothes, namely the photographs and newsreels showing her in the uniform of the U.S. army, supporting the allied troops in their fight against Nazi Germany. This was cross-dressing with real political consequences, for which the German public never forgave her. When in the early '60s Dietrich decided to tour Germany, she was greeted by an angry mob that was not willing to forget that she had deserted her homeland to fight with the enemy. In contrast to von Sternberg's mise-en-scène in a Moroccan cabaret, this crowd could not be appeased by a self-ironic play with gender roles, and until the end of her life, her position within the postwar ideology that governed the manner in which the German people came to fashion their imaginary relation to the consequences of World War II was laden with murky expressions of rejection.[41]

But for those on the other side, for the allies, Dietrich will be remembered as a more palatable modern-day Portia, not fighting against Shylock but, rather, on the side of his descendants for the rights of the Jewish people in a war against a totalitarian system whose revenge threatened a radical final solution to all Jewish claims on a right to existence. And like Shakespeare's heroine, Dietrich felt she was merely acting as a representative of a law she had inherited from her father—the Prussian officer's code of honor. She was joining the ranks of men not in order to introduce gender trouble but to be part of a simple opposition, where the Allies and the Nazis fought on clearly delineated moral grounds. Indeed, as a response to the question why she had changed her allegiance once the United States had declared war on the Axis powers, she came to construct a narrative that uncannily resonates with the one given by Shakespeare's heroine. It was a decision forced upon her, not one she had much freedom in, because for her it was the only decent thing she could do. Many years after the end of the war she explained to a journalist,

> Even today I receive letters from Germany, in which I am asked: "Given that you were a German and, as you repeatedly state, continue to be so today—why did you join the American army that fought against Germany?" I felt responsible for the war caused by Hitler. I wanted to help to bring this war to an end as quickly as possible. That was my only wish. When Japan attacked America I gave up everything I owned, I sold all my jewels and waited for my orders. I didn't have to wait very long. There weren't many "celebrities" who were willing to take upon themselves the discomforts of sharing the war with the soldiers. America had taken me in when I gave up Hitler and Germany. You can't simply take—you also have to give. That is already written in the Bible.[42]

Significantly, Marlene Dietrich considered the fact that she was awarded a medal of honor by the French government for her role as a simple allied soldier to be one of her most significant symbolic recognitions.

Uncanny Mimicry of a Less Wholesome Kind

In tandem with the critical attention paid to the cross-dressing enacted on the Shakespearean stage and its refiguration through the centuries, critics and artists alike have focused on drag culture as a postmodern moment of subversion.[43] Admitting that drag queens have been her obsession since the early '70s, when she first wanted to use photography to pay homage to the courage of her friends in recreating themselves according to their fantasies, Nan Goldin sees transvestites as a third sex, liberated from the constraints any homogeneous sexual definition entails. By using their bodies not only to materialize fantasies of what they want to look like but also to publicly declare that one can appropriate cultural formations of the feminine without relinquishing masculinity, they succeed in performing an astonishingly iridescent palette of genderings. "Some of my friends shift genders daily— from boy to girl and back again," Goldin explains. "Some are transsexual before or after surgery, and among them some live entirely as women while others openly identify themselves as transsexuals. Others dress up only for stage performances and live as gay boys by day. And still others make no attempt at all to fit in anywhere, but live in a gender-free zone, flaunting their third sex status." In Goldin's photographs, the transvestites seem to be saying, "Given that any existence within culture implies abiding by certain gender formations, then to consciously choose masquerades of the self can turn subjection before the law into a moment of agency." For Goldin, transvestites are the heroes in her saga about human relationships: "They are the real winners of the battle of the sexes because they have stepped out of the ring."[44]

However, leaving the battlefield of gender trouble behind can at best perform a utopic gesture, even while it continues to be riddled with uncanny ambivalence. Jennie Livingston's *Paris is Burning*, which documents her fascination with the drag balls in Harlem in the late 1980s where African American and Latino gay men competed in contests organized under predetermined categories, serves as another example for the vexed pleasures of drag. Seeking primarily to make visible the self-empowering creativity with which these contestants came to appropriate the image repertoire of the white world of fashion and celebrity, Livingston focuses on the competitions themselves and shows the contestants' almost parodic imitation of the clichés that characterize appearances in the white world of prosperity and fame, even while she interrupts these sequences with statements made by the contestants. Part of the resilience of this documentary material resides in the way in which "appearance" is resignified so as to become coterminous with realness. Although the mimicry is astonishingly perfect, the poignancy of the appropriation of the "executive look" or the "college student look" resides in a self-conscious staging of the fact that appearance is

precisely not to be understood as entertaining a transparent relation to existence. This is a foregrounding of utter appearances, of the imaginary relation over any social reality; it is a performance of ideology as pure fantasy,
empty but utterly poignant. The notion of "realness," one of a complex
array of concepts coined in the context of these balls, in fact describes the
ability "to be able to blend, to look as much as possible like your counterpart, to mimic the real woman/real man." At stake for most of these performers is not so much any one particular imitation; rather, the film foregrounds the agency involved in choosing one's dress and enacting the fact
that it is nothing but an appropriated appearance. The dictum performed by
the walkers in the heterotopia of these drag balls seems to be: "I can be what
I am not but want to be because I look it."

Commenting on her own unease with this documentary material, Judith
Butler notes that "there is both a sense of defeat and a sense of insurrection
to be had from the drag pageantry in *Paris Is Burning*, the drag we see, the
drag which is after all framed for us, filmed for us, is one which both appropriates and subverts racist, misogynist, and homophobic norms of oppression."[45] Indeed, Livingston's film offers a vibrant example for how a critical
appropriation of our cultural dictates involving normative definitions of
gender, class, and race might fruitfully perform a crisis in the very interpellation it also responds to. At the same time she also uncovers the blind spots
inherent to any imitation of hegemonic values on the part of drag culture.
Much as the attraction of the cross-dressed Shakespearean heroine revolved
around the manner in which this mode of dress could be instrumentalized
to contain the radical alterity of femininity within Renaissance culture, so
too, as Peggy Phelan argues, much of the appeal this film has for a white,
straight audience resides in "its ability to absorb and tame the so-called otherness of this part of black and Latino gay male culture."[46]

As Livingston herself explains, when she came to revisit Harlem two
years later, this particular moment in drag culture had already been eroded.
Two aspects of this change are particularly striking. Venus Xtravaganza, perhaps the most successful mimic in *Paris is Burning*, appears to have literally
experienced the dangers of identifying with the idealized images of a culture foreign to him/her. Having wanted nothing more than to become the
perfect white spoiled suburban housewife, s/he is found murdered in a hotel
room, killed by one of her/his clients, who, according to Livingston's suggestion, had been angered at the fact that s/he wasn't what s/he appeared
to be. But as Peggy Phelan conjectures, it is equally possible that Venus was

murdered because her passing was successful: "On the other side of the mirror which women are for men, women witness their own endless shattering. Never securely positioned within the embrace of heterosexuality or male homosexuality, the woman winds up *under* the bed, four days dead."[47]

At the same time, the success of the balls proved to be the other side of corrosion. The "voguing" celebrated at the drag balls had, in the course of two years, become a fashion trend; the parodic expressions of the marginalized had turned into an accepted mode of presentation at mainstream fashion shows, with some of the performers from these drag pageants suddenly transformed into the celebrities they were previously merely imitating. With subversion recuperated and diffused, Livingston's film ultimately closes with an acknowledgment of cultural constraint. Not only can we not choose the cultural norm interpellating us, but we can also not calculate the consequences that our appropriation and reformulation of this norm might take. Ironically, the toxic side-effects of thriving on a crisis in interpellation may be the utter success of this enterprise opened up, however, to two modes of destruction: "successful" cross-dressing can lead to the real killing off of the performing body, because the appearances are taken for being real (performance of femininity implying a real female), or to the complete dissolution of the performance, because the appearance is declared to be the real thing (the performance of femininity is all that counts).

Perhaps the most poignant lesson to learn, then, is that cross-dressing never fails as dramatically as when it fully succeeds. Indeed, Stephen Orgel astutely notes that the whole point of cross-dressing "is precisely for the audience to see through the impersonation." In contrast to the pleasure that a playful game with interpellation affords, "to be seriously deceived by cross-gendered disguising," he adds, "is for us deeply disturbing, the stuff of classic horror movies like *Psycho.*"[48] In order to explore the implications of this claim I want, by way of closure, to turn to Guillermo del Toro's science fiction thriller *Mimic* (1997). Genetic biologist Dr. Susan Tyler (Mira Sorvino) and her husband Dr. Peter Mann (Jeremy Northam), in charge of controlling infectious diseases in New York City, discover that an epidemic that threatens to kill an entire generation of children is being transmitted by the common cockroach. So as to contain it before it can spread beyond Manhattan, they design a new species, christened the "Judas breed," which secretes a poison fatal to the roaches. In an eerie scene of parturition, Susan, dressed in an armorlike white gown that completely shields her from her environment, sets free the killer-bugs and the epidemic is successfully overcome. Three years later, however, she finds herself confronted with a creature that, along the lines discussed by von Sternberg and Nan Goldin, constitutes a third species that defies clear definition. These nocturnal hybrid creatures, who look like big men dressed in black, become the symptoms of a far more dangerous xenophobic anxiety than the urban transvestite precisely because they render visible the toxic side-effect of successful appropriation. Far from dying, as they were designed to, they evolved to mimic their predators, namely the human species. Thinking about what the completion of this evolution will look like produces a nightmare. As Susan Tyler explains to the men who have gone out with her to destroy this brood, "They will imitate us, infiltrate us and breed a legion before anyone can notice." When one of the men, who has been listening to her conspiracy theory with incredulity, asks, "If that thing has been around, how come nobody has seen it?" Susan responds by giving voice to the horror that all too successful cross-dressing entails, precisely because it effaces all traces of incongruity between the posing subject and the attire it has chosen to appropriate: "I think we have [seen it]." In this scenario, cross-dressing can no longer be read for what it is. Her conjecture is that these cross-dressed killer-bugs will use the subway system to migrate out of the city and then spread across the entire country. Only the destruction of the one male living in the midst of this killer-bug colony that has placed its larvae all along the lower levels of the Delancey Street subway can stop this invasion.

Though Guillermo del Toro's *Mimic* follows along the same rhetoric of mistaken identities as Wilder's comedy, his nightmare scenario offers a less palatable rendition of how dominant culture uses the performance of cross-dressing to police its own boundaries against an invasion of queerness. Not only does del Toro's phobic fantasy scenario render more visible the violence underlying the act by which its representatives come once more to fortify the hegemonic regime, but he gives a significant turn to this performance of cultural panic. The mutated Judas breed, attacking humans and abducting them so as to feed on them in the safety of their subaltern realm, have usurped a foreign attire in a twofold sense. Only the female bugs can cross-dress, while the one male bug, the progenitor of the entire species, is unable to transform himself and must remain close to the larvae. The female bugs, furthermore, not only cross-dress as human beings but, more important, as tall men dressed in long black coats. The moment of *anagnorisis* occurs when Susan, on folding over a photograph that was taken of one of the bugs found dead in the sewer, suddenly finds herself looking at what by all appearances seems to be the image of a human skull. The toxic cross-dresser she has unwittingly created thus has several layers of dress: the nondistinctive urban male and the figure of human death. What is so compelling about *Mimic* is the fact that it plays through the consequences of a performance of cross-dressing, which produces panic by radically undercutting all attempts to distinguish the appropriator of foreign attire from those wearing appropriate attire. For the logic of del Toro's narrative is that the perfect mode of cross-dressing can only elicit an act of total eradication.

That he is not only interested in horror fantasies is, however, made poignantly clear by the explicit references to the iconography of Jewish immigration throughout the film. The blood-lusting Jew is more than a staple of anti-Semitic rhetoric. Beginning with the location—the Delancey Street subway—we recognize that del Toro is offering us a cruelly self-conscious parable about the way we police the boundary between ethnic groups by turning the unwelcome foreign body into a dangerous termite that can be eradicated. Delancey Street is, after all, the site of one of the most famous Jewish quarters during the big wave of immigration at the turn of the century, and, indeed, the show-down of Susan and her troop against the bugs takes place in the Old Armory subway shaft, built around 1900, where the subway line leads from lower Manhattan to Coney Island. Furthermore, as one of the men tries to return to the upper level to get help, he suddenly finds himself in rooms with old sewing machines, as though these abandoned objects were to recall for us the mode of production that allowed for the successful integration of Eastern European immigrants at the turn of the century. Crucially, for one brief moment, del Toro shows us Tom finding an old newspaper inside the stranded subway car in the Armory shaft and smiling obliquely at the date, May 4, 1945, as well as headline, which declares the end of the war in Europe and the surrender of the German troops.

The dictum at the heart of Jenny Livingston's drag queens—to look as much as possible like your counterpart—uncannily applies to both levels of del Toro's narrative about successful imitation, infiltration, and assimilation; it applies to the Jewish immigration he indirectly refers to as well as to its toxic refiguration, the threat of an invasion by killer-bugs. Resonating equally uncannily with the image of Marlene Dietrich joining the U.S. armed forces to move into a real battleground, much as Amy Jolly had cast off her shoes to follow her lover, Tom Brown, into battle at the end of *Morocco*, the form of cross-dressing played through by del Toro reaches far beyond the world of urban nightclub life. Having entered into the heart of the Judas breed's provisional home, the machine room underneath the Delancey Street subway, Peter strikes at the gas pipe he finds there, and, setting it on fire, causes a subaltern Holocaust that successfully destroys all the mimics.

Del Toro's tale poignantly illustrates how vexed the issue of cross-dressing remains, not least of all because the bugs are eradicated at precisely the site that, fifty years earlier, had served to signify the point of arrival for those Jews, who, by virtue of immigration, were able to escape the final solution of the Nazis. We are always steering between the Schylla of appropriation and the Charybdis of subversion. In this interzone a wide spectrum of negotiating scenarios can emerge, ranging from Billy Wilder's jubilatory celebration of a game of genders to del Toro's traumatic horror scenario, in which the violent wound, which the transgression of the law inflicts upon a hegemonic norm, necessarily calls for an equally violent act of injuring retribution, so that the law we all need in order to protect ourselves from unregulated violence can be reinstalled. The felled female Judas-bugs, who, once they are folded back onto themselves, give way to men dressed in black coats, are as resilient a trope for the way social laws deal with the pleasures of transgression as is the figure of Jack Lemmon, who, holding his wig in his hand, realizes with stunned sobriety that his lover has entered blissfully into the realm of romantic delusions and is no longer even looking at him.

NOTES

1. Edward Sikov, in *Laughing Hysterically: American Screen Comedy of the 1950s* (New York: Columbia University Press, 1986), highlights Wilder's *Some Like it Hot* as one of Hollywood's best example of the inability of human beings to construct themselves to the limit dictated by American social regulations.

2. As Michael Shapiro argues in *Gender in Play on the Shakespearean Stage: Boy Heroines and Female Pages* (Ann Arbor: University of Michigan Press, 1996), part of the fascination for cross-dressing on the Renaissance stage was that these figures were perceived neither as grotesque hybrids nor as static icons of androgyny; rather, they functioned as "a figure of unfused, discretely layered gender identities—playboy, female character, male persona. Any one of them could be highlighted at a given moment because all of them were simultaneously present at some level in the spectators' minds" (p. 4). Along these lines one could speculate whether the poignancy of Billy Wilder's comedy might not reside in the fact that the question of whether Osgood actually knows about Jeraldine's real sex, indeed whether Jerald really knows

about his sexual inclinations, remains open. The scenario of fused gender identities conforms with the fetishist's fantasy scenario, where to know one thing and to believe in another need not be mutually exclusive. It is as though Osgood were all along saying, "I know you are a man, but, in order to keep up the pretense you seem to desire, I will believe you are a woman," rather than the more conventional reading of mistaken identities: "I will believe you to be a woman, so as to cover up my clandestine and forbidden homoerotic desire."

3. Beyond the colloquial meaning of this terminating phrase, meant to emphasize that everybody lacks something, Osgood's statement can be read to mean "no body is perfect" in the sense that the sentience of the body alone is not enough to signify; it requires symbolic mediation. Equally the statement points to the fact that perfection may have to do with having not one body but several symbolically mediated bodies. Most crucially, however, someone by the name of Mr. Nobody is, indeed, perfect, in the sense that perfection is coterminous with having no manifest identity, and thus no troubling marks: "nobody" is perfect when the physical and symbolic body in question is in fact an empty human vehicle. The notion of cross-dressing at stake in my argument oscillates between these three positions.

4. See Marjorie Garber's study *Vested Interests: Cross-Dressing and Cultural Anxiety* (New York: Routledge, 1992), as well as Lesley Ferris's collection of essays, *Crossing the Stage: Controversies on Cross-Dressing* (New York: Routledge, 1993).

5. In her groundbreaking study *Gender Trouble: Feminism and the Subversion of Identity* (New York: Routledge, 1990), Judith Butler gestures toward the tension between, on the one hand, the unsolvable antagonism irrevocably inscribed in any performance of gender difference and, on the other, the way in which simple oppositions offer a mitigation of this friction, precisely by having recourse either to an overruling homogenous definition of gender or by subsuming one sex into the other. As Jan Freitag notes in "Impossible Geographies" (unpublished manuscript), men go to war to flee from the antagonism Hegel designates as the "abstract negativity" upon which all community is based. Freitag's reformulation of Hegel highlights the fact that, in the sense that war comes to stand for a simple opposition, it articulates the impossible plenitude of society, and it does so by articulating the antagonism that runs through the sedimented aspects of our objective everyday existence in the form of gender trouble. See also Slavoj Žižek's discussion of the tension between antagonism and fantasy work in *Plague of Fantasy* (London: Verso, 1997). Here he argues that narration emerges "in order to resolve some fundamental antagonism by rearranging its terms into a temporal succession." If we follow him in concluding that "the very form of narrative bears witness to some repressed antagonism" (p. 11), then an analysis of scenarios of cross-dressing involves exploring how the repressed antagonism resurfaces in this play with fixed gender identities: does it subversively resignify the antagonistic friction between the sexes, or does it elide this troubling friction of the sexes by appropriating the cross-dresser into a homoerotic or androgynous model?

6. I take the notion of sexual friction from Stephen Greenblatt's discussion of cross-dressing in Shakespeare's *Twelfth Night* in *Shakespearean Negotiations* (Berkeley: University of California Press, 1988), pp. 66–93, notably his speculation that even if the gender of the Shakespearean boy heroine was an open secret to the Renaissance audience, the narrative tension of these texts requires the friction between the sexes.

7. See Michel Foucault, "Of Other Spaces," *Diacritics* 16, no. 1 (Spring 1986): 22–27, where he discusses heterotopias as "countersites," effectively enacted utopias, places outside of all places, even though it is possible to indicate their location in reality. These are above all sites where crises are worked through and cultural memory is stored, exchanged, and imaginatively reworked.

8. Judith Butler, *Bodies that Matter: On the Discursive Limits of "Sex"* (New York: Routledge, 1993), p. 126.

9. Louis Althusser, "Ideological State Apparatuses (Notes Toward an Investigation)," in *Lenin and Philosophy and Other Essays*, trans. Ben Brewster (New York: Monthly Review Press, 1971).

10. Butler, *Bodies that Matter*, p. 121.

11. Ibid., p. 123.

12. Ibid., p. 124.

13. Mladen Dolar, "Beyond Interpellation," *Qui Parle* 6, no. 2 (Spring/Summer 1993): 76–78.

14. Ibid., p. 82.

15. See Jacques-Alain Miller's discussion of Lacan's reformulation of the uncanny, in "Extimité," trans. Françoise Massardier-Kennedy, *Prose Studies* 11 (December 1988): 121–30.

16. I use the adjective "chatoyant" to mean an object or a situation that has a changeable luster.

17. Though Lisa Jardine's argument in *Reading Shakespeare Historically* (London: Routledge, 1996) that one should never forget the difference between reading Shakespeare historically and reading him anachronistically is a crucial one, my own concern will be for the latter, given that at stake in my argument is what Julia Kristeva calls the transposition of one text into another, which is to say how later figurations of cross-dressing feed off of but also resignify the Shakespearean model.

18. See Stanley Cavell, *Pursuits of Happiness: The Hollywood Comedy of Remarriage* (Cambridge: Harvard University Press, 1981), p. 144.

19. Stephen Orgel, *Impersonations: The Performance of Gendering Shakespeare's England* (Cambridge: Cambridge University Press, 1996), p. 106. See also Orgel, "Nobody's Perfect, Or Why Did the English Stage Take Boys for Women," *South Atlantic Quarterly* 88, no. 1 (Winter 1989): 7–29. As Shapiro notes in *Gender in Play on the Shakespearean Stage*, pp. 199–204, tracing the manner in which Shakespearean comedies have been performed since the mid-eighteenth century, each historical

moment uses the cross-dressed woman to articulate the construction of femininity that is to be culturally privileged.

20. As Garber notes in *Vested Interests,* two trends can be noted in recent Renaissance scholarship on cross-dressing, the one "valorizing the female-to-male cross-dresser as a figure for emergent womanhood, either in economic or in psychological and social terms, the other privileging the historical facts of the playhouse, and the special role of the boy actor or boy actress as a sign of specifically homosexual energies in the theater, energies of male desire" (p.85). For a discussion of how cross-dressing allows for homoeroticism to be safely explored, see Valerie Traub, *Desire and Anxiety: Circulations of Sexuality in Shakespearean Drama* (New York: Routledge, 1992).

21. See Margaret Reynold's discussion of cross-dressing in early opera, "Ruggiero's Deceptions, Cherubino's Distractions," in *En Travesti: Women, Gender Subversion, Opera,* ed. Corinne E. Blackmer and Patricia Juliana Smith (New York: Columbia University Press, 1995), pp. 132–51.

22. Tracing the manner in which the subversive or transgressive potential of cross-dressing is recuperated and contained by the narrative solution offered by Shakespeare's plays, Jean E. Howard suggests that, while the unruly cross-dressed woman gives voice to an instability in the dominant gender system, it is ironically Olivia who poses as the real threat to the proposed hierarchy ("Crossdressing, the Theater, and Gender Struggle," *Shakespeare Quarterly,* 39, no. 4 [Winter 1988]: 431). For the story of containment of gender and class insurgency seems to "applaud a crossdressed woman who does not aspire to the positions of power assigned men, and to discipline a non-crossdressed woman who does."

23. Heinrich Heine, in his reading of Shakespeare's comedy in the context of the battle for emancipation on the part of German Jewry at the beginning of the nineteenth century, notes in *Shakespeares Mädchen und Frauen* (Munich: Winkler Verlag, 1972), pp. 652–66, that Bassanio is, indeed, nothing other than a fortune hunter, obsessed with money. As the young man admits to Antonio in the first act, he has much disabled his estate "by something showing a more swelling port than my fair means would grant continuance," so as to convince the older man to lend him more money, even though he has not yet paid back the earlier sum. Indeed his love interests can not be severed from his monetary ones. In the same speech he admits "to you, Antonio, I owe the most in money and in love" (I.i), much as his description of Portia lists wealth before beauty: "In Belmont is a lady richly left, and she is fair, and (fairer than that word), of wondrous virtues." Given that we are led from the start to see in Bassanio the proper suitor for Portia, Shakespeare thus obliquely gives voice to the cruelty of a law that privileges money over love, even while it dresses the pecuniary concerns in the theme of romantic comedy.

24. See Slavoj Žižek's discussion in *Looking Awry: An Introduction to Jacques Lacan through Popular Culture* (Cambridge: MIT Press, 1991) of how a rottenness subtend-

ing symbolic law is modulated by virtue of the splitting of the law into two representative figures, the first pointing to the necessary inconsistency of the symbolic register in a fallible figure of paternal authority who guarantees a certain stability to any given system of law, and the other, the figure of the obscene paternal function, the father who really enjoys in a transgressive and destructive manner. By pitting these two agencies against each other this rottenness of the law can be signified and then, in a second step, fixed onto a body that can once again be excluded or, as is the case of Shylock in *The Merchant of Venice*, radically assimilated.

25. As Jardine notes in *Reading Shakespeare Historically*, female cross-dressing in the Renaissance was readily conceived as a sign for prostitution, with the freely circulating woman considered to be "loose" or unconstrained in the sense of being "out of place." But this "looseness" also "eases the process of crossing the threshold into the male domain" (p. 67), or, as I am arguing for Jessica, crossing the boundary from one paternal domain into another. The correlation between cross-dressed woman, prostitute, and a female body having no fixed place will return in my discussion of Marlene Dietrich's first song in *Morocco*.

26. In the context of my discussion of forced choices one could note that it is astonishing how, in focusing his discussion on the motive of the three caskets, Sigmund Freud should have, perhaps willfully, overlooked the fact that accepting one's fate ultimately involves Portia and Shylock far more significantly than Bassanio. In Freud's discussion, the casket Bassanio chooses comes to represent the imaginative transformation of destiny into chance: "Choice stands in the place of necessity, of destiny. In this way man overcomes death, which he has recognized intellectually. No greater triumph of wish-fulfillment is conceivable. A choice is made where in reality there is obedience to a compulsion" ("The Theme of the Three Caskets," vol. 12 of *The Complete Psychological Works of Sigmund Freud*, ed. and trans. James Strachey [London: Hogarth Press, 1953–74], p. 299). Freud's oversight is significant because, while one could argue that for Portia a wishful reversal has taken place insofar as she refashions herself from disempowered daughter to an attorney-at-law, the same claim cannot be made for Shylock, forced to choose the psychic death Portia's law dictates. Furthermore, by reading the question of choice only in relation to Bassanio's romantic refiguration, Freud highlights only the manner in which romantic love deflects death by giving it the shape of a desirable beautiful woman. He thus relegates the issue of forced choices to the imaginary register and to the question of masculine recognition of death as a mode of disavowal. See Elisabeth Bronfen, *Over Her Dead Body: Death, Femininity, and the Aesthetic* (New York: Routledge, 1993). Shakespeare's text in fact offers two further instances where the Freudian formula holds, yet where the symbolic cut the law imposes on the subject cannot fully be recuperated into a happy imaginary tale of gendered love. Both Portia and Shylock know that their choice is a necessity, that any wishful reversal remains a fiction, and that this forced choice has nothing to do with their sexuality but with the position they are to assume in a symbolic realm.

27. In "Crossdressing," Howard notes how in the figure of Portia, Shakespeare has created "a fictional structure in which the ideology of male dominance breaks down. The woman," she argues, "is the only source of secure wealth, the only person in the courtroom capable of successfully playing the man's part and ousting the alien intruder" (p. 434).

28. In her article "Disrupting Sexual Difference: Meaning and Gender in the Comedies," in *Alternative Shakespeares*, ed. John Drakakis (London: Routledge, 1985), Catherine Belsey notes that the cross-dressed woman neither creates some "third, unified, androgynous identify which eliminates all distinctions," nor repudiates sexuality itself. Instead she gives body to a "plurality of places, of possible beings" (p. 189), which can be defined for each person by rendering visible the extimacy of the law of gender.

29. Josef von Sternberg, *Fun in a Chinese Laundry* (London: Columbus Books, 1965).

30. Initially we see her embarking on a boat leaving France for North Africa, a delicate lace veil attached to her hat covering her face. In the second and only other song scene of the film, she is dressed as the arch-seductress, Eve, selling apples to her clients. After performing these three dresses of feminine seduction she will finally cast off her high-heeled shoes and follow her lover barefoot into the desert, as though to signal a move beyond all imaginary self-fashionings.

31. In *Stars* (London: BFI, 1979), Richard Dyer offers a useful overview of the debate, focusing on the manner in which Dietrich was seen either as "an empty vehicle for Sternberg's erotic formalism" or as "resisting the construction of her as a goddess for male dreams" (p. 179). Seeking to arbitrate the various positions, he concludes that "the films can be seen as the traces of the complexities of their relationship rather than just the combination of two voices" (p. 180).

32. Quoted in Tom Flinn, "Joe, Where Are You? (Marlene Dietrich)," *Velvet Light Trap* 6 (Fall 1972): 9.

33. See Steven Bach's biography, *Marlene Dietrich: A Life and Legend* (New York: HarperCollins, 1993), for a discussion of the strange mixture between appropriation and dispossession that was written into the relation between von Sternberg and his star, Marlene Dietrich.

34. Writing about a different film from the same period, George Cukor's *Adam's Rib*, Mary Anne Doane suggests that it might be fruitful to speak about female spectators as spectatorial transvestites, when faced with cinematic performances of women cross-dressing as men (*Femmes Fatales: Feminism, Film Theory, Psychoanalysis* [New York: Routledge, 1991]).

35. See Gaylyn Studlar, *In the Realm of Pleasure: Von Sternberg, Dietrich, and the Masochistic Aesthetic* (New York: Columbia University Press, 1988), who privileges the position of the masochist in her discussion of the manner in which von Sternberg stages Dietrich. Dietrich's performance, she argues, refigures the position of the

maternal body, which is conceived as highly empowered, both dangerous as well as pleasurable, depending on the degree of proximity that the child has to it.

36. The critical engagement with this scene was, of course, inaugurated by Laura Mulvey's essay "Visual Pleasure and Narrative Cinema" (in *The Sexual Subject: A Screen Reader in Sexuality* [New York: Routledge, 1992]), in which she was the first to focus on the interplay of sadism and masochism at work in the von Sternberg-Dietrich couple, arguing that, insofar as the cinema satisfies a primordial wish for pleasurable looking, this pleasure splits between an active/male and a passive/female position. Within this economy women are "simultaneously looked at and displayed" so that they can be said to "connote to-be-looked-at-ness," while the man controls the film fantasy, and emerges as the representative of power, i.e., "as the bearer of the look of the spectator" (pp. 22–33). In the course of the last two decades Mulvey has herself reformulated her position on spectatorship; see for example *Fetishism and Curiosity* (Bloomington: Indiana University Press, 1996), p. 1.

37. Precisely the mise-en-scène of a sequence like this supports Molly Haskell's claim that Dietrich "comes closest to being a goddess, but she refuses to be one, refuses to take on the generalized aspects of love and suffering with which a mass audience could identify, and refuses to pretend for the sake of a man's ego that love will not die or that she will love only him. . . . Although she is a creature of myth—and not, in any sociological sense, a 'real woman'—she is also demystifying" (*From Reverence to Rape: The Treatment of Women in the Movies* [New York: Penguin, 1974], p. 109).

38. I want to thank Bodil Marie Thomsen for this interpretation of the final scene of *Morocco*.

39. See Andrea Weiss, " 'A Queer Feeling When I Look at You': Hollywood Stars and Lesbian Spectatorship in the 1930s," in *Stardom: Industry of Desire*, ed. Christine Gledhill (New York: Routledge, 1991). Weiss has argued that von Sternberg consciously plays with the possibility of a lesbian gaze, given that he allowed Paramount to use the publicity slogan, "Dietrich—the woman all women want to see." The song sequence thus not only opens up a privileging of heterosexuality, as was the intended reading of Hollywood comedies, where Dietrich's kiss comes to stand metonymically for her power of seduction, but also allows a queer reading that resists this intended reading. For a brief moment Marlene Dietrich seems to step out of her role as femme fatale so as to stage a different form of sexual desire, namely lesbian sexuality; but, more important, the chatoyant shift between seductress and seduced woman gives voice to a fluidity of positions that seduces all spectators, regardless of their proclivities.

40. Quoted in Renate Seydel, *Marlene Dietrich: Eine Chronik ihres Lebens in Bildern und Dokumenten* (Munich: Nymphenburger Verlag, 1984), p. 165.

41. Gertrud Koch, "Exorcised: Marlene Dietrich and German Nationalism," in *Women and Film: A Sight and Sound Reader*, ed. Pam Cook and Philip Dodd (Lon-

don: Scarlet Press, n.d.), pp. 10–15; Koch discusses how, because the Germans after the war continued to view Marlene Dietrich as a traitor to her own country, it caused great surprise that she asked to be laid to rest in Berlin, next to her mother. The grand funeral ceremony had, however, to be called off because the authorities were not sure how the Berlin audience would welcome the return of the international star. For a discussion of cross-dressing and the military, see Elizabeth Young, "Confederate Counterfeit: The Case of the Cross-Dressed Civil War Soldier," in *Passing and the Fictions of Identity*, ed. Elaine K. Ginsberg (Durham, N.C.: Duke University Press, 1996), pp. 181–217.

42. Quoted in Seydel, *Marlene Dietrich*, p. 223.

43. See the exhibition catalogue *Rrose Is a Rrose Is a Rrose: Gender Performance in Photography*, ed. Jennifer Blessing for the Guggenheim Museum, New York (January 17–April 27, 1997). See also Garber, *Vested Interests*, for a general discussion of contemporary expressions of drag.

44. Nan Goldin, *The Other Side* (Zürich: Scalo Verlag, 1993), pp. 8, 11.

45. Butler, *Bodies that Matter*, p. 128. See also Peggy Phelan, "Crisscrossing Cultures," in Ferris, ed., *Crossing the Stage*. In a similar mode to Butler's, Phelan notes that "walking in a ball is at once a celebration of one's grandest ambitions to charm, seduce, and attract, and an admission that what one most admires is perennially hostile and impervious to such admiration" (p. 162).

46. Emphasizing the manner in which these walkers are unavoidably complicitous with the cultural ideology they try to denounce, Phelan, in "Crisscrossing Cultures," cites bell hooks's scathing dismissal of the film: "What could be more reassuring to the white public than a documentary affirming that the victims of racism are all too willing to be complicit in perpetuating the fantasies of the ruling class white culture?" (p. 167).

47. Phelan, "Crisscrossing Cultures," p. 168.

48. Orgel, *Impersonations*, p. 19.

Chapter 10

Contingencies of Pleasure and Shame:
Jamaican Women's Poetry

ANITA HAYA PATTERSON

Complaints, sometimes virulent, against feminism are now commonplace in the mass media. We are told that feminists are immersed in obscure academic theory; they are out of touch with most women's concerns; their stridency has alienated a younger generation of would-be feminists; they are obsessed with male-bashing; they are neo-Puritans who deny the possibility of consensual sex; they promote reactionary stereotypes of women as victims, and so on.[1] Needless to say, it is far easier to show what was wrong with feminism in the 1990s than it is to propose constructive alternatives. But given such a climate of criticism in the media, it is not surprising that within the academy there has been a considerable effort to reassess feminist methods and goals.

A recent question raised in the debate has been whether the theoretical enterprise itself has created an impasse by blinding feminists to specific historical contingencies. Some critics, lamenting the fact that theorists tend to overlook local details, have tried to rectify the situation by resorting to what is now known as "autobiographical criticism." Two examples of this approach may be found in works by bell hooks and Trinh Minh-ha. Both hooks and Minh-ha try to offset the trend toward reductive generalization by appealing to the authority of their lived experience over and against the universal abstractions posited by feminist theory.[2]

But the practice of drawing on personal anecdotes, and relying on a minority perspective as legitimating ground, has also prompted a great deal of cogent criticism. Sara Suleri has suggested that, in certain instances, the "racially female voice" has been elevated into a metaphor for "the good" in what are ultimately thoughtless, simplistic celebrations of oppression. The proliferation of autobiographical anecdotes within feminist discourse does not help matters any, since they are usually accompanied by organicist rhetoric that implicitly reinforces racial separatism. According to Suleri, autobiographical criticism runs the risk of being "conceptually parochial," since it bars the possibility of globalization and intellectual exchange between feminists from different cultures.[3]

Ironically, in the race to affirm the importance of cultural specificity, autobiographical feminists in the previous decade have whittled away at all possible grounds, either for theory or for historiography. Trapped within the confines of uniquely situated subject-positions, bogged down in a quagmire of politically correct, skeptical relativism, we can no longer even affirm the existence of shared experiences that would allow us to describe and identify discrete cultures. As Judith Butler has observed, playing the identities game may have satisfied the requirements of political rhetoric but, in the eyes of many people both inside and outside the academy, it now poses the serious intellectual risk of solipsism.[4]

I agree with Gayatri Spivak, Chandra Mohanty, and other postcolonialist critics who have argued that the theoretical categories used by feminists in Europe and North America are misleading insofar as they lack historical specificity.[5] But harboring a critical, productive skepticism against sweeping generalizations does not mean we should do away with narratives of theory altogether. It simply means we should remember to scrutinize the applicability of any given theory each time we confront new conditions of analysis.[6]

In what follows, I will not rely on any anecdotal evidence. Nor will I offer a theory of the contingency of postcolonial agency, as Homi Bhabha has recently done.[7] Rather, I propose to show that many of the predictions raised by feminists in Europe and the United States have not been borne out by the distinctive history and literature of the Commonwealth Caribbean; and, conversely, that poetry by Jamaican women helps bring to light historical contingencies that significantly limit the applicability of central concepts in feminist theory. As we shall see, the history of women's economic development in Jamaica has shaped a distinctive set of attitudes toward gender equality, pleasure, and shame that are critical to understanding the emergence of women's poetry in the region. For years, literary works by Jamaican women have engaged with feminist ideas that originated in the United States and Europe and have been, as it were, "exported" to the Caribbean. In order to grasp the consequences of feminist theory in places such as Jamaica, we should attend to the ways in which women's poetry critically engages with some of the most orthodox assumptions and interpretative paradigms of feminism.

Let me begin with one very important example. Studies of women, work, and economic development in the Caribbean by Janet Momsen, Helen Safa, and others have shown that women in English-speaking Caribbean countries such as Jamaica have historically played a more important role in agriculture, and thus they have enjoyed conditions of greater socioeconomic equality than women have in either Latin America or the Hispanic Caribbean.[8] In fact, as the historian Sidney Mintz has argued, there has been, relatively speaking, more economic equality between the sexes in the Commonwealth Caribbean than in Europe and the United States. Mintz writes,

> The fact is that . . . Afro-Caribbean societies have been able, in some contexts, to achieve sexual equality still quite unheard of in Western societies for all of their vaunting of individual freedom. . . . With histories radically different from those of the Caribbean . . . , Europe and America have busily exported doctrines of equality rooted in their own past—their own primary-family, monogamous, male-property past. Meanwhile, West Africa and the Afro-Caribbean, influenced so profoundly and for so long by European power and domination, have demonstrated a version of equality in some population sectors that European societies, with their quite basic view of women as property, neither understand nor accept.[9]

The development of what Mintz identifies as a distinctively Afro-Caribbean "version" of gender equality dates back to the slavery era. In contrast to the American South—where planters, driven by economic incentives, often forced slave women to bear children—in places such as Jamaica women were denied any traditional reproductive and child-rearing roles. For most of Jamaican slave history, women were commonly used as field laborers, and pregnancy was no guarantee of a reduction in workload or punishment. This fact is not surprising, when we recall that, in contrast to the United States, slaves were being imported in substantial numbers from Africa until 1807, and there were much higher rates of infertility caused by malnutrition and overwork on Caribbean plantations.[10] As the historian Lucille Mair has argued in her groundbreaking work on Jamaican women, *The Rebel Woman*, there was a leveling effect on the occupational roles of women that took place during slavery. What this meant was that roles in agriculture were differentiated according to strength rather than gender. Mair writes, "Slavery, in many essentials, made men and women roughly equal in the eyes of the master. Their jobs on the plantation were distributed not according to sex but according to age and health. In theory men were supposed to do the backbreaking tasks of the field and factory; in fact as long as women were young and fit they were recruited into the same work force as men and shared more or less the same labor."[11] In addition to their role as field laborers, slave women also worked for one and a half days a week on "provision grounds," or marginal lands up in the hills where they were encouraged to supply their own foods. More recently, in a 1990 study called *Slave Women in Caribbean Society, 1650–1838*, Barbara Bush argued that because the economic organization of the provision grounds was based on a traditional African, rather than European, division of labor, Jamaican slave women not only participated fully in cultivation activities but also would exhibit a marked degree of entrepreneurial skill as prominent market sellers and "higglers" or commercial intermediaries, selling their crop surplus to other slaves.[12]

After emancipation took effect in 1838, Jamaican women continued to participate in the labor force—as cultivators and "higglers" selling fruit, vegetables, and other goods in the marketplace; as seamstresses; as domestic servants; as task workers on estates; or, in the late nineteenth century, as factory hands making straw goods or cigarettes. In all these activities, but especially in the marketplace, women exercised an unusual degree of independence, social authority, and control over their own capital. Between 1881 and 1921, high rates of unemployment for Jamaican men spurred mass migrations to Panama or parts of Central America, and this helps to explain the high number of female-headed households in the Commonwealth Caribbean during this period.[13] Afro-Jamaican women assumed the role and responsibilities of providing for themselves and their families economically, in part because men were economically marginalized and forced to migrate to find work.[14] As the Jamaican sociologist and novelist Erna Brodber has shown, at the turn of the century men did not play a large, visible role in the daily life of the second generation of Jamaican freedwomen.[15] In contrast to many parts of Europe and the United States, Latin America, and the Hispanic Caribbean, where patriarchal rules of inheritance often denied women access to family land, Afro-Jamaican women often inherited houses and land. If her plot of land, or "jonathan," was too small to allow for independent farming, a woman would often turn to "subsistence cultivation"—growing bananas, coffee, and yams for home consumption—and then supplement her income as a wage worker in a kitchen or cattle pen owned by her white neighbor. Although the tools and the "deep digging" activity required for yam planting were considered taboo for women, this task was often contracted out, or women would choose instead to plant traditionally "female" crops, such as oilnut and beans.

I have cited the foregoing examples to make the larger point that specific historical contingencies have shaped the development of gender equality in Jamaica. The fundamental differences between the historical experiences of women in Jamaica and the experiences of women in other, more economically developed societies in Europe and the United States must be acknowledged, if we are to address one of the prevailing criticisms of feminist theory raised at the outset: namely, the lack of specificity and limited applicability of existing paradigms.

In recent years there has been an emerging body of work done on Caribbean women's writing. Yet overall the intellectual response to feminism by Caribbean women—at least among many academic critics and activists—has been one of marked, tepid indifference. In the words of one critic, Carole Boyce Davies, "I am concerned that there is not sufficient excitement and passion about feminist issues being generated, at least in Caribbean intellectual and activist circles. By this I mean on either side of the question: the critique *or* application of feminist ideologies to the explication and/or analysis of Caribbean reality."[16] Given what we know about the history of women's development in the Caribbean, the difficulties of engaging Caribbean women's literature through contemporary feminist theory may seem obvious enough.

However, having stressed the mismatch between feminist theories of gender equality that are rooted in European and American culture, and the specific history of women in Jamaica, I do not mean to suggest that we should dispense with theory altogether. Rather, we should turn to the poems themselves, since they often probe the heterogeneous contingencies of history and, in some instances, explicitly engage with feminist orthodoxies that have already been globalized to even the farthest reaches of the Caribbean.

Paul de Man once said that, at its best, the enterprise of theory should entail a sustained and relentless "resistance," or questioning of its own methodological assumptions and possibilities: "The loftier the aims and the better the methods of literary theory, the less possible it becomes."[17] In order to come to terms with the consequences of feminism in places such as Jamaica, we should consider how women's poetry furthers the aims of this resistance by challenging the speculative expectations of feminist theory. A good poem may generate historical insights that eventually form the basis for a critique of familiar narratives in feminist theory; and the resulting task of making proper adjustments to theory may, in turn, lead to fresh perspectives on the historical contingencies that initially shaped the development of literature in the region. Instead of blinding ourselves to the surprising novelty of historical knowledge, we should pause and reflect on how poetry may oppose and thereby reinvigorate our theoretical proclivity for abstract generalization.

Consider, once again, the problem of women's socioeconomic equality. Whereas European and American feminists have unequivocally pushed this issue to the foreground of their literary, political, and social agendas, women in Jamaica such as the poet and popular media figure Louise Bennett have responded with a humorous, shrewd critique of these discourses on equality. The fact that Bennett was born in Kingston in 1919, and that her first volume of poems was published in the early 1940s, suggests that a sustained, creative, critical engagement with Western feminism by Jamaican women poets is not only possible, it is already well underway.[18]

For example, in a radio program aired in Jamaica called *Miss Lou's Views*, Bennett once delivered a witty monologue in creole dialect on the subject of women's liberation and the concept of "equality." Bennett begins by calling attention to the raucous, quarrelsome debate, or "kas-kas," raised by the globalization of the women's movement and then immediately proceeds to give some words of advice and caution about the term "equality." According to Bennett, we should take care (or "tickya") when dealing with foreign abstractions such as "equality," since this is a "croomoojin" or deceptive word that can ultimately be used to cheat us:

> Oonoo notice de whole heap a kas-kas Oman Liberation a kick up all over de worl nowadays? . . .

> But yet, still an for all, she woulda caution dem fi tickya dah wud "equality." Fur dat wud "equality" is a very croomoojin wud, mmmm.

What is particularly striking about Bennett's critique of feminism, is that she often calls upon traditional folk wisdom—drawing on old proverbs and the advice of her old Aunty Roachy—to drive home her main points.[19] As linguistic anthropologists have pointed out, the pervasive reference to proverbs throughout the modern Caribbean—as a technique of persuasion, and as a means of resolving conflict using figurative, indirect language—is a direct legacy of their importance in African societies. Peter Roberts has found that Jamaican proverbs often use humor to express skepticism, criticism, and other negative attitudes that reflect on past, negative experiences and a social history of struggle against oppression.[20]

Although Bennett strongly condemns injustices to women, she also cites the wisdom of an old proverb to express her skepticism about popular discourses on rights and equality. According to Bennett, women should beware of the limits and potential abuses of democratic rights rhetoric. In the words of the old proverb, "Pretty roses got macca jook"—which, roughly translated, means that the phrase "Equal Rights" may smell sweet, like a rose, but we should never forget that like a rose it also has sharp, painful thorns. What this suggests is that women should look out for the possibility that men might turn the same arguments for equality back against women and invoke the right to sue Jamaican women for child support:

> But oman haffi careful nuffi carry dis Equal Rights worries too far, for "Pretty roses got macca jook." An nex ting yuh know, man mighta seize de chance fi leggo all fi-dem rights pon oman an baps, whole heap a man start tun roun sue oman fi pickney supportance![21]

Bennett's lively, critical engagement with feminism and her reflections on the nature and limits of "equality" are also taken up in many of her poems. For example, in one of her best-known poems, "Jamaica Oman," she argues that the central issue of gender equality raised by feminists abroad does not reflect the concerns and historical contingencies of women's lives in Jamaica. The poem opens by celebrating the verbal prowess traditionally attributed to working women in Jamaica. The pleasure and power of rhetorical indirection, concealment, and artful cunning are evoked by the old creole term, "cunny." Jamaican women are so adept at concealment, the speaker contends, that their cunning borders on "jinnal," a word that has distinct overtones of obeah witchcraft practices.[22] The lyric speaker's diction suggests that these women managed to assert their freedom in such a cunning way that even Jamaican men were not aware of what was happening:

> Jamaica oman, cunny, sah!
> Is how dem jinnal so?
> Look how long dem liberated
> An de man dem never know![23]

Using a terse, vivid, creole idiom, Bennett refers to a broad array of historical and folk sources over the course of her poem. She points out that, over time, the influence of women in Jamaica extended well beyond the confines of the household (or "yard") and into public spaces, symbolized by the road to the market where they would sell their wares:

> Look how long Jamaica oman
> —Modder, sister, wife, sweetheart—
> Outa road an eena yard deh pon
> dominate her part!

In a 1983 study called *The Man of Words in the West Indies: Performance and the Emergence of a Creole Culture*, Roger Abrahams argued that, viewed within the distinctive linguistic culture and symbolic landscape of the Caribbean, the "yard" is a region identified with the constraints, concepts, and rules governing private family practices, whereas the active life of the "road" symbolizes a public world of socioeconomic mobility and freedom.[24] At the time Abrahams claimed that the world of the yard and road organized a central, symbolic opposition within the peasant culture: whereas the yard represented the domain of women and the private sphere, the road was traditionally dominated by men and was associated with "rudeness" (or sexual aggression), "gregariousness," and what Abrahams characterized as other "masculine values."[25] However, more recent sociological studies of women and work in Jamaica have called into question the strict binary oppositions entailed by Abrahams's theoretical schema.[26] The new, revisionary finding that Jamaican women have historically played an active role, both "outa road" and "eena yard," is supported by Bennett's ingenious use of these traditional folk symbols in her poem.

The intellectual scope of Bennett's "Jamaica Oman," and her insistence on the influence of Jamaican women both in public and private life, are ambitious insofar as she attempts to impose order on the chaotic panorama of women's history in Jamaica, from the earliest achievements of women in early slave rebellions to recent advances of women in education. The tradition of women's resistance and liberation began with the legendary figure of Maroon Nanny—a formidable obeah woman who was said to carry nine knives hanging down from her girdle, and who played a central role during the First Maroon Wars against the British colonials waged by the Jamaican Windward maroons in 1739—and continues up to the present day with young girls who win spelling bees:[27]

> From Maroon Nanny teck her body
> Bounce bullet back pon man,
> To when nowadays gal-pickney tun
> Spellin-Bee champion.

Ultimately, Bennett enlists the specific history of Jamaican women in order to stress what she regards as the limited applicability of "second wave" feminism, which emerged in Europe and the United States during the late 1960s and early 1970s, to the experience of women in Jamaica. Long before "Women's Lib" became a popular catchphrase in "foreign" lands, Bennett reminds us, Jamaican women had already been actively pursuing the project of economic equality and independence in their various trades:

> From de grass root to de hill-top
> In profession, skill and trade,
> Jamaica oman teck her time
> Dah mount an meck de grade.

An long before Oman Lib bruck out
Over foreign lan
Jamaica female wasa work
Her liberated plan!

I have dwelt at length on the fact of socioeconomic equality in Jamaica, because establishing this kind of detailed, historical specificity is a necessary step toward understanding the distinctive contingencies of pleasure—and, more generally, the organization of gender and ideas about sexuality—in the region. Earlier on I remarked that there are fundamentally different attitudes toward gender equality in Jamaica and in theories rooted in other, ostensibly more developed cultures in the United States and Europe. The same holds true for prevailing attitudes toward pleasure.

There is a wide disparity between, on the one hand, the predictions and assertions of feminist theories of sexuality developed in Europe and the United States and, on the other, the cultural shaping of sexuality in Jamaica. In Western societies, the tension between pleasure and the dangers of gender inequality in feminist thinking about sexuality is a longstanding and familiar one.[28] Pleasure and sexual freedom were central, divisive issues for feminists in Europe and the United States long before the Women's Liberation Movement challenged notions of biological determinism, criticized heterosexuality as a locus of male power, and generally tried to resist the moral double standards and traditional controls placed on women through marriage and the institutionalization of monogamy.[29] Subsequently, feminists have taken up a whole array of perspectives on the issue of pleasure, ranging from those that critique Freudian and Lacanian psychoanalytical approaches to more recent dissenters who have taken a so-called "libertarian" perspective on sexuality and insisted that by emphasizing sexual danger, feminists have missed out on the connection between pleasure and power.[30]

The fact of women's socioeconomic equality in Jamaica has meant that working women have also historically enjoyed considerable sexual freedom in the region. The relative degree of independence, socioeconomic participation, and social status achieved by women, both married and unmarried, helps explain why the experience of Jamaican women is fundamentally at odds with the feminist critique of the history of sexuality in Western societies. As Rhonda Cobham has argued, "The bourgeois role of the woman as wife and mother, removed from the productive sector of the economy and bound, by economic necessity rather than choice, to sexual fidelity to a

single man and a subsidiary role within the family unit, was not only unat-
tractive but also totally impractical for the Jamaican lower-class woman."[31]

The fundamental distinction being made here, between the history of gender equality in Jamaica, and the experiences of women in many Western societies, has broad implications for how we should study the development of cultural attitudes toward women's sexual pleasure in the Caribbean. The relative
freedom and social latitude enjoyed by Jamaican working women in the sexual domain are immediately evident, for example, when we turn to a 1973
study in which the anthropologist Peter Wilson found that, in modern
Caribbean societies, peasants have traditionally distinguished between a
woman's so-called "respectability" and her "reputation." Whereas "respectability" implied the internalization of the prevailing, British middle-class ideas
about women's sexual monogamy, virtue, and so on, the concept of "reputation" involved a traditional folk counterculture, in which peasants exercised
their own communal sanctions and developed a code of moral behavior that
was largely independent of European cultural norms. Although Jamaican
peasants may have paid lip service to the notion of women's "respectability,"
it turns out that, in fact, "reputation"—and adherence to the locally sanctioned
moral code of the village—were far more important in establishing the social
identity and worth of working women in the eyes of the community.[32]

The special contingencies of women's equality and pleasure in Jamaica
are all the more compelling when we realize that the nature of these freedoms were such that they contributed in important ways to the development of women's manner of speaking in Jamaica, as well as to the creation
of a rich, vibrant creole idiom. As Barbara Bush has pointed out, facility with
language, and especially forms of verbal abuse were commonly used by slave
women in the Caribbean as a means of resistance and self-defense, and this
practice continued after emancipation, as seen by the vast idiom of abuse
developed by working women and higglers in the marketplace.[33] The pleasures of competitive verbal play and indirection traditionally attributed to
Jamaican working women—and, in particular, the capacity for erotic pleasure and verbal play encoded in Louise Bennett's powerfully evocative use of
the creole term "cunny"—can only be understood within the historical
development of gender equality in Jamaica, a longstanding tradition in
which Jamaican women have always worked, competed, played, bartered,
and learned to defend and support themselves.

Broadly speaking, the process of literary emergence in Jamaica may be
attributed, at least in part, to the fact that one of the first major Jamaican

writers, Claude McKay, grasped the complex effects of economic mobility, sexual freedom, and the symbolic potential of women's pleasure. Wilson's distinction between "respectability" and "reputation"—and, more generally, the specific contingencies of women's pleasure at the turn of the century in Jamaica—have been vividly recorded in McKay's writings. Whereas many European and American novels and poems written at the turn of the century stigmatized prostitutes as symbols of degenerating morality and the failure of modern industrialization, McKay's works underscore the value of "reputation," and assert traditional, peasant-folk notions of morality that accommodated greater sexual freedom for women and signaled independence from bourgeois, European cultural norms. For example, in a short story called "The Strange Burial of Sue," he describes how a peasant woman, Sue, has a number of sexual partners in addition to her husband, but is nonetheless regarded as a "good" woman in the eyes of her community:

> Everybody in the village knew that Sue was free-loving. And there had never been any local resentment against her. She was remarkably friendly with all the confirmed concubines and the few married women, and she was a picturesque church member. . . . According to the peasant-folk idea of goodness Sue was a good woman. Which means she was kind.[34]

The verbal facility and racy, vituperative idioms of abuse developed by working women in the marketplace were such that, in McKay's first two volumes of poetry, *Songs of Jamaica* and *Constab Ballads*—which were both published in 1912 and, according to some scholars, marked the emergence of Caribbean poetry—Jamaican working women and their manner of speaking were often presented as powerful, central metaphors for the freedom, entrepreneurial spirit, and individuality that characterized peasant society as a whole. For example, in his 1912 poem, "A Midnight Woman to the Bobby," McKay creates a memorable portrait of a prostitute, or "midnight woman," who is giving a verbal lashing to the local policeman, or "bobby." Even when we bracket the question of the sociological accuracy of the poem, McKay's innovative, controversial thinking on the problem of gender equality and women's sexuality is striking given that the work was published in 1912, well over half a century before feminists began to critically examine the debate over commercial sex in the 1980s.[35] As the poem unfolds, the speaker, a midnight woman, presents a lengthy defense of prostitution as an honorable trade that ensures greater economic freedom and independence than farming, working as a day-laborer, or joining the police force. She points out that whereas farmers often fail to produce crops because they are dependent on unpredictable weather; and day-laborers or "come arounds" are migrants who are constantly on the move; and policemen are nothing more than poor country boys in new uniforms, who have put themselves in service of a white bureaucracy, the "buccra Police Force," a prostitute will always work for herself and never be forced to leave her home in search of employment. When the bobby tries to arrest her, she resists his advances by bombarding him with insults, first by making fun of the fact that his bad health has made all his teeth fall out, giving him an ugly "mash mouth"; and then by insisting that the legal authorities will eventually condemn his officiousness:

No palm me up, you dutty brute,
You' jam mout' mash like a ripe bread-fruit;
You fas'n now, but wait lee ya,
I'll see you grunt under de law.

You t'ink you wise, but we wi' see;
You not de fus' one fas' wid me;
I'll lib fe see dem tu'n you out,
As sure as you got dat mash' mout.'[36]

McKay's interest in the symbolic potential of women's sexual freedom in Jamaica is best understood in the context of a powerful repertoire of European stereotypes that distorted and maligned the sensuality of Afro-Jamaican women. As James Walvin has noted, Europeans have displayed a "curiosity bordering on the obsessional" about the sexual habits of Africans that dates back to the mid-sixteenth century.[37] During the heyday of Caribbean slavery, plantocratic historians such as Edward Long would habitually defend their racialist justifications for slavery by pointing out the animal sensuality of Afro-Jamaican women. For example, in his 1774 history of Jamaica, Long railed against the physical unattractiveness of these women, comparing them to "female orang-outangs," and then proceeded to blame them for the moral ruin of white men in the Caribbean.[38] Such stereotypes easily accommodated the prevailing view that the economic and sexual exploitation of slave women by European white men were in accordance with natural laws.

Moreover, whereas European ideals of womanhood tended to play up the difference between the physical appearance of men and women, planto-cratic accounts of slave women's bodies would emphasize their strong phys-ical and muscular build in order to justify their economic exploitation on slave plantations. As Barbara Bush has shown, the "corporeal equality of the sexes" amongst Afro-Caribbean people was a firmly entrenched European stereotype that endured well into the nineteenth century.[39]

In one poem, called "Pay Day," McKay confronts a long, ethnocentric tra-dition of images constructed by white observers, in which the aberrant, "uncivilized" behavior and repulsive physical appearance of Afro-Caribbean women were cited to justify slavery and affirm the unquestionable superi-ority of European moral and cultural values. In McKay's poem, the speaker addresses a European spectator who is "gazing" at the body of a Jamaican prostitute. Although the setting of the poem, and the presence of the white observer, are clearly reminiscent of what Saidiya Hartman has recently described as the "obscene theatricality" of the slave auction, McKay effec-tively uses the occasion of the poem to explore how the fact of women's socioeconomic equality and mobility in Jamaica contradicts the prevailing European stereotypes of Afro-Caribbean women as promiscuous, immoral, and always amenable to the sexual advances of white men:[40]

> See de waitin' midnight girl
> Wid her saucy cock-up lips,
> An' her strongly-built black hands
> Pressed against her rounded hips.
> She has passed de bound'ry line,
> An' her womanhood is sold;
> Wonder not then, as you gaze
> Dat, though young, she looks so bold.[41]

The poem effectively confronts and revises key aspects of the racialism inscribed in the visual culture. The body of the midnight girl is presented to the European spectator as beautiful and strangely androgynous. The figure is one that breaks down traditional social distinctions between "femininity" and "masculinity," and suggests that the midnight girl, like the poet, possesses a mysteriously autoerotic capacity for pleasure, or personal freedom, that is the direct result of material conditions of economic equality and geo-graphical mobility. The woman's deliberate gesture of pressing her "strongly-built black hands" to her hips expresses agency and self-possession, and has the visual effect of creating a distinct boundary line between her body and the world. Once drawn, the line allows the woman to transgress against conventions of middle-class respectability by "selling her womanhood" in the marketplace.

Throughout McKay's early writings, the figure of the working woman is a central, mediating term: she is simultaneously a metonymy for the Kingston marketplace and the growing effects of industrialization in Jamaica; and, even more important, her independence and transgressions against bourgeois European cultural norms make her a compelling, apt metaphor for McKay's own practices as an emergent poet. In this sense, the fact of gender equality—and the greater economic and sexual freedom of working women that resulted—had an enormous impact on the development of Jamaican literature.

But when we move away from McKay's celebration of women's economic freedom and sexual agency in works published just before World War I, and turn instead to some of the earliest poems written by Jamaican women, during the interwar period, an entirely different situation emerges. Instead of affirming the "free-loving" practices of working women and the distinctively Jamaican, peasant-folk attitudes toward women's pleasure encoded in the notion of village "reputation," the first Jamaican women poets seem instead to have embraced bourgeois European ideas of "respectability" and virtue. This makes sense when we consider the fact that the first women poets came from the Jamaican middle class, which was rapidly increasing in size in the early decades of the twentieth century. The changing nature of class stratification was such that the simple, "three-tiered" system that had developed under slavery and held on in the immediate postemancipation era—a system that included a white upper-class elite, a "colored" middle stratum, and the dark-skinned masses—was giving way to a much more complex system in which there was considerable movement up into the middle class. According to the historian Bridget Brereton, the predictable result of this wave of upward mobility was that the new Jamaican middle class renounced all connection to their peasant roots and folk attitudes toward women's sexuality and struggled obsessively to internalize European norms of family organization and sexual behavior. "Respectability," and not "reputation," became the critical factor in establishing social identity and worth of women in the eyes of this emerging middle-class community:

Often the children of ex-slaves or creole laborers were able to climb up
to middle-class status through teaching in the elementary schools: a secondary education was not necessary for this and so it was a favored chan-
nel of social mobility for young people from poor but "respectable,"
church oriented families. . . . Race was also significant, for members of
the middle stratum (who ranged in complexion from very fair to "pure"
black) tended to be obsessed with skin color and "good" (European-
type) features and hair. They emphasized the values of "respectability,"
which meant subscribing more or less to middle-class British . . . norms
of family organization, sexual behavior, and life-styles.[42]

Thus we are faced with a curious, but understandable paradox: that, despite
a long history of relative economic equality and considerable sexual freedom,
in the first poems written by Jamaican women—Eva Nicholas, Constance
Hollar, M. M. Ormsby, Stephanie Ormsby, and others, who all came from the
newly formed, educated Jamaican middle class—the word "pleasure" seems to
have vanished completely from the literary lexicon.[43] If feminists in Europe
and the United States read through these early writings by Jamaican women,
looking for grist for a theoretical mill that is dead set on exploring the power
and range of women's pleasure, they are bound to walk away empty-handed.

Instead of trying to impose existing theoretical paradigms of "pleasure"
on this literature, I have found that a related but distinct notion—namely,
that of "shame"—has a distinctive cultural resonance, and that the act of
putting a name to the experience of shame itself was a critical step in the
historical development of women's literary emergence in Jamaica. The history of women and work, and the distinctive constellation of attitudes
toward women's sexuality, have meant that there are specific contingencies
that surround the very idea of "shame" that is put forward in poems by
Jamaican women. By way of illustration, I will discuss the work of three
poets: Una Marson, Vera Bell, and Lorna Goodison. Each of these women
played an important role in a separate phase of the development of Jamaican
literature: Una Marson was the first major Jamaican poet to emerge after
Claude McKay and wrote during the interwar period; Vera Bell's work
marks the onset of the early nationalist phase; and Lorna Goodison is one
of the best-known contemporary poets. Although there are many other
excellent poets to choose from, I have selected Marson, Bell, and Goodison
because their poems discover and clarify the contingencies of shame.

The concept of shame has several facets. The first involves language:

shame, like pain, is language-destroying and often cannot be put into words.[44] The difficulty of putting a name to shame is vividly illustrated in the poetry of Una Marson. Early on in her career, Marson grappled with traditional literary forms, especially the Shakespearean sonnet and Romantic lyric forms, looking for the right word to describe a painful, nameless, incommunicable experience. Although none of these early poems are very good, they are all interesting insofar as they allow Marson to cast around for the right fit, experimenting with a range of emotions and genres, trying to locate and accurately describe the nameless source of her pain. In many of the poems that appear in her 1931 volume, Marson directly raises the central problem of inexpressibility or, as she says in the title poem, "Heights and Depths," the problem of wrestling with "thoughts too deep for speech." Although "Invocation" and "Waiting" address the more conventional theme of the poet's need for a compelling, divine source of inspiration, other poems, like "Perhaps," are odd, in that they are basically not about any specific emotion at all. At one point in the poem, Marson vaguely refers to fear of an unknown feeling lying deep inside her that is on the verge of bursting into flame:

> I am afraid of that which lies within
> My very soul, and like a smoldering fire
> Seems on the verge of bursting into flame
> And so consume my very being's might.
> I try to fathom what the urge may be.[45]

Another attribute of shame is that it has "low visibility"—in other words, it is often unacknowledged, and as a result people tend to confuse it with the distinct but related experience of guilt.[46] But the difference between shame and guilt is that whereas pangs of guilt result from the internalization of values and may thus be experienced in the absence of society, shame involves what psychologists have called "social monitoring"—an idea of the self in relation to others, a self that is seen by a real or imagined audience, who has the power to voice approval or disapproval.[47] Moreover, whereas guilt involves agency and transgression against social standards, shame is associated with a total lack of agency and a failure to live up to conventional and, in Marson's case, self-contradictory cultural norms.

Although "guilt" is a central theme in European literature, many of Marson's early poems illustrate the insufficiency and inapplicability of guilt as a concept that accurately accounts for her experience. In fact, the limited success of Marson's first two volumes of poetry may be attributed, at least in part, to her limited engagement with traditional genres and idioms that celebrate the sweetness of melancholy. It is clear that Marson attempted, early on in her career, to echo and, as it were, to "try on" the styles and sensibilities of these canonical poets: in her first book, *Tropic Reveries*, she parodies Kipling; in her second book, *Heights and Depths*, Marson repeatedly draws on epigraphs from Byron and Shelley; and in one poem on "Youth" she offers an interesting, but unsuccessful comparison between her experience of lost youth and that of Byron:

> The weight of the years has fallen upon me
> I think of fair Byron at thirty and three,
> Where are the flowers and fruit of the long years
> Tears, a dull ache, and just thirty and three.[48]

Over the course of her writings, Marson is searching for an alternative idiom that would allow her to express her painful inability to live up to the prevailing norm of "respectability" but at the same time to avoid the concept of agency and guilt.[49] In the great majority of poems collected in *Heights and Depths*, she seems stuck on the theme of melancholy—"The Heart's Cruelty," "Discord," "Poverty," "The Passing of the Year," "Conflict," "The Snare," "Sad Songs," and "My Heart Is Sad," to name just a few—but her apparent dissatisfaction with this concept makes her work sound agonizingly mechanical, repetitive, and tiresome to read through.

There is, however, an important turning point in Marson's third volume, *The Moth and the Star*, when she self-consciously breaks away from the literary culture of the metropole and explicitly comments on the limits of "sweetness in melancholy" as a theme that is deeply inscribed in the literature of colonial power:

> Is there sweetness in melancholy
> Some poets found it,
> Maybe they were stronger than I,
> Maybe they were wiser than I
> Maybe they were older than I. (*MS*, 90)

The Moth and the Star, which was published at Marson's own expense in 1937 after she had been living in England, reveals a transition from her intense introspection, her construction of an "open-ended" or historically unanchored lyric speaker, and her general use of lyric forms to dwell on feelings and crucial moments of private life, to a new, realist idiom that allows her to point out the social contingencies of her experience. Many of the poems written during this period also show the extent to which Marson's stay in London during the 1930s exposed her to the influence of African American modernism, including the blues poetry of Langston Hughes.

Another work of literature that Marson certainly read and may have been mulling over during this period is a dialect poem by Claude McKay, in which he lists a few of the most common emotional attitudes thematized in English and North American poetry—sadness, gaiety, mockery, and religious devotion—and then proceeds to contrast these traditional attitudes with the culturally distinctive worldview embodied in the poem's title, "Whe' Fe Do?," taken from the Jamaican creole expression meaning "What can one do?"

Life will continue so for aye,
Some people sad, some people gay,
Some mockin' life while udders pray;
But we mus' fashion-out we way
An' sabe a mite fe rainy day—
    All we can do.

We needn' fold we han' an' cry,
Nor vex we heart wid groan and sigh;
De best we can do is fe try
To fight de despair drawin' nigh:
Den we might conquer by an' by—
    Dat we might do.

The speaker concludes by quoting the creole expression "whe' fe do?" as a means of acknowledging unchangeable social forces that compel poor people to "batter" (or labor) endlessly, while at the same time asserting the need to ward off despair and participate in world history. The creole expression is an apt response to the poem's evocation of the harsh realities of social life in Jamaica, insofar as "whe' fe do?" affirms a fundamentally modern, existential worldview that developed out of the Afro-Jamaican experience of slavery, sustained colonial oppression, and industrialization in the Commonwealth Caribbean:

> We hab to batter in de sun,
> An' dat isn't a little fun,
> For Lard! 'tis hellish how it bu'n:
> Still dere's de big wul' to live do'n—
>   So whe' fe do?[50]

Marson's main insight was to identify a close correlation between the Jamaican creole expression "whe' fe do" and the existential worldview articulated by the modern folk idiom of African American blues. By turning to contemporary influences—most obviously McKay and Hughes—Marson was able to give up many of the traditional European idioms and forms she had been using with limited success. Rather than relying on poetic forms that centered on concepts of guilt and melancholy, in her later work Marson discovered the powerful impact of dialect and the stark, modern, rapidly globalizing idiom of the blues. For example, in "Brown Baby Blues," a blues poem written in Jamaican creole, Marson effectively mines the cultural resources of her own folk tradition and comes up with an important word, "shame," that represents a striking departure in the development of literary modernism in the Caribbean:

> I love me baby
> But she don't got no name.
> I love me baby
> She don't got no name.
> Well wha' fe do,
> Dat is not her shame. (*MS*, 97)

Earlier on, when I discussed Claude McKay's portrayal of the midnight woman in "Pay Day," I suggested that the speaker in the poem specifically addresses a European spectator and stages a volitional act of transgression against bourgeois sexual mores. The passing of a "boundary line" by the bold, androgynous midnight woman metaphorically represents the range of transgressions, both in content and form, required for McKay's critical engagement with the literary tradition of Europe and, more broadly, for his successful emergence as a poet.

Like McKay, who lived most of his life in exile, abandoned his wife and child, and is thought to have been bisexual, Marson's life and poetry show the extent to which she constantly transgressed dominant cultural norms: she never married, was highly educated, and became deeply involved in the anticolonial movement after migrating to England in 1932, where she worked for the Emperor Haile Selassie and the League of Colored People. And like McKay, in another late poem called "Black is Fancy," Marson uses her writing to transgress against a long, ethnocentric tradition of European racial stereotypes that stressed the ugliness of black people—and women in particular—in order to justify exploitative practices in the Caribbean and to assert the superiority of European cultural norms. Rather than viewing her body and culture through the "gaze" or perceptual lens of European literature, Marson uses the occasion of her poem to stage an act of critical revision and social self-construction:

Since Aunt Liza gave me
This nice looking glass
I began to be real proud
Of my own self.
I think I will take down
This white lady's picture,
It used to make me ashamed,
And all black folk
Seemed ugly. (MS, 75)

The act of taking down a "white lady's picture" and putting up a mirror from Aunt Liza symbolically conveys Marson's own effort to draw on a total heritage, to resolve the conflict between European ideals of feminine beauty and Afro-Jamaican cultural norms, and to make a new visual culture with her own hands. Viewed in symbolic terms, the scene suggests that Marson's ability to self-consciously interpret and revise the racialism inscribed in the visual culture is what ultimately led her to put a name to the experience of "shame," an experience that was central to her successful development as a poet.

I have been trying to show that Afro-Jamaican middle-class women such as Marson, who turned to poetry during the interwar period in Jamaica as a means of coming to terms with the cultural contradictions left to them by history, were encumbered by specific contingencies of shame. Poetry is a means of undoing the language-destroying capacity of shame, since it actively invents a name for an area of experience normally made inaccessible to language. The discovery of shame in Jamaican women's poetry marked a critical step in the historical development of poetry in the region, since it allowed these poets to acknowledge and reconcile the contradictory views of women's sexuality entailed by "reputation" and "respectability"; the insufficiencies of a literary tradition that focused on notions of agency and guilt; and a tradition of racialist stereotypes that distorted and maligned the sexuality of Afro-Caribbean women.

An important contingency of shame, viewed within the context of Caribbean history, is the extent to which shame is linked to the legacy of slavery. The history of slavery and the unique cultural resonance of shame in Jamaican society are clearly illustrated in a poem called "Ancestor on the Auction Block," by the poet Vera Bell. The poem was written in 1948 and reflects the rising tide of cultural nationalism, at a time when the Afro-Jamaican middle class was beginning to challenge the social norms and political power of the ruling white colonial elite. In this poem Bell explores the "gaze" of a slave on the auction block in order to understand the cultural baggage of the Afro-Jamaican middle class a century after emancipation. The poem opens by showing the negative effects of Bell's uncritical internalization of European cultural norms and, in particular, her blind belief in the stereotyped view of black people as "primitive," a view that was central to the self-negating ethos of middle-class society during the time Bell was writing:

> Ancestor on the auction block
> Across the years your eyes seek mine
> Compelling me to look
> I see your shackled feet
> Your primitive black face
> I see your humiliation
> And turn away
> Ashamed.[51]

The speaker of the poem discovers "shame" as a word that allows her to confront her connection to the Afro-Jamaican working class majority and to name the insecurities that would otherwise lead to "mental slavery" and uninspired derivativeness in her poetry. The setting of the poem invokes the humiliation of the ancestor on the auction block in order to suggest, without describing, the untold shameful humiliations of a colonial classroom

where, as one linguist put it, "literacy and education did not confer power
. . . ; what they did do was to make the educated feel powerless."[52] The
speaker describes her shame as a painful feeling of being "compelled," as if
she has suddenly found herself, through no agency of her own, in a situation of high visibility, a social situation of being seen and scorned by others. Drawing on the metaphor of slavery, the speaker discovers that her
shame—and, in particular, her sense of being "shackled" by ignorance—is
not just the historical consequence of slavery. Shame is itself a form of
mental enslavement to colonial values, insofar as it does not accommodate
agency or voluntary transgression against prescribed social codes:

> Across the years your eyes seek mine
> Compelling me to look
> Is this mean creature that I see
> Myself?
> Ashamed to look
> Because of myself ashamed
> Shackled by my own ignorance
> I stand
> A Slave.

The speaker feels shame when she is reminded of the legacy of slavery,
because the memory itself involves loss of honor and self-respect. But it is
important to notice that the shame she feels is, in at least one critical respect,
quite different from the moral and emotional experience of an ashamed
European woman in, say, a nineteenth-century British novel. Although Bell's
experience of shame is painful, it also has implications and consequences
that are surprisingly positive and life-affirming. Briefly put, Bell's ability to
experience shame is an indication of how far Afro-Jamaicans have come in
the century since emancipation. During the long period of Caribbean slavery, Jamaican slaves were ritually excluded from the social order in order to
enhance the honor of the slaveholders. As degraded or "socially dead" persons, slaves must have expressed their pained reactions to each other, but they
did not express their shame publicly, to the wider society, since this would
happen only to persons who had a position within the larger social order.[53]

The fact that Bell expresses shame in the poem suggests that she has a
sense of her position within and has embraced the values of a larger community. To feel shame in the past and present failures of a group or nation

means that she has a right to take pride in the success and honoring of that group. Although the experience of shame may at first seem to be profoundly negative, the main thrust of Bell's poem is that her capacity to express shame has opened her to new, profoundly self-affirming possibilities in language. Having moved beyond mental slavery and the conceptual impossibility of shame, at the end of the poem Bell effectively imagines the possibility of nationhood and belonging:

> Ancestor on the auction block
> Across the years
> I look
> I see you sweating, toiling, suffering
> Within your loins I see the seed
> Of multitudes
> From your labour
> Grow roads, aqueducts, cultivation
> A new country is born
> Yours was the task to clear the ground
> Mine be the task to build.[53]

In tracing the historical emergence of poetry by Afro-Jamaican women, I have sought to uncover the unique, cultural contingencies of both pleasure and shame in the region. I would like to conclude with the suggestion that the poet's task of putting the causes and effects of shame on display is not only a necessary step in the construction of a distinctively Caribbean lyric self. It is also an anticolonial gesture that illustrates the agonistic, competitive engagement of Caribbean poets with the literary culture of Europe and North America, a gesture that may help feminists to clarify and broaden existing theoretical paradigms of cultural translation.[54] I will give just one contemporary example to illustrate this last point, a poem by the Jamaican poet Lorna Goodison that illuminates the intricate entanglement of pleasure and shame entailed by her act of writing:

> Occasionally, an old chamber pot
> would be transformed, pressed into higher service.
> Battered and used, fallen into black holes
> dark cavities eaten into its white enamel surface
> it would become cleansed from years of low service

brought out from its shadow dwelling of nocturnal shame
and elevated to the level of respectable receptacle.

Necessary medicinal herbs, flowers easy to grow
no delicate blooms could survive here.[55]

The success of this poem lies, at least in part, in its demand for contextual specificity. Only the cultural shaping of shame in Jamaica will help explain the ambivalence being staged here, as well as Goodison's effort to strike a balance between two equally alluring possibilities: containment and revision. At the same time that we are made aware of the speaker's shame, and her acceptance of the constraints that language and history impose, her ability to strike a balance is also a source of pleasure, insofar as she proposes constructive, revisionary standards of beauty and "respectability." The passage memorably dramatizes the process of cultural translation as an effort to probe the historical contingencies of shame and to overcome the speaker's personal compulsion to look at herself through imperial eyes. The old chamber pot—a powerfully concrete, symbolic reminder of the historical legacy of slavery and colonial domination in the Caribbean, as well as the years of self-battery and unacknowledged shame endured by the lyric poet herself—has been literally translated and transformed by a volitional act of arrangement. Brought out from its shadow dwelling of shame into history, the pot, like the lyric poem itself, becomes a sturdy, unpretentious expressive vehicle that proffers the necessary pleasure of self-recognition.

NOTES

1. For a recent news article that discusses this "backlash ... of women against feminism," see Alex Kuczynski, "Enough About Feminism. Should I Wear Lipstick?" *New York Times*, March 28, 1999, p. 4.

2. bell hooks, *Yearning: Race, Gender, and Cultural Politics* (Boston: South End Press, 1990); Trinh T. Minh-ha, *Woman, Native, Other: Writing Postcoloniality and Feminism* (Bloomington: Indiana University Press, 1989).

3. Sara Suleri, "Woman Skin Deep: Feminism and the Postcolonial Condition," *Critical Inquiry* 18, no. 4 (Summer, 1992): 765.

4. Judith Butler, "Collected and Fractured: Response to Identities," in *Identities*, ed. A. K. Appiah and H. L. Gates (Chicago: University of Chicago Press, 1995), pp. 439–47.

5. Gayatri Spivak, *In Other Worlds: Essays in Cultural Politics* (New York: Routledge, 1998); Chandra T. Mohanty, "Under Western Eyes: Feminist Scholarship and Colonial Discourses," *Boundary* 2 (Spring/Fall, 1984): 333–58.

6. This, I take it, is Mohanty's main point when she polemically states that, in its current usage, the category "woman" lacks cultural specificity: "By women as a category of analysis, I am referring to the critical assumption that all of us of the same gender, across classes and cultures, are somehow socially constituted as a homogenous group identified prior to the process of analysis. This is an assumption that characterizes much feminist discourse. . . . Thus, for instance, in any given piece of feminist analysis, women are characterized as a single group on the basis of a shared oppression. What binds women together is a sociological notion of the 'sameness' of their oppression. It is at this point that an elision takes place between 'women' as a discursively constructed group and 'women' as material subjects of their own history" ("Under Western Eyes," p. 342).

7. Homi Bhabha, *The Location of Culture* (London: Routledge, 1994), pp. 186–90.

8. Janet Momsen, "Gender Roles in Caribbean Agriculture Labour," in *Caribbean Freedom: Economy and Society from Emancipation to the Present*, ed. H. Beckeles (Kingston, Jamaica: Ian Randle, 1993), pp. 216–24. Subsequent references are to *Caribbean Freedom*. For a discussion of the role of women in economic development that shows that there have historically been more women farmers in countries such as Jamaica and draws out contrasts between the Commonwealth Caribbean, Cuba, the Dominican Republic, and Puerto Rico, see Helen Safa, "Economic Autonomy and Sexual Equality in Caribbean Society," *Social and Economic Studies* 35, no. 3 (September 1986): 2.

9. Sidney Mintz, "Black Women, Economic Roles, and Cultural Traditions," in Beckeles, ed., *Caribbean Freedom*, p. 243.

10. Orlando Patterson, *The Sociology of Slavery: An Analysis of the Origins, Development, and Structure of Negro Slave Society in Jamaica* (Rutherford, N.J.: Fairleigh Dickinson University Press, 1967), pp. 105–12.

11. Lucille Mathurin Mair, *The Rebel Woman* (Kingston: Institute of Jamaica, 1975), p. 5.

12. Barbara Bush, *Slave Women in Caribbean Society, 1650–1838* (Bloomington: Indiana University Press, 1990), pp. 48–49.

13. Bonham Richardson, *The Caribbean in the Wider World, 1492–1992* (Cambridge: Cambridge University Press, 1992), pp. 132–57.

14. Janet Momsen, "Gender Roles in Caribbean Agricultural Labour," in Beckeles, ed. *Caribbean Freedom*, p. 219.

15. Erna Brodber, "Afro-Jamaican Women at the Turn of the Century," *Social and Economic Studies* 35, no. 3 (September 1986): 23–50.

16. Carole Boyce Davies, "Preface: Talking It Over: Women, Writing, and Feminism," in *Out of the Kumbla: Caribbean Women and Literature*, ed. C. B. Davies and E. S. Fido (Trenton, N.J.: Africa World Press, 1990), p. ix.

17. Paul de Man, *The Resistance to Theory* (Minneapolis: University of Minnesota Press, 1986), p. 19.

18. Bennett's first two collections of poems were published in Kingston, Jamaica, during the early 1940s. In 1943 the *Gleaner* newspaper began the regular practice of including a poem by Bennett in the Sunday edition. Although critics have been increasingly drawn to study Bennett's poems, in general her work has not been given the comprehensive analysis it deserves. See, for example, Mervyn Morris, "On Reading Louise Bennett Seriously," *Jamaica Journal* 1 (December 1967): 69–74; Rex Nettleford, "Introduction," in *Jamaica Labrish*, ed. Rex Nettleford (Kingston, Jamica: Sangster's Books Stores, 1966); and Gordon Rohlehr, "The Folk in Caribbean Literature," *Tapia* 2 (December 24, 1972): 8, 9, 15. See also Lloyd Brown, *West Indian Poetry* (London: Heinemann, 1984), pp. 100–117.

19. Carolyn Cooper has written a number of articles that refer to Bennett's use of a creole folk idiom: "Noh Lickle Twang: An Introduction to the Poetry of Louise Bennett," *World Literature Written in English* (April 1978): 324–29; "That Cunny Jamma Oman: The Female Sensibility in the Poetry of Louise Bennett," *Bulletin of Eastern Caribbean Affairs* 11, no. 1 (March/April 1985): 13–27; and "Proverb as Metaphor in the Poetry of Louise Bennett," *Jamaica Journal* 17 (May 1984): 21–27.

20. Peter Roberts, *West Indians and Their Language* (Cambridge: Cambridge University Press, 1988), pp. 156–58.

21. Louise Bennett, "Oman Equality," in *Aunty Roachy Seh*, ed. M. Morris (Kingston, Jamaica: Sangster's Book Stores, 1993), pp. 67, 69.

22. For a discussion of Bennet's poem that explores the necessary concealment of knowledge, see Opal Palmer Adisa, "I Must Write What I Know So I'll Know I've Known It All Along," in *The Woman, the Writer, and Caribbean Society*, ed. H. Pyne-Timothy (Los Angeles: UCLA Center for Afro-American Studies Publications, 1998), pp. 108–109.

23. Louise Bennett, "Jamaica Oman," in *Selected Poems*, ed. Mervyn Morris (Kingston, Jamaica: Sangster's Book Stores, 1982).

24. Roger Abrahams, *The Man of Words in the West Indies: Performance and the Emergence of a Creole Culture* (Baltimore: Johns Hopkins University Press, 1983), pp. 134–56.

25. Ibid., pp. 51–152.

26. There are, however, some regions and specific instances in the Commonwealth Caribbean that do conform to Abrahams's schema. For example, in one very recent study of the speech patterns and social organization of space in an Indo-Guyanese village, Jack Sidnell has found that among the descendants of East Indian immigrants to Guyana, "both men and women in the village are quick to note that it is not proper for a woman to spend too much time by the road. Women may use the road to travel from one place to another. . . . But they are expected not to socialize extensively on the road, as the behavior is usually associated with sexual impro-

priety and low class . . . origins" ("Organizing Social and Spatial Location: Elicitations in Indo-Guyanese Village Talk," *Journal of Linguistic Anthropology* 7, no. 2 [December 1977]: 147).

27. Bush, *Slave Women in Caribbean Society*, pp. 69–70.

28. There is a vast literature on this theme. See, for example, Kate Millett, *Sexual Politics* (New York: Doubleday, 1969); Catherine MacKinnon, "Feminism, Marxism, Method, and the State," *Signs* 7, no. 3 (1982); Susan Brownmiller, *Against Our Will: Men, Women, and Rape* (Harmondsworth, England: Penguin, 1976); and Carole Smart, *Feminism and the Power of Law* (London: Routledge, 1989).

29. See, for example, Ellen DuBois and Linda Gordon, "Seeking Ecstasy on the Battlefield: Danger and Pleasure in Nineteenth-Century Feminist Thought," in *Pleasure and Danger: Exploring Female Sexuality*, ed. Carole Vance (London: Routledge, 1984); Judith Walcowitz, *City of Dreadful Delight: Narratives of Sexual Danger in Late-Victorian London* (London: Virago, 1992); and Sheila Jeffreys, *The Spinster and Her Enemies* (London: Pandora, 1985).

30. A well-known psychoanalytic discussion of women's pleasure is put forward in Luce Irigaray's *This Sex Which Is Not One* (Ithaca, N.Y.: Cornell University Press, 1985). An example of the "libertarian" perspective may be found in Amber Hollibaugh, "Desire for the Future: Radical Hope in Passion and Pleasure," in Vance, ed., *Pleasure and Danger*.

31. Rhonda Cobham, "Women in Jamaican Literature, 1900–1950," in Davis and Fido, ed., *Out of the Kumbla*, p. 197.

32. Peter Wilson, *Crab Antics: The Social Anthropology of English-Speaking Negro Societies* (New Haven: Yale University Press, 1973).

33. Bush, *Slave Women in Caribbean Society*, pp. 56, 58.

34. Claude McKay, "The Strange Burial of Sue," in *My Green Hills of Jamaica*, ed. Mervyn Morris (Kingston, Jamaica: Heinemann Educational Book, 1979), pp. 145, 146.

35. An interesting set of feminist perspectives on the vexed issue of prostitution may be found in F. Delacoste and P. Alexander, eds., *Sex Work* (Pittsburgh: Cleis Press, 1988).

36. Claude McKay, "A Midnight Woman to the Bobby," in *The Passion of Claude McKay: Selected Poetry and Prose, 1912–1948*, ed. W. Cooper (New York: Schocken Books, 1973), p. 110.

37. James Walvin, *Black and White: The Negro in English Society, 1555 to 1945* (London: Allen Lane, Penguin Press, 1973), p. 54.

38. Edward Long, *The History of Jamaica* (London, 1774), 2:364, 380.

39. Bush, *Slave Women in Caribbean Society*, pp. 14–15.

40. Saidiya V. Hartman, *Scenes of Subjection: Terror, Slavery, and Self-Making in Nineteenth-Century America* (New York: Oxford University Press, 1997), p. 17. For a useful, revisionary discussion of European visual culture and stereotypes of black women during the period of slavery, see Bush, *Slave Women in Caribbean Society*, pp. 11–22.

41. Claude McKay, "Pay Day," in *The Dialect Poetry of Claude McKay*, ed. Wayne Cooper, Black Heritage Library Collection (Freeport, N.Y.: Books for Libraries Press, 1972), 2:53.

42. Bridget Brereton, "The British and French West Indies," in *The Modern Caribbean*, ed. F. Knight and C. Palmer (Chapel Hill: University of North Carolina Press, 1989), pp. 91–92.

43. As Cobham has noted, a "chaste idealized female figure" emerged in Jamaican literature during the interwar period, and "the black Jamaican woman who aspired to middle-class status was encouraged to see herself as being fulfilled in the role of wife and mother, or, if she could not marry, in chastity and good deeds" ("Women in Jamaican Literature," pp. 203, 205).

44. Compare Elaine Scarry's emphasis on the language-destroying capacities of pain in *The Body in Pain* (New York: Oxford University Press, 1985).

45. Una Marson, *Heights and Depths* (Kingston, Jamaica: Gleaner, 1931), p. 90.

46. H. Lewis, *Shame and Guilt in Neurosis* (New York: International University Press, 1971).

47. On this point, see Thomas Scheff, Suzanne Retzinger, and Michael Ryan, "Crime, Violence, and Self-Esteem: Review and Proposals," in *The Social Importance of Self-Esteem*, ed. M. Mecca, N. Smelser, and J. Vasconcellos (Berkeley: University of California Press, 1989), p. 179, and Helen Lynd, *On Shame and the Search for Identity* (London: Routledge & Kegan Paul, 1958), p. 21.

48. Una Marson, "Youth," in *The Moth and the Star* (Kingston, Jamaica: By the author, 1937), p. 95. Subsequent references are to this edition and will be cited parenthetically.

49. One poem, "A Moonlight Reverie," suggests that women should take on the burden of guilt even though they are not guilty; and at least six of the Shakespearean sonnets included in her first two volumes of poems— "In Vain," "Resignation," "Forgetfulness," "Some Day," "The Ingrate," "Love's Eclipse," and "Pleading"—explore Marson's failure to meet standards imposed on the aspiring black middle class in Jamaica during the interwar period, namely, a happy, stable, heterosexual love life.

50. Claude McKay, "Whe' Fe Do?" in Cooper ed., *Dialect Poetry of Claude McKay*, 1:27.

51. Vera Bell, "Ancestor on the Auction Block," *Focus* (1948): 187.

52. Peter Roberts, *From Oral to Literate Culture: Colonial Experience in the English West Indies* (Barbados: Press University of the West Indies, 1997), p. 266.

53. On this point, see Orlando Patterson, *Slavery and Social Death: A Comparative Study* (Cambridge: Harvard University Press, 1982), p. 79.

54. For a theoretical description of blasphemy as a "transgressive act of cultural translation," see Bhabha, *Location of Culture*, pp. 223–29.

55. Lorna Goodison, "In City Gardens Grow No Roses as We Know Them," in *To Us, All Flowers Are Roses* (Urbana: University of Illinois Press, 1995), p. 15.

Chapter 11

Fierce Pussies and Lesbian Avengers: Dyke Activism Meets Celebrity Culture

ANN CVETKOVICH

A Visual Archive

I want to reflect on the 1990s through a collection of images that stages the ongoing serial drama of encounters between feminism and mass culture. Although it's a historically significant collection, it's also a very personal one, accumulated according to the idiosyncratic dictates of pleasure; it includes the Lesbian Avengers' poster featuring blaxploitation star Pam Grier, *Vanity Fair*'s 1993 cover shot of k.d. lang and Cindy Crawford, Della Grace's photographs of butch-femme couples in sexy poses, and Nicole Eisenman's drawings of cartoon heroines such as Wilma and Betty. When I look at these images, I see some of the outcomes of the 1980s sex wars. I see the impact of queer politics and new lesbian cultures in redefining feminism. I see a resurgence of activism that ushered in the decade and that seems ultimately to have waned by its close. I see a complex dialogue between popular and

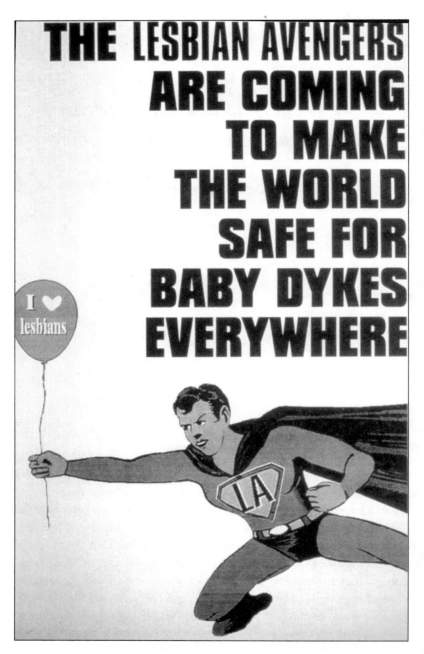

FIGURE 1. Lesbian Avengers flyer, 1992. Courtesy Carrie Moyer.

FIGURE 2. Lesbian Avengers flyer, 1992. Courtesy Carrie Moyer.

FIGURE 3. Dyke Action Machine poster, 1991. Courtesy DAM.

FIGURE 4. Dyke Action Machine poster, 1994. Courtesy DAM.

FIGURE 5. Dyke Action Machine poster, 1997. Courtesy DAM.

FIGURE 6. Fierce Pussy poster, 1993. Courtesy Fierce Pussy.

FIGURE 7. Fierce Pussy poster, 1993. Courtesy Fierce Pussy.

FIGURE 8. Zoe Leonard, "Untitled" (from a series of seven photographs), 1984–91. Courtesy Zoe Leonard and Paula Cooper Gallery.

FIGURE 9. Carrie Moyer, "I Don't Have a Name for This Yet," 1994.
Courtesy Carrie Moyer.

FIGURE 10. Nicole Eisenman, "Alice in Wonderland," 1996.
Courtesy Nicole Eisenman and Jack Tilton Gallery.

academic cultures, and between practice and theory. I see the commodification of identity politics. Indeed, one value of the images I will explore in this article is that they form an archive of history, condensing the 1990s into a visual scrapbook.[1] Although the apparent ease of access to history through such a catalogue can be deceptive, I am prepared to take seriously the pleasure of its power to translate complex, and often invisible, social forces and structures into the domain of the visual, as though it required nothing more than a pair of eyes that see to understand history. As a fan of one of mass culture's preeminent genres, the magazine, I will risk mimicking the convention of publications such as *Time* and *Life* that review years or decades in pictures in order to argue, contrary to critiques of commodity fetishism, that mass culture and the visible can be a valuable feminist and activist resource. Indeed, as products of the close of the nineteenth century—along with sexual identity—magazines, advertising, photography, and celebrity offer suggestive vehicles for considering the last decade's feminisms and our own century's close within a larger historical context, one that includes the history of popular culture.[2] My aim, though, is not just a nostalgic retrospective; while the images displayed here may not, and perhaps should not, predict the shape of things to come, the act of reviewing them can be a way of planning for the future.

One reason to take the risk of presuming that the historical complexity of a decade could be rendered visible in a series of images is that this process productively replicates one of this article's central concerns, the politics of lesbian visibility. Over the last decade the project of "promoting lesbian visibility" has asserted that political power can be linked to, and even equated with, the cultural power of visibility in representations.[3] Visibility has played a distinctive and prominent role in gay and lesbian culture and politics because, unlike gender or race, sexual identity is not so easily assumed to be marked on the body or to be something one is born with. It thus has given rise to a variety of codes and conventions, including a range of performances for "coming out" and for allowing lesbians, gay men, and same-sex partners to identify one another. Although, ultimately, the certainty of knowing, for example, what a woman or a white person looks like is open to challenge, the need to know what a lesbian or gay man looks like can be an urgent question not just for those outside that category but also for those inside of it. There are also important distinctions between lesbians and gay men, since the concept of "lesbian visibility" in the 1990s has carried a particular charge in the face of fears that lesbianism will be left out of constructions of gay identity. As gay men became more visible in the early 1990s in the context of media coverage of AIDS, gays in the military, and even queer activism, lesbians worried about remaining invisible. Visibility and political power, however, do not necessarily go hand in hand; one of the dubious consequences of increased visibility—niche-marketing to the privileged consumer—has made this especially clear. The tension between representational visibility and political visibility or power has been persistent and unpredictable in the 1990s and, even once they are distinguished from one another, questions remain about how they might be productively linked. Hence, the vitality, but also the conflicts, of a cultural politics of representation around lesbianism.

Even if one accepts, however provisionally, that images are a useful index of historical change, political struggle, and feminist thinking, there is still the question of what archive will do this work of representation. In the interest of preserving an archive that can be all too easily lost, one goal of this article will be to make visible the images produced by an activist group, the Lesbian Avengers, and two visual collectives based in New York, Fierce Pussy and Dyke Action Machine!. The Lesbian Avengers were active both nationally and in New York between 1992 and 1995; Fierce Pussy was active from 1991 to 1994; and Dyke Action Machine! began in 1991 and continues to do projects about once a year. Although the images these groups have created are representative of the 1990s, they are unimaginable without developments from prior decades, including feminism, AIDS activism, and the dialogue between artists and popular visual culture. Many members of these groups have histories with the group ACT UP, and they borrow its style of activism, including its sense of style *as* activism. Like other groups from the early 1990s influenced by AIDS activism, such as Queer Nation and Women's Action Coalition, these visual collectives forged a prominent place within activism for artists, who used performance, images, and media to create new forms of specifically cultural activism. As a center for both the art world and the culture industry, New York City provides a unique context for visual and cultural activism. Many activists use their ties to jobs at magazines, public relations firms, advertising corporations, and production companies to support their activism, and New York's pedestrian culture and urban geography make it a distinctive site for visual activism.

But these material conditions would not have been so richly productive had it not been for key conceptual breakthroughs in the encounter between feminism and visual culture, and I would argue that the influence of feminist artists such as Barbara Kruger and Cindy Sherman, as well as activist groups such as the Guerilla Girls, cannot be underestimated. These artists opened up new possibilities for feminist art and activism in the 1980s by engaging with mass culture rather than turning away from it. Borrowing from her experience as a graphic artist, Barbara Kruger, for example, imported the techniques of advertising, including the use of slogans, to make feminist images.[4] Cindy Sherman borrowed from film to pose herself in photographs that challenge the presumptions and impasses of the theory of the male gaze.[5] While there are certainly other important feminist artists from the 1980s, these two have had a popular and crossover appeal that is especially notable and that suggests the power of artistic practice to reframe both activism and theory.[6] Moreover, this important feminist prehistory for AIDS activism can often be lost as Douglas Crimp and Adam Rolston hint at when they write in *AIDS Demographics* that "Gran Fury adopted Barbara Kruger's seductive graphic style, which was subsequently, and perhaps less knowingly, taken up by other ACT UP graphic producers" (18).[7]

Both popular and academic feminisms were very much affected in the 1980s by the absence of any robust movement of feminism; not least of these effects was the increasing separation of academic feminism, especially feminist theory, from political activism. The link between feminist and post-structuralist theory and certain forms of visual practice was, however, quite fertile, and the feminist images that resulted can in turn be credited with playing a role in the activisms of the late 1980s and early 1990s.[8] One of the truly notable and lively aspects of academic queer theory has been its connections to activism, especially AIDS activism and in particular ACT UP.[9] The lesbian visual activism that is my focus thus stands at a crucial nexus of theory, activism, and visual culture, resolving some of the impasses and disconnections between these worlds that were the fallout of the 1970s.

I feel an additional urgency about capturing and chronicling the images and moments of 1990s visual activisms because they seem already to be irrevocably past and subject to incomplete and suspect retrospectives and revisionisms. For example, the story of the politics of lesbian visibility in the 1990s would not be complete without attention to "lesbian chic" as one of the media events of 1993, or the events surrounding the coming out of Ellen De Generes and Ellen Morgan in 1997 and the cancellation of the *Ellen* series just a year later on the grounds, according to some, of being "too gay," or, in other words, of making lesbianism too visible. But important as these media events might be for a history of the intersections of mass culture and alternative cultures, and of consumer culture and sexual cultures, I want to resist having the decade represented by its most mainstream images and events, and I will thus focus on an archive of images that might be less well known and certainly less widely distributed. Visibility is subject to uneven development; while any image seems, by definition, to be visible, some images are more visible than others because of the material conditions of their distribution.

In many ways the story of lesbian visibility in the 1990s is a story as old as capitalism, the story of the dialectic, that ongoing serial drama in which mainstream and alternative cultures are so intertwined that the work of analytical separation can seem doomed to infinite repetition. By the end of the 1990s, some critics are ready for something new. Assessing the impact of Foucault's work and related forms of theory, Eve Sedgwick has, with acerbic wit, described the routinized application of the lessons of theory, especially the repressive hypothesis, as resulting in "the good dog/bad dog rhetoric of puppy obedience school," in which all texts are read as "kinda subversive, kinda hegemonic."[10] Nowhere has this tendency been more prevalent than in readings of popular culture, motivated by the influence of a cultural studies interested in producing something more than a critique of popular culture but constantly under pressure to acknowledge the relentless logic of capital. I'm interested in considering how the images that are my focus might produce a different story because, within capitalism's conditions of uneven visibility, they are in danger of being invisible when the 1990s becomes only the story of the commodification of lesbian identity.

Feminism and the Politics of Visibility

In addition to forging new kinds of queer politics, lesbians promoting visibility as an agenda in the 1990s were responding to feminism's persistent concern with the visual, which is central to important debates about pleasure, fashion, pornography, and consumer culture. Contending with the hypervisibility of women within popular culture, feminists have had a significant history of iconoclasm toward visual representation, associating the representation of woman with objectification and voyeurism, both understood to be problematic.[11] Genres such as advertising and pornography have been particular targets of critique because they become the visible sign of sexism, their "explicitness" in representing the body equated with the explicitness of their sexism. Borrowing from Neil Hertz's analysis of male hysteria under political pressure, we could say that pornography has been feminism's Medusa head. Just as, in Hertz's model, the sexually charged image of a woman (lifting her skirts at the barricades to display her genitals) converts a political threat into a sexual one, so the sexualized image of women in popular culture converts the structural and political fact of sexism into the visible threat of objectification and degradation.[12]

It can be difficult to formulate a feminist visual politics around the representation of women when the available genres of cultural and visual representation seem to constitute a mode of domination. It has been equally difficult to formulate a visual politics around the racialized body, whether to call for representation in the face of invisibility or to contend with the stereotypical visibility of the racialized body (both male and female) that has historically accompanied a range of ideological agendas. In both cases, finding or producing a "politically correct" image becomes a fraught endeavor that is only reductively (or partially or problematically) addressed by calls for positive images or more images or accurate images.

Vexed as it might be in turn, the project of lesbian visibility has burst through many of the paradigms and impasses of the prosex and pornography debates by assuming that pornography and visual pleasure for women are possible and by using many of the conventions for the representation of women as though they were useful tools rather than strictly patriarchal ones. There is often a camp sensibility present in such appropriations and it should be acknowledged that this humorous distance has been enabled by the successful impact of 1970s feminism. The icons and fetishes of a prefeminist era, including images from Hollywood cinema, popular magazines, advertising, and girls' culture, now understood as fantasies rather than accurate representations, thus become available for reworking in the 1990s.

In addition to revising feminism's sexual politics, 1990s dyke visual activism offers new ways of thinking about the status of countercultures, refusing the separatist utopianism of the 1970s that is especially evident in lesbian feminist efforts to create an alternative women's culture. As we gain historical distance on the 1960s, including the benefit of hindsight provided by what are now many decades of the postwar marketing of youth cultures, it is increasingly clear that the relations between mainstream and countercultures—and between mass culture and subcultures—are dialectical, and that consumer culture has spawned oppositional cultures and vice versa. Nowhere is this more evident than in gay and lesbian cultures, which can be viewed as the offspring and wellspring of a consumer culture that is driven by sexuality and affect.[13] The intimate relation between consumer and popular culture is still very powerful even when it takes the form of repudiation or what José Muñoz calls "disidentification."[14]

Especially visible in the complex intersections of consumer culture and lesbian representation that give rise to my archive of images is celebrity culture, the hybrid product of consumer culture's crossing of identity with the commodity-form. The artists and activists explored here use celebrity images as a vehicle for lesbian representation, in some cases through the appropriation of existing images to make them images of lesbianism, and in other cases through the use of the conventions of celebrity representation to depict actual lesbians. An example of the first case would be Deborah Bright's appropriation of Hollywood press stills in which she inserts herself into the picture alongside Katharine Hepburn and others. An example of the second tactic would be Della Grace's very stylized portraits of lesbians in which fashion and sex merge in glamorous portraits.[15] It is important to note, however, that the goal is not realistic representation and thus many of these image makers, while promoting lesbian visibility, are doing so in a way that differs from the agenda of media activism and liberal politics, which tend to equate visibility with images of actual lesbians. The celebrity as icon or diva, an identity that is frequently a visual one produced through photographic genres that are fantastic and glamorous, is a highly stylized representation of woman and femininity. To fault such images for being unreal or inauthentic, as some feminist critics have done, is to miss the point. The artists and activists explored here embrace such images in order to promote lesbian representation by means other than realist or documentary idioms. They reappropriate icons of fashion and celebrity in order to produce not "real lesbians" but lesbians as larger-than-life superheros and divas.

The goal of many of the projects discussed here is to insert lesbians into one of modernity's central genres of public culture, the production of stars or celebrities. Images are crucial to this process, putting the body, and especially the face, of a person into public circulation and making people important by making them visible.[16] A countercultural politics of visibility is necessarily parasitic on the equation of citizenship with visibility that has achieved particular prominence in the context of celebrity culture. Fandom is one of the forms of reception that mobilizes this process, and the queer dimensions of fandom are one of the ways in which celebrity images can be inflected with lesbian desires and politics. At stake in current studies of celebrity is the claim that, rather than being dismissed for corrupting notions of personhood and identity, celebrity should be taken seriously as constituting them.[17] Lesbian uses of celebrity culture lend weight to this argument.

Lesbian Avengers

As its name suggests, the Lesbian Avengers actively invoke celebrity culture, using, for example, the image of Superman in a flyer advertising their first meeting and action (figure 1). Founded in 1992 in New York City, the Lesbian Avengers describe themselves as a "direct action group focused on issues vital to lesbian visibility and survival." Inspired by groups such as ACT UP and Queer Nation that many of the cofounders had participated in, the Avengers' agenda emerged from a lack of attention to specifically lesbian issues in those other groups and a desire to create a space for lesbians to address their own issues rather than working in coalition with others. The Avengers also respond to a history of feminist organizing, seeking to avoid the tendency to get bogged down in processing. In her book *My American History*, an important archive of Avengers' history, cofounder Sarah Schulman says, "One outstanding revelation has been to stay away from abstract theoretical discussion. It is so easy to create false polarities when there is nothing concrete on the table. . . . So in our meetings if you disagree with the proposal on the floor, instead of just tearing it apart, propose another way of realizing the goal" (290–91).[18] Responding critically to traditional organizing strategies, the Avengers seek to create a new style of action: "Avoid old stale tactics at all costs. Chanting and picketing no longer make an impression. Standing passively still and listening to speakers is boring and disempowering. Look for daring new participatory tactics depending on the nature of your action" (298). Building on the lessons of previous generations of activism (including the civil rights movement and feminist conscious-ness-raising), the Lesbian Avengers move forward into the 1990s with a style of activism that self-consciously includes style and that knowingly embraces the tactics of media culture.

In their first couple of years of activity, the Avengers inspired chapters in many U.S. cities, and their ongoing legacy includes the Dyke Marches that have become an annual event in New York, San Francisco, and other cities since the first one that preceded the March on Washington in 1993. Among their ambitious projects has been the transportation of their urban organizing skills to states such as Maine and Idaho in order to fight antigay legislation, and the development of the Civil Rights Organizing Project (CROP), which would build on these local struggles in order to create a national network of resistance. Although critical of some aspects of past activisms, the Avengers explicitly borrowed the model of the 1960s civil rights movement's Freedom Rides, even using the name, in an ambitious attempt to adapt the successful and widely mythologized strategies of that movement to the cause of gay and lesbian rights. Although many chapters have become less active as the initial participants have moved on to other things, the Avengers' relatively short lifespan was itself part of the initial game plan, a kind of planned obsolescence. One of the Avengers' initial goals—to train a new generation of activists—has definitely been achieved, making good on their popular slogan "we recruit."

The New York Lesbian Avengers, drawing especially on the skills of graphic artist Carrie Moyer, have made visual culture central to their activist style, taking literally the politics of visibility announced in their mission statement: "The visual design of our actions is a crucial part of Avenger work. In general we try to make each action look different from our previous events and have a style and presentation that has never been used by anyone before. Props play a huge part in this.... Demo-graphics need to be eye-catching, meaningful and visually exciting" (306). The Avengers, for example, have a logo, an image of a cartoonlike bomb, that has been reproduced on flyers, T-shirts, buttons, and other materials.[19] The Avengers produced two manifestos in which their views were presented in broadsheet style but with bold graphics and visuals rather than the fine print characteristic of many grassroots organizations. The first manifesto in particular emphasizes activism as fun, attempting to bring into the group those who might not otherwise think of themselves as potential organizers. The images come alive in the performative context of demonstrations, parties, and other events, serving as a vehicle for the orchestration of large groups into a visual, and hence visible, public.[20] In many instances, the Avengers also borrow from mainstream advertising culture as, for example, in the flyer for a 1994 party that reproduced a cropped version of Calvin Klein's CK One ads and pasted an Avengers logo onto Kate Moss's white T-shirt. Mass culture and alternative street culture are impossible to separate in this ongoing intertextuality since Calvin Klein is himself appropriating street culture both for his styles and for his ads, which juxtapose supermodels with regular hip people and sometimes, as in the case of dyke model Jenny Shimizu, those who live in both worlds.

Given the Avengers' interest in using the tactics of media culture, it is not surprising that images of celebrities appear in their visual repertoire. A particularly striking example is the 1993 poster that advertised a party with an image of blaxploitation star Pam Grier (from the 1973 film *Coffy*), accompanied by the slogan "we recruit" (figure 2). Participating in a widespread 1970s nostalgia through the specific genre of the blaxploitation film, the image has camp appeal as an emblem of both militancy and style, and style *as* militancy. Its intertextuality is densely layered since blaxploitation in its original context borrowed from the appeal of cultural nationalism and groups such as the Black Panthers, who in turn used symbols of subcultural style such as the beret and the leather jacket to promote their image. Thus the putative distinction between authentic activism and the culture industry's "exploitation" of it is hard to maintain in 1970s African American culture, and this confusion is part of the appeal of Pam Grier's image for 1990s lesbian culture as it turns to the fashion and culture industry to promote lesbian visibility.

Mobilizing a homoerotic visual pleasure for purposes of collective action, not just romance, the Avengers use the glamorized image of the female celebrity (and the girl with a gun) as a resource rather than a false stereotype or unattainable ideal. But the role of race in the homoerotic appeal of Pam Grier's recontextualization complicates its relation to feminist visual politics. At one point, I thought the image could represent the Lesbian Avengers' racial diversity as a group and that it was especially significant because it was not presuming to be mimetic; that is, an image of an African American woman could represent a group composed of a majority of white women. Because Pam Grier is not only African American but a celebrity, and because she appears as a fantastic superhero in her screen roles, the image announces itself as a fiction, opening the distance between the Avengers' representation and their reality more fully than an image of a white star might. But in reading the image this way, I was presuming the Lesbian Avengers' racial diversity. Over time, my reading has shifted as I have become aware of a history of Lesbian Avenger discussions and tensions around the issue of race, leading eventually in 1995 to a manifesto announcing the resignation of some women of color from the group. I have come to think of the Pam Grier image as representing a *fantasy* of racial diversity and commitment to antiracism that is indeed an important part of the Lesbian Avengers' visual and political style. It signifies the desire of white women for African American women as activist cohorts and their identification with a history of racial politics, especially the civil rights movement. In certain social circles, politics can be fetishized in the same way that commodities are, and the African American woman's body and her image circulate in an economy of tokenization.

But a fetish object can reveal, or make material, social contradictions, as well as obscuring them. The image of Pam Grier stands for the challenging and unresolved legacies of discussions of race in a range of white institutions in the 1990s. On the one hand, the use of an African American woman's image to signify all women of color runs the risk of reducing the U.S. color line to a simple black/white dichotomy, but, on the other hand, the category "woman of color" is a catachrestic fiction that can both enable the representation of racial identities and homogenize differences. The visual representation of the "woman of color" actually presents an interesting challenge; since any single "woman of color" is also something else more specific, the category is often represented by a group of women, who can render visible its multiplicity and open-endedness.[21] The domain of cultural representation is no simpler than the domain of political representation, and the image of Pam Grier takes certain risks in order to move past a strategy of political correctness that demands positive images. It must necessarily fail in some respects, however, because it can never match up to or represent a social and political reality in which racism does not exist, since that reality itself does not exist, particularly in institutions that are majority white. The Lesbian Avengers had a difficult time addressing the challenge of racism and ultimately foundered, as so many groups do, because a strategy of multiracial inclusion often seems better to serve the interests of white people in search of integration (although only as long as they are not confronted on their racism) than it does the people of color they are so eager to include. Better than any realistic portrait, the image of Pam Grier represents this white fantasy of overcoming racism by embracing the idealized image of an African American woman.[22]

For African American women and other women of color, Pam Grier's image also enables a fascinating range of possibilities for racial identification and disidentification. For example, one of the actual women who provided the inspiration for the image of Pam Grier—Angela Davis—draws attention to the potentially dangerous effects of the use of celebrity images to construct political fantasies. Writing about the appropriation of her image in a

fashion spread in *Vibe* magazine in which the models mimic the many photographs that circulated following her arrest in 1970, Davis objects to the
dehumanizing effects of having been made an icon and to the populariza-
tion of her activist image as a fashion statement.[23] The recent controversy,
especially among African American artists, surrounding the work of Kara
Walker, who has appropriated the nineteenth-century tradition of the sil-
houette to depict slaves and masters in a range of sexualized and transgressive poses, suggests that the reclaiming of racialized stereotypes can be even
more fraught than the reclaiming of sexist ones. Yet, there are also examples
of African American women artists, such as Etang Inyang in the short film
Badass Supermama (1996), embracing blaxploitation and other African American popular traditions as archives for cultural representation.[24]

It is precisely because of such debates that I like the Pam Grier image
and the Lesbian Avengers' use of it; its rich range of audiences and associations provides a compelling example of the celebrity image's overdetermined visibility. Ultimately the political meanings of the Pam Grier image
cannot be fully predicted, and they may be only utopian fantasy rather than
realizable goals. But these ambitions cannot be recognized at all unless we
acknowledge that the image is nonmimetic and that the power of such
images to signify activist goals, including antiracist ones, is crucial.

Dyke Action Machine!

In addition to her work for the Lesbian Avengers, Carrie Moyer has another
artist-activist identity as a member of the collective Dyke Action Machine!
(DAM!), which since 1991 has mounted a series of public art campaigns that
very directly engage with the genre of advertising. Most of their projects
have been poster campaigns, although they have infiltrated other distribution
networks as well; they have a web page in the form of a television guide to
the Girlie Network, and in 1996, they created a series of matchbook covers,
phone lines, and product flyers that borrow the visual style and distribution
techniques of lowbrow, low-budget advertising. Their most prominent targets have been the high-profile ad campaigns that evidence the overlapping
connections between celebrity culture, subcultures, and fashion. In 1991 they
borrowed the format of Gap ads to represent lesbian artists and activists (figure 3); their 1993 Gay Pride poster, "Do You Love the Dyke in Your Life?"
transformed Calvin Klein's Marky Mark campaign into a lesbian statement.

Functioning autonomously, rather than as the cultural arm of an activist group with a variety of goals, visual collectives insist that the transformation of the public visual landscape is itself a form of activism, that seeing and being seen are political acts. Distribution is as crucial as content. Groups such as Dyke Action Machine! and Fierce Pussy depend on the specifically urban landscape and the visual public culture brought into being by pedestrian traffic. New York's landscape of bus shelters, subway announcements, and billboards is their ideal, although perhaps limited, home.[25] They presume the spatialized relation between official and unofficial forms of publicity; to colonize the public print culture of the street is to be visible.

The series of posters adapted from the Gap ads prevalent in the early 1990s reveal the dense intertextualities of identity politics, consumer culture, and celebrity. They very dramatically articulate a politics of visibility in which lesbians are made visible by being represented as celebrities. Yet, the power of the original ads rests significantly on the reverse trend, showing even famous people dressed in the homogenizing and everyday style of T-shirts and jeans turned into a lifestyle commodity by the Gap. The ads use black-and-white photography with the Gap logo very discreetly installed in the corner of the image. The small print names not only the featured celebrity but the photographers, such as Herb Ritts, Annie Leibovitz, and Steven Meisel, who are themselves celebrities (partly through their association with such high-profile ad campaigns). Among the subjects who appeared in the ads were sports figures such as Mike Tyson, actors and actresses such as Dennis Hopper and Isabella Rossellini, supermodels such as Naomi Campbell, and even the drag queen Lypsinka. Indeed, the "supermodel" is another noteworthy product of 1990s celebrity culture, which, if it can turn models into household names who are as well known as other kinds of stars, inspires the fantasy that it can do the same for lesbians. The success of the supermodel as celebrity is also, though, the more specific result of the centrality of visual culture, and especially photography, to the creation of celebrity; already highly visible, models are perfect candidates for celebrity, part of the mechanisms by which those with the greatest visual power have become those with the greatest social power. The ad campaigns and celebrity culture of the 1990s, which have featured a mix of ordinary people as models, models as stars, and stars as ordinary people, are crucial sites for witnessing the representation of the public as a physical body. It is multiracial; it is beautiful; it encompasses a wide range of people.

When DAM! inserts lesbians into this context of visual celebrity culture, their presence can be both seamlessly assimilable and disruptive. Although lesbians such as k.d. lang and Martina Navratilova have been featured in celebrity advertising, and there are numerous gay men (including Andrew Sullivan) in the Gap campaigns, DAM!'s series features a particular kind of lesbian activist and artist who is likely to be unknown to the world at large but who may be a celebrity within a smaller lesbian public. DAM!'s ongoing policy, in fact, has been to use only their friends as models, and they thus make the intimate circle of their affections into a visible public culture. Although their images thus imply that anyone, including a lesbian, can be a model or a visual celebrity, to this viewer's eyes, DAM!'s versions of Gap models are beautiful, make hipness visible, and are not so very different from the celebrities featured in the original campaigns. In both cases, the black-and-white photography stylizes and aestheticizes the image. DAM! uses the conventions of corporate advertising to install lesbians within the public sphere and it closes the discrepancy between political and visual power by making lesbian activists as sexy and attractive as supermodels.

Like the Avengers' Pam Grier image, one of my favorite DAM! campaigns, the fake movie poster for *Straight to Hell*, which appeared on the streets of downtown New York during Stonewall 94, is important for its strategies of combining celebrity culture with racialized representation (figure 4). A posse of three girls is framed by the lines, "She came out. So the Army kicked her out. Now she's out for blood . . . *Straight to Hell.*" The small typeface credit lines are full of in-jokes—starring Clare "Don't Ask" Latelle, original concept by Valerie Solanis, Special Rights editor Armed and Ready, and director of cinematography Girl Ray. *Straight to Hell* is rated HG13 for "Homosexual Guidance Suggested," meaning "some material may be too challenging for heterosexuals over age 13." The poster constitutes a clever response to the debates about gays in the military that dominated national gay and lesbian politics in 1993. Throughout the 1990s, DAM! has distinguished itself in responding to issues current in gay and lesbian politics, using its advertising tactics to create messages that fit particular historical circumstances.

Visually the poster adapts the style of masculinist action movies, as the three girls strike a butch pose. Below the title, one of the girls embraces her girlfriend protectively; even without a dress in the picture, the look is butch-femme, and dyke style is central to the images. The dykes in these pictures are realistic, not far anyway from what one might see on the streets of the East Village, but also carefully stylized to the specifications of a conventional genre such as the fashion photograph. It is important to keep in mind that fashion photography has its own version of girl gangs; in fact, one of the reasons I love the *Straight to Hell* poster is that it visually echoes one of my most cherished fashion images of the 1990s: a Versace ad in which super-models Linda Evangelista, Christy Turlington, and Helena Christensen are wearing black leather jackets with jeweled Christian iconography, including virgins and crosses, and sporting sunglasses that give them a menacing look. In order to make the visual style of advertising available for lesbian representation, Dyke Action Machine! just has to add real lesbians.

Like other DAM! images, this one foregrounds racial diversity. The star is African American, her buddies are white and Asian, and her girlfriend is racially ambiguous, perhaps African American or Puerto Rican but definitely not white. Even this multiracial quality doesn't distinguish activist imagery since, for example, although she is not present in the Versace ad mentioned above, Naomi Campbell was part of photographer Steven Meisel's "Holy Trinity" of 1990s supermodels that also included Christy and Linda. Activism and advertising share the fantasy of diversity and inclusion, and images such as this one are an important reminder that consumer culture and activist cultures are not completely distinct. Indeed, activist cultures can use fantasy as effectively as advertising does. If visibility is ultimately a matter of political power and not just of positive images or the presence of images, then the images used to promote it can be freed from the obligation to be literal or realistic. Arguments for representation often lose this point, and Dyke Action Machine!'s work is important for its commitment to the codes of mass culture as genres for lesbian representation. But one of the reasons that advertising and activism converge is that both reach a certain impasse around racial representation; the staging of images that depict a multiracial group can as easily represent the containment of antiracism through "inclusion" and "diversity" as it does a challenge to the hegemony of whiteness. Ultimately this is a problem that cannot be solved by visual means alone; there is no one right path for cultural representation, nor can an inclusive cultural representation compensate for an absence of other forms of power. The same might be said for the conundrum of lesbian visibility in the 1990s.

Because, unlike the Lesbian Avengers and Fierce Pussy, DAM! has continued to produce work, its oeuvre makes an important archive of historical change. Its longevity is distinctive and it has proved remarkably adaptable to shifting circumstances, responding where criticism is necessary. If, in the early 1990s, it was possible to intervene in the assumption that lesbians were invisible by making them more literally visible, then by the end of the decade, increased visibility has shifted emphasis to the question of how lesbians are visible. Recent DAM! projects have included posters for the 1997 and 1998 Gay Pride seasons. In 1997, as Ellen's coming out was celebrated as a victory for queer representation and Clinton's Defense of Marriage Act created debate about gay marriage as a political goal, DAM! provided a message of dissent. An image of two women, both in wedding gowns, was accompanied by wedding invitation typescript bearing the slogan "Is It Worth Being Boring for a Blender?" (figure 5). In 1998 DAM! turned to the style of propaganda posters from the 1930s; an image of three wholesome lesbians and a dog on the farm, against a backdrop of the American flag, is accompanied by the slogan "Lesbian Americans, Don't Sell Out." The fine print warns, "Power to All the People or to None." Increasingly, then, in the late 1990s, DAM! has directed its campaigns to the mainstream gay community, rather than to mainstream culture, promoting a critical perspective on the marketing of gay politics and identities.[26] Such dissenting images and voices are important and DAM!'s ability to turn their political positions into accessible images and slogans is crucial.

Fierce Pussy

Fierce Pussy, another visual collective based in New York and active from 1991 to 1994, adopts a different tactic from DAM! in its engagement with the images of advertising and celebrity culture. Like DAM!, members of Fierce Pussy are both artists and activists, some with ties to ACT UP. But rather than insinuating themselves into celebrity and media culture by appropriating its strategies, as DAM! does, Fierce Pussy resists these tactics. Two notable strategies are their use of words as a form of visibility and their use of personal photographs. One of their most powerful visual campaigns was the 1992 series of posters and stickers bearing lists of words for lesbians, many of them stigmatized terms. One version reads: "I am a lezzie muffdiver mannish femme bulldagger amazon butch dyke AND PROUD," with the words listed in a column. A lesbian-specific incarnation of a "queer" politics, the images render lesbianism visible by rendering the words for it visible. As such they are a reminder that visibility is a metaphor, as much a function of names as faces. The fact that words can constitute an image is a reminder that images themselves are also stylized or conventional, rather than transparent, representations. Moreover, these words raise the possibility that lesbianism may not be visible in the form of a particular image or look but may be visible only through an act of self-nomination. Hence the list is prefaced with the words "I am a . . . " and ends with the reclaiming of the words as a source of pride. Affixed to walls, newspaper boxes, and light poles, the language of graffiti and harassment is circulated with a difference in the public sphere. Especially notable is the use of an old-fashioned typescript, signifying a rejection of the high-tech fonts of advertising and the word processor. The slightly uneven script with dots and smudges gives the words a materiality and tactility that emphasizes their status as image; this strategy actually constitutes an (un)canny version of advertising's power to exploit difference, including anachronisms, to draw attention to itself.

This insinuation of low-tech or anachronistic forms into the visual public sphere is also evident in Fierce Pussy's use of personal snapshots in some of their other series from this period. Drawing especially on childhood snapshots that nostalgically evoke the styles of the 1950s and 1960s, the slogans recirculate and rename these images as potentially lesbian. In one series, images of young girls are accompanied by labels, again in typescript, such as "dyke," "muffdiver," and "lover of women" (figure 6). In another series, group shots, such as family portraits and class pictures, carry captions such as "Find the lesbian in this picture" or "How many lesbians in this picture?" These images leave open the question of how lesbianism is visible—the childhood snapshot of a lesbian can be read as a predictor of her adult sexuality but it can just as easily testify to lesbianism's uncertain origins and the impossibility of rendering it visible in the childhood face or body. Even as these refunctioned images lesbianize the heteronormative family album and trouble presumptions of heterosexuality, they also indicate the impossibility of any predictable or mimetic relation between the photograph and lesbianism. The choice of the snapshot as genre is especially important because of its presumed power to act as a document of intimate history.[27] Capitalizing on its susceptibility to retroactive interpretation, Fierce Pussy suggests that the snapshot's meanings are not stable.

In choosing the snapshot, generally a private or intimate genre, for public distribution, Fierce Pussy adds another interesting dimension to Dyke Action Machine!'s choice of public genres for the dissemination of lesbian images. By circulating Xeroxed and blown-up family photos within the public sphere, Fierce Pussy suggests that these can be images of public persons and thus links them to celebrity images. Indeed the family snapshot is a way of making history, of representing every person as worthy of representation. Fierce Pussy places the ordinary person more overtly within the circuits of distribution of advertising and visual public culture. Because the label "lesbian" has often been presumed to exclude people from the status of public citizens, this circulation is crucial. The snapshot is not positioned as the antidote to the advertising image's mythic versions of femininity and lesbianism. Instead, it invades their domain, going public in order to suggest that lesbians can be public persons, celebrities even, and that lesbianism might be visible in any image.

The Hypervisibility of Lesbian Chic

Fierce Pussy intervened in 1993's lesbian chic phenomenon with a poster that displayed a crude line drawing of a butt and the scrawled slogan "Fuck lesbian chic. We want our civil rights now" (figure 7). An older model of a refusal of representation is present in the line drawing, which uses the style of graffiti to resist the increasing presence of glossy images of celebrity lesbians in the media. Fierce Pussy was not the only group to say "Fuck Lesbian Chic"; the Lesbian Avengers' second manifesto, distributed for 1994's Stonewall 25 festivities, also included that headline as part of its call for lesbian civil rights. Activists must adapt to shifting circumstances as rapidly as the fashion industry does, and the early 1990s activist slogan "Promote Lesbian Visibility," which was circulated on fluorescent crack-and-peel stickers by Queer Nation, had been replaced in 1994 by the slogan "Dyke Liberation: A Movement not a Market" (distributed by a group called Lesbian Contradiction). In between these two moments, accompanying the media coverage of gays in the military and the March on Washington, was the flurry of 1993 mainstream news stories announcing that lesbians were hot. This story was primarily a visual one, its message carried in the images of lesbians not as drab separatists or fierce butch dykes but as stars, lipstick lesbians, glamour dykes, and femmes. Underscored by the caption "lesbian chic," the story was that lesbians could be good models for the fashion and celebrity photographs so prized by the culture industry. Had the project of lesbian visibility become a victim of its own success, relegated to the status of consumer trend that merited its very own fifteen minutes of fame?

The answer to this question is not simple, especially given the resemblance between the forms of lesbianism manifest in lesbian chic's most visible moments and the activist images that had already forged connections between mass culture's celebrity genres and lesbianism. The 1993 cover stories about lesbianism that appeared in rapid succession in *New York*, *Newsweek*, and *Vanity Fair* have achieved an almost iconic status as emblems of the relation between lesbian chic and lesbian visibility, including its troubling aspects.[28] But a closer look at these cover images reveals significantly divergent approaches to the project of making lesbianism visible, a difference that turns on the use of celebrity photography. Whereas *Newsweek's* strategy is to make ordinary people into cover models (and to make lesbians into ordinary people), *New York* and *Vanity Fair* both choose a "celebrity lesbian," k.d. lang, as their subject, and *Vanity Fair*, in keeping with its tradition of spectacular covers, goes so far as to pair her with supermodel Cindy Crawford in a butch-femme barber shop scene. I'd like to explain why, even if the choice is a limited one, I'd take *Vanity Fair's* butch-femme queer-straight-girl-with-a-dyke fantasy over *Newsweek's* ordinary people realism.

Establishing its reputation as a source for serious journalism by distinguishing itself from celebrity culture, *Newsweek* displays two women (of somewhat uncertain ethnicity) in a demure embrace (just enough to indicate that they are lovers but not enough to be too overtly sexual). They serve as the poster girls who make the accompanying headline—"What are the limits of tolerance?"—intelligible as a claim for at least some measure of tolerance. Eschewing celebrity lesbianism, the cover encourages its (presumptively heterosexual) viewers to think of lesbians as normal people who are just like them because they look just like them; the photograph is crucial to a political strategy that has become a significantly visual one. This cover aptly exemplifies Eric Clarke's analysis of how homoeroticism is included in the public sphere at the price of normalization. The acceptable (or tolerable) images are the visible face of a process whereby economic and cultural representation comes to substitute for political representation.[29]

By merging celebrity and lesbianism, the *New York* and *Vanity Fair* covers arguably present a strategy for making lesbianism visible that doesn't make the same bid for normalization that has become so persistent and troubling in mainstream gay and lesbian politics. Throughout her career, k.d. lang has been a highly visual star, appearing in a broad range of photographs that make powerful use of the compatible visual powers of celebrity culture and genderbending. Like Madonna, who is one of the central photochameleons of the 1980s and 1990s, k.d. lang has been willing to play with the roles and poses demanded by studio photography, and both of them understand that the process need not be a form of objectification but can instead be a forum for queer drag. But lang's photogenic power is especially notable because it has not required that she hide her lesbianism or become feminine. Indeed, throughout her now lengthy career as a visual star, k.d. lang has never not looked like a lesbian, even though she has also looked like a celebrity. Instead, she has found ways to make butch lesbianism the material for glamour photography, and the *New York* cover, a head shot that shows her wearing a suit, is a good example of the results of this happy congruence between lesbian styles and celebrity culture. lang chooses not just masculinity but celebrity masculinity, and in doing so, participates in a long tradition of such fashion codes within lesbian cultures, including 1920s salon culture, 1940s and 1950s bar culture, and even, contrary to some stereotypes, 1970s lesbian feminist culture.[30] (Dykes in tuxedos and other dress suits are a staple on the stages of women's music festivals.)

The *Vanity Fair* cover takes lang's visual celebrity lesbianism one step further. The performative dimension of the photo shoot is even more pronounced as lang plays at being masculine in a series of poses with Cindy Crawford that enact a barber shop scene. Not only is lang dressed to play a part but the choice of supermodel Cindy Crawford as her partner places the scene into the domain of fantasy, since Crawford is another product of a specifically visual celebrity culture that has used the power of photography to make models into stars. *Vanity Fair*'s photos of a celebrity lesbian and a celebrity supermodel can thus be appreciated on a number of levels. k.d. lang might be seen as the lesbian who is powerful and sexy enough to attract straight girls; Crawford could be read as courageously challenging homophobia by being willing, as straight, to play a femme lesbian; she could be read as declaring herself as, if not lesbian, at least queer-identified.[31] Crawford's status in the image is ambiguous in both positive and negative ways, but her presence in a lesbian image as one of celebrity culture's most visible faces adds incalculable star power to lesbianism's visibility and its glamour. She helps make it possible for lang to be on the cover of *Vanity Fair*, one of the measures of celebrity success in contemporary media culture, and lang's image is remarkable for being visibly and indisputably lesbian at the same time as it is so emphatically that of a celebrity.

One of the reasons why lesbianism and celebrity can form such a glamorous partnership on the cover of *Vanity Fair* is that such images have always been queer. Magazines such as *Vanity Fair* and *Vogue* have been produced by gay and "queer" editors, art directors, and other staff members, including photographers such as Baron Adolph De Meyer, Cecil Beaton, Horst P. Horst, George Hoyningen-Huene, and Berenice Abbott, and, more recently, Annie Leibovitz, Bruce Weber, Steven Meisel, and Herb Ritts, the photographer for the lang/Crawford cover. In their queer celebrity-subjects, coverage of the arts and theater, and use of photographs that stage fantasy scenarios rather than providing realistic representation, these magazines forge a tradition of queer and gay and lesbian culture that has yet to be rendered fully visible as such.[32] Thus the visibility of lesbian chic in the 1990s is not necessarily new but draws on a longer history of sexual and celebrity cultures merging in the domain of the visible.

All of these cover photos could be construed as beside the point of the dyke visibility demanded by activists because they take "visibility" too literally as a matter of images. But if visibility is understood as a metaphor, then cultural visibility is freed from the obligation to be the equivalent of political representation or to be realistic, and we must ask anew what kind of images we want to represent us. One argument implicit in my account of activist images is that the answer to this question should not be to assume that the fashionable image of the glamour dyke can be replaced by some putative "real" dyke to be captured by a more documentary aesthetic. I dwell in some detail on this series of 1993 magazine covers because the differences among them are as important as their possible common effect of displacing political representation onto cultural representation and commodifying gay and lesbian politics through visual and celebrity culture. It should be remembered, for example, that both the *Newsweek* and the *Vanity Fair* covers are fictions, in which case there's no reason not to have fictions that are fantasies. In the struggle between facts and fantasy manifest in the difference between *Newsweek* and *Vanity Fair*, the claim is often made that real journalism and truth might be an antidote to the trivia circulated by celebrity culture. Given the central role of celebrity culture within politics and the news, such distinctions are questionable.

Ultimately, the differences between the lesbian chic images and the lesbian activist images may be less a matter of style, or something that can be seen, and more a matter of invisible factors, such as distribution. Some images are more visible than others, and the historical context provided by the activist images examined here can be hard to create because they are less widely circulated than the magazine covers that are the visible face of tremendous economic and material power. While I am entirely sympathetic to critiques of the magazine covers on the grounds that they represent the commodification of gay and lesbian culture in the 1990s,[33] there is a danger of critical analysis replicating this uneven visibility by neglecting to mention the lesbian activists, as well as photographers such as Della Grace (now Del LaGrace Volcano), Cathy Opie, Morgan Gwenwald, Deborah Bright, Jill Posener, and Honey Lee Cottrell, who have depicted lesbians through the stylized conventions of celebrity photography. If we look at the images carefully, the distinctions between activist images and magazine covers can be more, not less, difficult to see. Moreover, the juxtapositions and contextualizations provided here produce a kind of montage that temporarily evens out the discrepancies of power in which the images are institutionally located. One of the appeals of visual activism in an age of reasonably accessible technology (such as computer graphics programs, Xerox machines, and color printers) is that activists can level the visual playing field in some contexts, producing activist images that appear "equal" alongside corporate images. (This is especially true within the pedestrian culture of New York City, where the tradition of illegal wheatpasting makes it possible to compete with corporate ads; as the Giuliani administration's crackdown has shown, however, the unofficial public spaces of the street are fragile and contested terrain. The World Wide Web is rapidly emerging as another space in which corporate and activist images can be juxtaposed.) The simulation of the look of celebrity and advertising culture has been an important tool for making the lesbian visible. The archive of lesbian chic should not only become the visible sign of the commodification of queer culture in the 1990s; it also stands for an important struggle within lesbian cultural politics that has opened up the possibility of celebrity representation not as a model for authentic representation, as in the *Newsweek* cover, but as a model for fantasies of lesbianism that have yet to be fully explored.

The Return of the Artist

In the course of writing this article, I came upon another important archive of images—those produced by the many members of Fierce Pussy and Dyke Action Machine! who are also individual artists—that revealed art as an unexpected resource for radical visual thinking. These artists' simultaneous allegiance to mass culture and individual craft transforms the relation between lesbians and the public sphere and creates new possibilities for celebrity within both the art world and the activist world. Contrary to my initial expectations, the individual artist is not rendered obsolete by activism but is the creator of a spectrum of visual products that exploit the visual public sphere to create new ways of seeing the combined identities of celebrity and lesbian. My research into activists as artists began as the somewhat accidental byproduct of wondering how their artwork was affected by their activism. Dyke Action Machine!'s Carrie Moyer increasingly devotes her time to painting but also works as a graphic designer, and her partner, Sue Schaffner, is a photographer who does her own work as well as commercial work ranging from publicity photos for queer artists to fashion and advertising photography. Fierce Pussy's membership includes many visual artists, among them Suzanne Wright, Nancy Brody, Zoe Leonard, Joy Episalla, Carrie Yamaoka, Alison Froling, and Donna Evans, who work in a wide range of media and styles that are impossible to generalize.[34] Almost none of these activist-artists make a living exclusively from their art, but most of them would be happy to do so. Living simultaneously in the art world, the culture industry, and activist circles, they reconfigure these domains.

Encountering the material conditions within which these activist-artists work forced me to reexamine the assumptions I absorbed from theories of cultural activism that stressed the need to take art out of the problematic institutional context of the galleries and museums into the streets.[35] Although these women redefine what it means to be an artist through their activism, their lives also suggest the continued viability of the category rather than its disintegration. (Even those most vociferous critics of the art scene, the anonymous Guerilla Girls, are themselves professional artists.) My initial curiosity about whether and how the art work produced by activists shows the influence of their activism was supplemented by the sense that, not only has visual activism not meant the death of the artist but it has actually catalyzed the artistic ambitions of many visual activists, for whom their artwork enables forms of expression that cannot be provided by activism.[36]

One of the major surprises in my research has been the unpredictability of the relation between an artist's own work and her activist work. These artists maintain a flexibility of both style and content, adopting the visual strategies of advertising where necessary but also producing an incredible range of images that reveal, make visible even, the constraints of visibility within the public spheres of activism. The influence of popular and mass culture is often most visible in this work's freedom to depart from it. For example, as a photographer, Zoe Leonard, one of Fierce Pussy's members, uses the technology of mass culture, and her work engages with mass culture's commodification of women, beauty, and fashion. But the images combine disturbing and often unexpected forms of beauty; in a series from a Geoffrey Beene runway fashion show, the camera's awkward angle captures the model's legs below her raised skirt, and in a document from the Max Factor Beauty Museum, a photograph of the iron cage that takes facial measurements reveals the simultaneously beautiful and tyrannical technology behind the scene of beauty. Leonard uses the conventions of celebrity culture in her 1998 Bearded Lady Calendar, a collaborative project in which performance artist Jennifer Miller posed for her, and in her still photographs for Cheryl Dunye's *The Watermelon Woman* in which Leonard simulated the photo archive of an imaginary African American performer, a process that drew attention to the absence of black women from histories of celebrity and their accompanying archives.[37]

Some of Leonard's work has been quite polemical; for her 1992 Documenta installation, which dates from the period when she was active with ACT UP, GANG, and Fierce Pussy, she juxtaposed reproductions of old-master oil paintings with photographs of women's pussies, including an image that was used by Fierce Pussy in a postcard mailing about the 1992 elections. Haunted, however, by death, loss, and the affective dimensions of the social problems that activism addresses, Leonard's photographs are also significantly idiosyncratic and personal, and they exceed any account of their links to her activism. In a 1995 pamphlet entitled *Strange Fruit*, she references the history of lynching obliquely in an image of a huge and leafless tree that is improbably laden with fruit. Included as well are photographs of fruit whose empty peels have been sewn back together; Leonard has made installations of the fruit and photographs of the installations as a memorial to dead friends. The images constitute both an intensely personal archive and a means of addressing public concerns. In this respect, they resemble the tactics of Fierce Pussy's use of family photographs, and Leonard's series of photographs of two little girls in the Museum of Natural History seems particularly reminiscent of the Fierce Pussy projects. Dwarfed by the diorama scenes of stuffed animals and bones from other times, one of the girls stares at the windows, looking both lost and alive with curiosity (figure 8). The photographs reflect a vision that doesn't make it into either fashion magazines or political rallies, but they are nonetheless informed by the questions popular culture provokes about the use of spectacle and the gaze to produce gendered knowledge. Leonard's recent series of photographs of trees that have burst through the constraints of fences and sidewalks on New York City streets exemplifies her use of photography as a means of evading the constant barrage of images that structures our daily lives in order to produce new ways of seeing.[38] She revitalizes the potential of art and creative work to provide alternatives to popular imagery, but does so partly by including the remnants of popular culture's representation of women, girls, and fashion.

Little girls also show up in a series of paintings and drawings by Carrie Moyer whose unsettling violence and ambiguity make even her most outrageous activist images seem tame by comparison.[39] As if freed from the necessity to be attractive or persuasive on behalf of lesbian visibility, Moyer dares to depict the fundamentalist right's worst nightmares in "The Women/Girl Love Association," in which a suave butch-looking woman in a schoolyard holds open her trench coat and hovers over four schoolgirls who are only too eager for her attentions, and in "The Gay Gene (Heather Has Two Mommies)," in which a very young girl has each hand in the vaginas of two women who are mostly torsos and thighs. Moyer's references to political controversy announce her commitment to images of queer childhood sexuality that are uncompromising and unthreatened by taboo. In "I Don't Have A Name for This Yet," a mother and two little girls are dressed in the Sunday-school fashions of the 1960s—coat dresses, hats, hairbows, and white ankle socks with black patent leather shoes (figure 9). The drawing style, which is reminiscent of Dick and Jane grade-school readers, is also reminiscent of a historical period that promoted girlhood as pure and sexually innocent, often through popular culture's visual representations.[40] Moyer brings out the sinister potential of this visual style. Her eyes bulging, one little girl sticks out her red pointy tongue in an almost Satanic way. The other little girl is smoking a cigarette, and her facial expression and wicked gaze seem preternaturally worldly. Apparently oblivious to the little girls, Mom gazes outward with a smile that seems pasted on. But her face is also disturbing; the lining and smudging of the eyes brings out the creepy, even hostile side of feminine conventions of cheerfulness. In another similar image, "Pat the Bunny," an almost twinlike mother and daughter seem to be holding hands, but on closer inspection, we see that the little girl has her hand up mom's dress. The two paintings give mother-daughter intimacies a perverse twist, although part of what is unsettling is that Moyer reveals the queerness that is already present in the supposedly "normal" heterosexual family. Like Moyer's activist work, these images are concerned with how the visual technologies of popular culture affect girls and women, but her willingness to present disturbing and perverse versions of popular imagery is a reminder of activism's strategic emphasis on promoting visual pleasure.

The most pronounced difference between Moyer's activist work and her art work is not, however, her choice of subject matter but her choice of media. She eschews computer graphics and photographs in favor of the more archaic and handcrafted techniques of drawing and painting. This use of more traditional media creates an intimacy between the artist and the work and, by extension, between the artist and the viewer. The resulting body of work stands in intriguing contrast with Moyer's activist images, which are for the most part produced anonymously and in a more impersonal and public commercial style. The archaic modes that might seem to be rendered obsolete by the technologies of mass culture in fact have new life in Moyer's work (as well as that of other activist-artists), which turns to painting and drawing as a vehicle for the expression of messages that cannot be made visible in the genres of mass culture. But rather than crafting a modernist refuge or retreat from mass culture, Moyer develops a personal style that exists with full knowledge of its power. She seeks the more intimate spaces of the small drawing or painting, where visual expression is not limited by the need to be strategic that informs activism and advertising alike.

In this respect Moyer shares the sensibility of Nicole Eisenman, who does not have a history of public activism but who is notable for being one of the most recognized contemporary artists, including having a place in the 1995 Whitney Biennial, for work that is unabashedly, but not exclusively, lesbian.[41] Eisenman herself takes her distance from political art in statements such as, "What I value in other people's art and my own is imagination and personal things. Politics just seems to me to be mean-spirited and trendy. I don't see myself as being in a combative stance."[42] Nonetheless, the overlap between her work and that of activist-artists provides an important context for understanding both her rich body of work and the unpredictable links between art and activism. One of the charms of Eisenman's work, and no doubt one of the reasons for her critical success, is that her lesbian interests are combined with, and even indistinguishable from, her use of the traditions of high art. Her drawings, paintings, and installations invoke a variety of canonical figures including Picasso, Matisse, and Van Gogh. But Eisenman's tastes are extremely broad, and she frequently approaches art history like a popular culture fan, voraciously appropriating cultural references both high and low and reproducing them with both love and humor. For example, in "The Village People/La Dance," the disco heroes are depicted in the manner of Matisse's famous painting. For the Whitney Biennial exhibition, she spoofed the commercialism of the art world in a series of drawings titled the "Whitney Houston Buy Any Ol' Painting Show" that were part of a large installation. In the spirit of DAM! and Fierce Pussy, Eisenman incorporates an often highly sexualized lesbianism (as well as the perverse eroticism of peeing and other bodily functions) into the imagery of both high culture and popular culture, and she makes particular use of celebrities and famous artists (as the celebrities of the art world) to do so. Celebrities, brand-name figures, and cartoon heroes abound in her work, which includes images of the Tropicana Girl (who pees in cartons to make orange juice), Wilma butt-fucking Betty in "Betty Gets It," and, in a drawing titled "Alice in Wonderland," Alice with her entire head thrust into a towering Wonder Woman's pussy (figure 10).[43] In the Whitney installation, for example, her own self-portrait was the largest image surrounded by many other smaller drawings and paintings. Eisenman's work makes the artist, including the lesbian artist, a kind of celebrity in the current world of visual culture and she adapts the strategy of making art historical references through which artists situate themselves in a tradition by also referencing popular culture and lesbianism. She both spoofs artist-celebrity culture and insinuates herself into it, like the activists who have insinuated themselves into commercial and celebrity visual cultures in order to transform it.

The activist power of Eisenman's diverse range of references is supplemented by her penchant for unusual forms of installation. I first saw her work in a group show at Exit Art in New York City, where her drawings of nasty little girls, most notably a dog licking the puddle left by the Morton Salt girl peeing, were tacked up with push pins in odd corners of the gallery walls, as though she had put her sketchbook on public display. In addition to producing casual, small pieces in prolific numbers, Eisenman has also made large murals, and by working in a range of scales, she explodes distinctions between intimate and monumental space. She frequently combines both, as in the case of her Biennial project, where the large wall-size installation was composed of a cluttered collage of little drawings and paintings, including a number of images of herself. Her insistence on the small-scale dailiness of the production of images seems in keeping with the sensibility of lesbian activist-artists who turn to personal and intimate forms as an alternative to activism. Eisenman's use of drawing, like Moyer's, also suggests a return to more intimate media, one in which the artist has a manual connection to the paper and the materials. Yet like Fierce Pussy's insertion of family photographs into public space, Eisenman installations transform these small-format pieces into the stuff of public art. Thus, although she has sometimes resisted being constructed as a lesbian artist or connected to identity politics, Eisenman shares with artists who are more overtly activist the sensibility that comes from being a member of a girl gang.

Thinking about activists as artists is also a way to evaluate the gains constituted by lesbian visibility in the economic terms of who has made a profit from it. Crude and individualistic as this form of accounting might be, it is useful to remember that only a tiny number of lesbian artists support themselves through their art work, and their activist work is almost always unpaid labor. The category of the artist remains an important locus of ambition for earning a living from creative work, and a living wage for lesbian artists is one modest goal of lesbian visibility and the (supposed) marketability of queer culture that has yet to be achieved.

The Archive as Visual Demonstration and Visible Theory

It's a good thing that lesbian artists are producing interesting work at the close of the 1990s because the activist work that marked the beginning of the decade is much harder to find. But this state of affairs need not be cause for pessimism since it is important to remember that activist groups always wax and wane. As I noted earlier, for example, the founders of Lesbian Avengers expected their own obsolescence, seeing their task as the production of a new generation of activists who would go on to other projects more suited to shifting circumstances. Feminisms and activisms of the 1990s have been haunted by the legacy of the 1960s and 1970s, whether in seeking to recapture some of the same energy and impact or in seeking to do something different in order to avoid repeating earlier mistakes. The increasing awareness that both feminism and lesbianism, along with being marked by other forms of difference, are intergenerational has brought new historical challenges. While intergenerational dialogue can be schismatic, leading to reductive critiques of the past, destructive comparisons, or suspicion that authenticity has been lost over time, it can also be a productive way to negotiate differences. The presence now of multiple generations of activism since the 1960s serves as a reminder that there are multiple models for activism, that activism's time is never over, and that it always arises anew out of the myriad provocations of everyday life. The activism of the 1990s that publicized lesbian popular culture fandom and produced new images of lesbians, including even new stereotypes, was born out of the surprising discovery that private forms of consumption and reception could be the basis for a collective counterpublic. Even as the marketing of lesbianism has produced what Sarah Schulman calls a false picture of gay community, alternative counterpublics persist, including the archive of activism constructed here, the art being made by artists who may not be doing activism but are still working, and other unpredictable cultural formations.[44] I mean here to capture some of the messiness and invisibility of history that may not be apparent in single images, as well as to document the ongoing presence of alternative or counterpublics, which are constantly spawned and absorbed by capital.

I have also become aware that an article like this is its own kind of demonstration and that just publicizing these images is an accomplishment. I write in the spirit of Douglas Crimp and Adam Rolston's *AIDS Demo Graphics*, which has become an invaluable archive of AIDS activist graphics from the late 1980s. Criticism becomes its own way of extending the reach of these materials beyond their largely ephemeral origins as posters and publicity for very specific events and occasions. This conviction has been further confirmed by my contact with the artists whose work is presented here. I had been prepared for them to be wary of criticism that might remove the work from its original activist context; instead they were delighted to have it further publicized, expressing concern that it would be lost from the record even though only a few years old.

My display of images is also intended to contribute to this collection's concern with feminist theory at the turn of the new century. Although I said at the outset that it is risky to read images allegorically or emblematically as historically representative, it also seems especially appropriate to do so in this article because the artists and activists considered here self-consciously seek to pursue theoretical inquiry by visual means. The production of images reframes theoretical debates that might otherwise remain stuck in impasses. In reframing the relation between theory and practice by inventing "figurations" such as the cyborg, Donna Haraway, for instance, has actually collaborated with a visual artist, Lynn Randolph, whose images have appeared in conjunction with Haraway's writing, especially her most recent book *Modest Witness@Second Millennium*.[45] Randolph's images are not illustrations.

Haraway describes them as "performative images that can be inhabited" because they bring into being, through the act of making visible, a world that answers her theoretical questions.

The relation between image and theory in Haraway's work provides a model for understanding the images explored in this article as forms of politics and theory, not just illustrations of them. It seeks to reclaim the image from the iconoclasms of both ideology critique, which is suspicious of how images mystify or hide deeper social processes, and feminism, which is suspicious of the images of woman made endlessly visible by commodity culture. By some queer logic, those who have been most invisible in these regimes of representation, such as lesbians and people of color, may be most able to reclaim them. Or, in the words of Fierce Pussy, borrowing from Star Trek, "DYKE: The Final Frontier. To boldly go where no man has gone before." This slogan was used in a graphic design that was displayed on the side of a truck that drove through the streets of Manhattan and in the Dyke March during the weekend of Stonewall 94. Using the power of the image, a power that advertising has successfully deployed for the last century, Fierce Pussy and other activists allow us to "see" what happens when feminists take up the challenge of re-presenting images of women in popular culture. No longer, for example, does the theoretical question of the politics of visual pleasure or pornography or the male gaze remain confined to staking out whether the reversal of patriarchal modes of representation is conceptually possible. Instead feminists and lesbians have set out to reframe the relation between gender and the gaze by actually making pornography for women and images of lesbians that embrace the conventions of celebrity culture. The question is no longer "can it be done?" but "how has it been done?" If the archival evidence offered by this article is any indication, the answer to the first question is a resounding yes and the answers to the second question are many.

NOTES

I'd like to thank Avery Gordon, Eric Clarke, and Patty White for valuable readings, and Carrie Moyer, Sue Schaffner, Zoe Leonard, Joy Episalla, Carrie Yamaoka, and Nicole Eisenman for access to their visual archives and their behind-the-scenes stories. And special thanks to Misha Kavka, whose incisive editorial wisdom made this a better article.

1. For more on the concept of the archive in relation to lesbian culture and the value of popular culture for this archive, see my "In the Archives of Lesbian Feelings: Documentary and Popular Culture," *Wide Angle* (forthcoming, 2000). See also

Lauren Berlant on the popular culture archive and national culture in *The Queen of America Goes to Washington City: Essays on Sex and Citizenship* (Durham, N.C.: Duke University Press, 1997), esp. pp. 10–15, and José Muñoz, "Ephemera as Evidence: Introductory Notes to Queer Acts," *Women and Performance* 16 (1996): 5–18.

2. For an account of the magazine's central, and even originary, place in the history of mass culture, see Richard Ohmann, *Selling Culture: Magazines, Markets, and Class at the Turn of the Century* (London: Verso, 1993).

3. On the politics of visibility, see Lisa Walker, "How to Recognize a Lesbian: The Cultural Politics of Looking Like What You Are," *Signs* 18, no. 4 (Summer 1993): 866–90; Peggy Phelan, *Unmarked: The Politics of Performance* (New York: Routledge, 1993); Robyn Wiegman, "Introduction: Mapping the Lesbian Postmodern," in *The Lesbian Postmodern*, ed. Laura Doan (New York: Columbia University Press, 1994), pp. 1–20; Rosemary Hennessy, "Queer Visibility in Commodity Culture," *Cultural Critique* 29 (Winter 1994/95): 31–76; and Eric Clarke, *Virtuous Vice: Homoeroticism in the Public Sphere* (Durham, N.C.: Duke University Press, 2000). An exceptionally sophisticated account of the relation between lesbian representation and popular culture, published as this essay was going to press, can be found in Patricia White, *Uninvited: Classical Hollywood Cinema and Lesbian Representability* (Bloomington: Indiana University Press, 1999).

4. For a survey of images, see Barbara Kruger, *Love for Sale: The Text and Images of Barbara Kruger*, text by Kate Linker (New York: Abrams, 1990). Kruger has herself been an important source of cultural theory in her writing for art journals. See her collection of essays, *Remote Control: Power, Culture, and the World of Appearances* (Cambridge: MIT Press, 1993).

5. For surveys of Cindy Sherman's work, see *Cindy Sherman* (New York: Pantheon, 1984); *Cindy Sherman: Retrospective* (New York: Thames and Hudson, 1997); and Rosalind Krauss, *Cindy Sherman, 1975–1993* (New York: Rizzoli, 1993). A recent sign of Sherman's reputation has been the Museum of Modern Art's acquisition of her Untitled Film Stills series and an accompanying exhibit (sponsored by, among others, Madonna).

6. Among those who deserve further mention are Nan Goldin, for her crossover between queer culture and mass culture, as well as African American artists making use of popular culture and stereotypes, such as Carrie Mae Weems, Adrian Piper, and Lorna Simpson. For Nan Goldin's work, see *The Ballad of Sexual Dependency* (New York: Aperture, 1986), and Elizabeth Sussman, *Nan Goldin: I'll Be Your Mirror* (New York: Whitney Museum, 1996), the catalogue from her major retrospective at the Whitney in 1996.

7. See Douglas Crimp and Adam Rolston, *AIDS Demo Graphics* (Seattle: Bay Press, 1990). One of the most explicit queer appropriations of, and homages to, Kruger is Adam Rolston's revision of her "I Shop, Therefore I Am" image to create his 1989 "I Am Out, Therefore I Am" sticker and T-shirt. See *AIDS Demo Graphics*, p. 103.

8. See the catalogue from the important 1985 New Museum Show, *Difference: Sexuality and Representation*, organized by Kate Linker and Jane Weinstock. Rosalyn Deutsche mentions this show in the course of arguing that feminist art practice of the 1980s constituted an important form of activism. See *Evictions: Art and Spatial Politics* (Cambridge: MIT Press, 1996).

9. For the intersections of queer theory and popular culture, see Lauren Berlant and Elizabeth Freeman, "Queer Nationality," in *Fear of a Queer Planet: Queer Politics and Social Theory*, ed. Michael Warner (Minneapolis: University of Minnesota Press, 1993), pp. 193–229; Danae Clark, "Commodity Lesbianism," *Camera Obscura* 25/26 (1991): 181–201; and Lisa Duggan, "Making it Perfectly Queer" and "Queering the State," in *Sex Wars: Sexual Dissent and Political Culture*, ed. Lisa Duggan and Nan Hunter (New York: Routledge, 1995), pp. 155–72, 179–93.

10. See Eve Sedgwick, "Introduction," in *Shame and Its Sisters: A Silvan Tompkins Reader* (Durham, N. C.: Duke University Press, 1995), p. 5. See also her introduction, "Paranoid Reading and Reparative Reading; or, You're So Paranoid, You Probably Think This Introduction Is About You," in *Novel Gazing: Queer Readings in Fiction*, ed. Eve Sedgewick (Durham, N. C.: Duke University Press, 1997), and Sedgwick, "Queer Performativity: Henry James's *The Art of the Novel*," *GLQ* 1, no. 1 (1993): 1–16.

11. Susanne Kappeler's book, *The Pornography of Representation* (Minneapolis: University of Minnesota Press, 1986), is the most extreme example. For feminists more sympathetic to pornography, see Kate Ellis et al., *Caught Looking: Feminism, Pornography, and Censorship* (Seattle: Real Comet Press, 1988); Lynne Segal and Mary McIntosh, eds., *Sex Exposed: Sexuality and the Pornography Debate* (London: Virago, 1992); and Duggan and Hunter, *Sex Wars*.

12. Neil Hertz, "Medusa's Head: Male Hysteria Under Political Pressure," in *The End of the Line* (New York: Columbia University Press, 1985).

13. In addition to Hennessy, "Queer Visibility in Commodity Culture," and Clarke, *Virtuous Vice*, see John D'Emilio's early and prescient "Capitalism and Gay Identity," in *The Lesbian and Gay Studies Reader*, ed. Henry Abelove, Michele Aina Barale, and David Halperin (New York: Routledge, 1993), and Amy Gluckman and Betsy Reed, eds., *Homo Economics: Capitalism, Community, and Lesbian and Gay Life* (New York: Routledge, 1997).

14. See José Muñoz, *Disidentifications: Queers of Color and the Performance of Politics* (Minneapolis: University of Minnesota Press, 1999).

15. For work by Deborah Bright, as well as many other photographers, see Tessa Boffin and Jean Fraser, eds., *Stolen Glances: Lesbians Take Photographs* (London: Pandora, 1991), and Deborah Bright, ed., *The Passionate Camera* (New York: Routledge, 1998). For the work of Della Grace (now using the name Del LaGrace Volcano), see *Love Bites* (London: GMP, 1991), and Del LaGrace Volcano and Judith "Jack" Halberstam, *The Drag King Book* (London: Serpent's Tail, 1999). For work by other lesbian photographers, see Susie Bright and Jill Posener, *Nothing but the Girl: The Bla-*

tant Lesbian Image (New York: Freedom Editions, 1996). A crucial essay on the earlier decades of lesbian representation is Jan Zita Grover, "Dykes in Context: Some Problems in Minority Representation," in *The Contest of Meaning: Critical Histories of Photography*, ed. Richard Bolton (Cambridge: MIT Press, 1989), pp. 163–203.

16. See Michael Warner, "The Mass Public and the Mass Subject," in *Habermas and the Public Sphere*, ed. Craig Calhoun (Cambridge: MIT Press, 1992), pp. 377–401.

17. For work on celebrity culture from the perspective of cultural studies, see Joshua Gamson, *Claims to Fame: Celebrity in Contemporary America* (Berkeley: University of California Press, 1994), and P. David Marshall, *Celebrity and Power: Fame in Contemporary Culture* (Minneapolis: University of Minnesota Press, 1997). An extremely suggestive essay on feminism and celebrity is Jennifer Wicke, "Celebrity Material: Materialist Feminism and the Culture of Celebrity," *SAQ* 93, no. 4 (Fall 1994): 751–78.

18. Sarah Schulman's *My American History* (New York: Routledge, 1994) provides an important archive because it includes not only Schulman's journalism essays about activism during the period but also the Lesbian Avengers handbook. The more ephemeral materials of activism (including graphics and posters) and journalism are made more permanent through book publication. Also useful documentation is the video *Lesbian Avengers Eat Fire Too!*, directed and filmed by Friedrich and Janet Baus, 1993.

19. The bomb logo continues to be used, appearing in June 1999 publicity for New York's 7th Annual Dyke March that featured the slogan "Dykes: We're Da Bomb!"

20. For more on Lesbian Avengers activism as performance, see Carolyn Shapiro, "Performative Activism," unpublished essay. For discussion of queer AIDS activism's use of performance, see David Roman, *Acts of Intervention: Performance, Gay Culture, and AIDS* (Bloomington: Indiana University Press, 1998). For discussion of the use of bold graphics in ACT UP, see Crimp and Rolston, *AIDS Demo Graphics*. See also David Deitcher, "Gran Fury," in *Discourses: Conversations in Postmodern Art and Culture*, ed. Russell Ferguson, William Olander, Marcia Tucker, and Karen Fiss (New York: New Museum and MIT Press, 1990), pp. 196–208.

21. For more on the origins of the term "women of color" as an antiracist organizing strategy, see Norma Alarcon, "The Theoretical Subject(s) of *This Bridge Called My Back* and Anglo-American Feminism," in *Criticism in the Borderlands: Studies in Chicano Literature, Culture, and Ideology*, ed. Hector Calderon and José David Saldivar (Durham, N. C.: Duke University Press, 1991), pp. 28–39.

22. The ongoing power of Pam Grier's star image and the ongoing cult status of blaxploitation is evident in her recent appearances in Quentin Tarantino's *Jackie Brown* and Jane Campion's *Holy Smoke!*.

23. See Angela Davis, "Afro Images: Politics, Fashion, and Nostalgia," in *Soul: Black Power, Politics, and Pleasure*, ed. Monique Guillory and Richard C. Green (New York: New York University Press, 1998), pp. 23–31.

24. Other examples of independent film and videos that rework popular culture's representations of African Americans include Leah Gilliam, *Sapphire and the Slave Girl*, and Cheryl Dunye, *The Watermelon Woman* (1996). May Joseph's *Nomadic Identities* (Minneapolis: University of Minnesota Press, 1999) includes a fascinating discussion of the reception of blaxploitation among African and Asian Tanzanian audiences in the 1970s.

A roundtable, "More on Positive and Negative Images: The Case of Kara Walker, Artist," at the 1998 American Studies Association (ASA) meeting in Seattle produced a lively discussion. For more on the debate provoked by Walker's work, see the *International Review of African American Art* 14, no. 3 (1997): 3–29, and 15, no. 2 (1998): 44–52. My thanks to Avery Gordon, who was one of the ASA panelists, for drawing my attention to these sources.

25. Giuliani's repressive tactics as mayor of New York City have also affected the practice of illegal wheatpasting; the stricter enforcement of the law since he was elected in 1994 has severely curtailed this public mode of expression. The links between visual activism and sex cultures are revealed by Giuliani's persistent and multiheaded battle against all forms of public street culture. See Dangerous Bedfellows, *Policing Public Sex: Queer Politics and the Future of AIDS Activism* (Boston: South End Press, 1996).

26. DAM!'s 1999 project is a web site featuring FAQs about lesbians, such as "Are you two sisters?" and "Which one is the man?" See www.dykeactionmachine.com. (I myself have had the honor of posing for a video clip included in the web site.)

In a departure from previous projects, the 1999 campaign was not timed for release during Gay Pride, although DAM! distributed palm cards at the Dyke March announcing the future appearance of the web site. In the late 1990s, Gay Pride parades seem to have waned in significance as a site for activism or politics.

27. For more on the role of snapshots, especially in the gendered or minoritarian archive, see my "In the Archives of Lesbian Feelings," as well as Marianne Hirsch, *Family Frames: Photography, Narrative, and Postmemory* (Cambridge: Harvard University Press, 1997).

28. "Lesbian Chic: The Bold, Brave New World of Gay Women," *New York*, May 10, 1993; "Lesbians: Coming Out Strong. What Are the Limits of Tolerance?" *Newsweek*, June 21, 1993; *Vanity Fair*, August 1993.

29. See Clarke, *Virtuous Vice*.

30. I'm adapting here Judith Halberstam's notion of "female masculinity." See *Female Masculinity* (Durham, N.C.: Duke University Press, 1998).

31. In a prescient moment that also provides evidence of the overlaps between counterpublics and mainstream culture, the visual activist group GANG, also active in the early 1990s, designed a series of postcards that linked political slogans with celebrity images. (They were printed on the back cover of *Outlook* magazine and could be torn out for mailing.) One of the cards in the series features Cindy Craw-

ford's face accompanied by the slogan "I didn't know lesbians get bashed. That's so bad." (Among GANG's members was Zoe Leonard, also a member of Fierce Pussy.)

32. For an excellent example of this project, see Thomas Waugh, "Posing and Performance: Glamour and Desire in Homoerotic Art Photography," in Bright, ed., *Passionate Camera*, pp. 58–77.

33. Over the years since 1993, it has been interesting to see how frequently these cover images are cited or reproduced as a way of documenting this moment. See, for example, Rosemary Hennessy, "Queer Visibility in Commodity Culture"; Linda Dittmar, "The Straight Goods," in Bright, ed., *Passionate Camera*; and the introduction to *Homo Economics. Out* magazine commented on the cover images by incorporating them into a fashion layout, and San Francisco's *Bay Times* spoofed the image by changing the headline to "Heterosexuality: What Are the Limits of Tolerance?" Most recently, the *Newsweek* and *Vanity Fair* covers appear in the film *After Stonewall* (1999), which documents the last three decades of gay and lesbian history. They also appear in Deborah Bright's valuable survey of lesbian photography and visibility in the 1980s and 1990s, which came to my attention as this essay was going to press. See "Mirrors and Window Shoppers: Lesbians, Photography, and the Politics of Visibility," in *OverExposed: Essays on Contemporary Photography*, ed. Carol Squiers (New York: New Press, 1999), pp. 24–47.

Dittmar is critical of the image of lesbian chic promoted not just by the magazine covers but by many fashion photographs from this period, whereas Reina Lewis and Katrina Rolley have a lesbian fan's enthusiasm for them. See Lewis and Rolley, "Ad(dressing) the Dyke: Lesbian Looks and Lesbians Looking," in *Outlooks: Lesbian and Gay Sexualities and Visual Cultures*, ed. Peter Horne and Reina Lewis (New York: Routledge, 1996), pp. 178–90. My own approach is to reframe this impasse between appreciation and critique by placing the magazine images within the context of visual activism and art by lesbians.

34. I've met with Zoe Leonard, Carrie Yamaoka, and Joy Episalla. Yamaoka has been doing abstract paintings whose surfaces are metallic and reflective. See *Carrie Yamaoka* (New York: Debs and Co., 1997). Episalla does installations that include photography. A 1996 installation included found photographs of two women whom Episalla speculates might have been lesbians. See *Joy Episalla* (Hannover, Germany: Neue Galerie, 1996). I cannot here cover adequately all of the work done by these artists, and I feel the difficulty of making choices of both individual works and artists to cover in more depth. I hope this section will serve at least as a reminder of the importance of supporting work by lesbians that often still meets with the discrimination of invisibility in the art world.

35. For a polemical statement of this view, see Crimp and Rolston, *AIDS Demo Graphics*. For more on the politics of the museum and the art world, including a discussion of the Guerilla Girls, see Andrew Ross, "The Great Un-American Numbers Game," in *Real Love* (New York: New York University Press, 1998), pp. 117–48.

36. For a survey of recent work by lesbian artists, which is itself a valuable archive that includes work by Dyke Action Machine! and Fierce Pussy, as well as both Carrie Moyer and Nicole Eisenman, see Cherry Smyth, *Damn Fine Art by New Lesbian Artists* (London: Cassell, 1996).

37. Publications featuring Leonard's work include *Strange Fruit* (New York: Paula Cooper Gallery, 1995); *Secession: Zoe Leonard* (Wiener Secession, 1997); Zoe Leonard and Cheryl Dunye, *The Fae Richards Photo Archive* (San Francisco: Artspace Books, 1996); and *The 1998 Bearded Lady Calendar: Starring Jennifer Miller* (Kunsthaus Glarus, 1997).

38. I thank Leonard for discussion of this point.

39. Carrie Moyer's work is featured in Smyth's *Damn Fine Art*, and in Nayland Blake, Lawrence Rinder, and Amy Scholder, eds., *In a Different Light: Visual Culture, Sexual Identity, Queer Practice* (San Francisco: City Lights Books, 1995).

40. For more on the appropriation of visual images of girlhood from the 1950s and 1960s, especially drawings, see my "In the Archives of Lesbian Feelings."

41. Eisenman's work appears in Smyth, *Damn Fine Art,* and Blake et al., eds., *In a Different Light.*

42. See http://www.artseensoho.com/Art/TILTON/eisenman96/

43. Even a partial list of celebrities that Eisenman has depicted is too long to include here. When asked for one, she began with "all the Flintstones characters, Thelma from Scoobie-Doo, Mikhail Baryshnikov, Margot Fonteyn, Daisy-May" and ended with "Penelope Pitstop, Droop Along, Annette Funicello, Hitler, Mary Poppins, Mr. Peanut, Eloise, Gertrude Stein, Patty Hearst, Ule Brenner, John Lennon, Popeye." Correspondence with N. Eisenman, February 1999.

44. See Sarah Schulman, *Stagestruck* (Durham, N.C.: Duke University Press, 1998).

45. See Donna Haraway, *Modest Witness@Second Millennium* (New York: Routledge, 1997), which features a range of images by Randolph to accompany the different chapters. Randolph also made the cover illustration for Haraway's collection, *Simians, Cyborgs, and Women* (New York: Routledge, 1991), an image of a woman at a computer that combines indigenous and technocultures. Haraway also wrote about Randolph's work for an exhibition catalogue. See Lynn Randolph, *Millennial Myths: Paintings by Lynn Randolph* (Tempe: Arizona State University Art Museum, 1997).

PART 4

Where to Feminism?

Chapter 12

Enfolding Feminism

MIEKE BAL

Figuring It Out

In the seventies, defining femininity seemed so important because it enabled women to seek a ground for bonding. Somehow, it took me a long time to understand that ontological communalities don't necessarily lead to common politics.[1] In my experience, women had not been socialized to trust, and care for, other women. Their training had been obsessively to encourage jealousy and rivalry instead of trust, and all the care had to go to the men and the kids. Unlearning this turned out to be harder than we would have liked.[2] The tenacious presence of family metaphors—sisterhood cannot be thought of outside of the familial ideology—was a superficial but telling symptom.[3]

By the time I discovered the irresolvable contradictions between the two elements "identity" and "politics," common womanhood had been set aside in favor of difference. "Being a woman is not enough"; feminism as a common project had to surrender to the insight that "all the women are white, all the blacks are men, but some of us are brave."[4] The pain of that insight is not over, and solutions that don't get trapped in the overruling ideology that caused the problem in the first place—say, individualism—are still hard to find.

Through these well-rehearsed divides, another runs rampant and does damage by being reduced to slurs: the theoretical divide between concerns that fall under ontology, such as what opponents dismiss as "essentialist," and concerns of epistemology, which first justified and then unjustified special corners of the academy called "Women's Studies."[5] Roughly, post-Kantians and anti-Cartesians can't talk to each other, they can only scream. This division demonstrates that women are no smarter than other people. Which, I find, is too bad.

As much as these two approaches to feminism seem "naturally" incompatible, simply following as they do an age-old division in philosophy, it seems obvious to me that the question of whether women know differently[6] cannot be separated from the question of whether women are different.[7] Nor can either question be separated from the political issues that splice feminism into invisibility and, worse, ineffectivity, at the moment of its indisputable success.

The issue that lies at the heart of both epistemology and ontology is the bond between existence and knowledge.[8] In spite of brief moments and rallying cries such as "thinking through the body," today's debates in feminism are polarized around what such insights left behind long ago.[9] This bond is complicated by the consequence of the ensuing bond between subject and object. Feminism has not succeeded in articulating this bond beyond the divide that makes the endeavor to account for the intricate relationship between existence and knowledge itself unthinkable. Epistemology and ontology are both incompatible and inseparable.

Two examples must suffice. As the dénouement of Roman Polanski's 1994 film *Death and the Maiden* so troublingly suggests, you never know the truth even if you hear the accused say it himself. Uncertainty severs the bond between epistemology—knowing the truth, with confession as its ultimate end and lie—and ontology—the truth exists, even if it cannot be known. Yet, as Jodie Foster so utterly convincingly conveys in Jonathan Kaplan's 1988 film *The Accused*, it is urgent that the truth be recognized. The epistemological question is of vital importance for the ontological possibility of Jodie's character.

The tragic fate of feminism in the 1990s can be mapped out in the unresolved dispute between these two classic and controversial films. Mapped out more clearly there, one could argue, than it is in the disputes between FACT and MacKinnon, humanist and poststructuralist feminisms, political-activist and academic-theoretical feminisms, feminist metaphysics and scholarship, unreconstructedly white and antiracist feminisms, unreconstructedly straight and queer feminisms, and, for me the most tragic dispute, between victim speech and fun talk. If there is change from decade to decade, perhaps the most painful divide lies here. Rape, gender-based torture, pornography, and other forms of abuse got many feminists excited in the seventies. Rather suddenly, the tone of complaint that these issues seemed to entail became unbearable, and instead of the discourse and theory being changed, it was the thematics that was replaced. "Enough complaining" led to a focus on pleasure, as if the two areas of interest could not coexist.[10]

Some of these changes and divides are inevitable and even productive. I am all for a certain eclecticism, for multiple battles on various grounds to be fought simultaneously. The worst waste of energy for feminists is to fight other feminists on the ground of a difference of opinion. Much energy, I find, has been and continues to be wasted in this way. What can be done about it depends on insight into what went wrong. The indictment of a continued predominance of privileged groups has been heeded, at least verbally with lips, but also transformed into an uncritical celebration of differences—only acceptable in the plural. In the United States and its tentacles, differences have been co-opted into an individualist conception of identity as an accumulation of differences. Hence the slogan "race, class, and gender," which, countering its political grounding, became an obnoxious slur that exacerbated disagreements. It's a trap; as long as you don't omit a single difference from the list, we are all different enough again to keep us apart. In Europe, on the other hand, identity itself has been marked, if not erased, by difference within.

At the level of institutional feminism, this geopolitical difference has played itself out in the creation of campuswide programs, in which the faculty of all departments have united under the banner of women's studies, now renamed gender studies, thereby further expanding their reach but at the same time diluting feminism's visibility. In Europe, the creation of separate research institutes or departments has had a ghettoizing effect. In the United States, affirmative action has left some ineradicable traces, at least here and there. European women's studies centers, firm in their policy of

difference within identity, remain as massively white as mainstream departments remain massively male. This difference between American and European academic culture, immediately visible, is the best argument in favor of
some version or other of "I'd rather be accepted as a woman /as a black person than refused as one"—which is my bottom-line policy in these things.
And having failed to make the connections that—women's /gender studies
departments fear—would make them invisible, they are now available for
the taking, to economically exasperated administrators.

Now the hopes that rallied around femininity and difference have been
exhausted, and, ironically, female pleasure is beginning to become a boring
topic at a time when we can no longer ignore the fact that rape and other
violence against women have not diminished, a new rallying cry is needed.
I personally am longing for one that does not require consensus on priorities, or decisions on whether it matters what femininity is and, if there is
such a thing as femininity, what that is. I therefore propose to give that cry
the form not of a "position" to be defended and used to tighten the mazes
of the networks but of a metaphor.

Metaphor, as I have argued elsewhere, is a powerful tool for overcoming
the dichotomy between epistemology and ontology.[11] Moreover, a well-
chosen metaphor is semantically enriching, affectively powerful, and can be
so innovative that it offers an antidote against the temptation of recidivism.
This latter aspect is mightily productive. For the metaphor as rallying cry
must avoid the old traps, including the one that divides us up into generations to be left behind. Admitting that I turned away from institutional feminism when someone hissed "you Kantian!" instead of "you bitch!" in my
ear, my passionate commitment to the issues involved in feminism makes me
want to continue trying to think these on a different model. For now, a very
productive metaphor for what feminism has been, could become, and should
pursue, I submit, is the *fold*.

The fold is another of Gilles Deleuze's inventive concepts, through
which he tried to overcome the consequences of old concepts. It is the term
through which he actualized the thought of baroque philosopher Leibniz.[12]
To offer the new millennium a term with such a background may sound
hopelessly nostalgic. Yet I wish to give it a try. Despite Deleuze's current
popularity, the possibilities of the fold as a manner of thinking have not
been taken up by feminism. Rather, Deleuze has inspired ontologists and
epistemologists, although they have remained opposed to each other. His
antisubjectivity has led to a neo-ontology of the subject, an often senti-

mental, romantic plea for nomadic subjectivity that flies in the face of the same pernicious problem as sisterhood, and now seems scandalously exploitative in a world of real migration (Battersby 1998: 195). On the other hand, Deleuze's metaphor of the rhizome, attractive as it is, in a formal, primarily epistemological sense, for replacing structure, remains caught in an ontology of common genetic origin.[13] Hence, this metaphor is not fit to overcome the divide most in need of being bridged.

This Deleuzian metaphor of the fold, less romantically inclined than the nomadic, less biologically fixed than the rhizome, is more simply grounded in a material manner of thinking, yet has no genetic connotations, and is basically anti-originary. I will argue that the "fold" catches the nature of relationship beyond the rift between ontology and epistemology, and, politically speaking, beyond identity, essentialist stability, but also beyond the individualist pluralization that killed identity politics.

The move beyond subjectivity-only is necessary because the exclusive focus on subjectivity has encouraged a navel-gazing sterility that has benefited an ineradicable individualism. The fold's potential to overcome individualism derives from the way, as a figure, it helps us think, not the position of the subject caught in the abyss between victimhood and pleasure, or that of the object as, for example, in some sentimentalizing forms of ecofeminism, but the relationship between the two. This relationship is mutually transformative; it is neither static nor slippery but durative in a dynamic way. And, since the fold remains a rather banal, material figure, it deromanticizes the idea of relationship itself. At the same time, its visual appearance in the form of smooth, tactile, often appealing satin or velvet, while "catching" and hence imprisoning the look whose autonomy it threatens, also lures and seduces. Attracted to its inner secrets, we want to know (epistemically driven) what is in it. But there is nothing, so there is no ontological trap that can captivate us.

Thus, the figure of the fold has the capacity to enable us to suspend, or challenge, the divisions mentioned above. It neither cancels nor ignores the provisional interests that inform such divisions but enables us to probe, utilize, and then overcome, not them but their hold over feminism as a theoretical practice. Last but not least, it helps articulate the relationship between feminism as a movement of women and as a concern for issues, a way of thinking, that men can and must share.

Because of the fold's history as an emblem of baroque philosophy and visual art, I will draw upon works of visual art to make this argument. By doing so, I wish to demonstrate what I am arguing: to propose the fold not only as a model for argumentation, but *as* argument in and of itself. Of all the senses, vision has been the most deceptive one, used and abused for untenable claims about ontology as well as epistemology.[14] It is the sense that requires distance, separateness, and, at the same time, spatial proximity. It resists the direct communication of bodies implied by hearing and touch. It relies only on surface. As the primary sense of seduction, it colludes with both violence and pleasure. In all these respects, it seems, vision is not the most reliable sense at all.

Worse, this sense has been identified with a predominant model of vision—Renaissance perspective, the visual shape later articulated by the Cartesian *cogito*.[15] Yet, precisely because of all these dangers, vision can become the domain in which the feminist virtues of the fold can best be articulated, under the argument that what is gained with maximum difficulty will be easier to expand beyond itself. I will be suggesting such expansion of the reach of this theoretical figure by connecting visual folding to the dimension most alien to it: time. To avoid those simplifications that specifically affect temporality and that discussing such a figurative and material figure as the fold in theory entails, and in keeping with what I wish to argue, I can only put the issue forward through "cases." I will invoke these as allegories.

Beyond Representation

Let me first explain the fold through an allegorical example of a practice of looking, which is also an allegory of where we are now, feminists before our own results. For the most significant rift in feminism exists on a level that is both theoretical and utterly practical. It involves the subject and the object, and resolving it requires a rethinking of both. A rethinking is necessary between, on the one hand, an orientation in feminism toward the subject that probes the conditions of feminine or female subjectivity in or out of specific contexts and, on the other, an orientation—informed and motivated by feminism—toward the object that probes the potential productivity of an outward relation that, as such, is inflected by feminism. As long as the subject-object opposition remains in place, it is overlayered by the opposition between the (different, feminine) subject and the way it perceives the object: ontology and epistemology remain separate. In probing this opposition of orientation I am trying to articulate a way out of the double framing that comes with a focus on representation.

Anyone who has followed up on Spivak's founding article, "Can the Subaltern Speak?" has lost the innocent belief that speaking *about* and speaking *for* others is either possible or avoidable.[16] Representation, hovering as it does on the edge between these two incommensurable yet inextricable meanings, remains a glib and troubled notion. As a result, the point of feminist academic work, and of any political action that is not directly activist, has come under siege. Within the academy, both critical analysis and identity politics have begun to turn against themselves. Meanwhile, speaking *with* others, an old tradition in anthropology, can only be a false dialogue rife with power inequity.[17]

Spivak's indictment of representation's double bind should, of course, not be taken as a reason for giving up on analyzing representations. Instead, a more materially grounded search for at least partial solutions to the dilemma can yield a reconsideration of allegory. My own position toward allegory has always been one of deep suspicion, considering the cultural tendency to invoke this figure to explain away such disturbing representations as, for example, the rape of Lucretia.[18] More recently, and under the influence of deconstructive theory, I have been led to consider allegory not necessarily as escapist but, more literally, as a way of potentially speaking *through* the discourse of others.[19] If taken seriously, the preposition "through," unlike "for," "about," or "with," precludes an unmodified return of the subject to the state before speaking.

How can we mobilize the figure of the fold to make a decisive move here? I will argue that the fold stands for a different relation between subject and object, one that bypasses the problem of representation's ambiguity. It is able to do so thanks to the specific temporality it entails—one that refuses the divide between ontology and epistemology. As I will explain below, the specifically "baroque" point of view that the fold emblematizes engages the subject in a voyage through the field of the object that unhinges the distinction between those two positions.

My first allegory is the following case of a conflict between representation and presentation. In the Musée du Louvre, Caravaggio's *Death of the Virgin* cannot be viewed easily. This large canvas from 1605–6 hangs too high for comfort as well as opposite a window whose light reflects in the glass, preventing the humbled viewer, who cranes her neck to see it, from getting closer, and who then tries distance, all in vain. From a distance, the reflections blind you; close up, your neck hurts, the angle is too wide, the image too flat (figure 1).

But in the process of trying, you can become absorbed in the effort and end up seeing things that an easy glance would not reveal—if it were hung in ideal museal circumstances, invisible circumstances, that is. *Not so fast!* says this infelicitous installation; it requires time. During that time, the relation between the subject and object of looking hurts your body. Although it is obvious that visual images can *evoke* or *represent* time—the past, the future, or two or more moments simultaneously—it is more difficult to see how they can *be* in time without simultaneously unfolding that being in time as film and literature do: in a sequential development, a time axis whose continuity moves forward. The temporal realism that sticks to those media is tenacious, even if different rhythms can bring temporal variation into play, as in fact they routinely do in those media. It is, I contend, those naturalizations of time that make such works fictional, in the specific sense of the suspension of history; *ahistorical*. Conversely, art that foregrounds time, that alerts its viewers to their inhabiting of time, is *historically active*. Thus, it contributes to the current challenges of conceptions of history as safely remote. It enfolds the past within the present.[20]

In my attempt to understand the fold in action—in time—differentiating temporal existence became an urgent part of thinking the relationship between that object—the painting—and myself. The painting in its current installation unwittingly foregrounds four different aspects of time that the figure of the fold entails: *bodily experience, material corruption, virtual sensuality*, and *actualizing attention*.[21] These aspects of time all engage the subject's willingness to enfold within, or with, the object. None of them is compatible with either a spiritualized, idealist, or grossly materialist ontology. Caravaggio's work makes such a good kick-off point because it is hyperillusionistic, yet antirealist to the point of being almost nonfigurative, or hyperfigurative. It refuses to yield to the pressure to spiritualize. But it effectively refrains from telling stories the way classical Renaissance art did. Nor is his work descriptive of an object that can be represented as such. Its narrative dimension derives instead from its appeal to an interaction with the viewer, to its own processing in time rather than to representing time in a represented fabula.[22]

The frustration at trying to see Caravaggio's Louvre painting entails a physical realization of the difficulty of seeing. It inaugurates the oscillation between the object coming from the past and the viewer standing in the

FIGURE 1. Installation of Michelangelo Merisi da Caravaggio, *Death of the Virgin*, ca. 1605–6, oil on canvas. Musée du Louvre, Paris.

present. This image does not "give itself," although it pretends it does. The curtain that separates front from back; the apostles chatting in the wings behind the curtain; the subdued light coming from the back at the left and barely seeming to reach the front, as if underlying a depth that otherwise is not so convincing; a division in planes, each occupied by groups of figures: it all seems constructed to prove that the painter knew the history of his art, had studied Raphael, had mastered the ruses and paradoxes of perspective. Before Descartes, he stands here as a model of post-Cartesian thought.

For, if we take that large curtain literally, it is an embodiment of the baroque fold, an instruction for use that tells you that depth circles back to the surface, the only outcome of a voyage through a picture plane (figure 2). Once reassured that all is fine, as it should be in Italian art after the Renaissance, the viewer arrives at a big black hole, where the vanishing point should be, but isn't. This hole, literally, enfolds what it resists, encapsulating the expectation of linear perspective in its refusal to allow the illusion of objectivism that that mode of representation carries, exposing it as carrier only—as metaphor. Turning to the far left, one hits three faces—a close group, barely readable, excluding you from the conversation, making it forever impossible to find out if they are saints or actors. Rejected by this group, as by conventional realism, and turning back with the light, one arrives, finally, at the main character, so close to the picture plane that she is hard to see. Rather than contributing to the depth, this figure comes forward, into the viewing space that is already so uncomfortable. The nasty reflections of the Louvre window take on a meta-artistic sense. Not so much the face as the neck, whose wrinkles may indicate age for aficionados of realism but also "do" the Leibnizean fold, which dictates a cyclical look without outcome; not so much the face as the oversized hand without strength; not so much that hand as the other hand, resting on the stomach that has borne the child, preposterously dead, before its mother; not so much the virgin as the senseless neck of Mary Magdalene, bent in mourning. It is not quite possible to unify this image, whose elements send you on from one to the other, keeping your look busy.[23]

The body of the virgin, so indecently exposed, yet hard to see, dead, old, and scandalously corporeal, cannot be taken as a whole; it cannot be put safely at a diagonal, at an increasing distance from the viewer. Instead, the very line that inscribes linear perspective takes off in the opposite direction, toward us, not diminishing the size of the telescoped body but making it gradually larger, until it threatens to invade the viewing space. The con-

FIGURE 2. Caravaggio, *Death of the Virgin*.

frontation with the dead body would be easier to sustain if it were sent in the opposite direction, head in front, lower part of the body farther away. But no; if the direction of the light enhances some detached parts of the upper body, the inverse perspective foregrounds the feet, indecently dead, gray feet that emerge to sight at the end of a second, third, tour of the image. Feet that definitely impede a transcendental view of death in a spiritual appropriation of the events through an untenable split between body and mind. Those troubling feet point to the apostle standing in for the viewer, preventing the latter from approaching; preventing, also, any attempt to spiritualize death.

This painting declares the unity of image untenable. It shrinks the depicted space to the point of impeding the master gaze of a viewer kept at bay. The scene is cut off at both sides, and in front, establishing a threatening, absorbing continuity, imposing proximity with the space of the Louvre, of the late twentieth-century viewer. The painting does this, but only in relationship to the twentieth-century viewer in that situation in the Louvre, like a post-Albertian agent that unwittingly contributes to the articulation of a post-Cartesian definition of subjectivity.

What's the point of this arresting of time, as a performance of the legacy of a tradition of high art that was almost exclusively inhabited by male figures and inhabiting an institution that emanates a nationalistic power adverse to everything feminism stands for?[24] By way of the fold, it is possible, indeed, productive, to remain involved, albeit at the edge, in a culture that can neither exclude nor fully accept those it considers its "others." Let me suggest that feminism can only move on by riding precisely that position on the precarious crest of history's waves. Caravaggio in the Louvre, then, is my allegory of being at the margin of that institution, and of desiring, needing, to participate in the culture in place there. It is an allegory of the place many people occupy, whatever their ontological status and relative difference may be. It is also a position that can be transferred—metaphor does that—to a range of other situations.

Other art today similarly addresses questions regarding issues of space, the body, representation, and difference—through its work with time. And some of that art, I contend, proposes ways of seeing that are both baroque and ways of seeing the baroque: enfolding past within present, articulating what makes Caravaggio's paintings exempla of the fold. They are baroque *bodies* in the two senses of the word: ontologically corporeal more than ever before, and bodies of thought. And they involve an epistemology of what that could mean—the presence of the human body. Dead or alive, but present, while accounting for the impossibility of that presence.

From House-Wife to House-Woman

At the end of the nineties, we still stand there: confronted with a masterpiece too high for us, in an institution that will not accommodate us, prevented from having a clear view of the dead flesh of the icon of a hostile but culturally sanctioned femininity. The situation is allegorical and as such—as a discourse through the other—we must make the best of it. Is there a way to reach over time and gender gaps in one move? Through the fold, subjectivity and the object become codependent, folded into one another, and this puts the subject at risk. The object whose surface is grazed by the subject of point of view may require a visual engagement that can only be called microscopic and in relation to which the subject loses his or her mastery over it. In view of this codependency, it makes sense that any appeal to knowledge by either of the two in turn should be based on an awareness of a similar codependency between the sources of our insights into this matter. This already makes the divide between ontology and epistemology untenable.

If it matters that Caravaggio belongs to the ineradicable canon massively gendered male, a status the location of his *Virgin* in the Louvre only underscores, let me now begin at the other end. My second allegory is borrowed from a woman artist working today. French-American sculptor Louise Bourgeois makes a canny use of baroque folds to, so to speak, take art out of the Louvre into lived reality. Her interest in the fold translates into explicit and implicit references to Bernini, a sculptor as emblematically baroque as Caravaggio the painter. Bourgeois repeatedly responds explicitly to Bernini's thinking, through the fold.[25]

Less explicitly, but perhaps more clearly visible, her "theorizing" of the fold comes across in a work from 1983 that belongs to a series of related works, each titled *Femme Maison*. Over a number of years, the artist produced, in many drawings and sculptures, the semitransfiguration of a female figure into a house, which both imprisons and inhabits her body. But the common theme does not reify the meaning of each of these works. Some emphasize the anxiety of women locked up in the existence of the family, others foreground the liberation of a woman standing on the roof of the house. Still others suggest the power this confinement of women also yields. Most of them remain powerfully ambiguous. Many are square, rectangular, angular, in a nearly hostile way. All somehow address the condition of women in the Western family of the 1950s and 1960s. They are arguably feminist works.

By the same token, the figure of the woman whose head is replaced by a house neatly fits the art-historical category of surrealism. Quite literally, these works can be construed as critical responses to Max Ernst's series *La femme cent tête* and, by extension, as critiques of surrealism's sexist practices. Both these interpretations have some merit; neither is decisive or satisfactory. Both imprison the works in a prefabricated template, which reduces them, instead of deploying what they have to say "about" feminism and surrealism, and what have you.

In the most Berninesque work of this series, a hostile skyscraper voluptuously sinks into a royal robe of folds (figure 3).[26] These folds refuse all tendency toward regularity. On one side, toward the bottom, the folds confess to the deception of their illusory infinity as surface, when the base becomes sheer matter. Elsewhere, the folds detach themselves from the interior mass. The sculpture denies the core implied in the idea of depth but also of unification. Here and there, the folds are knotted, turning infinite texture into inextricable confusion and liberation into imprisonment. The cone-shaped body, sagging under its own and the house's weight, remains a body, refuses to go up in flames like Bernini's *Saint Teresa* or be elevated toward transcendence like his *Beata Ludovica*.[27] Firmly fixed on a visible disk-shaped bottom, this body is as heavy as Ludovica's, but it does not believe in miracles.

On top, like a head, stands the angular skyscraper of twentieth-century architecture. It looks forlorn, small, and lonely. The gigantic body of folds, folds of flesh, that surround and incorporate this building, states simultaneously mutual dependency and threat. This sculpture absorbs architecture in a secular, disenchanted, yet merry acceptance of the materiality of body, house, and sculpture between them. A house in which women are locked up but also given mastery, a house that confines and protects but can also be escaped, often fails to protect, weighs the body down. But lest we escape reality by bowing for transcendence and tragedy, the folds, knotted around the building as the body's neck, are also just what they appear to be. Between figuration and conceptualism, Bourgeois winks at us when, from one angle, the surface full of secrets is just a garment lovingly warming the lonely house. The architecture, here, in this exploration of frightful interventions in space, encompasses motherly care, humor, and companionship. In opposi-

FIGURE 3. Louise Bourgeois, *Femme Maison*, 1983. Marble. 25 x 19½ x 23 in.;
63.5 x 49.5 x 58.5 cm. Collection Jean-Louis Bourgeois. Courtesy Cheim & Read,
New York. Photo: Alan Finkelman.

tion to the Vitruvian tradition, this house-woman, while refusing the rigidity of classical symmetry, endorses the caprices of body and matter.[28]

The sculpture not only establishes an enfolded relationship between past and present, but it adopts, probes, and transforms the baroque fold. By playing out the "debate" about representation with Bernini, it also refuses to answer the question of whether it matters that it was made by a woman. In the years after this sculpture was made, feminism was deeply committed to the affirmative action sometimes called "gynocriticism" and dug up women artists whom the process of canonization had passed over. And whereas this seems a not very spectacular position today, like affirmative action in the "real world" Bourgeois's work makes a case for the complexity of that question, which, I contend, cannot so easily be left behind.

Again, then: does it matter that the artist is a woman? It does, which explains why so many revisionist art historians rush to celebrate this exceptional artist-as-woman. If the twentieth-century West is to have a heroine in the visual arts, Bourgeois is a good candidate. She, however, will have nothing to do with that recuperation. To Bourgeois, it doesn't matter if the artist is a woman, and rightly so, for the issue of recognition has fared poorly in the hands of affirmative action that makes a fashionable fetish out of art that deserves better.[29]

On another level, though, it does matter, for arguably, the experience of bodily confinement in the mud of housewifery called motherhood, can only be so acutely yet humorously rendered if one knows the experience from one's own body. It doesn't matter, though, because all those—men or women—who feel isolated, confined, by the very mastery deceptively given to them as a consolation prize, can align with this sculpture, fold themselves into it, seek shelter within its knot.

The point here, though, is that the work *was* made by a woman, just as Caravaggio's *Death* was made by a man; hence, engaging with it from the other gender on the model of the fold requires an embodied engagement with the other gender on *its* terms.

How can we envision such an engagement? For this, let me return to Deleuze. His account of Leibniz focuses less on that baroque philosopher's ideas of logic and fundamental laws than on his views of perception and sensation, identity, and the activity of matter. Deleuze mediates between the two domains, through the concept of point of view, using it as a guideline for engagement with the world, people, and objects. The figure of the fold shapes a kind of point of view unlike the one still in use. Instead, this point of view is derived from Renaissance perspective. But it also shapes a mode of argumentation. Take the following rendering, by Deleuze, of Leibnizian point of view:

> Leibniz's idea about point of view as the secret of things, as focus, cryptography, or even as the determination of the indeterminate by means of ambiguous signs: *what* I am telling to you, *what* you are also thinking about, do you agree to tell *him* about *it*, provided that we know what to expect of *it*, about *her*, and that we also agree about who *he* is and who *she* is?[30]

This complex sentence is easier to read through its rhythmic movement than through its syntax and proposition. In other words, it embodies, or does, what it states, thus itself enfolding epistemology within ontology. Following the paradox of "determination of the indeterminate" and the subsequent colon, its rhythm performs the movement back and forth between subject and object of point of view, emphasizing the mobility that characterizes it. Objects, seen as enfolded within the subject in a shared entanglement, are considered events rather than things—events of becoming rather than being. The sentence itself, then, presents what it also re-presents. Yet it neither speaks "for" nor "about" others. But I, as other to it, can choose to walk with, on, or in it.

The fold as a figure (of thought, of matter) insists on surface and materiality. This materialism of the fold entails the involvement of the subject within the material experience, thus turning surface into skin, in a relation that is *correlativist*. The fold within Caravaggio's painting sets in motion the process or performance of the painting that entangles the viewer across time; a process, moreover, that itself takes time, thus foregrounding the double temporality of the image and the look that takes hold over it. Deleuze's formulation folds into itself both the object—as in other kinds of perspectivism—and the subject: "If the status of the object is profoundly changed, so also is that of the subject. We move from inflection or from variable curvature to vectors of curvature that go in the direction of concavity."[31]

Unlike the individualist appropriation of difference, this baroque point of view is emphatically not a subjectivist relativism. In my opinion, such subjectivism has led to an excess of the "personal voice" in feminist writing. For all the importance this voice has had as a critical intervention, it does not offer a way out of scientistic generalization. It remains caught in individualism. It has first been dismissed, then simply appropriated, absorbed in male-stream discourse.[32]

Deleuze's formulation, here, demonstrates the epistemological weight of folds as the embodiment of a position beyond subjectivism yet far removed from objectivism:

> Such is the basis of perspectivism, which does not mean a dependence in respect to a pregiven or defined subject; to the contrary, a subject will be what comes to the point of view, or rather what remains in the point of view. That is why the transformation of the object refers to a correlative transformation of the subject.[33]

For a feminism that still cannot rest on the results of affirmative action, this may appear to be a tricky position. The subject is not pregiven. No stability can be derived from it. The fold emblematizes the point of view in which the subject must give up its autonomy.

In spite of the dangers of renewed obliteration, endorsing this wavering point of view fully yields new advantages that can help overcome individualist traps without romanticizing sacrifice or idealizing transcendence. Again, a work of art shows a possible direction. In addition to a slowdown due to the emblematic difficulty of seeing, the object/subject of my third allegory will sharpen our awareness of the spatial aspect of the fold: its power to suspend the apparently self-evident divisions between large and small, which encompasses the collectivity (of sisterhood) and the individuality (of difference).

The body that enfolds a house, as in Bourgeois's *Femme Maison*, is also an embodiment of a questioning of that other opposition that has bogged feminism down: that between private and public life, one of many political and ideological counterparts of individualism. If feminism is to deploy the figure of the fold to repair severed links, this one is waiting in the "workshop of possibilities."[34] That this opposition lies rock-hard between a theoretical feminism and an effective practice will become apparent through a third aspect of the fold, and a third allegory. Here, the relationship between women and house takes a radical turn.

Actualizing Attention

Going from a disenchantment with subjectivity to hypostatizing the object may be another trap of representation. The object comes to mirror the painful victimhood that subjectivity has been increasingly denied. Hence, to the extent that such a projection partakes of the binary opposition between subject and object that continues to wreak such havoc, I would agree with Christine Battersby when she claims that "the urgent problem for feminist theory to address is not the problem of the subject, but the problem of the *object*"[35]—if it were not for the binary opposition that such a claim maintains. Instead, it is in the relationship between the two, a relationship defined as enfolding and that all but suspends the very nature of subjectivity as severed from objecthood, that a different feminist position can best be articulated. Again, visual art can suggest ways to do this, but again, this is due to a "theoretization" of the limits of classical ideas of vision in a practice of enfolding. Here, there are no visible folds, only temporal, yet very material, ones.

Colombian artist Doris Salcedo makes the visualization of duration the crucial weapon in her art, which wages war against violence and for its obliteration. Her work demonstrates how we can think a temporality of the fold as an effective figure of thought beyond the oppositions that pester feminist theory. Her sculptures militate against forgetting by making used furniture the site of the presence of the dead. Salcedo attempts to break the wall between private and public by bringing the disappeared victims of violence into the public domain from which their murderous deaths have torn them away. Spatially, she does this by using old kitchen furniture as the ground for her sculptures. Temporally, she gives them, in ways I will try to indicate below, the duration of the fold, specifically, a *lasting actuality*.

Time is most often conceived on the axes of duration, sequentiality, and rhythm. Duration is measured according to outside standards, the vastly different experiences of it notwithstanding (*Einstein's dream*). Sequentiality continues to suffer from the twin diseases of the *post-hoc ergo propter-hoc* fallacy that conflates succession with causation, and the Oedipally inflected *post-hoc ergo contra-hoc ph*allacy that conflates succession with progress and generational antagonism, lived out in the hostile rejection of all that precedes it. Any attempt to understand feminism in terms of generations is inevitably entangled with, at least, the latter. In my personal experience, feminism has suffered great damage because of it, perhaps fatal. So, an attempt to think time differently, on the model of the fold, gets me thoroughly excited. Salcedo's work on time foregrounds, aggrandizes, to the point of hyperbole, a temporality least reckoned with yet most important for a lived feminism beyond all the divides mentioned earlier. This is the temporality of actuality.

Actuality is the most intense moment of presentness, which, by definition, passes unnoticed. In George Kubler's poetic account:

> Actuality is when the lighthouse is dark between flashes: it is the
> instant between the ticks of the watch: it is a void interval slipping for-
> ever through time: the rupture between past and future: the gap at the
> poles of the revolving magnetic field, infinitesimally small but ulti-
> mately real. It is the interchronic pause when nothing is happening. It
> is the void between events.[36]

Actuality, then, is the stretch of the fold where the eye risks itself inside, into
invisibility to itself, not to reach depth but to reemerge with or on the fabric, on the skin of the other. Salcedo promotes that risky voyage while fighting the anonymity of actuality. She fills its void, stretching its space to *make
time* for remembrance of the dead, who died in the past but are violently
dead *in actuality*. Beyond the everyday bombardments of fleeting images, art
seems a suitable place for us to stop and invest these deaths with cultural
duration.

Again, we are facing a problem of representation. Recent re-memorial-
izations of the Holocaust have made it increasingly clear that art cannot in
any simple way represent horror and violence. Representing the Holocaust
in art leads to charges of having made "beauty" out of horror and "fiction"
out of a reality whose realness it is so utterly important to maintain; also,
given the experiential intensity of horror, of representing the unrepresentable. Yet, important as these cautionary discussions are, it is equally
important that the Holocaust, for these very same reasons, not be allowed to
disappear from the cultural scene.[37]

Moralizing prescriptions of what art can or cannot focus on are out of
place—or should I say, out of time—in an era as riddled with violence as
ours. Activist art made and exhibited over the past two decades has made
that clear enough. Salcedo's art, although not as "loud" as most activist art,
cannot exist within the confines set by this prescriptive view, which is in fact
grounded in a resilient formalism. For, without the outside world and its
politics of violence, there is, in her sculptures—which are both big and discrete, ordinary and stunningly powerful—simply *nothing to see*. No image, no
beauty, no forms. No visual folds of smooth velvet. Her work requires living, not seeing, the fold.

If television news, newspaper headlines, and journalistic photographs are to be casual purveyors of the horrors that take place, then the Benjaminian anxiety about the amnesiac effect of visual speed is entirely justified. Yet, it is the same Benjamin who wrote: "Every image of the past that is not recognized by the present as one of its own concerns threatens to disappear irretrievably."[38] Salcedo's art, while sharing the interactive production of duration, enforces such recognition through a strong sense of mood—in this case, a tragic and rebellious one, tender even, and at times, humorous, but one that is always fighting melancholic paralysis. This makes me want to endorse it as an allegory of a surviving feminism (figure 4).

Exposing pieces of used furniture in an art gallery compels the viewer to think about time. For it positions the pieces in the past in which they were used, ensconced in the private sphere, unspectacular. What do we viewers do with these pieces? The sheer fact that they are now in a museum indicates that the private realm of the home has somehow been violated. This violation of the home is represented in Salcedo's early work. According to Charles Merewether, some of her early pieces *look like* wounded surfaces: "Chairs are covered by a fine skin of lace as if seared into the wood, bones are embedded into the side of a cabinet, a spoon forced between the seams of wood of a kitchen bureau."[39]

Thus, these early sculptures represent the violation of the private lives of the victims of violence, by displaying the violence itself on the objects that were taken out of their lives, just as they themselves were dragged out of their homes to be slaughtered. The furniture is stubbornly banal but at the same time slightly anthropomorphized, to enact the violence that depleted its territory, the home. It is as if the small things that evoke woundedness have taken up *mimicry* to adapt to the environment of the outside world in order to be less noticeable.

In contrast to her earlier works, though, the pieces in Salcedo's 1998 *Unland* exhibition (New Museum of Contemporary Art, New York) are committed to a fundamentally different mode of (re-?)presentation, one that understands, proposes, then rejects and offers alternatives to, the predicament of the art/horror connection that so worries contemporary thought, and to the double bind of representation caught between speaking for and speaking about. This work succeeds in overcoming the joint predicaments of speaking for, about, and with those who cannot speak. I use *Unland* to formulate the subject-object relationship in terms of a temporal "enfolding." Looking at Salcedo's earlier work in the light of this later work, we can see that there the violence was in a sense still represented and, therefore,

FIGURE 4. Doris Salcedo, *Unland:The Orphan's Tunic*, 1997. Wood, cloth, and hair. 31½ x 96½ x 38½ in.; 80 x 245 x 98 cm. Courtesy Alexander and Bonin, New York. Photo: David Heald.

inevitably repeating it. The relation between victim and violence was established on the basis of indexical signification—through the deployment of furniture and kitchen utensils as extensions of the victims, evoking them through these synecdoches of their lives—but the violence itself was perpetrated on the objects by means of other objects so that *it*, not the victims, was visually re-presented.

The later work—in the *Unland* exhibition—radically transforms not the theme but the mode of representation. The difference is that this work operates entirely by means of duration. Here, *duration* has become the major tool for turning the direction of the narrative from third-person, out-there, concerning the other, to second-person, here, to touch the viewer in the most concrete bodily way possible. The fold, although not materially represented—no curtains here—is physically enacted, and this, in ways that engage the subject—both maker and viewer—and the object, the violated victim.

Irreversible Witness (1995–98) and *The Orphan's Tunic* (1997), which are both included in this exhibition, are extremely fragile, nearly impossible to make, and nearly impossible to see. The material is still furniture—kitchen tables, a child's cot—but the signifying element is extreme in its finesse, fragility, and durability: human hair, and a bit of silk. It is important that the two materials are combined. Silk is as biological, as animal, as hair. Spun by mean creatures, it is reworked into decoration by humans, most likely women weaving clothes for their children.

The Orphan's Tunic combines the silk and hair to produce a surface that evokes—re-presents, without representation—death in its gray discoloration and endures in its shiny surface. *Irreversible Witness* has sewn a child's metal cot onto a table using an intricate fabric of silk and hair. The sheer number of hairs used, a hole drilled patiently into the thick wood for each hair, while irresistibly operating the existential contiguity of indexical meaning production, bears testimony to the time of the work's making as a homage to the dead, whose bodies remain remembered through their hair only.

This use of hair makes a statement about material and bodily corruption outside of representation. Hair is more durable than any bodily tissue, as durable as bone. But bone's relation to death is too ordinary and predictable. While also being a bodily synecdoche, bone can only represent death symbolically. Hair is what was once lovingly combed, what shone and framed the face now gone. The fragility imposes respect and distance as an extreme form of the "don't touch" taboo that applies in venerable art museums. Salcedo's recent works resonate, by contrast, with the clumsy hanging of Caravaggio's *Virgin*. But the most important performance of these pieces is the way they enfold their viewers by means of the near impossibility of seeing.

This is how, on the edge of visuality, it enfolds the subject and the object. In order to actually see what makes these ordinary tables different from the tables in our own homes, what makes them worth putting in a museum, the viewer needs to come closer, dangerously close, since awareness of the fragility of the objects makes approaching feel like violence. One gets closer and closer, feeling less and less comfortable and more and more voyeuristic, penetrating into the home of this bodily presence. And, even with forewarning, the actual perception of the details—the sewing, the braiding, the weaving of the hair—comes as a shock (figure 5). Actuality comes out of its dreariness, is stretched out like long hairs. Stepping backwards, then approaching again, the shock is just as intense.

Here, there is no longer any representational third-person narrative as it was present in the earlier works. The representation of the violation of lives, of homes, by the kitchen spoon or bones inserted into the wooden furniture is now replaced by the performance of *attention*. And, whereas the slow, myopic attention makes the viewer feel in her own body what intrusion into someone's life is, that keen and ambivalent attention does not repeat the violence; it counters it. Remembering the dead does not redeem them; reflecting on one's intrusion does not take the sting of voyeurism out of looking in. But between repetition and redemption lies the cultural activity of suspending the course of time that makes the passing of repetition too easy, offering it protection under the wings of redemption.

In a mode and mood that points most emphatically to a politics of embodied, enfolded vision, Salcedo's sculptures work on the basis of the *performance of duration*. They slow down to the extreme; make you dizzy from the back-and-forthness between microscopic and macroscopic looking where no eyeglasses or contact lenses will quite do the job. Looking itself becomes tortuous, almost torturous. Like Caravaggesque confinement in a space of shadows and luminosity where body parts are so foreshortened as to enter the viewer's space, making her recoil, these surfaces, whose structure of microscopic detail conjures up such massive violence as to make it impossible for any historical or journalistic account to encompass it, so foreshorten time as to enter the viewer's life-time, breaking its linearity and regularity. The viewer's enfolding in, and Salcedo's speaking through, the other that she has partly become and the encounter from which, through her, the

FIGURE 5. Salcedo, *Unland: The Orphan's Tunic* (detail).

viewer cannot escape, continue, long after the intense experience of time has faded back into everyday life.

De-allegorizing Feminism

But allegorical reasoning must not be deployed as an escapism from the harsh realities this volume is trying to address. Escapism threatens the productive power of allegory. Indeed, my grumpiness with much feminism that has come my way, as stated at the beginning of this article, has not been suspended. Nor do I wish to replace a philosophical or political argument with an enthusiasm for art. Allegory here is used on the model of the fold: as a way to enfold myself within what I perceive as objects that have something of crucial importance to say about a feminism that is defined neither by essentialist exclusivism nor by hyper-differentiating dilution but by an engagement in issues to which it has so decisively sensitized many people.

At first, Caravaggio's painting in situ helped me to articulate why history cannot be "reconstructed" as other than the present. The old masters are not disappearing, nor should they be, because we have uncovered the exclusions their adoration performed, and that discovery must help in preventing a relapse. Even the difficulty caused by the institutional elevation—here, also literalized by the hanging—need not prevent our engagement with the representation by a male artist of a dead woman, whose life as model is the most profoundly misogynistic fantasy imposed on our cultures. The Virgin is dead, but virginity is not. Nor is the Louvre and what it stands for.

Men have always spoken *for* and *about* women—representing them. From that mud, our cultures have been shaped. It has been extremely useful, indispensable, to mark women's ontological difference from the men that did this. In the name of that ontology an epistemological breakthrough has been possible, so that feminism can safely be said to have been one of the most important intellectual movements of the second half of the twentieth century. Against the second fallacy of sequentiality—the one that implies progress—I would not want to forget the provisional importance of even a naive essentialism. It was, after all, when that moment of common womanhood gained momentum that the differences that made it illusory became visible. Instead of casting out what is no longer satisfying, I would rather enfold it, or myself within it.

Bourgeois's marble folds enfold that cultural past, updating it, making it more experientially relevant for women who live today, and for men enfolded in that life. Is that an ontological or epistemological proposition? Just as her house is in the process of becoming enfolded within the body of the woman confined in it, so her ontology—being a woman artist—is only relevant epistemologically, to the extent that we must not stop recuperating women's voices. It would be doing Bourgeois an injustice, and by extension, all women who we thus, finally, take seriously, to posit her work as an *object* that is, ontologically, different.[40] Nor can her subjective ontological female-ness be either ignored or simply brought to bear on her work. It is only in the interstices of history in which women live different lives from men— not because they *are* different but because they are confined in difference— that, momentarily, the sex and gender of an artist matters.

Thanks to the forceful enfolding of object into subject through stretch-ing time, the dead enfolded in our lives by Salcedo can no longer be writ-ten off, passed over, under the banner of a refocusing of feminism toward "female pleasure," even if we can speak neither for nor about them, and even if lament is only a cultural song and dance. Men and women have the same confrontational difficulty in seeing the surface structure of these works, although what they see also depends on who they are. The dead whose vio-lation is actualized are women and men. Does this mean that gender is no longer an issue, that other, more burning problems require our attention?

Allow me to refrain from answering this question, which accepts no either/or. There is a small difference, though, that is neither ontological nor epistemological but enfolded in both. *The Orphan's Tunic* is made of human hair, and the silk from a dress a little girl wore day in and day out when the artist was working in the village where the little girl lived. Her mother had made the dress for her. Then the mother was killed. The dress, the material presence of it in Salcedo's work, remains stubbornly gendered in a multi-plicity of ways. Faced with this work, you can't even question if it matters whether the artist, the little girl, or the viewer is female or male.

In other, earlier writings, I have tried to deploy the metaphor of the navel as an alternative for phallic thought.[41] I still believe it has great analytical potential, and Elisabeth Bronfen's recent deployment makes an excellent case for this. At this point in history, I also feel inclined to try to think of alternatives for the exclusive interest in bodily metaphors and the obsession with the origins in feminist thought. In light of the dangers of clinging to subjectivity as the primary issue and origin as the only way to define it, the navel, for all the advantages this metaphor offers over the more usual ones, might suggest an essentializing not of the female body per se but still of the body, and of the mother's body of which the navel is an ineradicable index.

Where the navel, as Bronfen explains,[42] offers an adequate representation of the subject as knotted, there is something to say for the fold in feminism as an alternative to, or liberation from, the navel. Not one for us to stare at, delighted, embarrassed, self-enclosed, but one that refuses to obliterate the mother, including her sex and gender, yet that does not need the literal and perhaps fixating index to her body to keep her importance alive.

The relationship between these two key metaphors, the navel and the fold, can be envisaged as follows. The navel is a fold, but not every fold is a navel. The navel is inscribed in the body, the fold, hovering between touch and vision, necessitates some distance from it. The navel articulates the way cultural subjects are "knotted,"[43] the fold suggests ways to disentangle that knot. In that sense, the navel describes, the fold promises. Finally, the navel is a concept for a feminist critical analysis of representation, the fold is a concept for articulating a position beyond the inextricable knot of representation.

The silk of Salcedo's little girl's dress, made by her dead mother, replaces bodily essentialism with a reminder of materiality and work. Thus the fold can be a bodily index that reminds us, without sentimentality, of the importance of remembering. A scar of dependency that instills in every one of us the need to acknowledge that being is becoming, that the past is the only future we have.

NOTES

1. Long before this became a political issue, I began feeling increasingly bewildered by the use of "we" (see Marianna Torgovnick, "The Politics of 'We,' " in *Eloquent Obsessions: Writing Cultural Criticism*, ed. Marianna Torgovnick [Durham, N. C.: Duke University Press 1994], pp. 260–78). Not knowing who belongs to the group for which I am speaking, I will resort to the first-person singular as much as possible.

2. "We," here, is not used as a symptom of "the full deceptiveness of the false cultural 'we' " (Torgovnick, "Politics of 'We,' " p. 265), but refers to myself and my feminist friends of the seventies.

3. See Evelyn Fox Keller and Helen Moglen, "Competition and Feminism: A Problem for Academic Women," in *Competition Among Women: A Feminist Analysis*, ed. Helen Longino and Valerie Miner (Old Westbury, N.Y.: Feminist Press, 1987), pp. 21–37.

4. See Gloria T. Hull, Patricia Bell Scott, and Barbara Smith, eds., *All the Women Are White, All the Blacks Are Men, But Some of Us Are Brave* (Old Westbury, N.Y.: Feminist Press, 1983).

5. For a good account of conflicts in feminism, see Marianne Hirsch and Evelyn Fox Keller, eds., *Conflicts in Feminism* (New York: Routledge, 1990).

6. Lorraine Code, *What Can She Know? Feminist Epistemology and the Construction of Knowledge* (Ithaca, N.Y.: Cornell University Press, 1991).

7. Christine Battersby, *The Phenomenal Woman: Feminist Metaphysics and the Pattern of Identity* (Cambridge, England: Polity Press, 1998).

8. Perhaps the most important polemic against epistemology (read: epistemology only) is to be found in Theodor W. Adorno, *Against Epistemology*, trans. Willis Domingo (1956; rpt. Oxford: Blackwell, 1982). A useful collection of papers on feminist epistemology is Linda Alcoff and Elizabeth Potter, eds., *Feminist Epistemologies* (New York: Routledge, 1993). See also Helen E. Longino, *Science as Social Knowledge: Values and Objectivity in Scientific Inquiry* (Princeton: Princeton University Press, 1990) and "To See Feelingly: Reason, Passion, and Dialogue in Feminist Philosophy," in *Feminisms in the Academy*, ed. Domna C. Stanton and Abigail J. Stewart (Ann Arbor: University of Michigan Press, 1995), pp. 19–45; and Evelyn Fox Keller, *Reflections on Gender and Science* (New Haven: Yale University Press, 1984), and *Secrets of Life, Secrets of Death* (New York: Routledge, 1992) for excellent accounts of the inseparability in practice of epistemology and ontology.

9. Jane Gallop, *Thinking Through the Body* (New York: Columbia University Press, 1988).

10. Do I sound grumpy? I have often felt that the interest in female pleasure—whose importance I emphatically underwrite—has been used as a weapon to shut up feminists engaged in antiabuse activism, under the rather banal banner of fashion.

11. Mieke Bal, "Scared to Death," in *The Point of Theory*, ed. Mieke Bal and Inge E. Boer (Amsterdam: Amsterdam University Press; New York: Continuum, 1994), pp. 32–47. For the ontological consequences of metaphors in scientific practice, see, for example, Evelyn Fox Keller, *Refiguring Life: Metaphors of Twentieth-Century Biology* (New York: Columbia University Press, 1995).

12. See Gilles Deleuze, *The Fold: Leibniz and the Baroque*, trans. and foreword by Tom Conley (Minneapolis: University of Minnesota Press, 1993). For an extensive discussion and deployment of the fold, in particular in relation to visual art, see Mieke Bal, *Quoting Caravaggio: Contemporary Art, Preposterous History* (Chicago: University of Chicago Press, 1999).

13. Battersby, *Phenomenal Woman*, pp. 192–95.

14. See Evelyn Fox Keller and Christine R. Grontkowski, "The Mind's Eye," in *Discovering Reality*, ed. Sandra Harding and Merrill B. Hintikka (London: Reidel, 1983), pp. 207–24; see also Mieke Bal, *Double Exposures: The Subject of Cultural Analysis* (New York: Routledge, 1996).

15. Among many examples of the critical analysis of the *cogito*, see Vincent Descombes, "Apropos of the 'Critique of the Subject' and the Critique of this Critique," in *Who Comes After the Subject?*, ed. Eduardo Cadava, Peter Connor, and Jean-Luc Nancy (New York: Routledge, 1991). Erwin Panofsky already attempted to reason perspective as a cultural, not a natural, mode of representation in *Perspective as Symbolic Form*, trans. Christoffer Wood (1927; rpt. New York: Zone Books, 1991). For an excellent discussion of perspective, see Hubert Damisch, *L'Origine de la perspective* (Paris: Flammarion, 1987). (*The Origin of Perspective*, trans. John Goodman [Cambridge: MIT Press, 1994].)

16. Most accessible in Gayatri Chakravorty Spivak, *In Other Worlds: Essays in Cultural Politics* (New York: Methuen, 1987).

17. This has been convincingly argued by anthropologists. See for example, Johannes Fabian, *Power and Performance: Ethnographic Explorations Through Proverbial Wisdom and Theater in Shaba, Zaire* (Madison: University of Wisconsin Press, 1990).

18. See chapter 2 of my book on Rembrandt, *Reading "Rembrandt": Beyond the Word-Image Opposition* (New York: Cambridge University Press, 1991), and chapter 7 of my *Double Exposures*.

19. Classically, Paul de Man, *Allegories of Reading: Figural Language in Rousseau, Nietzsche, Rilke, and Proust* (New Haven: Yale University Press, 1979).

20. For an extensive argument for this view, see my *Quoting Caravaggio*.

21. The distinction among these four temporalities has been argued in detail elsewhere (see Bal, "Pour une interprétation intempestive," in *Où en est l'interprétation de l'oeuvre d'art?* ed. Michel Régis (Paris: Musée du Louvre and l'Ecole des Beaux-Arts, 2000).

22. For an extensive argument and demonstration, see my *Quoting Caravaggio*.

23. Some elements of this description have been borrowed from Pamela Askew's monographic study of the painting, *Caravaggio's "Death of the Virgin"* (Princeton: Princeton University Press, 1990).

24. See Carol Duncan, "Art Museums and the Ritual of Citizenship," in *Exhibiting Cultures: The Poetics and Politics of Museum Display*, ed. Ivan Karp and Steven D. Lavine (Washington: Smithsonian Institution Press, 1991), pp. 88–103, on the Louvre and nationalism, and Christine Battersby, *Gender and Genius: Toward a Feminist Aesthetics* (London: Women's Press, 1989), on the genderedness of the very notion of art.

25. For example, in sculptures such as *Baroque* (c. 1970) and *Homage to Bernini* (1967).

26. *Femme Maison*, marble, 63.5 x 49.5 x 58.5 cm, 1983.

27. On Bernini's Teresa, see Irving Lavin, *Bernini and the Unity of the Visual Arts* (New York: Oxford University Press for Pierpont Morgan Library, 1980); on his Ludovica, see Giovanni Careri, *Bernini: Flights of Love, the Art of Devotion*, trans. Linda Lappin (Chicago: University of Chicago Press, 1995).

28. This "fluid" or "viscous" view of architecture has been presented effectively

by Greg Lynn in "Body Matters," *Journal of Philosophy and the Visual Arts*, Special Issue: *The Body*, ed. Andrew Benjamin [no volume or issue number] (1993): 60–69, who took his inspiration from Luce Irigaray, *Speculum of the Other Woman* (1974), trans. Gillian C. Gill (Ithaca, N.Y.: Cornell University Press, 1985) and *This Sex Which Is Not One* (1977), trans. Catherine Porter and Carolyn Burke (Ithaca, N.Y.: Cornell University Press, 1985) (esp., "Volume Without Contours" and "The Mechanics of Fluids").

29. A particularly painful case is the current celebration of Charlotte Salomon, an unjustly neglected artist who is now "benefiting" from her status as a female artist who suffered trauma—an emblem in the "trauma industry." This is not to argue against the serious study of trauma or of Salomon (e.g., Ernst van Alphen, *Caught by History: Holocaust Effects in Contemporary Art, Literature, and Theory* [Stanford: Stanford University Press, 1997]), but against superficial and exploitative trendiness in academic topics, including in feminism.

30. Deleuze, *The Fold*, p. 22.

31. Ibid., p. 19.

32. Just recently, a book appeared with the enticing title *Philosophy in the Flesh: The Embodied Mind and Its Challenge to Western Thought*, which might be expected to take up Gallop's title *Thinking Through the Body* fifteen years later. Alas, it turns out to reiterate the universalist claims attached by "cognitive linguists" to male-inflected metaphors from capitalist America. Just try getting away with making such a claim for the metaphor "life is a box of chocolates" (George Lakoff and Mark Johnson, *Philosophy in the Flesh: The Embodied Mind and Its Challenge to Western Thought* [New York: Basic Books, 1999])!

33. Deleuze, *The Fold*, pp. 19–20.

34. Søren Kierkegaard, *Stages on Life's Way* (1845), ed. and trans. Howard V. Hong and Edna H. Hong, in *Kierkegaard's Writings* (Princeton: Princeton University Press, 1988), 11:76, cited by Battersby, *Phenomenal Woman*, p. 162.

35. Battersby, *Phenomenal Woman*, p. 127.

36. George Kubler, *The Shape of Time: Remarks on the History of Things* (New Haven: Yale University Press, 1962), p. 17.

37. See Van Alphen, *Caught by History*, for an extensive and clear discussion of issues pertaining to Holocaust representation.

38. Walter Benjamin, "Theses on the Philosophy of History," Thesis V, in *Illuminations*, ed. Hannah Arendt, trans. Harry Zohn (New York: Schocken Books, 1968), p. 255.

39. Charles Merewether, "To Bear Witness," in *Doris Salcedo*, ed. Charles Merewether (New York: New Museum of Contemporary Art, 1998), pp. 20–21.

40. In this respect, I completely agree with Rosalind Krauss when she writes: "art made by women needs no special pleading, and in the essays that follow I will offer none" (*Bachelors* [Cambridge: MIT Press, 1999], p. 50).

41. See my *Reading "Rembrandt."* The metaphor had been elaborated in close interaction with Elisabeth Bronfen, who also used it (*Over Her Dead Body: Death, Femininity, and the Aesthetic* [Manchester: Manchester University Press, 1992]) and offered an extensive theorization through it (*The Knotted Subject: Hysteria and Its Discontents* [Princeton: Princeton University Press, 1998]).

42. Bronfen, *Knotted Subject*, pp. 1–98.

43. See Bronfen, *Knotted Subject*.

Chapter 13

Success and Its Failures

BIDDY MARTIN

If Women's Studies has reached a point of stasis on some campuses, it is due in no small measure to its success. Women's Studies has succeeded in defining and delimiting objects of knowledge, authorizing new critical practices, significantly affecting scholarship in a number of disciplines, defining important political issues, and establishing itself as a legitimate academic and administrative unit on hundreds of college and university campuses. With these kinds of successes come problems. Having delimited a proper object and carved out particular domains, having generated and disseminated specific analytic practices, having developed consensus about at least some key political problems, and having been institutionalized on equal footing with other academic and administrative units, Women's Studies has lost much of its critical and intellectual vigor.[1] Women's Studies has now settled in. It has

This essay first appeared in *differences* 9, no. 3 (Fall 1997): 102–31.

and is a location, and the business it conducts could not be more usual. Many of the terms of political analysis and debate, some key critical procedures, and our modes of interacting with one another across disciplines have become so entrenched as to be stultifying; however conventionalized they have become, they are often protected from challenge and change by the piety with which they are repeatedly invoked and the familiarity they have come to enjoy.

In an intellectual and educational environment, endless repetitions of the already known eventually begin to fall on deaf ears. Many feminist scholars find their departmental homes more capacious and invigorating than Women's Studies. Of course, in some of those departments, Women's Studies scholarship deserves credit for having reanimated the discipline. In some domains, the conceptual tools developed in interdisciplinary feminist exchange have been refined by subjection to larger disciplinary debates and methodological rigor. However, many of the "refinements" could now stand to be challenged from outside the comfort of disciplinary homes. Unfortunately, Women's Studies is in no position to lead such a challenge because Women's Studies itself has succumbed to the insularity and then to the wars of the disciplines. To be exciting again, Women's Studies would have to assume leadership in making significant transformations of university curricula and interdisciplinary scholarship and learning.

Women's Studies has been plagued from the outset by the exclusions its self-definition entails. We have become habituated to a language that associates such exclusions with the sexual, racial, ethnic, and, to a lesser extent, class differences which are obfuscated by uncritical invocations of an internally consistent category of "woman." We have at our disposal enormously sophisticated theoretical and critical analyses of the exclusionary work that identity categories do.[2] Still, what we enact in our intellectual and institutional interactions with one another admits of little nuance. Righteousness accrues to positions with apparent claims to marginality, while the privilege of unknowing continues to protect those who choose single-mindedly to pursue only their own career successes. Still others use guilt to absolve themselves of the responsibility to engage one another or themselves in ways that would change hopelessly rigid suppositions and rhetorical habits.

Crisscrossing and exacerbating the often routinized ways of representing race, class, sex, and transnationalism are forms of difference that have received very little discussion. These are differences in institutional and professional status, for example, that are inevitable once significant numbers of women gain a foothold in their universities and their disciplines, and once feminist scholarship has professional cache. In the days when "love of women" and Women's Studies resonated with one another, we seemed capable of eroticizing individual women's strengths, authority, even power, and of enjoying seduction without abandoning claims to justice. (Some people still can.) In these sparer days, when institutional transferences and their accompanying eroticisms have given way to a much more insistent vigilance about abuse (or to equally or even more problematic claims to have transgressed feminist puritanisms), a more exclusively negative competitiveness reigns. I realize, of course, that these "days of old" are mythical, but they help highlight the bind for feminist intellectuals in an environment that requires, or perhaps it would be more honest to say allows, us finally to distinguish ourselves, but only if distinctions do not introduce differences that we find difficult to square with our political biases against institutional authority and its assessments of merit. The mixed messages we get and pass on to each other about distinctions in merit, status, visibility, and influence need to be fully acknowledged and then abandoned in favor of serious discussions about how to introduce into the institution greater differentiation in views of and rewards for different strengths and functions. As long as the current system of rewards and privileges dominates, certain talents and commitments will continue to be undervalued and the present system of values will continue to have gendered implications. We tell ourselves that resentment and relentless competitiveness can be blamed on the scarcity and unfair distribution of rewards and recognition, and this defense can never fail since it always contains truth. But there are also other sources of negativity such as the mistrust we seem at times to think we owe ourselves as oppositional intellectuals of the possibility of even minimally legitimate forms of authority and distinction, a cynical mistrust that can excuse us from acknowledging how, as educators, we inevitably exercise both. Oppositional stances can sometimes become rigid defenses against political participation.

I want to focus on how and why knowledge and learning need to be more significantly reorganized, not only in Women's Studies, but in the university as a whole. As I suggested above, Women's Studies' scholarship and curricula have come over time to replicate rather than challenge entrenched wars between the disciplines with the consequence that neither Women's Studies programs nor feminist scholarship are in a particularly good position to take the lead in completing transformations they helped begin. Because assumptions about what it means to "study women" have constrained fem-

inist scholarship across a range of disciplines, many feminists and queer theorists have long advocated a shift from the identity politics that inhere in
Women's Studies to the apparently more expansive terms of Gender and
Sexuality Studies. I have supported that shift, but for some time I have also
been teaching, speaking, and writing about the excesses of "social constructionism" and the repetitive and predictable analyses of gender that constructionist languages have inspired.[3] Here I want to suggest that Gender
Studies does not necessarily hold out the promise it has been assigned. Gender, too, may have outlived its usefulness, requiring of us more substantive
forms of reflection and change if interdisciplinary feminist studies are to
contribute again to the changes that are occurring and need to occur in our
modes of thinking and writing in higher education. Every field in which
feminist analysis has had a significant impact has a similar story. Putting
"women" at the center of inquiry initially opened canonical works to questions about their often troubling images and, later, added writing by women
to curricula and to the canon. The centering of woman and of feminist concerns also exposed the "sexist" premises at the heart of a range of traditional
and oppositional approaches, putting their adequacy into question and generating exciting revisions and transformations of Marxist, neo-Marxist and
liberal theories of (in my field of German Studies) socio-economic and cultural relations. Formalist, structuralist, and Marxist approaches to literary
texts were appropriated, negated, and reformulated. The influences of
"French feminist" theory introduced new terms and practices from deconstruction and psychoanalysis and expanded the scope of inquiry to phallocentric and repressed workings of "the feminine." But the exclusive focus on
"women" and "the feminine" also constrained feminist work. Significant
developments in the field with no immediately apparent relationship to
"women" or gender received little attention from feminist scholars with the
result that both feminist criticism and larger theoretical debates have been
impoverished by ignorance of one another.

At the same time, the shift from the study of women to analyses of gender and sexuality has opened up new fields of interest and made feminist
work central to the emerging field of cultural studies. But the alliance of
gender studies with cultural studies has also had leveling effects. Cultural
studies' projects on gender and sexuality have produced innovative synthe-
ses of different disciplinary methods and objects, but are organized by a split
that has come to seem one of the most symptomatic and disabling—the split
between theories of culture and its construction of gender on the one hand,

and developments in the biological sciences on the other. Some cultural studies work on gender defines its critical agenda precisely by way of the exclusion of science, even of the social sciences, and of biology, in particular. As a result gender studies is caught between traditional ways of organizing knowledge (humanities and social science versus the so-called hard sciences) and more innovative modes of interdisciplinary inquiry that cross these lines.

My concern about the radical critique of science in the humanities and some social sciences has intensified over the past three years for several reasons. First, collaborative work with a child psychologist on theories of clinical intervention and play has forced me to question a tendency in the humanities to adopt what we take to be properly Freudian, Lacanian, and to a lesser extent, Kleinian theory and then to produce dogma, dismissing out of hand revisionist psychoanalytic or alternative psychological approaches to psychic life, psycho-pathology, and clinical intervention—not necessarily or even primarily on the basis of our knowledge of those alternatives, and certainly not on the basis of clinical or research experience in psychology, but simply because we *know* there is nothing adequate to the task of explaining psychic life except specific psychoanalytic theories and their anti-essentialist forms. (For their part, social scientists dismiss not only psychoanalysis but increasingly all interpretive approaches to emotion, cognition, and behavior with horribly leveling consequences.) A second reason for my concern comes from contact with a neurobiologist with whom I shared administrative duties in the College of Arts and Sciences, and whose interests overlapped significantly with my own. I also spent most of my administrative time chairing a task force charged with a structural review of the Division of Biological Sciences at Cornell, and, hence, speaking with biologists about their work and the future of the biological sciences in general.

From neurobiologists I have learned that cognitive and neuroscientists work with model systems in their efforts to map neural networks, not with what they take to be one-to-one relations between observation and underlying facts about causation. Few of them harbor the illusion that the neural connections they can now activate or see authorize simple causal explanations. Even the most reductionist biologists, with their faith in the possibility that human cognition and emotion can be localized once and for all, acknowledge that they are a long way from being able to explain human emotions, cognition, or behavior with recourse to specific, putatively determinative parts of the brain or even with recourse to the pathways and networks they are increasingly able to map. A less reductionist interpretation would hold that the whole is always greater than the sum of its parts and that what emerges and manifests human consciousness, affect, and behavior will never finally be located, but will instead prove to be over-determined and explicable only in the relative terms of "differentness" methods, i.e. assessments about the differently weighted intensities of activation across or within networks.[4]

In the humanities, we have defended against the dominance of the sciences in the university and outside it by nominating ourselves critics of empiricism and anti-essentialist watchdogs. Radical challenges to objectivity, empiricism, and essentialism have had important consequences, but we have also permitted them to absolve us of the responsibility to recognize scientists' own anti-foundationalisms or to acquaint ourselves with what is going on in science at all. The resistance among many feminist scholars to the notion that "biology" might play any role at all in the construction of subjectivity is indicative of a defensive rather than a genuinely curious and interrogative procedure. The social sciences seem split between the harder social sciences with their claims to be a science and hence, outside the overly narrow parameters of (humanities) feminist inquiry, and the soft, interpretive social sciences which risk falling into the underfunded humanities. The only way to sustain the vital tensions among the not knowable, the inferential and the empirically verifiable is to lower or make permeable the defensive boundaries, to cease and desist from the "wars of the faculties," to interrogate the interpretive for its explanatory adequacy and to study the scientific for its embeddedness in the inferential, the interpretive. To reiterate the most important points, in order to reorganize education and scholarly exchange around problems so that we bring our different areas of expertise to bear on one another's assumptions, we have to become curious again, curious about what different disciplinary formations and knowledge can contribute to problems or questions that we share. Whether Women's Studies, as it is currently organized, can generate productive forms of curiosity and reorganization remains an open question. I will venture an answer at the end of this essay.

In the humanities, we research, write, and teach in an environment in which technology and information threaten, so we are told, to make literature and the book obsolete, in which resources for education continue to diminish, in which the imperative to prepare students for a rapidly changing job market makes the humanities an expensive and unduly time-consuming luxury in the eyes of many and, in the eyes of the far right, a decadent lux-ury represented by the "ne'er do wells" and advocates of cultural devolution. In such an environment, we cannot afford to be smug, complacent, or defensive. What options do we have? Let us consider two different recent approaches to changes in the educational environments in which we work.

In *The University in Ruins*, Bill Readings provides an historical and political analysis of the crisis in university education and our responses to it.[5] According to Readings, we live and teach in a posthistorical, transnational era in which the traditional mission of the university has declined, even disappeared. The transmission of culture and the production of national citizens who share a general education has given way to "the pressures of the cash nexus." The university has changed from being "an ideological arm of the state" to "an autonomous, bureaucratic corporation whose internal regulation is entirely self-interested without regard to wider ideological imperatives" (p. 40).

Readings emphasizes the pressures on universities to integrate fully into bureaucratic, administrative, information-based systems which demand efficiency in the transmission of information from one level of administration to another, and also from teacher to student. Transparency is enjoined everywhere in the system and between systems, and decisions about inclusion and exclusion are made on the basis of the relative opacity/transparency of one system to another. Organizational and intellectual complexity are abandoned, not for ideological reasons but because of the need for simple sequential processing. When it costs more for the [computer] system to create or accommodate non-transparencies or opacities, for example, decisions are negotiated at least in part around questions of cost. Evidence for Readings' point is provided everyday in university planning and program reviews where the infatuation with the measurable and with instruments for measurement have reached all-time highs. Perhaps the most pointed example of Readings' view is the emergence and growing popularity of distance learning and "Drive-Thru universities" as substitute for on-campus, classroom learning. At a recent presentation about the benefits of distance learning, I noted with some alarm that the decreased need for faculty and for classrooms was being sold to universities as one of the major advantages even for traditional liberal arts and research campuses. Rather than merely lamenting or worrying about such developments, humanities faculty need to think seriously about the technological and economic forces that drive them and respond with something other than refusal, dismissal, or invocations of tradition.

Readings argues that we live in a "de-referentialized" university, one in which the discourse of excellence has replaced the discourse of culture and familiar ideological battles are replaced with struggles for administrative rationalization. "Excellence" is an empty term and for that very reason marks the moment when "nation-state is no longer the major site at which capital reproduces itself. What we teach or write now "matters less than having it taught excellently." "Excellence," writes Readings, "serves as a unit of currency within a closed field, and allows for the maximum of internal administration" (p. 13). The discourse of excellence, he concludes, "draws only one boundary: the boundary that protects the unrestricted power of the bureaucracy" (p. 27). The university, in other words, is saturated with an antihumanism far more radical than any theory produced in the Humanities. I could not help but think of Bill Reading's argument while I watched an interview on cable NBC with Mike Wallace prior to the airing of his "Sixty Minutes" report on queer studies in the university. Wallace was asked how he responded to his "adventure" into the world of queer studies. His first line of defense against the interviewer's obvious skepticism and critical amusement was to say: "You know, there are really first-rate, excellent people involved in this." Alumni calls to universities on the Monday morning after the show demonstrated that ideological battles or culture wars are not entirely over, but the discourse of excellence, about which comedian Mike Meyers has produced the "most excellent" commentary, does have significant purchase and may even provide new opportunities for resistance, given its capacity to evacuate substance.

Readings maintains that the differentialized university produces more and more internal administration without reflecting on substantive questions of value. Program reviews, strategic planning, academic leadership workshops, "Quality Improvement" do seem designed to bring deans and faculty into our proper roles as assessors, measurers, regulators and promoters of efficiency, transparency, and excellence. The fact that all this activity creates enormous inefficiency seems to have escaped Readings' and many university administrators' notice. According to Readings, "all the system requires is for activity to take place" because activity produces the appearance of accountability in the form of accounting (p. 39). Activity generates visibilities, the visibility of excellence which attracts student tuition and outside funding, despite or because of the difficulty ascertaining the bases for assessments of merit. In such a universe, there is always the threat that everything substantive will be dissolved in the "acid bath of specularity."[6] Readings insists, however, that there is also opportunity in this universe.

What are our options, then, if we do not wish more frantically to do what can be measured more excellently, or do more excellently what can be measured? Readings argues that we have three possibilities: we can return to national culture; we can reinvent cultural identity in changing circumstances; and/or, we can abandon the notion of redemptive education altogether, and challenge the idea that the social mission for the university is linked to realizing a national, or cultural identity, even a resistant or oppositional one (p. 90). To choose the third option would mean dedicating ourselves instead to the incompleteness of Thought and the interminability of pedagogy, opposing them to the imperative to produce an excellence that can be measured, easily administered, made transparent to consumers, and learned/acquired once and for all.

The return to national culture is not off the table, certainly not in Congress or even in the NEH, but for our purposes it seems more important to dwell on the second of Readings' three possible strategies, "The Reinvention of Cultural Identity For Changing Circumstances," because this is the project to which Women's Studies and feminist cultural studies have at least tacitly committed themselves. In Readings' view, this strategy is doomed to failure. Women's Studies, even Queer Studies, can succeed in establishing themselves in the university; they can even become significant trends because ideology has given way to administrative transparency, integrated (market) systems and claims to "excellence." In an environment where a unified culture no longer matters, cultural studies and multiculturalism can become all the rage, but for Readings the claims to marginality and the appeals addressed to the center demonstrate a clear failure to see that there is no center, or, at most, an empty one. "Representation is no longer the battleground," Readings writes, and "if the ideological has become visible, it is because the high-stakes game has moved on to another table" (p. 104). This is an important, if controversial argument. "In general," he writes, "the effect of multiculturalism is necessarily to homogenize differences as equivalently deviant from a norm" (p. 113).

The ideological has become visible, the marginal has achieved a measure of representational significance, and cultural politics appear salient at the very moment when the center of culture has been evacuated. We enter the fray, demanding representation when there is no Other to whom we might represent ourselves and no center to disrupt. Without adjudication or even prohibition at the hands of the traditional bearers and protectors of culture, our cries for a hearing will neither be suppressed nor heard since there is no place from which we could continue to be excluded. This is not to say that wrongs have been righted or problems solved, only that our approaches to wrongs and to problems may require new strategies.

The evacuation of a center has generated a great deal of confusion in Women's Studies at Cornell where much recent activity has been concentrated in "Gender and Global Change" and in "Lesbian, Bisexual, Gay and Transgender Studies." Some faculty members have wondered out loud where Women's Studies stands or where it is in relation to what were once sub-groups or offshoots of the Program and now seem to have moved into the center. How should we interpret these questions? It is possible that there are no "women" left, no unmarked or "normal" women to occupy the center of our programs or our analyses. This could be seen as a conceptual and political triumph, but many would argue that a number of significant problems that affect women as women have dropped out of serious deliberation and debate. It may also be the case that the most helpful analyses of women's situation and of gender as a construct are being generated within these only apparently specialized fields within Women's Studies. Or we could imagine, with Readings, that the demands of the competitive market system (of ideas) requires constant movements of specialization and unceasing presentations of "the new" with the result that domains located on the "cutting edge" merely obscure critical questions or issues that remain at the heart of things because they have gone out of intellectual fashion. All these interpretations have some merit and I would add that entrenched analytic procedures characteristic of specific domains within Women's Studies and disciplinary stand-offs contribute significantly to the fragmentation of enclaves. Only where scholarship and teaching are problem-based and genuinely curious can fragmentation along disciplinary or theoretical lines be challenged. For now I fear that center-periphery arguments are bound to continue inside Women's Studies programs and assaults from the outside on transnational and sexuality studies will exacerbate, but not necessarily clarify the tensions.

Political theorist Wendy Brown argues that the failure to understand how power works inevitably leads to ever more hyperbolic claims to injury on all sides and fewer efforts to negotiate social and political relations.[7] And she has extended the force of her analysis to the specific question of Women's Studies in the special volume of *differences* devoted to the fate of Women's Studies.[8] Our ideological struggles with and against one another, particularly in the context of identity politics and representation, can at times seem remarkably parochial given what appear to be larger forces at work in the university and in education as a whole.

Readings reserves a particularly strong set of criticisms for cultural studies work that appears less obviously politicized and more "scientific." About the more academic forms of cultural studies, Readings asks us to notice:

1. "how little it needs to determine its object" (p. 99), since it defines culture as signifying practice, and explains nothing in terms of anything *in particular* (p. 97)
2. how little it *can* determine an object or mission since it has "committed to the generalized notion of signifying practice, to the argument that everything is culture [and] can only oppose *exclusions* from culture—which is to say, specifications of culture" (p. 102)
3. how it has academicized culture, "taking culture as the object of the university's desire for knowledge, rather than the object the university produces" (p. 99)
4. how it has misdiagnosed the situation, "focusing on exclusions from culture for understanding our abiding sense of non-participation *despite the fact that we are no longer excluded*" (p. 103).

I have reproduced this critique because, I too, lament the relentless "becoming science" not only of the social sciences, but also of the humanities and the abandonment of any commitment to sophisticated thinking about the gap between first and third-person knowledge. It seems important to link Readings' emphasis on the institutional will to transparency with what he calls the "academicizing" of culture in our calls for interdisciplinarity. For Readings, pressures to be interdisciplinary may serve only to turn more and more material into culture and to render it non-resistant to the leveling effects of a non-referential excellence. In what spaces in the university or in its accounting logic is there room for complexity, depth, pleasure, or for the intensities that cannot be made transparent, not even as transparent as desire can be made? Do feminist studies keep them alive?

Martha Nussbaum's recent effort to make Women's Studies central to a new redemptive mission and a reinvented cultural identity does not answer these questions, but it does allow us to explore another approach to changes in the university. Nussbaum's project, *Cultivating Humanity*, defends curricular reform against right-wing attacks by reorienting liberal education toward the preparation of transnational citizens.[9] Nussbaum's study casts itself as a response to the right-wing's assaults on university curricula and research and she defends curricular reform in terms that challenge conservatives' claims.

Nussbaum makes a strong case for what she calls Socratic education, by which she means reasoned debate, systematic questioning and self-questioning, and forms of achieved objectivity which "transcend the play of forces" (p. 38). She is concerned to distinguish between a general preparation for citizenship and a specialized preparation for a career (p. 294) and she makes a strong case for preparing students to deliberate and negotiate with curiosity, respect, knowledge, and reason. Her principles for Socratic education are designed to encourage critical thought without moral relativism and without intellectual elitism. She favors a curriculum that is problem-oriented rather than department or discipline-based, and she emphasizes the positive potential in new curricular areas that have generated the most criticism on the far right—African-American Studies, Women's Studies, Sexuality Studies, and Transnational Studies (to which she refers, symptomatically and problematically, as the study of "non-Western cultures").

Nussbaum could be said to agree with Readings' skepticism about equal representation, given her disdain for identity politics and for the institutionalization of academic projects organized around identity or reparation. In the rigorous and thoughtful study of difference, however, she sees signs of progress in the struggle against prejudice and bias and she distinguishes between reasonable and unreasonable constructions of difference in each of the new curricular areas. For Nussbaum, each of the reform projects in American universities has not only produced new knowledge at the level of content, but refinements of the techniques of reason themselves. Women's Studies' emphasis on relational as opposed to absolute knowledge receives a great deal of attention. And Nussbaum spends somewhat more time distinguishing between viable and non-viable approaches in the fields of critical race studies and the study of sexuality than she does on their potential for redefining what critical and rigorous thought might mean. In all three cases, however, she stresses that new information or knowledge is crucial, but that rigorous, critical thinking is even more essential if the university is to fulfill its purpose to help young people learn "how to situate their own tradition within a highly plural and interdependent world" (p. 299).

Nussbaum's version of a curriculum that will cultivate humanity for a transnational world includes the integrated study of gender, sexuality, race and racism, and the study of non-Western cultures. She insists that these projects be moved into the core of undergraduate studies and demands that we provide students not only with new in-depth knowledge but also with certain principles of critical reason and debate to ensure that the teaching of difference is ethical and transferable from one learning experience to another. Nussbaum enjoins us to provide students with a more integrated education, rather than asking them to swallow whole the fragments that constitute our separate areas of research specialization. These, it seems to me, are all injunctions worthy of our attention.

Nussbaum's support for making the study of non-Western cultures part of the core of an integrated, undergraduate curriculum and her insistence on modes of thinking about differences rather than on modes of appropriation provides an important intervention into the culture wars over curriculum. But she draws predictably rigid boundaries between reason and its others. Her axioms for the study of difference do not unsettle the assumption that Western culture can serve as ground and referent for reason, even if, as she argues, reason is not an exclusively Western possession. "Our tradition" remains homogeneous enough for her to represent it as "ours," and to imagine that heterogeneities have been introduced by virtue of specific and recent historical developments rather than having operated all along. She reserves her greatest contempt and criticism for those on any point of the political spectrum who claim or imply that logic and reason are specifically Western, phallogocentric or colonial attributes. About the claim that particular forms of reason are white, male, and Western, Nussbaum counters that "such criticisms [of logic] typically show ignorance of the logical traditions of non-Western cultures and a condescending attitude to the logical abilities of women and racial minorities" (p. 38). While Nussbaum's warning against excessively rigid oppositions between phallogocentric and feminine, or Western and Africanist modes of thinking have merit, she assumes too much authority for reason, for the possibility that with reason we can determine where the line between reason and unreason lies and too much self-evidence for the boundaries she draws tacitly and pointedly between Western and non-Western. Nussbaum rules trenchant critiques of logic out of bounds by accusing them all of being unreasonable. In the context of Women's Studies, Nussbaum credits feminist scholarship with having helped transform conceptions of reason through critical examination of received notions of autonomy. However, those feminist critiques of reason that make its rehabilitation more difficult (the work, for example, of a Luce Irigaray on the relentlessly phallic construction of logic) do not make it into Nussbaum's discussion except as negative example.

It is indicative of her implicit definition of reason that Nussbaum makes no mention of queer theory in her chapter on the study of sexuality. Nussbaum defends the centrality of sexuality to core undergraduate curricula by arguing that:

> Human sexuality is an important topic of scholarly inquiry, as it is an important aspect of life; indeed, this is one of the most lively research areas in the current academy, in part because it is so unusual to find a central area that has not been thoroughly studied.   (p. 223)

As she has in every other case, Nussbaum contends here as well that "any program in the study of sexuality is a failure if it remains isolated from the rest of the campus," or "when sexuality studies are dominated by literary theory" (p. 248), or are "initiated more or less entirely from within the Humanities" (p. 254). Nussbaum focuses a significant portion of her program for the study of sexuality on history but also generates tools for the analysis of our culture's prejudices. What her definitions of value and reason exclude are the more radically critical dimensions of critical race, sexuality, and postcolonial studies, not to mention the insights of psychoanalysis about unconscious motivations or desires. While emphasizing the compatibility of social constructionism and "normative moral evaluation" (p. 230), she stresses the dangers of postmodern critiques of normalization and fails, in my view, to do justice to the difficult relations between normalization and normativity. Not even sexuality interrupts Nussbaum's anxiety-free guidelines for enlightened transnational citizenry.

Nussbaum offers a normative definition of a cultivated transnational citizen, one free from hatred, prejudice, and irrationality, capable of empathic identification and reasoned debate. Given the nature of her project, its implicit and actual audience, and its visibility in public debate, Nussbaum's definitions can be considered expansive within certain obvious limits. Her call for empathy and reason suppresses the more stubborn and less pleasant aspects of our humanity. And she assumes, at least for the sake of argument, that the project of cultivating humanity will synchronize with the availability of time and resources and with the capabilities and desires of the human beings she wishes to cultivate. Her conception of an integrated education elevates philosophy to the master of all others, prohibiting thought that occurs outside the parameters of the good and the intelligible. Her proposals are important, but depressingly tame and premised upon surprisingly traditional boundaries between disciplines, replicating the terms that have become familiar from recent "wars of the faculties" in just the ways Readings had predicted the elevation of "reason" as the new referent would. In Nussbaum's proposal, literary study is reduced to the status of handmaiden to a philosophical/historical study of the universal and the good, useful for expanding students' narrative imagination and their capacity for empathy. Such a reduction displays the problems with universal claims to reason or logic that assume and reproduce self-interested forms of rank ordering. Literary theory, and its poststructuralist variants, are cast as the devil because of their assaults on truth, their putative lack of rigor, and what Nussbaum sees as their purposeful unintelligibility.[10]

Nussbaum gives little ground on the availability of truth, refuting "the idea that we can have access to the way things are in the universe entirely independently of the workings of our minds." Citing advances in the philosophy of quantum mechanics and the philosophy of language, she argues:

> Some philosophers hold, with Kant, that we can still defend a single conceptual scheme as the most adequate to reality; some hold that there is a small plurality of adequate schemes governed by stringent criteria of rightness; some adopt a still more elastic pluralism. All with the exception of Rorty still think we can establish claims as true by arguments that rightly claim objectivity and freedom from bias. (p. 39)

For Nussbaum, challenges to realism and empiricism can be contained and cast as "new articulations of the goals of objectivity and truth" (p. 40). Her language functions to make her the arbiter here of "rightful claims" to objectivity and entertains no apparent worries about her own objectivity. But she forecloses possibilities for reinvigorating interdisciplinary inquiry by closing the gap between what we consider reasonable and what we fear as unreason and she suppresses much of what is valuable and specific about literary study—its aesthetic, analytic, and political attentiveness to language and rhetoric, to the performative dimensions of their use, and their capacity to open up unforeseen possibilities. In her introduction to *The Feminist Difference*, Barbara Johnson argues that "literature is important for feminism because literature can best be understood as the place where impasses can be kept and opened for examination, where questions can be guarded and not forced into a premature validation of the available paradigms."[11]

Over against Nussbaum's plea for education in national or transnational values, or even in the reasonable negotiation of those values, Readings suggests that we think in terms of "the University as a space for a structurally incomplete practice of thought" (p. 19), and that we think community without recourse to notions of unity, consensus, or communication. It is useful to compare Readings and Nussbaum on these questions.

Readings suggests that we should resist the pressure toward transparency, mindless activity, and total integration into bureaucratic, administrative information systems, that we should resist the empty signifier of "excellence," and refuse to make "reason" the new referent. He embraces dereferentialization rather than indulging nostalgia for a time when the university appeared to have a "general culture" to transmit or values to which it could refer. In the place of "excellence," Readings suggests substituting questions of value and promoting "reflection upon the intersection of community and communication that *culture* names" (p. 123). Rather than "academicizing culture," Readings insists that we remain mindful of the fact that we produce the forms of community and communication that culture names, and he urges us to reflect upon them together.

Nussbaum, too, focuses concretely on classroom situations in which the putative object of study is produced even as it is discussed, where ethical interactions are as central to the work of the university as the content of any course. She continues to support a redemptive mission in the name of reason, and her text is replete with stories of contemporary heroes of education, primarily teacher-heroes, but also students. She urges us to resolve all internal conflict and negative affect through reason, a tool that begins to sound strangely outside us in that transcendental realm where the individual is only an abstraction and bodies have been rendered fully virtual or outside us, but somehow nonetheless *in* the speaker who enjoins us to be reasonable. Readings, on the other hand, urges us to abandon "the subject" and think of human beings in the terms of peripheral singularities, "aggregated in multiple demographic bands," in a pedagogical relation that is "dissymmetrical and endless." "The parties," he writes, "are caught in a dialogic web of obligations to thought. Thought appears as the voice of an Other that no third term, such as 'culture,' can resolve dialectically" (p. 145), and we must answer to thought as to the Other, to an unknowable, unmasterable network of obligations. Citing the Italian philosopher, Giorgio Agamben, Readings suggests that religion is "the discursive sphere in which the awareness of the possibility of an incalculable (and hence unpayable) debt has been preserved in modernity" (p. 188). We do not know in advance the nature of our obligations to others, and the community in formation is always a community of heteronomy and dependence, not emancipation.

To argue that we cannot know in advance the nature of our obligations to one another is to challenge an identity politics which assumes that we already know our obligations to one another, that we know the lines along which they run and the nature of the debt we owe or the payment we deserve. To suggest that we reflect on the culture we are in the process of building, rather than simply turning culture into an apparently fully academic, inert object whose meanings and implications we are positioned to know, introduces a space of deferral into our work, a pause or a break that interrupts the smooth workings of the productivity machine. Reinventing Women's Studies would mean suspending, in that breach, what we think we know about our debt, and developing a new attentiveness to the relations and the forms of community we enact. Holding open a space for not knowing would permit the study of gender, race, and sexuality to become an exploration again, rather than a contestation over what is already known and already owed. For Readings, this requires the third term of "Thought" as an Other to which we have an unanswerable debt, a third term onto which the differences, equivalences or debts we have distributed among us can be displaced and revisited. This is not a way to unknow what we already know—about forms of oppression, subordination, and discrimination. It is a way to suspend or defer what we know long enough to reflect on a responsibility to that which exceeds, though it ought not to exclude, actual others. The deferral cannot be left uninterrupted or unspaced by efforts at change, efforts based on a belief in what philosopher Gillian Rose calls "a good enough justice" in her critiques of postmodernism.

Nussbaum's university leaves too much intact, makes critical projects too safe, and subjects us all to Reason, to logical argumentation through which our proper positions can be established. Nussbaum's university still has a referent, a center, a redemptive mission and leaves too little to chance, to play, to unreason, and to the possibility that the effects of the forces of transnationalism may not be so easily contained by reason or by liberal education. In Nussbaum's case, the gap between objective knowledge and subjective experience is filled with ignorance or bias that can be eliminated, since ignorance, for Nussbaum, appears not to be motivated in the strong sense. In Readings, the gap between objective knowledge and subjective experience cannot be closed and the subject is dissolved in the play of forces out of which subjects and objects take form. It is difficult to see in Readings' postmodern language how that gap can be negotiated, what kinds of thought and interaction might go on in the here and now of our exchanges with one another. Nussbaum continues to promote interdisciplinary transparency to reason while Readings advocates that we create opacities.

To some degree, despite their very different political and intellectual foundations, both analyses risk too little. Both stay safely within the confines of discourses that have become conventionalized and predictable, Readings within the safety of impossibility and Nussbaum in the security of an easy resolution. In *Love's Work: A Reckoning With Life*, Gillian Rose argues against both the elevation of reason and its denigration. The "authority of reason," she writes, "is not the mirror of the dogma or superstition, but risk. Reason, the critical criterion, is forever without ground." [12] Rose likens the exercise of reason to children's aggressive play at the borders between fantasy and actuality and laments what she considers to be a simplistic tendency among postmodern thinkers to blame reason for violence. "The child who is locked away from aggressive experiment and play will be left terrified and paralyzed by its emotions, unable to release or face them, for they may destroy the world and himself or herself. The censor," according to Rose, "aggravates the syndrome she seeks to alleviate; she seeks to rub out in others the border which has been effaced inside herself." [13] Neither Reason nor dissemination can save us from the difficult pleasures and violences of limits, encounters, and conflict.

To dismiss either or both Readings and Nussbaum for these reasons would replicate horrifyingly easy gestures. I am convinced that we need them both and that they inform each other in productive ways. Where Readings permits himself to get more and more abstract and to emphasize the impossible, Nussbaum reminds us that we have a responsibility to an at least medium-level specificity about what a liberal education in the humanities entails. Readings' commitment to Thought and resistance to consumerism open up the space in which possibilities for less easily imagined and less contained languages, ideas, and interactions might occur, prying us loose from now routinized investments and closures. Nussbaum takes the risk of formulating a positive project, one that responds to a market which demands to know what value the humanities still have, something many postmodern thinkers are loathe to do. Nussbaum assumes responsibility for defining a set of problems around which our students' education and, to some extent, our work ought to be focused. Unless we want to dismiss the need for humanities education entirely, I do not see how we can do without some version or at least some degree of provocation from both Nussbaum's redemptive and Readings' disseminatory approaches.

Reinvigoration, however, requires that we do more, that we enter domains that have been excluded by the humanities in general, and by our approaches to gender in particular. In the process of engaging what has been disavowed, refused, or ignored, we might unsettle what have become routine and, thus, impoverished practices. In addition to transforming critical practices, we need to educate ourselves about developments in technology, knowledge, and administrative systems in and outside the university, suspending or deferring questions about what they have to do with women or gender long enough to make our analyses of gender and sexuality new again and supple enough to help us intervene usefully in those developments. However, we do not need to abandon our focus on language and its capacities to open new worlds or renounce our focus on poststructuralist accounts of subjectivity nor do we need to adopt an uncritical belief in the scientist's access to truth. In fact, our literary training and focus on language may hold out the greatest promise for new interdisciplinary discussions since it is at level of language, of metaphor, and of rhetoric that new connections across fields can begin to be imagined.

In the space remaining, I want to hint at one kind of interdisciplinary exploration that may have the potential to move theories of gender in a different direction. I begin again with my objections to forms of social constructionism that indulge a social determinism of psychic life and a psychic determinism of the body, to what Slavoj Žižek, drawing on Frederic Jameson, has characterized as constructionism's "vertiginous progression of universal virtualization" with the consequent loss "of our anchorage in the contracted physical body."[14] Žižek writes that "we can never cut the links with our real body and float freely in cyberspace; since, however, our bodily self-experience itself is always already 'virtual,' symbolically mediated, this body to which we are forced to return is not the constituted body of the full self-experience, of 'true reality,' but the formless remainder, the horror of the Real" (pp. 66–76). Žižek holds open a theoretical or metaphorical space between the reductionist assumption of "the constituted body of the full self-experience," on the one hand, and the positing of "the formless remainder," or the "horror of the real" on the other. In that space he insists on the philosophical subject, irreducible to positive knowledge or social construction. According to Žižek's Lacanian account, "*the empty screen onto which we project fantasies*," the "big Other" of symbolic authority provides the idealizing frame which guarantees internal (because apparent external) consistency and possibility, even as it renders unmediated self-relations and conflict-free intersubjective encounters unthinkable (p. 77). To achieve consistency and coherence requires alienation, alienation from the "formless remainders which resist symbolic integration" (p. 24) and from imaginary assumptions of full self-presence. Intersubjectivity occurs in what Gillian Rose has called the "broken middle," the space of redoubled alienation and contingency where both consensus and contestation become far more complex than Nussbaum or Readings would have it. "Ugliness," writes Žižek, "stands for existence itself, for the resistance of reality, which never simply lends itself effortlessly to our molding." Ugliness is also "the site of unbearable, filthy, excessive pleasure—of *jouissance*" (p. 24). What permits us to approach the real or *jouissance*, the physical reminders of what is truly other in the Other and in ourselves? For Žižek, the psychoanalytic cure and its "traversal of fantasies" returns us from the misrecognitions of our desires to the (sublimated) drives. Presumably, awareness at an affective as well as more cognitive level of the necessary alienation / separation from formless remainders that has made our own self-consistency possible, if constraining, permits us to integrate rather than *only* abject what is other in the other. Or, perhaps, in Žižek's universe, no more capacious bearings are possible:

> In order to render this notion [the *jouissance* of the Other] palpable, suffice it to imagine an intersubjective encounter: when do I effectively encounter the Other "beyond the wall of language," in the real of his or her being? Not when I am able to describe her, not even when I learn her values, dreams and so on, but only when I encounter the Other in her moment of *jouissance*: when I discern in her a tiny detail—a compulsive gesture, an excessive facial expression, a tic—that signals the intensity of the real of *jouissance*. This encounter of the real is always traumatic, there is something at least minimally obscene about it, I cannot simply integrate it into my universe, there is always a gap separating me from it.   (p. 25)

Here Žižek succeeds both in making palpable the difficulties of intersubjectivity and in elevating a certain impossibility to an absolute. That we cannot completely integrate the *jouissance* of the other into our universes, that the encounter is "always traumatic" or "minimally obscene" does not necessarily entail that it be unalterably unbearable in its intensity or that forms of incomplete integration are not possible, but subjectivity requires the holding open of a gap. For Žižek, sexual difference ultimately stands for the imposition of a limit, a limit that puts obstacles in the way of virtualization or desire even as it separates us from the unbearable real to which *jouissance* is bound.

For Judith Butler, our relation to the physical body is not determined by a primordial lack for which sexual difference stands or which it mediates, but by the operation of the social and discursive fields which naturalize their exclusionary workings.[15] Butler argues for a less rigid closure and for more capacious configurations of the social and symbolic fields, *not* a return to a body before the law, to formless remainders, or to the constraining and enabling screens of sexual division. Butler remains dedicated to the always unfinished, non-redemptive, difficult work of contestation, of politics which facilitate the emergence of unforeseen possibilities. Butler has been charged, nonetheless, with deriving the body from the psyche and the psyche too directly from the socio-symbolic in her effort to refute arguments that sexual difference is a necessary and inevitable organizing principle that protects us both from social and biological determinism. We continue to have a set of apparently irreconcilable arguments about how bodies matter and how subjectivity is to be conceived.[16]

In her introduction to the English translation of Niklas Luhmann's *Social Systems*, Eva Knodt suggests that work at the intersections of the humanities and sciences remains blocked "as long as difference is modeled upon linguistic difference," as long as difference and language are defined too narrowly.[17] She advocates shifting from the "Kantian question of how a subject can have objective knowledge of reality" to the question "how is organized complexity possible?"[18] Neuro-cognitive scientists might ask how rhythms get generated out of potential chaos and how the proliferation and complexity of rhythms get bound, rendered systematic.

My purpose is not to find a (pseudo) scientific account, but to think about what kinds of conceptual emphases might open our projects on to "their potential convergences" or even more productive impasses with social sciences and sciences, the exclusion of which has been formative for some constructionist projects. In his essay on "The Cartesian Subject versus Cartesian Theater," Žižek points to convergences and to paradigm breaks between cognitive science and psychoanalytic thought. "Among today's cognitive scientsts," he writes, "the preferred model for the emergence of (self-)consciousness is that of the multiple parallel networks whose interaction is not dominated by any central controller."[19] Though not centrally controlled either by a god, a human capacity for mastery, or by the laws of the unconscious, self-consciousness, to paraphrase Žižek, ought not to be conceived as a mere effect or another manifestation of empirical reality. Self-consciousness is not the patterning of or in the brain that spontaneously emerges but the negative of such spontaneous emergence, that which cannot be explained and is irreducible to "the positive order of the world." Happy to join cognitive scientists when they abandon top-down controls, Žižek parts with them over what he sees as a positivist desire to close the gap that ensures that " 'reality' is never a complete, self-enclosed, positive order of being."[20] It would go beyond the limited aims of this essay to analyze the significance of Žižek's thinking with and against cognitive science but his efforts to hold open a gap beyond scientific understanding seem crucial. One need not find Žižek's particular conceptualization of the gap or void that is the subject to be completely satisfying but he makes a compelling case for the psychoanalytic subject over against or a reductionist neuroscientific account. Interacting with the biological sciences requires that their practitioners reconfigure their presuppositions and analytic practices in ways that acknowledge the limits of what they can explain. Potential convergences and mutual reconfigurations are beautifully developed in Elizabeth Wilson's new book on feminism and cognitive science, *Neural Geographies: Feminism and the Microstructure of Cognition*.[21] Wilson puts connectionist theories of cognition, Freudian neurology, and Derridean conceptions of the trace to work on one another, demonstrating their inter-implication and providing the immanent transcendental weave through which they take their distance from one another.

Wilson begins her book with a challenge to what she calls feminism's "naturalized antiessentialism" and she sets out to "rethink our reflexive critical recoil from neurological theories of the psyche" (p. 14). Taking psychology as her focus, Wilson argues that the psychology of women and, later, feminist theories of gender have been enormously constrained in large part because definitions of what it means to do feminist psychology have ruled so much of mainstream psychology irrelevant, reproducing age-old and disabling splits between the putatively more objective knowledge and those pertaining to women. She also contends that feminism's "own internal con-figurations" have excluded biology and that the exclusion of biology is what "render[s] theories of gender intelligible in our current political context" (p. 52). As Pheng Cheah does in his work on mattering,[22] Wilson challenges the premise in gender theory and in social constructionism, more generally, that "sex and biology naturally incite the need for critical supplementation" and that "biology requires modification and supplementation in order to be analytically viable" (p. 54).

Wilson does not make the mistake of countering such assumptions about supplementation with a return to "the Real," or to a body as full presence. She works instead to put the essentialist tendencies in neurology into ques-tion even as she forces gender theory, including feminist appropriations of psychoanalytic theory, out of their now unearned dependence on the nega-tion of the biological sciences, unearned because theories of gender and antiessentialist rewriting of psychoanalysis so consistently fail to acknowl-edge "the possibility that biology is always already rewriting itself according to a morphological complexity of difference—that biology's outside is already within, its interiority already scattered" (p. 63).

Wilson uses Derrida to expose the "constitutive equivocation over inter-pretation" in cognitive science, and specifically, in the connectionist theories which lend themselves in any case to comparisons with deconstruction. Wil-son acknowledges that she is not the first scholar to bring deconstruction and connectionist psychology into contact with one another; her goal is to show that "biology can be rearticulated as a site of play" once neurological, biochemical, or genetic discourses are refused their tendency to "constitute the biological as fixed, locatable, and originary" (pp. 95–96).

The neurological trace becomes the key to restoring mobility and force to analyses in which organic localization has been made the key to causal-ity. Distinguishing connectionist network models from computer or infor-mation-processing models, on the one hand, and essentialist neurological models, on the other, Wilson explains that "connectionist models are com-posed of a web of interconnections between units or between groups of units rather than being arranged in simple linear systems." "Cognitive pro-cessing," she continues, "is assumed to be distributed and parallel rather than sequential and linear" (p. 159) and "knowledge is implicit, stored in the con-nections rather than the units—stored in the spatial and temporal differences between connection weights" (p. 160). It is worth quoting at some length Wilson's efforts to emphasize "force" over topography:

Rather than a presence-structure, which processes present and locatable traces, the connectionist network is a trace-structure, wherein the familiar and fixed space of cognition is realized through the mediation of location and mobility, place and force. This refiguring the cognitive trace and architecture inevitably forces a refiguration of cognition itself. Put technically, it is unclear whether cognitive processing in a connectionist system should be construed as a spatial-structural transformation (the propagation of activation through the network, from input to output, and the correlative back-propagation of feedback) or as a change of state in the network as a whole. Put colloquially, cognition is neither reducible to place nor an abstract process floating free from it.   (pp. 195–96)

Freud's *Project for a Scientific Psychology*, often read as a pre-psychoanalytic, neurological work, becomes differently significant when Wilson restores to Freud's work its "mediation of the impossible space between biology and psychology" (p. 184). Wilson shows how contemporary with connectionism Freud's conception of the trace may turn out to have been, and, in turn, how deconstructively psychoanalytic connectionist theories can be shown to be. But Wilson is not interested in turning neurology into psychoanalysis, or biology into deconstruction. She is committed instead to having them transform one another with the ultimate goal of restoring to feminist theories of gender a conception of over-determination which is not reduced by relying on the rejection of science. She stresses over and over that her account of the potential in connectionist theories is only potential and that work in neuro-cognitive science drifts, perhaps inevitably, in a more reductionist direction. She continues throughout to lament the assumption among constructionists that biology requires supplementation by a notion of culture which then becomes the ultimate determinant of "the body." In one of her provocations to neuro-cognitive scientists, she suggests that "the facilitating movements and effects of neuro-cognitive breaching are libidinal." She then draws out the conceptual implications of this claim:

The flow of activation across a neural network is an affective movement that could be described in terms of microintensities, tensions, repetitions, and satisfactions. "Pain," Freud reminds us, "passes along all pathways of discharge." So rather than considering the vicissitudes of libidinal force (sexuality) to be secondary effects or "constructions"

around, after, or upon the materiality of cognition or neurology, they
could more acutely be taken to be the very stuff of cognition or neurology. One strategic reversal that would be worth considering in this
context is that sexuality is not just one manifestation of cognitive
functioning; instead, cognitive functioning is one manifestation of the
sexualized breaching of neurocognitive matter.   (p. 204)

In her welcome efforts to challenge the often unthoughtful ways in
which something called "culture" has become determining in the first and
last instance for many constructionists, Wilson leaves questions about the
openness of psychic systems to social systems or, to put it another way, their
mutual production of one another underarticulated. Despite Wilson's own
objections to Butler's putative psychic determinism, it is here in the inter-
penetration of psychic and social systems that Butler's work on gender and
sexuality would be required, if not as a supplement, then as a kind of rerout-
ing. Still her critique of "culture" understood as the necessary supplement
to an otherwise inert or infinitely malleable biology provides a helpful challenge to current trends in cultural studies with its "academicizing" and paradoxically scientistic claims. When she asserts that "cognition is neither
reducible to place nor an abstract process floating free from it" she opens a
space that may well be compatible with Žižek's insistence on the ethical
necessity of assuming *the ontological incompleteness of "reality" itself.* Wilson's
work opens gender theory and theories of sexuality onto discursive worlds
that much of it has either excluded or ignored, demonstrating in the process
that the science onto which it is opened is itself a richer, more mobile
metaphoric field than many social constructionists, not to mention many
cognitive and neuroscientists, have ever permitted themselves to imagine.
Such openings do not necessarily lead to theories more adequate to Truth
in the traditional sense. Finding ways to make apparently opposed or mutually exclusionary discursive domains converge does have the potential, however, for challenging doxa, re-enlivening our languages, and generating theory that is more adequate than many available accounts of discursive construction for understanding complexity.

Wilson's work is salutary not only because of its overt and effective
assault on the opposition between gender theory and science, but also
because it introduces non-psychoanalytic scholarly work in psychology
into psychoanalytic and deconstructionist debates which have become tire-
somely arrogant with their assertions that there is nothing intellectually

interesting in the field of psychology, in non-psychoanalytic psychology, or even psychoanalysis in the United States, whether in academic or clinical domains. Given the sorry state of mental health care coverage in this country and the accompanying decline of clinical approaches other than the stabilizing combination of drug and behavioral therapies, given, too, the political consequences of an economic imperative to stabilize and control rather than treat, even heal, it seems crucial that we shift our focus from the often dogmatic theoretical debates within or between disciplines and intervene from informed positions open to the range of practices that might be usefully brought to bear on shared questions. The field of psychology is obviously but one example of a domain in transition both in and outside the university.

If feminist studies of gender are to remain vital, or even take the lead in reorganizing our approaches to knowledge and learning, we have to recognize and resist defensive refusals to be moved out of entrenched positions, whether disciplinary or political. Where in our universities and in our professional worlds is the *not known* treated creatively? Where do we find curiosity, risk, and a sense of responsibility to Thought? Where does Thought appear to unsettle dogma or to set aside disciplinary turf wars, yet remain engaged in the risk of the political? Where, when, under what conditions does the demand for excellence and visibility give way to an effort to interact and build the intellectual connections, with all their pleasures, that Women's Studies once promised, and at times, has even delivered?

As long as feminist and queer analysis is excluded, even prohibited, in our primary and secondary schools, and misogyny and homophobia continue to do so much work in the culture as a whole, university education in feminist and queer studies remains absolutely vital. Does the provision of feminist education require or benefit from freestanding Women's Studies programs? I think the answer to that question will depend on conditions on specific campuses. It would be naive and dangerous to think that the work of Women's Studies, or of feminism, is over. The question is whether the work we need to do can be done in the context of the programs and intellectual formations we have established and institutionalized. Perhaps the work cannot go on in the absence of the placeholder we call Women's (or Gender) Studies even when some of the liveliest scholarship and teaching is conducted outside its official parameters. At the very least, a healthy ambivalence now seems to flourish and may be the key to our best thinking. To use Readings' terms, we can begin discussions that enact the relationships to self and to others that we tell ourselves we are only studying. This would mean a certain fearlessness about the differences within feminist studies, even those that appear to threaten its identity as a field or a political project. It would also entail curiosity about how different, even apparently opposing, fields are implicated in feminist studies, how they challenge it, and expose its various limits. This kind of interdisciplinarity goes beyond merely additive and excessively combative or dismissive approaches to what threatens the identity and putative coherence of the formations we call disciplines and what we adopt as theories.

NOTES

1. For an exemplary analysis of the dangers of delimiting "proper objects," see Judith Butler, "Against Proper Objects," in *More Gender Trouble* (Bloomington: Indiana University Press, 1997).

2. Again, the work of Judith Butler is exemplary of such sophistication and has had far-reaching consequences. See, in particular, *Gender Trouble: Feminism and the Subversion of Identity* (New York: Routledge, 1990).

3. See my *Femininity Played Straight: The Significance of Being Lesbian* (New York: Routledge, 1996).

4. I am indebted to Ron Hoy, Professor of Neurobiology and Behavior, for the discussions that helped me generate this characterization. He is not responsible for any inaccuracies.

5. Bill Readings, *The University in Ruins* (Cambridge: Harvard University Press, 1996). All further page references appear in the text.

6. I owe this formulation to Trevor Hope, Visiting Assistant Professor at Cornell University, who used it to characterize my concerns about postmodern critiques of interiority.

7. Wendy Brown, *States of Injury: Power and Freedom in Late Modernity* (Princeton: Princeton University Press, 1995).

8. "Women's Studies on the Edge," *differences* 9, no. 3 (1997).

9. Martha Nussbaum, *Cultivating Humanity: A Classical Defense of Reform in Liberal Education* (Cambridge: Harvard University Press, 1997). All further page references appear in the text.

10. Though I wrote this essay before Nussbaum's attack on Judith Butler appeared in the *New Republic* (February 1999), that attack demonstrates that the language I use here to characterize her view of literary theory was not exaggerated.

11. Barbara Johnson, *The Feminist Difference* (Cambridge: Harvard University Press, 1998), p. 13.

12. Gillian Rose, *Love's Work: A Reckoning with Life* (New York: Schocken Books, 1995), p. 128.

13. Ibid., p. 126.

14. Slavoj Žižek, *The Abyss of Freedom: Ages of the World*, with F. W. J. von Schelling, *Die Weltalter*, trans. Judith Norman (Ann Arbor: University of Michigan Press, 1997), pp. 67–68. All further page references appear in the text.

15. See Judith Butler's critique of Žižek in *Bodies that Matter: On the Discursive Limits of "Sex"* (New York: Routledge, 1993).

16. For a sustained critique of what he takes to be Butler's linguistic determinism, see Pheng Cheah, "Mattering," *Diacritics* 26, no. 1 (1996): 108–39.

17. Eva Knodt, "Introduction," in Niklas Luhmann, *Social Systems* (Stanford: Stanford University Press, 1995).

18. Ibid.," p. xvii.

19. Slavoj Žižek, "Cartesian Subject Versus Cartesian Theater," in *Cogito and the Unconscious*, ed. Slavoj Žižek (Durham, N. C.: Duke University Press, 1998), p. 269.

20. Ibid., p. 270.

21. Elizabeth Wilson, *Neural Geographies: Feminism and the Microstructure of Cognitio* (New York: Routledge, 1998). All further page references appear in the text.

22. Cheah, "Mattering." pp. 108–39.

Chapter 14

Becoming-Woman: Rethinking the Positivity of Difference

ROSI BRAIDOTTI

Introduction

By the end of the last century of the second millennium one cannot even attempt generalizations about the state of feminist theory in the West, let alone in the rest of the globe. If this is to go down in history as the century of women, then diversity and the respect of differences among women are not optional, but are a real epistemological and ethical necessity. All one can offer is a reasoned map, or a politically invested cartography of one's situated perspective or location. These politics of location aim at expressing account-ability for one's own implication within the very power relations one is committed to critiquing and undoing. Feminist practice at the end as at the start of this century remains eminently political: it is the practice of accountability in a relational and collective mode that aims at unveiling power relations and reducing power differentials.

Taking this into account, if I were to sketch one aspect of feminist culture in the 1990s that I consider particularly relevant it would be the extent to which feminism came to show some of the same "perverse" features as late postindustrial societies in the West. In terms of what I would call the existential temperature as well as the mood of feminism, a marked generational shift took place by the end of the millennium.

Toward a Monstrous Social Imaginary?

In general, feminism came to share the flair for sexual indeterminacy, hybrid identities, transgendered bodies, and mutant sexualities that so much of the contemporary "technoculture" also promoted. "Queer" stopped being the noun that marks an identity they taught us to despise, to become a verb that destabilizes any claim to identity. The anorexic body replaced the hysteric as the fin-de-siècle psychopathological symptom for femininity and its discontents. The abject drug-addicted bodies of *Trainspotting* met with unprecedented public success. A colder, more ironic sensibility with a distinct flair for sadomasochism became the nineties' version of "no more nice girls." Mae West has replaced Rebecca West as feminist mother, as Madonna claimed in her *Sex* photo album. Bad girls are in and they go for mutant others. Cyberfeminism in all its multiple rhizomatic variables also promoted a monstrous or hybrid imaginary. As Marina Warner put it, "in rock music, in films, in fiction, even in pornography, women are grasping the she-beast of demonology for themselves. The bad girl is the heroine of our times, and transgression a staple entertainment."[1] Marcia Tucker proudly announced it: we have entered the age of the "Giant Ninja Mutant Barbies."[2]

What is important to note is that this represents a marked change from the previous decade. In the eighties feminist theory celebrated both the ambiguities and the intensity of the "gynocentric" or "mother-daughter" bond in positive terms—*écriture féminine* and Irigaray's paradigm of "labial or specular politics" being somewhat the epitome of this trend. By the late nineties, however, the maternalist/feminine paradigm was well under attack, if not discarded. This shift away from gynocentric psychoanalytic feminism toward a definitely bad attitude to the mother coincides, as often is the case in feminism, with a generation gap.

Melanie Klein's "bad" mother has replaced the Lacanian-inspired "vanilla sex" representation of the M/other as object of desire. Accordingly, parodic politics has replaced strategic essentialism and other forms of affirmative mimesis in feminist theories of difference.[3] Nixon[4] reads the anti-Lacanian climate of the '90s, best illustrated by the revival of interest in Melanie Klein's theory of the aggressive drives, "in part as a critique of psychoanalytic feminist work of the '70s and '80s, privileging pleasure and desire over hatred and aggression" (p.72). I would like to situate the new alliance that is currently being negotiated between feminists and Deleuze in this context of historical decline of Lacan's theory of desire as lack.[5] As for the emphasis on aggression, I see it as the cultural trend that expresses, among others, the rejection of the myth of global sisterhood and of inherent female feminist empathy. A more selective approach has become established, also in feminist politics.

Feminism shares the social imaginary of late postmodernity in the West by being in the grip of a teratological imaginary.[6] The monstrous, the grotesque, the mutant, and the downright freakish have gained widespread currency in postindustrial cultures.[7] The freak, the geek, the androgyne, and the hermaphrodite crowd the space of multiple urban, suburban, televised and on-line Rocky Horror shows. Drugs, mysticism, satanism, various brands of insanity are also on the catalogue. Liminal or borderland figures that mark the intersection between the human and the animal or the beast-figure, especially replicants, zombies, and vampires, including lesbian vampires and other queer mutants, seem to enjoy special favor in these post-AIDS days.

Although cultural critics tend to reduce the impact of this imaginary by consigning it to a very unclear category called "youth culture"—or, especially in Europe, "popular culture"—the teratological imaginary is also rampant in "high" cultural genres. Authors such as Angela Carter, Kathy Acker, Martin Amis, and Fay Weldon, as well as new genres such as science fiction, cyberpunk, horror, and crime stories, constitute a broad "posthumanist" techno-teratological landscape that privileges the deviant techno-bodies and the mutant others over the more conventional versions of the human.

Contemporary cyberspace culture simply intensifies this trend. Biotechnology has also contributed to shifting the issue of genetic mutations from the high-tech laboratories into popular culture, thus raising the idea of meta(-1-)morphosis to the status of a cultural icon. Jackie Stacey recommends that we link this social imaginary to the surge in classical and relatively newer killer diseases, of which cancer remains the deathly trademark.[8]

Let me clarify one important point here. By "social imaginary" I mean a set of socially mediated practices that function as the anchoring point—albeit contingent—for framing and shaping the constitution of the subject and therefore for identity formation. These practices are interactive structures where *desire* as a subjective yearning and *agency* in a broader sociopolitical sense are mutually shaped by one another. Neither "pure" imagination—locked in its classical opposition to reason—nor "fantasy" in the Freudian sense, the imaginary marks a space of transitions and transactions. It's inter- and intra-personal. Dynamic, it flows like a symbolic glue between the social and the self, the "constitutive outside" and the subject, the material and the ethereal.

It flows, but it is sticky: it catches on as it goes. It possesses fluidity, but it distinctly lacks transparency, let alone purity. I use the term "desire"—following poststructuralism—to connote the subject's own investment or enmeshment in this sticky network of interrelated social and discursive effects. This network constitutes the social field as a libidinal—or affective—landscape, as well as a normative—or disciplinary—framework.

Considering its structure, the imaginary cannot be unitary or have a generalized meaning. All we can do is offer philosophically reasoned diagrams or cartographies of it. Nor is it the case that an immediate Nietzschean transmutation of values can be implemented. Rather, it is the case that critiques of the social imaginary have provided—since the sixties—the arena in which different theories of representation have clashed, fueling the discourse of the crisis of representation.

The notion of the social imaginary thus owes a lot to poststructuralist political theory since Althusser and to Lacanian psychoanalysis, up to Deleuze's intervention. I also want to argue that it stretches beyond the confines of these respective discourses. It helps relate the process of constitution of the subject to the webs of discourses that circulate in culture and society in such a way as to avoid the dichotomous opposition between the "inner self" on the one hand and the "outside cultural codes" on the other. I think that the idea of a fluid, albeit nontransparent imaginary can account for the productive yet contradictory ways in which a nonunitary and consequently heterogeneous subject is formed in the feedback exchanges between the inside and the outside. It is these spaces in-between that are interesting.

The pronounced preference expressed by poststructuralist thinkers such as Foucault and Deleuze for surfaces rather than depths expresses this notion very powerfully. In this essay, therefore, I will speak of the subject as an intensive or dynamic field of intersecting forces that not only propel him/her back and forth but also provide a frame in which to "contain" this same subject. More on this later.

I define the social imaginary accordingly as a network of forces and interconnections that constitute subjects in multiple, complex, and multi-layered ways. Subjects are consequently simultaneously constructed and destabilized by interpellations that hit them at all levels simultaneously. I care particularly for emphasizing and granting due specificity to prediscursive and unconscious processes by which subjectivity is invested and decentered by the constant and ultimately productive encounter with cultural codes, forces, affects, norms, and other "events" with which the subject grows coextensive.

To apply this to the teratological imaginary, there is a clear resonance between the social manifestations of the fascination for the hybrid, or the mutant, and the ways in which they activate the "monsters within." This is also known as the "metamorphic effect" of the monstrous other upon the self.[9] Diane Arbus noted, way back in the sixties, the strangely reassuring function that freaky bodies and monstrous others fulfill in the anxiety-ridden contemporary imagination.[10] Freaks have already had their traumas and have come out at the other end; they are ontological aristocrats resilient in their capacity to endure at a time when many early twenty-first-century humans may instead have serious doubts as to what exactly happens next.

In other words, at times of fast-changing social and cultural conditions the mutant, hybrid, monstrous others accelerate to an almost vertiginous degree the destabilization of the subject. They both express and enhance the subjects' confrontations with the pain of transition and transformation. They stress the inevitability of negotiations, shifts, and restructuring that lie at the heart of the process of change and how they imply both pain and exhilaration and can never avoid conflict.

These processes of change need to be read in the context of the historical decline or decentering of Europe (West and East) as a world power. It is also intrinsic to the postnuclear predicament of an advanced world whose social realities become virtual—or dematerialized—under the pressure and the acceleration of a digitally-clad economy. One is tempted to link these factors to the "postnuclear sensibility" of advanced societies where science and technology have led to the implosion of the Enlightenment promise of progress *by* and *through* reason. Far from being the leading principle in a teleological process aimed at the perfectibility of the human, science and tech-

nology have sort of "spilled over" and have turned into sources of permanent anxiety over our present and future. In other words, this historical context has definitely contributed to making the "end" thinkable.

A culture that can rationally contemplate the spectacle of its own extinc-
tion, by technological overkill and environmental collapse, is not only
postindustrial /nuclear /modern, but also posthuman. And this goes well
beyond the loss of the materialistic paradigm, such as it is often celebrated
in structuralist and poststructuralist circles. It actually approaches a collective
case of machine-envy in the humans and the desire to imitate the inorganic.

In an age where, as Donna Haraway astutely observes,[11] the machines are
so restless while the humans are so inert, the issue is not only how to overcome the modernist divide between technophobia and technophilia, but
also—for me—especially how to redefine the enfleshed structure of the
subject, which we used to call "the body" in the old days, in such a way as
to account for its being immersed in the techno-industrial-military media
apparatus while preserving a sense of its singularity. This singularity allows
for accountability and for political practice amidst the collective renegotia-
tions of identity that are going on around us. Essential traits of this project
are the posthumanistic and antianthropocentric mode of representing the
new subject-positions that have emerged in the teratological technoland-
scapes of late postmodernity.

Consuming the Others

A second set of reasons that cast an interesting light on the monstrous social
imaginary is the reappraisal of difference—some would say the remarketing
of difference—which has taken place in late postmodernity.

Sexualized, racialized, "marked" differences return to the center of the
philosophical debate with the force of a return of the repressed. This proliferation of discursive practices of "otherness" cannot and should not be separated from material and geopolitical power relations in the age of postin-
dustrialism, postcoloniality, and postcolonialism. I am endorsing here a definition of late postmodernity in terms of the systematic construction and
marketing of consumable, representable, and tradable "differences" that are
shot through with structural power relations. These power relations result in
a proliferation of social as well as discursive practices that result in the "marketing" of pluralistic differences and the "commodification" of the "others"

in the mode of consumerism and neocolonial romantic appropriation of their "difference."[12] In the tradition of philosophical materialism within which I situate myself, I do not see any contradiction between the geopolitical and historical context, which engenders the practices of otherness, and the philosophical and discursive interest in both the politics and the theories of "difference." It is in fact to the credit of politically minded philosophies such as poststructuralism that they both register and intersect with historically relevant and politically poignant issues such as "difference."

I want to argue that this proliferation of discourses about difference, about "otherness," exposes the dichotomous economy of a philosophical *reason* that historically has posited itself as much by what it excludes as by what it *includes* within the apparatus of entitlements and power that lays the groundwork for subjectivity. In other words, the promotion of different differences is assured and governed by the empowered "Majority subject," as Deleuze would call Him (and the gender is anything but coincidental). These are the "others" of the Same, as Irigaray would more pointedly put it. This "familiarity of difference" is precisely what grants to monstrous others a metamorphic, peculiarly reassuring quality, to which I will return.

This proliferation of "pejorative others" is internally contradictory and fraught with tensions. Looked at from the angle of "different others," in fact, this inflationary production of different differences also and simultaneously expresses the emerging subjectivities of positive and self-defined others. It all depends on one's locations or situated perspectives. Far from seeing this as a form of relativism, I see it as an embedded and embodied form of enfleshed materialism.

Translated into a Deleuzian feminist perspective, this means that these differences may be quantitatively small, but they are qualitatively major in that they tend *not* to alter the logic or the power of that Same, the Majority, the phallogocentric master code. In late postmodernity the center merely gets fragmented, but that does not make it any less central, or dominating. It is against the uncritical reproduction of sameness on a molecular, global, or planetary scale that Deleuze proposes a different take; instead of the Majority-driven proliferation of difference, we need a theory of active becoming that would allow us to transgress and ultimately exit from the entire dialectical frame of opposition Majority-versus-minorities.

Black, postcolonial, and feminist critics have rightfully *not* spared criticism of the paradoxes as well as the rather perverse division of labor that has emerged in postmodernity and poststructuralist philosophy. According to

this paradox, it is the thinkers who are located at the *center* of past or present empires who are actively deconstructing the power of the center—thus
contributing to the discursive proliferation and consumption of former
"negative others"—while those same others—especially in postcolonial, but
also in postfascist and postcommunist societies—are rather more keen to
reassert their identity, rather than to deconstruct it.

The irony of this situation is not lost on any of the interlocutors; think
for instance of the feminist philosophers saying, "How can we undo a subjectivity we have not even historically been entitled to *yet?*" Or the black
and postcolonial subjects who argue that it is now their historical turn to be
self-asserting. And if the white, masculine, ethnocentric subject wants to
"deconstruct" himself and enter terminal crisis, then—so be it! The point
remains that "difference" emerges as a central—albeit contested and paradoxical—notion; this implies that the confrontation with the notion of
"negative difference," or "pejorative others," is historically inevitable, as
we—postmodern subjects—are historically condemned to our history.

Thus the monstrous or teratological imaginary expresses the social, cultural, and symbolic mutations that are taking place in the context of technoculture in the age of postcolonial, postfeminist, and other insurrected and
emerging subjectivities. They are highly contested, multilayered, and internally contradictory subjectivities, but this does not make them any less materially embedded, concretely embodied, or any less ridden with power relations.

Sexualized and racialized monstrous others are signs of an embodied difference that had historically been coined negatively—by the metaphysical
cannibalism of a subject that feeds upon its specular, structurally excluded
others. Pejorative otherness thus helps to illuminate the dissymetrical power
relation within Western theories of subjectivity. By virtue of its organic, as
well as structural, proximity to the dominant subject-position, the monstrous other helps define "sameness." Normality is, after all—as Canguilhem
teaches us—the zero-degree of monstrosity.

In such a context, I want to resist two complementary trends:

The first is the euphoric celebration of the intrinsically liberatory power
of the major dislocation of subject positions (the "Majority-driven" proliferation of differences mentioned before) that our historicity is enacting—
including the fascination for monstrous techno-bodies, for "postgender"
bodies, and other hyped figurations that circulate in this end of century.
Technocultures in postcoloniality are political regimes of acute visualiza-

tion. From the panoptical eye explored by Foucault, to the disembodied satellite eye /I of Haraway's cyborgs—without forgetting, at a more sociological level, the ubiquitous presence of television and surveillance videos and the wired computer screens—it is the visual dimension of contemporary technoculture that defines its all-pervading power.

Some of the masters of the postmodern "aesthetics of disappearance" tend to launch euphoric celebrations of the "evaporation of reality," to speak like Ernst Gellner, and to celebrate the reduction of the embodied subject to a mere "surface of representation," placing all hope in potential multiple and virtual reembodiments. I would prefer to issue a more sober message, alerting us not only to the danger of "visual politics" but also to the challenge that it throws our way, namely of how to recompose an ethical and political sense of agency of the subject, without falling into nostalgic reappraisals of an authentic or essential "human nature"—or, on the contrary, an orientalist glorification of deviant others.

The second trend that I want to resist consists in giving in to a celebration of nihilism. To go back to the example of the monstrous social imaginary, I refuse the rather nostalgic position that consists in reading it as the symptom of the cultural decadence of our times, or the much celebrated decline of "master narratives," or the loss of the canon and standards of "high culture."

There is no denying the fact that, in late postmodernity, various brands of nihilism are circulating. A whole philosophical style based on "catastrophe" is popular among several prophets of doom, who contemplate the implosion of humanism with tragic joy.[13] Nothing could be further removed from the ethics of affirmation and the political sensibility of posthumanist subjects than the "altered states" proposed by what I facetiously call the "narcophilosophers": those who celebrate the implosion of sense, meaning, and values for their own sake. They end up producing histrionic renditions of that delirious megalomania against which Deleuze proposes firmly and rigorously a sustainable definition of the self.

It is against these contemporary forms of nihilism that a critical philosophy of immanence needs to disintoxicate us and to reset the agenda in the direction of affirmation and sustainable subjectivity.

What I see as the theoretical stake of the debate is the question of the status of difference, certainly, but more specifically the issue of how to elaborate adequate forms of representation of the contemporary subject-positions. At stake is how to reconfigure the positivity of difference, stressing the

potentially affirmative aspects of a philosophy of becoming, of active transformations in the age of posthumanist subjectivity.

Becomings

Deleuze emphasizes processes, dynamic interaction, and fluid boundaries in
a materialist, postmodernist brand of vitalism. The emphasis on actuality
must be read against the background of Deleuze's stern rejection of the role
of rational consciousness in our culture. Phallogocentric reason's Medusa-
like head has the power to captivate and intimidate its beholders.

In his effort to move beyond the dogmatic image of thought, its oedipal
foundations and the anxiety of influence it arouses, Deleuze redefines philosophy as the nonreactive activity of thinking the present, the actual
moment, so as to account adequately for change and changing conditions.

In his quest for a postmetaphysical discourse about the thinking subject,
Deleuze also redefines the practice of theory-making in terms of flows of
affects and the capacity to draw connections. Accordingly, thinking is not for
Deleuze the expression of the in-depth interiority of a "knowing" subject,
or the enactment of transcendental models of reflexive consciousness. Pursuing to a radical degree the insight of psychoanalysis about the noncoincidence of the subject with his/her consciousness, Deleuze posits the subject
as an affective or intensive entity.

Deleuze describes ideas as events, active states that open up unsuspected
possibilities of life. In other words, beyond the propositional content of an
idea, there lies another category: the affective force, the level of intensity that
ultimately determines its truth-value. The truth of an idea is less in its propositional content or referential value than in the kind of affects that it releases;
ideas are noble or lowly, active or reactive, depending on whether they mobilize one's powers of affirmation and joy over the forces of denial and negation.

In juxtaposition with the linear, self-reflexive mode of thought that is
favored by phallologocentrism, Deleuze defines this new style of thought as
"rhizomatic" or "molecular." These new figurations of the activity of thinking are chosen for their capacity to suggest weblike interaction and inter-
connectedness, as opposed to vertical distinctions, in a manner of speech
that can be compared to Donna Haraway's figuration of the cyborgs.[14]

Deleuze defends this view of the subject as a flux of successive becomings by positing the notion of a "minority" consciousness.

This "intensive" redefinition of the activity of thinking entails a vision of subjectivity as a bodily entity. The embodiedness of the subject is not of the natural, biological kind; rather, Deleuze deessentializes the body, which thus appeases this complex interplay of constructed social and symbolic forces. The body is not an essence, let alone a biological substance; it is a play of forces, a transformer and relay of energy, a surface of intensities. The embodied subject is a term in a process of intersecting forces (affects) and spatiotemporal variables (connections).

Applied to feminist discussions of gendered identity, this means that Deleuze's work does not rest upon a dichotomous opposition of masculine and feminine subject positions but, rather, on a multiplicity of sexed subject positions. The differences in degree between them mark different lines of becoming, in a web of rhizomatic connections:

> For us . . . there are as many sexes as there are terms in symbiosis, as many differences as elements contributing to a process of contagion. We know that many beings pass between a man and a woman; they come from different worlds, are born on the wind, form rhizomes around roots; they cannot be understood in terms of production, only in terms of becoming.[15]

These different degrees of becoming can be rendered as diagrams of thought, typologies of ideas, politically informed maps, variations on intensive states. Multiplicity does not reproduce one single model—as in the Platonic mode—but, rather, creates and multiplies differences. This has dire consequences for sexual difference.

In identifying the points of exit from the phallocentric modes of thought, toward a new, intensive image of philosophy, Deleuze stresses the need for new images for these subject-positions. This results in the elaboration of a set of postmetaphysical figurations of the subject. The notion of the *figural* (as opposed to the more conventional aesthetic category of the "figurative") is central to this project.[16] Figurations such as rhizomes, becomings, lines of escape, flows, relays, and bodies without organs release and express active states of being, which break through the conventional schemes of theoretical representation.

Alternative figurations of the subject, including different feminine and masculine subject-positions, are figural modes of expression, which displace the vision of consciousness away from phallogocentric premises.

Deleuze's central figuration is a general becoming-minority, or becoming-nomad, or becoming-molecular. The minority marks a crossing or a trajectory; nothing happens at the center, for Deleuze, but at the periphery there roam the youthful gangs of the new nomads:

> All becomings are already molecular. That is because becoming is not to imitate or identify with something or someone. Nor is it to proportion formal relations. Neither of these two figures of analogy is applicable to becoming: neither the imitation of a subject nor the proportionality of a form. Starting from the forms one has, the subject one is, the organs one has, or the functions one fulfills, becoming is to extract particles between which one establishes the relations of movements and rest, speed and slowness that are *closest* to what one is becoming, and through which one becomes.[17]

The space of becoming is therefore a space of affinity and symbiosis between adjacent particles. Proximity is both a topological and a quantitative notion, which marks the space of becoming of subjects as sensitive matter. The space of becoming is one of dynamic marginality.

Deleuze's theory of becoming-minority, however, displays a problematic double pull. On the one hand, the becoming-minority/nomad/molecular/bodies-without-organs/woman is posited as the general figuration for the kind of subjectivity that Deleuze advocates. On the other hand, not all the forms taken by the process of becoming are equivalent. Let us analyze this stage of his argument carefully.

In so far as man, the male, is the main referent for thinking subjectivity, the standard-bearer of the Norm, the Law, the Logos, woman is dualistically, i.e., oppositionally, positioned as his "other." The consequences are that

1. there is no possible becoming-minority of man;
2. the becoming-woman is a privileged position for the minority-consciousness of all.

Deleuze states that all the lines of deterritorialization go necessarily through the stage of "becoming-woman," which is not just any other form of becoming minority, but rather is the key, the precondition and the necessary starting point for the whole process of becoming.

The reference to "woman" in the process of "becoming-woman," however, does not refer to empirical females but, rather, to topological positions. The becoming-woman is the marker for a general process of transformation; it affirms positive forces and levels of nomadic, rhizomatic consciousness:

> There is a becoming-woman, a becoming-child, that do not resemble the woman or the child as clearly distinct entities. . . . What we term a molecular entity is, for example, the woman as defined by her form, endowed with organs and functions and assigned as a subject. Becoming-woman is not imitating this entity or even transforming oneself into it. . . . Not imitating or assuming the female form, but emitting particles that enter the relation of movement and rest, or the zone of proximity, of a microfemininity, in other words, that produce in us a molecular woman, create the molecular woman.[18]

Clearly, the woman occupies a troubled area in this radical critique of phallocentrism: insofar as woman is positioned dualistically as the other of this system, she is also annexed to it. Deleuze—not uncharacteristically ignorant of basic feminist epistemological distinctions between Woman as representation and women as concrete agents of experience—ends up making distinctions internal to the category of woman herself. At this point his difference from Irigaray's sexual difference theory grows wider and more irreparable than ever.

Deleuze, just like Derrida and other poststructuralists, opposes to the "majority/sedentary/molar" vision of Woman as a structural operator of the phallogocentric system the woman as "becoming/minority/molecular/nomadic." Concludes Deleuze: all becomings were equal, but some were more equal than others. As against the molar or sedentary vision of woman as an operator of the phallologocentric system, Deleuze proposes the molecular or nomadic woman as process of becoming.

In so far as the male/female dichotomy has become the prototype of Western individualism, the process of decolonisation of the subject from this dualistic grip requires as its starting point the dissolution of all sexed identities based on the gendered opposition. In this framework, sexual polarisations and gender-dichotomy are rejected as the prototype of the dualistic reduction of difference to a subcategory of Being. Thus, the becoming-woman is necessarily the starting point for dissolving the overemphasis on masculine sexuality; the persistence of sexual dualism and the positioning of woman as the privileged figure of otherness are constitutive of Western thought. In other words, "becoming-woman" triggers off the deconstruction of phallic identity, because of historical and cultural and not biologically essentialist reasons.

Sexuality being the dominant discourse of power in the West, as Foucault taught us,[19] it requires special critical analysis. Thus, the generalized becoming-woman is the necessary starting point for the deconstruction of phallogocentric identities precisely because sexual dualism and its corollary—the positioning of Woman as figure of Otherness—are constitutive of Western thought. In other words, it is because of historical and not biological reasons that sexed identities are foregrounded in the process of deconstruction.

More significant still for feminist theory is Deleuze's next step: Deleuze's ultimate aim with respect to sexual difference is to move toward its final overcoming. The nomadic or intensive horizon is a subjectivity "beyond gender" in the sense of being dispersed, not binary; multiple, not dualistic; interconnected, not dialectical; and in a constant flux, not fixed. This idea is expressed in figurations such as "polysexuality," the "molecular woman," and the "bodies without organs," which are the figurations for this world beyond gender, to which Deleuze's de-phallic style actively contributes.

Deleuze uses also the becoming-woman of women as the basis for a critique of certain kinds of feminism. Some feminists—among whom I do not hesitate to situate myself—display in fact the irritating tendency to refuse to dissolve the subject "woman" into a series of transformative processes that pertain to a generalized and "gender-free" becoming. In other words, feminists are conceptually mistaken, though they may be politically correct, in their assertion of specific rights and entitlements for women. They are even more misguided when they argue for a specifically feminine sexuality: emphasis on the feminine is restrictive. Deleuze suggests that they should instead draw on the multisexed structure of the subject and reclaim all the sexes of which women have been deprived.

Ultimately, what Deleuze finds objectionable in feminist theory is that it perpetuates reactive, molar, or majority thinking: in Nietzsche's scale of values, feminists have a slave morality.[20] Thus, women would be revolutionary if, in their becoming, they contributed both socially and theoretically to constructing a nonoedipal woman, by freeing the multiple possibilities of desire meant as positivity and affirmation. Women, in other words, can be revolutionary subjects only to the extent that they develop a consciousness that is not specifically feminine, dissolving "woman" into the forces that structure her.

This new general configuration of the feminine as the post- or, rather, unoedipal subject of becoming is explicitly opposed to the feminist config-uration of a new universal based on extreme sexualization or, rather, an exacerbation of the sexual dichotomy, such as Luce Irigaray proposed. It is important to keep in mind, at this point, that Deleuze's understanding of the embodied nature of the subject and of the structures of the unconscious and of sexuality are based on his "intensive" notion of the subject. Vitalism; empiricism; affectivity; desire as positivity, not lack; typology of passions and machinic connections constitute the backbone of Deleuze's critique of Lacanian psychoanalysis, or, more specifically, of its Hegelian legacy. The lat-ter overemphasizes dialectical oppositions, the metaphysical illusion of sub-stance and the teleological structures of identity.

I do wonder whether Deleuze's objection to the Hegelian legacy in fem-inist thinking, and the oppositional logic it entails, which is quite manifest in the case of de Beauvoir, does justice to sexual difference theorists such as Irigaray.[21] Be that as it may, in Deleuze's framework all feminists are lumped together, and in his opinion emphasis on any one of the gender polarities, whether masculine or feminine, achieves the equally undesirable aim of reasserting all that he is critical of: binary thinking as the support of phallo-centrism as the dominant image of thought.

Following Luce Irigaray and the bulk of feminist political practice, I feel doubtful about Deleuze's call for the dissolution of sexed identities by the neutralization of gender dichotomies, because I think that it is both theo-retically and historically dangerous for women. I am also, however, quite aware of the potentially paranoid undertones of this position in that it expresses a reactive attachment to the very identity—woman—that, as a feminist, I am committed to deconstructing. I would rather approach the issue of subjectivity in terms of a constructive paradox.[22] I see the concept of "becoming" as central to this project.

We have seen that Deleuze stresses the element of affectivity and desire that constitute the structural core of the subject. Thus, the subject is off-cen-ter in relation to the flow of affects that invest it. Psychoanalysis starts from the same assumption that the subject is not master in *his* house, but according to Deleuze it fails to destabilize the power of consciousness as the moral and rational agency. Both in the *Anti-Oedipus* and in subsequent works, Deleuze (with Guattari) radicalizes the critique of psychoanalysis that Foucault had initiated on more sociopolitical grounds. In a more conceptual vein, Deleuze praises the psychoanalytic emphasis on the primacy of the "drives," but he also argues that psychoanalytic theory and practice end up closing the very door they had initially opened. The whole economy of the unconscious is resubjugated in-the-Name-of-the-Father and under the moral and political supervision of a self-regulating, socially enforced conscious and moral rationality. Freud's moment of genius, according to Deleuze, is the discovery of the theory of the drives. His failing is to have indexed them back toward a regulatory and normative scheme of subject, governed by compulsory heterosexuality, oedipal reproduction, and the cost-effective transmission of property best guaranteed by the socioeconomic and legal structure of the family. In other words, according to Deleuze, psychoanalysis reinvests the affective foundations of the subject in a libidinal economy dominated by the phallologocentric principle that equates consciousness with control or the despotic domination of the "dark continents within."

Contrary to this a nomadic or Deleuzian Spinozist approach stresses that the affectivity (*conatus*) is indeed the heart of the matter, but that it is equally the case that this desire is not internalized, but external—or rather, it happens in the encounter between different embodied and embedded subjects who are joined in the sameness of the forces that propel them. Intensive, affective, external resonances make desire that which remains unthought at the heart of thinking, because it is that which triggers and sustains the power of thinking in the first place.

A slice of matter activated by a fundamental drive to life, a *potentia* (rather than *potestas*)—neither by the will of God nor the secret encryption of the genetic code—this subject is yet psychologically embedded in the corporeal materiality of the self. The enfleshed intensive or nomadic subject is rather an in-between: a folding-in of external influences and a simultaneous unfolding-outward of affects. A mobile entity in space and time, an enfleshed kind of memory (I will return to this concept), this subject is in-process but is also capable of lasting through sets of discontinuous variations, while remaining extraordinarily faithful to itself.

This idea of the "faithfulness" of the subject is central to the project of the "sustainable self" that I want to defend here. This "faithfulness to one-

self" is not to be understood in the mode of the psychological or sentimental attachment to an "identity" that often is little more than a social
security number and a set of photo albums. Nor is it the mark of authenticity of a self that is a clearing house for narcissism and paranoia—the great
pillars on which Western identity predicates itself. It is, rather, the faithfulness of duration, the expression of one's continuing belonging to certain
dynamic spatiotemporal coordinates.

As I said earlier, the subject lies at the intersections with external, relational forces. It's about assemblages. Encountering them is almost a matter
for geography; it's a question of orientations, points of entry and exit, a constant unfolding. In this field of transformative forces, sustainability is a very
concrete practice—not the abstract ideal that some of our development and
social-planning specialists often reduce it to. It is a basic concept about the
embodied and embedded nature of the subject. The sensibility to and availability for changes or transformation are directly proportional to the subject's ability to sustain the shifts without cracking. The border, the framing
or containing practices are crucial to the whole operation, one that aims at
affirmative and not dissipative processes of becoming—joyful-becoming or
potentia—as a radically ontological force of empowerment.

Becoming is an intransitive process; it's not about becoming anything in
particular—only what one is capable of and attracted to and capable of sustaining its life on the edge, but not over it (exit Bataille). It's not deprived of
violence, but deeply compassionate. It's an ethical and political sensibility
that begins with the recognition of one's limitations as the necessary counterpart of one's forces or intensive encounters with multiple others. It has to
do with the adequacy of one's intensity to the modes and time of its enactment. It can only be embodied and embedded, because it's inter-relational
and collective.

Memory and the Imagination

Remembering is about repetition or the retrieval of information. In the
human subject, that information is stored throughout the physical and experiential density of the embodied self and not only in the "black box" of the
psyche. I find Deleuze's distinction between a "majority" and a "minority"
memory very useful in illuminating the paradoxes and the riches of repetition as the engine of identity and coherence of the self.

Again, Freud's early psychoanalytic insights had caught a glimpse of two crucial notions. First, he understood that processes of remembrance extend well beyond the rationalistic control of consciousness. In fact, consciousness is merely the tip of the iceberg of a far more complex set of resonances, echo, and data-processing that we commonly call "memory." Second, these processes of remembrance are enfleshed: they encompass the embodied self as a whole and therefore rest on somatic layers that call for a specific form of (psycho) analysis.

According to Deleuze and Guattari, however, Freud immediately closes the very door that he had half-opened by reindexing this vitalistic and time-bound definition of the subject onto the necessity to conform to dominant sociocultural expectations about civilized adult human behavior. Lacan, argue Deleuze and Guattari, operates a sort of kidnapping of the subject from the solid bodily or somatic grounds of Freudian psychoanalysis. This has the advantage of radicalizing the politics of psychoanalysis by attacking conventional morality, expectations about bourgeois propriety, and the reformist impact of American-dominated "ego-psychology." It also has the disadvantage, however, of introducing into the conceptual framework of the psychoanalytic subject a heavier dose of Hegelian dialectics, mostly through the idea of desire as lack and the role of negativity in the constitution of consciousness. These emerge as major points of disagreement between Lacan and Deleuze.

In his own work on the philosophy of "becoming," Deleuze is committed to rescuing the concept of "memory" from the metaphysical trappings into which psychoanalysis had thrown it. With reference to Bergson, Spinoza, and Nietzsche, Deleuze radicalizes and unhinges the role of memory in subject-formation.

In Deleuze's becomings, the Bergsonian continuous present is set in opposition to the tyranny of the past—in the history of philosophy, for instance, but also in the psychoanalytic notion of remembrance, repetition, and the retrieval of repressed psychic material. Deleuze, via Bergson, disengages memory from its indexation on a fixed identity, predicated upon a majority-subject. The memory of the logocentric or "molar" subject is a huge data bank of centralized information, which is relayed through every aspect of His activities (again, the gender is anything but coincidental).

The majority subject holds the key to the central memory of the system, thus reducing to an insignificant, or rather "a-signifying" role the memories of the minorities—subjugated, marginal, alternative "countermemories," as Foucault used to call them. In reaction to this centralized, monolithic memory, Deleuze activates a minority-memory, which is a power of remembrance without a priori prepositional attachment to the centralized data bank. This intensive, zig-zagging, cyclical, and messy type of re-membering does not even aim at retrieving information in a linear manner. It simply intuitively endures. It rather functions as a deterritorializing agency that dislodges the subject from his unified and centralized location. It destabilizes identity by opening up spaces where virtual possibilities can be actualized. It's a sort of empowerment of all that was not programmed within the dominant memory.

Re-membering in this mode requires composition, selection, and dosage, that is, the careful layout of empowering conditions that allow for the actualization of affirmative forces. Like a choreography of flows or intensities that reprieve adequate framing in order to compose into a form, intensive memories reprieve empathy and cohesion between their constitutive elements. They operate like a constant quest for temporary moments when a balance can be sustained, before the forces dissolve again and move on. And on it goes, never equal to itself, but faithful enough to itself to endure, and to pass on.

Memory is fluid and flowing; it opens up unexpected or virtual possibilities and it is transgressive in that it works against the programs of the dominant memory system. This continuous memory is, however, not necessarily or inevitably linked to "real" experience. In what I consider as one of the more radical conceptual attacks on the authority of "experience" and the extent to which the appeal to experience both confirms and perpetuates the belief in steady and unitary identities, Deleuze links memory, rather, to the imagination.

The imagination plays a crucial role in enabling the whole process of becoming-minority. The imaginative, affective force of remembrance—that which returns and is re-membered/re-peated—is the propelling force in this idea of becoming-intensive. When you re-member in the intensive or minority-mode, you in fact open up spaces of movement—of de-territorialization—that actualize virtual possibilities that had been frozen in the image of the past. Opening up these virtual spaces is a creative effort. When you re-member to become what you are—i.e., a subject-in-becoming—you actually reinvent yourself on the basis of what you hope you could become with a little help from your friends!

It is crucial in fact to see to what an extent processes of becoming are collective, intersubjective, and not individual or isolated. "Others" are the integral element of one's successive becomings. Again, my quarrel here is with any notion of the subject that would imply an ethics of individual responsibility in the bourgeois liberal model. A Deleuzian feminist approach would rather favor the destitution of the sovereign subject altogether and consequently the overcoming of the dualism Self/Other, Sameness/Difference which that vision of the subject engenders. Subjects are fields of forces that aim at duration and joyful self-realization and that, in order to fulfill them, need to negotiate their way across the pitfalls of negativity that phallogocentric culture is going to throw in the way of the fulfillment of their intrinsic positivity.

As far as I am concerned, this means exit Hegel and Lacan; enter Spinoza and Nietzsche, reread with Deleuze.

Re-membering in this nomadic mode is the active reinvention of a self that is joyfully discontinuous—as opposed to being mournfully consistent, as programmed by phallogocentric culture. The tense that best expresses the power of the imagination is the future perfect, "I will have been free," shifting away from the reassuming platitudes of the past to the openings hinted at by the future perfect. This is the tense of a virtual sense of potential. Memories need the imagination to empower the actualization of virtual possibilities in the subject. They allow the subject to differ from oneself as much as possible while remaining faithful to oneself, i.e., while enduring.

A personalized overthrowing of the internal simulacra of the self, this kind of imaginative recollection of the self is about repetition, but it is less about forgetting to forget (Freud's definition of the neurotic symptoms) than about retaking, as in refilming a sequence. The imaginative force of this operation is central to what I would consider as a vitalist, yet antiessentialist theory of desire.

Desire is the propelling and compelling force that is attracted to self-affirmation, i.e., the transformation of negative into positive passions. The desire is not to preserve but to change; it is a deep yearning for transformation or a process of affirmation. To enact the different steps of this process of becoming, one has to work on the conceptual coordinates. These are not elaborated by voluntaristic self-naming but, rather, through processes of careful revisitations and retakes. Empathy and compassion are key features of this nomadic yearning for in-depth transformation. The space of becoming is a space of affinity and a correlation of elements between compatible and mutually attractive forces.

It is a space of sympathy between the constitutive elements of the process.

Proximity or intellectual sympathy is both a topological and a qualitative notion, both geography or meteorology and ethical temperature. It is an affective framing for the becoming of subjects as sensible or intelligent matter. The affectivity of the imagination is the motor for these encounters and the conceptual creativity they trigger off. It is a transformative force that propels multiple, heterogeneous "becomings" of the subject.

Running with Virginia Woolf

Throughout his work, Deleuze quotes Virginia Woolf as a perfect example of the process of becoming. Woolf's "stream-of-consciousness" style expresses with uncanny precision the seriality, as well as the radical immanence and the structural contingency, of the patterns of repetition by which differences occur. In *The Waves*, for instance, Woolf captures the concrete multiplicity—as well as the shimmering intensity—of becoming-molecule, becoming-animal, becoming-imperceptible.[23] The sheer genius of Woolf rests in her ability to present—and, I would add, also to experience—her life as a passing through. She is the writer of multiple and intransitive becomings, in-between ages, sexes, elements, characters. Woolf's texts enact a flow of positions, a crossing of boundaries, an overflowing into a plenitude of affects where life is asserted to its highest degree. Woolf also provides Deleuze with a model for the "plane of immanence," where different elements can encounter one another, producing those assemblages of forces without which there is no becoming. As I have said, these assemblages are geographical and even meteorological—they organize space and time around them. The "haecceity" is the specific and highly contingent actualization of a field of forces stable enough, and consolidated by their structural affinity, so as to be able to constitute a phase of immanence.

Woolf's prose expresses the vitalistic interconnections that make the whole process of becoming into a concrete and actualized event. I think that this process of composition and assemblage of forces is what desire is all about, as an ontological layer of affinity and sympathy between different enfleshed subjects.

Although Deleuze recognizes the extraordinary position of Woolf as a conveyor or relay-point for this passionate process of becoming in both *Dialogues* and *A Thousand Plateaus*, he is very careful to dis-engage Woolf's work from her being-a-woman, and even more from the "écriture féminine" style made popular by sexual-difference feminism.

There is something in what feminists of sexual difference like myself call the "feminine libidinal economy" of excess without self-destruction and desire as plenitude, not lack, that is central to the whole Deleuzian project of becoming.[24] As it is to his aesthetics and theory of art. Nonetheless, Deleuze cannot resolve his ambivalence toward it.

To challenge Deleuze's desexualization of Woolf's style and of her power of affirming positive passions, and thus to provide a diagram of possible becomings, I will turn to one *topos* in her work that I consider of the highest significance and whose sexual connotations and specificity are beyond doubt.

Throughout Woolf's letters and diaries as well as in her fictional works, the figure of Vita Sackville-West—the real-life model for *Orlando*—looms large. What makes it particularly striking is the highly defined field of perception that she enacts and, in some ways, organizes.

From their very first encounter in 1923, which was dutifully recorded in Woolf's diaries, through to the end of her life, Vita stands for a life force of mythical proportions. Clearly magnified through the lens of erotic desire but stretching beyond the whimsical tricks of Eros (that cruel god), Vita endures in a field of her own that is one of perpetual becomings.

Spatiotemporal coordinates gather around her; carried by her statuesque legs, the arch of her shoulders, the specific hue of her complexion, Vita organizes Virginia's cosmos around Vita. There's a specific quality of light around her, which is recorded and repeated in the diaries with mathematical precision. It has to do with the porpoise radiance and the luster of pink and of pearls.[25]

There's an acceleration of life about Vita—due to the speed of desire, but also to the more bearable lightness of being. The space gets filled with warmth, with that shimmering intensity that we also find in Woolf's novels. There's a heightening of sensorial perception, the flowing of deep-seated affinity, of immense compassion, to the very end.

Diary, February 16, 1930

Vita was here: and when she went, I began to feel the quality of the evening—how it was spring coming; a silver light; mixing with the early lamps; the cabs all rushing through the streets; I had a tremendous sense of life beginning; mixed with that emotion, which is the essence of my feeling, but escapes description. . . . I felt the spring beginning and Vita's life so full and flush; and all the doors opening; and this is I believe the moth shaking its wings in me.[26]

Virginia will remember these affects, and be able to retrieve their spatiotemporal coordinates throughout her life, even when the actual (I would be tempted by "empirical," except that it may backfire by evoking the phenomenological distinction empirical/transcendental, which Deleuze is absolutely committed to undo and to replace with multiple becomings in/of radical immanence) relationship with Vita has lost its brilliance.

I want to argue that these spatiotemporal, geographical, historical, and meteorological features are Vita, such as she exists as the phase of immanence where she and Virginia activate a process of becoming that goes beyond their psychological, amorous, and sexual relationship. Something much more elemental, rawer, is at stake.

The best way to assess the scale and magnitude of this encounter, and the fields of possible becomings it activates, is by turning to the literature itself: the letters and diaries as well as the fictional work. This is neither a biography nor a mere love letter—it is the unfolding, with meticulous regularity, of the virtual layers of *potentia* contained in the encounter between Virginia & Vita. It is the actualization of multiple and virtual realities, possibilities such as they are perceived, recognized, and amplified by the writer of genius that was Mrs. Woolf. In her study of Virginia Woolf's correspondence, Kate Stimpson argues that the epistolary genre is very specific—and can best be defined as an in-between space, bridging the public and the private.[27] As such, Woolf's letters possess a fluid quality that allows the readers to catch a glimpse of the fleeting state of the writer's mind. Moreover, the letters are interactive exchanges that construct an intersubjective space with her (privileged) interlocutor. They draw a space of flow and becoming through a set of "epistolary performances" that are expressed in order to be shared in a communal—albeit volatile—communicative space. Today's equivalent would be E-mail exchanges.

Moreover, the intense and deep affectivity that is expressed in these letters opens a space of freedom that allows simultaneously for experiments with different writing techniques and for depositing residual and complex emotions. These letters occupy a psychological and rhetorical middle space between what she wrote for herself and what she produced for a general audience. They are a brilliant, glittering encyclopedia of the partially-said . . . the materials or a full autobiography of consciousness, a mediation between life and work. . . . They concern social worlds that she needed and wanted. They form an autobiography of the self with others, a citizen/denizen of relationships.[28]

It is the link, the affinity, the bond of *potentia* and recognition between them that results in setting the frame for the affirmation of this joyful potency—i.e., in being able to sustain it.

This is all the more remarkable if you consider that, in real life, the actual V & V were far from the life forces that they happened to become together. Virginia could hardly sustain, in her frail body and even more vulnerable psychic balance, the intensity of the forces that she registered, evoked and recorded. As for Vita, Virginia put her finger on it, with the disarming cruelty of her superior intelligence: "you lack transparency. There's something that doesn't vibrate in you; it may be purposely—you don't let it: but I see it with other people as well as with me: something reserved, muted."[29]

That she hit the mark is testified by Vita's comments in her correspondence to her husband Harold Nicolson:

Damn the woman! She has put her finger on it. There is something that . . . doesn't come alive . . . it makes everything I do (i.e.: write) a little unreal; it gives the effect of having been drawn from the outside. It is the thing which spoils me as a writer; destroys me as a poet. . . . It is what spoils my human relationships too.[30]

But this fundamental opacity of Vita's soul is compensated and sustained by a feminine magnificence about her.

Diary, July 1927

Vita very free & easy, always giving me great pleasure to watch & recalling some image of a ship breasting a sea, nobly, magnificently, with all sails spread & the gold sunlight on them.[31]

A Deleuzian feminist reader could draw a cartography of the affective forces that frame the encounters between Virginia and Vita, such as they are reported in the diaries and the letters (literature and work of remembrance) as well as in the fiction (literature and work of the imagination).

The most recurrent images are that of the porpoise, pink light, the pearls: images of radiance and vitality that occur systematically throughout Woolf's writings. Vita produces a diagram that contains forces of the utmost intensity: a quality of the light, coupled with a degree of intensity that may alternatively generate desire or trigger an outburst of comic laughter. Vita becomes a factor that introduces an acceleration in the pulse of life, the opening up of possibilities, like the fluttering of wings before one takes the flight. Vita not merely re-presents, but actually enacts and organizes physically as well as in writing the becoming-woman of Virginia Woolf, a becoming-woman that has a distinctly marine quality about it, so ubiquitous are the images of fluidity, flowing, waves, and sea animals. It does mark a fundamental moment in Woolf's race against time, which is the space where she could finally write.

The assemblage of forces that activate the becoming-Orlando of Vita requires a careful phase of composition of forces that go through the becoming-woman of Virginia and the becoming-lesbian of both Vita and Virginia—but only in order to move on, to keep on becoming—to that last recognition of the bond to Vita as an imperceptible and all-encompassing life force. A pattern of de-territorialization takes place between them, which runs parallel to and in-and-out of their respective and mutual existences, but certainly does not stop there.

It will have been a joyful and towering passion, though not entirely Virginia's or Vita's or my own, or yours. You cannot have your own "phase of immanence" (or of transcendence, for the phenomenologically-minded) and still hold onto it; you can only share in the composition of one, in the company of others. One does not run with Woolf alone—women, even Virginia Woolf herself—must learn to run with other (s/he)-wolves.

The real-life Vita recognizes this, much as she had acknowledged from the start her friend's superior literary genius. After reading *Orlando*, for which she is the model, she actually fails to cope with the shock:

Vita to Virginia, November, 10, 1928

How could you hang so splendid a garment on so poor a peg? . . . Also, you have invented a new form of narcissism—I confess—I am in love with Orlando—this is a complication I had not foreseen.[32]

The life that Virginia sees in her is something that Vita herself deeply aspires to. This is nothing to do with narcissistic delight—it is actually a sort of yearning on Vita's part for the potential that lies not so much in her as in the encounter between herself and Virginia. It is simultaneously the slightly ashamed recognition of her own limitations ("I'm not that good, really!") and the grateful recognition of what she owes to her lover's passionate enhancement of the life that is in her ("Thank God you saw that in me !").

In other words, the relation between what in psychoanalysis is called the empirical level (the real-life Vita) and its symbolic representation (the leading character in *Orlando*) is no longer adequate to make sense of the intense transformation that takes place around the field of forces that is activated by Virginia & Vita. The empirical psychology of the two women has nothing to do with this; the psychoanalytic notion of identifications is equally inadequate to account for the magnitude of the exchange that takes place between these two high-powered subjects. We are better off seeing Virginia & Vita as a common block of becoming, a plane for the realization of forces that transcend them both and yet require their presence and affinity in order to become actualized. Forces are concentrated, focused, and activated in the space *between* them and aim at the fulfillment of their own *potentia*. These forces are the acceleration of pure becoming.

Vita herself does justice to this process by accepting to become a mere reader and not the main star of the process of becoming-Orlando. Being an aristocrat and a much celebrated author herself in her own right, this displacement required some humility and flexibility on Vita's part, qualities in which we know that she was notoriously deficient. Yet she displays surprising skills of adaptation by letting her narcissism be simultaneously gratified—"I love myself as Orlando!"—and blown to smithereens—"Orlando is the literary creation of a woman who is a much greater writer than I will ever be!"

In the framework of an ethics of joyful affirmation, the dilemma is clear. One oscillates between positive and negative passions: gratification and resentment, gratitude and envy, as Melanie Klein—one of Deleuze's main sources of inspiration—would put it. Ultimately I find that Vita settles for the more ethical option; she transforms negative into positive passions and accepts to go along with the process of alchemical transformation of her own life and image, which Virginia has actualized. Vita, too, goes running with Woolves.

Neither Virginia nor Vita's life was like that; this becoming is not about being faithful to the authority of past experience and the solidity of foundations. It is about inventing it together in the space that is framed by the encounter between the two of them, out of the transitory flows of multiple and incoherent experiences of all kinds, speeds, and intensity, in the spaces where transformation can occur. The life that flew between Vita and Virginia certainly was an intensified and accelerated space of becoming.

In the brand of antiessentialist vitalism that I adopt from Deleuze, that life has no brand name on it. Nor does it flow within the constraints of a phallogocentric scheme of signification that imposes its own code: desire as lack; alterity and /as negativity; the burden of Being that coincides with consciousness. None of this applies any longer. This is why psychoanalysis cannot do justice to the kind of concrete and highly singular process of becoming that I am trying to account for, bending Deleuze for my own needs.

Thus, it is Vita's shameful recognition of her failing, not the jubilant assertion of her triumph that opens the gates through which flows the intensity that shapes the encounter between Virginia & Vita. The moment of negative passion (envy, resentment, feeling of dispossession) is the prelude to the ethical gesture that involves transcending the negativity and accepting the displacement of the self through the impact of an other that is so very close. This is a case of destitution of the ego, not of its triumphant apotheosis. This is also the ethical moment in their interaction, which rescued *Orlando* from being an act of cannibalistic consumption of the other and turns it into one of the greatest love stories of all times. Similarly, Virginia's self-effacement is crucial to the whole process of being able to sustain, provoke, record, and return the life that is in Vita, amplified to the nth power. Such is the task of *potentia*, and such is the genius of Virginia Woolf's writing.

In other words, one's affirmation of the life that one is shot through with is materially embodied and embedded in the singularity that is one's enfleshed self. But this singular entity is collectively defined, interrelational and external; it is impersonal but highly singular because it is crossed over with all sorts of "encounters" with cultural codes, bits and pieces of that sticky social imaginary I mentioned earlier and that constitutes the subject by literally gluing it together, for a while at least. This is not an atomized individual but a moment in a chain of being that passes on, goes through the instance of individuation, but does not stop there; it moves on nomadically, by multiple becomings.

Commenting on Primo Levi's and Virginia Woolf's suicides Deleuze—who will himself choose this way to terminate his own existence—put it very clearly: you can suppress your own life, in its specific and radically immanent form and still affirm the potency of life, especially in cases where deteriorating health or social conditions may seriously hinder your power to affirm and to endure joyfully. This is no Christian affirmation of Life nor transcendental delegation of the meaning and value system to categories higher than the embodied self. Quite on the contrary, it is the intelligence of radically immanent flesh that states with every single breath that the life in you is not marked by any signifier and it most certainly does not bear your name. So what will the skeptic say at this point? Is it not the specific property and quality of the imagination to magnify reality, especially in situations that, as Virginia would put it, are "not untinged with amorosity"?[33] There is something extremely familiar and almost self-evident about these processes of transformation of the self through an other that triggers processes of metamorphosis of the self.

That is precisely the point: this theory of radical immanence is very simple at heart and it is intuitively accessible. What happens is really a relocation of the function of the subject through the joining of memory and the imagination into propelling a vital force that aims at transformation. As a rigorous reader of Spinoza, Deleuze suggests a positive and equal relationship between reason and the imagination. Overthrowing the traditional hierarchy of intellectual and mental faculties, which had discriminated against the imaginative and the oneiric, Deleuze locates the *potentia* of affirmation firmly on the side of the imagination. In so doing, he produces a new theory of desire.

Hence the importance that literature, the arts, theater, music, and film play in his work. They do not fulfill merely an illustrative function; they are rather the privileged field of application for the kind of conceptual creativity that Deleuze would like to make operative also within philosophy. I agree with Deleuze: the result of this process is not (just) feminine writing, or the assertion of feminine specificity. What is expressed is a force of affirmation, the potency of a joy that goes beyond the metaphysical divide of sexual differentiation. And yet, the affirmation of that life force requires as its unalienable and inevitable starting point the process of becoming-woman. It requires it of Virginia & Vita, as it does of Deleuze and any of the readers; sexual difference as a threshold of differentiation remains primary to this process.

The question of the trace of sexual difference and the privileged location of "the feminine" in Deleuze's account of becoming is therefore a very fundamental issue. There are moments, especially in Deleuze's work on literature and art, when he clearly codes as "feminine" that vitalistic, antiessentialist power of affirmation, no matter who or where it happens to actualize itself. Of course the aim is not to affirm the feminine but to open up fields of multiple becomings. It is nonetheless the case that the kind of style and sensibility that sustain this process are unequivocally closer to the feminine.

My conclusion can only be one of sustained ambivalence, in return. The paradoxes of Deleuze's theory of becoming are productive and dynamic. While pleading that they should be inscribed in the contemporary scholarly agenda, I also want to recommend that we all linger a little longer on these productive paradoxes, without rushing headlong into a hasty resolution. Let us endure, instead!

Conclusion

So what does all this have to do with the monstrous social imaginary I started off with? Have we not come too far? I rather think that we are right around the corner. It seems clear to me that a culture that is in the grip of a techno-teratological imaginary at a time of deep social and historical changes is a culture that badly needs *less* abstraction and less hype. We have received our prosthetic promises of perfectibility; now let's hand over our pound of flesh, shall we?

I believe that a concretely embedded reading of the subject as a material, vitalistic, antiessentialist but sustainable entity can be a profoundly sane reminder of the positive virtualities that lie in store in the crisis and transformation we are currently going through. But there is also a question of style, in the sense of a political and aesthetic sensibility. It is crucial to nurture a culture of affirmation and joy, if we are to pull out of the end of millennium stagnation. And there has to be something mere rigorous than "new age" celebration of bodily harmony!

What I also want to argue for in this conclusion is a conceptual, not a polemical recognition of a structural and—in my eyes at least—productive paradox in Deleuze's thought on the issue of the becoming-woman, at a time when the question of his legacy is a very contested one. I am struck by a pattern that is beginning to emerge in the reception of Deleuze's work, which displays such conventional genderized features: is it not astonishing that it is mostly from the areas of feminism and through the voices of

women that the positivity of Deleuze's re-composition of the subject outside the humanistic frame is being asserted? And that the intoxicating,
nihilistic contemplation of the dissipation of life forces is mostly the work
of men? To what an extent does this highly genderized reception merely
restate the genderized dimension of labor that is so dominant in Western
societies: women as the savior of *mankind?*

The *Alien* film series is a perfect example of this trend. It turns the "new
feminist monsters" engendered by late postindustrial technosocieties into
the subjects who are most likely to save humanity from its technoactivated
annihilation. The feminist is the last of the humanists. It would be too sad
an ending, were an intergalactical Joan of Arc bearing Sigourney Weaver's
face to come to represent all that feminism can do for a condemned species.
And what a defeat for the feminists who work with sexual difference, to
have the dialectics of the sexes merely reserved for the benefit of women—
while leaving the power structures completely in place. I wonder whether it
may not be more productive all-round if, practicing a philosophy of enduring sustainable subjectivity, some of us could work toward raising this tension to the level of a genuine paradox and explode it as such.

Feminism is not about a quest for authenticity, or the Golden Fleece of
truth. I think that at the dawn of the new millennium we need to acquire a
flair for complicating the issues so as to live up to the complexities of our
age. I would like feminism to avoid the flat-out recomposition of genderized and racialized power differences on the one hand, and, on the other, the
equally unsatisfactory assumption of a triumphant feminine as showing the
way to the future. Cultivating the art of complexity—and the specific aesthetic and political sensibilities that sustain it—I plead for working with an
idea of the subject as the plane of composition for multiple becomings.

What is at stake, ultimately, is an acceleration that would allow us to jump
over the high fence of the ruins of metaphysics. Not in a utopian mode, but
in a very embodied and embedded way, actualized in the here and now. We
need a process by which "Being" gets dislodged from its fundamentalist
pedestal, starts whirling off its logocentric base—and gets a beat. Losing its
dogmatic authority, "Being" can expose at last the multiple "differences
within"—exposing also its function as the great pretender and stitching
together the different moments it enacts but that it does *not* encompass into
a unity that "Being" would then supervise.

As in Gertrude Stein's operatic prose, the swift exhilaration that
emanates from texts that are clearly indexed on the *potentia* of life, and not

on its diminishment or negation, has to put wings on our feet and infuse joyfulness. If it doesn't have the right beat, it will not work—but if it blasts our minds with excessive intensity, it will not be much good either. Let us just opt for the staggering intelligence of "just a life," as Deleuze put it in the last text he wrote before ending his own slice of life. Just a life in its radical immanence, in affirmation and sets of discontinuous but sustainable becomings.

It may be a way of returning the subject back to the specific complexity of one's singularity—and returning the activity of "thinking" to a lightness of touch, a speed that many of us passionately aspire to. Becoming, over and over again.

NOTES

1. Marina Warner, *Managing Monsters: Six Myths of Our Time*, The 1994 Reith Lectures (London:Vintage Press, 1994), p. 11.

2. Marcia Tucker, "The Attack of the Giant Ninja Mutant Barbies," in *Bad Girls* (New York: New Museum of Contemporary Art/ MIT Press, 1994).

3. See Rosi Braidotti, "Feminist Deleuzian Tracks, or Metaphysics and Metabolism," in *Gilles Deleuze and the Theatre of Philosophy*, ed. C. Boundas and D. Olkowski (London: Routledge, 1995).

4. Mignon Nixon, "Bad Enough Mother," *October* 71 (1995): 71–92.

5. Gilles Deleuze and Félix Guattari, *A Thousand Plateaus: Capitalism & Schizophrenia*, trans. Brian Massumi (Minneapolis: University of Minnesota Press, 1987).

6. I am using "teratological" in the classical sense of a discourse about monstrous beings, from the Greek *teras*, meaning "monster" or "marvel." For more details, see Rosi Braidotti, "Mothers, Monsters, and Machines," in *Nomadic Subjects: Embodiment and Sexual Difference in Contemporary Feminist Theory* (New York: Columbia University Press, 1994) and "Signs of Wonder and Traces of Doubt: On Teratology and Embodied Differences," in *Between Monsters, Goddesses and Cyborgs*, ed. Nina Lykke and Rosi Braidotti (London: Zed Books, 1996).

7. Rosi Braidotti, "Teratologies," in *Deleuze and Feminism*, ed. Claire Colebrook and Ian Buchanan (Edinburgh: Edinburgh University Press, 2000).

8. See Jackie Stacey, *Teratology* (London: Routledge, 1997).

9. The best psychoanalytic rendition of this idea in feminism is to be found in Jane Gallop, "The Monster in the Mirror: The Feminist Critic's Psychoanalysis," in *Feminism and Psychoanalysis*, ed. Richard Feldstein and Judith Roof (Ithaca, N.Y.: Cornell University Press, 1989).

10. Diane Arbus, *Diane Arbus* (New York: Millerton, 1972).

11. Donna Haraway, *Simians, Cyborgs, and Women* (London: Free Association Books, 1990) and "The Promises of Monsters: A Regenerative Politics for Inappropriate/d Others," in *Cultural Studies*, ed. Lawrence Grossberg, Cary Nelson, and Paula A. Treichler (New York: Routledge, 1992).

12. Avtrah Brah, *Cartographies of the Diaspora* (London: Routledge, 1999); Caren Kaplan and Ingrepal Grewal, *Scattered Hegemonies* (Minneapolis: University of Minnesota Press, 1994).

13. See, for instance, Arthur Kroker and Marilouise Kroker, *Body Invaders: Panic Sex in America* (New York: St. Martin's Press, 1987).

14. I have explored further the lines of intersection between Deleuze's polysexuality and feminist attempts to think subjectivity beyond gender polarities in "Feminist Deleuzian Tracks."

15. Deleuze and Guattari, *Thousand Plateaus*, p. 242.

16. I am grateful to Roland Bogue for elucidating this point.

17. Deleuze and Guattari, *Thousand Plateaus*, p. 272.

18. Ibid., p. 275.

19. Michel Foucault, *Surveiller et punir* (Paris: Gallimard, 1975); *Histoire de la sexualité, I: La Volonté de savoir* (Paris: Gallimard, 1976); *Histoire de la sexualité, II: L'Usage des plaisirs* (Paris: Gallimard, 1984); *Histoire de la sexualité, III: Le Souci de soi* (Paris: Gallimard, 1984). For a feminist analysis, see Irene Diamond and Lee Quinby, eds., *Foucault and Feminism* (Boston: Northeastern University Press, 1988), and Lois McNay, *Foucault and Feminism: Power, Gender, and the Self* (Boston: Northeastern University Press, 1993).

20. On this point, see Wendy Brown, "Feminist Hesitations, Postmodern Exposures," *differences* 3 (1991): 63–84.

21. On this point, see Judith Butler, *Subjects of Desire* (New York: Columbia University Press, 1987).

22. Teresa de Lauretis, "The Essence of the Triangle, or Taking the Risk of Essentialism Seriously," in *The Essential Difference*, ed. Naomi Schor and Elizabeth Weed (Bloomington: Indiana University Press, 1994), pp. 1–39.

23. See Virginia Woolf, *The Waves* (Harmondsworth, England: Penguin, 1992), pp. 5–6.

24. For a synthetic introduction to the feminism of sexual difference, see my chapter "Sexual Difference Theory," in *A Companion to Feminist Philosophy*, ed. Iris Young and Alison Jaggar (Oxford: Blackwell, 1998).

25. See the letters of December 13, 1933; February 15, 1935; and November 15, 1937, in *The Letters of Virginia Woolf*, ed. Nigel Nicolson and Joanne Trautmann (London: Hogarth Press, 1975–80); see also the diary entry for July 1934 in *The Diary of Virginia Woolf*, vol. 4, ed. Anne Olivier Bell (London: Hogarth Press, 1977–82).

26. *Diary of Virginia Woolf*, vol. 3, 1925–1930.

27. Catharine R. Stimpson, "The Female Sociograph: The Theater of Virginia

Woolf's Letters," in *Where the Meanings Are: Feminism and Cultural Spaces* (New York: Methuen, 1988).

28. Deleuze and Guattari, *Thousand Plateaus*, p. 130.

29. Quoted in a letter from Vita to Harold, November 20, 1926, in *Vita and Harold: The Letters of Vita Sackville-West and Harold Nicolson*, ed. Nigel Nicolson (New York: Putnam, 1992), p. 173.

30. Letter from Vita to Harold, November 20, 1926, in Nicolson, ed., *Vita and Harold*, p. 173.

31. *Diary of Virginia Woolf*, vol. 3.

32. *The Letters of Vita Sackville-West to Virginia Woolf*, vol. 3, 1923–1928, ed. L. de Salvo and M. A. Leaska (London: Macmillan, 1984).

33. *Diary of Virginia Woolf*, vol. 3, December 12, 1925.

Chapter 15

The End of Sexual Difference?

JUDITH BUTLER

I am not sure that the millennium is a significant way to mark time or, indeed, to mark the time of feminism. But it is always important to take stock of where feminism is, even as that effort at reflection is necessarily marred. No one stands in the perspective that might afford a global view of feminism. No one stands within a definition of feminism that would remain uncontested. I think it is fair to say that feminists everywhere seek a more substantial equality for women, and that they seek a more just arrangement of social and political institutions. But as we make room to consider what we mean, and how we might act, we are confronted quite quickly with the difficulty of the terms that we need to use. Differences emerge over whether

This essay was written in 1996 and has appeared in shorter form, in German, in Jörg Huber and Martin Heller, eds., *Konturen des Unentschiedenen*, Interventionen, 6 (Basel: Strömfeld/Roter Stern; Zürich: Museum für Gestaltung, 1997), and, in Italian, in *Genera e sessualita negli studi critici*, ed. Lucia Re (Milan: Fetrinelli 1997).

equality means that men and women ought to be treated interchangeably. The Parity movement in France has argued that that is not an appropriate notion of equality, given the social disadvantages that women suffer under current political circumstances. We will surely argue as well over justice, and by what means it ought to be achieved. Is it the same as "fair treatment"? Is justice distinct from the conception of equality? What is its relation to freedom? And which freedoms are desired, how are they valued, and what do we make of serious disagreements among women on the question of how sexual freedom is to be defined, and whether it can receive a meaningful international formulation?

Add to these zones of contestation continuing questions about what a woman is, how we are to say "we," who is to say it and in the name of whom, and it seems that feminism is in a mess, unable to stabilize the terms that facilitate a meaningful agenda. Criticisms of feminism as inattentive to questions of race and to the conditions of global inequality that condition its Euro-American articulation continue to put into doubt the broad coalitional power of the movement. And in the United States, the abuse of sexual harassment doctrine by the Conservative Right in its persecutorial inquiries into sex in the workplace presents a serious public-relations problem for feminists on the Left. Indeed, the relation between feminism *and* the Left is another thorny matter, since there are now probusiness forms of feminism that focus on actualizing women's entrepreneurial potential, hijacking models of self-expression from an earlier, progressive period of the movement.

One might be tempted to despair, but I believe that these are among the most interesting and productive unsolved issues at the end of the century. The program of feminism is not one in which we might assume a common set of premises and then proceed to build in logical fashion a program from those premises. Instead, this is a movement that proceeds precisely by bringing critical attention to bear on its premises in an effort to become more clear about what it means, and to begin to negotiate the conflicting interpretations, the irrepressible democratic cacophony of its identity. As a democratic enterprise, feminism has had to forfeit the presumption that at base we can all agree about some things or, equivalently, to embrace the notion that each of our most treasured values are under contestation and that they will remain contested zones of politics. This may sound as if I am saying that feminism can never build from anything, that it will be lost to reflection upon itself, that it will never move beyond this self-reflective moment toward an active engagement with the world. On the contrary, it is precisely in the course of engaged political practices that these forms of internal dissension emerge. And I would argue emphatically that resisting the desire to resolve this dissension into unity is precisely what keeps the movement alive.

I work in the area of feminist theory, which is not distinct from feminism as a social movement. Feminist theory would have no content were there no movement, and the movement, in its various directions and forms, has always been involved in the act of theory. Theory is an activity that does not remain restricted to the academy. It takes place every time a possibility is imagined, a collective self-reflection takes place, or a dispute over values, priorities, and language emerges. I believe that there is importance in overcoming the fear of immanent critique and in maintaining the democratic value of producing a movement that can contain, without domesticating, conflicting interpretations on fundamental issues. As a latecomer to the second wave, I approach feminism with the presumption that no undisputed premises are to be agreed upon in the global context. And so, for practical and political reasons, there is no value to be derived in silencing disputes. The only question is how best to have them, how most productively to stage them, and how to act in ways that acknowledge the irreversible complexity of who we are.

I propose to consider a set of terms in this essay that have come into conflict with one another: sexual difference, gender, and sexuality. My title suggests perhaps that I am announcing the end to "sexual difference" in its presumed facticity or as a useful theoretical entry into questions of feminism. My title is intended as a citation of a skeptical question, one that is often posed to theorists who work on gender or sexuality, a challenge I wish both to understand and to which I propose a response. My purpose is not to win a debate, but to try to understand why the terms are considered so important to those who use them, and how we might reconcile this set of felt necessities as they come into conflict with one another. I am here as interested in the theoretical reasons proffered for using one framework at the expense of another as in the institutional possibilities that the terms alternately open and foreclose in varying contexts.

I do not ask the question about the end of sexual difference in order to make a plea for that end. I do not even propose to enumerate reasons why I think that framework, or that "reality," depending on your take, is no longer worth pursuing. For many, I think, the structuring reality of sexual difference is not one that one can wish away or argue against, or even make claims about in any reasonable way. It is more like a necessary background to the possibility of thinking, of language, of being a body in the world. And those who seek to take issue with it are arguing with the very structure that makes their argument possible. There is sometimes a laughing and dismissive response to the problem: you think that you might do away with sexual difference, but your very desire to do away with it is only further evidence of its enduring force and efficacy. Defenders of sexual difference make dismissive reference to the famous feminine "protest" elaborated by psychoanalysis, and in this way the protest is defeated before it is articulated. To challenge the notion of femininity is the consummately feminine act, a protest that can be read as evidence for that which it seeks to contest. Sexual difference—is it to be thought of as a framework by which we are defeated in advance? Anything that might be said against it is oblique proof that it structures what we say. Is it there in a primary sense, haunting the primary differentiations or structural fate by which all signification proceeds?

Luce Irigaray makes clear that sexual difference is not a fact, not a bedrock of any sorts, nor the recalcitrant "real" of Lacanian parlance. On the contrary, it is a question, a question for our times. As a question, it remains unsettled and unresolved, that which is not yet or not ever formulated in terms of an assertion. Its presence does not assume the form of facts and structures but persists as that which makes us wonder, that which remains not fully explained and not fully explicable. If it is the question for our time, as she insists in *The Ethics of Sexual Difference,*[1] then it is not one question among others but a particularly dense moment of irresolution within language, one that marks the contemporary horizon of language as our own. Like Drucilla Cornell, the ethics that Irigaray has in mind is not one that follows *from* sexual difference but is a question that is posed by the very terms of sexual difference itself: how to cross this otherness? How to cross it without crossing it, without domesticating its terms? How to remain attuned to what remains permanently unsettled about the question?

Irigaray then would not argue for or against sexual difference, but, rather, she offers us a way to think about the question that sexual difference poses, or the question that sexual difference *is*, a question whose irresolution forms a certain historical trajectory for us, those who find ourselves asking this question, those of whom this question is posed. The arguments in favor and against would be so many indications of the persistence of this question, a persistence whose status is not eternal but one, she claims, that belongs to *these times*. It is a question that Irigaray poses of modernity, a question that marks modernity for her. Thus, it is a question that inaugurates a certain problematic of time, a question whose answer is not forthcoming, a question that opens up a time of irresolution and marks that time of irresolution as our own.

I think for many of us it is a sad time for feminism, even a defeated time. A friend recently asked what I would teach in a feminist theory course right now, and I found myself suggesting that feminist theory has no other work than in responding to the places where feminism is under challenge. And by responding to those challenges, I do not mean a defensive shoring up of terms and commitments, reminding ourselves of what we already know, but something quite different, something like a submission to the demand for rearticulation, a demand that emerges from crisis. It makes no sense, I would argue, to hold fast to theoretical paradigms and preferred terminologies, to make the case for feminism on the basis of sexual difference, or to defend that notion against the claims of gender, the claims of sexuality, the claims of race, or the umbrella claims of cultural studies. I begin with Irigaray because I think her invocation of sexual difference is something other than foundational. Sexual difference is not a given, not a premise, not a basis on which to build a feminism; it is not that which we have already encountered and come to know; rather, as *a question* that prompts a feminist inquiry, it is something that cannot quite be stated, that troubles the grammar of the statement, and that remains, more or less permanently, to interrogate.

When Irigaray refers to the question of sexual difference as a question for our times, she appears to refer to modernity. I confess to not knowing what modernity is, but I do know that many intellectuals are very worked up about the term, defending it or decrying it. Most recently, I note that those who are considered at odds with modernity, or are considered postmodern, get characterized in the following way: "calls into question or debunks terms such as reason, the subject, authenticity, universality, the progressive view of history." What always strikes me about these kinds of generalizations is that "calling into question" is assumed to mean "debunk" (rather than, say, revitalize) and that the question of the question is never given much play. If one calls such terms into question, does that mean that they cannot be used anymore? Does it mean that one is now prohibited from such a term by the superego of theoretical postmodernism or that they are proclaimed as exhausted and finished? Or is it simply that the terms do not function in quite the same way as they once did?

Recently, at a panel in which I had the occasion to discuss Leo Bersani's book *Homos*, I realized that he was no longer sure whether he could say that lesbians were women, and I found myself reassuring him that no one had issued a prohibition on the use of the word. I certainly have no qualms about using such terms, and will end this essay, after a reflection on some international debates, with a reflection on how one might continue *at the same time* to interrogate and to use the terms of universality. If the notion of the subject, for instance, is no longer given, no longer presumed, that does not mean that it has no meaning for us, that it ought no longer to be uttered. On the contrary, it means only that the term is not simply a building block on which we rely, an uninterrogated premise for political argument. Rather, the term has become an object of theoretical attention, something for which we are compelled to give an account. I suppose that this places me on the divide of the modern/postmodern in which such terms remain in play, but no longer in a foundational mode.

Others have argued that all the key terms of modernity are premised on the exclusion of women, of people of color, that they are wrought along class lines and with strong colonial interests. But it would also be important to add, following Paul Gilroy in *The Black Atlantic: Modernity and Double Consciousness*,[2] that the struggle against those exclusions very often end up reappropriating those very terms from modernity, appropriating them precisely to initiate an entrance into modernity as well as the transformation of modernity's parameters. Freedom comes to signify what it never signified before; justice comes to embrace precisely what could not be contained under its description.

Gilroy argues that the exclusion of people of African descent from European modernity is not a sufficient reason to reject that modernity, for the terms of modernity have been and still can be appropriated from their exclusionary Eurocentrism and made to operate in the service of a more inclusive democracy. At stake in his subtle historiography is the question of whether the conditions of reciprocal recognition by which the "human" comes into being can be extended beyond the geopolitical sphere presumed by the discourse of equality and reciprocity. And though Hegel gives us the strange scene of the lord and bondsman, a scene that vacillates between a description of serfdom and slavery, it is not until the work of W. E. B. Du Bois, Orlando Patterson, and Paul Gilroy that we start to understand how the Hegelian project of reciprocal recognition might be renarrated from the history of slavery and its diasporic effects.

Gilroy argues that the perspective of slavery "requires a discrete view not just of the dynamics of power and domination in plantation societies dedicated to the pursuit of commercial profit but of such central categories of the Enlightenment project as the idea of universality, the fixity of meaning, the coherence of the subject, and, of course, the foundational ethnocentrism in which these have all tended to be anchored."[3] Less predictably, Gilroy then argues that it would be a great mistake to dismiss the project of modernity. Citing Habermas, he notes that even those who have been most radically excluded from the European project of modernity have been able to appropriate essential concepts from the theoretical arsenal of modernity to fight for their rightful inclusion in the process. "A concept of modernity worth its salt," he writes, "ought, for example, to have something to contribute to an analysis of how the particular varieties of radicalism articulated through the revolts of enslaved people made selective use of the ideologies of the Western Age of Revolution and then flowed into social movements of an anti-colonial and decidedly anti-capitalist type."[4]

Gilroy takes issue with what he calls postmodern forms of skepticism that lead to a full-scale rejection of the key terms of modernity and, in his view, a paralysis of political will. But he then also takes his distance from Habermas, noting that Habermas fails to take into account the relationship between slavery and modernity. Habermas's failure, he notes, can be attributed to his preference for Kant over Hegel. Gilroy writes, "Habermas does not follow Hegel in arguing that slavery is itself a modernising force in that it leads both master and servant first to self-consciousness and then to disillusion, forcing both to confront the unhappy realisation that the true, the good, and the beautiful do not have a shared origin."[5] Gilroy proceeds to read Frederick Douglass, for instance, as "lord and bondsman in a black idiom" and then to read the contemporary black feminist theorist Patricia Hill Collins as seeking to extend the Hegelian project into that of a racialized standpoint epistemology. In these and other instances, he insists that the Eurocentric discourse has been taken up profitably by those who were traditionally excluded from its terms, and that the subsequent revision carries radical consequences for the rethinking of modernity in nonethnocentric terms. Gilroy's fierce opposition to forms of black essentialism, most specifically, Afrocentrism, makes this point from another angle.

One of the most interesting philosophical consequences of Gilroy's work is that he provides a cultural and historical perspective on current debates in philosophy that threaten to displace its terms. Whereas he rejects the hyperrationalism of the Habermasian project, even as he preserves certain key features of its description of the Enlightenment project, he also rejects forms of skepticism that reduce all political positioning to rhetorical gesture. The form of cultural reading he provides attends to the rhetorical dimension of all sorts of cultural texts and labors under the aegis of a more radically democratic modernity. Thus, his, I would suggest, is a position that is worth considering as one rehearses the debates between the defenders and detractors of the Enlightenment project.

Such debates clearly predominate discussions in feminist theory, which are not always distinct from the subject of race. The terms that we use in the course of political movements that have been appropriated by the Right or for misogynist purposes are not, for that reason, strategically out of bounds. These terms are never finally and fully tethered to a single use. The task of reappropriation is to illustrate the vulnerability of these often compromised terms to an unexpected progressive possibility; such terms belong to no one in particular; they assume a life and a purpose that exceed the uses to which they have been consciously put. They are not to be seen as merely tainted goods, too bound up with the history of oppression, but neither are they to be regarded as having a pure meaning that might be distilled from their various usages in political contexts. The task, it seems, is to compel the terms of modernity to embrace those they have traditionally excluded, where the embrace does not work to domesticate and neutralize the newly avowed term; such terms should remain problematic for the existing notion of the polity, should expose the limits of its claim to universality, compel a radical rethinking of its parameters. For a term to be made part of a polity that has been conventionally excluded is for it to emerge as a threat to the coherence of the polity, and for the polity to survive that threat without annihilating the term. The term would then open up a different temporality for the polity, establishing for that polity an unknown future, provoking anxiety in those who seek to patrol its conventional boundaries. If there can be a modernity without foundationalism, then it will be one in which the key terms of its operation are not fully secured in advance, one that assumes a futural form for politics that cannot be fully anticipated, a politics of hope and anxiety.

The desire not to have an open future can be a strong one, threatening one with loss, loss of certainty about how things are. It is important, however, not to underestimate the force of the desire to foreclose futurity and the political potential of anxiety.[6] This is one reason that asking certain questions is considered dangerous. Imagine the situation of reading a book and thinking, I cannot ask the questions that are posed here because to ask them is to introduce doubt into my political convictions, and to introduce doubt into my political convictions could lead to the dissolution of those convictions. At such a moment, the fear of thinking, indeed, the fear of the question, becomes moralized as the defense of politics. And politics becomes that which requires a certain anti-intellectualism. To remain unwilling to rethink one's politics on the basis of questions posed is to opt for a dogmatic stand at the cost of both life and thought.

To question a term, a term such as "feminism," is to ask how it plays, what investments it bears, what aims it achieves, what alterations it undergoes. The changeable life of that term does not preclude its use. If a term such as "feminism" becomes questionable, does that mean it cannot be used any longer, and that we can only use terms that we *already know how to master*? Why is it that posing a question about a term is considered the same as effecting a prohibition against its use? Why is it that we sometimes do feel that if a term is dislodged from its foundational place, we will not be able to live, to survive, to use language, to speak for ourselves? What kind of guarantee does the foundational fix exercise, and what sort of terror does it forestall? Is it that in the foundational mode, terms are assumed, terms such as "the subject" and "universality," and the sense in which they "must" be assumed is a *moral* one, taking the form of an imperative, and like some moral interdictions, a defense against what terrifies us most? Are we not paralyzed by a kind of moral compulsion that keeps us from interrogating the terms, taking the risk of living the terms that we keep in question?[7]

As a way of showing how passions for foundations and methods sometimes get in the way of an analysis of contemporary political culture, I propose to consider the way in which the efforts to secure a theoretical basis for political struggle often read precisely in opposition to the travels of certain key political signifiers within contemporary public culture. The most confusing for me has to do with the status of the term "gender" in relation to feminism, on the one hand, and lesbian and gay studies, on the other. I was surprised, perhaps naively, to understand from my queer studies friends that a proposed methodology for gay and lesbian studies accepts the notion that whereas feminism is said to have *gender* as its object of inquiry, lesbian and gay studies is said to have *sex and sexuality* as its "proper" objects. Gender, we are told, is not to be mistaken for sexuality, which seems right in a certain way, but imagine then my shock when the Vatican announced that "gender" ought to be struck from the NGO (Non-Governmental Organization) platform on the status of women because it is nothing other than a code for homosexuality![8] Added to my worries is that some of my closest associates within feminist theory scorn the notion of gender. They claim that sexual difference is the preferred term to gender, that "sexual difference" indicates a fundamental difference, and that gender indicates a merely constructed or variable effect.

The United Nations Meeting on the Status of Women in Beijing in 1995 exhibited yet another challenge to academic commitments. In particular, what is the status of universal claims within the domain of international human rights work? Although many feminists have come to the conclusion that the universal is always a cover for a certain epistemological imperialism, insensitive to cultural texture and difference, the rhetorical power of claiming universality for, say, rights of sexual autonomy and related rights of sexual orientation within the international human rights domain appears indisputable.

Consider first the surprising use of gender in the UN context. The Vatican not only denounced the term "gender" as a code for homosexuality but insisted that the platform language return to the notion of sex, in an apparent effort to secure a link between femininity and maternity as a naturally and divinely ordained necessity. In late April 1995, in preparation for the Non-Governmental Organization meetings in Beijing (or, rather, outside Beijing)—called the prepcom—several member states, under the guidance of the Catholic Church, sought to expunge the word "gender" from the Platform for Action and to replace it with the word "sex"; this was called by some on the prepcom committee an "insulting and demeaning attempt to reverse the gains made by women, to intimidate us and to block further progress."[9] They wrote further: "We will not be forced back into the 'biology is destiny' concept that seeks to define, confine, and reduce women and girls to their physical sexual characteristics. We will not let this happen—not in our homes, our workplaces, our communities, our countries and certainly not at the United Nations, to which women around the world look for human rights, justice, and leadership."

The statement goes on to note:

The meaning of the word "gender" has evolved as differentiated from the word "sex" to express the reality that women's and men's roles and status are socially constructed and subject to change. In the present context, "gender" recognizes the multiple roles that females fill through our life cycles, the diversity of our needs, concerns, abilities,

life experiences and aspirations.... The concept of "gender" is embedded in contemporary social, political and legal discourse. It has been
integrated into the conceptual planning, language, documents and
programmes of the UN system. The infusion of gender perspectives
into all aspects of UN activities is a major commitment approved at
past conferences and it must [be] reaffirmed and strengthened at the
4th world conference.[10]

This debate led Russell Baker in the *New York Times* to wonder if the term
"gender" hasn't so supplanted the notion of sex that we will soon find ourselves in relation to our erotic lives confessing to having had "gender" with
someone.

As gender became intensified at the UN discussion as a code for homosexuality, the local fields of queer theory and feminism were taking quite a
different direction—at least apparently. The analogy offered by methodolog-
ically minded queer theorists in which feminism is said to be concerned
with gender, and lesbian and gay studies with sex and sexuality, seems far
afield from the above debate. But it is surprising to see that in the one case
gender appears to stand for homosexuality, and in the other, it seems to be
its opposite.

My point is not simply that academic debate seems woefully out of sync
with the contemporary political usage of such terms, but that the effort to
take distance from gender marks two political movements that are in many
ways opposed to one another. In the international debate, the Vatican
denounces the use of the term "gender" because it is either (1) a code for
homosexuality, or (2) offers a way for homosexuality to be understood as one
gender among others, threatening to take its place among masculine, feminine, bisexual, and transsexual or, more likely, threatening to take the place of
male and female altogether. The Vatican fears—and they cite Anne Fausto-
Sterling[11] on this matter—that homosexuality implies the proliferation of
genders. (*La Repubblica* claims that in the United States the number of genders has leaped to five: masculine, feminine, lesbian, homosexual, transsexual.)
This view of homosexuality as proliferating gender seems to be based on the
notions that homosexuals have in some sense departed from their sex, that in
becoming homosexuals, they cease to be men or women, and that gender as
we know it is radically incompatible with homosexuality; indeed, it is so
incompatible that homosexuality must become its own gender, thus displacing the binary opposition between masculine and feminine altogether.

Interestingly, the Vatican seems to share a certain presupposition with those who would make queer studies into a methodology distinct from feminism: whereas the Vatican fears that sexuality threatens to displace sex as the reproductive aim and necessity of heterosexuality, those who accept the methodological division between queer theory and feminism hold out the promise that sexuality might exceed and displace gender. Homosexuality in particular leaves gender behind. The two are not only separable but persist in a mutually exclusive tension in which queer sexualities aspire to a utopian life beyond gender, as Biddy Martin has so ably suggested.[12] The Vatican seeks to undo gender in an effort to rehabilitate sex, but method-oriented queer theory seeks to undo gender in an effort to foreground sexuality. The Vatican fears the separation of sexuality from sex, for that introduces a notion of sexual practice that is not constrained by putatively natural reproductive ends. And in this sense it appears that the Vatican, in fearing gender, fears the separation of sexuality from sex, and so fears queer theory. Queer methodology, however, insists on sexuality and even, in *The Lesbian and Gay Studies Reader*, on "sexuality and sex," evacuating gender as well, but only because gender stands for feminism and its presumptive heterosexuality.[13]

In both contexts, there are debates about terminology: whether the term "gender" could be allowed into the platform language for the non-governmental organization meetings, whether the term "sexual orientation" would be part of the final language of the UN conference resolutions (the answer to the first is "yes" and to the second "no," but language regarding sexual autonomy was deemed acceptable). Terms such as "gender," "sexual orientation," and even "universality" were contested publicly precisely on the question of what they will mean, and a special UN meeting was convened in July 1996 to come up with an understanding of what "gender" means.

My view is that no simple definition of gender will suffice, and that more important than coming up with a strict and applicable definition is the ability to track the travels of the term through public culture. As I write this, the term "gender" has become a site of contest for various interests. Consider the domestic U.S. example in which "gender" is often perceived as a way to defuse the political dimension of feminism, so that "gender" becomes a merely discursive marking of masculine and feminine, understood as constructions that might be studied outside a feminist framework or simple self-productions, manufactured cultural effects of some kind. Gender Studies programs (and not only in the United States) were sometimes established as ways to legitimate an academic domain by refusing to

engage recent polemics against feminism. The introduction of gender studies programs and centers in Eastern Europe made sense to many as a way to
overcome the alliance of "feminism" with a Marxist state ideology that held
that feminist aims were understood to be achievable only on the condition
of the realization of communist aims.

As if that struggle internal to the gender arena were not enough, the
challenge of an Anglo-European theoretical perspective within the academy
casts doubt on the value of the overly sociological construal of the term:
"gender" is thus opposed in the name of sexual difference precisely because
gender endorses a socially constructivist view of masculinity and femininity, displacing or devaluing the *symbolic* status of sexual difference and the
political specificity of the feminine. Here I am thinking of criticisms that
have been leveled against the term by Naomi Schor, Rosi Braidotti, Elizabeth Grosz, and others.

In the meantime, sexual difference is clearly out of favor within some
reigning paradigms in queer theory. Indeed, even as queer theory is seeking
to establish the anachronism of feminism, feminism is described as a project
unambiguously committed to gender. Within critical race studies one finds,
I believe, very little reference to "sexual difference" as a term.[14]

But what is this sexual difference? It is not a simple facticity, but neither
is it simply an effect of facticity. If it is psychic, it is also social, and in a sense
that is not yet elaborated. Much recent scholarship seeks to understand how
psychic structure becomes implicated in dynamics of social power. How are
we to understand this conjuncture or disjuncture, and what has it to do with
the theorization of sexual difference?

I want to suggest that the debates concerning the theoretical priority of
sexual difference to gender, of gender to sexuality, of sexuality to gender, are
all cross-cut by another kind of problem, a problem that sexual difference
poses, namely, the permanent difficulty of determining where the biological, the psychic, the discursive, the social begin and end. If the Vatican seeks
to replace the language of gender with the language of sex, it is because the
Vatican wishes to rebiologize sexual difference, that is, to reestablish a biologically narrow notion of reproduction as women's social fate. And yet,
when Rosi Braidotti, for instance, insists that we return to sexual difference,
it is rather different than the Vatican's call for such a return; if for her sexual
difference is a "difference" that is irreducible to biology and irreducible to
culture or to social construction, then how are we to understand the ontological register of sexual difference? Perhaps it is precisely that sexual differ-

ence registers ontologically in a way that is permanently difficult to determine.[15] Sexual difference is neither fully given nor fully constructed, but partially both. If that sense of "partially" resists any clear sense of "partition," then sexual difference operates as a chiasm, but the terms that overlap or blur are perhaps less importantly masculine or feminine than the problematic of construction itself; what is constructed is of necessity prior to construction, even as there appears no access to this prior moment except through construction.

As I understand it, sexual difference is the site where a question concerning the relation of the biological to the cultural is posed and reposed, where it must and can be posed, but where it cannot, strictly speaking, be answered. Understood as a border concept, sexual difference has psychic, somatic, and social dimensions that are never quite collapsible into one another but are not for that reason ultimately distinct. Does sexual difference vacillate there, as a vacillating border, demanding a rearticulation of those terms without any sense of finality? Is it, therefore, not a thing, not a fact, not a presupposition, but, rather, a demand for rearticulation that never quite vanishes—but also never quite appears?

What does this way of thinking sexual difference do to our understanding of gender? Is what we mean by gender that part of sexual difference that *does* appear as the social (gender is thus the extreme of sociality in sexual difference), as the negotiable, as the constructed; is it precisely what the Vatican seeks to restore to "sex"—to the site of the natural, where the natural itself is figured as fixed and nonnegotiable? Is the Vatican's project as unrealizable as the project to produce gender ex nihilo either from the resources of culture or from some fabulous will? Is the queer effort to override gender, or to relegate it to the superseded past as the proper object of some other inquiry, feminist, that is not its own, is this not an effort to still sexual difference as that which is radically separable from sexuality? The regulation of gender has always been part of the work of heterosexist normativity, and to insist upon a radical separation of gender and sexuality is to miss the opportunity to analyze that particular operation of homophobic power.[16]

From quite separate quarters, the effort to associate gender with nefarious feminist aims continues along other lines. In a disturbing cooptation of anti-imperialist discourse, the Vatican went so far as to suggest that "gender" was an import from decadent strains within Western feminism, one imposed on "third world countries," often used interchangeably with the term "developing countries."

Although it is clear that "gender" did become a rallying point for some feminist organizing at the UN conferences, it became most tense as an issue that emerged when a Honduran women's group objected to the appointment of an ultraconservative Christian delegation to represent the Honduran government at the September conference. Led by Oscar Rodriguez, the president of the Latin American Episcopal conference, the attempt to oppose a kind of feminism labeled as "Western" was opposed by grass-roots movements within the country, including the vocal Women's Rights Centre in Honduras.[17] Thus, the state apparatus, in conjunction with the Church, appropriates an anticultural imperialist language in order to disempower women in its own country. Apart from claiming that Beijing was going to represent a feminism that was "a culture of death" and one that viewed "motherhood as slavery," this still unnamed form of feminism also claimed that the concerns of the Beijing conference represented a false feminism (the Vatican as well, in its letter of apology for its own patriarchalism, sought to distinguish between a feminism that remained committed to the essence of the dignity of women and a feminism that would destroy maternity and destroy sexual difference). Both Rodriguez and the Vatican took aim at "unnatural genders" as well, homosexuals and transsexuals. The Women's Rights Centre (CDM) responded by pointing out that it was not interested in destroying maternity, but was fighting for mothers to be free of abuse, and that the focus of the Beijing conference was not "unnatural genders" but "the effects of structural adjustment plans on women's economic status, and violence against women." Significantly, the Christian group representing Honduras was also vocally antiabortion; for them, the link between unnatural genders, the destruction of maternity, and the promotion of abortion rights was clear.

In the platform language, "gender" was finally allowed to stay, but "lesbian" had to remain in "brackets." Indeed, I saw some delegates in San Francisco preparing for the meetings by wearing T-shirts with "lesbian" in brackets. The brackets are, of course, supposed to signal that this is disputed language, that there is no agreement on the appropriate use of this term, and though they are supposed to relieve the word of its power, calling into question its admissability, they offer up the term as a diacritically compounded phrase, one that achieves a kind of hypervisibility by virtue of its questionability.

The term "lesbian" went from this bracketed form to being dropped from the language altogether. But the success of this strategy seemed only to stoke the suspicion that the term was reappearing at other linguistic sites: through the word "gender," through the discourse of motherhood, through references to sexual autonomy, and even to the phrase "other status"—understood as a basis on which rights could be violated. The "other status" indicated a status that could not be named directly but that designated lesbians through the obliquity of the phrase: you know, that status that is "other," the one that is not speakable here, the one that has been rendered unspeakable here, the status that is not one.

Within the discursive frame of this international meeting, it seems crucial to ask what it is that occasions the linking of the inclusion of lesbian rights with the production of unnatural gender and the destruction of maternity as well as with the introduction of a "culture of death" (presumably antilife; a familiar Rightist translation of what it is to be prochoice). Clearly, those who would oppose lesbian rights on this basis (and there were others who opposed them on other bases) either assume that lesbians are not mothers or, if they are, they are nevertheless participating in the destruction of maternity. So be it.

Importantly, though, I think we see in this scene a number of issues simultaneously at play that are not easily separable from one another. The presumption that "gender" is a code for "homosexuality," that the introduction of "lesbian" is the introduction of a new gender, an unnatural one, and that it will result in the destruction of maternity, understood as linked with feminist struggles for reproductive rights, is at once irreducibly homophobic and misogynist. Moreover, the argument that sexual rights are a Western imposition, advanced by a church/state alliance and echoed by the U.S. delegation as well, was used most forcefully to debunk and contain the claims of the grass-roots women's movement in Latin America to represent women at the conference. Hence, we see an augmentation of church/state ideological power over the women's movement precisely through the appropriation of an anti-imperialist discourse from such movements.

Over and against a church/state alliance that sought to rehabilitate and defend traditional ethnic purities in an effort to impede claims of sexual autonomy, an alliance emerged at the meetings between feminists seeking language supporting reproductive rights, women's rights to be free of abuse within marriage, and lesbian rights.

Significantly, the organizing at both conferences on the issue of sexual orientation did not, as the Vatican presumed it would, take cover behind the term "gender"; "sexual orientation," for all its legal and medical strangeness as a term, and "lesbian" became the language that the International Gay and Lesbian Human Rights Commission sought to have included among the bases on which human rights violations against women can take place.

What does seem noteworthy, though, is that the UN conference did achieve consensus on language. The language is rhetorically important because it represents the prevailing international consensus on the issue and can be used by both governmental and non-governmental agencies in various countries to advance policies that are consistent with the wording of paragraph 97:

> the human rights of women include their right to have control over and decide freely and responsibly on matters related to their sexuality, including sexual and reproductive health, free of coercion, discrimination, and violence. Equal relationships between women and men in matters of sexual relations and reproduction, including full respect for the integrity of the person, require mutual respect, consent and shared responsibility for sexual behaviors and its consequences.

Lastly, then, it seems important to ask about the status of the UN language itself, a language that is supposed to be wrought from international consensus, not unanimity, one that is supposed to represent the consensus on what are universally acceptable claims, universally presumed rights. That what is permitted within the term "universal" is understood to be dependent on a "consensus" appears to undercut some of the force of universality itself. But perhaps not. The process presumes that what will and will not be included within the language of universal entitlement is not settled once and for all, that its future shape cannot be fully anticipated at this time. The UN deliberations became the site for the public ritual that articulates and rearticulates this consensus on what will be the limits of universality.

The meaning of "the universal" proves to be culturally variable, and the specific cultural articulations of "the universal" work against its claim to a transcultural status. This is not to say that there ought to be no reference to the universal or that it has become, for us, an impossibility. On the contrary. All it means is that there are cultural conditions for its articulation that are not always the same, and that the term gains its meaning for us precisely through the decidedly less than universal cultural conditions of its articulation. This is a paradox that any injunction to adopt a universal attitude will encounter. For it may be that in one culture a set of rights are considered to be universally endowed, and that in another those very rights mark the limit to universalizability, i.e., "if we grant those rights to those people we will be undercutting the foundations of the universal as we know it." This has become especially clear to me in the field of lesbian and gay human rights where "the universal" is a contested term and where various governments and various mainstream human rights groups voice doubt over whether lesbian and gay humans ought properly to be included in "the human," whether their putative rights fit within the existing conventions governing the scope of rights considered universal.

It is for me no surprise that the Vatican refers to the possible inclusion of lesbian rights as "antihuman." Perhaps that is true; to admit the lesbian into the realm of the universal might be to undo the human, at least in its present form, but it might also be to imagine the human beyond its conventional limits.

Here the notion of universality is not a foundation upon which to build nor is it a presumption that allows us to proceed; it is a term that has become scandalous, threatening to include in the human the very "other" against which the human was defined. In this sense, in this more radical usage, "universality" works against and destroys the foundations that have become conventionally accepted as foundations. "Universality" becomes an antifoundationalism. To claim a set of rights as universal, even when existing conventions governing the scope of universality preclude precisely such a claim, is both to destroy a concept of the universal, by admitting what has been its "constitutive outside," and in so doing to perform the reverse of any act of assimilation to an *existing* norm. I would insist that such a claim runs the productive risk of provoking and demanding a radical rearticulation of universality itself, forcing the universal into brackets, as it were, into an important sense of unknowingness about what it is, what it might include.

To be excluded from the universal, and yet to make a claim within its terms, is to utter a performative contradiction of a certain kind. One might seem foolish and self-defeating, as if such a claim can only be met with derision; or the wager might work the other way, as part of what is most crucial to the continuing revision and elaboration of historical standards of universality proper to the futural movement of democracy itself. To claim that the universal has not yet been articulated is to insist that the "not yet" is proper to an understanding of the universal itself: that which remains "unrealized" by the universal constitutes it essentially. The universal begins to become articulated precisely through challenges to its *existing* formulation, and this challenge emerges from those who are not covered by it, who have no entitlement to occupy the place of the "who," but who, nevertheless, demand that the universal as such ought to be inclusive of them. The excluded, in this sense, constitutes the contingent limit of universalization. This time around, the brackets fell from "lesbian" only to be consigned to "other status," the status of what remains other to language as we speak it, the otherness by which the speakable is instituted, that haunts its boundaries, threatens to enter the speakable through substitutions that cannot always be detected. Although gender was not the means by which homosexuality entered the official UN language, sexual freedom did become such a term, a rubric that brought lesbians and heterosexual women together for a time, one that gave value to autonomy and refused a return to any notion of fated biology. The sexual freedom of the female subject challenged the humanism that underwrites universality, suggesting that we might reconsider the power of social forms, such as the patriarchal heterosexual family, that still underwrite our "formal" conceptions of universality.

The human, it seems, must become strange to itself, even monstrous, to reachieve the human on another plane. This human will not be "one," indeed, will have no ultimate form, but it will be one that is constantly negotiating sexual difference in a way that has no natural or necessary consequences for the social organization of sexuality. By insisting that this will be a persistent and open question, I mean only to suggest that we make no decision on what sexual difference is, but leave that question open, troubling, unresolved, propitious.

NOTES

1. Luce Irigaray, *An Ethics of Sexual Difference*, trans. Carolyn Burke and Gillian C. Gill (Ithaca, N.Y.: Cornell University Press, 1993).

2. Paul Gilroy, *The Black Atlantic: Modernity and Double Consciousness* (Cambridge: Harvard University Press, 1993).

3. Ibid., p. 55.

4. Ibid., p. 44.

5. Ibid., p. 50.

6. I thank Homi Bhabha for this point.

7. Part of this discussion appeared in Judith Butler, *Excitable Speech: A Politics of the Performative* (New York: Routledge, 1997).

8. "La Chiesa si prepara alle guerre dei 5 sessi," *La Repubblica*, May 20, 1995, p. 11.

9. "IPS: Honduras Feminists and Church," InterPress Service, May 25, 1995.

10. *Report of the Informal Contact Group on Gender,* July 7, 1995.

11. See Anne Fausto-Sterling, "The Five Sexes: Why Male and Female Are Not Enough," *The Sciences* 33, no. 2 (1993): 20–25.

12. Biddy Martin, "Extraordinary Homosexuals and the Fear of Being Ordinary," *differences* 6, nos. 2 and 3 (1994): 100–125.

13. Henry Abelove, Michele Aina Barale, and David M. Halperin, eds., *The Lesbian and Gay Studies Reader* (New York: Routledge, 1993).

14. Whereas feminism is key, and the concept of "women" and even "womanist" are often central, the emphasis—in the work of Kimberle Crenshaw and Mari Matsuda—is more pervasively on the epistemological vantage point of those who are structurally subordinated and marginalized through their racialization. The emphasis on the social character of this subordination is nearly absolute, except for some psychoanalytic efforts to delineate the psychic workings of racialization, which understand becoming "raced" as an interpellation with resounding psychic effects. The salience of this last issue is found, I think, in what has become a veritable return to Fanon within contemporary race studies. And there, the emphasis is not social in a restricted sense but on a socially articulated imaginary, the specular production of racial expectations, the visual estrangement and visceral workings of the racial signifier. Where sexual difference enters, as it does, say, in the work of Rey Chow, it is to underscore the misogynistic consequences of Fanon's resistance to racism. More recently, Homi Bhabha has suggested in a Fanonian analysis of the white male subject that the splitting is to be understood in terms of a homophobic paranoia, one in which the threatened and externalizing relation to alterity forecloses homosexuality and sexual difference at once.

15. This was a suggestion made to me by Debra Keates's entry on sexual difference in *Psychoanalysis and Feminism: A Critical Dictionary,* ed. Elizabeth Wright (Oxford: Blackwell, 1992).

16. I have recently laid out my theoretical difficulties with this way of understanding the disjunctive relation between gender and sexuality in *differences.* I will try, though, to recapitulate briefly the terms of that argument. Whereas "sex and sexuality" have been offered as the proper objects for lesbian and gay studies, and this has been analogized with feminism whose proper object is described as "gender," it seems to me that most feminist research would not fall under this description, and that feminism for the most part insists that sexual and gender relations, although in no sense causally linked, are structurally linked in important ways. A characterization of feminism as an exclusive focus on gender also misrepresents the recent history of feminism in several significant ways: (1) the history of radical feminist sexual politics is erased from the proper characterization of feminism; (2) the various antiracist positions developed within feminist frameworks for which gender is no more central than race, or for which gender is no more central than colonial positionality, or

class—the entire movements of socialist feminism, postcolonial feminism, Third World feminism—are no longer part of the central or proper focus of feminism; (3) MacKinnon's account of gender and sexuality is taken as paradigmatic of feminism, the one in which she does understand gender as the categories "women" and "men" that reflect and institutionalize positions of subordination and domination within a social arrangement of sexuality that is always presumed to be heterosexual; the strong feminist opposition to her work is excluded from the offered definition of feminism; (4) gender is reduced to sex (and sometimes to sex-assignment), rendered fixed or "given," and the contested history of the sex/gender distinction is displaced from view; (5) the normative operation of gender in the regulation of sexuality is denied; and (6) the sexual contestation of gender norms is no longer an "object" of analysis within either frame, as it crosses and confounds the very domains of analysis that this methodological claim for lesbian and gay studies strains to keep apart.

The significant differences between feminists who make use of the category of gender, and those who remain within the framework of sexual difference is erased from view by this intellectually untenable formulation of what feminism is. And how would we understand the history of black feminism, the pervasive intersectionality of those concerns, were we to accept what is a white feminist concern with gender as an isolable category of analysis?

17. InterPress Third World News Agency, Internet.

Chapter 16

A Return for the Future:
Interview with Drucilla Cornell

DRUCILLA CORNELL
ELISABETH BRONFEN
MISHA KAVKA

MK: What has been your own experience of feminism? What are the issues and debates that have shaped your thinking as a feminist?

DC: I come from a very different background than many academic feminists, and I think my experience of feminism was shaped by that difference. I was very active in the antiwar movement and in the civil rights movement, which I shared with many other women of my generation. I took it perhaps one step further, as I was a union organizer for six years and worked in factories. My experience of feminism was shaped by the basic class understanding that underlies a union. During this period I was in a number of different Marxist-Leninist organizations, including one that did armed self-defense for the Black Panther Party. Part of my notion of what I have now come to call "imperial feminism" was shaped by my understanding of imperialism as something that was not just a "foreign policy" but that deeply affected the way we treated African Americans as well as Caribbean African Americans, Chicanos, Puerto Ricans, and Cubanos. I saw national difference, ethnic difference, and class struggle as being at the very heart of what feminism was about and I never thought of feminism or gender separately from these issues. Obviously, when you decide to involve yourself in an organization that does armed self-defense for the Black Panther Party, you have chosen not to be part of a safe or reform feminism.

When I was a union organizer and I developed my "feminist" consciousness, I joined a consciousness-raising group in which I was the only white woman. One of the women in that organization was a prostitute, who organized prostitute collectives and was also in the Young Lords Party. It was a time in which profound social transformation and real collective action seemed possible; we never thought of relying mainly on the state to help us out. I can give an example of an action our consciousness-raising group undertook. One of the women, an African American, had problems with her husband paying child support. Rather than taking legal action against him, we went down to Harlem Hospital where he worked and passed out leaflets asking all of our sisters to express their disapproval of his behavior. As a result, he was pelted with food in the cafeteria and got stink bombs in his locker; this went on for weeks. And I'm very proud to say that almost twenty-five years later, he hasn't missed a child-support payment. I still keep up with the woman and we still laugh about it. Our collective action made a big impression on him.

EB: What year would this be?

DC: I was in this consciousness-raising group in 1974. We thought we could really change things. And changing things meant doing it radically: fighting for socialism, ending the kind of racism that existed, and engaging in an anti-imperialist politics that we called "helping along the demise of the empire."

MK: What would you say has become of feminism as a political project? In the '60s and '70s feminism was engaged with some very concrete, material issues and you believed that you could change the world. But clearly there has been a shift. One could argue that feminism is more apolitical now. What would you say has become

of the political project that was once feminism? Or has feminist
politics perhaps taken on a different resonance?

DC: For me feminism is still very much a political project. And
some of these same issues remain as burning for me today as they
were then. Feminism does call for radical transformation of our
form of social organization. Whether you want to call it socialism or come up with some other word for it, I don't think that
we can effectively struggle for the kinds of goals shared by my
consciousness-raising group without raising the issue of social
transformation. We *are* a demising empire. I am as determined
now as I was in 1974 to continue to put the end of the CIA on
a meaningful political agenda. What business do we have running
a secret police that runs amok and plunders and murders in the
rest of the world? Our analysis of imperialism informed the
demands of our consciousness-raising group. For instance, the
way we addressed the political issue of prostitution on military
bases was to demand that the military bases get out of the Philip-
pines. Yes, it's true that military bases are collective sites for the
organization of prostitution, but we always saw it from the anti-
imperialist, or what would now be called the "postcolonial," perspective. Today when you talk about having a postcolonial horizon, it still means taking anti-imperialist positions. The struggle
against imperialism is still so much a part of my feminist politics.
When you have alliances with the Puerto Rican feminists, you
can't imagine a feminism that isn't also fighting for some form of
social transformation. The status of Puerto Rico as a commonwealth raises some of the most interesting questions about the
relationship between the nation, the state, and cultural and social
transformation. Its ambivalent status has promoted innovative
discussions among leftists about the relationship between status
and social change. This is why it seems so wrong-headed to me
to say that these questions are outdated: I am still a supporter of
the Independista movement in Puerto Rico, and they still don't
have independence. In fact, but for one vote our House nearly
passed a law prohibiting Puerto Rico from becoming a state
unless they suppressed Spanish. Here we again confront United
States' brutality to a country that is not a former colony but is
colonized in the depth of its being.

I say this because I think that if there is a feminism that's apolitical, it may reflect a deep class bias within feminism, and it may also reflect a pessimism about whether we can actually change the world. But we can't know whether we can change it or not. No one can get us off the hook, so even if we say, "Well, look, socialism has failed; what kinds of things are we going to put in its place?," we are still left with the ethical responsibility for social transformation.

EB: If you were asked, in the context of the fall of the German wall and the end of so-called communism or socialism in Eastern European countries, whether the entire socialist project has proven defunct, would you say "no"?

DC: I would say that the form of socialism that became philosophically justified as a kind of utilitarianism has obviously shown itself to be a failure. It never succeeded in democratizing its own concept of the socialist redistribution of goods. Do I think that there were fundamental problems in the way that Marxism conceived of socialism, or in the way that communist parties conceived of socialism? Absolutely. But do I think that capitalism is the answer? No. We still have a political and ethical responsibility to figure out what form of distributive justice we might be able to combine with democratic politics. And I don't think we are in any way off the hook simply because of the blatant failure of communist governments. Of course, we're in a very complicated position, and we may have to "go back to the drawing board."

EB: Can you give us a sense of where you would start with "the drawing board"? In light of the discussion about the end of master narratives, would you advise looking for a new master narrative?

DC: I would not look for a "new master narrative," if what you mean by that is a new form of Marxism or Hegelianism, the two great master narratives of our time. What I would look for is what I have called "ethical feminism," which would try to examine the components of feminist theory, and its relationship to a feminist practice, in terms of the relationship between the aesthetic, the ethical, the political, the moral, and the legal. Do I think there's going to be an overarching "geist" that will allow us to put these categories into neat boxes? Or do I think that communicative rationality in Habermas's sense will allow us to do so? No. But I do think that feminism demands an articulation of the realm of the aesthetic and what we mean by it, and how that aesthetic affects what we think of as our understanding of the material world. We need an understanding of ethics and of the way ethics should be connected to politics, and politics in turn to some idea of legal right. All of these questions to me ultimately turn on the different levels of the meaning of the word "representation": what are the conditions of representability; who represents whom to whom, when; and what relations of representation are possible? These three levels of representation for me are very much part of how one would begin to reexamine the aesthetic, the ethical, the moral, the political, and the legal as categories.

EB: One of the crucial concepts around which feminism has evolved is the notion of subjectivity. Does that continue to be an important concept today, and what notion of subjectivity would you find useful for feminist theory at the end of the millennium, when systems theory tries to get rid of the subject entirely or cyborg theory claims that we're no longer subjects? In my own work, I have been making a plea for a return to the notion of the subject.

DC: For me, there is no way we can have political philosophy, let alone a meaningful political practice, without some consideration of the subject, so I'm in agreement with you there. I get a little choked up about this because my mother died in August 1998, and on the last day of her life she said, "I believe I understand now what you mean by the phrase 'laying claim to my own person.' And I only wish that I had more time, now that I finally understand what it means, to do something about it." She died that evening. That is one of the phrases that I use, and it had a deep influence on my mother with respect to the moral right to die. I have reclaimed "the person" as part of a theory of right that I develop in the book *At the Heart of Freedom*.[1] I basically argue that "the person," particularly in a legal theory of right, is a mark of freedom that has to be recognized by the state. What is "true" of this person is thus not really the question; we should ask instead what is the right relation of the state to what you're calling subjectivity. I have chosen the phrase "the right to lay claim to your own person" to make it clear that the person is not just a given. If it were, the history of my mother's life would make no sense, since she could not have realized on the last day of her life that this was something she had never done. My

ideal of the "person" is not individualistic. Indeed, we need the protection of this ideal because we are interconnected at the core of
our being, not only to other people but also to the symbolic order
that either affords us the space to make this claim or undermines
our entitlement to make it.

In the realm of sexuality, I have called for what I call the *imaginary domain*, which recognizes that as persons we have many basic
identifications: language, race, ethnicity, sexual difference. What I
call "sexuate being" is almost like a transcendental orientation for
human beings; it recognizes that you have to do something with
your sexuality. It doesn't mean that it has to be in the Western form
of individualism; it doesn't mean that you even have to choose to
"have sex," let alone orient yourself to one object or the other. But
you do have to orient yourself to sexuality. The imaginary domain
is meant to be paradoxical in that it is both a domain and imaginary, meaning that the horizon can always be reimagined and
therefore, although there are parameters to your life that I am calling basic identifications, they, too, can always be reimagined. I claim
that our imaginary domain should be protected, and the protection
of the imaginary domain would also allow us, against the state, to
make sense of our own identifications. Although I would mainly
defend this in the realm of sexual difference, I have also used it in
defending Spanish-language rights in the United States. The point
of the phrase "sexuate being" is not to give it any form either in
gender or sex, but to keep it at this level of abstraction. To lay claim
to your own person means that *you* represent your own sexuate
being and not the state. This means in part, of course, that like
Hegel I understand having or not having a right to personhood as
inseparable from the symbolic order that shapes the extent to
which you are able to have those things called agency and subjectivity. All of this is an attempt in the realm of the legal to think
through the remaining place of the person.

I have also been concerned with the idea of self-representation
in terms of what I have called the minimum conditions of individuation, which is part of the broader project of reconceiving a
legal sense of right of personality. The idea of self-representation
recognizes that the self is always already constituted by its basic
identifications—its political position, its moral position, its ethical

position—but still insists that you are endlessly involved in the process of representing yourself, and in fact inescapably so. We can't get away from representing ourselves, and I mean representing ourselves in the most basic way. For instance, if I'm asked whether I feel that I have to take responsibility for the fact that I am white and Anglo and that those identifications mean something in the United States at this time, the answer is "yes"; I feel I *must* identify as white and Anglo. This process of self-representation is inseparable from another way that I have conceived of responsibility, which has been shaped very much by my interpretation of some of Heidegger's work on Kant. Hannah Arendt took this work into the political realm, while I've tried to take it into the ethical realm by saying that to recognize that we are always already constituted in no way takes away from the possibility of our re-representing ourselves, nor does it get us away from the fact that we're responsible for how we represent ourselves. In other words, in a society in which white is what renders itself invisible, if I say to you, "Well, I don't really have any identifications; I'm not white; I'm not Anglo," then I would be engaging in a representation. It is in the sense of responsibility going hand in hand with self-representation that I've tried to rethink the most sophisticated philosophical critiques of the self-generating autonomous subject.

EB: Is that a way to bring together Kristeva's notion of the subject as part of a signifying process, and Butler's idea of the subject as something that has to constantly renegotiate itself toward the Law? Or would you differentiate your position from them when you suggest that we can't get outside of representation and yet that it is also our responsibility?

DC: I think it's close to both Butler's and Kristeva's ideas, with perhaps one difference. Perhaps the main difference between myself and Judith Butler is the understanding we have of the role of ideality and the ideal, and at the same time of the responsibility to accept the fact that certain representations are morally binding, meaning that I don't in any foreseeable future see myself getting out of having to tell you that I'm white and I'm Anglo. I'd like to think that someday I'm going to live in a world where that could be meaningfully renegotiated, but I don't see it happening soon. In other words, I think there are "slippages" in Stuart Hall's sense, but for me to not make that identification would be, as I said, to try to render this identification invisible exactly according to the received symbolic meaning of whiteness. I do not see us moving towards a time when I'm not going to have to tell you I'm white and I'm Anglo.

EB: Would you say there's any value in us coming to a point where that would no longer be crucial? Is this actually something desirable?

DC: I can imagine a world in which what we think of as "race" would not matter. In fact, one of the things that I have been against is the way we use "race" as a constitutional matter because race has become reduced to an "immutable" attribute of the person. For me, I could imagine a world without race, since I don't think race exists without imperialism and the degradation of persons who are racialized. But can I imagine a world without national and ethnic difference? The answer is "no." Would I want to imagine a world without linguistic difference? On the contrary, every time I hear my daughter speak her beautiful Spanish, I regret that I am mono-lingual. I see it as such a disability. And I see my daughter pass into worlds that I will never be able to pass into. In that sense, I would speak of race very differently than I would speak of ethnic and national origin. Yes, we're always going to be renegotiating those categories, and this brings me back to the question of who represents whom, when. As a white, Anglo woman, I am not going to be renegotiating the meaning of "Latina"; my daughter might, but I'm not. That's not my "place."

MK: If any single issue marks feminist debates of the '90s, then it must be the construction (or deconstruction) of sexual, racial, and political identities. Speaking critically, one might say that the tendency to mark "differences" has gone so far as to fragment feminism beyond recognition or efficacy. Would you agree with this criticism? Or would you say that particularization has served the feminist project, since we no longer speak about feminism but feminisms?

DC: Part of what I'd hoped to do with the project on the imaginary domain, at least as a means of legal reform, was to try to find a way of talking about a shared project of legal reform that would include the transgendered, transsexuals, gays, and lesbians, and also, in a very different arena, would allow us to make claims for language rights. This would be part of a struggle against what, following David Richards, I call moral servitude. The crucial question would not be how you were oppressed and how you experienced your oppression, but rather whether I have the right to represent my own basic identifications, my own sexuate being. My argument is that the state has no right to tell me how to organize my sexuate being, whether I identify as a woman, transgendered, transsexual, lesbian, gay, or none of the above. It seems to me that all of us, because we have the right to lay claim to our own person, can join together in the struggle against moral servitude and make that struggle the heart of a meaningful platform of legal reform. Particularism, on the other hand, is ironically turning us back to an old-fashioned notion of truth. People are battling about what's really "true"—about this, that, or the other identity—but no one wants to say that, whatever your conception of queer identification is, queers have rights in this country. Lesbian mothers in most states can't legally adopt their own children, which is ridiculous. If you say, I have a claim here that I want you to join with because you, like me, have an interest in struggling against moral servitude, then we could find a platform for legal reform that would not be reduced to interest group or identity politics. Nor would it turn us back to the truth of shared experiences or to the truth of "real" identifications. Rather, it would return us to something like subjectivity. It would allow people to say, there is a wrong being done, not in the sense that I claim myself as a victim but that I claim myself as someone who can lay claim to their own person.

EB: For various reasons, rather than talking about the way the symbolic is breaking down, we've discovered that, as Slavoj Žižek or Renata Salecl would say, perhaps there isn't a kind of paternal authority in the center at all. This has moved on the one hand to conspiracy theories—there is no order, so that one starts to identify with the mad figure of authority—or, what I think went on in the Clinton affair, a complete flooding (in Lacanian terms) of the Symbolic through the Imaginary. That is to say, people had forgotten that our relationship to the president is ideological and not personal. Part of the problem I have with identity politics is that it means turning private issues into public issues and forgetting that the ground-zero of collective action can't be a private, intimate issue. Is this an issue for you as well, a concern that we are turning public discourse into "family romances"?

DC: Let me try to break this complicated question into several parts. Tom Nagel has called for what he terms a "new civility," which would allow us to make this division between public discourse and private discourse. On one level, you can understand laws against sexual harassment as being part of the "new civility" or "new reticence" because in fact feminists have wanted to keep certain forms of discourse out of public interaction, say, for instance, in workplaces, government offices, and educational institutions. So, for instance, if you went in to speak to your lawyer you should not be asked to give him a blow job underneath the desk. Or if you were a student going into a professor's office, you should not be asked to do that either. Many of us who were once students have had the experience of going into exactly those kinds of offices and having that suggested to us as an alternative to discussion. If you read feminism as insisting that a certain kind of "private" moment not be made public, then you can understand the phrase "the personal is political" in a way that doesn't require that all "personal" questions be politicized. I understand the issue of sexual harassment as meaning that you have the right to your own imaginary domain and to the dignity of your person, which is coherent with what someone like Nagel calls the "new civility."

On the other hand, the danger of marking this division is that we may reinstate simplistic notions of the personal and the political, and thereby miss something crucial, which is Hegel's insight that the way the state defines kinships is (a) always a public act, (b) almost always a legal act, and (c) inseparable from the ensuing definition of other spheres of life (i.e., ethical life, the sphere of right, civil society). As you know, Hegel came to the conclusion that kinship had to be articulated within heterosexuality and then set women certain established duties as the result of their "nature." Where he is right is that the enactment of kinship relations is crucial for how the state will define itself. Thus, for me a radical feminism has to call the law of kinship into question. I don't think we have the mad father, in Žižek's Lacanian sense, or that the place of the Father has now been displaced by some kind of raving madman, thereby allowing the Imaginary to flood the Symbolic and getting us into such social and political turmoil. What's getting us into trouble, in my opinion, is patrilineal lineage and institutionalized heterosexuality. So I would call for the end of state support for patriarchal institutions as the basis for a normal "private" life and try to elaborate what legitimate state interests in the support of families might be. These reforms would still mean a public enactment of kinship, which in that way would still "do the work" of psychic laws, but it would do that work very differently from flooding the public space by the Lacanian Imaginary. I have basically argued that there is no reason and no justification whatsoever, if you take the Kantian notion of the person seriously, for the institutionalization of the Law of the Father. Period. So could there still be legitimate state interest in protecting children? Yes. But there could be *no* legitimate state interest in connecting reproduction to patrilineal lineage and to the idea of lineage in general. The right to represent your own sexuate being thus means that we would no longer have the legally enforced nuclear family. We would still have institutions that would protect "families," but families could be three women friends who all have children and who call themselves a family, and then the state would be able, as in Sweden, to deliver them the family package. What I want to make clear in this discourse, including Nagel's notion of the "new civility," is that as radical as some of my ideas on kinship might seem, they still take seriously Hegel's insight that the state will be in part shaped by how it establishes the point at which kinship ends and the state begins. In the sense of creating for ourselves much greater freedom in our family forms, I would say that the radical reshaping of "psychoanalytic law" is crucial to a feminist project at the end of the century.

EB: So you would say "yes" to law, but "no" to the Law of the Father, thereby decoupling the family triad from notions of legality. I fully agree with you and I think that bemoaning the dysfunctional family neglects the fact that the nuclear family, which begins in the early part of the nineteenth century, has been—as Foucault says and as so much opera and literature shows—a moment of disaster for women and men and children. Do you actually see a possibility of our moving into different forms of family structures?

DC: You know, I do. In her lecture yesterday on *Antigone*, Judith Butler (who is also working on issues of kinship) joked that after the
sexual revolution of the '60s many of us became disillusioned.
During the 1960s I was still looking for reciprocal recognition, so
in some ways I never went through the sexual revolution. I was
such a Hegelian at the age of sixteen that—I thought I was heterosexual—when boys didn't act the way that I thought they
should according to relations of reciprocal symmetry, I would pass
out books of Hegel to the boys, beautifully bound by my grand-
mother, who was a printer. I won't say this effort was a smashing
success, but it certainly gives you the history of my belief that we
don't have to accept certain ways of engaging in sexual relations.
I'm constantly involved in this project, because I have a daughter.
I'd like to think that I have created a kind of different, alternative
family structure for her, and it's one that I'm constantly engaged
with and constantly rethinking. She has several adopted uncles who
help me with child care. She has her Spanish teacher. She has
another person whom she calls her sister, Irena, who's someone I
love almost as a daughter. And none of this has to do with biological connection, but they've been crucial to me in actually raising
her and allowing me to do things like give interviews and write
books. I see the maintenance of this family as a day-to-day political struggle. This is particularly true when money is involved, but
also when that's not the case, and it's about trying to carve out an
understanding with one of her gay uncles who wants to cut back
his hours of committed time to child care. To deal with those conflicts the concept of commitment itself has to be reexamined
because he's not "the father" in the traditional sense or even the
biological uncle in the traditional sense. And because I am not my
daughter's "biological mother," it has helped us to recognize that
she's not "abnormal," and that our kind of family is valuable
because we're trying to make love be a part of it.

EB: How important would you say gender continues to be in the
debate about different and shifting identifications? I go to quite a
few gender studies conferences in Europe, and I hear from people
who've made their name in gender studies saying that no one's
interested in gender anymore, that it's not really an issue anymore,
that we no longer need the concept of gender. Even as people say

that, of course, gender studies continues to thrive in academic departments and books on gender studies make up some of the most successful titles. There is clearly ambivalence about the usefulness of the term, even on the part of the people involved with gender studies. Is gender still a crucial concept for you, along with class and ethnicity?

DC: Ironically, I've never used the word "gender" much, and now I use the term "sexuate being" when talking about a program of legal reform. In my book *Beyond Accommodation*,[2] where I articulated the aesthetic heart of feminism in terms of the endless re-representation of feminine sexual difference, I argued against the idea that there is any set identity that is gender or that is fixed. At the same time, because of the Lacanianism that still remains part of my work, I saw the masculine and feminine as positions that had to be worked through, at least in our symbolic order at this time. So when I said the "feminine within sexual difference" I meant not an essence or a "thing" but a symbolic code that both imposes limits on "who you are" as a person and at the same time is always open to what I've called re-imagination, or re-representation. Thus the feminine within sexual difference, if one doesn't want to take it up as repudiation, is a necessary political and ethical engagement. This is "the feminine" understood not as femininity but as that which is marked in our symbolic order not just as lack but as a whole set of imposed limitations. Using Butler's terms, if it's the case that we only experience ourselves as having an essential gender core because of performance, I also argued that the performance is already staged within a symbolic order, and therefore it is necessary to re-represent this staging. In order to do this without having to reinstate the traditional philosophical position of repudiating the feminine, you would have to "work it through" *knowing it* not to be anything that actually exists. Given all that, I still think that gender is an important category, and I think the most succinct and eloquent work on the subject has been done by Joan Scott, perhaps because she's a historian. She both shows the problems of using gender without looking at the specific context in which it has taken on a particular historical meaning and, at the same time, shows why in certain kinds of histories it can be a very important category. I think that my own lack of engagement with the term "gender" is that I'm not very engaged with what in the United States we call the category of the social, precisely because of the way I think of the aesthetic as being at the heart of feminism. Still, I would never say that gender is over with as a useful category, given what I've just said about a symbolic code that presents us with a whole set of limits or deep prohibitions, as well as internalized costs to those who try to perform differently. We can't just throw it out. So that's why I think Scott's work about how to use gender cautiously is exemplary. We have to theorize gender and not just use it as a descriptive category. If gender isn't theorized but is just descriptive, like "women in the 1950s and their earnings," then it can become a conservative project. I think that's the political drive that has caused some people to question this issue.

EB: Would you suggest that it might be useful to distinguish between gender and something else—as you suggested distinguishing between race and ethnicity?

DC: I have always preferred to speak of sexual difference—that is, the masculine and the feminine as symbolic positionings—because I think that what is being reworked in these re-representations is the feminine within in sexual difference. And, as I said, I do not conceive of it as a "thing" that can be adequately represented but as an endless process of resignifying. I also use the word "re-imagining." In that sense, although I accept Hegel's point about the state and its relationship to kinship, a certain amount of flooding of the symbolic order by the imaginary is desirable. I want a little bit of that flood.

EB: Why?

DC: Because I think that there is an "unrepresentable" thing that we can, for our political and ethical purposes, call the feminine imaginary, which is one of the sources for our re-representation of the feminine within sexual difference. And calling for the reenactment of a different line between the state and kinship is in part to allow some flooding to take place.

EB: I'm getting rather bored with the phallus and the way that it necessarily positions femininity and the maternal as lack within or as the beyond of the symbolic order. I wonder whether there couldn't be more than one position of accepting the law within the symbolic—not the Law of the Father, but just the law. This may be a way of breaking open the incredible split between masculine and feminine positions. I have argued that the radical, in the sense of the ethical, position would be to say that the feminine subject is also on the side of the law, but has to rethink what its relation to the law is. I've been talking about ethics for the last eight years, and in the beginning people were throwing metaphorical eggs at me. Now when I say the word "ethics" people at least are willing to listen. How does the question of ethics relate to your work on female agency in the judicial and cultural sphere? Why is it an important concept for you?

DC: At least for the last seven or eight years, since I've been asked to give a name to my feminism, I've called it ethical feminism. There are two things that I want to emphasize. First, let's just stick with the feminine as a site of representation within the law. Some of my most speculative thinking about this—again, as almost a day-to-day practice—is how to re-represent the maternal and my relationship to my daughter, and perhaps most daringly, the erotic transference between us. A poem that's daring still, written two thousand years ago by Sappho, begins, "O my daughter, / whose skin of burnished gold pales the magnificence of the sun, / I cower before your beauty. / In your footprints, I stand. / As you twirl in the sun, / for a moment there, / I thought you might be mine. Now you have left me behind / I celebrate that distance."[3] The moment when she "forgets" that this is her daughter is an admittance of something you see nowhere in the psychoanalytic literature, but something that I have experienced—the profound erotic transference between mother and daughter. What that might mean, if we were to allow ourselves to articulate it, is that the daughter and the mother would represent a kind of place where the daughter could work through her transference to the mother rather than disavow it. If in Butler's terms gender has traditionally meant that a woman becomes a woman by disavowing her love for the other woman, and thus disavowing herself as one who loves other women, then we must ask what it would mean if we said, "No, let us articulate and represent, as Sappho did, the profound erotic transference between mother and daughter." Could we even dare to utter words so close to incestuous attachment, if not incestuous enactment? In the poem, of course, Sappho celebrates it in the distance; she doesn't act on it. That's the moment of the law. Everything in that poem for me is revolutionary and tangibly important; my daughter also has skin of burnished gold that pales the magnificence of the sun, so the poem is very dear to me in that way, too. Everything in that poem is about challenging the idea that this eroticism cannot be articulated. But the law is still there because the mother remains symbolically distant. She celebrates the very distance at the same moment that she articulates the highly eroticized nature of her transference. For me, then, one of our tasks in rearticulating kinship is to allow for this kind of re-representation of a relationship that we think is so fundamental.

EB: In part, I'm compelled to say that once we look for the mother/daughter transference, we may find it more often than we think. What you're saying now offers a way of distantiating ourselves from that body which, if too close, becomes all-engulfing, even as we must preserve a bond to it . . .

DC: . . . and yet we allow desire to circulate between mother and daughter. You see, this is a relationship that is never conceptualized as one in which desire circulates. That's what makes Sappho's poem so revolutionary. And certainly, no one knows better than I do just how much desire circulates between me and my daughter. Though the Lacanians may now be thinking, "oh my god, the Symbolic will be bloodied everywhere!," this doesn't mean that there is a destruction of ethically desirable psychic laws of individuation and symbolic distance between mother and daughter. To the extent that there is any enactment of a symbolizable relationship, it is that which allows the articulation of the desire between mother and daughter, so that mother is no longer just a body but a person who, for the moment when she sees her daughter in the distance, expresses her desire and then steps back from it. But she doesn't step back from the expression of desire. In one form of Lacanianism that expression of desire would have to be so buried that Sappho could have never written that poem.

EB: So in a sense you're suggesting that by rethinking the maternal, one may be able to bring desire and ethics closer together than we tend to see them?

DC: Absolutely. And in fact, that's part of what I think is at the core of ethical feminism: a challenge to the way the state enacts kinship and, with it, the reopening of the space where we might actually contest the idea that the feminine is either "beyond" or is lack. Making ourselves within a different kind of legal space—what I have called the imaginary domain—would give us a way of articulating this notion that Sappho had of the mother and daughter as a relationship of desire. In terms of the broader question of ethics, I have always seen part of my project to be inverting the positive and the ethical, so that questions of identification are ethical questions. I just finished a paper called "Antiracism, Multiculturalism, and the Ethics of Identification," which I coauthored with Sara Murphy, where I basically argue that it's precisely because our identities are not captured by any set of identifications that we are engaged in ethics when we do make identifications. It's not like we can just say, I *am* this, so we're stuck with ethics whenever we begin to talk about identification. I have tried to invert the ethical meaning of many of the debates about identity and identifications, insisting that though what one says may be "positively true," this only means that ethically we are always going to be responsible for how we represent these identifications—precisely because there is no set of attributes of identity that are just there. There must always be a moment when we internalize the identities and represent them; even though we are constituted by them, that doesn't get us off the hook. For me, ethics is the ultimate criterion by which we judge whether an identification is one that should be taken up, or needs to be reappropriated, renegotiated, or re-represented.

EB: Let me add to that. I've started rereading Althusser, who claims that we become subjects when we accept the position that we have to the one calling us. I would add that we are always already interpellated, but it is possible for us to make a choice, because we're interpellated in a more complex sense. It's not just one call, but many different calls, which are sometimes in fact contradictory. Agency may have to do with the fact that we either choose an interpellation, or we choose not to choose that interpellation.

DC: I would put it in terms of what I call "basic identifications": even if we see ourselves as constituted by them, we at the same time enunciate them as identifications that we "identify" with or affirm. Your point is that in a sense there's a moment of "agency" when you have to do one thing or the other when you are called. This is very much what I felt when I got involved in the organization to do armed self-defense for the Black Panther Party. I assumed that the police wouldn't fire on whites the way they would on African Americans, and, although it's perfectly true that they do not fire on whites the same way, I was in enough Black Panther offices to know that they do fire on whites once those whites are no longer in the position of the "white person," which means that the white person has no business being in the Black Panther office in the first place. You lose white-skin privilege if you take certain kinds of political actions; that I learned very vividly. So where you say "choice," I would use the phrase "a process of assuming responsibility" that is inevitable precisely because these basic identifications can never have descriptive fullness. You might say that the failure of this descriptive fullness is exactly the place where the ethical begins, which is why, for me, the ethical always inverts the positive. The failure doesn't mean that you're not responsible; the failure means that you are *ethically* responsible. This is something that Althusser never attempted to think through.

MK: Do you see a split between academic and mainstream feminism, understood either as a split between theory and praxis or perhaps as a split between those who "understand" what feminism's about and those who don't, either because they privilege thinking OR because they privilege doing?

DC: I see it in two ways. First of all, my consciousness-raising group only had one woman who had ever gone to college, and I hadn't finished college at the time that I was in it. And we read Hegel, we read Marx. One of the academic fantasies is that these texts are only of interest to academics. You see, when I was sixteen and passing out Hegel to boys, I wasn't a Hegel scholar, I was a Hegelian; I believed that the ideas would capture the hearts of these young men who just hadn't been exposed to them. The idea of being involved in a discipline may be something that distinguishes feminists in the academy from feminists who engage with the same texts but who take those texts to heart in a very different way.

The other comment I want to make is about the obsession with law (meant as the legal system, not psychoanalytically—though they're always connected). The second wave of feminism did get some of us "girls" into law schools. But the legalization of feminism and the obsession with law went way beyond the legal academy, and I think that's in part because the second wave of feminism turned to law as opposed to direct action, and I see this as part of its class bias. In the pornography debate, for instance, there was a union movement going on in the early '90s in the porn industry, but feminists didn't ally with the union movement; instead, we debated whether or not Dworkin and MacKinnon's ordinance was constitutional. Now, I knew when I started writing on pornography that I'd find a union organizer somewhere, and I did. But she got no press, no attention. I think that one conservative element of feminism has been its failure to take seriously the fact that we are an experiment in radical democracy. This gets me back to my three levels of representation. The split between feminists who primarily look to law and feminists who primarily look to collective action is rarely articulated because in a sense feminism has become, at least in the United States, very tied into civil rights victories. And yet for me it was always so much more than that.

EB: How would you position that in relation to the question of political correctness and the tendency to come up with legal language to describe relationships?

DC: That would take me back to Tom Nagel and the "new civility" or "new reticence." Since in the Lacanian terms you were using, I see feminism as instating a kind of "reticence" in certain public situations, I don't see it as instating political correctness. The fact that a female student walks into her professor's office and doesn't have to hear "nice knockers" anymore is not politically correct, but is about maintaining a "publicness" to public space. So when feminists are accused of being the problem behind the Clinton affair, I would argue that's a complete misunderstanding of sexual harassment.

EB: I hear this point very rarely made, that "political correctness" is the wrong language. What we're talking about is people dealing with each other in a responsible and dignified manner. It's simply because one hasn't up until now dealt with women and with people who are not white in this manner that it has been necessary to insist on this. I say this as a Jewish person living in Europe.

MK: Finally, what do you think are the relevant issues for feminism in the next decade? Do you think that feminism has a continuing relevance?

DC: First, the struggle, as Elisabeth put it, to keep the feminine within the law as a site of representation is going to be crucial—which for me means a radical rearticulation of the relationship of the state to the borderline with kinship, or what used to be called the "bloodline" of kinship. Politically, this will lead to the practical issue of struggling to reformulate our civil rights away from ideas of gender, where the term "gender" has become very conservative; this involves struggles for gay and lesbian rights, for the rights of the transgendered, for the rights of the transsexual. The political struggle should also involve an intergenerational solidarity to resymbolize the place of the maternal and to make desire something that can be expressed between mothers and daughters, and between women in feminist politics. If you were to take seriously the idea of making the feminine within sexual difference a site within the law, then you would have to radically rearticulate a lot of the political struggles going on now because you'd be challenging the acceptance of a certain kind of kinship structure. That would open up a whole space for collective action and different kinds of alliances, which could be reformulated or reconnected to what was once called the struggle against patriarchy. I would thus say that there are ways in which we can connect up some of the earlier radical insights of the second wave of feminism in the struggle against patriarchy, with the newer, more sophisticated psychoanalytic language we have been using in this interview, in such a way as to give us sites of actual struggle.

Second, I think that the struggle against imperialism is equally crucial. Any kind of politics we take up, including a theoretical or practical critique of identity politics, must always be done within the context of an ethical commitment to take up an anti-imperialist position within the United States. Otherwise, as Toni Morrison rightly comments, it's pretty odd for white people to be calling for the end of other people's affirmation of their identifications. I think that we have to be very aware of exactly what kinds of politics are possible, but for me the struggle against imperialism is far from a local struggle. We are left with our responsibility to change the world in accordance with an appeal to universality, which begins with the exclusion of hierarchies of colonial status.

NOTES

1. Drucilla Cornell, *At the Heart of Freedom: Feminism, Sex, and Equality* (Princeton: Princeton University Press, 1988).

2. Drucilla Cornell, *Beyond Accommodation: Ethical Feminism, Deconstruction, and the Law* (New York: Routledge, 1991; rpt. Boulder, Colo.: Rowman and Littlefield, 1999).

3. Sappho, unpublished translation, on file with the author.

CONTRIBUTORS

MIEKE BAL is professor of the theory of literature at the University of Amsterdam, a founding director of the Amsterdam School of Cultural Analysis, and A. D.White professor-at-large at Cornell University. Her recent books on visual art include *Schweben zwischen Gegenstand und Ereignis: Begegnungen mit Lili Dujourie* (exhibition catalogue, 1998) (English edition: *Hovering Between Thing and Event: Encounters with Lili Dujourie* [1998]), *Jeannette Christensen's Time* (1998), *Quoting Caravaggio* (1999), and *Looking In:The Art of Viewing* (2000).

LAUREN BERLANT teaches English at the University of Chicago. She has completed two thirds of a trilogy on national sentimentality, *The Anatomy of National Fantasy: Hawthorne, Utopia, and Everyday Life* (1991) and *The Queen of America Goes to Washington City: Essays on Sex and Citizenship* (1997). Her current work, *The Female Complaint*, focuses on sentimental modes of address in subaltern public sphere building in the twentieth century in the United States, taking "women's culture" as its central case.

ROSI BRAIDOTTI is professor of women's studies at the University of Utrecht and visiting professor at the Gender Institute, London School of Economics. She has written widely on feminist theory, French philosophy, and teratology, including the book *Nomadic Subjects: Embodiment and Sexual Difference in Contemporary Feminist Theory* (1994), and was coeditor of the anthology *Between Monsters, Goddesses, and Cyborgs* (1996). Her next book is entitled *Metamorphoses: Towards a Materialist Theory of Becoming*.

ELISABETH BRONFEN is professor of English and American studies at the University of Zurich. Her books include *Over Her Dead Body* (1992), *The Knotted Subject* (1998), a monograph on Sylvia Plath (1998), and a book on the notion of home in Hollywood films entitled *Heimweh: Illusionsspiele in Hollywood* (2000) [English edition: *Critical Nostalgia: Construction of Home in Hollywood Cinema* (forthcoming)]. Her current research projects include a cultural history of the night and a cultural reconsideration of the 1950s.

JUDITH BUTLER is Maxine Elliot professor in the departments of rhetoric and comparative literature at the University of California, Berkeley. She is the author of *Gender Trouble* (1990), *Bodies That Matter* (1993), *The Psychic Life of Power* (1997), and *Excitable Speech* (1997), as well as numerous articles on philosophy, feminist theory, and queer theory. Her most recent work is *Antigone's Claim: Kinship Between Life and Death* (2000).

REY CHOW is Andrew W. Mellon professor of the humanities at Brown University, where she teaches in the departments of modern culture and media, and comparative literature. She is the author of a number of books, the latest of which is *Ethics after Idealism*. She is currently guest editor of a special issue of the journal *differences*, entitled "Writing in the Realm of the Senses."

DRUCILLA CORNELL is a professor of women's studies and political science at Rutgers University. She is the author of *Beyond Accommodation* (1991), *Transformations* (1993), *The Imaginary Domain* (1995), and *At the Heart of Freedom* (1998), as well as coeditor of *Feminist Contentions* (1994). In addition, she has coedited anthologies and written numerous articles on feminist theory, legal theory, and philosophy.

ANN CVETKOVICH is associate professor of English at the University of Texas at Austin. She is the author of *Mixed Feelings: Feminism, Mass Culture, and Victorian Sensationalism* (1992), as well as articles on lesbian culture. She is currently completing her book *In the Archive of Lesbian Feelings: Trauma, Sexuality, and Lesbian Public Culture*.

JANE GALLOP teaches feminist theory in the modern studies interdisciplinary graduate program at the University of Wisconsin, Milwaukee. She is the author of several books, including *Thinking Through the Body, Around 1981: Academic Feminist Literary Theory*, and *Feminist Accused of Sexual Harassment*. She is currently at work on a book on family and photography to be entitled *Living With His Camera*.

BEATRICE HANSSEN was trained in comparative literature at the Humanities Center, Johns Hopkins University, and is associate professor of German at Harvard University, where she also teaches in comparative literature and the literature program. She is the author of *Walter Benjamin's Other History: Of Stones, Animals, Human Beings, and Angels* (1998), *Critique of Violence: Between Poststructuralism and Critical Theory* (2000), and an editor of *The Turn to Ethics* (2000).

CLAIRE KAHANE is a professor of English at the University at Buffalo and a member of the Center for the Study of Psychoanalysis and Culture. She has written widely in the area of feminist-psychoanalytic criticism. Her publications include *Passions of the Voice* (1995) and *In Dora's Case* (2d ed., 1990), coedited with Charles Bernheimer. Her most recent project is a collection of essays on Holocaust trauma and its effects on literary representation.

MISHA KAVKA teaches English literature, film, and media culture at the University of Zurich. She has published essays on the theory and history of hysteria, feminist and queer theory, contemporary Hollywood film, and New Zealand film. Her current project is a book on the affective basis of reality effects in American television, entitled *As Seen on TV: Reality in America*.

RANJANA KHANNA is assistant professor of English and adjunct professor of women's studies at the University of Washington, Seattle, where she teaches postcolonial and feminist theory and literature. She is currently completing two books, *Dark Continents: Psychoanalysis and Colonialism* and *Algeria Cuts: Women and Representation, 1830 to the Present*.

BIDDY MARTIN is professor of German studies and women's studies at Cornell University, and the provost of the university. She is the author of *Woman and Modernity: The (Life)styles of Lou Andreas-Salome* (1991) and *Femininity Played Straight: The Significance of Being Lesbian* (1996), as well as numerous articles on gender, sexuality, and German studies.

JULIET MITCHELL is lecturer in gender and society at the University of Cambridge, visiting professor in comparative literature at Yale University, and a practicing psychoanalyst. She is the author of numerous books, including *Psychoanalysis and Feminism* (1975) and *Women: The Longest Revolution* (1984), and has also edited the essays of Jacques Lacan, Melanie Klein, and Enid Balint. Her most recent book is *Mad Men and Medusas: Reclaiming Hysteria and the Effects of Sibling Relations on the Human Condition* (2000).

ANITA PATTERSON is assistant professor of English at Boston University. She is author of *From Emerson to King: Democracy, Race, and the Politics of Protest* (1997), and has published essays on Fanon, Du Bois, Douglass, and Harriet Jacobs. She is currently writing *Passage to the Americas: The Poetics of Migration from Whitman to Walcott*, a book about literary emergence in the New World.

VALERIE SMITH is professor of English and chair of the program in Afro-American studies at UCLA. She is the author of *Self-Discovery and Authority in Afro-American Narrative* (1987) and *Not Just Race, Not Just Gender* (1998), as well as the editor of *Representing Blackness* (1997), *New Essays on* Song of Solomon (1994), and *African American Writers* (1991). At present she is working on a study of narratives of race in the "post-Civil Rights" era.

INDEX

abortion, 131, 140, 141, 143, 188n. 24

Abraham, Nicolas, 122n. 4

activism: and advertising, 297; against AIDS, 285, 286, 311; and artists, 304–10; and lesbians, 283–318; and pleasure, 291; and snapshots, 299–300; and style, 285–90

actuality, 339–40, 344, 390

advertising, 287, 294, 297, 298, 300, 304

affect, xix, 105–7, 111, 119, 121, 132, 163, 165, 176, 182–83, 289, 358, 376, 401, 403; Deleuze on, 390, 395, 396; and event, 107, 111; and history, 105; negative, 368; and social imaginary, 384; and temporality, 112; traumatic, 177

agency, xxi, 41, 88, 128, 135, 153, 218, 226, 229, 237, 241, 268, 384, 389, 440, 451

AIDS, 155n. 6, 285, 286, 311

allegory, 326, 327, 332, 346

Althusser, Louis, 12, 112, 217–18, 223, 384, 451

antifoundationalism, 61, 62, 66, 73–74, 81, 92n. 9; and politics, 74; and universality, 431

archive, 116, 120; and lesbian culture, 312n. 1; visual, 283–87, 310–12

Arendt, Hannah, 183, 441

banality, 134, 136, 139, 147, 157n. 17

Barrett, Michèle, xii, xiii